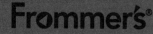

KU-182-147

British Columbia & the Canadian Rockies

6th Edition

by Bill McRae

with Donald Olson

WILEY

Wiley Publishing, Inc.

Published by:

WILEY PUBLISHING, INC.

111 River St.
Hoboken, NJ 07030-5774

ISBN 978-0-470-59153-6 (paper); ISBN 978-0-470-64589-5 (ebk)

Editor: Ian Skinnari
Production Editor: Katie Robinson
Cartographer: Guy Ruggiero
Photo Editor: Richard Fox
Production by Wiley Indianapolis Composition Services
Front cover photo: Mountain Lake in Elk Lakes Provincial Park ©Carson Ganci / Design Pics/Corbis
Back cover photo: Carmanah Walbran Provincial Park, Vancouver Island ©Ron Watts / Corbis

For information on our other products and services or to obtain technical support, please contact our Customer Care Department within the U.S. at 877/762-2974, outside the U.S. at 317/572-3993 or fax 317/572-4002.

Wiley also publishes its books in a variety of electronic formats. Some content that appears in print may not be available in electronic formats.

Manufactured in the United States of America

5   4   3   2   1

CONTENTS

4 SUGGESTED ITINERARIES IN BRITISH COLUMBIA & THE CANADIAN ROCKIES 48

5 VANCOUVER 57

6 VICTORIA 103

7 SOUTHERN VANCOUVER ISLAND & THE GULF ISLANDS 131

8 CENTRAL VANCOUVER ISLAND 166

9 NORTHERN VANCOUVER ISLAND   203

10 THE SUNSHINE COAST & WHISTLER   223

11 NORTHERN BRITISH COLUMBIA   246

12 THE CARIBOO COUNTRY & THE THOMPSON RIVER VALLEY   272

13 THE OKANAGAN VALLEY   293

14 SOUTHEASTERN BRITISH COLUMBIA & THE KOOTENAY VALLEY 312

15 GATEWAYS TO THE CANADIAN ROCKIES: CALGARY & EDMONTON 337

16 THE CANADIAN ROCKIES: BANFF & JASPER NATIONAL PARKS & MORE 371

17 FAST FACTS 421

LIST OF MAPS

HOW TO CONTACT US

In researching this book, we discovered many wonderful places—hotels, restaurants, shops, and more. We're sure you'll find others. Please tell us about them, so we can share the information with your fellow travelers in upcoming editions. If you were disappointed with a recommendation, we'd love to know that, too. Please write to:

Frommer's British Columbia & the Canadian Rockies, 6th Edition
Wiley Publishing, Inc. • 111 River St. • Hoboken, NJ 07030-5774

AN ADDITIONAL NOTE

Please be advised that travel information is subject to change at any time—and this is especially true of prices. We therefore suggest that you write or call ahead for confirmation when making your travel plans. The authors, editors, and publisher cannot be held responsible for the experiences of readers while traveling. Your safety is important to us, however, so we encourage you to stay alert and be aware of your surroundings. Keep a close eye on cameras, purses, and wallets, all favorite targets of thieves and pickpockets.

ABOUT THE AUTHORS

Bill McRae was born and raised in rural eastern Montana, though he spent the better years of his youth attending university in Great Britain, France, and Canada. He has previously written about Montana, Utah, and Oregon for Moon Publications and about the Pacific Northwest and Seattle for Lonely Planet. Other publications he has written for include *National Geographic,* Microsoft Expedia, and *1,000 Places to See in the U.S.A. and Canada Before You Die* for Workman Press. Bill makes his home in Portland, Oregon.

Donald Olson is a novelist, playwright, and travel writer who has lived and worked in London. His newest novel, *Memoirs Are Made of This,* was published in the U.K. by Hodder-Headline in 2007 under the pen name Swan Adamson and translated into Russian in 2008. Two earlier Swan Adamson novels, *My Three Husbands* and *Confessions of a Pregnant Princess,* were published in the U.S. and translated into French, and his essay, "Confessions of a Faux Pa," is featured in the new anthology *What I Would Tell Her: 28 Fathers on the Joys and Challenges of Raising their Daughters.* Donald Olson's novel, *The Confessions of Aubrey Beardsley,* was published in the United Kingdom by Bantam Press, and his play, *Beardsley,* was produced in London. His travel stories have appeared in the *New York Times, Travel + Leisure, Sunset, National Geographic* books, *Town & Country,* and many other publications. His additional guidebooks *England For Dummies, Best Day Trips from London, Irreverent London, Germany For Dummies, Germany Day by Day,* and *Frommer's Vancouver & Victoria* are all published by Wiley. *England For Dummies* won a 2002 Lowell Thomas Travel Writing Award for best guidebook.

FROMMER'S STAR RATINGS, ICONS & ABBREVIATIONS

Every hotel, restaurant, and attraction listing in this guide has been ranked for quality, value, service, amenities, and special features using a **star-rating system.** In country, state, and regional guides, we also rate towns and regions to help you narrow down your choices and budget your time accordingly. Hotels and restaurants are rated on a scale of zero (recommended) to three stars (exceptional). Attractions, shopping, nightlife, towns, and regions are rated according to the following scale: zero stars (recommended), one star (highly recommended), two stars (very highly recommended), and three stars (must-see).

In addition to the star-rating system, we also use **seven feature icons** that point you to the great deals, in-the-know advice, and unique experiences that separate travelers from tourists. Throughout the book, look for:

(**Finds**)	Special finds—those places only insiders know about
(**Fun Facts**)	Fun facts—details that make travelers more informed and their trips more fun
(**Kids**)	Best bets for kids, and advice for the whole family
(**Moments**)	Special moments—those experiences that memories are made of
(**Overrated**)	Places or experiences not worth your time or money
(**Tips**)	Insider tips—great ways to save time and money
(**Value**)	Great values—where to get the best deals

The following **abbreviations** are used for credit cards:

AE	American Express	**DISC**	Discover	**V**	Visa
DC	Diners Club	**MC**	MasterCard		

TRAVEL RESOURCES AT FROMMERS.COM

Frommer's travel resources don't end with this guide. Frommer's website, **www.frommers. com**, has travel information on more than 4,000 destinations. We update features regularly, giving you access to the most current trip-planning information and the best airfare, lodging, and car-rental bargains. You can also listen to podcasts, connect with other Frommers.com members through our active-reader forums, share your travel photos, read blogs from guidebook editors and fellow travelers, and much more.

The Best of British Columbia & the Canadian Rockies

British Columbia and the Canadian Rockies, which stretch across the provincial border into Alberta, are extravagantly scenic and quietly sophisticated. The diversity of landscapes is astounding: You'll travel from cactus-studded desert to soaring mountaintops and on to wilderness ocean beaches. You can visit traditional First Nations (Native Canadian) villages, thread through market stalls in the largest Chinese community outside of Asia, and cheer on cowboys at an old-fashioned rodeo.

As for creature comforts, British Columbia and the Rockies are famed for their luxury hotels, rustic guest ranches, quiet inns, and B&Bs. And the food? With Alberta beef, Pacific salmon, and some of the world's most fertile farm and orchard land, these two provinces champion excellent regional cuisine.

Finally, there's no better place to get outdoors and enjoy yourself. These areas are flush with ski resorts and golf courses, hiking is a near universal passion, and you'll find no better spot on earth to try your hand at adventure sports like sea kayaking, trail riding, or scuba diving.

This guide is chock-full of recommendations and tips to help you plan and enjoy your trip to western Canada; the following are the best of the best, places and experiences you won't want to miss.

1 THE BEST TRAVEL EXPERIENCES

- **Wandering Vancouver's West End:** Vancouver is one of the most cosmopolitan cities in the world, and wandering the streets, people-watching, and sipping cappuccinos at street cafes can fill an entire weekend. Stroll up Robson Street with its busy boutique-shopping scene, turn down cafe-lined Denman Street, then stride into 405-hectare (1,001-acre) Stanley Park, a gem of green space with old-growth cedars, miles of walkways, and the city's excellent aquarium. See chapter 5.
- **Taking Tea in Victoria:** Yeah, it's a little corny, but it's also fun—and delicious. Tea, scones, clotted cream—who said the British don't know good food? The

afternoon tea at the Empress is world-renowned, a little stuffy, and very expensive; if that doesn't sound like fun to you, we'll show you other places where tea is more reasonably priced and a lot less formal. See chapter 6.
- **Ferrying through the Gulf Islands:** The Gulf Islands, a huddle of cliff-lined, forested islands between Vancouver Island and the British Columbia mainland, can be reached only via ferry. Hop from island to island, staying at excellent country inns and B&Bs; pedal the quiet farm roads on your bike, stopping to visit artists' studios or to quaff a pint in a cozy rural pub. The romantic getaway you've been dreaming of starts

and ends right here on these idyllic islands. See chapter 7.

- **Traveling the Inside Passage:** The 15-hour Inside Passage ferry cruise aboard the MV *Northern Adventure* takes you from Vancouver Island's Port Hardy along an otherwise inaccessible coastline north to Prince Rupert, near the southern tip of the Alaska Panhandle. Orcas swim past the ferry, bald eagles soar overhead, and the dramatic scenery—a narrow channel of water between a series of mountain islands and the craggy mainland—is utterly spectacular. See chapter 11.

- **Wine Tasting in the Okanagan Valley:** The Okanagan Valley in central British Columbia has some of the most arid climatic conditions in Canada, but with irrigation, grape varietals like merlot, cabernet sauvignon, and pinot blanc flourish here. Vineyards line the edges of huge, glacier-dug lakes and clamber up the steep desert-valley walls. Taste delicious wines, go for a swim, play some golf, eat at excellent restaurants, and do it all again tomorrow. See chapter 13.

- **Skiing the Canadian Rockies:** You can hit all three ski areas in Banff National Park with a one-price ticket, using the frequent shuttle buses to ferry you and your skis from resort to resort. The skiing is superlative, the scenery astounding, and—best of all—you can stay at Banff's luxury hotels for a fraction of their astronomical summer rates. See chapter 16.

- **Riding Herd at a Guest Ranch:** The edge of the Great Plains nudges up to the face of the Canadian Rockies in Alberta, making this some of the most fertile and beautiful ranching country anywhere. For more than a century, ranches have welcomed guests to their rustic lodges and cabins, offering trail rides, cattle drives, evening barbecues, and barn dances that'll keep you entertained whether you're a greenhorn or an old hand. See p. 381.

2 THE BEST ACTIVE VACATIONS

- **Hiking the West Coast Trail:** Hiking the entire length of the rugged 69km (43-mile) West Coast Trail, from Port Renfrew to Bamfield on Vancouver Island, takes 5 to 7 days, but it's truly the hike of a lifetime. This wilderness coastline, edged with old-growth forest and lined with cliffs, is utterly spectacular, and can be reached only on foot. If you're not up for it, consider an 11km (6¾-mile) day trip on the more easily accessible stretch just south of Bamfield. See p. 182.

- **Scuba Diving off Vancouver Island:** According to no less an authority than Jacques Cousteau, the waters off Vancouver Island offered some of the best diving in the world. And they still do. Nanaimo and Port Hardy are popular departure points, with outfitters ready to drop you into the briny world of the wolf eel, yellow-edged cadlina, and giant Pacific octopus. See chapters 8 and 9.

- **Kayaking Clayoquot Sound:** Paddle a kayak for 4 or 5 days through the waters of Clayoquot Sound on Vancouver Island's wilderness west coast, from the funky former fishing village of Tofino to a natural hot-springs bath near an ancient Native village. Along the way, you'll see thousand-year-old trees and glaciers, whales, and bald eagles. See p. 188.

- **Salmon Fishing from Campbell River:** Even though salmon fishing is not what it once was, Campbell River is still the "Salmon-Fishing Capital of the

World." Join a day trip with an outfitter and fish the waters of Discovery Passage. Get ready to hook the big one! Even if your trophy salmon gets away (or you're required to release it), you'll see plenty of wildlife: bald eagles, seals, even orcas and porpoises. See p. 207.

- **Rafting the Chilcotin and Fraser Rivers:** This 3-day white-water extravaganza flushes you from the slopes of the glaciered Coast Range down through shadowy canyons to the roiling waters of the mighty Fraser River, second in North America only to the Columbia River in power and size. A number of outfitters in Williams Lake offer river options ranging from half-day thrill rides to multiday trips with catered camping. See p. 279.

- **Canoeing Bowron Lakes Provincial Park:** Every summer, canoeists and kayakers set out to navigate a perfect 120km (75-mile) circle of six alpine lakes, with minimal portages in between. There are no roads or other signs of civilization beyond the launch point, except some well-placed cabins, campsites, and shelters. The full circuit is a 7-day trip, but the memories will last a lifetime. See p. 284.

- **Mountain Biking the Kettle Valley Rail Trail:** This rails-to-trails hiking and biking route travels from Okanagan Lake up and over Okanagan Mountain and Myra Canyon, crossing 17 trestles and traversing two tunnels on its 175km (109-mile) route. The entire circuit, which takes from 3 to 5 days, provides lots of challenging grades and excellent scenery. See p. 299.

- **Heli-Skiing near Golden:** Helicopters lift adventurous skiers to the tops of the Selkirk and Purcell mountains that rise just west of Golden, accessing acres of virgin powder far from the lift lines and crowds of traditional ski resorts. **CMH Heli-Skiing** (② **800/661-0252**) offers a variety of holidays, most based out of its private high-country lodges and reached only by helicopter. See p. 322.

- **Cross-Country Skiing at Canmore:** The 1988 Olympic cross-country skiing events were held at Canmore, on the edge of Banff National Park. The routes at the **Canmore Nordic Centre** (② **403/678-2400**) are now open to the public and offer 70km (43 miles) of world-class skiing. See p. 379.

- **Lodge-to-Lodge Trail Riding in Banff National Park:** See the park's backcountry without getting blisters on your feet. Instead, get saddle-sore as you ride horseback on a 3-day excursion, spending the nights in remote but comfortable mountain lodges. **Warner Guiding and Outfitting** (② **800/661-8352**) provides all meals and lodging, plus oats for Silver. See p. 385.

3 THE BEST NATURE- & WILDLIFE-VIEWING

- **Tide Pools at Botanical Beach near Port Renfrew:** Waves have eroded potholes in the thrust of sandstone that juts into the Pacific at Botanical Beach, which remain water-filled when the waves ebb. Alive with starfish, sea anemones, hermit crabs, and hundreds of other sea creatures, these potholes are some of the best places on Vancouver Island to explore the rich intertidal zone. See p. 152.

- **Bald Eagles near Victoria:** Just a few miles north of Victoria is one of the world's best bald eagle–spotting sites: Goldstream Provincial Park. Recent counts put the number of eagles wintering here at around 4,000. (Jan is the best month for viewing, though there are eagles here year-round.) See p. 155.

- **Gray Whales at Pacific Rim National Park:** Few sights in nature match observing whales in the wild. March is the prime viewing time, as the whales migrate north from their winter home off Mexico. During March, both Tofino and Ucluelet celebrate the Pacific Rim Whale Festival; outfitters offer whale-watching trips out onto the Pacific. See chapter 8.

- **Orcas at Robson Bight:** From whale-watching boats out of Telegraph Cove or Port McNeill, watch orcas (killer whales) as they glide through the Johnstone Strait in search of salmon, and rub their tummies on the pebbly beaches at Vancouver Island's Robson Bight. See p. 216.

- **Spawning Salmon at Adams River:** Every October, the Adams River fills with salmon, returning to their home water to spawn and die. While each autumn produces a large run of salmon, every fourth year (the next is 2010), an estimated 1.5 to 2 million sockeye salmon struggle upstream to spawn in the Adams River near Squilax. Roderick Haig-Brown Provincial Park has viewing platforms and interpretive programs. See p. 286.

- **Songbirds and Waterfowl at the Columbia River Wetlands:** Between Golden and Windermere, the Columbia River flows through a valley filled with fluvial lakes, marshes, and streams—perfect habitat for hundreds of species, including moose and coyotes. Protected as a wildlife refuge, the wetlands are on the migratory flyway that links Central America to the Arctic; in spring and fall, the waterways fill with thousands of birds—over 270 different species. Outfitters in Golden operate float trips through the wetlands. See p. 323.

- **Elk in Banff National Park:** You won't need to mount an expedition to sight elk in Banff: They graze in the city parks and on people's front lawns. To see these animals in their own habitat, take the Fenlands Trail just west of Banff to Vermillion Lakes, another favorite grazing area. See chapter 16.

- **Black Bears in Waterton Lakes National Park:** There are black bears throughout the Canadian west, but chances are good you'll spot a bear or two along the entry road to Waterton Lakes National Park, where the open grasslands of the prairies directly abut the sheer faces of the Rocky Mountains. (Remember, bears were originally prairie animals.) See p. 417.

4 THE BEST FAMILY-VACATION EXPERIENCES

- **The Beaches near Parksville and Qualicum Beach:** The sandy beaches near these towns warm in the summer sun, then heat the waters of Georgia Strait when the tides return. Some of the warmest ocean waters in the Pacific Northwest are here, making for good swimming and family vacations. See chapter 8.

- **The MV *Lady Rose* (℗ 800/663-7192):** This packet steamer delivers mail and merchandise to isolated marine communities along the otherwise inaccessible Alberni Inlet, the longest fjord on Vancouver Island's rugged west coast. Along the way, you may spot eagles, bears, and porpoises. The MV *Lady Rose* is large enough to be stable, yet small enough to make this daylong journey from Port Alberni to Bamfield and back seem like a real adventure. See p. 181.

- **The Okanagan Lakes:** Sunny weather, sandy lake beaches, and miles of clean, clear water: If this sounds like the ideal family vacation, then head to the lake-filled Okanagan Valley. Penticton and Kelowna have dozens of family-friendly hotels, watersports rentals, and lakeside parks and beaches. Mom and Dad can enjoy the golf and wineries as well. See chapter 13.

- **Fort Steele Heritage Town** (© **250/ 426-7352**): Once a 19th-century frontier boomtown turned ghost town, Fort Steele again bustles with life. Now a provincial heritage site, the town has been rebuilt, other historic structures have been moved in, and daily activities with living-history actors give this town a real feel of the Old West. See p. 327.

- **Fort Calgary Historic Park** (© **403/ 290-1875**): This reconstruction of the Mountie fort on the banks of the Bow River—and the genesis for the city of Calgary—has always been interesting, as volunteers have been in the process of rebuilding the original fort. In the last couple years, critical mass has been reached and new/old Fort Calgary is really taking shape: It's gone from a good idea to a great attraction. But what's really cool is that the labor has been volunteer and that all the work was done using tools and techniques

from the 1880s. Take the kids and give them a lesson in history and volunteer-ism! See p. 344.

- **The Kicking Horse River:** One of the best white-water rafting trips in the Rockies is on the Kicking Horse River near Golden. While it's the treacherous Class IV rapids that give the river its fame, there are also stretches gentle enough for the entire family. Better yet, most outfitters run simultaneous trips on both sections of the river, so part of your brood can run the rapids while the other enjoys a leisurely float through lovely Rocky Mountain scenery. See p. 323.

- **West Edmonton Mall** (© **800/661-8890**): Okay, so it's a mall. But what a mall! Within its 483,000 sq. m (5.2 million sq. ft.) are 800 stores and a mammoth entertainment center that contains a complete amusement park, roller coaster, bungee-jumping platform, and lake-size swimming pool with real sand beaches and rolling waves. You can also ice-skate, watch performing dolphins, ride a submarine, attend movies at 19 theaters—oh, and get your shopping done, too. See p. 360.

5 NATIVE CANADIAN CULTURE & HISTORY

- **Quw'utsun' Cultural Centre** (Duncan; © **877/746-8119**): North of Victoria, this facility contains a theater, carving shed, ceremonial clan house, restaurant, and art gallery, all dedicated to preserving traditional Cowichan history and culture. Try to visit when the tribe is preparing a traditional salmon bake. See p. 158.

- **Nuyumbalees Cultural Centre** (formerly the Kwakiutl Museum and Cultural Center, Quadra Island;

© **250/285-3733**): To the Native peoples along the Northwest coast, the potlatch was one of the most important ceremonies, involving the reenactment of clan myths and ritual gift giving. When Canadian officials banned the potlatch in the 1920s, the centuries-old costumes, masks, and artifacts of the Kwagiulth tribe were confiscated and sent to museums in eastern Canada and England. When the items were repatriated in the early 1990s, the tribe built this handsome museum to showcase this incredible collection of Native art. See p. 210.

- **Alert Bay** (off Vancouver Island): One of the best-preserved and still vibrant Native villages in western Canada, Alert Bay is a short ferry ride from northern Vancouver Island. Totem poles face the waters, and cedar-pole longhouses are painted with traditional images and symbols. The **U'Mista Cultural Centre** (© 250/974-5403) contains a collection of carved masks, baskets, and potlatch ceremonial objects. See p. 218.

- **Gwaii Haanas National Park Reserve** (Queen Charlotte Islands): A UNESCO World Heritage Site and a Canadian national park, this is the ancient homeland of the Haida people. Located on the storm-lashed Queen Charlottes, it isn't easy or cheap to get to: You'll need to kayak, sail, or fly in on a floatplane. But once here, you'll get to visit the prehistoric village of Ninstints, abandoned hundreds of years ago and still shadowed by decaying totem poles. See p. 258.

- **'Ksan Historical Village** (Hazelton; © 877/842-5518): The Gitxsan people have lived for millennia at the confluence of the Skeena and Bulkley rivers, hunting and spearing salmon from the waters. On the site of an ancient village near present-day Hazelton, the Gitxsan have built a pre-Contact replica village, complete with longhouses and totem poles. No ordinary tourist gimmick, the village houses a 4-year carving school, Native-art gift shop, traditional-dance performance space, artists' studios, restaurant, and visitor center. See p. 263.

- **Secwepemc Museum & Heritage Park** (Kamloops; © 250/828-9801): This heritage preserve contains a Native Secwepemc village archaeological site from 2,400 years ago, plus re-creations of village structures from five different eras. It's not all just history here: The Shuswap, as the Secwepemc are now called, also perform traditional songs and dances and sell art objects. See p. 286.

6 THE BEST MUSEUMS & HISTORIC SITES

- **Museum of Anthropology** (Vancouver; © 604/822-5087): Built to resemble a traditional longhouse, this splendid museum on the University of British Columbia campus contains one of the finest collections of Northwest Native art in the world. Step around back to visit two traditional longhouses. See p. 84.

- **Royal British Columbia Museum** (Victoria; © 888/447-7977): The human and natural history of coastal British Columbia is the focus of this excellent museum. Visit a frontier main street, view lifelike dioramas of coastal ecosystems, and gaze at ancient artifacts of the First Nations peoples. Outside, gaze upward at the impressive collection of totem poles. See p. 119.

- **The Museum at Campbell River** (Campbell River; © 250/287-3103): The highlight of this regional museum is a multimedia presentation that retells a First Nations myth using carved ceremonial masks. Afterward, explore the extensive collection of contemporary aboriginal carving, then visit a fur trapper's cabin and see tools from a pioneer-era sawmill. See p. 206.

- **North Pacific Historic Fishing Village** (Port Edward; © 250/628-3538): Located on the waters of Inverness Passage, this isolated salmon cannery built an entire working community of 1,200 people—complete with homes, churches, and stores—on boardwalks and piers. Now a national historic site, the mothballed factory is open for tours, and you can even spend a night at the old hotel. See p. 251.

- **Fort St. James National Historic Site** (Vanderhoof; © **250/996-7191**): In summer, the rebuilt log Fort St. James trading post hums with activity, as actors play the roles of explorers, traders, and craftspeople. This open-air museum of frontier life is a replica of the first non-Native structure in British Columbia, constructed in 1806. See p. 266.

- **Barkerville** (83km/52 miles east of Quesnel; © **250/994-3332**): Once the largest city west of Chicago and north of San Francisco—about 100,000 people passed through during the 1860s—the gold-rush town of Barkerville is one of the best-preserved ghost towns in Canada. Now a provincial park, it comes to life in summer, when costumed "townspeople" go about their frontier way of life amid a completely restored late-Victorian pioneer town. See p. 283.

- **Glenbow Museum** (Calgary; © **403/268-4100**): One of Canada's finest museums, the Glenbow has fascinating displays on the Native and settlement history of the Canadian Great Plains, plus changing art shows and thematic exhibitions. The gift shop is a good place to find local crafts. See p. 344.

7 THE MOST SCENIC VIEWS

- **Vancouver from Cloud Nine** (© **604/662-8328**): Situated on the top floor of one of the tallest hotels in Vancouver, towering 42 floors above the city, the rotating restaurant/lounge Cloud Nine has 360-degree views that go on forever. See p. 100.

- **The Canadian Rockies from Eagle's Eye Restaurant** (© **250/344-8626**): The Kicking Horse Mountain Resort isn't just one of the newest skiing areas in the Canadian Rockies. This exciting development also boasts the highest-elevation restaurant in all of Canada. The Eagle's Eye sits at the top of the slopes, 2,410m (7,907 ft.) above sea level. Ascend the gondola to find eye-popping views of high-flying glaciered crags—and excellent cuisine. See p. 325.

- **Calgary Tower** (© **403/266-7171**): At 191m (627 ft.), this is one landmark that you'll want to get on top of. From the windows of this revolving watchtower, you'll see the face of the Rocky Mountains to the west and the endless prairies to the east. If you like the view, stay for dinner or a drink. See p. 342.

- **Sulphur Mountain in Banff National Park:** Ride the gondola up to the top of Sulphur Mountain for tremendous views of the cliff-faced mountains that frame Banff. Hike the ridge-top trails, have lunch in the coffee shop, or fill your camera's memory chip with shots of ground squirrels and glaciers. See p. 387.

- **Moraine Lake in Banff National Park:** Ten snow-clad peaks towering more than 3,000m (9,843 ft.) rear up dramatically behind this tiny, eerily green lake. Rent a canoe and paddle to the mountains' bases. See p. 396.

- **Waterton Lakes from the Garden Court Restaurant at the Prince of Wales Hotel** (© **403/859-2231**): There are lots of great views of the Canadian Rockies, but perhaps the most singular is the view from the Prince of Wales Hotel, high above Waterton Lake. With blue-green water stretching back between a series of rugged snow-capped peaks, the view is at once intimate and primeval. See p. 420.

8 THE MOST DRAMATIC DRIVES

- **The Sea-to-Sky Highway:** Officially Hwy. 99, this drive is a lesson in geology. Starting in West Vancouver, the amazing route begins at sea level at Howe Sound and the Squamish Cliffs—sheer rock faces rising hundreds of feet—then up a narrowing fjord, climbing up to Whistler, near the crest of the rugged, glacier-clad Coast Mountains. Continue over the mountains and drop onto Lillooet. Here, on the dry side of the mountains, is an arid plateau trenched by the rushing Fraser River. See p. 228.

- **The Sunshine Coast:** Hwy. 101 follows the mainland British Columbia coast from West Vancouver, crossing fjords and inlets twice on ferries on its way to Powell River. On the east side rise the soaring peaks of the Coast Mountains, and to the west lap the waters of the Georgia Strait, with the green bulk of Vancouver Island rising in the middle distance. From Powell River, you can cross over to Vancouver Island on the BC Ferries service to Comox. See chapter 8.

- **Williams Lake to Bella Coola:** Start at the ranching town of Williams Lake, and turn your car west toward the looming Coast Mountains. Hwy. 20 crosses the arid Fraser River plateau, famed for its traditional cattle ranches, until reaching the high country near Anaheim Lake. After edging through 1,500m (4,921-ft.) Heckman Pass, the route descends what the locals simply call "The Hill": a 32km (20-mile) stretch of road that drops from the pass to sea level with gradients of 18%. The road terminates at Bella Coola on the Pacific, where summer-only ferries depart for Port Hardy on northern Vancouver Island. See p. 280.

- **The Icefields Parkway** (Hwy. 93 through Banff and Jasper national parks): This is one of the world's grandest mountain drives. On a road trip back to the ice ages, you'll climb past glacier-notched peaks to the Columbia Icefields, a sprawling cap of snow, ice, and glacier at the very crest of the Rockies. See p. 399.

9 THE BEST WALKS & RAMBLES

- **Vancouver's Stanley Park Seawall:** Stroll, jog, run, blade, bike, skate, ride—whatever your favorite mode of transport is, use it, but by all means get out here and explore this wonderful park. See p. 89.

- **Victoria's Inner Harbour:** Watch the boats and aquatic wildlife come and go while walking along a pathway that winds past manicured gardens. The best stretch runs south from the Inner Harbour near the Parliament Buildings, past the Royal London Wax Museum. See chapter 6.

- **Strathcona Provincial Park:** Buttle Lake, which lies at the center of Strathcona Provincial Park, is the hub of several hiking trails that climb through old-growth forests to misty waterfalls and alpine meadows. Return to the trailhead, doff your hiking shorts, and skinny-dip in gem-blue Buttle Lake. See p. 212.

- **Johnston Canyon in Banff National Park:** Just 24km (15 miles) west of Banff, Johnston Creek cuts a deep, very narrow canyon through limestone cliffs. The trail winds through tunnels, passes waterfalls, edges by shaded rock faces, and crosses the chasm on footbridges before reaching a series of iridescent pools, formed by springs that bubble up through highly colored rock. See p. 384.

- **Plain of Six Glaciers Trail in Banff National Park:** From Chateau Lake Louise, a trail rambles along the edge of emerald-green Lake Louise, then climbs up to the base of Victoria Glacier. At a rustic teahouse, you can order a cup of tea and scones—each served up from a wood-fired stove—and gaze up at the rumpled face of the glacier. See p. 396.

- **Maligne Canyon in Jasper National Park:** As the Maligne River cascades from its high mountain valley to its appointment with the Athabasca River, it carves a narrow, deep chasm in the underlying limestone. Spanned by six footbridges, the canyon is laced with trails and interpretive sites. See p. 401.

10 THE BEST LUXURY HOTELS & RESORTS

- **The Fairmont Hotel Vancouver** (Vancouver; ✆ **800/441-1414**): Built by the Canadian Pacific Railway on the site of two previous Hotel Vancouvers, this landmark opened in 1929. The château-style exterior, the lobby, and even the guest rooms—now thoroughly restored—are built in a style and on a scale reminiscent of the great European railway hotels. See p. 68.

- **The Fairmont Empress** (Victoria; ✆ **800/441-1414**): Architect Francis Rattenbury's masterpiece, the Empress has charmed princes (and their princesses), potentates, and movie moguls since 1908. If there's one hotel in Canada that represents a vision of bygone graciousness and class, this is it. See p. 109.

- **Hastings House Country House Hotel** (Salt Spring Island; ✆ **800/661-9255**): This farm matured into a country manor and was then converted into a luxury inn. The manor house is now an acclaimed restaurant; the barn and farmhouse have been remade into opulent suites. You might feel like you've been transported to an idealized English estate, if it weren't for those wonderful views of the Pacific. See p. 142.

- **Poets Cove Resort and Spa** (South Pender Island; ✆ **888/512-7638**): Poets Cove may be on a remote bay on a rural island, but don't let the isolation fool you. New and dazzling, the resort has beautifully furnished rooms, villas, and cottages, all overlooking a peaceful harbor. The spa, restaurant, and facilities are absolutely first class. See p. 149.

- **The Wickaninnish Inn** (Tofino; ✆ **800/333-4604**): Standing stalwart in the forest above the sands of Chesterman Beach, this log, stone, and glass structure boasts incredible views over the Pacific and extremely comfortable luxury-level guest rooms. The dining room is equally superlative. See p. 192.

- **Four Seasons Resort Whistler** (Whistler; ✆ **888/935-2460** or 604/935-3400): This grand—even monumental—hotel is the classiest place to stay in Whistler, which is saying something. This is a hotel with many moods, from the Wagnerian scale of the stone-lined lobby to the precise gentility of the guest rooms to the faint and welcome silliness of the tiled and backlit stone fixtures of the restaurant. This is a hotel that's not afraid to make big statements. See p. 238.

- **Grand Okanagan Lakefront Resort** (Kelowna; ✆ **800/465-4651**): You can't get much closer to Okanagan Lake than this marina-fronted hotel, and you won't find more luxurious lodgings either, particularly the new **Royal Private Villas.** In their own building, these sumptuous guest units are essentially luxury apartments, with access to a private rooftop infinity pool. See p. 308.

- **The Fairmont Palliser** (Calgary; ☎ **800/441-1414**): Calgary's landmark historic hotel, the Palliser is permeated with good breeding and high style. The magnificent lobby looks like an Edwardian gentlemen's club, and the guest rooms are large and luxurious. See p. 346.

- **Fairmont Hotel Macdonald** (Edmonton; ☎ **800/441-1414**): When the Canadian Pacific bought and refurbished this landmark hotel, all of the charming period details were preserved, and the inner workings were modernized and brought up to snuff. The result is an elegant but still-friendly small hotel. From the tuxedoed bellman to the gargoyles on the walls, this is a real class act. See p. 362.

- **Rimrock Resort Hotel** (Banff; ☎ **800/661-1587**): Banff is known for its scenery and its high prices; this is one of the few luxury hotels whose rates are actually justified. New and architecturally dramatic, it steps nine stories down a steep mountain slope. A fantastic marble lobby, great restaurant, and handsomely appointed bedrooms complete the package. See p. 391.

- **The Fairmont Chateau Lake Louise** (Lake Louise; ☎ **800/441-1414**): First of all, there's the view: Across a tiny gem-green lake rise massive cliffs, shrouded in glacial ice. And then there's the hotel: Part hunting lodge, part palace, the Chateau is its own community, with sumptuous boutiques, sports-rental facilities, nine dining areas, and beautifully furnished guest rooms. See p. 397.

- **Post Hotel** (Lake Louise; ☎ **800/661-1586**): Quietly gracious hospitality in a dramatic Canadian Rockies setting is the hallmark of this luxurious lodge. The original log-built dining room and bar remain from the 1940s, now joined by a new hotel wing with extremely comfortable and beautifully furnished rooms. The "F" suites are the most desirable. See p. 398.

11 THE BEST B&BS & COUNTRY INNS

- **West End Guest House** (Vancouver; ☎ **604/681-2889**): This 1906 heritage home is filled with an impressive collection of Victorian antiques. Fresh-baked brownies accompany evening turn-down service, and the staff is thoroughly professional. See p. 72.

- **Andersen House Bed & Breakfast** (Victoria; ☎ **250/388-4565**): Your hosts outfit their venerable 1891 Queen Anne home in only the latest decor, from raku sculptures to carved-wood African masks. Their taste is impeccable—the old place looks great. See p. 110.

- **Old Farmhouse B&B** (Salt Spring Island; ☎ **250/537-4113**): The Old Farmhouse is an 1894 farmstead with a newly built guesthouse. The welcome you'll get here is as engaging and genuine as you'll ever receive, and the breakfasts are works of art. See p. 143.

- **Galiano Oceanfront Inn & Spa** (Galiano Island; ☎ **877/530-3939**): Combine a magical island view, a wonderfully inventive restaurant, a full-service spa, plus luxury-level rooms, and you get this very handsome inn. Flanked by gardens and filled with major Northwest Native art, the Galiano Inn wears its high style very comfortably. See p. 146.

- **Oceanwood Country Inn** (Mayne Island; ☎ **250/539-5074**): Overlooking

Navy Channel, this inn offers top-notch lodgings and fine dining in one of the most extravagantly scenic locations on the West Coast. Admirably, the inn maintains an array of prices ranging from affordable and cozy garden-view rooms to luxury-level suites that open onto hot-tub decks and hundred-mile views. See p. 148.

- **Fairburn Farm Culinary Retreat & Guesthouse** (Duncan; ℭ 250/746-4637): This rambling farmhouse B&B sits amid some of the most bountiful farmland in Canada—so start cooking. This unusual operation is part culinary school, part country inn, and part pilgrimage site for Slow Food–movement devotees. Come here for the comfy guest rooms, and stay for the *terroir*. See p. 160.

- **Urban Villa** (Kelowna; ℭ 866/961-2220): This swank guesthouse is just a stroll from Lake Okanagan beaches and minutes from the crush of downtown Kelowna. You get the hands-on attentiveness of a B&B but without the fuss. Plus, the decor and fittings match those of a top-end hotel. See p. 309.

- **Mulvehill Creek Wilderness Inn and Bed & Breakfast** (Revelstoke; ℭ 877/837-8649): Equidistant to a waterfall and Arrow Lake, this remote inn in the forest has everything going for it: nicely decorated rooms with locally made pine furniture, a beautiful lounge with

fireplace, decks to observe the pool and garden, and gracious hosts who exemplify Swiss hospitality. Swimming, boating, fishing—it's all here, even a wedding chapel. See p. 317.

- **Vagabond Lodge** (Golden; ℭ 866/944-2622): Right at the base of the lifts at Kicking Horse Mountain Resort, this log lodge is more of a small boutique hotel, except with lots of Western-style friendliness. With log-built furniture and an enormous stone fireplace, the Vagabond looks right out of a North Woods fantasy, except for the fastidious level of comfort in the guest rooms. See p. 325.

- **Union Bank Inn** (Edmonton; ℭ 780/423-3600): Not quite a B&B, not quite a hotel, the absolutely charming Union Bank Inn is something in between. Right downtown, this marble-faced 1910 bank sat vacant for many years before being redeveloped as an inn and restaurant. Each bedroom was individually decorated by one of Edmonton's top interior designers. See p. 365.

- **Thea's House** (Banff; ℭ 403/762-2499): A vision of stone, pine, and antique carpets, Thea's is a newly built bed-and-breakfast just 5 minutes from downtown Banff. "Elegant Alpine" is Thea's style, a cross between a log lodge and a vision out of *Architectural Digest.* Perfect for a romantic getaway. See p. 391.

12 THE BEST RUSTIC ACCOMMODATIONS: LODGES, WILDERNESS RETREATS & LOG-CABIN RESORTS

- **Tigh-Na-Mara Resort Hotel** (Parksville; ℭ 800/663-7373): Comfortably rustic log cabins in a forest at beach's edge: Tigh-Na-Mara has been welcoming families for decades, and the new luxury log suites are just right for romantic getaways. See p. 179.

- **Strathcona Park Lodge** (Strathcona Provincial Park; ℭ 250/286-3122): A summer camp for the whole family is what you'll find at Strathcona Park Lodge, with rustic lakeside cabins and guided activities that range from sea kayaking and fishing to rock climbing and mountaineering. See p. 214.

- **Rockwater Secret Cove Resort** (Half Moon Bay; ✆ **877/296-4593**): Stroll the boardwalk above the waters of the Strait of Georgia to your platform tent—filled with all the luxuries of a high-end hotel room. "Glamour Camping" is all the vogue, and it's hard to imagine a more scenic locale to rediscover tenting joys, particularly from the resort's outdoor "spa without walls." See p. 227.

- **Buffalo Mountain Lodge** (Banff; ✆ **800/661-1367**): Rustic charm meets upscale comfort on the Tunnel Mountain bluff behind Banff. Buffalo Mountain Lodge is centered on a large, handsome log lodge building with an intimate fireplace-dominated bar and elegant dining room. The woodsy, holiday-card-perfect atmosphere extends to the guest rooms, with fireplaces, slate-tiled bathrooms, and balconies overlooking the forests. Definitely worth the splurge. See p. 390.

- **Tekarra Lodge** (Jasper; ✆ **888/962-2522**): Quaint little cabins ring a central lodge building at this well-loved getaway. The cabins are atmospherically rustic; best of all, you're a mile distant from Jasper's busy town center. See p. 408.

- **Becker's Chalets** (Jasper; ✆ **780/852-3779**): These very attractive new cabins are set right along the Athabasca River. Some units are as large as houses. Jasper's best restaurant is here as well. See p. 407.

- **Overlander Mountain Lodge** (Jasper East; ✆ **877/866-2330**): Forget the wildly overpriced rooms in Jasper Townsite and stay here, just .5km (⅓ mile) outside the park gates. Lovely new cabins plus a handsome older lodge with a good restaurant make this an in-the-know favorite. See p. 409.

- **The Emerald Lake Lodge** (Yoho National Park; ✆ **800/663-6336**): Location, location, location: Sumptuous lakeside cabins at the base of the Continental Divide make this a longtime favorite family-vacation spot. See p. 415.

13 THE BEST NORTHWEST REGIONAL CUISINE

See "A Taste of British Columbia & the Canadian Rockies," in chapter 2, for more information on the style of cuisine unique to this region.

- **West** (Vancouver; ✆ **604/738-8938**): In a sleek, jewel-box dining room, absolutely fabulous West starts with classic techniques and the finest Pacific seafood, fish, and other regional ingredients to provide an up-to-the-second dining experience. Book the "chef's table" in the kitchen to watch the chefs at work. See p. 79.

- **The Blue Crab Bar and Grill** (Victoria; ✆ **250/480-1999**): You might think that the food would have a hard time competing with the view at this

restaurant in the Coast Hotel, but you'd be wrong. The creative chef serves up the freshest seafood, the presentation is beautiful, and the dishes are outstanding. See p. 113.

- **Sooke Harbour House** (Sooke; ✆ **250/642-3421**): This small country inn has one of the most noted restaurants in all of Canada. Fresh regional cuisine is the specialty, with an emphasis on local seafood. Views over the Strait of Juan de Fuca to Washington's mighty Olympic Mountains are spectacular, nearly matching the wine list. See p. 153.

- **Masthead Restaurant** (Cowichan Bay; ✆ **250/748-3714**): Sitting above a busy marina, with islands and mountains rising in the distance, the Masthead's views are mesmerizing and its trappings—the century-old clapboard structure was built as a fine hotel—are charming. But the food here is absolutely up-to-date, an exploration of Vancouver Island's rich *terroir*. See p. 162.

- **Shelter** (Tofino; ✆ **250/725-3353**): Fine dining in Tofino has always been synonymous with the Pointe, the wonderful restaurant at the Wickaninnish Inn. But the tourist boom in Tofino created an explosion of fantastic new places in this remote corner of Vancouver Island. Check out Shelter for its youthful vigor and absolutely fresh and authentic flavors—everything is right off the boat or just off the land. See p. 193.

- **Araxi Restaurant & Bar** (Whistler; ✆ 604/932-4540): A longtime Whistler favorite that just keeps on getting better. Chef James Walt is capable of gastronomic alchemy, producing dishes that are inventive yet tradition-based and full of flavor. Choose one of the tasting menus; then face the wondrous stupefaction by selecting something delicious from the 12,000-bottle wine inventory. See p. 243.

- **Bearfoot Bistro** (Whistler; ✆ 604/932-3433): The food scene in Whistler is extremely dynamic, as you'd expect at North America's top ski resort and recent Olympic host. To get noticed amid Whistler's many restaurants requires something special—and Bearfoot Bistro's got it. With very inventive food served in three- or five-course meals, this is like having a cutting-edge Iron Chef in charge of your dinner. See p. 243.

- **All Seasons Café** (Nelson; ✆ **250/352-0101**): Innovative preparations and rich, hearty flavors are the hallmarks of the cuisine at this superlative restaurant in a downtown Nelson heritage home. Food this stylish and up-to-date would pass muster anywhere; to find it in Nelson is astonishing. See p. 333.

- **Belvedere** (Calgary; ✆ **403/265-9595**): The moody, noirish atmosphere of this elegant fine-dining room lights up when the food arrives: Easily one of western Canada's top restaurants, Belvedere offers an inventive dining experience focused on Pan-Canadian ingredients and impeccable French-by-way-of-Tokyo technique. See p. 350.

- **River Café** (Calgary; ✆ **403/261-7670**): You'll walk through a quiet, tree-filled park on an island in the Bow River to reach this bustling place. At the restaurant's center, an immense wood-fired oven and grill produce smoky grilled meats and vegetables, all organically grown and freshly harvested. On warm evenings, picnickers loll in the grassy shade. See p. 351.

- **Hardware Grill** (Edmonton; ✆ **780/423-0969**): Although located in one of Edmonton's first hardware stores, there's nothing antique about the food at the Hardware Grill. A very broad selection of inventive appetizers makes it fun to snack your way through dinner. See p. 366.

- **Maple Leaf Grille & Spirits** (Banff; ✆ **403/760-7680**): In a soaring, two-story dining room that's at once rustic and classy, the Maple Leaf serves up Banff's most sophisticated mountain cuisine. The menu focuses on regional ingredients, fresh preparations, and a friendly unstuffy welcome that lets you relax into having a great time with inventive, delicious food. See p. 394.

- **Vancouver's Three F Festivals:** The Folk, the Fringe, and the Film are the three F's in question. The Folk Fest (p. 33) brings folk and world-beat music to a waterfront stage in Jericho Park. The setting is gorgeous, the music great, and the crowd something else. Far more urban is the Fringe (604/637-6380; www.vancouverfringe.com), a festival of new and original plays that takes place in the arty Commercial Drive area. The plays are wonderfully inventive; better yet, they're short and cheap. In October, the films of the world come to the Vancouver International Film Festival (www.viff.org). Serious film buffs buy a pass and see all 500 flicks (or as many as they can before their eyeballs fall out).

- **Celebration of Light** (Vancouver): This 3-night fireworks extravaganza takes place over English Bay in Vancouver. Three of the world's leading fireworks manufacturers are invited to represent their countries in competition against one another, setting their best displays to music. On the fourth night, all three companies launch their finales. See p. 33.

- **Market in the Park** (Salt Spring Island): The little village of Ganges fills to bursting every Saturday morning, as local farmers, craftspeople, and flea marketers gather to talk, trade, and mill aimlessly. With all ages of hippies, sturdy housewives, fashion-conscious Eurotrash, and rich celebrities all mixed together, the event has the feel of a weird and benevolent ritual. See p. 141.

- **World Championship Bathtub Race** (Nanaimo): Imagine guiding a claw-foot tub across the 58km (36-mile) Georgia Strait from Nanaimo to Vancouver: That's how this hilarious and goofily competitive boat race began. Nowadays, dozens of tubbers attempt the crossing as part of July's weeklong Marine Festival, with a street fair, parade, and ritual boat burning and fireworks display. See p. 169.

- **Calgary Stampede:** In all of North America, there's nothing like the Calgary Stampede. Of course it's the world's largest rodeo, but it's also a series of concerts, an art show, an open-air casino, a carnival, a street dance—you name it, it's undoubtedly going on somewhere here. In July, all of Calgary is a party—and you're invited. See p. 343.

- **Edmonton International Fringe Theatre Festival** (Edmonton): Every August, Edmonton plays host to North America's largest fringe theater festival, an 11-day spectacular offering theatrics, performance, and a nonstop street party atmosphere. The festival attracts 150 theater companies and performing troupes from around the world, plus an audience of over 600,000. See p. 359.

2

British Columbia & the Canadian Rockies in Depth

The more you know about British Columbia and the Canadian Rockies, the more you're likely to enjoy and appreciate everything the region has to offer. The pages that follow include a brief history, a range of highly recommended books, a primer on the unique cuisine of the area, and more.

1 BRITISH COLUMBIA & THE CANADIAN ROCKIES TODAY

Canada's westernmost region has a lot to offer travelers, including dramatic landscapes, a vibrant arts culture, and unparalleled access to outdoor recreation. British Columbia and the Canadian Rockies, which stretch across the provincial border into Alberta, are obviously part of Canada, and have a thoroughly Canadian infrastructure and political system. However, these two giant provinces—British Columbia covers 948,600 sq. km (366,257 sq. miles), Alberta 661,188 sq. km (255,286 sq. miles)—are separated from the nation's capital, Ottawa, and the political and cultural centers of eastern Canada by thousands of miles of farmland.

Much closer is the northwestern tier of the United States. Although British Columbia and Alberta are definitely part of Canada, they are much closer in spirit to the Pacific Northwest states than to, say, Quebec or Nova Scotia. The states of Washington, Oregon, Idaho, and Montana share their northern neighbors' climate, economies, and cultural histories. These regions of Canada and the United States have more in common with each other than with the rest of their respective countries—a reality that seems to please everyone in both the Canadian and the American Pacific Northwest.

There's another cultural overlay at work here, not quite at odds with the above observation, but simultaneously true: In the United States, the westering urge—that uniquely North American drive to keep moving west toward unspecified freedom and opportunity—was diffused across a dozen or so states, each of which developed its own culture and institutions. In Canada, only British Columbia and Alberta absorbed all the hopes, idealism, and pragmatism of 150 years' worth of western migration.

British Columbia is often called the California of Canada, with Canada's most temperate climate, a vibrant film industry, a visible and powerful gay and lesbian community, and a soft-focus New Age patina. However, British Columbia is also the Idaho of Canada, the Washington state of Canada, and, incidentally, the Asia of Canada. In terms of cultural diversity and competing interests, there's a lot happening here.

Likewise, the Alberta of prosperous Edmonton and Calgary may seem like an oil- and agriculture-fueled monoculture, but dozens of its rural communities began as colonies of religious refugees whose stories have a lot in common with the Mormons of Utah. And with its nouveau-riche wealth and well-rehearsed swagger, Alberta is more like Texas than anywhere else on earth.

As if these factors weren't enough to explain the schizoid nature of the two westernmost provinces, the populace is further divided by highly politicized environmental issues. Although Canadians in general seem more environmentally conscious than Americans, that doesn't mean that individual Canadians want to lose their salmon-fishing jobs to some vague international treaty, or that they want to close down the mine that's employed their families for generations just because of a little mud in the river. Environmental issues—especially those surrounding logging, agriculture, mining, and fishing—are especially contentious, often pitting urban and rural residents against each other.

It's easy to think of Canada as North America's Scandinavia—well ordered, stable, and culturally just a little sleepy. In fact, during your own travels across British Columbia and the Rocky Mountains, you'll likely find this corner of Canada a fascinating amalgam of cultures, histories, and conflicting interests.

2 LOOKING BACK AT BRITISH COLUMBIA & THE CANADIAN ROCKIES

NATIVE WESTERN CANADA According to generally accepted theories, the Native peoples of North America arrived on this continent about 15,000 to 20,000 years ago from Asia, crossing a land bridge that spanned the Bering Strait. At the time, much of western Canada was covered with vast glaciers. Successive waves of these peoples moved south down either the coast or a glacier-free corridor that ran along the east face of the Rockies. As the climate warmed and the glaciers receded, the Native peoples moved north, following game animals like the woolly mammoth.

The ancestors of the tribes and bands that now live on the prairies of Alberta didn't make their year-round homes here in the pre-Contact era. The early Plains Indians wintered in the lake and forest country around present-day Manitoba, where they practiced basic agriculture. In summer and fall, hunting parties headed to the prairies of Alberta and Saskatchewan in search of buffalo. The move to a year-round homeland on the Great Plains was a comparatively recent event, caused by Native displacement as the eastern half of North America became increasingly dominated by European colonists. Thus, a number of linguistically and culturally unrelated tribes were forced onto the prairies at the same time, competing for food and shelter.

The Native peoples of the prairies relied on the buffalo for almost all their needs. The hide provided tepee coverings and leather for moccasins; the flesh was eaten fresh in season and preserved for later consumption; and the bones were used to create a number of tools.

The Native peoples along the Northwest coast had a very different culture and lifestyle, and in all likelihood migrated to the continent much later than the Plains Indians. Living at the verge of the Pacific or along the region's mighty rivers, these early people settled in wooden longhouses in year-round villages, fished for salmon and shellfish, and used the canoe as their primary means of transport. The Pacific Northwest coast was one of the most heavily populated areas in pre-Contact America, and an extensive trading network developed. Because the temperate coastal climate and abundant wildlife made this a relatively hospitable place to live, the tribes were reasonably well-off, and the arts—carving and weaving in particular—flourished. Villages were organized according to clans, and elaborately carved totem poles portrayed ritual clan myths.

EUROPEAN EXPLORATION The first known contact between Europeans and the Native peoples of western Canada came in the last half of the 18th century, as the Pacific Northwest coast became a prize in the colonial dreams of distant nations. Russia, Britain, Spain, and the United States each would assert a claim over parts of what would become British Columbia and Alberta.

In 1774, the Spanish explorer Juan Perez landed on the Queen Charlotte Islands and then on the western shores of Vancouver Island, at Nootka Sound. England's James Cook made a pass along the Pacific Northwest coast, spending a couple weeks at Nootka Sound in 1778, where the crew traded trinkets for sea otter pelts. Later in the same journey, Cook visited China and discovered that the Chinese would pay a high price for otter furs.

Thus was born the Chinese trade triangle that would dominate British economic interests in the northern Pacific for 30 years. Ships entered the waters of the Pacific Northwest, their crews traded cloth and trinkets for pelts of sea otters, and then the ships set sail for China, where the skins were traded for tea and luxury items. After the ships returned to London, the Asian goods were sold.

Since the Spanish and the English had competing claims over the Pacific Northwest coast, these nations sent envoys to the region—the Spaniard Don Juan Francisco de la Bodega y Quadra and the British Captain George Vancouver—to further explore the territory and resolve who controlled it. The expeditions led by these explorers resulted in a complete mapping of the region, though the ownership of the territory wasn't resolved until 1793, when Spain renounced its claims.

Fur traders also explored the interior of British Columbia and the Alberta prairies. Two British fur-trading companies, the Hudson's Bay Company (HBC) and the North West Company, began to expand from their bases along the Great Lakes and Hudson's Bay, following mighty prairie rivers to the Rockies. Seeking to gain advantage over the Hudson's Bay Company, the upstart North West Company sent traders and explorers farther inland to open new trading posts and to find routes to the Pacific. Alexander Mackenzie became the first white man to cross the continent when he followed the Peace River across northern Alberta and British Columbia, crossing the Rockies and the Fraser River Plateau to reach Bella Coola, on the Pacific, in 1793.

Simon Fraser followed much of Mackenzie's route in 1808, though he floated down the Fraser River to its mouth near present-day Vancouver. Another fur trader and explorer was David Thompson, who crossed the Rockies and established Kootenay House trading post on the upper Columbia River. In 1811, Thompson journeyed to the mouth of the Columbia, where he found Fort Astoria, an American fur-trading post, already in place. Competing American and British interests would dominate events in the Pacific Northwest for the next 2 decades.

By the 1820s, seasonal fur-trading forts were established along the major rivers of the region. Cities like Edmonton, Kamloops, Prince George, and Hope all had their beginnings as trading posts. Each of the forts was given an assortment of trade goods to induce the local tribes to trap beaver, otter, fox, and wolf. Although the fur companies generally treated the Native populations with respect and fairness, there were tragic and unintentional consequences to the relationships that developed. While blankets, beads, and cloth were traded for furs, nothing was as popular or as effective as whiskey: Thousands of gallons of alcohol passed from the trading posts to local tribes, corrupting traditional culture and creating a cycle of dependence that enriched the traders while poisoning the Native peoples. The traders also unwittingly introduced European diseases to the local population, who had little or no resistance to such deadly scourges as smallpox and measles.

The Louisiana Purchase, which gave the U.S. control of all the territory along the Missouri River up to the 49th parallel and to the Continental Divide, and the Lewis and Clark Expedition from 1804 to 1806 gave the Americans a toe-hold in the Pacific Northwest. As part of the settlement of the War of 1812, the Pacific Northwest—which included all of today's Oregon, Washington, and much of British Columbia—was open to both British and American exploitation, though neither country was allowed to set up governmental institutions. In fact, Britain had effective control of this entire area through its proxies in the Hudson's Bay Company, which had quasi-governmental powers over its traders and over relations with the Native peoples, which included pretty much everyone who lived in the region.

B.C. CONSOLIDATES & JOINS CANADA

From its headquarters at Fort Vancouver, on the north banks of the Columbia River near Portland, Oregon, the Hudson's Bay Company held sway over the river's huge drainage, which extended far into present-day Canada. However, with the advent of the Oregon Trail and settlement in what would become the state of Oregon, the HBC's control over this vast territory began to slip. In 1843, the Oregon settlers voted by a slim majority to form a government based on the American model. The HBC and Britain withdrew to the north of the Columbia River, which included most of Washington and B.C.

The U.S.-Canada boundary dispute became increasingly antagonistic. The popular slogan of the U.S. 1844 presidential campaign was "54/40 or fight," which urged the United States to occupy all of the Northwest up to the present Alaskan border. Finally, in 1846, the British and the Americans agreed to the present border along the 49th parallel. The HBC headquarters withdrew to Fort Victoria on Vancouver Island; many British citizens moved north as well. In order to better protect its interests and citizens, Vancouver Island became a crown colony in 1849—just in case the Americans grew more expansionist-minded. However, population in the Victoria area was still small: In 1854, the population counted only 250 white people.

Then, in 1858, gold-rush fever struck this remote area of the British Empire. The discovery of gold along the Fraser River, and in 1862 in the Cariboo Mountains, brought in a flood of people. By far the vast majority of the estimated 100,000 who streamed into the area were Americans who came north from the by-now-spent California gold fields. Fearing domination of mainland Canada by the United States, Britain named the mainland a new colony, New Caledonia, in 1858. In 1866, the two colonies—Vancouver Island and the mainland—merged as the British colony of British Columbia.

As population and trade increased, the need for greater political organization grew. As a colony, British Columbia had little local control, and was largely governed by edict from London. In order for British Columbia to have greater freedom and self-determination, the growing colony had two choices: join the prosperous United States to the south, with which it shared many historic and commercial ties, or join the new Dominion of Canada far to the east. After Ottawa promised to build a railroad to link eastern and western Canada, B.C. delegates voted in 1871 to join Canada as the province of British Columbia.

Meanwhile, the rule of the HBC over the inland territory known as Ruperts Land relaxed as profits from trapping decreased, and in 1869, the Crown bought back the rights to the entire area. The border between the United States and Canada in the prairie regions was hazy at best, lawless at worst. Although selling whiskey to Native people was illegal, in the no man's land between Montana and Canada, trade in alcohol was rife.

In response to uprisings and border incursions, the Canadian government created a new national police force, the Royal Canadian Mounted Police. In 1873, a contingent of Mounties began their journey across the Great Plains, establishing Fort Macleod (1874) in southern Alberta along with three other frontier forts, including Fort Calgary at the confluence of the Bow and Elbow rivers. The Mounties succeeded in stopping the illegal whiskey trade and creating conditions favorable for settlement. By 1875, there were 600 residents at Fort Calgary, lured by reports of vast and fertile grasslands.

However, for the prairies and the interior of Canada to support an agrarian economy, these remote areas needed to be linked to the rest of Canada. In 1879, the Canadian Pacific Railroad reached Winnipeg, and in 1883 arrived at Banff. Finding a route over the Rockies proved a major challenge: The grades were very steep, the construction season short, and much of the rail bed had to be hacked out of rock.

Canada's transcontinental railway needed a mainland coastal terminus in British Columbia, as the new province's population center and capital, Victoria, was on an island. Railroad engineers set their sites on the sheltered Burrard Inlet, then a sparse settlement of saloons, lumber mills, and farms. The first train arrived from Montreal in 1886, stopping at a thrown-together, brand-new town called Vancouver. A year later, the first ship docked from China, and Vancouver began its boom as a trading center and transportation hub.

All along the railroad's transcontinental reach, towns, farms, and other industries sprang up for the first time. In Alberta, huge ranches sprawled along the foothills of the Rockies, and Calgary boomed as a cow town. The railroads also brought foreign immigration. Entire communities of central and eastern European farmers appeared on the prairies overnight, the result of the railroads' extensive promotional campaign in places like the Ukraine. Other settlers came to western Canada seeking religious tolerance; many small towns on the prairies began as utopian colonies for Hutterites, Mennonites, and Dukhobors. Alberta became a province in 1905, and in 1914 the Grand Trunk Railroad, Canada's second transcontinental railroad, opened up the more northerly prairies, linking Saskatoon and Edmonton to Prince George and Prince Rupert. By 1920, Alberta was Canada's leading agricultural exporter.

All this development demanded lumber for construction, and in Canada, lumber—then as now—meant British Columbia. In return for building the transcontinental railroad, the CPR was granted vast tracts of land along its route. As the demand for lumber skyrocketed, these ancient forests met the saw.

As the population, industry, logging, farming, and shipping all increased in western Canada, it was not just the local ecosystem that took a hit. Although European diseases wiped out enormous numbers of Native peoples, they had reasonably cooperative relations with the HBC trappers, who did little to overtly disturb their traditional life and culture.

That awaited the arrival of agriculture, town settlements, and Christian missionaries. After the HBC lost its long-standing role in Indian relations, authority was wielded by a federal agency in Ottawa. The Native peoples received no compensation for the land deeded over to the CPR, and increased contact with the whites who were flooding the region simply increased contact with alcohol, trade goods, and disease. The key social and religious ritual of the coastal Indians—the potlatch, a feast and gift-giving ceremony—was banned in 1884 by the provincial government under the influence of Episcopal missionaries. The massive buffalo herds of the open prairies were slaughtered to near-extinction in the 1870s and 1880s, leaving the once proud Plains Indians little choice but to accept confinement on reservations.

THE 20TH CENTURY   The building of the Panama Canal, which was completed in 1914, meant easier access to markets in Europe and along North America's East Coast, bringing about a boom for the western Canadian economy. As big business grew, so did big unions. In Vancouver in the 1910s, workers organized into labor unions to protest working conditions and pay rates. A number of strikes hit key industries, and in several instances resulted in armed confrontations between union members and soldiers. However, one area where the unions, the government, and business could all agree was racism: The growing Chinese and Japanese populations were a problem they felt only punitive legislation and violence could solve. Large numbers of Chinese had moved to the province and were instrumental in building the CPR; they were also important members of hard-rock mining communities and ran small businesses such as laundries. Japanese settlers came slightly later, establishing truck farms and becoming the area's principal commercial fishermen. On several occasions, Vancouver's Chinatown and Little Tokyo were the scene of white mob violence, and in the 1920s, British Columbia passed legislation that effectively closed its borders to non-white immigration.

The period of the world wars was turbulent on many fronts. Settlers with British roots returned to Europe to fight the Germans in World War I, dying in great numbers and destabilizing the communities they left behind. Following the war, Canada experienced an economic downturn, which led to further industrial unrest and unemployment. After a brief recovery, the Wall Street crash of 1929 brought severe economic depression and hardship. Vancouver, with its comparatively mild climate, became a kind of magnet for young Canadian men—hungry, desperate, and out of work. The city, however, held no easy answers for these problems, and soon the streets were filled with demonstrations and riots. Vancouver was in the grip of widespread poverty.

With the beginning of World War II, anti-German riots took hold of the city streets; and German-owned businesses were burned. In 1941, Japanese-Canadians were removed from their land and their fishing boats and interned by the government on farms and work camps in inland British Columbia, Alberta, and Saskatchewan.

Perversely, for other Canadians, social calm and prosperity returned as World War II progressed: the unemployed enlisting as foot soldiers against the Axis nations, and the shipbuilding and armaments-manufacturing industries bolstering the region's traditional farming, ranching, and lumbering.

Alberta's wild oil boom began in 1947, when drillers struck black gold near Leduc and a period of tremendous economic growth ensued. By the 1960s, Alberta was supplying most of Canada's crude oil and natural gas. In the 1970s, as oil-producing nations joined together to form the Organization of Petroleum Exporting Countries (OPEC) and oil shortages hit North America, Alberta was left holding the hose. The value of the province's petroleum resources tripled almost overnight;

by the end of the 1970s, their value had quadrupled again, allowing for a period of nearly unlimited building and infrastructure development. Calgary morphed from a sleepy ranchers' town into a brand-new city of soaring office towers, the financial and business center of Canada's oil industry. Edmonton, the capital of Alberta, boomed as the center of oil technology and refining.

After the war years, British Columbia generally boomed economically as well, especially under the leadership of the Social Credit Party, supposedly the party of small business. Father and son premiers, W. A. C. and Bill Bennett, effectively ruled the Social Credit Party and the province from 1952 until 1986. With close ties between government ministers and the resources they oversaw, business—especially manufacturing, mining, and logging—certainly boomed, but along with prosperity came significant governmental scandals, opportunistic financial shenanigans, and major resource mismanagement. Social Credit Premier Bill Vander Zalm was forced to resign in 1991. Reform-minded governments have been in place in Victoria since, although corruption still seems rampant in both government and business.

The 1990s saw a vast influx of Hong Kong Chinese to the Vancouver area, the result of fears accompanying the British handover of Hong Kong to the mainland Chinese in 1997. Unlike earlier migrations of Chinese to North America, these Hong Kong Chinese were middle- and upper-class merchants and business leaders. Real-estate prices shot through the roof, and entire neighborhoods became Chinese enclaves. Currently, Vancouver has one of the world's largest Chinese populations outside of Asia.

Asians are not the only people bolstering western Canada's fast-growing population. Canada has relatively open immigration laws, resulting in a steady flow of newcomers from the Middle East, the Indian subcontinent, and Europe. Additionally, many young Canadians from the economically depressed eastern provinces see a brighter future in the west. With their strong economies and big-as-all-outdoors setting, Vancouver, Edmonton, and Calgary serve as magnets for many seeking new lives and opportunities.

3 THE LAY OF THE LAND

Canada's westernmost province, British Columbia, and the Canadian Rockies region, which stretches into the province of Alberta, are incredibly diverse, with distinct regions that vary both in geography and culture.

Vancouver is one of the most beautiful and cosmopolitan cities in the world. While there are certainly good museums and tourist sights, what we love most are the incredible mosaic of people and languages, the bustle of the streets, the mountains reaching down into the sea, and the wonderful food. Kayaking and canoeing are just off your front step in False Creek and the Georgia Strait, and skiing just up the road at **Whistler/Blackcomb Mountain Resorts,** one of the continent's greatest ski areas.

Vancouver Island is a world apart from busy urban Vancouver. At the island's southern tip is the British Columbia capital of **Victoria,** a small, charming city that makes a lot of fuss about its Merry Olde Englishness. In summer, the crowds can be off-putting, the sham Britishness intolerable. But in the off season, Victoria is just a beautifully preserved frontier town in a magnificently scenic seaside location.

The rest of the mountainous island ranges from rural to wild. It would be easy to spend an entire vacation just on Vancouver Island, especially if you take a few days for **sea kayaking** on the island's wilderness west coast near **Tofino,** or off the east coast in the beautiful **Gulf Islands.** Or you can learn to **scuba dive:** No less an authority than Jacques Cousteau has claimed that these waters are some of the best diving environments in the world. Vancouver Island is also home to dozens of First Nations Canadian bands. If you're shopping for **Native arts,** this is the best single destination in western Canada.

From the northern tip of Vancouver Island, you can take the 15-hour BC Ferries trip through the famed **Inside Passage** to Prince Rupert, a port town just shy of the Alaska Panhandle. Getting a glimpse of the dramatically scenic Inside Passage is what fuels the Alaska-to-Vancouver cruiseship industry; by taking this route on BC Ferries, you'll save yourself thousands of dollars and catch the same views. From Prince Rupert, you can journey out to the mystical **Queen Charlotte Islands,** the ancient homeland of the Haida people, or turn inland and drive up the glacier-carved Skeena River valley to **Prince George,** on the Fraser River.

You can also reach the upper reaches of the Fraser River from Vancouver by following Hwy. 99 north past Whistler and Lillooet to the **Cariboo Country.** This route follows the historic Cariboo Trail, a gold-rush stage-coach road blazed in the 1860s. The road now leads through cattle- and horse-covered grasslands, past 19th-century ranches, and by lakes thick with trout. The gold rush started at **Barkerville,** which is now one of the best-preserved ghost towns in North America. In addition to this great family destination, the Cariboo Country offers the province's best **guest ranches** and rustic lakeside **fishing resorts.**

The Thompson River meets the Fraser River south of Lillooet. This mighty river's southern fork has its headwaters in the **Shuswap Lakes,** a series of interconnected lakes that are favorites of houseboaters. The north fork Thompson River rises in the mountains of **Wells Gray Provincial Park,** one of British Columbia's neglected gems. Hiking and camping are as compelling as in the nearby Canadian Rockies, but without the overwhelming crowds.

One of the best summer family destinations in western Canada is the **Okanagan Valley.** Stretching from the U.S.-Canadian border nearly 200km (124 miles) north to Vernon, this arid canyon is filled with glacier-trenched lakes, which in summer become the playground for all manner of watersports. The summer heat is also good for wine grapes: This is the center for British Columbia's growing wine industry. Add to that a dozen golf courses and excellent lodging and dining in the cities of **Penticton** and **Kelowna,** and you've got the makings for an excellent vacation.

The **Canadian Rockies** are among the most dramatically scenic destinations in the world. Unfortunately, this is hardly a secret—you'll find the entire area dripping with tourists in summer and early fall. **Banff** and **Jasper** national parks in Alberta are especially busy; however, it's hard to find fault with the sheer beauty of these places. The British Columbia side of the Rockies contains much less busy mountain parks, including **Yoho, Glacier,** and **Kootenay** national parks, plus **Mount Robson Provincial Park.** Another spectacular mountain retreat is **Waterton Lakes National Park,** which adjoins the United States' Glacier National Park.

Spending several days in the Rockies should remain a part of any western Canadian itinerary. Despite the crowds, the town of **Banff** is charming and filled with great hotels and fine restaurants; **Lake Louise** is a magical sight; and the **Icefields Parkway,** which joins Banff and Jasper parks, is completely spellbinding. Throughout this area, chances are good you'll see lots of **wildlife,** like black bears, moose, bighorn sheep, mountain goat, and elk. The parks all offer marvelous outdoor recreation, including **hiking, mountain biking, climbing,** and **skiing.**

Calgary, the city that oil built, is a friendly town in the foothills of the Rockies. One of the most prosperous cities in all of Canada, it's still a ranchers' town, and the disparity between its role as a cow town and world oil center is one of its charms. The dichotomies are never more apparent than during the **Calgary Stampede,** the world's largest rodeo and an excuse for turning the city into one huge party. You can also thank Calgary's prosperity for its wonderful restaurant scene.

Edmonton, the capital of Alberta, sits high above the North Saskatchewan River at the center of a vast, farm-covered plain. This welcoming city's historic district is great for strolling and eating. While Edmonton lacks the high spirits and urbane attitude of Calgary, it's no slouch when it comes to fine dining and excellent hotels. And if you enjoy shopping—or swimming, carnival rides, or performing dolphins—then you must visit the **West Edmonton Mall,** one of the world's largest shopping centers. Like a cross between Disneyland, Las Vegas, and Gap, West Ed Mall is unlike any mall you've ever seen.

4 BOOKS, FILM & MUSIC: BRITISH COLUMBIA & THE CANADIAN ROCKIES IN POPULAR CULTURE

BOOKS

The following books on British Columbia and Alberta provide background information, and can add immeasurably to your enjoyment of your trip. The following list contains books both in print and out of print—all are easily available in bookstores and Internet shopping sites.

CANADIAN HISTORY A basic primer on the country's complex history is *The Penguin History of Canada,* by Kenneth McNaught. *The Canadians,* by Andrew H. Malcolm, is an insightful and highly readable rumination on what it is to be Canadian, written by the former *New York Times* Canada bureau chief.

Peter C. Newman has produced an intriguing history of the Hudson's Bay Company, *Caesars of the Wilderness,* beginning with the early fur-trading days. *The Great Adventure,* by David Cruise and Alison Griffiths, tells the story of the Mounties and their role in the subduing of the Canadian west.

Pierre Berton is the preeminent popular historian of Canada. He has written nearly 50 books on Canada's rich past, all well researched and well written. His books cover many subjects, from the days of the Hudson's Bay Company and the fur trade to pondering on what it means to be Canadian in the 21st century.

For a specific history of British Columbia, try *British Columbia: An Illustrated History,* by Geoffrey Molyneux, or *The West Beyond the West: A History of British Columbia,* by Jean Borman. Review Vancouver's past with *Vancouver: A History in Photographs,* by Aynsley Wyse and Dana Wyse.

Alberta: A History in Photographs, by Faye Reinebert Holt, is a good introduction to the history of that province, though the engaging *Alberta History Along the Highway: A Traveler's Guide to the Fascinating Facts, Intriguing Incidents and Lively Legends in Alberta's Remarkable Past,* by Ted Stone, is the book you'll want to take along in the car. (The same author has a companion volume on British Columbia.)

To learn about Canada's Native peoples, read *Native Peoples and Cultures of Canada,* by Alan D. McMillan, which includes both history and current issues. The classic book on Canada's indigenous peoples, *The Indians of Canada,* was written in 1932 by Diamond Jenness. The author's life is an amazing story in its own right, as he spent years living with various indigenous peoples across the country.

NATURAL HISTORY Two good general guides to the natural world in western Canada are the Audubon Society's *Pacific Coast,* by Evelyn McConnaghey, and *Western Forests,* by Stephen Whitney.

British Columbia: A Natural History, by Richard Cannings, is an in-depth guide to the province's plants, animals, and geography. *Plants and Animals of the Pacific Northwest: An Illustrated Guide to the Natural History of Western Oregon, Washington, and British Columbia,* by Eugene N. Kozloff, is another good general resource.

For information on the natural history of Alberta's southern prairies, pick up *From Grasslands to Rockland: An Explorers Guide to the Ecosystems of Southernmost Alberta,* by Peter Douglas Elias.

Bird-watchers might want to dig up a copy of *Familiar Birds of the Northwest,* by Harry B. Nehls.

Read about the natural history of extinct wildlife in *A Wonderful Life: The Burgess Shale and the Nature of History,* by Stephen Jay Gould, which details the discovery and scientific ramifications of the fossil beds found in Yoho National Park.

OUTDOOR PURSUITS Edward Weber's *Diving and Snorkeling Guide to the Pacific Northwest* is a good place to start if you're planning a diving holiday in the Northwest.

Mountain Bike Adventures in Southwest British Columbia, by Greg Maurer and Tomas Vrba, is just one of a cascade of books on off-road biking in western Canada.

A good hiking guide to western British Columbia is *Don't Waste Your Time in the B.C. Coast Mountains: An Opinionated Hiking Guide to Help you Get the Most from this Magnificent Wilderness,* by Kathy Copeland. *A Guide to Climbing and Hiking in Southwestern British Columbia,* by Bruce Fairley, also includes Vancouver Island.

The *Canadian Rockies Access Guide* by John Dodd and Gail Helgason is an excellent resource for hikers and cross-country skiers in the national parks of Alberta.

Hiking Alberta, by Will Harmon, covers 75 hikes along the eastern face of the Rockies. Chris Dawson's *Due North of Montana: A Guide to Flyfishing in Alberta* will point you toward favorite fishing holes.

FICTION & MEMOIR Alice Munro's short fiction captures the soul of what it is to be Canadian in brief, though often wrenching, prose. Some of the stories in *The Love of a Good Woman* take place in Vancouver. Another good selection of short stories as well as poetry is *Fresh Tracks: Writing the Western Landscape,* a collection of writings by western Canadian authors.

The frontier-era conflicts in southern Alberta form the backdrop for the award-winning *The Englishman's Boy,* by Guy Vanderhaeghe, an atmospheric western with a story that travels from Fort Macleod to Hollywood.

Richard P. Hobson, Jr., writes of his experiences as a modern-day cowboy on the grasslands of central British Columbia in an acclaimed series of memoirs titled *Grass Beyond the Mountains: Discovering the Last Great Cattle Frontier on the North American Continent, The Rancher Takes a Wife,* and *Nothing Too Good for a Cowboy.*

Vancouver and southwestern British Columbia is and has been home to a number of noted international authors. Mystery writer Laurali R. Wright lived in Vancouver, and her Karl Alberg mystery series usually took place in and around Vancouver. Jane Rule's *Desert of the Heart* was a breakthrough in lesbian fiction when it was published in 1964.

Generation X chronicler Douglas Coupland lives in Vancouver. Science-fiction writer William Gibson's dark vision of the cyber-future attracts a large young audience. W. P. Kinsella *(Shoeless Joe)* writes about baseball and First Nations issues from his home in the Lower Mainland.

FILM & TV

British Columbia is one of the centers of film in Canada, and many Canadian features are set in Vancouver. Numerous Hollywood films have also been shot in the province: *Twilight* and *New Moon, Legends of the Fall, Little Women, Jumanji,* and *Rambo: First Blood* give an idea of the range of films done here. Television's groundbreaking series *The X-Files* was shot in and around the city for its first 4 years of production. (Vancouver doubles as many American cities, notably Washington, D.C.)

The Canadian Rockies feature frequently in movie Westerns, though often they stand in for other locals. *Brokeback Mountain* was filmed in Alberta, with the Canadian Rockies standing in for Wyoming. *The Assassination of Jesse James by the Coward Robert Ford* and *Unforgiven* were also filmed in Alberta.

MUSIC

Vancouver is a major trendsetter in Canadian music, particularly in the realms of folk and post-punk pop music. The music scene in Calgary and Edmonton is also vibrant, though with significantly more country music overlays: k.d. lang is the province's most famous musical export.

Vancouver's leading role in Canadian rock stylings doesn't mean that the city lacks a full array of classical music institutions, including the well-respected Vancouver Symphony Orchestra and Vancouver Opera Association. The city's love of music is also on display in its many music festivals, particularly the beloved Vancouver Folk Music Festival, one of the largest and most laid-back folk festivals in North America. The Vancouver International Jazz Festival is another major musical event featuring a diverse line-up of musicians from around the world.

Vancouver is extremely ethnically diverse, providing a League-of-Nations-like multiplicity to its music scene, which moves beyond typical World Beat internationalism. You'll find Chinese, East Indian, and Russian punk bands, and lots of rock groups that blend central European and Eastern Mediterranean influences. Muslim punk, often referred to as "taqwacore" (a neologism formed from taqwa, Arabic for piety, and hardcore) is another genre popular in some Vancouver clubs. Secret Trial Five, an all-female punk band with its roots in Vancouver, has caused a sensation with its politically pointed, hard-edged sounds.

One of Vancouver's defining moments in folk-rock history is Joni Mitchell's "Big Yellow Taxi," which was a commentary on the city's rapid urbanization. Other early rock bands with Vancouver and B.C. roots were Bachman Turner Overdrive, Loverboy, and the Boomtown Rats.

Vancouver is currently a hotbed for Indie Rock and singer songwriters that blend folk and rock. Notably recent bands with B.C. roots include The New Pornographers, with its side acts Destroyer and singer Neko Case; Ladyhawk; Said The Whale; and Left Spine Down.

5 A TASTE OF BRITISH COLUMBIA & THE CANADIAN ROCKIES

Western Canada is home to an excellent and evolving regional cuisine that relies on local produce, farm-raised game, grass-fed beef and lamb, and fresh-caught fish and shellfish. These high-quality ingredients are matched with inventive sauces and accompaniments, often based on native berries and wild mushrooms. In attempting to capture what the French call the *terroir,* or the native taste of the Northwest, chefs from Edmonton and Calgary to Victoria and Vancouver are producing a delicious school of cooking with distinctive regional characteristics.

One of the hallmarks of Northwest cuisine is freshness. In places like Vancouver Island, chefs meet fishing boats to select the finest of the day's catch. The lower Fraser Valley and the interior of British Columbia are filled with small specialty farms and orchards. Visit Vancouver's Granville Island Market or stop at a roadside farmer's stand to have a look at the incredible bounty of the land.

Cooks in western Canada are also very particular about where the food comes from. Menus often tell you exactly what farm grew your asparagus, what ranch your beef was raised on, which orchard harvested your peaches, and what bay your oysters came from. To capture the distinct flavor of the Northwest—its *terroir*—means using only those products that swam in the waters or grew in or on the soil of the Northwest.

Once you've assembled your extra-fresh, locally produced foodstuffs, you need to cook them according to some kind of aesthetic. This is where Northwest cooks get inventive. While many chefs marry the region's superior meat, fish, and produce to traditional French or Italian techniques, other cooks turn elsewhere for inspiration. One popular school of Northwest cooking looks west across the Pacific to Asia. Pacific Rim or Pan-Pacific cuisine, as this style of cooking is often called, matches the North American Pacific Coast's excellent fish and seafood with the flavors of Pacific Asia. The results can be subtle—the delicate taste of lemon grass or nori—or intense, with lashings of red curry or wasabi. However, don't expect Pacific Rim cuisine to follow the rules of Asian cooking: One memorable meal at Calgary's Belvedere restaurant (p. 350) matched grilled Alberta beef tenderloin with a sauce of Japanese seaweed and reduced red wine, served with heirloom potato cakes.

Other attempts to find the authentic roots of Northwest cooking look back to frontier times or to Native American techniques. There's no better way to experience salmon than at a traditional salmon bake at a Native village—most First Nations communities have an annual festival open to the general public—and many restaurants replicate this method by baking salmon on a cedar plank. Several restaurants in Vancouver and on Vancouver Island specialize in full Northwest Native feasts.

FRUITS OF THE FIELD & FOREST Although there's nothing exotic about the varieties of vegetables available in western Canada, what will seem remarkable to visitors from distant urban areas is the freshness and quality of the produce here. Many fine restaurants contract directly with small, often organic, farms to make daily deliveries. Heirloom varieties—old-fashioned strains that are often full of flavor but don't ship or keep well—are frequently highlighted.

Fruit trees do particularly well in the hot central valleys of British Columbia, and apples, peaches, apricots, plums, and pears do more than grace the fruit basket. One of the hallmarks of Northwest cuisine is its mixing of fruit with savory meat and chicken dishes. And as long as the chef is slicing apricots to go with sautéed chicken and thyme, she might as well chop up a few hazelnuts (filberts) to toss in: These nuts thrive in the Pacific Northwest.

Berries of all kinds do well in the milder coastal regions. Cranberries grow in low-lying coastal plains. The blueberry and its wild cousin, the huckleberry, are both used in all manner of cooking, from breads to savory chutneys. In Alberta, another wild cousin, the Saskatoonberry, appears on menus to validate regional cooking aspirations. The astringent wild chokecherry, once used to make pemmican (a sort of Native American energy bar), is also finding its way into fine-dining restaurants.

Wild mushrooms grow throughout western Canada, and harvesting the chanterelles, morels, porcinis, and myriad other varieties is big business. Expect to find forest mushrooms in pasta, alongside a steak, in savory bread puddings, or braised with fish.

MEATS & SEAFOOD Easily the most iconic of the Northwest's staples is the Pacific salmon. For thousands of years, the Native people have followed the cycles of the salmon, netting or spearing the fish, then smoking and preserving it for later use. The delicious and abundant salmon became the mainstay of settlers and early European residents as well. Although salmon fishing is now highly restricted and some salmon species are endangered, salmon is still very available and easily the most popular fish in the region. Expect to find a salmon dish on practically every fine-dining menu in the Northwest.

However, there are other fish in the sea. The fisheries along Vancouver Island and the Pacific Coast are rich in bottom fish like sole, flounder, and halibut, which grow to enormous size here. Fresh-caught rock and black cod (also called sablefish) are also delectable, and the Pacific has plentiful tuna, especially ahi and albacore.

Although shellfish and seafood are abundant in the Pacific, it is only recently that many of the varieties have appeared on the dinner table. Oysters grow in a number of bays on Vancouver Island, and while wild mussels blanket the length of the coast, only a few sea farms grow mussels commercially. Fanny Bay, north of Qualicum Beach on Vancouver Island, is noted for both its oysters and its mussels. Another Northwest shellfish delicacy is the razor clam, a long, thin bivalve with a nutty and rich flavor. Shrimp of all sizes thrive off the coast of British Columbia, and one of the clichés of Northwest cooking is the unstinting use of local shrimp on nearly everything, from pizza to polenta. Local squid and octopus are beginning to appear on menus, while sea urchin—abundant along the coast—is harvested mostly for export to Japan, though it does appear in high-end sushi restaurants.

Both British Columbia and Alberta have excellent ranch-raised beef and lamb. Steaks are a staple throughout the region, as is prime rib. You'll see lamb on menus more often in western Canada than in many areas of the United States. Game meats are increasingly popular, especially in restaurants dedicated to Northwest cuisine. Buffalo and venison are offered frequently enough to no longer seem unusual, and farm-raised pheasant is easily available. You'll look harder to find meats like caribou or elk, however. Savor it when you can.

FRUITS OF THE VINEYARDS British Columbia wines remain one of western Canada's greatest secrets. Scarcely anyone outside of the region has ever heard of these wines, yet many are delicious and, while not exactly cheap, still less expensive than comparable wines from California. There are wineries on Vancouver and Saturna islands and in the Fraser Valley, but the real center of British Columbia's wine-making is the Okanagan Valley. In this hot and arid climate, noble grapes like cabernet sauvignon, merlot, and chardonnay thrive when irrigated. You'll also find more unusual varietals, like Ehrenfelser and Marechal Foch. More than 100 wineries are currently producing wine in the Okanagan Valley; when combined with excellent restaurants in Kelowna and Penticton, this region becomes a great vacation choice for the serious gastronome.

DINING IN RESTAURANTS Canadians enjoy eating out, and you'll find excellent restaurants throughout British Columbia and Alberta. Many of the establishments recommended in this guide serve Northwest regional cuisine, the qualities of which are outlined above.

However, there is also a wealth of other kinds of restaurants available. If you're a meat eater, it's worth visiting a traditional steakhouse in Calgary or Edmonton. In many smaller centers, Greek restaurants double as the local steakhouse. Don't be surprised when you see a sign for, say, Zorba's Steakhouse; both the steaks and the souvlaki will probably be excellent.

Vancouver is one of the most ethnically diverse places on earth, and the selection of restaurants is mind-boggling. You'll find some of the best Chinese food this side of Hong Kong, as well as the cooking of Russia, Mongolia, Ghana, and Sri Lanka, along with every other country and ethnic group in between.

Several Canadian chain restaurants are handy to know about. White Spot restaurants serve basic but good-quality North American cooking. Often open 24 hours, these are great places for an eggs-and-hash-browns breakfast. Tim Horton's is the place to go for coffee and doughnuts, plus light snacks. Earl's serves a wide menu and frequently has a lively bar scene. Expect grilled ribs and chicken, steaks, and gourmet burgers. The Keg is another western Canadian favorite, and is a bit more sedate than Earl's, with more of a steakhouse atmosphere.

3

Planning Your Trip to British Columbia & the Canadian Rockies

The westernmost provinces of Canada, British Columbia and Alberta, are the two most popular tourist destinations in a country that is itself one of the world's favorite vacation getaways. Both provinces have very well organized tourism infrastructures, which makes trip planning both simple and a pleasure: Piecing together a trip through Banff National Park or the coastal forests of B.C. can be a highly pleasant diversion in and of itself.

Planning a trip to B.C. and the Canadian Rockies requires little in the way of precaution, as Canada is remarkably safe and civilized. However, before setting out, there are a few points to consider. Due to its northerly location, Canada presents very distinct seasons: You'll have a very different experience if you travel in western Canada in summer than in winter. While summer in the north is glorious, there are ample reasons to travel outside of the peak July through September tourist season: Prices are lower and crowds much thinner, for starters. As for winter, if you're a skier, then you'll find that B.C. and Alberta boast some of the top ski resorts in the world.

Which brings up another consideration. The urban attractions of B.C. and Alberta are very compelling, and plenty of travelers come here largely to enjoy the dazzling culture and dining in cities such as Vancouver, Victoria, and Calgary. However, even if you are by inclination an urban kind of person, you should plan to get outdoors and experience the truly astonishing land- and seascapes of western Canada. Outfitters and resorts make it easy to head out into the wilderness, whether on a kayak, in snowshoes, or atop a horse.

And that's what's truly remarkable about Canada. Its cities and towns are the very model of civilized culture, but at the city limits, the wilderness begins. As you plan your trip, be sure to make time to experience both sides of Canada.

For additional help in planning your trip and for more on-the-ground resources in B.C. and the Canadian Rockies, please turn to chapter 17, "Fast Facts."

1 WHEN TO GO

When to go to B.C. and the Canadian Rockies depends largely on what you intend to do when you get there. Summer brings warm weather and largely sunny skies, and also the most festivals and events. Unsurprisingly, this is also when the most tourists choose to visit, and many areas, particularly the Canadian Rockies, are absolutely thronged. However, even if you travel during the heavily touristed months of summer, this guide offers suggestions for less-frequented parks and activities where you can experience the solitary pleasures of the Canadian outback.

By and large, winter means skiing, which is big business here. Both B.C.

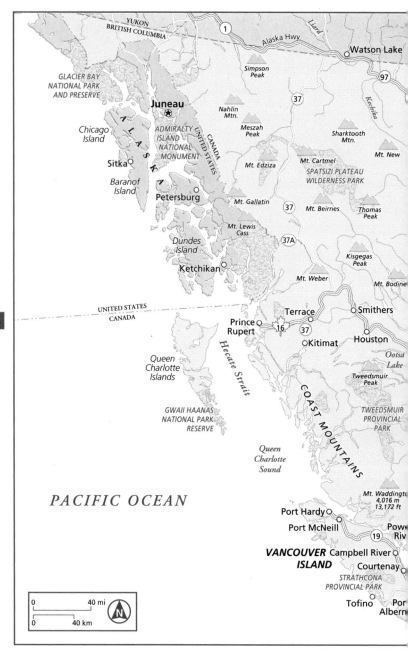

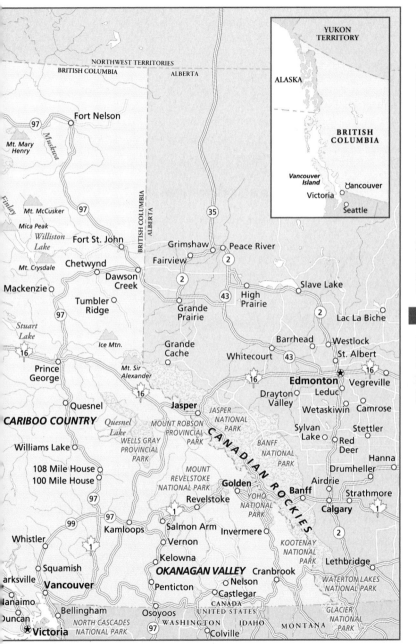

(Vancouver and Whistler) and the Canadian Rockies (Calgary and Nakiska) have hosted the Winter Olympics, and recent years have seen the opening of ever more upscale resorts, particularly in the mountains of southeast B.C. Winter can be a fun time to visit B.C. and the Canadian Rockies, as it's literally a winter wonderland, and all the top restaurants and hotels are running at high gear.

Spring (Apr and May) and late fall (Oct through early Dec) are definitely off season, and in many ways can be the nicest times to visit. Hotel prices are often one-third to one-half of high-season rates, and you'll have dining rooms to yourselves. Come prepared for changeable weather, but otherwise this can be a low-key, budget-pleasing time to visit.

THE WEATHER

Canada west of the Rocky Mountains has generally mild winters, with snow mostly at the higher elevations. Even though spring comes early—usually in March—gray clouds can linger through June. Dry summer weather is assured only after July 1, but often continues through October. The Canadian Rockies and the mountains of the B.C. interior are often socked in with clouds and rain throughout the summer; plan to spend several days here to assure that you'll catch at least some good weather. In winter, the Rockies fill with snow, but frequently the weather is not as cold as you'd expect. Chinook winds from the prairies can bring warm-air systems, boosting temperatures up to early spring levels. On the prairies of Alberta, winters can be fiercely cold and windy. If you plan to travel across the prairies or through the Rockies in winter, be sure to have snow tires and chains.

Remember that your car should be winterized through March and that snow sometimes falls as late as May. Evenings tend to be cool everywhere, particularly on or near water. In late spring and early summer, you'll need a supply of insect repellent if you're planning bush travel or camping.

Coastal B.C. can be very rainy in winter, and even in high summer (July and Aug) rain and fog are not uncommon. However, it's never very cold due to offshore currents.

For up-to-date weather conditions, check out http://weatheroffice.ec.gc.ca or www.theweathernetwork.com.

Daily Mean Temperature & Total Precipitation for Vancouver, B.C.

	Jan	Feb	Mar	Apr	May	June	July	Aug	Sept	Oct	Nov	Dec
Temp (°F)	37	41	45	39	46	63	66	66	61	43	48	39
Temp (°C)	3	5	7	4	8	17	19	19	16	6	9	4
Precipitation (in.)	5.9	4.9	4.3	3.0	2.4	1.8	1.4	1.5	2.5	4.5	6.7	7.0

Daily Mean Temperature & Total Precipitation for Calgary, Alberta

	Jan	Feb	Mar	Apr	May	June	July	Aug	Sept	Oct	Nov	Dec
Temp (°F)	25	32	37	52	61	70	73	73	63	55	37	28
Temp (°C)	−4	0	3	11	16	21	23	23	17	13	3	−2
Precipitation (in.)	.5	.4	.6	1	2.1	3	2.8	1.9	1.9	.6	.5	.5

CALENDAR OF EVENTS

Canadians love a festival, and not even the chill of winter will keep them from celebrating. The Canadian festival calendar is jammed with events celebrating ethnic cultures, food and wine, historical events and characters, the arts, rodeos, music and theater, even salmon and whales. Following is a seasonal list of festival highlights from British Columbia and Alberta. Each community's special events are listed in the regional chapters that follow.

WINTER

Reino Keski-Salmi Loppet (www.skilarchhills.ca), January, held in Salmon Arm, is one of Canada's largest cross-country ski races.

TELUS Winter Classic (www.whistlerblackcomb.com), January, brings the world's top skiers and snowboarders, and lots of youthful energy, to Whistler.

SPRING

Pacific Rim Whale Festival (© 250/726-4641; www.pacificrimwhalefestival.org), March, celebrates the yearly return of up to 20,000 gray whales to the waters off Tofino and Ucluelet, Vancouver Island, B.C.

SUMMER

Calgary Stampede (© 800/661-1767; www.calgarystampede.com), July, the world's largest and richest rodeo, and Calgary's opportunity to celebrate its cowboy past.

Banff Summer Arts Festival (© 800/413-8368; www.banffcentre.ca), July and August, a celebration of classical and jazz music in the heart of the Canadian Rockies.

Vancouver Folk Festival (© 604/602-9798; www.thefestival.bc.ca), July, one of North America's top folk music events, Vancouver's festival brings Summer of Love musical stylings to a gorgeous bayside park.

Marine Festival (www.bathtubbing.com), in Nanaimo, in late July, is highlighted by the World Championship Bathtub Race, in which unusual watercraft (originally claw-foot bathtubs) motor from Nanaimo to Vancouver.

HSBC Celebration of Light (www.celebration-of-light.com), late July and early August, is a fireworks competition culminating with a huge pyrotechnical display accompanied by live music, all at Vancouver's English Bay Beach.

Edmonton International Fringe Festival (www.fringetheatreadventures.ca), August, is the world's second-largest fringe theater festival (after Edinburgh), offering over 1,000 performances in the Old Strathcona neighborhood.

FALL

Okanagan Wine Festival (© 250/861-6654; www.thewinefestivals.com), October, celebrates B.C.'s Okanagan Valley's fall harvest with wine tastings, winery open houses, and dining events.

Great Canadian Beer Festival (www.gcbf.com), November, brings the country's top brewers to Victoria.

For an exhaustive list of events beyond those listed here, check http://events.frommers.com, where you'll find a searchable, up-to-the-minute roster of what's happening in cities all over the world.

2 ENTRY REQUIREMENTS

PASSPORTS

All persons traveling between the United States and Canada are required to present a passport or other valid travel document. A birth certificate and photo ID are **no longer accepted** for crossing the border by land or sea, as of June 1, 2009.

Other valid travel documents include passport cards (a new high-tech identity card, which can speed up entry at U.S. land and sea ports of entry); enhanced driver's licenses; trusted traveler cards such as NEXUS, FAST, or SENTRI; a valid Merchant Mariner Document (MMD) when traveling in conjunction with official maritime business; or a valid U.S. Military identification card when traveling on official orders.

Permanent U.S. residents who aren't U.S. citizens must be prepared to present their Alien Registration Cards (green cards). If you plan to drive into Canada, be sure to bring your car's registration papers and proof of insurance.

Children under the age of 16 (or anyone under 19, if traveling with a school, religious group, or other youth group) need only present a birth certificate or naturalization certificate. Birth certificates can be an original, photocopy, or certified copy.

An important point: Any person under 18 traveling alone requires a letter from a parent or guardian granting him or her permission to travel to Canada. The letter must state the traveler's name and the duration of the trip. It's essential that teenagers carry proof of identity, usually a passport, though see the above website for alternatives; otherwise, their letter is useless at the border.

VISAS

Citizens of the U.S., most European countries, most former British colonies, and certain other countries (Israel, Korea, and Japan, for instance) do not need visas but must carry passports to enter Canada. Entry visas are required for citizens of more than 130 countries. Entry visas must be applied for and received from the Canadian embassy in your home country. For more information on entry requirements to Canada, see the Citizenship and Immigration website visitors' services page at **www.cic.gc.ca/english/visit/index.asp**.

CUSTOMS
What You Can Bring into Canada

Customs regulations are very generous in most respects but get pretty complicated when it comes to firearms, plants, meats, and pets. You can bring in free of duty up to 50 cigars, 200 cigarettes, and 200 grams (about a half-pound) of tobacco, providing you're over 18. Those of age (18 or 19, depending on the province) are also allowed about 1.15 liters (39 oz.) of liquor, 1.5 liters (51 oz.) of wine, or 24 355-milliliter (12-oz.) containers of beer or ale. Dogs, cats, and most pets can enter Canada with their owners, though you must have proof of rabies vaccinations within the last 36 months for pets over 3 months old.

Canada has complex requirements, restrictions, and limits that apply to importing meat, eggs, dairy products, fresh fruits and vegetables, and other food from around the world. You can avoid problems by not bringing such goods into Canada.

As for firearms, visitors can bring rifles into Canada during hunting season and for the purposes of hunting. Handguns and automatic rifles are generally not allowed. Fishing tackle poses no problems, but the bearer must possess a nonresident license for the province or territory where

Bringing Children into Canada

If you are traveling with children under age 18, you must carry identification for each child. Passports are best, though birth certificates are still accepted for children under 16. Divorced parents who share custody of their children should carry copies of the legal custody documents. Adults who are not parents or guardians should have written permission from the parents or guardians to supervise the children. When traveling with a group of vehicles, parents or guardians should travel in the same vehicle as the children when arriving at the border. Customs officers are looking for missing children and may ask questions about the children who are traveling with you.

he or she plans to use it. For a clear summary of Canadian rules, write for the booklet I Declare, issued by the Canada Border Service Agency (© 800/461-9999 within Canada, or 204/983-3500; www.cbsa-asfc.gc.ca). It's available as a download at www.cbsa-asfc.gc.ca/publications/pub/bsf5056-eng.html#P021.

What You Can Take Home from Canada

U.S. Citizens: Returning **U.S. citizens** who have been away for at least 48 hours are allowed to bring back, once every 30 days, US$800 worth of merchandise duty-free. You'll be charged a flat rate of 3% duty on the next US$1,000 worth of purchases. Be sure to have your receipts handy. With some exceptions, you cannot bring fresh fruits and vegetables into the United States. Travelers 18 and older are allowed to bring back 100 cigars, or 200 cigarettes duty-free, and those over 21 can bring back 1 liter of alcohol, as well. For specifics on what you can bring back and the corresponding fees, download the invaluable free pamphlet *Know Before You Go* online at **www.cbp.gov**. (Click on "Travel," and then click on "Know Before You Go!") Or contact the **U.S. Customs & Border Protection (CBP),** 1300 Pennsylvania Ave., NW, Washington, DC

20229 (© **877/287-8667;** www.cbp.gov), and request the pamphlet.

U.K. citizens returning from Canada have a Customs allowance of 200 cigarettes or 50 cigars or 250 grams of smoking tobacco; 2 liters of still table wine; 1 liter of spirits or strong liqueurs (over 22% volume); 2 liters of fortified wine, sparkling wine, or other liqueurs; 60cc (mL) perfume; 250cc (mL) of toilet water; and £145 worth of all other goods, including gifts and souvenirs. People under 17 cannot have the tobacco or alcohol allowance. For more information, contact **HM Customs & Excise** at © **0845/010-9000** (from outside the U.K., 020/8929-0152), or consult their website at www.hmce.gov.uk.

Australian Citizens: The duty-free allowance in Australia is A$900 or, for those under 18, A$450. Citizens can bring in 250 cigarettes or 250 grams of loose tobacco, and 2.25 liters of alcohol (for travelers 18 and older). If you're returning with valuables you already own, such as foreign-made cameras, you should file form B263. A helpful brochure available from Australian consulates or Customs offices is *Know Before You Go*. For more information, call the **Australian Customs Service** at © **1300/363-263,** or log on to www.customs.gov.au.

New Zealand Citizens: The duty-free allowance for New Zealand is NZ$700. Citizens over 17 can bring in 200 cigarettes, 50 cigars, or 250 grams of tobacco (or a mixture of all three if their combined weight doesn't exceed 250g), plus 4.5 liters of wine and beer, or 1.125 liters of liquor. New Zealand currency does not carry import or export restrictions. Fill out a certificate of export, listing the valuables you are taking out of the country; that way, you can bring them back without paying duty. Most questions are answered in a free pamphlet available at New Zealand consulates and Customs offices: *New Zealand Customs Guide for Travellers,*

Notice no. 4. For more information, contact **New Zealand Citizens: New Zealand Customs,** The Customhouse, 17–21 Whitmore St., Box 2218, Wellington (℃ **04/473-6099** or 0800/428-786; www.customs.govt.nz).

MEDICAL REQUIREMENTS

Unless you're arriving from an area known to be suffering from an epidemic (particularly cholera or yellow fever), inoculations or vaccinations are not required for entry into Canada. If you are traveling under a South African passport and intend to stay more than 6 months in Canada, you may be asked to pass a medical exam.

3 GETTING THERE & GETTING AROUND

GETTING TO B.C. & THE CANADIAN ROCKIES
By Plane

Western Canada is linked with the United States, Europe, Australia, and Asia by frequent nonstop flights. Calgary (YYC) and Vancouver (YRV) are the major air hubs; regional airlines connect to smaller centers.

Air Canada (℃ **888/247-2262;** www.aircanada.ca), Canada's dominant airline, has by far the most flights between the United States and Canada, and also offers service to the U.K. out of Calgary and Vancouver. Air Canada also has a number of partner airlines, such as **Air Canada Jazz,** that fly to secondary cities. Flights on these airlines can be booked from the main Air Canada website.

Most major U.S. carriers also fly daily between cities in Canada and the States—these include **American Airlines** (℃ 800/433-7300; www.aa.com), **Continental** (℃ 800/525-0280; www.continental.com), Delta (℃ 800/221-1212; www.delta.com), **Northwest** (℃ 800/447-4747; www.nwa.com), **United** (℃ 800/241-6522;

www.ual.com), and **US Airways** (℃ 800/428-4322; www.usair.com).

International airlines with nonstop service to Vancouver include **British Air** (℃ 800/247-9297 in the U.S. and Canada, 0845/773-3377 in the U.K.; www.ba.com), **KLM** (℃ 800/447-7747 in the U.S. and Canada for KLM partner Northwest Airlines), **Lufthansa** (℃ 800/581-6400 in Canada, 800/563-5954 in the U.S., or 0803/803-803 in Germany; www.lufthansa.com), and **SAS** (℃ 800/221-2350 in the U.S. or Canada; www.scandinavian.net). Asian airlines that fly into Vancouver include **China Airlines** (℃ 800/227-5118 or 604/682-6777 in Vancouver; www.china-airlines.com), **Cathay Pacific** (℃ 800/233-2742; www.cathay-usa.com), **Japan Air Lines** (℃ 800/525-3663; www.jal.com), and **Korean Air** (℃ 800/438-5000; www.koreanair.com). Additionally, **Air Canada** offers international flights from Mexico, most cities in northern Europe, and many centers in Asia. Canada's **Air Transat** (℃ 866/847-1112; www.airtransat.com) offers still more options from Europe and Latin

America. From the southern hemisphere, both **Qantas** (© 800/227-4500 in the U.S. and Canada; www.qantas.com) and **Air New Zealand** (© 800/663-5494; www.airnewzealand.ca), offer flights into Vancouver.

Calgary offers nonstop flights to a number of European cities, including London on Air Canada and British Air; Amsterdam on KLM and Air Transat; and Paris on Air Transat.

Another option is to fly into Seattle, Washington. Airfares are frequently less expensive to Seattle, and the difference in distance to destinations such as the Okanagan Valley, the Canadian Rockies, and Vancouver Island is negligible (driving from Seattle to Vancouver, for instance, takes about 2½ hr.). Seattle's **Sea-Tac Airport** has nonstop flights from London, Copenhagen, Frankfurt, Seoul, Tokyo, and Hong Kong, among other cities.

By Car

Because Canada and the U.S. share the longest open border on earth, it makes sense that many U.S.-based travelers will consider taking their own car to Canada as a road-trip destination. There are scores of border crossings between Canada and the U.S. (The U.S. freeway system enters at 13 different locations.) However, not all border crossings keep the same hours, and many are closed at night. Before you set off to cross the border at a remote location, ascertain if it will be open when you arrive there.

In addition to having the proper ID to cross into Canada, drivers may also be asked to provide proof of car insurance and show the car registration. If you're driving a rental car, you may be asked to show the rental agreement. It's always a good idea to clean your car of perishable foodstuff before crossing the border; fruit, vegetables, and meat products may be confiscated and may lead to a full search of the car. Remember that firearms are allowed across the border only in special

circumstances; handguns are almost completely outlawed.

Once in Canada, you'll find that roads are generally in good condition. There are two major highway routes that cross Canada east to west. **Hwy. 1,** which is largely four lanes, travels from Victoria on the Pacific to St. John's in Newfoundland, a total of 8,000km (4,971 miles)—with some ferries along the way. The **Yellowhead Highway (Hwy. 16)** links Winnipeg to Prince Rupert in B.C. along a more northerly route.

RENTAL CARS Canada has scores of rental-car companies, including **Hertz** (© 800/654-3001; www.hertz.com), **Avis** (© 800/331-1084; www.avis.com), **Dollar** (© 800/800-3665; www.dollar.com), **Thrifty** (© 800/847-4389; www.thrifty.com), **Budget** (© 800/527-0700 in the U.S., or 800/268-8900 in Canada; www.budget.com), **Enterprise** (© 800/261-7331; www.enterprise.com), and **National Car Rental** (© 877/222-9058; www.nationalcar.com). Nevertheless, rental vehicles tend to get tight during the tourist season, from around mid-May through August. It's a good idea to reserve a car as soon as you decide on your vacation.

Members of the **American Automobile Association (AAA)** should remember to take their membership cards since the **Canadian Automobile Association (CAA)** (© 800/222-4357; www.caa.ca) extends privileges to them in Canada.

By Train

Amtrak (© 800/USA-RAIL [872-7245]; www.amtrak.com) can get you into Canada at a few border points, where you can connect up with Canada's **VIA Rail** (© 888/VIA-RAIL [842-7245]; www.viarail.ca) system. On the West Coast, the *Cascades* runs from Eugene, Oregon, to Vancouver, British Columbia, with stops in Portland and Seattle. Amtrak-operated buses may also connect segments of these routes.

Amtrak and VIA Rail both offer a North American Railpass, which gives you 30 days of unlimited economy-class travel in the U.S. and Canada. Remember that the Railpass doesn't include meals; you can buy meals on the train or carry your own food.

The problem with traveling on VIA Rail, particularly in western Canada, is that the train runs only 3 days a week. If you want to link your visit between destinations in Alberta and B.C. with a train journey, you may be out of luck unless your schedule is very flexible. Also, if sightseeing, and not just transport, is part of your vacation agenda, then you may also find that your train journey takes place overnight. Because of the way the train is scheduled in many parts of rural Canada, there's just one schedule per train, so the leg between Winnipeg and Edmonton, for instance, will always be overnight, no matter which train you take.

By Bus

Greyhound (*C* **800/661-8747** in Canada, www.greyhound.ca; in the U.S. *C* 800/231-2222, www.greyhound.com) operates the major intercity bus system in Canada. In recent years, several of the Greyhound routes between the U.S. and Canada have been terminated. The only international route still in operation in the West is the crossing between Seattle and Vancouver.

International visitors intending to travel across Canada (and/or the U.S.) should consider the **Greyhound North American Discovery Pass.** The pass, which offers unlimited travel and stopovers in the U.S. and Canada, can be obtained from foreign travel agents or through www.discoverypass.com.

By Boat

Ocean ferries operate from Seattle, Anacortes, and Port Angeles, Washington, to Victoria, British Columbia. For details, see the relevant chapters.

GETTING AROUND

B.C. in particular has an admirable public transportation system, and it would be possible to see most of the sites covered by this guide by linking buses, trains, and ferries—actually a very pleasant prospect. However, having your own wheels will increase your options.

By Plane

It's actually cheaper now to fly between Canadian cities than take the bus or train, as deregulation has resulted in a number of excellent new airlines that offer no-frills but perfectly comfortable air travel. These airlines rely on the Internet to create savings in booking flights and other information gathering, so you'll want Internet access to learn about these flights. **WestJet** (*C* **888/937-8538;** www.westjet.com) offers the largest service area, with flights spanning the country from Victoria to St. John's.

In addition to Air Canada flights between major western Canadian cities, the regional **Air Canada Jazz** (*C* **888/247-2262;** www.flyjazz.ca) flies to smaller centers. Regularly scheduled floatplane service links Victoria and Vancouver harbors, and many island communities in the Strait of Georgia; see those chapters for more information.

By Car

Canadian highways are well maintained, and most are open year-round. For instance, Hwy. 1, which links Vancouver to Calgary, and the Icefields Parkway, which links Lake Louise and Jasper, are both open all winter long. Even though Canada is a major oil producer, you'll find that gasoline there is generally more expensive than in the U.S.

DRIVING RULES Wearing seat belts is compulsory for all passengers. Children under 5 must be in child restraints. Motorcyclists must wear helmets. In British Columbia and Alberta, it's legal to turn right at a red light after you've come to a full stop. Pedestrians have the right of way. The speed limit on express routes (limited-access highways) ranges from 62 to 68 mph (100–110kmph). Drivers must carry proof of insurance at all times.

By Train

In addition to the transcontinental VIA Rail, Vancouver Island offers the **Malahat,** a passenger train that makes a daily run between Victoria and Courtenay. This is a rather charming way to progress up and down the eastern shores of Vancouver Island, and it's easy to link to ferries to make loop trips along the B.C. coast. Another marvelous B.C. route is the **Skeena,** which links Prince Rupert on the Pacific with Jasper, in the Canadian Rockies. For information on both, contact **VIA Rail** (*C* **888/VIA-RAIL** [842-7245]; www.viarail.ca).

By Bus

While many Americans may not relish the option of traveling by bus while in Canada, in fact **Greyhound Canada** (*C* **800/661-8747;** www.greyhound.ca) offers far superior service and coverage than does Greyhound in the U.S. Not only are the buses newer and cleaner, and the bus stations better kept up than in the U.S., but

Greyhound is also often the only option for land transport in many parts of Canada due to the relatively minimal coverage by VIA Rail.

Greyhound and its affiliates provide the primary transportation infrastructure among communities in British Columbia. On Vancouver Island, a number of private carriers also offer services, particularly on the run between Victoria and Tofino.

In the Canadian Rockies, **Brewster Transportation** (*C* **866/606-6700** or 403/762-6700) offers bus transport among Calgary, Banff, and Jasper in addition to running tours.

By Boat

BC Ferries (*C* **888/223-3779** or 250/386-3431; www.bcferries.com) operates an extensive car and passenger ferry network along the British Columbia coast. These ferries link the B.C. mainland to Vancouver Island, and also provide service to dozens of smaller island communities. Also notable is the Inland Passage route, which links Port Hardy on the northern tip of Vancouver Island with Prince Rupert, just south of the Alaska Panhandle. This service can be joined with other public transport options to make a really great loop around B.C.

4 MONEY & COSTS

The Value of the Canadian Dollar vs. Other Popular Currencies

C$	US$	UK£	Euro €	A$	NZ$
1.00	0.94	0.59	0.67	1.05	1.33

Frommer's lists exact prices in the local currency. The currency conversions quoted above were correct at press time. However, rates fluctuate, so before departing consult a currency exchange website such as **www.oanda.com/convert/classic** to check up-to-the-minute rates.

Prices for goods and services are comparable between Canada and the U.S.—particularly now that the Canadian dollar is largely at par with its U.S. counterpart. On a day-to-day basis, traveling in Canada will cost about the same as traveling in the U.S., as long as restraint is used when making hotel and dining selections. European travelers using euros and the British pound will find that Canadian prices for comparable goods and services are generally lower than those in their home countries.

CURRENCY

Canadian currency is counted in dollars and cents, just like the currency system in the U.S. However, in addition to pennies, nickels, dimes, and quarters, there are one- and two-dollar coins (there are no dollar or two-dollar bills). Dollar coins are bronze-plated coins and bear the picture of a loon—hence their nickname "loonies." There's also a two-toned $2 coin sometimes referred to as a "toonie." Paper currency begins with $5 bills.

Exchanging currency is pretty straightforward, particularly if you are changing U.S. dollars into Canadian. The easiest way to procure Canadian currency is simply to withdraw money from an ATM, which are as omnipresent as they are in the U.S.

Often, Canadian businesses will accept U.S. dollars in payment, making the currency value exchange, if any, at the till.

It's always advisable to bring money in a variety of forms on a vacation: a mix of cash, credit cards, and traveler's checks. You should also exchange enough petty cash to cover airport incidentals, tipping, and transportation to your hotel before you leave home, or withdraw money upon arrival at an airport ATM.

5 HEALTH

STAYING HEALTHY
General Availability of Health Care

Canada's healthcare system is similar to that in the U.S. except that health insurance for Canadian citizens is managed nationally by the federal government. Hospitals, clinics, and pharmacies are as common as in the U.S. and western Europe. Contact the **International Association for Medical Assistance to Travelers (IAMAT)** (© **716/754-4883** or, in Canada, 416/652-0137; www.iamat.org) for tips on travel and health concerns in Canada. **Travel Health Online** (www.tripprep.com), sponsored by a consortium of travel-medicine practitioners, also offers helpful advice on traveling abroad. You can find listings of reliable medical clinics overseas at the **International Society of Travel Medicine** (www.istm.org).

WHAT TO DO IF YOU GET SICK AWAY FROM HOME

Canadian hospitals have emergency rooms open 24 hours for emergency care. In addition, most cities also have walk-in clinics where nonemergency treatment is available.

Pharmacies are common, and most large cities have at least one 24-hour operation. You'll have no trouble having prescriptions filled; in fact, you may note that prescription drugs are substantially cheaper in Canada than in the U.S. Also, certain drugs are available over-the-counter in Canada that are available only by prescription in the U.S.

In most cases, your existing health plan will provide the coverage you need, though you may need to pay upfront and request reimbursement later. But double-check; you may want to buy **travel medical insurance** instead. Bring your insurance ID card with you when you travel.

If you require additional medical insurance, try **MEDEX Assistance** (℃ 410/453-6300; www.medexassist.com) or **Travel Assistance International** (℃ 800/821-2828; www.travelassistance.com; for general information on services, call the company's **Worldwide Assistance Services, Inc.,** at ℃ 800/777-8710).

We list additional **emergency numbers** in "Fast Facts," chapter 17.

6 SAFETY

Canada is one of the least violent countries on Earth—at least off the hockey ice. Using common sense, most travelers should experience few if any threatening situations during a trip to Canada. In fact, most Canadians are unfailingly polite and helpful.

The weather and wildlife are probably a greater threat to the average traveler than violence from other human beings. If driving in winter, be sure to carry traction devices such as tire chains in your vehicle, plus plenty of warm clothes and a sleeping bag.

Wildlife is really only dangerous if you put yourself into their habitat in the wrong place at the wrong time. Elk can often seem tame, particularly those that live near human civilization. However, during calving season, mother elk can mistake your doting attention as an imminent attack on her newborn. Hiking trails are often closed to hikers during calving season, so be sure to obey all trail postings.

Moose are more dangerous, as they are truly massive and when surprised are apt to charge first and ask questions later. Give a moose plenty of room, and resist the temptation to feed them snacks. Chances are they will come looking for more.

Bears are the most dangerous wilderness denizens to humans. Canada is home to grizzly bears, one of the largest carnivores in North America, and to black bears, a smaller, less fearsome cousin (unless you're traveling along the polar ice floes, you're extremely unlikely to see a polar bear). Grizzly bears tend to keep their distance from humans, preferring mountain meadows to human garbage dumps. However, black bears can coexist much more readily with humans, and in some ways pose a more persistent threat. Never come between a bear and its cub, or its food source. Never hike alone in the back woods, and if camping keep food items away from tents.

7 SPECIALIZED TRAVEL RESOURCES

In addition to the destination-specific resources listed below, please visit Frommers.com for additional specialized travel resources.

GAY & LESBIAN TRAVELERS

Canada is one of the most gay-tolerant travel destinations in the world. Witness the fact that gay marriage is legal in Canada and that the entire nation has nondiscrimination protection for gays and lesbians. While not every rural village is ready for the circuit party set, most gay travelers will encounter little adversity.

A good clearinghouse for information on gay Canada is the website **www.gaycanada.com**, which features news and links to gay-owned or -friendly accommodations and businesses across Canada.

Most disabilities shouldn't stop anyone from traveling. There are more options and resources for travelers with disabilities than ever before.

A clearinghouse of official Canadian federal government information on disability issues, including those related to travel and transportation, is available from Persons with Disabilities Online, **www.pwd-online.ca**. The Canadian Paraplegic Association (🕾 **613/723-1033;** www.canparaplegic.org) can offer advice for travelers with limited mobility as well as address issues for those with spinal cord injuries or other physical disabilities. From the national website, you can click to find provincial organizations.

Organizations that offer a vast range of resources and assistance to travelers with disabilities include **MossRehab** (🕾 **800/CALL-MOSS** [225-5/667]; www.mossresourcenet.org); the **American Foundation for the Blind** (AFB; 🕾 **800/232-5463;** www.afb.org); and **SATH** (Society for Accessible Travel & Hospitality) (🕾 **212/447-7284;** www.sath.org).

Access-Able Travel Source (🕾 **303/232-2979;** www.access-able.com) offers a comprehensive database on travel agents from around the world with experience in accessible travel; destination-specific access information; and links to such resources as service animals, equipment rentals, and access guides.

Many travel agencies offer customized tours and itineraries for travelers with disabilities. Among them are **Flying Wheels Travel** (🕾 **507/451-5005;** www.flyingwheelstravel.com); and **Accessible Journeys** (🕾 **800/846-4537** or 610/521-0339; www.disabilitytravel.com).

The "Accessible Travel" link at **MobilityAdvisor.com** (www.mobility-advisor.com) offers a variety of travel resources to people with limited mobility.

British travelers should contact **Tourism for All** (🕾 **0845/124-9971** in the U.K. only; www.tourismforall.org.uk) to access a wide range of travel information and resources for seniors and travelers with disabilities.

FAMILY TRAVEL

Destinations such as the Canadian Rockies are especially attractive for families, as outfitters make it easy to arrange guided hiking, biking, white-water rafting, and horseback riding adventures simply by talking to your hotel's concierge. Outfitters on the Pacific coast provide opportunities to learn to sea kayak or to journey out onto the seas to view marine wildlife, while the Rockies' foothills and the B.C. interior feature guest ranches and Old West activities.

Remember that even children traveling with parents will be required to have some sort of official ID. This can either be a passport or a birth certificate. Children under the age of 18 traveling alone to Canada will need to have a signed letter from parents.

To locate accommodations, restaurants, and attractions that are particularly kid-friendly, refer to the **"Kids" icon** throughout this guide.

If your travel plans take you to Vancouver, consider buying a copy of *Frommer's Vancouver with Kids* (Wiley Publishing, Inc.).

SENIOR TRAVEL

Mention the fact that you're a senior while traveling in Canada, and frequently you can receive discounted admission prices to cultural and tourist attractions. In most of Canada, people age 65 and older qualify for reduced admission to theaters, museums, and other attractions, as well as discounted fares on public transportation. It is less common to receive discounts on lodging, though it does happen, so it is worth asking when you make your lodging reservations.

Members of **AARP,** 601 E St. NW, Washington, DC 20049 (© **888/687-2277;** www.aarp.org), get discounts on hotels, airfares, and car rentals. Anyone 50 or older can join.

Many reliable agencies and organizations target the 50-plus market. **Exploritas** (formerly Elderhostel, © **800/454-5768;** www.exploritas.org) arranges worldwide study programs for those aged 55 and over. **ElderTreks** (© **800/741-7956** or 416/558-5000 outside North America; www.eldertreks.com) offers small-group tours to off-the-beaten-path or adventure-travel locations, restricted to travelers 50 and older.

8 SUSTAINABLE TOURISM

Although one could make the case that any journey that includes travel in a car or airplane can't truly be "green," there are several ways that you can make your trip to western Canada more sustainable. The **Hotel Association of Canada** (© **613/237-7149;** www.hotelassociation.ca) offers a voluntary program called the Green Key Program (www.greenkeyglobal.com) that recognizes hotels and lodgings that are taking steps to reduce environmental impacts. Lodgings are rated from one to five Green Keys based on their performance in such areas as energy and water conservation, land use, and environmental management.

Canadagreentravel.com is another reference for green accommodations, activities, and restaurants in Canada.

In addition, both B.C. and the Canadian Rockies offer eco-tourism opportunities that join adventure and recreation with sustainable travel practices. **Ecotour** (www.ecotourdirectory.com) is a Web directory that provides listings for eco-tourism operators in Canada (and around the world).

Another valuable website is **www.green livingonline.com**, which offers extensive content on how to travel sustainably, including a travel and transport section and profiles of the best green shops and services in Toronto, Vancouver, and Calgary.

9 ACTIVE VACATION PLANNER

See the individual destination chapters for specific details on how and where to enjoy the activities below.

BIKING Most of western Canada's highways are wide and well maintained, and thus well suited for long-distance bicycle touring. Most resort areas offer rentals (it's a good idea to call ahead and reserve a bike).

While most hiking trails are closed to mountain bikes, other trails are developed specifically for backcountry biking. Ask at national park and national forest information centers for a map of mountain-bike trails.

Probably the most rewarding biking anywhere is in Banff and Jasper national parks. The Icefields Parkway is an eye-popping route that leads past soaring peaks and glaciers.

CANOEING & KAYAKING Low-lying lakes and rivers form vast waterway systems across the land. Multiday canoeing trips make popular summer and early fall expeditions; you'll see lots of wildlife and keep as gentle a pace as you like. The Bowron Lakes in the Cariboo Country make an excellent weeklong paddle through wilderness.

DIVING An amazing array of marine life flourishes amid the 2,000 shipwrecks off the coast of British Columbia. Divers visit the area year-round to see the Pacific Northwest's unique underwater fauna and flora, and to swim among the ghostly remains of 19th-century whaling ships and 20th-century schooners.

The Pacific Rim National Park's Broken Group Islands are home to a multitude of sea life; the waters off the park's West Coast Trail are known as "the graveyard of the Pacific" for the hundreds of shipwrecks. Nanaimo and Campbell River, on Vancouver Island, are both centers for numerous dive outfitters.

FISHING Angling is enjoyed across western Canada. However, the famed salmon fisheries along the Pacific Coast face highly restricted catch limits in most areas, and outright bans on fishing in others. Not all salmon species are threatened, though, and rules governing fishing change quickly, so check locally with outfitters to find out if a season will open while you're visiting. Trout are found throughout the region, some reaching great size in the lakes in the British Columbia interior.

Fishing in Canada is regulated by local governments or tribes, and appropriate licenses are necessary. Angling for some fish is regulated by season; in some areas, catch-and-release fishing is enforced. Be sure to check with local authorities before casting your line.

If you're looking for a great fishing vacation with top-notch accommodations, contact **Oak Bay Marine Group,** 1327 Beach Dr., Victoria (© **800/663-7090** or 250/598-3366; www.obmg.com), which operates nine different resorts. Three are on Vancouver Island; the other lodges are on remote islands and fjords along the north coast.

HIKING Almost every national and provincial park in western Canada is webbed with trails, ranging from easy nature hikes to long-distance backcountry trails. Late summer and early fall are good times to visit, since trails in the high country may be snowbound until July. For many people, the Canadian Rockies, with their abundance of parks and developed trail systems, provide the country's finest hiking. Before setting out, request hiking and trail information from the parks and buy a good map.

HORSEBACK RIDING Holidays on horseback have a long history in western Canada, and most outfitters and guest ranches offer a variety of options. Easiest are half-day rides on an easygoing horse, with sufficient instruction to make you feel comfortable no matter what your previous riding ability. Multiday pack trips take riders off into the backcountry, with lodging in tents or at rustic camps. These trips are best for those who don't mind roughing it: You'll probably go a day or two without showers and end up saddle sore and sunburned. The Canadian Rockies in Alberta and the Cariboo district in B.C. are filled with guest ranches offering a wide range of horseback activities.

SEA KAYAKING One of the best places to practice sea kayaking is in the sheltered bays, islands, and inlets along the coast of British Columbia; kayaks are especially good for wildlife-viewing. Most coastal towns have rentals, instruction, and guided trips. Handling a kayak isn't as easy as it looks, and you'll want to have plenty of experience in sheltered coves before heading out into the surf. Be sure to check the tide schedule and weather forecast before setting out, as well as what the coastal rock formations are. You'll need to be comfortable on the water and ready to get wet, as well as be a strong swimmer.

SKIING Canada, a mountainous country with heavy snowfall, is one of the world's top ski destinations. Both downhill and cross-country skiing are open to all ages, though downhill skiing carries a higher price tag: A day on the slopes, with rental gear and lift ticket, can easily top C$150.

For downhill skiing, the Canadian Rockies and the Winter-Olympics-vetted Whistler/Blackcomb resort near Vancouver are the primary destinations. Readers of *Condé Nast Traveler* repeatedly award Whistler/Blackcomb the title of best ski resort in North America.

The 1988 Winter Olympics were held at Nakiska, just outside Banff National Park, and the park itself is home to three other ski areas. If you're just learning to ski, then the easier slopes at Banff's Mount Norquay are made to order. Almost all downhill areas also offer groomed cross-country ski trails. Canmore Nordic Centre, in Alberta, was the site of the 1988 Olympic cross-country competition, and is now open to the public.

WHITE-WATER RAFTING Charging down a mountain river in a rubber raft is one of the most popular adventures for many people visiting Canada's western mountains. Trips range from daylong excursions, which demand little of a participant other than sitting tight, to long-distance trips through remote backcountry. Risk doesn't correspond to length of trip: Individual rapids and water conditions can make even a short trip a real adventure. You should be comfortable in water, and a good swimmer, if you're floating an adventurous river.

Jasper National Park is a major center for short yet thrilling white-water trips. Another excellent destination is the Kicking Horse River near Golden, British Columbia.

10 ESCORTED GENERAL-INTEREST TOURS

Brewster Transportation and Tours, P.O. Box 1140, Banff, AB T0L 0C0 (© 877/791-5500; www.brewster.ca), offers a wide variety of tours throughout the Canadian Rockies, both escorted and independent. Their offerings include motorcoach and train excursions, ski and other winter vacations, city and resort combination packages, chartered day tours by bus, and independent driving tours. Highlights include a visit to the Columbia Icefield in Jasper National Park. Many packages in the Rockies include stays at guest ranches.

Travel by train lets you see the Rockies as you never would in a bus or behind the wheel of a car. The **Rocky Mountaineer Vacations,** 1150 Station St., First Floor, Vancouver, BC V6A 2X7 (© 877/460-3200; www.rockymountaineer.com), bills its *Rocky Mountaineer* as "The Most Spectacular Train Trip in the World." During daylight hours between mid-April and mid-October, this sleek blue-and-white train winds past foaming waterfalls, ancient glaciers, towering snowcapped peaks, and roaring mountain streams. The *Rocky Mountaineer* gives you the options of traveling east from Vancouver; traveling west from Jasper, Calgary, or Banff; or taking round-trips. Another rail service offers travel to/from Vancouver and Jasper via Whistler and Quesnel.

John Steel Railtours (© 800/988-5778 or fax 604/886-2100; www.johnsteel.com) offers both escorted and independent tour packages, many through the Rockies and the West and a few in other regions, which combine train and other forms of travel. VIA Rail operates the train portions of John Steel tours. Packages run from 5 to 12 days, at all times of year, depending on the route, and combine stays in major cities and national parks.

For more information on escorted general-interest tours, including questions to ask before booking your trip, see www.frommers.com/planning.

3

TELEPHONES

The Canadian phone system is exactly the same as the system in the United States. Canadian phone numbers have 10 digits: The first three numbers are the area code, which corresponds to a province or division thereof, plus a seven-digit local number. To call a number within the same locality, usually all you have to dial is the seven-digit local number. If you're making a long-distance call (out of the area or province), you need to precede the local number with "1" plus the area code.

For directory assistance: Dial 411 if you're looking for a number inside Canada or the U.S. Fees for these directory assistance calls range from C$1.50 to C$3.50. You can get the same service for free by dialing 1-800/FREE-411 (473-3411). If you're looking for a business phone number, try 1-800/GOOG-411 (466-4411), a free service from Google. For international directory assistance, dial "00" and ask for the international directory assistance operator. These calls cost C$7.95 plus taxes each. It is free to use Web-based phone directories, such as www.whitepages.com or www.anywho.com, to research phone numbers.

Toll-free numbers: Numbers beginning with 800, 888, 877, and 866 within Canada are toll-free.

CELLPHONES

The good news for most U.S. travelers with cellphones: Your phones will probably work just fine in Canada. Call your service provider to make certain, but nearly all U.S. providers have reciprocal relationships with national Canadian networks. Calls on a U.S. phone using a Canadian network can be expensive, however, usually more than the standard roaming charges incurred within the U.S.

For cellphone users from Asia, Australia, and Europe, the situation is a bit more complicated. The three letters that define much of the world's wireless capabilities are **GSM** (Global System for Mobile Communications), a seamless network that makes for easy cross-border cellphone use throughout Europe and dozens of other countries worldwide. In Canada and the U.S., however, the typical cellular network operates on the CDMA protocol, which is incompatible with GSM phones.

However, visitors to the Vancouver and Lower Mainland with GSM cellphones are in luck. As part of the infrastructure buildout for the 2010 Winter Olympics, all three major Canadian cellular phone services providers (Rogers, Bell Mobility, and Telus) have unveiled GSM networks. So visitors with GSM phones should be able to make and receive calls and obtain data services anywhere in the Vancouver area and in other urban areas in B.C. GSM services are also available in much of Alberta, including Calgary and Edmonton. Cellphone service in general is sketchy in the Rockies.

If you have never used your GSM phone internationally before, you may want to contact your service provider in advance. Just call your wireless operator and ask for "international roaming" to be activated on your account. Unfortunately, per-minute charges can be high in Canada.

For some, **renting** a phone when visiting Canada may be a good idea. A quick search of the Internet reveals many cellphone rental companies that provide service in Canada, including Cellular Abroad (✆ **800/287-5072;** www.cellularabroad. com) and Planet Omni (✆ **877/327-5076;** www.planetomni.com). Cellphone rental charges begin at C$18 to C$24 a week, but fees can quickly mount as you'll also need to buy a SIM card and pay for outgoing calls. To rent a phone, you'll need to contact the rental company in advance of your departure and await the arrival of your phone.

Buying a phone once you arrive in Canada can be more economically attractive. Two of Canada's largest carriers, Rogers (www.shoprogers.com) and Telus Mobility (www.telusmobility.com) offer pay-as-you-go plans, which don't require users to sign up for lengthy contracts.

INTERNET & E-MAIL

The vast majority of Canadian hotels, resorts, airports, cafes, and retailers offer **Wi-Fi** (wireless fidelity) services. It's usually free, but sometimes a small fee is charged for usage.

To find public Wi-Fi hotspots at your destination, go to **www.jiwire.com**; its Hotspot Finder holds the world's largest directory of public wireless hotspots.

For dial-up access, most business-class hotels also offer dataports for high-speed wired access. If you're uncertain about Wi-Fi access, be sure to bring a **connection kit** of the right power and phone adapters, a spare phone cord, and a spare Ethernet network cable—or find out whether your hotel supplies them to guests. (Both phone and electrical cables in Canada are exactly the same as in the U.S.)

If you're not traveling with your own laptop or mobile device, you'll find that most hotels will have a computer terminal with Internet access available for customer use. Cybercafes and public libraries are other options for computer access. To find a cybercafe, try www.cybercafe.com.

4

Suggested Itineraries in British Columbia & the Canadian Rockies

Canada's two westernmost provinces are not only large, but they are also packed with amazing must-see scenery and destinations. The following itineraries focus on the top areas covered by this book: the Canadian Rockies, and especially Banff and Jasper national parks; Vancouver, Victoria, the Pacific coast, and the islands of British Columbia; and the route between these areas. Many travelers make the journey between the Canadian Rockies and Vancouver in a couple days of driving, but there are very good reasons to slow down and linger in B.C.'s highly photogenic interior, particularly if you're a golfer or wine aficionado.

1 THE CANADIAN ROCKIES IN 1 WEEK

An outdoor-oriented exploration of the gateway cities and national parks of the Rockies can begin in either Calgary or Edmonton—simply reverse this itinerary to begin in Alberta's capital.

Day ❶: Exploring Calgary

Take a day to explore Calgary, the energetic city that Albertan oil built, beginning at the Eau Claire Market and the adjacent **Prince's Island Park** (p. 344). The **Stephen Avenue** area (p. 345), about all that remains of the city's historic downtown, is now a pedestrian area and home to many restaurants, street performers, and nightclubs. The **Glenbow Museum** (p. 344), one of Canada's top art and cultural institutions, is also here, and is a good destination if the weather turns.

If you have kids along, consider a visit to the **Canada Olympic Park** (p. 342), where some of the competition for the 1988 Winter Olympics took place. In addition to visiting the top of the ski jump platform, you can also take a ride down the luge slope year-round.

Days ❷ & ❸: Banff & Environs

From Calgary, follow Hwy. 1 W. toward the Rockies. Within an hour, you'll pass beneath the soaring peaks at Canmore and enter **Banff National Park** (chapter 16). **Banff Townsite** (chapter 16) is filled with grand hotels, modern lodges, B&B inns, plus innumerable restaurants and pubs. You could easily spend most of a day just exploring the town, particularly if you like to shop. However, you'll also want to spend another day exploring the natural sites around Banff, which include boat tours on **Lake Minnewanka** (p. 387), float trips down the **Bow River** (p. 385), day-hiking **Johnston Canyon** (p. 384), and riding the gondola to the top of **Sulphur Mountain** (p. 387).

Day ❹: Lake Louise

Although just an hour to the west of Banff, **Lake Louise** (p. 396) is its own destination. Explore the lake, with its fantastic château-style hotel going eye-to-eye with a glacier. Hiking trails lead to the toe of the glacier where you can replenish yourself with tea and scones at a wilderness teahouse. In the next valley over, Moraine Lake is perhaps even more dramatic, with 10 spirelike peaks rising above a placid lake. The year-round **gondola** at Lake Louise Ski Resort transports hikers to alpine meadows (p. 396). (From Lake Louise, road trippers with a westering urge can follow Hwy. 1 over the Rockies' Kicking Horse Pass and head toward Vancouver; see next itinerary.)

Day ❺: Traveling the Icefield Parkway

It will take a full day to travel the phenomenal **Icefields Parkway** between Lake Louise and Jasper (p. 399), which crosses Sunwapta Pass beneath the massive Columbia Icefields. Stop to view waterfalls, hike to hidden lakes, and have tea at mountain lodges. Explore the Columbia Icefield, at the very crest of the Rockies, aboard specially built Snocoaches, which can safely venture out onto the surface of the icefield.

Day ❻: Jasper & Environs

The town of **Jasper** (p. 402) doesn't offer the alpine shopping mall experience of

Banff, so after strolling through the small town center, head out on a hiking or biking trail to explore the mountains—trails start right in town. Driving to **Maligne Lake** (p. 404) for a boat tour of the Canadian Rockies' largest glacier lake is another option, as is signing up for a white-water raft trip on one of the area's many rivers. If you're a golfer, the course at Jasper Park Lodge is among the most noted in Canada.

Day ❼: Edmonton

Leave the park by heading east on the Yellowhead Highway to **Edmonton,** Alberta's capital (p. 356). Spend the afternoon exploring the city's trendy **Old Strathcona** neighborhood (p. 360), the domed **legislative building** (p. 358), and the art gallery district around High Street. Spend your final evening in Alberta in one of Edmonton's excellent restaurants. In the morning, return to Calgary via Hwy. 2 to catch your flight back home.

2 THE BACK ROADS OF INTERIOR B.C. IN 1 WEEK

Don't just zoom between the Canadian Rockies and Vancouver—take time to explore the significantly less crowded Purcell and Selkirk mountains, the Okanagan wine country, and detour through Whistler on your way to Vancouver.

Day ❶: Exploring B.C.'s Mountain Parks

Savvy outdoor enthusiasts know that just west of crowded Banff and Jasper parks are three much less busy but equally stunning national parks, Yoho, Glacier, and Revelstoke. From Lake Louise, follow Hwy. 1 west over the Continental Divide, where **Yoho National Park** (p. 413) offers Canada's second-highest waterfall, **Glacier National Park** (p. 319) features hiking trails to the base of icefields, and Revelstoke boasts the **Meadows in the Sky Parkway** (p. 318), leading to flower-spangled alpine meadows. Spend the night in the charming mountain town of **Revelstoke** (p. 312).

Days ❷ & ❸: The Okanagan Wine Country

Head west from Revelstoke, then drop south on Hwy. 97A at Sicamous. The landscape quickly changes from lush forests to arid desert highlands. The **Okanagan Valley** (chapter 13), filled with 128km-long (80-mile) Okanagan Lake, is

a fruit-growing paradise now famous for its burgeoning wine industry. After arriving in **Kelowna** (p. 302), relax at the city's sandy lake beachfront and check out the bustling restaurant scene. The following day, explore the valley's more than 100 **wineries** (p. 295), many of them south of Kelowna toward Penticton. The same irrigation that supports wine grapes sprinkles golf courses—some of B.C.'s top courses overlook Okanagan Lake.

Day ❹: West to Whistler

This is a road-trip day, starting on the so-called Peachland Connector (Hwy. 97C) that connects the Okanagan Valley to Merritt. From Merritt, leave the freeway and follow secondary roads to **Lillooet** (p. 274). At this historic town on the Fraser River begins one of the most dramatic mountain roads in British Columbia, climbing up the Cayoosh Valley, cresting the Coastal Mountains, and dropping into Whistler, one of the continent's top mountain resorts.

Days ❺ & ❻: Whistler

Whistler (see chapter 10) gained its fame as a ski destination—there's a reason that the 2010 Winter Olympics ski events were held at the exemplary **Whistler/Blackcomb Resort** (p. 231)—but today Whistler is as busy in summer as winter. If you're a shopper, exploring the shops in **Whistler Village** (p. 236) can take most of a day, and with four championship golf courses nearby, duffers will find plenty of challenges. In summer, there's **glacier skiing** through August (p. 231), and hiking and biking trails start at the village edge. **Nightlife** in Whistler is very lively (p. 245), with a **dining** scene (p. 242) to rival Vancouver's.

Day ❼: Drive to Vancouver

From Whistler, Hwy. 99 drops from mountain heights to sea level along the scenic **Sea-to-Sky Highway** (p. 228), before entering Vancouver from the north.

3 THE WILD & THE SOPHISTICATED ON VANCOUVER ISLAND IN 1 WEEK

Vancouver Island is home to rugged, nearly inaccessible rainforests and wilderness coastlines; the island also offers very sophisticated dining and lodging, often in the remote backcountry itself. This is the allure of exploring coastal British Columbia: After a challenging day sea-kayaking remote archipelagoes or hiking old-growth forest, you return to three-star lodging and dining.

Day ❶: The Gulf Islands

Begin your journey in Vancouver, driving to the ferry terminal at Tsawwassen to cross to the **Gulf Islands** (see chapter 7). BC Ferries links to five of these charmingly rural islands, and which island you choose will depend on your interests and inclinations. We recommend Salt Spring Island for its broad range of facilities and multiple ferry routes.

Day ❷: Duncan & the Cowichan Valley

Catch the morning **BC Ferries** (p. 132) run to Vancouver Island (from Salt Spring Island, take the Vesuvius/Crofton ferry) and travel north to **Duncan and the Cowichan Valley** (see chapter 7). This beautiful agricultural area is home to excellent wineries and organic farms and dairies. Just outside Duncan, the **Quw'utsun' Cultural Centre** (p. 158) preserves native Cowichan traditional ways of life, and downtown Duncan is studded with totem poles.

Days ❸, ❹ & ❺: Tofino

From Duncan, drive north to Parksville and the junction with Hwy. 4. This road to Tofino and Vancouver Island's wild west coast is long and windy, so allow 3 hours to make the journey from Parksville. However, Tofino and the **Long Beach** portion of the Pacific Rim National Park (p. 181) are certainly worth the journey. Outfitters make it simple to get out onto calm and isolated bays on sea kayaks—a popular trip crosses a sound to visit a natural **hot springs** (p. 188). Rainforest **hikes,** deep-sea **fishing** trips, ocean **wildlife**-viewing tours, and lingering on the splendid sandy **beaches** are other options (p. 187).

The B&Bs and lodges in Tofino are first-rate. Many are nestled above remote beaches at the edge of the forest; others cling to rocky headlands. Some of Vancouver Island's most notable restaurants are here, and the local seafood is exquisite.

Legend:
1. Gulf Islands
2. Duncan
3. Parksville
4. Long Beach (Pacific Rim Nat'l Park)
5. Tofino
6. Courtenay
7. The Sunshine Coast

Day ⑥: Courtenay

Cross back to the east side of Vancouver Island from Tofino, but turn north at Parksville and drive up Hwy. 19 to the twin cities of **Courtenay** and **Comox** (see chapter 8). If you have kids in tow, consider signing them up for a fossil dig tour with the local museum; golfers might play a round on the excellent local course, while the eco-minded will relish a sunset kayak tour on the wildlife-rich Courtenay River estuary.

Day ⑦: Returning to Vancouver

The following day, cross from Comox via BC Ferries to the mainland and Powell River, and journey to Vancouver along the scenic **Sunshine Coast** (see chapter 10).

This tour is meant to show off Vancouver as a whole, giving you an overview of what makes it so uniquely appealing. There are some places where you'll be exploring on foot, others where you'll drive to reach your destination. Nature, art, culture, and coffee are all part of today's itinerary. **Start:** Tourism Vancouver Touristinfo Centre, Burrard and Cordova streets.

❶ Canada Place

Start your day outside, on the upper (deck) level of the city's giant **convention center** and **cruise-ship terminal** (p. 62), which juts out into Burrard Inlet across from the Touristinfo Centre. From here you'll get a good sense of Vancouver's natural and urban topography, with the North Coast Mountains rising up before you; low-rise, historic Gastown to the east; Stanley Park to the west; and a forest of glass residential towers in between. Canada Place is busiest in summer, when up to four giant cruise ships may dock in 1 day.

❷ Stanley Park ★★★

You can't really appreciate **Stanley Park** (p. 81) by driving through it in a car, so park your vehicle and head in on foot via Lagoon Drive. Surrounded by a famed pedestrian seawall, this giant peninsular park invites hours of exploration. A 1-hour carriage ride is the perfect way to see the highlights, including an amazing collection of totem poles, giant trees, and landscaped areas.

❸ Vancouver Aquarium Marine Science Centre ★★

One of the best aquariums in North America is located right in Stanley Park. Have a look especially at the Arctic Canada exhibit with its beluga whales, and the Marine Mammal Deck, where you can see Pacific white-sided dolphins, sea otters, and other denizens of Pacific Northwest waters. See p. 82.

❹ ENGLISH BAY BEACH ★★
If the weather is warm, take off your shoes and enjoy the grass, sand, and sunshine at **English Bay Beach** (p. 86), an all-season gathering spot on the south side of Stanley Park. You can pick up picnic eats or find takeout food on nearby Denman Street.

❺ Robson Street & the West End

How you explore the West End is up to you. You can walk from English Bay Beach down Denman Street and then turn south on **Robson Street** (p. 81), taking in as much of the throbbing shopping and cafe scene as you want. It's also fun to explore the West End as a living neighborhood— the most densely populated in North America!

❻ CAFFÈ ARTIGIANO ★★
For the best latte in town, as well as grilled Italian sandwiches and snacks, stop in at this busy cafe right across from the Vancouver Art Gallery. There's a perfect people-watching patio in front.

❼ UBC Museum of Anthropology ★★★

Hop in your car for the 20-minute drive to the outstanding **Museum of Anthropology at the University of British Columbia** (p. 84). Here, in one of North America's preeminent collections of First Nations Art, you'll encounter powerful totem poles, spirit masks, and totemic objects, all richly carved and profoundly mysterious.

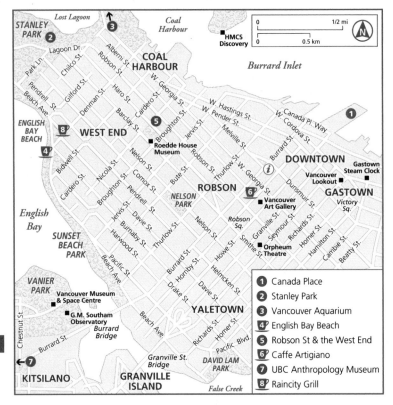

- ❶ Canada Place
- ❷ Stanley Park
- ❸ Vancouver Aquarium
- ❹ English Bay Beach
- ❺ Robson St & the West End
- ❻ Caffe Artigiano
- ❼ UBC Anthropology Museum
- ❽ Raincity Grill

❽ Dinner

In the last decade, Vancouver has become one of the top dining cities in the world, filled with superb restaurants of all kinds. For a romantic dinner that will introduce you to the best of Vancouver's "eat local" food philosophy, reserve a table at **Raincity Grill,** where the windows overlook English Bay, and the regional cuisine is a perfect excuse to linger (p. 77).

5 THE BEST OF VICTORIA IN 1 DAY

Victoria is less than a quarter of the size of Vancouver, and you can easily hit the highlights in 1 day if you arrive on an early ferry. The scenic ferry ride—from Vancouver, Seattle, Anacortes, or Port Angeles—is part of the fun. Although it's easy to experience Victoria on foot, by bike, and using public transportation, having a car will help to maximize your sightseeing.

1 Inner Harbour
2 Royal B.C. Museum
3 Fairmont Empress
4 Butchart Gardens
5 Il Terrazzo Ristorante

Information ⓘ

SUGGESTED ITINERARIES IN BRITISH COLUMBIA

4

THE BEST OF VICTORIA IN 1 DAY

❶ Inner Harbour

Victoria's official facade, epitomized by a pair of landmark buildings designed by Francis Rattenbury, is reminiscent of an era that promoted the idea of a British Empire. A stroll along the Inner Harbour takes you past the **Provincial Legislature ★**, a massive stone edifice completed in 1898, and the famous Fairmont Empress Hotel, which dates from 1908 (p. 118 and 109, respectively). Along the busy waterfront you'll also find information on whale-watching excursions (p. 124), a popular Victoria pastime.

❷ Royal British Columbia Museum ★★★

The highlight of this excellent museum (p. 119) is the First Peoples Gallery, an absorbing and thought-provoking showplace of First Nations art and culture. The other exhibits pale by comparison, but do have a look at the life-size woolly mastodon if he's on display.

☕ THE FAIRMONT EMPRESS ★★
Tea at the Empress (p. 115) is a traditional affair that has remained a real treat despite its fame. Make it your main meal of the day (seatings at 12:30, 2, 2:30, and 5pm), and be sure to reserve in advance.

④ Butchart Gardens ★★★

This century-old garden (p. 117) is one of the gardening wonders of the world, meticulously planned and impeccably maintained. Though hordes of tourists can jam the paths in the summer months, time your visit for late afternoon and you'll have more room; plus you can stay for the fabulous summer fireworks display.

⑤ Dinner

If there's time, have dinner at **Il Terrazzo Ristorante** ★★ (p. 114). Victoria's best Italian restaurant serves delicious, northern-Italian dishes and has a lovely patio for outdoor, summertime dining.

Vancouver

by Donald Olson

The setting is majestic and the city exciting, so it's no wonder that **Vancouver** lures visitors from around the globe. The rest of the world has taken notice of the blessed life people in these parts lead, and surveys generally list Vancouver as one of the 10 best cities in the world to live in. It's also one of the 10 best to visit, according to *Condé Nast Traveler,* and it won that magazine's Readers' Choice Award in 2005, 2006, and 2007 as "Best City in the Americas." In 2003, the International Olympic Committee named Vancouver the host of the 2010 Olympic and Paralympic Winter Games. Heady stuff for a spot that less than 20 years ago was routinely derided as the world's biggest mill town.

---

1 ESSENTIALS

GETTING THERE
By Plane
Daily direct flights between major U.S. cities and Vancouver are offered by **Air Canada** (© 888/247-2262; www.aircanada.com), **Alaska Airlines** (© 800/252-7522; www.alaska air.com), **American Airlines** (© 800/433-7300; www.aa.com), **Continental** (© 800/231-0856; www.continental.com), **Frontier Airlines** (© 800/432-1359; www.frontier airlines.com), **Northwest Airlines** (© 800/225-2525; www.nwa.com), and **United Airlines** (© 877/932-4259; www.united.com).

GETTING INTO TOWN FROM THE AIRPORT   **Vancouver International Airport (YVR;** © **604/207-7077;** www.yvr.ca) is 13km (8 miles) south of downtown.

 Tourist Information Centres (© **604/683-2000**), on Level 2 of the Main and International arrival terminals, are open daily from 8am to 11pm.

 The easiest, fastest, and cheapest way to get into Vancouver from the airport is by the brand-new **Canada Line SkyTrain** operated by Translink (© **604/953-3333;** www. translink.ca). The train zips into Vancouver in 22 minutes, stopping at stations in Yaletown, City Centre (downtown), and Waterfront (the SeaBus Terminal, near the Canada Place cruise-ship terminal). Prices for the SkyTrain run from C$2.50 to C$5 (depending on time of day and the number of zones you travel). However, an additional C$5 surcharge will be tacked on to the single fare price when you travel from the airport to downtown Vancouver (this surcharge does not apply to return trips to the airport). A DayPass (C$9), which you can purchase from any authorized FareDealer location at the airport, might be a better alternative if you plan on doing any sightseeing the same day you fly in.

 The **YVR Airporter** (© **800/668-3141** or 604/946-8866; www.yvrairporter.com) provides **airport bus service** to downtown Vancouver's major hotels and cruise-ship terminal. It leaves from Level 2 of the Main Terminal every 15 minutes daily from 8:20am to 9:45pm. Fares for the 30-minute ride across the Granville Street Bridge into

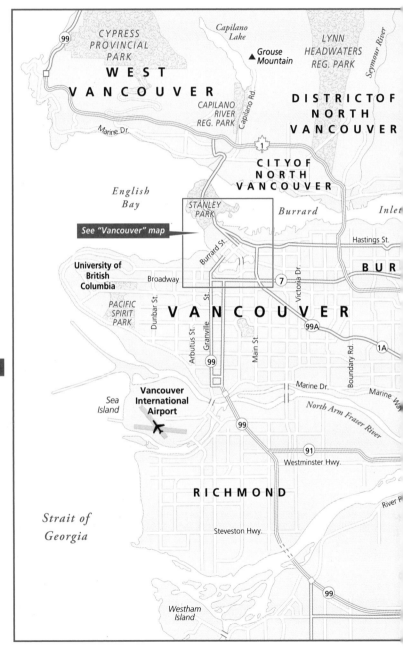

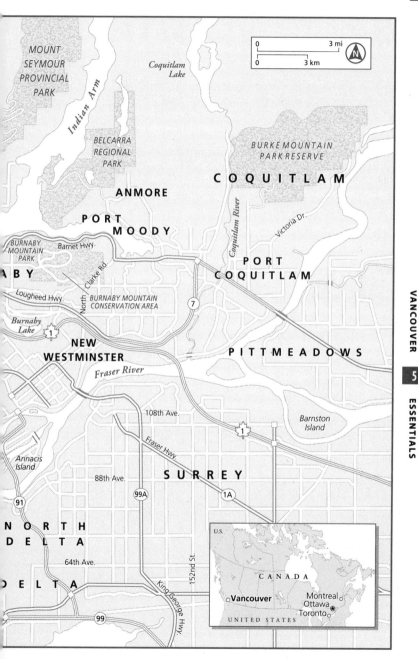

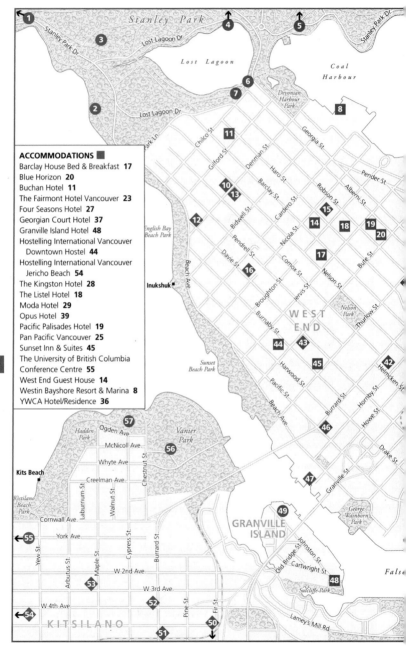

ACCOMMODATIONS ■
Barclay House Bed & Breakfast **17**
Blue Horizon **20**
Buchan Hotel **11**
The Fairmont Hotel Vancouver **23**
Four Seasons Hotel **27**
Georgian Court Hotel **37**
Granville Island Hotel **48**
Hostelling International Vancouver
  Downtown Hostel **44**
Hostelling International Vancouver
  Jericho Beach **54**
The Kingston Hotel **28**
The Listel Hotel **18**
Moda Hotel **29**
Opus Hotel **39**
Pacific Palisades Hotel **19**
Pan Pacific Vancouver **25**
Sunset Inn & Suites **45**
The University of British Columbia
  Conference Centre **55**
West End Guest House **14**
Westin Bayshore Resort & Marina **8**
YWCA Hotel/Residence **36**

VANCOUVER

5

ESSENTIALS

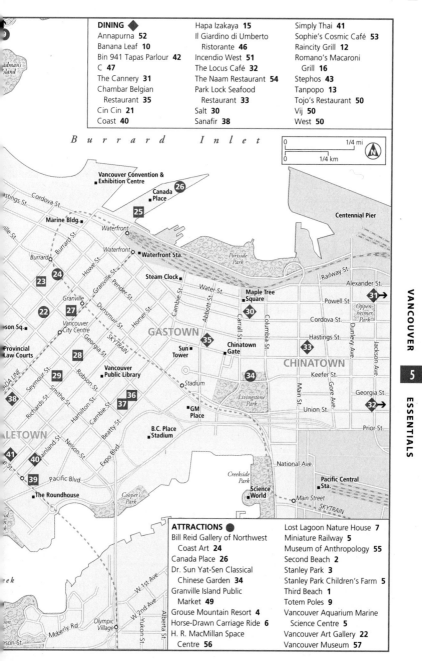

DINING ◆
Annapurna **52**
Banana Leaf **10**
Bin 941 Tapas Parlour **42**
C **47**
The Cannery **31**
Chambar Belgian
  Restaurant **35**
Cin Cin **21**
Coast **40**

Hapa Izakaya **15**
Il Giardino di Umberto
  Ristorante **46**
Incendio West **51**
The Locus Café **32**
The Naam Restaurant **54**
Park Lock Seafood
  Restaurant **33**
Salt **30**
Sanafir **38**

Simply Thai **41**
Sophie's Cosmic Café **53**
Raincity Grill **12**
Romano's Macaroni
  Grill **16**
Stephos **43**
Tanpopo **13**
Tojo's Restaurant **50**
Vij **50**
West **50**

Burrard   Inlet

0 ———— 1/4 mi
0 ———— 1/4 km

VANCOUVER

5

ESSENTIALS

ATTRACTIONS ●
Bill Reid Gallery of Northwest
  Coast Art **24**
Canada Place **26**
Dr. Sun Yat-Sen Classical
  Chinese Garden **34**
Granville Island Public
  Market **49**
Grouse Mountain Resort **4**
Horse-Drawn Carriage Ride **6**
H. R. MacMillan Space
  Centre **56**

Lost Lagoon Nature House **7**
Miniature Railway **5**
Museum of Anthropology **55**
Second Beach **2**
Stanley Park **3**
Stanley Park Children's Farm **5**
Third Beach **1**
Totem Poles **9**
Vancouver Aquarium Marine
  Science Centre **5**
Vancouver Art Gallery **22**
Vancouver Museum **57**

downtown Vancouver are C$14 for adults, C$11 for seniors, C$6.50 for children, and C$28 for families (two adults, two children). Buses leave from selected downtown hotels every half-hour between 7:30am and 9pm. Scheduled pickups serve the bus station, cruise-ship terminal, Four Seasons, Hotel Vancouver, Georgian Court, Sutton Place, Landmark, and others. Ask the driver on the way in or ask your hotel concierge for the nearest pickup stop and time.

Getting to and from the airport with **public bus** is much slower and requires at least one transfer. Public buses are operated by **Translink** ((C) **604/953-3333;** www.translink.ca).

The average **taxi** fare from the airport to a downtown Vancouver hotel is approximately C$30 plus tip, but the fare can run up to C$40 if the cab gets stuck in traffic. **LimoJet** ((C) **604/273-1331;** www.limojetgold.com) offers flat-rate sedan or stretch-limousine service at C$39 per trip (not per person) to the airport from any downtown location, plus tax and tip, for up to three people (C$45 for up to six passengers).

Most major **car-rental firms** have airport counters and shuttles. Drivers heading into Vancouver from the airport should take the Arthur Laing Bridge, which leads directly to Granville Street, the most direct route to downtown.

By Ship & Ferry

Vancouver is the major embarkation point for cruises going up British Columbia's Inland Passage to Alaska. In the summer, up to four cruise ships a day berth at **Canada Place** cruise-ship terminal ((C) **604/665-9000;** www.portmetrovancouver.com). Public transit buses and taxis greet new arrivals, but you can also easily walk to many major hotels.

If you're arriving from Vancouver Island or Victoria, **BC Ferries** ((C) **888/223-3779** or 250/386-3431; www.bcferries.com) has three daily routes.

By Train & Bus

BY TRAIN   **VIA Rail Canada,** 1150 Station St., Vancouver ((C) **888/842-7245;** www. viarail.ca), connects with Amtrak at Winnipeg, Manitoba. From there you can transfer to the Canadian, the western transcontinental train that travels between Vancouver and Toronto. For travel within Canada only, the 12-day **Canrailpass** (C$576 off-peak; C$923 peak) is available through www.viarail.com.

Amtrak ((C) **800/872-7245;** www.amtrak.com) offers daily service from Seattle, though there's currently only one train in the morning (departing Seattle 7:10am, arriving Vancouver 11:35am); otherwise, the Seattle-Vancouver route is covered by an Amtrak bus.

BY BUS   **Greyhound Bus Lines** ((C) **800/231-2222** or 604/482-8747; www.greyhound. ca) offers daily bus service between Vancouver and all major Canadian cities, and between Vancouver and Seattle (at the border crossing, passengers disembark the bus and take their luggage through Customs). For information on Greyhound's cost-cutting **Canada Pass,** which allows for unlimited travel within Canada, and **Discovery Pass,** which allows for unlimited travel in the U.S. and Canada, consult their website.

By Car

You'll probably be driving into Vancouver along one of two routes. **U.S. I-5** from Seattle becomes **Hwy. 99** when you cross the border at the Peace Arch. The 210km (130-mile) drive from Seattle takes about 2½ hours. On the Canadian side of the border, you'll drive through the cities of White Rock, Delta, and Richmond, pass under the Fraser River through the George Massey Tunnel, and cross the Oak Street Bridge. The highway ends there and becomes Oak Street, a busy urban thoroughfare heading toward downtown. Turn left at the first convenient major arterial (70th, 57th, 49th, 41st, 33rd, 16th, and 12th aves. will all serve) and proceed until you hit the next major street, which will be Granville Street. Turn right on Granville Street. This street heads directly into downtown Vancouver via the Granville Street Bridge.

Trans-Canada Hwy. 1 is a limited-access freeway that runs to Vancouver's eastern boundary, where it crosses the Second Narrows Bridge to North Vancouver. When traveling on Hwy. 1 from the east, exit at Cassiar Street and turn left at the first light onto Hastings Street (Hwy. 7A), which is adjacent to Exhibition Park. Follow Hastings Street 6.4km (4 miles) into downtown. When coming to Vancouver from parts north, take exit 13 (the sign says TAYLOR WAY, BRIDGE TO VANCOUVER) and cross the Lions Gate Bridge into Vancouver's West End.

VISITOR INFORMATION

The Vancouver Touristinfo Centre, 200 Burrard St., Plaza Level (© **604/683-2000;** www.tourismvancouver.com), has an incredibly helpful and well-trained staff who are able to provide information, maps, and brochures, and can help you with all your travel needs, including hotel, cruise-ship, ferry, bus, and train reservations.

The free weekly tabloid *Georgia Straight* (© **604/730-7000;** www.straight.com), found in cafes, bookshops, and restaurants, provides up-to-date schedules of concerts, lectures, art exhibits, plays, recitals, and other happenings. Not free but equally good— and with more attitude—is the glossy city magazine *Vancouver* (© **604/877-7732;** www.vanmag.com), available on newsstands. The free guide called *Where Vancouver* (© **604/736-5586;** www.where.ca) is available in many hotels and lists attractions, entertainment, upscale shopping, and fine dining. It also has good maps.

CITY LAYOUT

With four different bodies of water lapping at its edges and miles of shoreline, Vancouver's geography can seem a bit complicated. **Downtown Vancouver** is on a peninsula: Think of it as an upraised thumb on the mitten-shaped Vancouver mainland. **Stanley Park,** the **West End, Yaletown,** and Vancouver's business and financial center (downtown) are located on this thumb of land bordered to the north by Burrard Inlet, the city's main deepwater harbor and port, to the west by English Bay, and to the south by False Creek. Farther west beyond English Bay is the Strait of Georgia, part of the Pacific Ocean. Just south across False Creek is **Granville Island,** famous for its public market, and the beach community of **Kitsilano.** This part of the city, called the **West Side,** covers the mainland, or the hand of the mitten. Its western shoreline looks out on the Strait of Georgia with the Pacific beyond, and the north arm of the Fraser River demarcates it to the south. Pacific Spirit Park and the University of British Columbia (UBC), a locus for visitors because of its outstanding Museum of Anthropology, take up most of the western tip of the West Side; the rest is mostly residential, with a sprinkling of businesses along main arterial streets. Both the mainland and peninsula are covered by a simple rectilinear street pattern. **North Vancouver** is the mountain-backed area across Burrard Inlet from downtown.

2 GETTING AROUND

BY PUBLIC TRANSPORTATION

Vancouver's public transportation system is the most extensive in Canada and includes service to all major tourist attractions, so it's not really necessary to have a car (especially if you're staying in the downtown area).

The **Translink** (otherwise known as B.C. Transit; ℂ **604/521-0400;** www.translink. ca) system includes electric buses, the SeaBus catamaran ferry, and the light-rail SkyTrain. It's an ecologically friendly, highly reliable, inexpensive system that allows you to get everywhere, including the beaches and ski slopes. Regular service runs from 5am to 2am.

Schedules and routes are available online, at tourist information centers, at many major hotels, and on buses. Pick up a copy of *Discover Vancouver on Transit* at one of the tourist information centers (see "Visitor Information," above). This publication gives transit routes for many city neighborhoods, landmarks, and attractions.

Fares are based on the number of zones traveled, and are the same for buses, the Sea-Bus, and the SkyTrain. One ticket allows you to transfer from one mode of transport to another, in any direction, within 90 minutes. A one-way, one-zone fare (everything in central Vancouver) costs C$2.50. A two-zone fare—C$3.75—is required to travel to the airport or to nearby suburbs such as Richmond or North Vancouver, and a three-zone fare—C$5—is required for travel to the far-off city of Surrey. After 6:30pm on weekdays and all day on weekends and holidays, you can travel anywhere in all three zones for C$2.50. **DayPasses,** good on all public transit, cost C$9 for adults and C$7 for seniors, students, and children. They can be used for unlimited travel on weekdays or weekends and holidays.

Tip: Keep in mind that drivers do not make change, so you need the exact fare or a valid transit pass. Pay with cash or buy tickets and passes from ticket machines at stations, tourist information centers, both SeaBus terminals, and convenience stores, drugstores, and outlets displaying the FAREDEALER sign; most of these outlets also sell a transit map showing all routes.

BY BUS Both diesel and electric-trolley buses service the city. Regular service on the busiest routes is every 12 minutes from 5am to 2am. Wheelchair-accessible buses and bus stops are identified by the international wheelchair symbol. From June until the end of September, the Vancouver Parks Board operates a **free bus through Stanley Park,** which stops at 14 points of interest. Call ℂ **604/953-3333** for general public-transportation information.

BY SKYTRAIN The SkyTrain is a fast, light-rail service between downtown Vancouver and the suburbs. The **Expo Line** trains operate from Waterfront to King George station, running along a scenic 27km (17-mile) route from downtown Vancouver east to Surrey through Burnaby and New Westminster in 39 minutes. There are 20 stations along this route; four downtown stations are underground and marked at street level. The **Millennium Line,** which opened in fall 2002, makes the same stops from Waterfront to Columbia, then branches to Sapperton, Braid, Lougheed town center, and beyond to Commercial Drive. All stations except Granville are wheelchair accessible; trains arrive every 2 to 5 minutes. **Canada Line,** the newest SkyTrain, began operating in October 2009, and links the Vancouver Airport to Yaletown, City Centre, and Waterfront Station (SeaBus terminal).

BY SEABUS The SS *Beaver* and SS *Otter* catamaran ferries take passengers, cyclists, and wheelchair riders on a scenic 12-minute commute across Burrard Inlet between downtown's Waterfront Station and North Vancouver's Lonsdale Quay. On weekdays, a SeaBus leaves each stop every 15 minutes from 6:15am to 6:30pm, then every 30 minutes until 1am. SeaBuses depart on Saturdays every half-hour from 6:30am to 12:30pm, then every 15 minutes until 7:15pm, then every half-hour until 1am. On Sundays and holidays, runs depart every half-hour from 8:30am to 11pm. Note that the crossing is a two-zone fare on weekdays until 6:30pm.

BY TAXI

Cab fares start at C$2.85 and increase at a rate of C$1.66 per kilometer. In the downtown area, you can expect to travel for less than C$12 plus tip. The typical fare for the 13km (8-mile) drive from downtown to the airport is C$30.

Taxis are easy to find in front of major hotels, but flagging one down can be tricky. Call for a pickup from **Black Top** (© **604/731-1111**), **Yellow Cab** (© **604/681-1111**), or **MacLure's** (© **604/731-9211**).

BY CAR

If you're just sightseeing around town, public transit and cabs will easily see you through. However, if you're planning to visit the North Shore Mountains or pursue other out-of-town activities, a car is necessary. Car insurance is compulsory in British Columbia. *Note:* The speed limit in Vancouver is 50kmph (31 mph); highway speed limits vary from 90 to 110kmph (56–68 mph).

All major downtown hotels have guest parking, either in-house or at nearby lots. Valet secure parking at most hotels costs about C$25 per day. Public parking is found at **Robson Square** (enter at Smithe and Howe sts.), the **Pacific Centre** (Howe and Dunsmuir sts.), and **the Bay** department store (Richards near Dunsmuir St.). You'll also find larger **parking lots** at the intersections of Thurlow and Georgia, Thurlow and Alberni, and Robson and Seymour streets.

Street meters accept C$2 and C$1 coins. Rules are posted and strictly enforced; generally, downtown and in the West End, metered parking is in effect 7 days a week. (*Note:* Drivers are given about a 2-min. grace period before their cars are towed away when the 3pm no-parking rule goes into effect on many major thoroughfares.) Unmetered parking on side streets is often subject to neighborhood residency requirements: Check the signs. If you park in such an area without the appropriate sticker on your windshield, you'll get ticketed and towed. If your car is towed away or you need a towing service and aren't a CAA or an AAA member, call **Unitow** (© **604/251-1255**) or **Busters** (© **604/685-8181**). If you are parking on the street, remove all valuables from your car; break-ins are not uncommon.

BY BIKE

Vancouver is a biker's paradise. Along Robson and Denman streets near Stanley Park are plenty of places to rent bikes. (For specifics, see p. 87.) Paved paths crisscross through parks and along beaches. Helmets are mandatory, and riding on sidewalks is illegal except on designated bike paths.

You can take your bike on the SeaBus anytime at no extra charge. Bikes are not allowed in the George Massey Tunnel, but a tunnel shuttle operates four times daily from mid-May to September to transport you across the Fraser River. From May 1 to Victoria Day (the third weekend of May), the service operates on weekends only. All of the West

Vancouver blue buses (including the bus to the Horseshoe Bay ferry terminal) can carry two bikes, first-come, first-served, free of charge. In Vancouver, only a limited number of suburban bus routes allow bikes on board: no. 351 to White Rock, no. 601 to South Delta, no. 404 to the airport, and the no. 99 Express to UBC.

BY MINIFERRY

Crossing False Creek to Granville Island or beautiful Vanier Park on one of the zippy little miniferries is cheap and fun. These small, covered boats connect various points of interest; they are privately operated, so your public transit pass or ticket is not valid. It's well worth the extra money, though.

The **Aquabus** (© **604/689-5858;** www.theaquabus.com) docks at the south foot of Hornby Street, the Arts Club on Granville Island, Yaletown at Davie Street, Science World, and Stamp's Landing. Ferries operate daily from 6:40am to 10:30pm (9:30pm in winter) and run every 15 minutes to half-hour from 10am to 5pm (later in May and June). One-way fares are C$3 for adults and C$1.50 for seniors and children. A day pass is C$14 for adults and C$8 for seniors and children. You can take a 25-minute scenic boat ride (one complete circuit) for C$7 adults, C$4 seniors and children.

(*Fast Facts* **Vancouver**

Business Hours Vancouver **banks** are open Monday through Thursday from 10am to 5pm and Friday from 10am to 6pm. Some banks, like Canadian Trust, are also open on Saturday. **Stores** are generally open Monday through Saturday from 10am to 6pm. Last call at **restaurant bars** and **cocktail lounges** is 2am.

Child Care If you need to rent cribs, car seats, playpens, or other baby accessories, **Cribs and Carriages** (© **604/988-2742;** www.cribsandcarriages.com) delivers them right to your hotel.

Dentists Most major hotels have a dentist on call. **Vancouver Centre Dental Clinic,** Vancouver Centre Mall, 11-650 W. Georgia St. (© **604/682-1601**), is another option. You must make an appointment. The clinic is open Monday to Friday 8:30am to 5pm (Wed until 6pm).

Doctors Hotels usually have a doctor on call. **Vancouver Medic Centre,** Bentall Centre, 1055 Dunsmuir St. (© **604/683-8138**), is a drop-in clinic open Monday through Friday 8am to 4pm. Another drop-in medical center, **Carepoint Clinic,** 1175 Denman St. (© **604/681-5338**), is open Monday through Thursday from 9am to 9pm, Friday through Sunday 9am to 8pm. See also "Hotlines," below.

Hospitals **St. Paul's Hospital,** 1081 Burrard St. (© **604/682-2344**), is the closest facility to downtown and the West End. West Side Vancouver hospitals include **Vancouver General Hospital Health and Sciences Centre,** 855 W. 12th Ave. (© **604/875-4111**), and **BC Children's Hospital,** 4480 Oak St. (© **604/875-2345**). In North Vancouver, there's **Lions Gate Hospital,** 231 E. 15th St. (© **604/984-5785**).

Hotlines Emergency numbers include **Crisis Centre** (© 604/872-3311), **Rape Crisis Centre** (© 604/255-6228), **Rape Relief** (© 604/872-8212), **Poison Control Centre** (© 604/682-2344), **Crime Stoppers** (© 800/222-8477), and **SPCA** animal emergency (✆ 604/879-3571). Or dial ✆ **911** for any emergency police, fire, or ambulance service.

Internet Access Free Internet access is available at the Vancouver **Public Library** Central Branch, 350 W. Georgia St. (✆ **604/331-3600**). **Cyber Space Internet Café,** 1701 Robson St. (✆ **604/684-6004**), and **Internet Coffee,** 1104 Davie St. (✆ **604/682-6668**), are both open until at least midnight.

Laundry & Dry Cleaning **Davie Laundromat,** 1061 Davie St. (✆ **604/682-2717**), offers self-service, drop-off service, and dry cleaning. **Laundry & Suntanning,** 781 Denman St. (✆ **604/689-9598**), doesn't have dry-cleaning services, but you can work on your tan while you wait. Also, almost all hotels have laundry service.

Luggage Storage & Lockers Lockers are available at the main Vancouver railway station (which is also the main bus depot), **Pacific Central Station,** 1150 Station St., near Main Street and Terminal Avenue south of Chinatown (✆ **604/661-0328**).

Newspapers & Magazines The two local papers are the *Vancouver Sun* (www. vancouversun.com), published Monday through Saturday, and the *Province* (www.theprovince.com), published Sunday through Friday mornings. The free weekly entertainment paper, the *Georgia Straight* (www.straight.com), comes out on Thursday.

Pharmacies **Shopper's Drug Mart,** 1125 Davie St. (✆ **604/669-2424**), is open 24 hours. Several Safeway supermarket pharmacies are open late; the one on Robson and Denman is open until midnight.

Police For emergencies, dial ✆ **911**. This is a free call. Otherwise, the **Vancouver City Police** can be reached at ✆ **604/717-3535.**

Post Office The **main post office,** 349 W. Georgia St. at Homer Street (✆ **800/267-1177**), is open Monday through Friday from 8am to 5:30pm. You'll also find post office outlets in Shopper's Drug Mart and 7-Eleven stores with longer opening hours.

Weather Call ✆ **604/664-9010** for weather updates. Each local ski resort has its own snow report line: **Cypress Mountain** ✆ 604/419-7669; **Whistler/Blackcomb** ✆ **604/687-7507.**

3 WHERE TO STAY

Most of Vancouver's hotels are in the downtown area or the West End. Central Vancouver is small and easily walkable, so in both of these neighborhoods you'll be close to major sights, services, and nightlife.

Quoted prices don't include the 10% **hotel room tax,** the 7% **provincial accommodations tax,** or the 6% **goods and services tax (GST).** I list the rack rates, the rates you would receive if you walked in off the street and requested a room. By checking the hotel's website, you'll almost always find lower rates, including special "romance packages" and weekend-getaway specials. The highest price I list is for high season (mid-June to Sept).

Bus and/or public transportation information is given only for those hotels listed below that are outside of the Vancouver city center.

If you prefer to stay in a B&B, **Canada-West Accommodations,** P.O. Box 86607, North Vancouver, B.C. V7L 4L2 (*©* **800/561-3223** or 604/990-6730; www.b-b.com), specializes in matching guests with establishments that best suit their needs.

DOWNTOWN & YALETOWN
Very Expensive

The Fairmont Hotel Vancouver ★★ (Kids) A landmark in the city since it first opened in 1939, the Fairmont Hotel has been brought up to 21st-century standards but retains its traditional, old-fashioned elegance. The rooms are spacious, quiet, and comfortable, if not particularly dynamic in layout or finish. The bathrooms (with tub/shower combinations) look a bit dated when compared with those at other downtown hotels in this price range, but that's part of the charm. Courtyard suites feature a luxuriously furnished living room, separated from the bedroom by French doors. Guests can use the state-of-the-art gym with heated indoor pool. The hotel is family friendly and even has two resident dogs (former Seeing Eye dogs) that can be taken out for walks.

900 W. Georgia St., Vancouver, BC V6C 2W6. *©* **866/540-4452** or 604/684-3131. Fax 604/662-1929. www. fairmont.com. 556 units. C$299–C$439 double. Children 17 and under stay free in parent's room. AE, DC, DISC, MC, V. Parking C$33. **Amenities:** 2 restaurants; bar; babysitting; concierge; executive-level rooms; health club; Jacuzzi; indoor pool; room service; sauna; rooms for those w/limited mobility; rooms for hearing-impaired guests. *In room:* A/C, TV w/pay movies, hair dryer, high-speed Internet (C$15/day), minibar.

Four Seasons Hotel ★★★ (Kids) For over 30 years now, the Four Seasons has reigned as one of Vancouver's top hotels. From the outside, this huge high-rise hotel across from the Vancouver Art Gallery is rather unappealing. But the large, light-filled rooms are wonderfully comfortable, with superb beds and interesting views of downtown with glimpses of the mountains. The marble bathrooms are on the small side but well designed. For a slightly larger room, reserve a deluxe corner room with wraparound floor-to-ceiling windows. One of the glories of this hotel is its health club with an enormous heated pool—half indoor, half outdoor—on a terrace. The Four Seasons kicked off the first stage of its top-to-bottom renovation in 2008 with the opening of its hip new bar/lounge/restaurant Yew.

791 W. Georgia St., Vancouver, BC V6C 2T4. *©* **800/819-5053** or 604/689-9333. Fax 604/684-4555. www. fourseasons.com/vancouver. 376 units. Nov–Apr C$250–C$330 double; May–Oct C$370–C$555 double. AE, DC, MC, V. Parking C$31. **Amenities:** 2 restaurants; bar; babysitting; concierge; exercise room; indoor and heated outdoor pool; room service; sauna; rooms for those w/limited mobility. *In room:* A/C, TV/VCR, hair dryer, minibar, Wi-Fi (C$17/day).

Opus Hotel ★★★ If you want to stay in a hip, happening, luxury hotel, try the Opus—in 2005, *Condé Nast Traveler* voted it one of the world's top 100 hotels. It's the only hotel in Yaletown, the trendiest area for shopping, nightlife, and dining. Each room is furnished according to one of five "personalities," with its own layout, color, and flavor—the luscious room colors are eye candy if you're tired of blah hotel interiors. Bathrooms are fitted with high-design sinks, soaker tubs, or roomy showers (or both). The cool Opus Bar serves an international tapas menu, and on weekends it becomes one of Yaletown's see-and-be-seen scenes. (Be forewarned: This area of Yaletown is "club central" and can be noisy until the wee hours; book a Courtyard Room if you don't want to be disturbed.) Opus's top-notch restaurant, Elixir, serves modern French bistro food.

322 Davie St., Vancouver, BC V6B 5Z6. *©* **866/642-6787** or 604/642-6787. Fax 604/642-6780. www. opushotel.com. 96 units. May–Oct C$359–C$549 double, C$815 and up suite; Nov–Apr C$229–C$429

double, C$739 and up suite. Children 17 and under stay free in parent's room. AE, DC, MC, V. Valet parking C$29. **Amenities:** Restaurant; bar; bikes; concierge; small exercise room; room service. *In room:* A/C, TV w/pay movies, hair dryer, minibar, Wi-Fi (C$16/day).

Pan Pacific Vancouver ★★★ This 23-story luxury hotel atop Canada Place is a key landmark on the Vancouver waterfront. Despite its size, the hotel excels in comfort and service, and it provides spectacular views of the North Shore Mountains, Burrard Inlet, and cruise ships arriving and departing from the terminal below. The rooms are spacious and comfortable, with contemporary furnishings and a soothing color palette. Bathrooms are large and luxurious. Guests have use of a heated outdoor pool and Jacuzzi overlooking the harbor. Spa Utopia offers a full array of pampering treatments. Café Pacifica puts on one of the best breakfast buffets in Vancouver.

300-999 Canada Place, Vancouver, BC V6C 3B5. ℂ **877/324-4856** in the U.S., or 604/662-8111. Fax 604/685-8690. www.panpacific.com. 504 units. May–Oct C$540–C$640 double, C$700–C$5,000 suite; Nov–Apr C$410–C$480 double, C$520 and up suite. AE, DC, DISC, MC, V. Valet parking C$30. **Amenities:** 2 restaurants; bar; babysitting; concierge; health club; Jacuzzi; outdoor heated pool; room service; sauna; spa. *In room:* A/C, TV w/pay movies, hair dryer, high-speed Internet (C$15/day), minibar.

Moderate

Georgian Court Hotel ★ (Value) This modern, 14-story brick hotel is extremely well located, just a block or two from B.C. Place Stadium, GM Place Stadium, the Queen Elizabeth Theatre, the Playhouse, and the Vancouver Public Library. You can walk to Robson Square in about 10 minutes. The guest rooms are relatively large, nicely decorated, and have good-size bathrooms. And while the big-time celebs are usually whisked off to the glamorous top hotels, their entourages often stay at the Georgian Court, as it provides all the amenities and business-friendly extras such as two phones in every room, brightly lit desks, and complimentary high-speed Internet access—a service that other hotels almost always charge for.

773 Beatty St., Vancouver, BC V6B 2M4. ℂ **800/663-1155** or 604/682-5555. Fax 604/682-8830. www. georgiancourt.com. 180 units. May–Oct 15 C$199–C$279 double; Oct 16–Apr C$150–C$209 double. AE, DC, MC, V. Parking C$13. **Amenities:** Restaurant; bar; babysitting; concierge; exercise room; Jacuzzi; room service; sauna. *In room:* A/C, TV, fridge, hair dryer, free high-speed Internet.

Moda Hotel ★ (Finds) Situated downtown, across from the Orpheum Theatre and close to the clubs on Granville Street, the Moda offers lots of style and excellent value. Rooms and suites in this 1908 heritage building feature a sleek, tailored, European look with dramatic colors, luxury beds and linens, flatscreen TVs, nice tiled bathrooms with a tub/shower, and double-glazed windows to dampen the traffic noise. The only thing the refurbers couldn't change was the slant in some of the old floors. For years, this hotel was called the Dufferin and catered to a mostly gay clientele; it's still gay friendly, but anyone with a spirit of adventure and a taste for something out of the ordinary will enjoy a stay here. Suites offer an extra half-bathroom, corner locations with more light, and upgraded amenities.

900 Seymour St., Vancouver, BC V6B 3L9. ℂ **877/683-5522** or 604/683-4251. Fax 604/683-0611. www. modahotel.ca. 57 units. C$119–C$229 double; C$219–C$289 suite. AE, DC, MC, V. **Amenities:** 2 restaurants; bar. *In room:* A/C, TV, high-speed Internet.

Inexpensive

In addition to the establishments listed below, Downtown is home to the **Hostelling International Vancouver Downtown Hostel,** 1114 Burnaby St. (at Thurlow St.), Vancouver, BC V6E 1P1 (ℂ **888/203-4302** or 604/684-4565; fax 604/684-4540;

www.hihostels.ca). Rates for nonmembers run from C$30 (dorm) to C$88 (double) and include a full breakfast. Another HI hostel, the **Vancouver Jericho Beach,** can be found on the West Side, 1515 Discovery St., Vancouver, BC V6R 4K5 (℗ **888/203-4303** or 604/224-3208).

The Kingston Hotel (Value An affordable downtown hotel is a rarity for Vancouver, but if you can do without the frills, the Kingston offers a clean, safe, inexpensive place to sleep and a complimentary continental breakfast to start your day. You won't find a better deal anywhere, and the premises have far more character than you'll find in a cookie-cutter motel. The Kingston is a Vancouver version of the kind of small budget B&B hotels found all over Europe. Just 9 of the 55 rooms have private bathrooms and TVs; the rest have hand basins and shared showers and toilets on each floor. The premises are well kept, and the location is central, so you can walk everywhere. The staff is friendly and helpful, and if you're just looking for a place to sleep and stow your bags, you'll be glad you found this place.

757 Richards St., Vancouver, BC V6B 3A6. ℗ **888/713-3304** or 604/684-9024. Fax 604/684-9917. www.kingstonhotelvancouver.com. 52 units, 13 with private bathroom. C$85–C$95 double with shared bathroom; C$125–C$170 double with private bathroom. Additional person C$10. Rates include continental breakfast. AE, MC, V. Parking C$20 across the street. **Amenities:** Restaurant; bar; sauna. *In room:* TV (in units w/private bathrooms), free Wi-Fi.

YWCA Hotel/Residence ★ (Value This attractive 12-story residence next door to the Georgian Court Hotel is an excellent choice for travelers on limited budgets. Bedrooms are simply furnished; some have TVs. Quite a few reasonably priced restaurants and a number of grocery stores are nearby. Three communal kitchens are available for guests' use, and all rooms have minifridges. The Y has three TV lounges and free access to the best gym in town, the nearby coed YWCA Fitness Centre.

733 Beatty St., Vancouver, BC V6B 2M4. ℗ **800/663-1424** or 604/895-5830. Fax 604/681-2550. www.ywcahotel.com. 155 units, 53 with private bathroom. C$66–C$94 double with shared bathroom; C$80–C$125 double with private bathroom. Weeklong discounts available. AE, MC, V. Parking C$14. **Amenities:** Access to YWCA facility. *In room:* A/C, TV, fridge, hair dryer, Wi-Fi (C$10/day).

THE WEST END
Expensive
The Listel Hotel ★★ (Finds What makes the Listel unique is its artwork. Hallways and suites on the top two Gallery floors are decorated with original pieces from the Buschlen Mowatt Gallery or, on the Museum floor, with First Nations artifacts from the UBC Anthropology Museum (p. 84). Also unique is the fact that the Listel is the first Vancouver hotel to really go "green" with the use of solar power-generating panels. The hotel is luxurious without being flashy, and all the rooms and bathrooms feature top-quality bedding and handsome furnishings—though some bathrooms are larger than others, with separate soaker tub and shower. The roomy upper-floor suites facing Robson Street, with glimpses of the harbor and the mountains beyond, are the best bets. Rooms at the back are quieter but face the alley and nearby apartment buildings. In the evenings, you can hear live jazz at O'Doul's, the hotel's restaurant and bar. Downtown or Stanley Park is a 10-minute walk away.

1300 Robson St., Vancouver, BC V6E 1C5. ℗ **800/663-5491** or 604/684-8461. Fax 604/684-7092. www.thelistelhotel.com. 129 units. C$229–C$269 standard to Gallery room double; C$400–C$600 suite. AE, DC, DISC, MC, V. Parking C$26. **Amenities:** Restaurant; bar; concierge; executive-level rooms; exercise room; Jacuzzi; room service; free Wi-Fi. *In room:* A/C, TV w/pay movies, hair dryer, minibar.

Pacific Palisades Hotel ★★★ (Kids) (Finds)   It's hard not to like this place. Sherbet yellows and apple greens, pastel-colored fabrics, bright splashes of color, and whimsical touches make the hotel bright and welcoming (although the rock music playing in the lobby can be upbeat or annoying, depending on your mood), and the "green" policies are probably the most comprehensive in Vancouver. The rooms feature low-flow water valves, energy-efficient light bulbs, and the hotel as a whole uses eco-conscious cleaning products and has its own carbon-offset initiative. Guest rooms are spacious, airy, and equipped with kitchenettes (with minibar items priced at corner-store prices). The one-bedroom suites include large living/dining rooms and balconies. Other perks include the complimentary afternoon wine tasting in the attached art gallery, the large indoor pool and fitness rooms, and the fact that pets stay free. Zin is a cool spot for a drink and dinner. Internet is free if you sign up for the free Kimpton InTouch loyalty program.

1277 Robson St., Vancouver, BC V6E 1C4. © 800/663-1815 or 604/688-0461. Fax 604/688-4374. www. pacificpalisadeshotel.com. 233 units. C$150–C$425 double. AE, DC, DISC, MC, V. Valet parking C$25. **Amenities:** Restaurant; bar; babysitting; concierge; health club; Jacuzzi; indoor pool; room service; spa services; basketball court; yoga program. *In room:* A/C, TV, fridge, hair dryer, high-speed Internet (C$10/day), kitchenette, minibar, robes.

Westin Bayshore Resort & Marina ★★★ (Kids)   This is Vancouver's only resort hotel with its own marina, and the views from all but a handful of its rooms are stunning. The Bayshore overlooks Coal Harbour and Stanley Park on one side, and Burrard Inlet and the city on the other. The hotel is in two buildings, the original low-rise from 1961 and a newer tower, with a giant pool, restaurant, and conference center between them. All the rooms received a makeover in 2009 with comfortable, contemporary West Coast decor and floor-to-ceiling windows that open wide. In the newer tower, the rooms are a bit larger and have narrow balconies. The bathrooms in both buildings are nicely finished but fairly small. A new spa opened in October 2009. Children receive their own welcome package and love the pools.

1601 Bayshore Dr., Vancouver, BC V6G 2V4. © 800/937-8461 or 604/682-3377. Fax 604/687-3102. www. westinbayshore.com. 510 units. C$460 double. Children 17 and under stay free in parent's room. AE, DC, MC, V. Self-parking C$23; valet parking C$28. **Amenities:** 2 restaurants; bar; Starbucks; babysitting; concierge; health club; Jacuzzi; 2 pools (indoor and outdoor); room service; sauna. *In room:* A/C, TV w/pay movies, hair dryer, minibar, Wi-Fi (C$15/day).

Moderate

Barclay House Bed & Breakfast ★ (Finds)   The Barclay House is located on one of the West End's quiet maple-lined streets a block from historic Barclay Square. Built in 1904, this beautiful house is furnished in Victorian style; a number of the pieces are family heirlooms. The penthouse offers skylights, a fireplace, and a claw-foot tub; the south room contains a queen-size brass bed and an elegant sitting room. The parlors and dining rooms are perfect for lounging on a rainy afternoon or sipping a glass of complimentary sherry before dinner. On a summer day, the front porch, with its wooden Adirondack chairs, is a comfy spot to read and relax.

1351 Barclay St., Vancouver, BC V6E 1H6. © 800/971-1351 or 604/605-1351. Fax 604/605-1382. www. barclayhouse.com. 5 units. C$155–C$295 double. Rates include breakfast. AE, MC, V. Free parking. **Amenities:** Access to nearby fitness center. *In room:* TV/VCR w/pay movies, movie library, CD player, fridge, hair dryer, free Wi-Fi.

Blue Horizon (Value)   This 31-story high-rise built in the 1960s has a great location on Robson Street, just a block from the trendier Pacific Palisades and the tonier Listel Vancouver (see above for both). It's cheaper than those places and has views that are just as good if not better, but it lacks their charm and feels a bit like a high-rise motel. The rooms are fairly spacious, with a contemporary look, and every room is on a corner with wraparound windows and a small balcony; superior rooms on floors 15 to 30 offer the best views. The decor could use some updating, but overall these rooms are a good deal for this location. The hotel uses energy-efficient lighting, low-flow showerheads, and recycling bins, and the entire hotel is nonsmoking.

1225 Robson St., Vancouver, BC V6E 1C3. (© **800/663-1333** or 604/688-1411. Fax 604/688-4461. www. bluehorizonhotel.com. 214 units. C$109–C$219 double; C$119–C$219 superior double; C$199–C$329 penthouse suite. Children 15 and under stay free in parent's room. AE, DC, MC, V. Self-parking C$16. **Amenities:** Restaurant; concierge; exercise room; Jacuzzi; indoor pool; sauna. *In room:* A/C, TV w/pay movies, fridge, hair dryer, free high-speed Internet, minibar.

Sunset Inn & Suites ★ (Value) (Kids) Just a couple of blocks from English Bay on the edge of the residential West End, the Sunset Inn offers roomy studios or one-bedroom apartments with balconies and fully equipped kitchens. Like many other hotels in this part of town, the Sunset Inn started life as an apartment building, meaning the rooms are larger than at your average hotel. Request an upper floor since the views are better but the price remains the same. For those traveling with children, the one-bedroom suites have a separate bedroom and a pullout couch in the living room. All of the rooms were refurbished in 2008. The beds are comfy, the staff is helpful and friendly, and the location is great for this price.

1111 Burnaby St., Vancouver, BC V6E 1P4. (© **800/786-1997** or 604/688-2474. Fax 604/669-3340. www. sunsetinn.com. 50 units. Low season C$99–C$239 double; high season C$159–C$475 double. Additional person C$10. Rates include continental breakfast in lobby. Children 11 and under stay free in parent's room. Weekly rates available. AE, DC, MC, V. Free parking. **Amenities:** Small exercise room. *In room:* TV, kitchen, free Wi-Fi.

West End Guest House ★ (Finds) A heritage home built in 1906, the West End Guest House is a handsome example of what the neighborhood looked like before concrete towers and condos replaced the original Edwardian homes in the early 1950s. Decorated with early-20th-century antiques and a serious collection of vintage photographs of Vancouver taken by the original owners, this gay-friendly B&B is a calm, charming respite from the hustle and bustle of the West End. The seven guest rooms feature feather mattresses and down duvets; the Grand Queen Suite, an attic-level bedroom with a brass bed, fireplace, sitting area, claw-foot bathtub, and skylights, is the best and most spacious room. Owner Evan Penner and his partner, Ron Cadurette, pamper their guests with a scrumptious breakfast and serve iced tea and sherry in the afternoon.

1362 Haro St., Vancouver, BC V6E 1G2. (© **888/546-3327** or 604/681-2889. Fax 604/688-8812. www. westendguesthouse.com. 9 units. Low season C$90–C$195 double; high season C$200–C$275 double. Rates include full breakfast. AE, DISC, MC, V. Free off-street parking. **Amenities:** Bikes. *In room:* TV/DVD, hair dryer, free Wi-Fi.

Inexpensive

Buchan Hotel (Value) Built in 1926, this three-story building is tucked away on a quiet residential street in the West End, 2 blocks from Stanley Park and Denman Street. Like the Kingston (see above) downtown, this is a small European-style budget hotel that doesn't bother with frills or charming decor; unlike the Kingston, it isn't a B&B, so don't expect the second B. The standard rooms are quite plain; be prepared for cramped quarters and tiny bathrooms, half of which are shared. The best rooms are the executive

rooms: four nicely furnished front-corner rooms with private bathrooms. The hotel also
has in-house bike and ski storage, and a reading lounge.

1906 Haro St., Vancouver, BC V6G 1H7. © **800/668-6654** or 604/685-5354. Fax 604/685-5367. www.
buchanhotel.com. 60 units, 30 with private bathroom. C$53–C$86 double with shared bathroom; C$80–
C$135 double with private bathroom; C$110–C$138 executive room. Children 12 and under stay free in
parent's room. Weekly rates available. AE, DC, MC, V. Limited street parking available. **Amenities:** Lounge.
In room: TV, no phone.

THE WEST SIDE
Expensive
Granville Island Hotel ★ (Finds) One of Vancouver's best-kept secrets, this hotel is
tucked away on the edge of Granville Island in a unique waterfront setting, a short stroll
from theaters, galleries, and the fabulous Granville Island Public Market (p. 83). Rooms
in the original wing are definitely fancier, so book these if you can, but the new wing is
fine, too. Rooms are fairly spacious with traditional, unsurprising decor and large bathrooms with soaker tubs; some units have balconies and great views over False Creek. If
you don't have a car, the only potential drawback to a stay here is the location. During
the daytime when the False Creek ferries are running, it's a quick ferry ride to Yaletown
or the West End. After 10pm, however, you're looking at a C$15 to C$20 cab ride or an
hour walk. The Island after dark is reasonably happening, and the hotel's waterside restaurant and brewpub are good-weather hangout spots with outdoor seating.

1253 Johnston St., Vancouver, BC V6H 3R9. © **800/663-1840** or 604/683-7373. Fax 604/683-3061. www.
granvilleislandhotel.com. 85 units. Oct–Apr C$170 double, C$399 penthouse; May–Sept C$250 double,
C$499 penthouse. AE, DC, DISC, MC, V. Parking C$12. **Amenities:** Restaurant; brewpub; babysitting;
concierge; small fitness room w/Jacuzzi and sauna; room service; access to nearby tennis courts. *In room:*
A/C, TV w/pay movies, hair dryer, minibar, free Wi-Fi.

Inexpensive
The University of British Columbia Conference Centre ★ (Value) The Univer-
sity of British Columbia Conference Centre is in a pretty, forested setting on the tip of
Point Grey, convenient to Kitsilano and the University itself. If you don't have a car, it's
a half-hour bus ride from downtown. Although the on-campus accommodations are
actually student dorms most of the year, rooms are usually available. The rooms are nice,
but don't expect luxury. The 17-story Walter Gage Residence offers comfortable accommodations, many on the upper floors with sweeping views of the city and ocean. One-
bedroom suites come equipped with private bathrooms, kitchenettes, TVs, and phones.
Each studio has a twin bed; each one-bedroom features a queen-size bed; a six-bed Towers room—a particularly good deal for families—features one double bed and five twin
beds. The West Coast Suites, renovated in 2007, are the most appealing, and have a very
reasonable price.

5961 Student Union Blvd., Vancouver, BC V6T 2C9. © **888/822-1030** or 604/822-1000. Fax 604/822-
1001. www.ubcconferences.com. Approx. 1,500 units. Gage Towers units available May 10–Aug 26;
Pacific Spirit Hostel units available May 15–Aug 15; West Coast Suites and Marine Drive Residence units
(adjacent to the Gage Residence) available year-round. Gage Towers and Marine Drive Residences: C$39–
C$53 single with shared bathroom; C$99–C$119 studio; C$119–C$139 1-bedroom suite. Pacific Spirit
Hostel: C$33 single; C$66 double. West Coast Suites: C$159–C$199 suite. AE, MC, V. Parking C$7. Bus: 4,
17, 44, or 99. **Amenities** (on campus): Restaurant; cafeteria; pub; weight room; access to campus Olympic-size swimming pool; sauna (C$5 per person); tennis courts. *In room:* A/C, TV, hair dryer.

4 WHERE TO DINE

For travelers who love to dine out and dine well, Vancouver is a delightful discovery. It's so good, in fact, that you could come here just to eat. And here's the capper: A fabulous meal at one of Vancouver's top restaurants costs about a third less than a similar meal would cost in New York, London, or San Francisco.

Restaurant meals in British Columbia carry no provincial tax, but venues add the **6% goods and services tax (GST).** Restaurant hours vary. Lunch is typically served from noon to 1 or 2pm; Vancouverites begin dinner around 6:30pm, later in summer. Reservations are recommended at most restaurants and are essential at the city's top tables.

DOWNTOWN & YALETOWN
Very Expensive
C ★★★ SEAFOOD/PACIFIC NORTHWEST   Since opening in 1997, the popularity of this award-winning trendsetter hasn't flagged. The dining room is a cool white space with painted steel and lots of glass; the waterside location on False Creek is sublime (book an outside table if the weather is fine). Ingredients make all the difference here: The chef and his highly knowledgeable staff can tell you not only where every product comes from, but also the name of the boat or farm. Expect exquisite surprises and imaginative preparations: For appetizers, sample the fresh B.C. oysters with tongue-tingling sauces, candied salmon belly, or poached pear cannelloni. Mains are artfully created and might include twice-cooked sablefish with porcini fondue or crispy trout with black truffle puree. Give chef Robert Clark a chance to show off, and order a 6- or 10-course tasting menu as you watch the sun set over the marina. Excellent wine pairings, too.

1600 Howe St. ✆ **604/681-1164.** www.crestaurant.com. Reservations recommended. Main courses C$29–C$41; tasting menus C$98–C$130. AE, DC, MC, V. Dinner daily 5:30–11pm; lunch Mon–Fri 11:30am–2:30pm (May to Labour Day). Valet parking C$10. Bus: 1 or 2.

Expensive
Chambar Belgian Restaurant ★★ (Finds) BELGIAN   One of Vancouver's favorite restaurants, Chambar occupies an intriguing space in a kind of no man's land on lower Beatty Street between Yaletown and Gastown. Michelin-trained chef Nico Scheuerman and his wife, Karri, have worked hard to make the place a success, and plenty of plaudits have come their way. The menu features small and large plates. Smaller choices typically include mussels cooked in white wine with bacon and cream (or with fresh tomatoes), beef carpaccio, or prosciutto and grilled pear. Main dishes feature tagine of braised lamb shank with honey, and roasted halibut with curried saffron risotto. For dessert, try the Belgian chocolate mousse or the mocha soufflé. Chambar specializes in Belgian beers, with some 25 varieties in bottles and on tap.

562 Beatty St. ✆ **604/879-7119.** www.chambar.com. Reservations recommended. Small plates C$15–C$21; main courses C$28–C$29; 3-course set menu C$60. AE, MC, V. Daily 6pm–midnight. Bus: 5 or 17.

Coast ★★★ (Finds) SEAFOOD/INTERNATIONAL   This dashing restaurant moved from Yaletown to its new downtown location in 2009 and re-established itself as a culinary and people-watching spot of note. The concept at Coast is to offer an extensive variety of fresh and non-endangered seafood from coasts around the world. The dining room is a handsomely designed affair with a special "community table" that allows diners to watch the chef prepare culinary teasers such as the delicious lobster corn dog or the

Dungeness crab-and-cucumber roll. The signature coastal platter with oysters, crab claws, clams, mussels, and more is a fabulous appetizer. Then, from the grill, you could order wild B.C. salmon, B.C. lingcod, or a seafood brochette. Other temptations include Creole lobster and prawn fettuccine, Arctic char over Alsatian sauerkraut, and (always) Liverpool-style fish and chips. Accompany your meal with a recommended wine from Coast's large cellar.

1054 Alberni St. (✆) **604/685-5010.** www.coastrestaurant.ca. Reservations recommended. Main courses C$17–C$34. AE, DC, MC, V. Daily 4:30–11pm. Bus: 1 or 22.

Il Giardino di Umberto Ristorante ★★ ITALIAN   Restaurant magnate Umberto Menghi started this small restaurant, tucked away in a yellow heritage house at the bottom of Hornby Street, about 3 decades ago. It still serves some of the best Italian fare, and has one of the prettiest garden patios in town. A larger restaurant now adjoins the original house, opening up into a bright, spacious dining room that re-creates the ambience of an Italian villa. The menu leans toward Tuscany, with dishes that emphasize pasta and game. Entrees usually include classics such as *osso buco* with saffron risotto, and that Roman favorite, spaghetti carbonara. A daily list of specials makes the most of seasonal fresh ingredients, often offering outstanding seafood dishes. The wine list is comprehensive and well chosen.

1382 Hornby St. (btw. Pacific and Drake). (✆) **604/669-2422.** Fax 604/669-9723. www.umberto.com. Reservations recommended. Main courses C$15–C$35. AE, DC, MC, V. Mon–Fri noon–3pm and 6–11pm; Sat 6–11pm. Closed holidays. Bus: 1 or 22.

Moderate

Bin 941 Tapas Parlour ★ TAPAS/CASUAL   Still booming after nearly a decade, Bin 941 remains the place for trendy tapas dining. True, the music's too loud and the room's too small, but the food that alights on the bar and eight tiny tables is delicious and fun, and the wine list is great. Look especially for local seafood such as scallops and tiger prawns tournedos. In this sliver of a bistro sharing is unavoidable, so come prepared for socializing. A second Bin, dubbed Bin 942, opened at 1521 W. Broadway ((✆) **604/ 734-9421**). The tables start to fill up at 6:30pm at both spots, and by 8pm, the hip and hungry have already formed a long and eager line.

941 Davie St. (✆) **604/683-1246.** www.bin941.com. Reservations not accepted. All plates are C$16. MC, V. Daily 5pm–1:30am. Bus: 4, 5, or 8.

Sanafir ★★ (Finds) INTERNATIONAL   Influenced by the exotic dining and decor found along the Silk Road, Sanafir creates an opulent and fun dining experience that doesn't cost a fortune. The first-floor dining room is loud and buzzily exciting, but parties can also drink and dine upstairs while reclining on pillows beneath sexy harem-style draperies. The tapas-style plates come in three of five possible Silk Road variations: Asian, Mediterranean, Middle Eastern, Indian, or North African. And the trio of tastes costs only C$14. Order the chicken, for instance, and your three-dish tapas plate might contain Moroccan chicken tagine with saffron herb couscous, Indonesian chicken satays with lemon grass and peanut sauce, and Kashmir-style Tandoori chicken with mango chutney. Larger chef's specials are also available, such as the super-rich oxtail cappelletti with white truffle cream, Parmigiano-Reggiano, and shaved black truffle. There's no sign outside, so just look for the most glamorous place on gentrifying Granville Street, and you'll be there.

1026 Granville St. (at Nelson). (✆) **604/678-1049.** www.sanafir.ca. Reservations recommended. Tapas C$14; chef's specials C$17. AE, DC, MC, V. Daily 5pm–midnight. Bus: 4 or 7.

Simply Thai ★ THAI   At this small restaurant in trendy Yaletown, you can watch chef and owner Siriwan in the open kitchen as she cooks up a combination of northern and southern Thai dishes with some fusion sensations. The appetizers are perfect finger foods: *Gai satay* features succulent pieces of grilled chicken breast marinated in coconut milk and spices and covered in a peanut sauce, while the delicious *cho muang* consists of violet-colored dumplings stuffed with minced chicken. Main courses run the gamut of Thai cuisine: noodle dishes and coconut curries with beef, chicken, or pork, as well as a good number of vegetarian options. Don't miss the *tom kha gai,* a deceptively simple-looking coconut soup with chicken, mushrooms, and lemon grass. The set menu is a good way to sample a bit of everything.

1211 Hamilton St. ✆ **604/642-0123.** www.simplythairestaurant.com. Reservations recommended on weekends. Main courses C$13–C$18; set menu C$40. AE, DC, MC, V. Mon–Fri 11:30am–3pm and 5–10:30pm; Sat–Sun 5–10:30pm. Bus: 2.

GASTOWN & CHINATOWN
Expensive
The Cannery ★ SEAFOOD   At least some of the pleasure of eating at The Cannery comes from the adventure of finding the place. (Drive or take a cab because it's impossible to get there on foot or by public transportation.) Hop the railroad tracks, thread your way past a harbor security checkpoint, pass container terminals and fish-packing plants, and there it is—a timber-framed rectangular building hanging out over the waters of Burrard Inlet. The interior, with its exposed beams and seafaring memorabilia, adds to the charm, but many come here for the view, one of the best in Vancouver. You'll find good, solid, traditional seafood, and ever-changing specials. Famous dishes include salmon Wellington (salmon, shrimp, and mushrooms baked in a puff pastry), smoked Alaskan black cod, and roasted mussels. Meat lovers can get a grilled New York steak or Alberta beef tenderloin. Chef Frederic Couton has been getting more inventive lately, but when an institution founded in 1971 is still going strong, no one's ever *too* keen to rock the boat. The wine list is stellar, and the desserts are wonderfully inventive.

2205 Commissioner St. (near Victoria Dr.). ✆ **877/254-9606** or 604/254-9606. www.canneryseafood. com. Reservations recommended. Main courses C$24–C$41. AE, DC, DISC, MC, V. Tues–Fri 11:30am–2:30pm and 5:30–9pm; Sat 5–9:30pm; Sun 5–9pm. Closed Dec 24–26. From downtown, head east on Hastings St., turn left on Victoria Dr. (2 blocks past Commercial Dr.), then right on Commissioner St.

Moderate
Park Lock Seafood Restaurant (Kids) CHINESE/DIM SUM   If you've never done dim sum, this large, second-floor dining room in the heart of Chinatown is a good place to give it a try, even though you'll have to listen to schlocky Western music while you dine. From 8am to 3pm daily, waitresses wheel little carts loaded with Chinese delicacies past the tables. When you see something you like, just point and ask for it. The final bill is based upon how many little plates are left on your table. Dishes include spring rolls, *hargow* (shrimp dumplings), *shumai* (steamed shrimp, beef, or pork dumplings), prawns wrapped in fresh white noodles, small steamed buns, sticky rice cooked in banana leaves, curried squid, and lots more. Parties of four or more are best—that way you get to try each other's food.

544 Main St. (at E. Pender St., on the 2nd floor). ✆ **604/688-1581.** Reservations recommended. Main courses C$10–C$25; dim sum C$3–C$7. AE, MC, V. Mon–Thurs 7:30am–4pm; Fri–Sun 7:30am–4pm and 5–9:30pm. Bus: 19 or 22.

Inexpensive

Salt ★ CHARCUTERIE   The location of this new dining spot in Gastown's Blood Alley might put some visitors off, and that's really a shame because Salt is unique, and it's a wonderful place to get a good, inexpensive meal. The minimalistically modern room is set with communal spruce dining tables. Salt has no kitchen per se, as it serves only cured meats and artisan cheeses plus a daily soup, a couple of salads, and grilled meat and cheese sandwiches. For the tasting plate, you mix and match three of the meats and cheeses listed on the blackboard. To drink, choose from a selection of beers, and several good wines and whiskeys, or opt for a wine flight. As Blood Alley has no apparent street numbers, look for the salt shaker flag over the doorway. Try it for lunch if you're in Gastown.

45 Blood Alley, Gastown. ℂ **604/633-1912.** www.salttastingroom.com. Tasting plates C$15; lunch specials C$12. AE, MC, V. Daily noon–midnight. Bus: 1 or 8.

THE WEST END
Expensive

Cin Cin ★★★ MODERN ITALIAN   Vancouverites looking for great food and a romantic atmosphere frequent this award-winning, second-floor restaurant on Robson Street. The spacious dining room, done in a rustic Italian-villa style, surrounds an open kitchen built around a huge wood-fired oven and grill; the heated terrace is an equally pleasant dining and people-watching spot. The dishes, inspired by Italy but using locally sourced ingredients, change monthly, but your meal might begin with house-made Dungeness crab sausage with herb salad and lemon vinaigrette, followed by bison-filled gnocchi or biodynamic rice with scallops. Mouthwatering main courses include local fish and meat cooked in the wood-fired oven or on the wood grill, and a delicious pizza with sautéed wild mushrooms, peppercorn pecorino, and caramelized onions. The wine list is extensive, as is the selection of wines by the glass. The service is as exemplary as the food.

1154 Robson St. ℂ **604/688-7338.** www.cincin.net. Reservations recommended. Main courses C$21–C$36; fixed-price menu (5–6pm) C$45. AE, DC, MC, V. Mon–Fri 11:30am–2:30pm and 5–11pm; Sat–Sun 5–11pm. Bus: 5 or 22.

Raincity Grill ★★★ PACIFIC NORTHWEST   This top-starred restaurant on a busy, buzzy corner across from English Bay is a gem—painstaking in preparation, arty in presentation, and yet completely unfussy in atmosphere. Raincity Grill was one of the very first restaurants in Vancouver to embrace the "buy locally, eat seasonally" concept and pioneered the OceanWise sustainable seafood organization. The menu focuses on seafood, game, poultry, and organic vegetables from British Columbia and the Pacific Northwest. The room is long, low, and intimate. To sample a bit of everything, I recommend the seasonal "100 miles" tasting menu, a bargain at C$70, or C$80 with wine pairings. One recent tasting menu included wild B.C. salmon with smoked turnip and potato roulade; roasted Berkshire pork belly with pear and parsnip puree; and spiced cider soup—all of it made with ingredients found within 161km (100 miles) of the restaurant. The wine list is huge and, in keeping with the restaurant's philosophy, sticks pretty close to home. From May through Labour Day, Raincity opens a takeout window on Denman Street, where you can get a gourmet sandwich, salad, and sweet to go for C$10.

1193 Denman St. ℂ **604/685-7337.** www.raincitygrill.com. Reservations recommended. Main courses C$17–C$33. AE, DC, MC, V. Mon–Fri 11:30am–2:30pm and 5–10:30pm; Sat–Sun 10:30am–3pm (brunch) and 5–10:30pm. Bus: 1 or 5.

Hapa Izakaya ★ JAPANESE   Dinner comes at almost disco decibels in Robson Street's hottest Japanese "eat-drink place" (the literal meaning of Izakaya), where chefs call out orders, servers shout acknowledgments, and the maitre d' and owner keep up a running volley to staff about the (often sizable) wait at the door. The menu features inventive nontraditional dishes such as bacon-wrapped asparagus, *negitori* (spicy tuna roll), and fresh tuna belly chopped with spring onions and served with bite-size bits of garlic bread. Inventive appetizers and meat dishes and a scrumptious Korean hot pot are also on the menu, for the non–raw fish eaters in your party. The crowd is about a third expat Japanese, a third Chinese (both local and expat), and a third Westerners. The service is fast and obliging, and the price per dish is reasonable. A second location is in Kitsilano at 1516 Yew St. (📞 **604/738-4272**).

1479 Robson St. 📞 **604/689-4272.** www.hapaizakaya.com. No reservations accepted 6–8pm. Main courses C$8–C$14. AE, MC, V. Sun–Thurs 5:30pm–midnight; Fri–Sat 5:30pm–1am. Bus: 5.

Romano's Macaroni Grill (Kids) FAMILY STYLE/ITALIAN   It's almost worth eating here just to see the interior. Housed in a stone mansion built in 1900 by sugar baron B. T. Rogers, Romano's is a fun and casual chain restaurant with an Italian-influenced menu. This isn't high-concept Italian; the food is simple, understandable, and reliably good. The pastas are definitely favorites. The children's menu features lasagna, mac and cheese, spaghetti with meatball, and tasty pizzas. In the summer it's fun to dine outside on the beautiful garden patio, but the stunning interior, filled with handcrafted wood detailing and stained glass, is pretty amazing.

1523 Davie St. 📞 **604/689-4334.** www.macgrillbc.com. Reservations recommended. Main courses C$12–C$23; children's courses C$5. AE, DC, MC, V. Mon–Thurs noon–10pm; Fri–Sat noon–11pm. Bus: 5.

Tanpopo (Value) JAPANESE   Occupying the second floor of a corner building on Denman Street, Tanpopo has a partial view of English Bay, a large patio, and a huge menu of hot and cold Japanese dishes. But the line of people waiting 30 minutes or more every night for a table are here for the all-you-can-eat buffet. The unlimited fare includes the standards—makis, tuna and salmon sashimi, California and B.C. rolls—as well as cooked items such as tonkatsu, tempura, chicken kara-age, and broiled oysters. The quality is okay, a bit above average for an all-you-can-eat place. A couple of secrets to getting seated: You might try to call ahead, but they take only an arbitrary number of reservations for dinner each day. Otherwise, ask to sit at the sushi bar.

1122 Denman St. 📞 **604/681-7777.** Reservations recommended for groups. Main courses C$7–C$20; all-you-can-eat buffet C$22 for dinner, C$14 for lunch. AE, DC, MC, V. Daily 11:30am–10pm. Bus: 5.

Inexpensive

Banana Leaf ★ MALAYSIAN   One of the city's best spots for Malaysian food, Banana Leaf is just a hop and a skip from English Bay. The menu includes inventive specials such as mango and okra salad, delicious South Asian mainstays such as *gado gado* (a salad with hot peanut sauce), *mee goreng* (fried noodles with vegetables topped by a fried egg), and occasional variations such as an assam curry (seafood in hot-and-sour curry sauce), with okra and tomato. Must-tries are sambal green beans and a signature chile crab. For dessert, don't pass up *pisang goreng*—fried banana with ice cream. The seven-course tasting menu (C$30) lets you sample a bit of everything. The small room is tastefully decorated in dark tropical woods; service is very friendly. Other locations are at

1096 Denman St. © **604/683-3333**. www.bananaleaf-vancouver.com. Main courses C$11–C$20. AE, MC, V. Sun–Thurs 11:30am–10pm; Fri–Sat 11:30am–11pm. Bus: 5.

Stephos (Value) GREEK   A longtime fixture on the Davie Street dining scene, Stephos offers Greek food at its simplest and cheapest. Customers line up outside for a seat amid Greek travel posters, potted ivy, and whitewashed walls (the average wait is about 10–15 min., but it could be as long as 30 min., as once you're inside, the staff will never rush you out the door). Order some pita and dip (hummus, spicy eggplant, or garlic spread) while you peruse the menu. An interesting appetizer is the *avgolemono* soup, a delicately flavored chicken broth with egg and lemon, accompanied by a plate of piping hot pita bread. When choosing a main course, keep in mind that portions are huge. The roasted lamb, lamb chops, fried calamari, and a variety of souvlaki are served with rice, roast potatoes, and Greek salad. The beef, lamb, or chicken pita come in slightly smaller portions served with fries and *tsatsiki* (a sauce made from yogurt, cucumber, and garlic).

1124 Davie St. © **604/683-2555**. Reservations accepted for parties of 5 or more. Main courses C$6– C$11. AE, MC, V. Daily 11am–11:30pm. Bus: 5.

THE WEST SIDE
Very Expensive

Tojo's Restaurant ★★★ JAPANESE   Tojo's is considered Vancouver's top Japanese restaurant, the place where celebs and food cognoscenti come to dine on the best sushi in town. It's expensive, but the food is absolutely fresh, inventive, and boy is it good. The dining room's main area wraps around Chef Tojo and his sushi chefs with a giant curved maple sake bar and an adjoining sushi bar. Tojo's ever-changing menu offers such specialties as sea urchin on the half shell, herring roe, lobster claws, tuna, crab, and barbecue eel. Go for the Chef's Arrangement—tell them how much you're willing to spend (per person), and let the good times roll.

1133 W. Broadway. © **604/872-8050**. www.tojos.com. Reservations required. Main courses C$16–C$30; sushi/sashimi C$8–C$28; Chef's Arrangement C$50–C$100. AE, DC, MC, V. Mon–Sat 5–10pm. Closed Christmas week. Bus: 9.

West ★★★ FRENCH/PACIFIC NORTHWEST   Every meal I've had at this award-winning restaurant—it was voted "Best Restaurant in Vancouver" by *Vancouver* magazine 4 years in a row—has been memorable. The credo at West is deceptively simple: "True to our region, true to the seasons." That means fresh, organic, locally harvested seafood, game, and produce are transformed into extraordinary creations. The menu changes three to four times a week, but first courses might include lightly poached B.C. spot prawns in a rhubarb and watermelon essence or quail tortellini with roasted sweet corn puree. For a main course you might find fillet of smoked sablefish, seared Qualicum Bay scallops with smoked veal tongue, or crisp sliced porchetta with black garlic and toasted gnocchi. For the ultimate dining experience, try one of the seasonal tasting menus—a multicourse progression through the best the restaurant has to offer. A carefully chosen wine list includes a selection of affordable wines by the glass and half-bottle. If you're really into cooking, reserve one of the two "chef tables" adjacent to Chef Warren Geraghty's bustling kitchen.

2881 Granville St. © **604/738-8938**. www.westrestaurant.com. Reservations recommended. Main courses C$22–C$32 lunch, C$37–C$44 dinner; tasting menus C$85–C$98. AE, DC, MC, V. Mon–Fri 11:30am–2:30pm and 5:30–11pm; Sat–Sun 5:30–11pm. Bus: 8.

Vij ★★★ INDIAN   Vij doesn't take reservations, as is apparent by the line outside every night, but patrons huddled under the neon sign don't seem to mind since they're treated to tea and *papadums* (a thin bread made from lentils). Inside, the decor is as warm and subtle as the seasonings, which are all roasted, hand-ground, and used with studied delicacy. The menu changes monthly, though some of the more popular entrees remain constant. Recent offerings included beef short ribs in a cinnamon and red-wine curry; eggplant and papaya curry with chickpeas and roasted almonds; and chicken breast in clove, garlic, and yogurt curry. Vegetarian selections abound, including curried vegetable rice pilaf with cilantro cream sauce, and Indian lentils with naan and *raita* (yogurt-mint sauce). The wine and beer list is short but carefully selected. And for teetotalers, Vij has developed a souped-up version of the traditional Indian chai, the chaiuccino. Vij recently opened Rangoli, right next door, for lunch and takeout.

1480 W. 11th Ave. ⓒ **604/736-6664.** www.vijs.ca. Reservations not accepted. Main courses C$23–C$26. AE, DC, MC, V. Daily 5:30–10pm. Closed Dec 24–Jan 8. Bus: 8 or 10.

Inexpensive

Annapurna ★ ⟨**Value**⟩ INDIAN/VEGETARIAN   A Kitsilano favorite. The menu is all vegetarian, but with the amazing combinations of Indian spices, herbs, and local vegetables, the dishes are rich and satisfying. The wine list is small but very reasonably priced.

1812 W. 4th Ave. ⓒ **604/736-5959.** Main courses C$11–C$13. AE, MC, V. Daily 11:30am–10pm. Bus: 4 or 7.

Incendio West ★ ⟨**Finds**⟩ PIZZA   If you're looking for something casual and local that won't be full of other tourists, this Kitsilano pizzeria is just the spot. The 22 pizza combinations are served on fresh, crispy crusts baked in a wood-fired oven; pastas are homemade. The wine list is decent; the beer list is inspired.

2118 Burrard St. ⓒ **604/736-2220.** Main courses C$14–C$24. AE, MC, V. Mon–Thurs 11:30am–3pm and 5–10pm; Fri 11:30am–3pm and 5–11pm; Sat 5–11pm; Sun 4:30–10pm. Closed Dec 23–Jan 3. Bus: 1 or 8.

The Naam Restaurant ★ ⟨**Kids**⟩ VEGETARIAN   Back in the '60s, when Kitsilano was Canada's hippie haven, the Naam was tie-dye central. Things have changed since then, but Vancouver's oldest vegetarian and natural-food restaurant still retains a pleasant granola feel, and it's open 24/7. The decor is simple, earnest, and welcoming, and includes well-worn wooden tables and chairs, plants, an assortment of local art, a nice garden patio, and live music every night. The brazenly healthy fare ranges from all-vegetarian burgers, enchiladas, and burritos to tofu teriyaki, Thai noodles, and a variety of pita pizzas. The sesame spice fries are a Vancouver institution.

2724 W. 4th Ave. ⓒ **604/738-7151.** www.thenaam.com. Reservations accepted on weekdays only. Main courses C$7–C$12. AE, MC, V. Daily 24 hr. Live music every night 7–10pm. Bus: 4 or 22.

Sophie's Cosmic Café ⟨**Kids**⟩ FAMILY STYLE/AMERICAN   For a fabulous home-cooked, diner-style breakfast in a laid-back but buzzy atmosphere, come to this Kitsilano landmark. On Sunday morning get here early, or you may have to wait a half-hour or more to get in. You can also have a good, filling lunch or dinner here. Every available space in Sophie's is crammed with toys and knickknacks from the 1950s and 1960s, so, understandably, children are inordinately fond of the place. Crayons and coloring paper are always on hand. The menu is simple and includes pastas, burgers and fries, great milkshakes, and a few classic Mexican and "international" dishes, but it's the breakfast menu that draws the crowds.

2095 W. 4th Ave. ⓒ **604/732-6810.** www.sophiescosmiccafe.com. Main courses C$5–C$17. MC, V. Daily 8am–9:30pm. Bus: 4 or 7.

Moderate

The Locus Café CASUAL/SOUTHWESTERN   Even if you arrive by your lone-some, you'll soon have plenty of friends because the Locus is a cheek-by-jowl kind of place, filled with a friendly, funky crowd of artsy Mount Pleasant types. The big bar is overhung with "swamp-gothic" lacquer trees and surrounded by a tier of stools with booths and tiny tables. The cuisine originated in the American Southwest and picked up an edge along the way, as demonstrated in the roasted half-chicken with a cumin-corian-der crust and sambuca citrus demi glace. Keep an eye out for fish specials, such as grilled tomba tuna with a grapefruit and mango glaze. The pan-seared calamari makes a perfect appetizer. Bowen Island Brewing Company provides the beer, so quality's high. Your only real problem is catching the eye of the busy bartender.

4121 Main St. *C* **604/708-4121.** www.locusonmain.com. Reservations recommended. Main courses C$10–C$16. MC, V. Mon–Sat 11am–1:30am; Sun 11am–midnight. Bus: 3.

---

5 EXPLORING VANCOUVER

A city perched on the edge of a great wilderness, Vancouver offers unrivaled opportuni-ties for exploring the outdoors. But within the city limits, Vancouver is intensely urban, with buzzy sidewalk cafes and busy shopping streets. The forest of high-rises ringing the central part of the city reminds some visitors of New York or Shanghai, and Chinatown inevitably invites comparisons to San Francisco. But similarities with other places begin to pall as you come to realize that Vancouver is entirely its own creation: a young, self-confident, sparklingly beautiful city like no other place on Earth.

THE TOP ATTRACTIONS
Downtown & the West End

Bill Reid Gallery of Northwest Coast Art ★★   This downtown museum-gallery showcases the work of the great Northwest coast First Nations artist Bill Reid, who died in 1994. Permanent installations include the Raven's Trove: Gold Masterworks by Bill Reid; the monumental bronze sculpture Mythic Messengers, Reid's masterful composi-tion of 11 intertwined figures recounting traditional Haida myths; a monumental cedar tribute pole carved by Haida Chief 7idansuu (Jim Hart) honoring Reid.

639 Hornby St. *C* **604/682-3455.** www.billreidgallery.ca. Admission C$10 adults, C$7 seniors and stu-dents, C$5 children 6–17, C$25 families. Summer Tues–Fri 10am–5pm, Sat–Sun 11am–5pm; winter Wed–Sun 11am–5pm.

Stanley Park ★★★ **(Kids)**   The green jewel of Vancouver, Stanley Park is a 400-hect-are (988-acre) rainforest jutting out into the ocean from the edge of the busy West End. Exploring the second-largest urban forest in Canada is one of Vancouver's quintessential experiences.

The park, created in 1888, is filled with towering western red cedar and Douglas fir, manicured lawns, flower gardens, placid lagoons, and countless shaded walking trails that meander through it all. The famed **seawall** ★★★ runs along the waterside edge of the park, allowing cyclists and pedestrians to experience the magical interface of forest, sea, and sky. One of the most popular free attractions in the park is the **collection of totem poles** ★★★ at Brockton Point, most of them carved in the 1980s to replace the original ones that were placed in the park in the 1920s and 1930s. The area around the totem poles features open-air displays on the Coast Salish First Nations and a small gift shop/ visitor information center.

The park is home to lots of wildlife, including beavers, coyotes, bald eagles, blue herons, cormorants, trumpeter swans, brant geese, ducks, raccoons, skunks, and gray squirrels imported from New York's Central Park decades ago and now quite at home in the Pacific Northwest. (No, there are no bears.) For directions and maps, brochures, and exhibits on the nature and ecology of Stanley Park, visit the **Lost Lagoon Nature House** (© **604/257-8544;** daily 10am–7pm July 1 to Labour Day, weekends only outside this period; free admission). On Sundays at 1pm, rain or shine, they offer Discovery Walks of the park (pre-registration recommended). Equally nature-focused but with way more wow is the **Vancouver Aquarium** ★★ (see below). The **Stanley Park Children's Farmyard** (© **604/257-8531**) is a petting zoo with peacocks, rabbits, calves, donkeys, and Shetland ponies. Next to the petting zoo is **Stanley Park's Miniature Railway** ★ (© **604/257-8531**), a diminutive steam locomotive that pulls passenger cars on a circuit through the woods.

Swimmers head to **Third Beach** and **Second Beach** (p. 86), the latter with an outdoor pool beside English Bay. For kids there's a free **Spray Park** near Lumberman's Arch, where they can run and splash through various water-spewing fountains. Perhaps the best way to explore the park is to rent a bike (p. 87) or in-line skates, and set off along the seawall. If you decide to walk, remember the free shuttle bus that circles the park every 15 minutes, allowing passengers to alight and descend at most of the park's many attractions. The wonderful **horse-drawn carriage ride** ★★★ operated by **AAA Horse & Carriage Ltd.** (© **604/681-5115;** www.stanleypark.com) is one of the most enjoyable ways to tour the park. Carriage tours depart every 20 minutes mid-March through October from the lower aquarium parking lot on Park Drive near the Georgia Street park entrance. The ride lasts an hour and covers portions of the park that many locals have never seen. Rates are C$27 for adults, C$25 for seniors and students, and C$15 for children 3 to 12.

Of the three restaurants located in the park, the best is the Fish House in Stanley Park, where you can have lunch, afternoon tea, or dinner.

Stanley Park. © **604/257-8400.** http://vancouver.ca/parks. Free admission; charge for individual attractions. Park does not close. Bus: 23, 35, or 135; free "Around the Park" shuttle bus circles the park at 15-min. intervals mid-June to late Sept (visitors can get off and on at 14 points of interest). Parking entire day C$7 summer, C$4 winter.

Vancouver Aquarium Marine Science Centre ★★ (Kids)

One of North America's largest and best, the Vancouver Aquarium houses more than 8,000 marine species. From platforms above or through underwater viewing windows you can watch the white beluga whales flashing through their pools. (One of the belugas gave birth in June 2008, and as of press time another one is expecting.) There are also sea otters, Steller sea lions, and a Pacific white-sided dolphin.

Stanley Park. © **604/659-FISH** (3474). www.vanaqua.org. Admission C$20 adults; C$15 seniors, students, and youths 13–18; C$12 children 4–12; free for children 3 and under. Summer daily 9am–7pm; winter daily 9:30am–5pm. Bus: 135; "Around the Park" shuttle bus June–Sept only. Parking C$7 summer, C$4 winter.

Vancouver Art Gallery ★★

Designed as a courthouse by B.C.'s leading early-20th-century architect Francis Rattenbury (the architect of Victoria's Empress Hotel and the Parliament buildings), and renovated into an art gallery by B.C.'s leading late-20th-century architect Arthur Erickson, the Gallery is an excellent stop to see what sets

Canadian and West Coast art apart from the rest of the world. Along with an impressive collection of paintings by B.C. native **Emily Carr** ★★★ are examples of a unique Canadian art style created during the 1920s by members of the "Group of Seven," which included Vancouver painter Fred Varley. The Gallery also hosts rotating exhibits of contemporary sculpture, graphics, photography, and video art from around the world. Geared to younger audiences, the Annex Gallery offers rotating presentations of visually exciting educational exhibits.

750 Hornby St. (**C**) **604/662-4719.** www.vanartgallery.bc.ca. Admission C$18 adults, C$13 seniors, C$12 students, C$7 children 5–12, C$47 families, Tues 5–9pm by donation. Wed and Fri–Mon 10am–5:30pm; Tues and Thurs 10am–9pm. SkyTrain: Granville. Bus: 3.

Gastown & Chinatown
Dr. Sun Yat-Sen Classical Chinese Garden ★★
This small reproduction of a Classical Chinese scholar's garden truly is a remarkable place, but to get the full effect, it's best to take the free guided tour. Untrained eyes will only see a pretty pond surrounded by bamboo and oddly shaped rocks. The engaging guides, however, can explain this unique urban garden's Taoist yin-yang design principle, in which harmony is achieved through dynamic opposition. To foster opposition (and thus harmony) in the garden, Chinese designers place contrasting elements in juxtaposition: Soft-moving water flows across solid stone; smooth, swaying bamboo grows around gnarled immovable rocks; dark pebbles are placed next to light pebbles in the paving. Moving with the guide, you discover the symbolism of intricate carvings and marvel at the subtle, ever-changing views from covered serpentine corridors.

578 Carrall St. www.vancouverchinesegarden.com. Admission C$9 adults, C$7 seniors and students, free for children 5 and under, C$20 family pass. Free guided tour included. May–June 14 and Sept daily 10am–6pm; June 15–Aug daily 9:30am–7pm; Oct–Apr Tues–Sun 10am–4:30pm. Bus: 19 or 22.

The West Side
Granville Island ★★★ (Kids)
Almost a city within a city, Granville Island is a good place to browse away a morning, an afternoon, or a whole day. You can wander through a busy public market jammed with food stalls, shop for crafts, pick up some fresh seafood, enjoy a great dinner, watch the latest theater performance, rent a yacht, stroll along the waterfront, or simply run through the sprinkler on a hot summer day; it's all there and more. If you only have a short period of time, make sure you spend at least part of it in the **Granville Island Public Market** ★★★, one of the best all-around markets in North America.

Once a declining industrial site, Granville Island started transforming in the late 1970s when the government encouraged new, people-friendly developments. Maintaining its original industrial look, the former warehouses and factories now house galleries, artist studios, restaurants, and theaters; the cement plant on the waterfront is the only industrial tenant left. Access to Granville Island is by Aquabus from the West End, Yaletown, or Kitsilano, or by foot, bike, or car across the bridge at Anderson Street (access from W. 2nd Ave.). Avoid driving over on weekends and holidays—you'll spend more time trying to find a parking place than in the galleries. Check the website for upcoming events or stop by the information center, behind the Kids Market.

Located on the south shore of False Creek, under the Granville St. Bridge. For studio and gallery hours and other information about Granville Island, contact the information center at (**C**) **604/666-5784.** www.granvilleisland.com. Public market daily 9am–7pm. For information on getting to Granville Island, see "By Miniferry," earlier in this chapter. Bus: 50.

H. R. MacMillan Space Centre ★ **Kids**   In the same building as the Vancouver Museum (see below), the space center and observatory has hands-on displays and exhibits that will delight budding astronomy buffs and their parents (or older space buffs and their children). Displays are highly interactive: In the Cosmic Courtyard, you can try designing a spacecraft or maneuvering a lunar robot. Or, punch a button and get a video explanation of the *Apollo 17* manned-satellite engine that stands before you. The exciting **Virtual Voyages Simulator** ★★ takes you on a voyage to Mars—it's a thrilling experience for kids and adults. In the GroundStation Canada Theatre, video presentations explore Canada's contributions to the space program and space in general. The Star Theatre shows movies—many of them for children—on an overhead dome. The Planetarium Star Theatre features exciting laser shows in the evening.

1100 Chestnut St., in Vanier Park. ✆ **604/738-7827.** www.hrmacmillanspacecentre.com. Admission C$15 adults; C$11 seniors, students, and children 5–10; C$7 children 4 and under; C$45 families (up to 5, maximum 2 adults). Evening laser shows C$11 each. Tues–Sun 10am–5pm; evening laser shows Fri–Sat 8, 9:15, and 10:20pm. Closed Dec 25. Bus: 22.

Museum of Anthropology ★★★ **Kids**   In 1976, B.C. architect Arthur Erickson created a classic Native post-and-beam-style structure out of poured concrete and glass to house one of the world's finest collections of Northwest coast Native art. A major renovation in 2009 more than doubled the gallery space and added new luster to this remarkable showplace.

Enter through doors that resemble a huge, carved, bent-cedar box. Artifacts from different coastal communities flank the ramp leading to the Great Hall's **collection of totem poles.** Haida artist Bill Reid's cedar bear and sea wolf sculptures sit at the Cross Roads; Reid's masterpiece, *The Raven and the First Men,* is worth the price of admission all by itself. The huge carving in glowing yellow cedar depicts a Haida creation myth, in which Raven—the trickster—coaxes humanity out into the world from its birthplace in a clamshell. Some of Reid's fabulous jewelry creations in gold and silver are also on display.

6393 NW Marine Dr. (at Gate 4). ✆ **604/822-3825.** www.moa.ubc.ca. Admission C$9 adults; C$7 seniors, students, and children 6–18; free for children 5 and under; free Tues 5–9pm. Summer Wed–Mon 10am–5pm, Tues 10am–9pm; winter Wed–Sun 11am–5pm, Tues 11am–9pm. Closed Dec 25–26. Bus: 4 or 99 (10-min. walk from UBC bus loop).

Vancouver Museum   Located in the same building as the H. R. MacMillan Space Centre (see above), the Vancouver Museum is dedicated to the city's history, from its days as a Native settlement and European outpost to its 20th-century maturation into a modern urban center. The exhibits have been remounted and revitalized to make them more interesting to the casual visitor. Of most importance here is the wonderful collection of First Nations art and artifacts. Hilarious, campy fun abounds in the 1950s Room, where a period film chronicles "Dorothy's All-Electric Home." Next to this is another fun, and socially intriguing, room devoted to Vancouver's years as a hippie capital, with film clips, commentary, and a replica hippie apartment.

1100 Chestnut St. ✆ **604/736-4431.** www.museumofvancouver.ca. Admission C$11 adults, C$9 seniors, C$7 youths 4–19. Fri–Wed 10am–5pm; Thurs 10am–9pm. Closed Mon Sept–Apr. Bus: 22, then walk 3 blocks south on Cornwall Ave. Boat: Granville Island Ferry to Heritage Harbour.

North Vancouver & West Vancouver

Grouse Mountain ★★ **Kids**   Once a local ski hill, Grouse Mountain has developed into a year-round mountain recreation park that claims to be the number-one attraction in Vancouver. It's fun if you're sports minded or like the outdoors; if not, you might find it disappointing. Located only a 15-minute drive from downtown, the **SkyRide gondola** ★★ transports you to the mountain's 1,110m (3,642-ft.) summit. (Hikers can take a near vertical trail called the Grouse Grind.) On a clear day, the **view** ★★★ from the top is the best around: You can see the city and the entire lower mainland, from far up the Fraser Valley east across the Strait of Georgia to Vancouver Island. In the lodge, **Theater in the Sky** ★ shows wildlife movies. Outside, in the winter, you can ski and snowboard (26 runs, 13 runs for night skiing/snowboarding; drop-in ski lessons available), go snow-shoeing, skate on the highest outdoor rink in Canada, take a brief "sleigh ride" (behind a huge snow-cat), and the kids can play in a special snow park. In warmer weather, you can wander forest trails, take a scenic chair ride, enjoy a lumberjack show or Birds in Motion demonstrations, visit the Refuge for Endangered Wildlife, or ride on the moun-tain-bike trails. Most of these activities are included in the rather exorbitant price of your SkyRide ticket; you have to pay extra for a lift ticket and equipment rentals. Casual and fine-dining options, and a Starbucks, are in the lodge.

6400 Nancy Greene Way, North Vancouver. ✆ **604/984-0661.** www.grousemountain.com. SkyRide C$35 adults, C$33 seniors, C$21 youths 13–18, C$13 children 5–12, free children 4 and under. Full day ski-lift tickets C$50 adults, C$40 seniors and youths, C$22 children, C$150 families (2 adults, 2 children 17 and under). SkyRide free with advance Observatory Restaurant reservation. Daily 9am–10pm. Bus: 232, then transfer to bus 236. SeaBus: Lonsdale Quay, then transfer to bus 236. Car: Hwy. 99 north across Lions Gate Bridge, take North Vancouver exit to Marine Dr., then up Capilano Rd. for 5km (3 miles). Parking C$3 for 2 hr. in lots below SkyRide.

VANCOUVER'S PARKS

Park and garden lovers are in heaven in Vancouver. The wet, mild climate is ideal for gardening, and come spring the city blazes with blossoming cherry trees, rhododendrons, camellias, azaleas, and spring bulbs—and roses in summer. Gardens are everywhere. For general information about Vancouver's parks, call ✆ **604/257-8400,** or try http://vancouver.ca/parks. For information on **Stanley Park** ★★★, the queen of them all, see p. 81.

On the West Side you'll find the magnificent **UBC Botanical Garden,** one of the largest living botany collections on the West Coast, and the sublime **Nitobe Japanese Garden.**

In Chinatown, the **Dr. Sun Yat-Sen Classical Chinese Garden** ★★ (p. 83) is a small, tranquil oasis in the heart of the city, built by artisans from Suzhou, China; right next to it, accessed via the Chinese Cultural Centre on Pender Street, is the pretty (and free) **Dr. Sun Yat-Sen Park,** with a pond, walkways, and plantings.

On the West Side, **Queen Elizabeth Park**—at Cambie Street and West 33rd Ave-nue—sits atop a 150m-high (492-ft.) extinct volcano and is the highest urban vantage point south of downtown, offering panoramic views in all directions. Along with the rose garden in Stanley Park, it's Vancouver's most popular location for wedding-photo ses-sions, with well-manicured gardens and a profusion of colorful flora. There are areas for lawn bowling, tennis, pitch-and-putt golf, and picnicking. The **Bloedel Conservatory** (✆ **604/257-8584**) stands next to the park's huge sunken garden, an amazing reclama-tion of an abandoned rock quarry. A 42m-high (138-ft.) domed structure, the conserva-tory (daily 10am–5pm) houses a tropical rainforest with more than 100 plant species as well as free-flying tropical birds. Admission to the conservatory is C$5 for adults, with discounts for seniors, children, and families. Take bus no. 15 to reach the park.

Vancouver's 22-hectare (54-acre) **VanDusen Botanical Gardens,** 5251 Oak St., at West 37th Avenue (© **604/878-9274;** www.vandusengarden.org), located just a few blocks from Queen Elizabeth Park and the Bloedel Conservatory, concentrates on whole ecosystems. From towering trees to little lichens on the smallest of damp stones, the gardeners at VanDusen attempt to re-create the plant life of a number of different environments. Should all this tree gazing finally pall, head for the farthest corner of the garden to the devilishly difficult Elizabethan garden maze. Admission April through September: C$9 adults, C$6.50 seniors and youths 13 to 18, C$5 children 6 to 12, C$20 families, and free for children 5 and under. Admission is about C$2 less from October through March. Open daily 10am to dusk. Take bus no. 17. *Note:* The garden lost hundreds of trees in the December 2006 windstorm that also devastated Stanley Park.

Adjoining the University of British Columbia (UBC) on the city's west side at Point Grey, **Pacific Spirit Regional Park,** called the **Endowment Lands** by longtime Vancouver residents, is the largest green space in Vancouver. Comprising 754 hectares (1,863 acres) of temperate rainforest, marshes, and beaches, the park includes nearly 35km (22 miles) of trails ideal for hiking, riding, mountain biking, and beachcombing.

6 OUTDOOR ACTIVITIES

An excellent resource for outdoor enthusiasts is **Mountain Equipment Co-op,** 130 W. Broadway (© **604/872-7858;** www.mec.ca).

BEACHES   Only 10% of Vancouver's annual rainfall occurs during June, July, and August; 60 days of summer sunshine is not uncommon, although the Pacific never really warms up enough for a comfortable swim. Still, **English Bay Beach ★★**, at the end of Davie Street off Denman Street and Beach Avenue, is a great place to see sunsets. The bathhouse dates to the turn of the 20th century, and a huge playground slide is mounted on a raft just off the beach every summer.

On **Stanley Park**'s western rim, **Second Beach ★** is a short stroll north from English Bay Beach. A playground, a snack bar, and an immense heated oceanside **pool ★** (© **604/ 257-8370**), open from May through September, make this a convenient and fun spot for families. Admission to the pool is C$5.15 for adults, C$3.60 for seniors and youths 13 to 18, and C$2.60 for children 6 to 12. Farther along the seawall, due north of Stanley Park Drive, lies secluded **Third Beach.** Locals tote along grills and coolers to this spot, a popular place for summer-evening barbecues and sunset-watching.

South of English Bay Beach, near the Burrard Street Bridge, is **Sunset Beach ★**. Running along False Creek, it's actually a picturesque strip of sandy beaches filled with enormous driftwood logs that serve as windbreaks and provide a little privacy for sunbathers and picnickers. A snack bar, a soccer field, and a long, gently sloping grassy hill are available for people who prefer lawn to sand.

On the West Side, **Kitsilano Beach ★★★**, along Arbutus Drive near Ogden Street, is affectionately called Kits Beach. It's an easy walk from the Maritime Museum and the False Creek ferry dock. If you want to do a saltwater swim but can't handle the cold, head to the huge (135m/443-ft.) heated (25°C/77°F) **Kitsilano Pool ★★**. Admission is the same as for Second Beach Pool, above.

For information on any of Vancouver's many beaches, call © **604/738-8535** (summer only).

BOATING   With thousands of miles of protected shoreline along B.C.'s West Coast, boaters enjoy some of the finest cruising grounds in the world. You can rent powerboats for a few hours or up to several weeks at **Bonnie Lee Boat Rentals,** 1676 Duranleau St., Granville Island (✆ **866/933-7447** or 604/290-7447; www.bonnielee.com), a company that has been renting boats and offering chartered fishing expeditions since 1980. Rates for a 5.8m (19-ft.) sport boat with 115-horsepower motor begin at C$60 per hour (plus C$9 insurance fee and fuel), or C$375 for an 8-hour package. **Jerry's Boat Rentals,** Granville Island (✆ **604/696-5500**), is steps away and offers similar deals. **Delta Charters,** 3500 Cessna Dr., Richmond (✆ **800/661-7762** or 604/273-4211; www.delta charters.com), has weekly and monthly rates for skippered boats that sleep four.

CANOEING & KAYAKING   Both placid, urban False Creek and the incredibly beautiful 30km (19-mile) North Vancouver fjord known as Indian Arm have launching points that can be reached by car or bus. Prices range from about C$40 per 2-hour minimum rental to C$70 per 5-hour day for single kayaks and about C$60 for canoe rentals. Customized tours range from C$75 to C$150 per person.

Ecomarine Ocean Kayak Centre, 1668 Duranleau St., Granville Island (✆ **888/425-2925** or 604/689-7575; www.ecomarine.com), has 2-hour, daily, and weekly kayak rentals, as well as courses and organized tours. The company also has an office at the **Jericho Sailing Centre,** 1300 Discovery St., at Jericho Beach (✆ **604/224-4177;** www. jsca.bc.ca). In North Vancouver, **Deep Cove Canoe and Kayak Rentals,** 2156 Banbury Rd. (at the foot of Gallant St.) (✆ **604/929-2268;** www.deepcovekayak.com), is an easy starting point for anyone planning an Indian Arm run. It offers hourly and daily rentals of canoes and kayaks, as well as lessons and customized tours.

Lotus Land Tours, 2005-1251 Cardero St. (✆ **800/528-3531** or 604/684-4921; www.lotuslandtours.com), runs guided kayak tours on Indian Arm that come with hotel pickup, a barbecue salmon lunch, and incredible scenery. The wide, stable kayaks are perfect for first-time paddlers. One-day tours cost C$165 for adults, C$119 for children 4 to 12.

CYCLING & MOUNTAIN BIKING   Cycling in Vancouver is fun, amazingly scenic, and very popular. Cycling maps are available at most bicycle retailers and rental outlets. Some West End hotels offer guests bike storage and rentals. Hourly rentals run around C$7 for a one-speed "Cruiser" to C$17 for a top-of-the-line mountain bike or tandem; C$30 to C$80 for a day, helmets and locks included. Popular shops that rent city and mountain bikes, child trailers, child seats, and in-line skates (protective gear included) include **Spokes Bicycle Rentals & Espresso Bar,** 1798 W. Georgia St. (✆ **604/688-5141;** www. spokesbicyclerentals.com), at the corner of Denman Street at the entrance to Stanley Park; **Alley Cat Rentals,** 1779 Robson St., in the alley (✆ **604/684-5117**); and **Bayshore Bicycle and Rollerblade Rentals,** 745 Denman St. (✆ **604/688-2453;** www. bayshorebikerentals.ca). *Note:* Be advised that wearing a helmet is mandatory, and one will be included in your bike rental.

The most popular cycling path in the city runs along the **seawall** ★★★ around the perimeter of Stanley Park. Offering magnificent views, this flat, 10km (6¼-mile) pathway attracts year-round bicyclists, in-line skaters, and pedestrians. Another popular route is the **seaside bicycle route,** a 15km (9⅓-mile) ride that begins at English Bay and continues around False Creek to the University of British Columbia. Some of this route follows city streets that are well marked with cycle-path signs.

Serious mountain bikers also have a wealth of world-class options within a short drive from downtown Vancouver. The trails on **Grouse Mountain** (p. 84) are some of the lower mainland's best. The very steep **Good Samaritan Trail** on **Mount Seymour** connects to the Baden-Powell Trail and the Bridle Path near Mount Seymour Road. Local mountain bikers love the cross-country ski trails on **Hollyburn Mountain** in **Cypress Provincial Park,** just northeast of Vancouver on the road to Whistler on Hwy. 99. Closer to downtown, both **Pacific Spirit Park** and **Burnaby Mountain** offer excellent beginner and intermediate off-road trails.

FISHING   Five species of salmon, rainbow and Dolly Varden trout, steelhead, and sturgeon abound in the local waters around Vancouver. To fish, anglers over the age of 16 need a **nonresident saltwater or freshwater license.** Licenses are available province-wide from more than 500 vendors, including tackle shops, sporting-goods stores, resorts, service stations, marinas, charter-boat operators, and department stores. Saltwater (tidal waters) fishing licenses for nonresidents cost C$7.50 for 1 day, C$20 for 3 days, and C$33 for 5 days. Fly-fishing in national and provincial parks requires special permits, which you can get at any park site for a nominal fee. Permits are valid at all Canadian parks.

The B.C. *Tidal Waters Sport Fishing Guide* and *B.C. Sport Fishing Regulations Synopsis for Non-Tidal Waters,* and the *B.C. Fishing Directory and Atlas,* available at many tackle shops, are good sources of information. Another good source of general information is the **Fisheries and Oceans Canada** website (www.pac.dfo-mpo.gc.ca).

Hanson's Fishing Outfitters, 102-580 Hornby St. (© **604/684-8988**), and **Bonnie Lee Fishing Charters Ltd.,** 1676 Duranleau St., Granville Island (© **866/933-7447** or 604/290-7447; www.bonnielee.com), are outstanding outfitters that also sell fishing licenses.

GOLF   With five public 18-hole courses, half a dozen pitch-and-putt courses in the city, and dozens more nearby, golfers are never far from their love. For discounts and short-notice tee times at more than 30 Vancouver-area courses, contact the **A-1 Last Minute Golf Hot Line** (© **800/684-6344** or 604/878-1833; www.lastminutegolfbc.com).

A number of excellent public golf courses, maintained by the **Vancouver Board of Parks and Recreation** (© **604/280-1818** to book tee times; http://vancouver.ca/parks), can be found throughout the city. **Langara Golf Course,** 6706 Alberta St., around 49th Avenue and Cambie Street (© **604/713-1816**), built in 1926 and recently renovated and redesigned, is one of the most popular golf courses in the province. Depending on the course, summer greens fees range from C$24 to C$49 for an adult, with discounts for seniors, youths, and off-season tee times.

The public **University Golf Club,** 5185 University Blvd. (© **604/224-1818;** www.universitygolf.com), is a great 6,560-yard, par-71 course with a clubhouse, pro shop, locker rooms, bar and grill, and sports lounge.

Leading private clubs are situated on the North Shore and in Vancouver. Check with your club at home to see if you have reciprocal visiting memberships with one of the following: **Capilano Golf and Country Club,** 420 Southborough Dr., West Vancouver (© **604/922-9331;** www.capilanogolf.com); **Marine Drive Golf Club,** West 57th Avenue and SW Marine Drive (© **604/261-8111;** www.marine-drive.com); **Seymour Golf and Country Club,** 3723 Mt. Seymour Pkwy., North Vancouver (© **604/929-2611;** www.seymourgolf.com); **Point Grey Golf and Country Club,** 3350 SW Marine Dr. (© **604/261-3108;** www.pointgreygolf.com); and **Shaughnessy Golf and Country Club,** 4300 SW Marine Dr. (© **604/266-4141;** www.shaughnessy.org). Greens fees range from C$42 to C$75.

HIKING   Great trails for hikers of all levels run through Vancouver's dramatic environs. You can pick up a local trail guide at any bookstore. Good trail maps are also available from **International Travel Maps and Books,** 12300 Bridgeport Rd., Richmond (② 604/273-1400; www.itmb.com), which also stocks guidebooks and topographical maps. The retail store is open daily from 9:30am to 5pm or you can order maps online.

If you're looking for a challenge without a long time commitment, hike the aptly named **Grouse Grind** from the bottom of **Grouse Mountain** (p. 84) to the top; then buy a one-way ticket down on the Grouse Mountain SkyRide gondola.

For a bit more scenery with a bit less effort, take the Grouse Mountain SkyRide up to the **Grouse chalet** and start your hike at an altitude of 1,100m (3,642 ft.). The trail north of **Goat Mountain** is well marked and takes approximately 6 hours round-trip, though you may want to build in some extra time to linger on the top of Goat and take in the spectacular 360-degree views of Vancouver, Vancouver Island, and the snowcapped peaks of the Coast Mountains.

ICE-SKATING   The highest ice-skating rink in Canada is located on **Grouse Mountain** (p. 84). In the city, the **West End Community Centre,** 870 Denman St. (② 604/257-8333), rents skates at its enclosed rink, open January through March, as is the **Kitsilano Ice Rink,** 2690 Larch St. (② 604/257-6983; http://vancouver.ca/parks). The enormous **Burnaby 8 Rinks Ice Sports Centre,** 6501 Sprott St., Burnaby (② 604/291-0626), is the Vancouver Canucks' official practice facility. It has eight rinks, is open year-round, and offers lessons and rentals. Call ahead to check hours for public skating at all these rinks.

IN-LINE SKATING   All over Vancouver, you'll find lots of locals rolling along beach paths, streets, park paths, and promenades. If you didn't bring a pair of blades, try **Bayshore Bicycle and Rollerblade Rentals,** 745 Denman St. (② 604/688-2453; www.bayshorebikerentals.com). Rentals run C$5 per hour or C$20 for 8 hours. For information on in-line skating lessons and group events, visit www.inlineskatevancouver.com.

JOGGING   Local runners traverse the **Stanley Park seawall** ★★★ and the park paths around **Lost Lagoon** and **Beaver Lake.** If you're a dawn or dusk runner, take note that this is one of the world's safer city parks. However, if you're alone, don't tempt fate—stick to open and lighted areas. Other prime jogging areas are **Kitsilano Beach, Jericho Beach,** and **Spanish Banks** (see "Beaches," earlier in this chapter); all of them offer flat running paths along the ocean. You can also take the seawall path from English Bay Beach south along **False Creek.** If you feel like doing a little racing, competitions take place throughout the year; ask for information at any runners' outfitters such as **Forerunners,** 3504 W. 4th Ave. (② 604/732-4535), or **Running Room,** 679 Denman St. (corner of Georgia; ② 604/684-9771). Check www.runningroom.com for information on clinics and events around Vancouver and British Columbia.

SKIING & SNOWBOARDING   World-class skiing lies outside the city at the **Whistler Blackcomb Ski Resort,** 110km (68 miles) north of Vancouver; see chapter 10 However, you don't have to leave the city to get in a few runs. It seldom snows in the city's downtown and central areas, but Vancouverites can ski before work and after dinner at the three ski resorts in the North Shore Mountains. These local mountains played host to the freestyle and snowboard events in the 2010 Winter Games.

Grouse Mountain Resort, 6400 Nancy Greene Way, North Vancouver (② 604/984-0661, snow report 604/986-6262; www.grousemountain.com), is about 3km (1¾ miles) from the Lions Gate Bridge and overlooks the Burrard Inlet and Vancouver skyline. Four chairs, two beginner tows, and two T-bars take you to 24 alpine runs. The resort has night skiing, special events, instruction, and a spectacular view, as well as a 90m (295-ft.) half-pipe for snowboarders. All skill levels are covered, with two beginner trails, three blue trails, and five black-diamond runs. Rental packages and a full range of facilities are available.

Mount Seymour Provincial Park, 1700 Mt. Seymour Rd., North Vancouver (© **604/986-2261;** www.mountseymour.com), has the area's highest base elevation; it's accessible via four chairs and a tow. In addition to day and night skiing, the facility offers snowboarding, snowshoeing, and tobogganing along its 22 runs, as well as 26km (16 miles) of cross-country trails. The resort specializes in teaching first-timers. Camps for children and teenagers, and adult clinics, are available throughout the winter. Shuttle service is available during ski season from various locations on the North Shore, including the Lonsdale Quay SeaBus. For more information, call © **604/953-3333.**

Cypress Bowl, 1610 Mt. Seymour Rd. (© **604/926-5612,** snow report 604/419-7669; www.cypressmountain.com), has the area's longest vertical drop (525m/1,722 ft.), challenging ski and snowboard runs, and 16km (10 miles) of track-set cross-country ski trails (including 5km/3 miles set aside for night skiing). Snowshoe tours and excellent introductory ski packages are available. *Note:* Cypress was home to the 2010 Winter Olympics freestyle skiing (moguls and aerials), snowboarding (half-pipe and parallel giant slalom), and brand-new skicross events. In winter 2008, Cypress opened nine new runs for intermediate and expert skiers and snowboarders, accessed by a new quad chairlift. A new day lodge opened for the winter 2008/2009 season.

SWIMMING The **Vancouver Aquatic Centre,** 1050 Beach Ave., at the foot of Thurlow Street (© **604/665-3424**), has a heated, 50m (164-ft.) Olympic pool, saunas, whirlpools, weight rooms, diving tanks, locker rooms, showers, child care, and a tot pool. Admission is C$5.65 for adults, C$2.80 for children 2 to 12. The new, coed **YWCA Fitness Centre,** 535 Hornby St. (© **604/895-5800;** www.ywcavan.org), in the heart of downtown, has a 6-lane, 25m (82-ft.), ozonated (much milder than chlorinated) pool, steam room, whirlpool, conditioning gym, and aerobic studios. A day pass is C$18 for adults. UBC's **Aquatic Centre,** 6121 University Blvd. (© **604/822-4522;** www.aquatics. ubc.ca), located next door to the Student Union Building and the bus loop, sets aside time for public use. Admission is C$5 for adults, C$4 for youths and students, and C$3 for seniors and children 3 to 12.

See also "Beaches," p. 86.

TENNIS The city maintains 180 outdoor hard courts that have a 1-hour limit and accommodate patrons on a first-come, first-served basis from 8am until dusk. Local courtesy dictates that if people are waiting, you surrender the court on the hour. (Heavy usage times are evenings and weekends.) With the exception of the Beach Avenue courts, which charge a nominal fee in summer, all city courts are free.

Stanley Park has four courts near Lost Lagoon and 17 courts near the Beach Avenue entrance, next to the Fish House Restaurant. During the summer season (May–Sept), six courts are taken over for pay tennis and can be pre-booked by calling © **604/605-8224.** **Queen Elizabeth Park**'s 18 courts service the central Vancouver area, and **Kitsilano Beach Park**'s ★ 10 courts service the beach area between Vanier Park and the UBC campus.

Play at night on the **Langara Campus** of Vancouver Community College, on West 49th Avenue between Main and Cambie streets. The **UBC Coast Club,** 6160 Thunderbird Blvd. (© **604/822-2505;** www.tennis.ubc.ca), has 10 outdoor and four indoor courts. Indoor courts are C$12 to C$22 per hour, depending on the time; outdoor courts are C$5 per person.

WHITE-WATER RAFTING　A 2½-hour drive from Vancouver, on the wild Nahatlatch River, **Reo Rafting,** 845 Spence Way, Anmore (© **800/736-7238** or 604/461-7238; www.reorafting.com), offers some of the best guided white-water trips in the province, at a very reasonable price. One-day packages—including lunch, all your gear, and 4 to 5 hours on the river—start at C$105 for adults. Multiday trips and group packages are available, and they can provide transportation from Vancouver.

Only a 1½-hour drive from the city is **Chilliwack River Rafting** (© **800/410-7238;** www.chilliwackriverrafting.com), which offers half-day trips on the Chilliwack River and in the even hairier Chilliwack Canyon. The cost is C$89 for adults and C$69 for children.

WILDLIFE-WATCHING　Orcas, or killer whales, are the largest mammals to be seen in Vancouver's waters. Three pods (families), numbering about 80 whales, return to this area every year to feed on the salmon that spawn in the Fraser River starting in May and continuing into October. The eldest female leads the group; the head of one pod is thought to have been born in 1911. From April through October, daily excursions offered by **Vancouver Whale Watch,** 12240 2nd Ave., Richmond (© **604/274-9565;** www.vancouverwhalewatch.com), focus on the majestic whales plus Dall's porpoises, sea lions, seals, eagles, herons, and other wildlife. The cost is C$125 per person (slightly lower rates for a semi-covered boat). **Steveston Seabreeze Adventures,** 12551 No. 1 Rd., Richmond (© **604/272-7200**), also offers whale-watching tours for about the same price. Both companies offer a shuttle service from downtown Vancouver.

Thousands of migratory birds following the Pacific flyway rest and feed in the Fraser River delta south of Vancouver, especially at the 340-hectare (840-acre) **George C. Reifel Bird Sanctuary,** 5191 Robertson Rd., Westham Island (© **604/946-6980;** www.reifel birdsanctuary.com), which was created by a former bootlegger and wetland-bird lover. Many other waterfowl species have made this a permanent habitat. More than 263 species have been spotted. The **Snow Goose Festival,** celebrating the annual arrival of the huge, snowy white flocks, is held here during the first weekend of November. The snow geese stay in the area until mid-December. (High tide, when the birds are less concealed by the marsh grasses, is the best time to visit.) An observation tower, 3km (1¾ miles) of paths, free birdseed, and picnic tables make this wetland reserve an ideal outing spot from October to April, when the birds are wintering in abundance. The sanctuary is wheelchair accessible and open daily from 9am to 4pm. Admission is C$4 for adults and C$2 for seniors and children.

The **Richmond Nature Park,** 11851 Westminster Hwy. (© **604/718-6188**), was established to preserve the Lulu Island wetlands bog. It features a Nature House with educational displays and a boardwalk-encircled duck pond. On Sunday afternoons, knowledgeable guides give free tours. Admission is by donation.

To hook up with local Vancouver birders, try the **Vancouver Natural History Society** (© **604/737-3074;** www.naturevancouver.ca). This all-volunteer organization runs birding field trips most weekends; many are free.

During the winter, thousands of bald eagles—in fact, the largest number in North America—line the banks of the **Squamish, Cheakamus,** and **Mamquam** rivers to feed on spawning salmon. To get there by car, take the scenic **Sea-to-Sky Highway** (Hwy. 99) from downtown Vancouver to Squamish and Brackendale; the trip takes about an hour. Alternatively, you can take a **Greyhound** bus from Vancouver's Pacific Central Station, 1150 Station St. (© **604/482-8747;** www.greyhound.ca); trip time is 1¼ hours. Contact

Squamish & Howe Sound Visitor Info Centre (✆ 604/815-4994; www.squamish chamber.com) for more information.

The annual summer salmon runs attract more than bald eagles. Tourists also flock to coastal streams and rivers to watch the waters turn red with leaping coho and sockeye. The salmon are plentiful at the **Capilano Salmon Hatchery Goldstream Provincial Park** out on Vancouver Island, and numerous other fresh waters.

Stanley Park (p. 81) and **Pacific Spirit Park** (p. 86) are both home to heron rookeries. You can see these large birds nesting just outside the Vancouver Aquarium. Ravens, dozens of species of waterfowl, raccoons, skunks, beavers, gray squirrels (imported from New York's Central Park decades ago), and even coyotes are also full-time residents. The **Stanley Park Ecology Society** (✆ 604/257-8544) runs regular nature walks in the park. Call or check their website (www.stanleyparkecology.ca) for more information, or drop by the **Lost Lagoon Nature House** in Stanley Park (p. 82).

7 VANCOUVER SHOPPING

Vancouver's a fun place to shop because it's international and cosmopolitan but hasn't lost its funky, fun-loving edge. There are stores galore, and most of them are not in malls. Blessed with a climate that seems semitropical in comparison to the rest of Canada, Vancouverites never really developed a taste for indoor malls (though there is one, the Pacific Centre, right downtown). Below are a few thoughts on where to start your shopping expeditions.

SHOPPING A TO Z

ANTIQUES **Bakers Dozen Antiques,** 3520 Main St. (✆ 604/879-3348; www. dodaantiques.com), specializes in antique toys, model ships and boats, folk art, and unusual 19th- and early-20th-century furniture.

Part museum and part subcontinental yard sale, **Mihrab,** 4578 Main St. (✆ 778/737-5959), specializes in one-of-a-kind Indian antiques for the house and garden. Think intricately carved teak archways or tiny jewel-like door pulls, all selected by partners Lou Johnson and Kerry Lane on frequent trips to the subcontinent.

The **Vancouver Antique Centre,** 422 Richards St. (✆ 604/684-9822), is housed in a heritage commercial building; inside is a maze containing about a dozen separate shops on two levels, specializing in everything from china, glass, and jewelry to military objects, sports, toys, retro '50s and '60s collectibles, home furnishings, and watches. Neighboring buildings house even more shops.

BOOKS **Duthie Books Fourth Avenue,** 2239 W. 4th Ave. (✆ 604/732-5344; www. duthiebooks.com), a well-known local bookstore on Granville Island, has been in business since 1957. It's a good place to find local authors and stocks an excellent inventory of Canadian and international titles.

International Travel Maps and Books, 12300 Bridgeport Rd., Richmond (✆ 604/273-1400), has the best selection of travel books, maps, charts, and globes in town, plus an impressive selection of special-interest British Columbia guides. This is the hiker's best source for detailed topographic charts of the entire province. The only problem is that they've closed their handy downtown store and moved out to Richmond.

Kidsbooks, 3083 W. Broadway (✆ 604/738-5335; a second location is at 3040 Edgemont Blvd., North Vancouver, ✆ 604/986-6190; www.kidsbooks.ca), features the largest and most interesting selection of children's literature in the city, and also has an amazing collection of puppets and holds regular readings.

CERAMICS   The **Gallery of B.C. Ceramics,** 1359 Cartwright St. (© **604/669-3606;** www.bcpotters.com), is owned and operated by the Potters Guild of British Columbia and features a collection of sculptural and functional ceramic works from 100 B.C. potters. Gallery hours change seasonally, so phone ahead. Closed on Mondays in January and February.

DEPARTMENT STORES   From the establishment of its early trading posts during the 1670s to its modern coast-to-coast department-store chain, **The Bay (Hudson's Bay Company),** 674 Granville St. (© **604/681-6211;** www.hbc.com), has built its reputation on quality goods. You can still buy a Hudson's Bay woolen "point" blanket (the colorful stripes originally represented how many beaver pelts each blanket was worth in trade), but you'll also find Tommy Hilfiger, Polo, DKNY, and more.

Hills of Kerrisdale, 2125 W. 41st Ave. (© **604/266-9177;** www.hillsofkerrisdale. com), the neighborhood department store in central Vancouver, is a city landmark. Carrying full lines of quality men's, women's, and children's clothes, as well as furnishings and sporting goods, it's a destination for locals because the prices are often lower than those in the downtown core.

FASHION   Vancouver has the Pacific Northwest's best collection of clothes from Paris, London, Milan, and Rome, in addition to a great assortment of locally made, cutting-edge fashions. It seems that almost every week a new designer boutique opens in Yaletown, Kitsilano, or Kerrisdale. International designer outlets include **Chanel Boutique,** 900 W. Hastings St. (© 604/682-0522); **Salvatore Ferragamo,** 918 Robson St. (© 604/669-4495); **Gianni Versace Boutique,** 757 W. Hastings St. (© 604/683-1131); **Polo/Ralph Lauren,** the Landing, 375 Water St. (© 604/682-7656); and **Plaza Escada,** Sinclair Centre, 757 W. Hastings St. (© 604/688-8558).

Designed to look like a Pacific Northwest longhouse, **Dorothy Grant,** 138 W. 6th Ave., Unit 1B. (© **604/681-0201;** www.dorothygrant.com), is where First Nations designer Dorothy Grant exhibits her unique designs as well as her husband's (acclaimed artist Robert Davidson) collection of exquisitely detailed Haida motifs, which she appliqués on coats, leather vests, jackets, caps, and accessories. The clothes are gorgeous and collectible. She also carries contemporary Haida art and jewelry.

Big-name designs can be found anywhere, but **Dream 311,** 311 W. Cordova St. (© **604/683-7326**), is one of the few places to show early collections—clothing and jewelry—of local designers.

Please Mum, 2951 W. Broadway (© **604/732-4574;** www.pleasemum.com), sells attractive Canadian-made toddler's and children's cotton clothing.

Proudly Canadian, **Roots Canada,** 1001 Robson St. (corner of Burrard St.; © **604/ 683-4305;** www.roots.com), features sturdy casual clothing, including leather jackets and bags, footwear, outerwear, and athletic wear for the whole family.

Specializing in unique retro clothing, **Legends Retro-Fashion,** 4366 Main St. (© **604/875-0621**), is well known among vintage purists for its cache of one-of-a-kind pieces. Most of the clothes, such as evening dresses, shoes, kid gloves, and other accessories, are in immaculate condition. Closed Monday and Tuesday.

True Value Vintage Clothing, 710 Robson St. (© **604/685-5403**), has a collection of funky fashions from the 1930s through the 1990s, including tons of fake furs, leather jackets, denim, soccer jerseys, vintage bathing suits, formal wear, smoking jackets, sweaters, and accessories.

FIRST NATIONS ART & CRAFTS You don't have to purchase a pricey antique to acquire original Coast Salish or Haida work. As the experts at the **Museum of Anthropology** explain, if an item is crafted by any of the indigenous Pacific Northwest artisans, it's a real First Nations piece of art. Galleries will tell you about the artist, and explain how to identify and care for these beautifully carved, worked, and woven pieces. Bold, traditional, and innovative geometric designs, intricate carvings, strong primary colors, and rich wood tones are just a few of the elements you'll find in First Nations crafts.

Even if you're not in the market, go gallery-hopping to see works by Haida artists **Bill Reid** (the province's best-known Native artist) and **Richard Davidson,** and by Kwakwaka'wakw artist and photographer **David Neel.**

Coastal Peoples Fine Arts Gallery, 1024 Mainland St. (© 604/685-9298; www. coastalpeoples.com), showcases an extensive collection of fine First Nations jewelry. The motifs—Bear, Salmon, Whale, Raven, and others—are drawn from local myths and translated into 14-karat or 18-karat gold and sterling silver creations. Inuit sculptures and items made of glass or wood are also worth a look. Custom orders can be filled quickly and shipped worldwide.

In a re-creation of a trading post interior, **Hill's Native Art,** 165 Water St. (© 604/685-4249; www.hillsnativeart.com), established in 1946 and claiming to be North America's largest Northwest coast Native art gallery, sells ceremonial masks; Cowichan sweaters; moccasins; wood sculptures; totem poles; silk-screen prints; soapstone sculptures; and gold, silver, and argillite jewelry.

Images for a Canadian Heritage, 164 Water St. (at Cambie St.) (© 604/685-7046; www.imagesforcanada.com)—and the Inuit Gallery of Vancouver, 206 Cambie St. (© 604/688-7323; www.inuit.com)—are government-licensed First Nations art galleries, featuring traditional and contemporary works such as Native designs on glass totems and copperplates. With a museum-worthy collection, this shop deserves a visit whether you're buying or not.

The **Lattimer Gallery,** 1590 2nd Ave. (© 604/732-4556; www.lattimergallery.com), showcases museum-quality Pacific Northwest First Nations art, including ceremonial masks, totem poles, limited-edition silk-screen prints, argillite sculptures, and expensive gold and silver jewelry.

FOOD You'll find **salmon** everywhere in Vancouver. Many shops package whole, fresh salmon with ice packs for visitors to take home. Shops also carry delectable smoked salmon in travel-safe, vacuum-packed containers. Some offer decorative cedar gift boxes; most offer overnight air transport. Try other salmon treats such as salmon jerky and Indian candy (chunks of marinated smoked salmon), which are available at public markets such as **Granville Island Public Market** and **Lonsdale Quay Market.**

If you want some salmon to take home, **Salmon Village,** 779 Thurlow St. (© 604/685-3378; www.salmonvillage.com), has a good selection to choose from. Smoked salmon or jerky are vacuum sealed for travel, and fresh salmon can be packed in an ice box or (for a price) shipped to you anywhere on the planet.

The works at **Chocolate Arts,** 2037 W. 4th Ave. (© 604/739-0475; www.chocolate arts.com), are made with exquisite craftsmanship. Seasonal treats include pumpkin truffles around Halloween or eggnog truffles for Christmas. They even make chocolate toolboxes filled with tiny chocolate tools. Look for the all-chocolate diorama in the window—it changes every month or so.

Live lobsters, Dungeness crabs, oysters, mussels, clams, geoducks, and scallops are just a few of the varieties of seafood swimming in the saltwater tanks at the **Lobsterman,**

1807 Mast Tower Rd. (© **604/687-4531;** www.lobsterman.com). The staff steams the food fresh on the spot, free. Salmon and other seafood can also be packed for air travel.

Murchie's Tea & Coffee, 970 Robson St. (© **604/669-0783;** www.murchies.com), has been the city's main tea and coffee purveyor for more than a century. You'll find everything from Jamaican Blue Mountain and Kona coffees to Lapsang Souchong and Kemun teas. The knowledgeable staff will help you decide which flavors and blends fit your taste. A fine selection of bone china and crystal serving ware, as well as coffeemakers and teapots, are also on sale.

The South Seas have always been a source of intrigue. The **South China Seas Trading Company,** Granville Island Public Market (© **604/681-5402;** www.southchinaseas.ca), re-creates a bit of that wonder, with a remarkable collection of rare spices and hard-to-find sauces. Look for fresh Kaffir lime leaves, Thai basil, young ginger, sweet Thai chile sauce, and occasional exotic produce like mangosteens and rambutans. Pick up recipes and ideas from the knowledgeable staff.

JEWELRY At **Costen Catblue,** 1832 W. 1st Ave. (© **604/734-3259;** www.costen catblue.com), one-of-a-kind pieces in platinum and gold are made on the premises by a team of four goldsmiths and artists Mary Ann Buis and Andrew Costen. The two artists' styles complement each other; Buis favors contemporary and clean lines, and Costen's designs tend toward a more ornate Renaissance style.

If you've never seen West Coast Native jewelry, it's worth making a trip to **The Raven and the Bear,** 1528 Duranleau St. (© **604/669-3990**). Deeply inscribed with stylized creatures from Northwest mythology, these rings, bangles, and earrings are unforgettable. (See also "First Nations Art & Crafts," above.)

SHOES **John Fluevog Boots & Shoes Ltd,** 837 Granville St. (© **604/688-2828;** www.fluevog.com), has a growing international cult following of designers and models clamoring for his under-C\$200 urban and funky creations. You'll find outrageous platforms and clogs, Angelic Sole work boots, and a few bizarre experiments for the daring footwear fetishist. You may even meet the designer, who often spends his time at this flagship store on Granville. A new store has now opened in Gastown at 65 Water St.

SPECIALTY Want money to burn? At Chinese funerals, people burn *joss*—paper replicas of earthly belongings—to help make the afterlife for the deceased more comfortable. **Buddha Supply Centre,** 4158 Main St. (© **604/873-8169**), has more than 500 combustible products to choose from, including \$1-million notes (drawn on the bank of hell), luxury penthouse condos, and that all-important cellphone.

Beautifully displayed, the large collection of soaps, bath oils, shampoos, and other body products at **Escents,** 1744 Commercial Dr. (© **604/255-4505;** www.escents aromatherapy.com), come in a variety of scents, such as the fresh ginger-citrus twist or the relaxing lavender sea. Locally produced and made with minimal packaging, the all-natural, environmentally friendly products come in convenient sizes and prices and can be individually blended to fit your mood. An additional store is at 2579 W. Broadway.

Lush, 1025 Robson St. (© **604/687-5874;** www.lush.ca), has the look of an old-fashioned deli with big wheels of cheese, slabs of sweets, and vats of dips and sauces, but all those displays are really soaps (custom cut from a block), shampoos, skin treatments, massage oils, and bath bombs made from all-natural ingredients.

If you want to bring home a few gifts from the sea, then select from the **Ocean Floor**'s, 1522 Duranleau St. (© **604/681-5014**), collection of seashells, ship models, lamps, chimes, coral, shell jewelry, stained glass, and marine brass.

A family business since 1935, the **Umbrella Shop,** 526 W. Pender St. (© **604/669-1707;** factory store at 1106 W. Broadway, © 604/669-9444; www.theumbrellashop.com), carries an amazing assortment of quality umbrellas in every size, shape, and color.

TOYS   Probably the only mall in North America dedicated to kids, the **Kids Market,** 1496 Cartwright St. (© **604/689-8447;** www.kidsmarket.ca), on Granville Island, features a Lilliputian entryway; toy, craft, and book stores; play areas; and services for the younger set, including a "fun hairdresser."

Kites on Clouds, The Courtyard, 131 Water St. (© **604/669-5677**), has every type of kite. Prices range from C$10 to C$20 for nylon or Mylar dragon kites to around C$200 for more elaborate ghost clippers and nylon hang-glider kites.

WINE   Ten years of restructuring, reblending, and careful tending by French and German master vintners have won the province's vineyards world recognition. When buying B.C. wine, look for the VQA (Vintner Quality Alliance) seal on the label; it's a guarantee that all grapes used are grown in British Columbia and meet European standards for growing and processing.

Summerhill, Cedar Creek, Mission Hill, and **Okanagan Vineyards** are just a few of the more than 50 local estates producing hearty cabernet sauvignons, honey-rich ice wines, and oaky merlots. These wines can be found at any government-owned **BC Liquor Store,** such as the one at 1716 Robson St. (© **604/660-9031**), and at some privately owned wine stores.

If you're looking for a particular B.C. vintage, try **Marquis Wine Cellars,** 1034 Davie St. (© **604/684-0445;** www.marquis-wines.com), first. The owner and staff of this West End wine shop are dedicated to educating their patrons about wines. They conduct evening wine tastings, featuring selections from their special purchases. They also publish monthly newsletters. In addition to carrying a full range of British Columbian wines, the shop also has a large international selection.

The Okanagan Estate Wine Cellar, The Bay, 674 Granville St. (© **604/681-6211**), sells a great selection of British Columbian wines by the bottle and the case.

8 VANCOUVER AFTER DARK

For the best overview of Vancouver's nightlife, pick up a copy of the weekly *Georgia Straight* (www.georgiastraight.com). The Thursday edition of the *Vancouver Sun* contains the weekly entertainment section *Queue.* The monthly *Vancouver* magazine (www.vanmag.com) is filled with listings and strong views about what's really hot in the city. Or, get a copy of *Xtra! West* (www.xtra.ca), the free gay and lesbian biweekly tabloid, available in shops and restaurants throughout the West End.

The **Alliance for Arts and Culture,** 100-938 Howe St. (© **604/681-3535;** www.allianceforarts.com), is a great information source for all performing arts, literary events, and art films. The office is open Monday through Friday from 9am to 5pm.

Half-price tickets for same-day shows and events are available at the **Tickets Tonight** (www.ticketstonight.ca) kiosk (Tues–Sat 11am–6pm) in the **Vancouver Touristinfo Centre,** 200 Burrard St. (© **604/684-2787** for recorded events info). The Touristinfo Centre is open from May to Labour Day daily from 8am to 6pm; the rest of the year, it's open Monday through Saturday from 8:30am to 5pm.

Three major theaters in Vancouver regularly host touring performances. The **Orpheum Theatre,** 801 Granville St. (© **604/665-3050;** www.vancouver.ca/theatres), is a 1927 theater that originally hosted the Chicago-based Orpheum vaudeville circuit. The theater now hosts the Vancouver Symphony and pop, rock, and variety shows. The Queen Elizabeth Theatre and the Vancouver Playhouse comprise the **Queen Elizabeth Complex,** 600 Hamilton St., between Georgia and Dunsmuir streets (© **604/665-3050;** www.vancouver.ca/theatres), home to the Vancouver Opera and Ballet British Columbia. The 670-seat Vancouver Playhouse presents chamber-music performances and recitals. Located in a converted turn-of-the-20th-century church, the **Vancouver East Cultural Centre** (the "Cultch" to locals), 1895 Venables St. (© **604/251-1363;** www.thecultch. com), coordinates an impressive program that includes avant-garde theater productions, performances by international musical groups, and children's programs.

On the UBC campus, the **Chan Centre for the Performing Arts,** 6265 Crescent Rd. (© **604/822-2697;** www.chancentre.com), showcases the work of the UBC music and acting students and hosts a winter concert series. Designed by local architectural luminary, Bing Thom, the Chan Centre's crystal-clear acoustics are the best in town.

THEATER An annual summertime Shakespeare series, **Bard on the Beach,** is presented in Vanier Park (© **604/737-0625;** www.bardonthebeach.org). You can also bring a picnic dinner to Stanley Park and watch **Theatre Under the Stars** (see below), which features popular musicals and light comedies.

The **Arts Club Theatre Company** (© **604/687-1644;** www.artsclub.com; tickets C$25–C$45), presents dramas, comedies, and musicals at the 425-seat Granville Island Stage (1585 Johnston St.), with post-performance entertainment in the Backstage Lounge. The Arts Club **Revue Stage** is an intimate, cabaret-style showcase for small productions, improvisation nights, and musical revues. The Art Deco **Stanley Industrial Alliance Theatre** (2750 Granville St.) plays host to longer-running plays and musicals. The box office is open 9am to 7pm.

Some students at UBC are actors in training, and their productions at **Frederic Wood Theatre,** 6354 Crescent Rd., Gate 4, University of British Columbia (© **604/822-2678;** www.theatre.ubc.ca; tickets C$20 adults, C$14 seniors, C$12 children), are extremely high caliber.

From mid-July to mid-August, favorite musicals like *Annie, West Side Story,* and *Thoroughly Modern Millie* are performed outdoors at **Theatre Under the Stars,** Malkin Bowl, Stanley Park (© **604/734-1917** or 604/687-0174; www.tuts.ca; tickets C$30 adults, C$25 seniors and youths, C$20 children 6–10, C$85 families [2 adults and 2 children]), by a mixed cast of amateur and professional actors. Bring a blanket (it gets chilly once the sun sets) and a picnic for a relaxing evening.

CLASSICAL MUSIC & OPERA Western Canada's only professional choral ensemble, **Vancouver Chamber Choir,** 1254 W. 7th Ave. (© **604/738-6822;** www.vancouver chamberchoir.com; tickets C$15–C$35 adults, C$13–C$25 seniors and students), presents an annual concert series at the Orpheum Theatre, the Chan Centre, and Ryerson United Church.

I've always been impressed with the quality of the stagings and performances at the **Vancouver Opera,** 835 Cambie St. (© **604/683-0222;** www.vancouveropera.ca; tickets C$24–C$140). The company produces both concert versions and fully staged operas, often sung by international stars. The season runs October through May, with most performances in the Queen Elizabeth Theatre.

VANCOUVER

5

VANCOUVER AFTER DARK

At its home in the Orpheum Theatre during the fall, winter, and spring, the **Vancouver Symphony,** 601 Smithe St. (☎ **604/876-3434;** www.vancouversymphony.ca; tickets C$20–C$75; discounts available for seniors and students), under the baton of maestro Branwell Tovey, presents a variety of year-round concerts. The box office is open from 6pm until showtime.

DANCE   For fans of modern dance, the time to be here is early July, when the **Dancing on the Edge Festival** (☎ **604/689-0926;** www.dancingontheedge.org) presents 60 to 80 original pieces over a 10-day period. For more information about other festivals and dance companies around the city, contact the **Dance Centre** at ☎ **604/606-6400** or www.thedancecentre.ca.

Ballet British Columbia, 1101 W. Broadway (☎ **604/732-5003;** www.balletbc.com; tickets C$25–C$60), strives to present innovative works along with more traditional productions by visiting companies. Performances are usually at the Queen Elizabeth Theatre, at 600 Hamilton St.

LAUGHTER & MUSIC

COMEDY CLUB/IMPROV SHOW   Part comedy, part theater, and partly a take-no-prisoners test of an actor's ability to think extemporaneously, **Vancouver TheatreSports League,** New Revue Stage, 1601 Johnston St. (☎ **604/738-7013;** www.vtsl.com; tickets C$11–C$20), involves actors taking suggestions from the audience and spinning them into short skits or full plays, often with hilarious results. Since moving to the Arts Club Stage, Vancouver's TheatreSports leaguers have had to rein in their normally raunchy instincts for the more family-friendly audience—except, that is, for Friday and Saturday at 11:45pm, when the Red-Hot Improv show takes the audience into the R-rated realm. Shows are Wednesday and Thursday at 7:30pm and Friday and Saturday at 8, 10, and 11:45pm.

STRICTLY LIVE   The **Vancouver International Jazz Festival** (☎ **604/872-5200;** www.coastaljazz.ca) takes over many venues and outdoor stages around town every June. The festival includes a number of free concerts.

The **Vancouver Folk Music Festival** (☎ **604/602-9798;** www.thefestival.bc.ca) is one of the big ones on the West Coast. It takes place outdoors in July on the beach at Jericho Park.

Live bands play every day of the week at the **Roxy,** 932 Granville St. (☎ **604/331-7999;** www.roxyvan.com; cover C$5–C$15), a raucous, no-holds-barred club, which also features bartenders with Tom Cruise *Cocktail*-style moves. On weekends, the lines are long, the patrons often soused. Dress code: No bags, no backpacks, no track suits, no ripped jeans.

In the far-off reaches of East Vancouver (okay, Commercial Dr. area), the **WISE Club,** 1882 Adanac St. (☎ **604/254-5858;** www.wisehall.ca; cover depends on show, but C$15 for most bands), was unplugged long before MTV ever thought of reaching for the power cord. Bands are local and international.

Yale Hotel, 1300 Granville St. (☎ **604/681-9253;** www.theyale.ca; cover Thurs–Sat C$15–C$28), is a century-old tavern on the far south end of Granville, and is Vancouver's one-and-only home of the blues. Shows are Monday through Saturday at 9:30pm. On Saturday and Sunday is an open-stage blues jam from 3 to 7pm.

BARS, PUBS & OTHER WATERING HOLES

City policy has been to concentrate the city's pubs and clubs into two ghettos—er, *entertainment zones*—one along **Granville Street** and the other along **Water and Pender**

streets in Gastown. **Yaletown** has recently become a third, more upscale, bar/lounge/ club zone. Pubs and clubs can be found in other places, and many are listed below, but if you just want to wander out for a serendipitous pub-crawl, the Granville or Water Street strips are best. Granville Street tends more to Top 40 discos and upscale lounges, while down in Gastown, it's dark cellars spinning hip-hop and house. Yaletown is the newest late-night entertainment/drinking area, a place where martinis reign and some of the restaurants turn into cocktail lounges at 11pm.

BARS MASQUERADING AS RESTAURANTS   One holdover from the bad old days of the liquor license drought is the relatively large number of restaurants that look suspiciously like pubs. You can order food in these places. Indeed, it used to be a condition of drinking (wink, wink), but most patrons stick to a liquid diet.

The Alibi Room, 157 Alexander St. (at Main St.) (© **604/623-3383;** www.alibi.ca), a high-end, trendy restaurant/bar, has new owners and a new chef creating modern-British-pub-style cuisine, but there's still a DJ and a dance floor. Located on the eastern edge of Gastown.

At the **Atlantic Trap and Gill,** 612 Davie St. (at Seymour St.) (© **604/806-6393;** www.trapandgill.com), regulars in this sea shanty of a pub know the words to every song sung by the Irish and East Coast bands that appear onstage Thursday and Saturday night.

Located just off busy Davie Street in the West End, the **Jupiter Café,** 1216 Bute St. (at Davie St.; © **604/609-6665**), combines a postapocalyptic industrial look with lounge chic. Black ceilings, exposed pipes, and roof struts mix surprisingly well with chandeliers, velvet curtains, and plush chairs. The crowd is diverse: gay and straight, funky and preppy, casual and dressed to kill. A huge outdoor patio provides a pleasant refuge from the street, but on colder nights, it's the exclusive domain of die-hard smokers.

What **Monsoon Restaurant,** 2526 Main St. (at Broadway; © **604/879-4001**), does really well is beer and fusion-inspired tapas, accompanied by a buzzing atmosphere generated by interesting and sometimes beautiful people. The kitchen is open noon until 11pm on weekdays, later on weekends.

The taut and tanned from nearby Kits Beach drop into the **Urban Well,** 1516 Yew St. (© **604/737-7770;** www.urbanwell.ca), as the sun goes down, and often don't emerge until the next day. Monday and Tuesday features stand-up comedy, while a DJ keeps things groovy the rest of the week.

ACTUAL BARS   A bright, pleasant Irish pub in the dark heart of Gastown, the **Irish Heather,** 210 Carrall St. (© **604/688-9779;** www.irishheather.com), boasts numerous nooks and crannies, some of the best beer in town, and a menu that does a lot with the traditional Emerald Isle spud. The clientele is from all over the map, from artsy types to urban pioneers.

Part of the renewal of Granville Street, the **Lennox Pub,** 800 Granville St. (© **604/ 408-0881**), fills a big void in the neighborhood; it's a comfortable spot for a drink without having to deal with lines or ordering food. The beer list is extensive, featuring hard-to-find favorites.

A SPORTS BAR   The city's premier sports bar, **The Shark Club Bar and Grill,** 180 W. Georgia St. (at Beatty St.; © **604/687-4275;** www.sharkclubs.com; cover Fri–Sat C$6–C$8)—in the Sandman Inn—features lots of wood and brass, TVs everywhere, and on weekend evenings, lots of young women who don't look terribly interested in sports.

BARS WITH VIEWS You're in Vancouver. Odds are you're aware that this is a city renowned for its views. The entire population could make more money living in a dull, flat place like Toronto, but they stay here because of the seductive scenery. As long as that's your raison d'être, you may as well drink in style at one of the places below.

On the water at the foot of Cardero Street, **Cardero's Marine Pub,** 1583 Coal Harbour Quay (℃ **604/669-7666**), offers a great view of Stanley Park, the harbor, and the North Shore. Overhead heaters take away the chill when the sun goes down.

As **Cloud Nine,** 1400 Robson St. (42nd floor of the Empire Landmark Hotel; ℃ **604/662-8328;** cover Fri–Sat after 8:30pm C$5), a sleek hotel-top lounge, rotates 6 degrees a minute, your vantage point circles from volcanic Mount Baker, the Fraser estuary, and English Bay to Stanley Park, the towers of downtown, the harbor, and East Vancouver. Live entertainment Friday and Saturday nights.

The Dockside Brewing Company, 1253 Johnson St. (℃ **604/685-7070;** www. docksidebrewing.com), is located in the Granville Island Hotel and looks out across False Creek to Yaletown and Burnaby Mountain far in the distance. The grub's not much to write about, but the beer is among the best in town—brewed-on-the-premises lagers, ales, and porters. It's a good idea not to arrive too late: An hour or two after the sun goes down, the mostly 30-something patrons remember that they have homes to go to.

Located beneath the flyway of Vancouver International, the **Flying Beaver Bar,** 4760 Inglis Dr., Richmond (℃ **604/273-0278**), offers nonflyers great views of incoming jets, along with mountains, bush planes, river craft, and truly fine beer.

LOUNGES At **Afterglow,** 350 Davie St. (℃ **604/602-0835**), intimate couches and a soft soundtrack (which gets cranked up to deafening decibels as the evening wears on) make for candlelit foreplay to a meal at glowbal grill; you can also stay in the low-slung love seats for a long evening's cuddle.

The Arts Club Backstage Lounge, 1585 Johnston St. (℃ **604/687-1354;** www. thebackstagelounge.com), has a fabulous location under the Granville Bridge by the water on the edge of False Creek. The crowd is a mix of tourists and art-school students from neighboring Emily Carr College. A live band plays on Friday and Saturday evenings. Most other times, if the sun's out, the waterfront patio is packed.

George Ultra Lounge, 1137 Hamilton St. (℃ **604/628-5555;** www.georgelounge. com), is small, loud, crowded, and hedonistic. Look for local glitterati and primo cocktails from the mixologist who started Vancouver's high-end cocktail trend.

A mix of lounge, restaurant, and club, **Ginger Sixty-Two,** 1219 Granville St. (℃ **604/688-5494;** www.ginger62.com), is the darling of the fashion-industry trendsetters who love to be spotted here. The room is funky warehouse-chic-meets-adult-recroom. Comfy crash pads are strategically placed throughout the room, and plenty of pillows help prop up those less-than-young in the joints.

Supertrendy decor, great drinks, and a succulent small-plates menu have helped the **Opus Bar,** 50 Davie St. (℃ **604/642-0577;** www.elixir-opusbar.com), in the cool **Opus Hotel** (p. 68) become a Yaletown hot spot for a pre-dinner martini or an extended evening schmooze.

BREWPUBS In addition to the brewpubs listed below, don't forget the **Dockside Brewing Company,** 1253 Johnson St. (℃ **604/685-7070**), in the Granville Island Hotel, listed under "Bars with Views," above.

Winding your way from room to room in **Steamworks Pub & Brewery,** 375 Water St. (℃ **604/689-2739;** www.steamworks.com), is almost as much fun as drinking. Upstairs, by the doors, it's a London city pub. Farther in by the staircase, it's a refined old-world club, with wood paneling, leather chairs, and great glass windows overlooking the harbor. Down in the basement, it's a Bavarian drinking hall with long lines of benches, set up parallel to the enormous copper vats. Fortunately, the beer's good. Choose from a dozen in-house beers.

Every Sunday at **Yaletown Brewing Company,** 1111 Mainland St. (at Helmcken St.; ℂ **604/681-2739;** www.markjamesgroup.com), all pints of brewed-on-the-premises beer are C$3.75, and pizzas are half-price. The excellent beer is complemented by an extremely cozy room, a great summertime patio, and a good appetizer menu.

DANCE CLUBS Generally clubs are open until 2am every day but Sunday, when they close at midnight. In the summer months (mid-June through Labour Day), opening hours are extended to 4am.

Au Bar, 674 Seymour St. (ℂ **604/648-2227;** www.aubarnightclub.com; cover C$5–C$8), is packed with beautiful people milling from bar to dance floor to bar (there are two) and back again.

The Cellar, 1006 Granville St. (ℂ **604/605-4350;** www.cellarvan.com; cover C$5–C$8), inhabits that netherworld between dance club, bar, meat market, and personals ads. Dance-club characteristics include a cover charge, small dance floor, and a DJ who mostly spins Top 40. But Cellar patrons are far less interested in groovin' than they are in meeting other Cellar dwellers, a process facilitated by a wall-length message board upon which pickup lines are posted.

Located in the heart of Gastown, one of Vancouver's biggest and most legendary rooms (it was formerly Sonar) has been revitalized and reborn as **Fabric Nightclub,** 66 Water St. (ℂ **604/683-6695;** www.fabricvancouver.com; cover C$10–C$20). With a 500-plus capacity, couches, a VIP balcony section that overlooks the giant dance floor, plus some of the biggest-name DJs in the world, the club doesn't disappoint.

For years, **Richard's on Richards,** 1036 Richards St. (ℂ **604/687-6794;** www.richards onrichards.com; cover Fri–Sat C$8 for the club, C$10–C$30 for concerts), was a notorious pickup spot. Things have mellowed since then, but as the line of limos out front on busy nights attests, Dick's is still hot. Inside are two floors, four bars, a laser light system, and lots of DJ'ed dance tunes and concerts.

Shine, 364 Water St. (ℂ **604/408-4321;** www.shinenightclub.com; cover C$5–C$10), located in a downstairs cellar in Gastown, plays house and hip-hop, with occasional forays into other genres such as reggae.

At the **Stone Temple,** 1082 Granville St. (ℂ **604/488-1333;** www.stonetemplenight club.com; cover weeknights C$5, weekends C$10), frat boys from America are tickled pink that the drinking age in B.C. is only 19. And dude, the beer's so cheap! Opens at 9pm.

Squeeze past the well-endowed door bunnies at **Tonic,** 919 Granville St. (ℂ **604/669-0469;** www.thetonicclub.com; cover C$6–C$10), and you're in a narrow room with a soaring ceiling, oversize paintings of hard-liquor bottles, and an impressive-looking disco ball. The crowd is post-university but as yet unmated. Music is Latin, Brazilian, and Top 40 mix on weekends.

GAY & LESBIAN BARS The "Gay Village" is in the West End, particularly on Davie and Denman streets. Many clubs feature theme nights and dance parties, drag shows are ever popular, and every year in early August, as Gay Pride nears, the scene goes into overdrive. For information on the current hot spots, pick up a free copy of *Xtra West!,* available in most downtown cafes.

Reflecting the graying and—gasp!—mellowing of Vancouver's boomer-age gay crowd, the hottest hangout for gays is the **Fountain Head,** 1025 Davie St. (ℂ **604/687-2222;**

VANCOUVER

5

VANCOUVER AFTER DARK

www.thefountainheadpub.com), a pub located in the heart of the city's gay ghetto on Davie Street. The Head offers excellent microbrewed draft, good pub munchies, and a pleasant humming atmosphere until the morning's wee hours.

Once among the most disreputable of Gastown gay bars, **Lotus Hotel,** 455 Abbott St. (© **604/685-7777;** cover Milk and Lotus C$5–C$12 some nights; Honey C$7 Sat only), was given a face-lift and is now home to three bars and lounges, all with a largely but not exclusively gay clientele. Downstairs, the Lotus Lounge is one of the hottest house music venues in town, particularly on Straight Up Fridays with an all-female DJ team on the turntables. Milk, on the main floor, is a lesbian bar. The third venue, also on the main floor, is Honey, a comfortable lounge where a mixed crowd gathers for cocktails or beers.

Odyssey, 1251 Howe St. (© **604/689-5256;** www.theodysseynightclub.com; cover Thurs–Tues C$3–C$5), is the hottest and hippest gay/mixed dance bar in town (alley entrance is for men; women go in by the front door). The medium-size dance space is packed. Shows vary depending on the night.

Victoria

by Donald Olson

Once a little patch of the British Empire, Victoria is now wading into the shoals of a highly internationalized 21st century, and doing it with an appealing vitality that tweaks nostalgia for the past with a thoroughly modern sensibility.

As in Vancouver, you'll be amazed at how nice the people of Victoria are. Of course, you'd be nice, too, if you lived in such a pleasant place surrounded by such generous doses of natural beauty. Victoria, after all, with a population of about 325,000, occupies just a tiny corner of an island one-fifth the size of England but far more wild—so wild, in fact, that parts of it still have no roads and the only way to get around is by boat or on foot.

The city is one thing, its location something else. Only in the past decade or so has Victoria finally begun to capitalize on its stunning physical surroundings. Whale-watching is now a major industry, kayak tours are becoming ever more popular, mountain bikes have taken to competing for road space with the bright-red double-decker tour buses, eco-tourism is big, and "outdoor adventures" are available in just about every form you can think of. Your trip will be even more memorable if you move a bit beyond "Tourist Central" (the Inner Harbour area) and put yourself in touch with Mother Nature.

---

1 ESSENTIALS

GETTING THERE
By Plane
The **Victoria International Airport** (© 250/953-7500; www.victoriaairport.com) is near the Sidney ferry terminal, 22km (14 miles) north of Victoria off the Patricia Bay Highway (Hwy. 17).

Air Canada (© 888/247-2262 or 800/661-3936; www.aircanada.com) and **Horizon Air** (© 800/547-9308; www.alaskaair.com) offer direct connections from Seattle, Vancouver, Portland, Calgary, Edmonton, Saskatoon, Winnipeg, and Toronto. Canada's low-cost airline **WestJet** (© 888/WEST-JET [937-8358]; www.westjet.com) offers flights to Victoria from Kelowna, Calgary, Edmonton, and other destinations; WestJet service now extends to a few U.S. cities as well.

Commuter airlines, including floatplanes that land in Victoria's Inner Harbour, provide service to Victoria from Vancouver and destinations within B.C. They include **Air B.C.** (reached through Air Canada at © 888/247-2262), **Harbour Air Sea Planes** (© 604/274-1277 in Vancouver, or 250/384-2215 in Victoria; www.harbour-air.com), and **West Coast Air** (© 800/347-2222; www.westcoastair.com).

Kenmore Air (© 800/543-9595; www.kenmoreair.com) and **Helijet** (© 800/665-4354; www.helijet.com) offer flights between Seattle, Port Angeles, and Victoria.

Many **car-rental** firms have desks at the airport. If you're driving from the airport, take Hwy. 17 south to Victoria; it becomes Douglas Street as you enter downtown.

The **Akal Airporter shuttle bus** (© 250/386-2525; www.victoriaairportshuttle.com) has a ticket counter at the airport, and makes the trip downtown in about a half-hour. Buses leave every 30 minutes daily from 4:30am to midnight; the fare is C$16 one-way, C$10 per person for groups of four or more. Drop-offs are made at most hotels and bed-and-breakfasts, and pickups can be arranged as well. A limited number of hotel courtesy buses also serve the airport. A cab ride into downtown Victoria costs about C$45 plus tip. **Empress Cabs** and **Blue Bird Cabs** (p. 107) make airport runs.

By Ferry

Car-carrying **BC Ferries** (© 888/223-3779 or 250/386-3431; www.bcferries.com) has three routes from Vancouver to Vancouver Island and Victoria. In the summer, if you're driving, it's a good idea to reserve a space beforehand, especially on long weekends. Call BC Ferries reservations at © 888/724-5223 (in B.C. only) or 604/444-2890.

By Train

VIA Rail's **E&N Railiner** departs from Nanaimo and winds down Vancouver Island's Cowichan River valley through Goldstream Provincial Park and to Victoria. The trip takes 2½ hours and ends at **E&N Station,** 450 Pandora Ave. (© 800/561-8630 in Canada), near the Johnson Street Bridge. For more information, contact **VIA Rail Canada** (© 888/842-7245; www.viarail.ca).

By Bus

Pacific Coach Lines (© 604/662-7575; www.pacificcoach.com) provides service between Vancouver and Victoria with daily departures between 5:45am and 7:45pm. Pacific Coach Lines will pick up passengers from the Vancouver cruise-ship terminal and from most downtown hotels. For more information, call or visit their website.

VISITOR INFORMATION

Tourism Victoria Visitor Centre, 812 Wharf St. (© 800/663-3883 or 250/953-2033; www.tourismvictoria.com), is located on the Inner Harbour, across from the Fairmont Empress hotel. The center is open daily September through June 5 from 9am to 5pm, and June 6 through August from 9am to 8:30pm.

For details on the after-dark scene, pick up a copy of *Monday Magazine,* available free in cafes around the city; it's an excellent guide to Victoria's nightlife. The online version (www.mondaymag.com) has detailed entertainment listings.

CITY LAYOUT

Victoria was born at the edge of the Inner Harbour in the 1840s and spread outward from there. The areas of most interest to visitors, including **downtown** and **Old Town,** lie along the eastern edge of the **Inner Harbour.** (North of the Johnson St. Bridge is the **Upper Harbour,** which is largely industrial but taking on new life as old buildings are redeveloped.) A little farther east, the **Ross Bay** and **Oak Bay** residential areas around Dallas Road and Beach Drive reach the beaches along the open waters of the Strait of Juan de Fuca.

Victoria's central landmark is the **Fairmont Empress** hotel on Government Street, right across from the Inner Harbour. If you turn your back to the hotel, downtown and

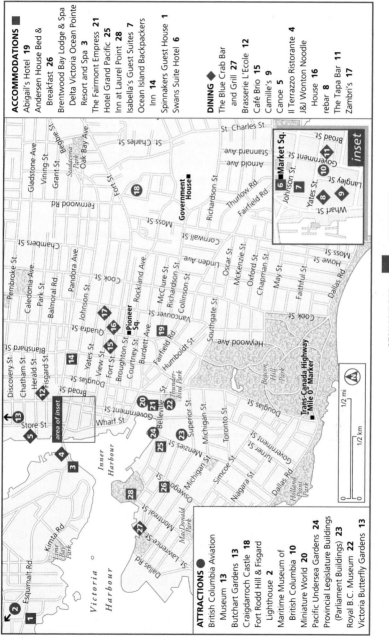

ACCOMMODATIONS ■

Abigail's Hotel **19**
Andersen House Bed & Breakfast **26**
Brentwood Bay Lodge & Spa **25**
Delta Victoria Ocean Pointe Resort and Spa **3**
The Fairmont Empress **21**
Hotel Grand Pacific **25**
Inn at Laurel Point **28**
Isabella's Guest Suites **7**
Ocean Island Backpackers Inn **14**
Spinnakers Guest House **1**
Swans Suite Hotel **6**

DINING ◆

The Blue Crab Bar and Grill **27**
Brasserie L'Ecole **12**
Café Brio **15**
Camille's **9**
Canoe **5**
Il Terrazzo Ristorante **4**
J&J Wonton Noodle House **16**
rebar **8**
The Tapa Bar **11**
Zambri's **17**

ATTRACTIONS ●

British Columbia Aviation Museum **13**
Butchart Gardens **13**
Craigdarroch Castle **18**
Fort Rodd Hill & Fisgard Lighthouse **2**
Maritime Museum of British Columbia **10**
Miniature World **20**
Pacific Undersea Gardens **24**
Provincial Legislature Buildings (Parliament Buildings) **23**
Royal B.C. Museum **22**
Victoria Butterfly Gardens **13**

Old Town are on your right, while the **Provincial Legislature Buildings** and the **Royal B.C. Museum** are on your immediate left. Next to them is the dock for the **Seattle–Port Angeles ferries,** and beyond that the residential community of **James Bay,** the first neighborhood in the city to be developed.

2 GETTING AROUND

BY PUBLIC TRANSPORTATION

BY BUS The **Victoria Regional Transit System (B.C. Transit;** *©* **250/382-6161;** www.bctransit.com) operates 40 bus routes through greater Victoria as well as the nearby towns of Sooke and Sidney. Buses run to both the Butchart Gardens and the Vancouver Ferry Terminal at Sidney. Regular service on the main routes runs daily from 6am to just past midnight.

Fares are good throughout the Greater Victoria area. One-way fares are C$2.25 for adults and students and C$1.40 for seniors and children 5 to 13. Transfers are good for travel in one direction only, with no stopovers. A **DayPass,** C$7 for adults and students, and C$5 for seniors and children 5 to 13, covers unlimited travel throughout the day. You can buy passes at the Tourism Victoria Visitor Centre (see "Visitor Information," above), convenience stores, and ticket outlets throughout Victoria displaying the FARE-DEALER sign.

BY FERRY Crossing the Inner, Upper, and Victoria harbors by one of the blue 12-passenger **Victoria Harbour Ferries** (*©* **250/708-0201;** www.victoriaharbourferry.com) is cheap and fun. May through September, the ferries to the Fairmont Empress, Coast Harbourside Hotel, and Ocean Pointe Resort hotel run about every 15 minutes daily from 9am to 9pm. In March, April, and October, ferry service runs daily 11am to 5pm. November through February, the ferries run only on sunny weekends 11am to 5pm. The cost per hop is C$4 for adults and C$2 for children.

BY CAR

You can easily explore the downtown area of Victoria on foot. If you're planning out-of-town activities, you can rent a car in town or bring your own on one of the car-passenger ferries from Vancouver, Port Angeles, or Anacortes. Traffic is light in Victoria, largely because the downtown core is so walkable.

RENTALS Car-rental agencies in Victoria include the following: **Avis,** 1001 Douglas St. (*©* **800/879-2847** or 250/386-8468; www.avis.ca; bus no. 5 to Broughton St.); **Budget,** 757 Douglas St. (*©* **800/668-9833** or 250/953-5300; www.budgetvictoria.com); **Hertz,** 655 Douglas St., in the Queen Victoria Inn (*©* **800/654-3131** or 250/952-3765; www.hertz.com); and **National,** 767 Douglas St. (*©* **800/227-7368** or 250/386-1213; www.nationalvictoria.com). These latter three can be reached on the no. 5 bus to the Convention Centre.

PARKING Metered **street parking** is available downtown, but be sure to feed the meter because rules are strictly enforced. Unmetered parking on side streets is rare. All major downtown hotels have guest parking. Parking lots can be found at **View Street** between Douglas and Blanshard streets, **Johnson Street** off Blanshard Street, **Yates Street** north of Bastion Square, and **The Bay** on Fisgard at Blanshard Street.

via gravel logging roads, on which logging trucks have absolute right of way. If you're on a logging road and see a logging truck coming from either direction, pull over to the side of the road and stop to let it pass.

BY BIKE

Biking is the easiest way to get around the downtown and beach areas. The city has numerous bike lanes and paved paths in parks and along beaches. Helmets are mandatory, and riding on sidewalks is illegal, except where bike paths are indicated. You can rent bikes starting at C$7 per hour and C$24 per day (lock and helmet included) from **Cycle B.C.,** 707 Douglas St. (© **866/380-2453** or 250/380-2453; www.cyclebc.ca).

BY TAXI

Within the downtown area, you can expect to travel for less than C$10, plus tip. It's best to call for a cab; you won't have much luck if you try to flag one down on the street. Drivers don't always stop, especially when it's raining. Call for a pickup from **Empress Cabs** (© **250/381-2222**) or **Blue Bird Cabs** (© **250/382-2222**).

BY PEDAL-CAB

You get to sit while an avid bicyclist with thighs of steel pedals you anywhere you want to go for C$1 per minute (C$2 per min. if there are four of you). You'll see these two- and four-seater bike cabs along the Inner Harbour at the base of Bastion Square, or you can call **Kabuki Kabs** (© **250/385-4243;** www.kabukikabs.com) for 24-hour service.

VICTORIA

6

FAST FACTS: VICTORIA

(Fast Facts) Victoria

Business Hours Victoria **banks** are open Monday through Thursday 10am to 3pm and Friday 10am to 6pm. **Stores** are generally open Monday through Saturday 10am to 6pm. Some establishments are open later, as well as on Sundays, in summer. Last call at the city's **bars** and **cocktail lounges** is 2am.

Currency Exchange The best exchange rates in town can be found at banks and by using ATMs. **Royal Bank,** 1079 Douglas St., at Fort Street, is in the heart of downtown. Take bus no. 5 to Fort Street.

Dentist Most major hotels have a dentist on call. **Cresta Dental Centre,** 3170 Tillicum Rd., at Burnside Street in the Tillicum Mall (© **250/384-7711;** bus no. 10), is open Monday through Friday 8am to 9pm, Saturday 9am to 5:30pm, and Sunday 11am to 5pm.

Doctor Hotels usually have doctors on call. The **Tillicum Mall Medical Clinic,** 3170 Tillicum Rd., at Burnside Street (© **250/381-8112;** bus no. 10 to Tillicum Mall), accepts walk-in patients daily 9am to 9pm.

Hospitals Local hospitals include the **Royal Jubilee Hospital,** 1952 Bay St. (© **250/370-8000,** emergency 250/370-8212), and the **Victoria General Hospital,** 1 Hospital Way (© **250/727-4212,** emergency 250/727-4181). You can get to both hospitals on bus no. 14.

Internet Access In the heart of Old Town, **Stain Internet Café,** 609 Yates St. (© **250/382-3352**), is open daily 10am to 2am (C$2.50 per half-hour). Closer to the Legislature, try **James Bay Coffee and Books,** 143 Menzies St. (© **250/386-4700**), open daily 7:30am to 10pm (C$1 per 10 min.). Most hotels have Internet access, as does the Victoria Public Library; see below.

Library The **Greater Victoria Public Library** (© **250/382-7241**; bus no. 5 to Broughton St.) is at 735 Broughton St., near the corner of Fort and Douglas streets.

Luggage Storage & Lockers Coin lockers are available outside the bus station (behind the Fairmont Empress). Take bus no. 5 to the Convention Centre.

Pharmacies **Shopper's Drug Mart,** 1222 Douglas St. (© **250/381-4321**; bus no. 5 to View St.), is open Monday through Friday 7am to 8pm, Saturday 9am to 7pm, and Sunday 9am to 6pm.

Police Dial © **911.** This is a free call. The **Victoria City Police** can also be reached by calling © **250/995-7654.**

Post Office The **main post office** is at 714 Yates St. (© **250/953-1352**; bus no. 5 to Yates St.). There are also postal outlets in **Shopper's Drug Mart** (see "Pharmacies," above) and in other stores displaying the CANADA POST postal outlet sign. Supermarkets and many souvenir and gift shops also sell stamps.

3 WHERE TO STAY

You'll save big-time if you schedule your holiday from October to May. When the high summer season starts in June, rates tend to skyrocket.

Reservations are essential in Victoria June through September. If you arrive without a reservation and have trouble finding a room, **Tourism Victoria** (© **800/663-3883** or 250/953-2033; www.tourismvictoria.com) can make reservations for you at hotels, inns, and B&Bs. It deals only with establishments that pay a fee to list with them; fortunately, most do.

Another good resource is **Canada-West Accommodations Bed & Breakfast Registry,** P.O. Box 86607, North Vancouver, BC V7L 4L2 (© **800/561-3223** or 604/990-6730; www.b-b.com), which specializes in matching guests to the B&Bs that best suit their needs.

Prices quoted here don't include the 10% **hotel room tax,** the 7% **provincial accommodations tax,** or the 6% **goods and services tax (GST).**

THE INNER HARBOUR & NEARBY
Very Expensive
Delta Victoria Ocean Pointe Resort and Spa ★★ (Kids) The "OPR," located across the Johnson Street Bridge on the Inner Harbour's north shore, is a big, bright, modern hotel with commanding views of downtown, the Legislature, the Fairmont Empress, and the busy harbor itself. The rooms here are nice and big, and so are the bathrooms. The decor, like the hotel itself, is a blend of contemporary and traditional. All guests have use of the big indoor pool, a really good whirlpool, and a fully equipped gym with racquetball and tennis courts. Lots of guests come for the new spa, one of the best in Victoria. Kids receive a free welcome kit, and they'll love the pool.

45 Songhees Rd., Victoria, BC V9A 6T3. ℰ **800/667-4677** or 250/360-2999. Fax 250/360-1041. www.
deltavictoria.com. 239 units. C$119–C$499 double; C$449–C$999 suite. Children 16 and under stay free
in parent's room. AE, DC, MC, V. Underground valet parking C$15. Bus: 24 to Colville. **Amenities:** Restau-
rant/lounge; babysitting; concierge; executive-level rooms; health club; Jacuzzi; indoor pool; room service; sauna; spa; outdoor tennis courts; rooms for those w/limited mobility. *In room:* A/C, TV/VCR w/pay
movies, hair dryer, free high-speed Internet, minibar.

The Fairmont Empress ★★★ Kids   The world-renowned Empress is the most
famous celebrity on the Victoria waterfront, and staying at this full-service landmark
hotel makes for a memorable experience. But to get the most out of your stay, it's a good
idea to book a room at the Gold level, which comes with larger rooms, a dedicated concierge, breakfast, and evening hors d'oeuvres; it's like a smaller hotel within the hotel. The
hotel's 256 standard rooms are smallish and offer little in the way of views. The Deluxe
rooms are bigger, with high ceilings, and most of them have a view of the harbor. The
Signature rooms are large corner rooms. The hotel's fabulous location and first-class
amenities—including a kid-friendly indoor pool and luxurious Willow Stream spa—add
to the pleasure of staying here. The enormous Empress is firmly traditional (old-fashioned) in terms of decor. If you don't stay here, you may want to come for the famous
afternoon tea (see "Taking Afternoon Tea," later in this chapter), a relaxing session at the
spa, or a cocktail in the wood-paneled Bengal Lounge (which also serves a lunchtime
curry buffet).

721 Government St., Victoria, BC V8W 1W5. ℰ **866/540-4429** or 250/384-8111. Fax 250/381-4334. www.
fairmont.com/empress. 477 units. C$169–C$569 double; C$269–C$769 Gold level double. AE, DC, DISC,
MC, V. Underground valet parking C$28. Bus: 5. **Amenities:** 2 restaurants; bar/lounge; tearoom; babysit-
ting; concierge; executive-level rooms; high-quality health club; Jacuzzi; indoor lap pool; room service;
sauna; spa; rooms for those w/limited mobility. *In room:* TV w/pay movies, hair dryer, high-speed Internet
(C$15/day).

Expensive

Hotel Grand Pacific ★★   On Victoria's bustling Inner Harbour, directly across the
street from the Port Angeles–Victoria ferry dock, the Grand Pacific is more luxurious
than the Delta Ocean Pointe, and has rooms that are generally more spacious than standard rooms at the Fairmont Empress. Like those other two hotels on the Inner Harbour,
the Grand Pacific has its own spa; its health club is better than the others and features a
huge ozonated indoor pool. All rooms have balconies and are attractively and comfortably furnished. Suites provide the best views, overlooking the harbor and the Empress.
Bathrooms throughout are fairly small.

463 Belleville St., Victoria, BC V8V 1X3. ℰ **800/663-7550** or 250/386-0450. Fax 250/380-4475. www.
hotelgrandpacific.com. 304 units. C$159–C$289 double; C$219–C$399 suite. Additional person C$30. AE,
DC, DISC, MC, V. Self-parking C$12; valet parking C$24. Bus: 30 to Superior and Oswego sts. **Amenities:**
2 restaurants; cafe; bar; concierge; superior health club; Jacuzzi; indoor pool; room service; spa; squash
courts. *In room:* A/C, TV w/pay movies, hair dryer, free high-speed Internet, minibar.

Inn at Laurel Point ★★★   The three stars are for the Erickson Wing suites featuring stylish, contemporary furnishings, Asian artwork, balconies overlooking a Japanese
garden, shoji-style sliding doors, and luxurious marble bathrooms with deep soaker tubs
and glassed-in showers. This art-filled, resort-style hotel occupies a prettily landscaped
promontory jutting out into the Inner Harbour, and consists of the original north wing
and the newer south wing designed by noted Vancouver architect Arthur Erickson in
1989. The overall design reflects the elegant simplicity of Japanese artistic principles and
is a refreshing change from the chintz and florals found in so many Victoria hotels.

Rooms in the older north wing come with pocket balconies (every room in the hotel has a water view) and nice bathrooms—but the Erickson Wing is where you want to be. The hotel's Aura restaurant is a new dining hot spot.

680 Montreal St., Victoria, BC V8V 1Z8. ℂ **800/663-7667** or 250/386-8721. Fax 250/386-9547. www.laurel point.com. 200 units. C$149–C$269 double; C$249–C$369 suite. Additional adult C$25. Children 17 and under stay free in parent's room. AE, DC, DISC, MC, V. Secure parking C$12. Bus: 30 to Montreal and Superior sts. **Amenities:** Restaurant; bar; babysitting; concierge; free access to YMCA facilities; indoor pool; room service; rooms for those w/limited mobility. *In room:* A/C, TV, hair dryer, free high-speed Internet.

Moderate

Andersen House Bed & Breakfast ★
The art and furnishings in Andersen House are drawn from the whole of the old British Empire and a good section of the modern world beyond. Each room has a unique style: the sun-drenched Casablanca room on the top floor, for example, boasts Persian rugs, a four-poster queen-size bed, and a boxed window seat. All rooms have private entrances and come with two-person Jacuzzis, books, CD players and CDs, and complimentary Wi-Fi.

301 Kingston St., Victoria, BC V8V 1V5. ℂ **877/264-9988** or 250/388-4565. Fax 250/388-4508. www.andersenhouse.com. 4 units. C$125–C$285 double. Rates include breakfast. AE, MC, V. Free off-street parking. Bus: 30 to Superior and Oswego sts. Children 11 and under not accepted. *In room:* TV/VCR, hair dryer, Jacuzzi, free Wi-Fi.

Spinnakers Guest House ★ (Value)
This bed-and-breakfast-style guesthouse offers good accommodations at a moderate price. The two separate buildings are owned and operated by the same local entrepreneur who runs Spinnakers Brewpub. The 1884 heritage building on Catherine Street is the more luxurious. Rooms feature queen-size beds, lovely furnishings, in-room Jacuzzis, fireplaces, high ceilings, and lots of natural light. The four Garden Suites units on Mary Street are really self-contained apartments, with separate bedrooms and full kitchens, perfect for longer stays or for families. Guests at both buildings get an in-room breakfast.

308 Catherine St., Victoria, BC V9A 3S8. ℂ **877/838-2739** or 250/384-2739. Fax 250/384-3246. www.spinnakers.com. 10 units. C$129–C$279 double. Rates include breakfast. AE, MC, V. Free parking. Bus: 24 to Catherine St. *In room:* Kitchen (some units), free Wi-Fi, fireplace (some units), Wi-Fi.

Inexpensive

Admiral Inn (Value) (Kids)
The family-operated Admiral is in a three-story building on the Inner Harbour, near the Port Angeles–bound ferry terminal and close to restaurants and shopping. The combination of clean, comfortable rooms and reasonable rates attracts young couples, families, seniors, and other travelers in search of a harbor view at a moderate price. The rooms are pleasant and comfortably furnished, a bit motel-like, with small bathrooms and balconies or terraces. The more expensive rooms come with a kitchenette with a small fridge and stove. The suites come with full kitchens. Some units can sleep up to six (on two double beds and a double sofa bed).

257 Belleville St., Victoria, BC V8V 1X1. ℂ **888/823-6472** or ℂ/fax 250/388-6267. www.admiral.bc.ca. 29 units. C$99–C$199 double; C$139–C$229 suite. Additional person C$10. Children 11 and under stay free in parent's room. Rates include continental breakfast. AE, DC, MC, V. Free parking. Bus: 5 to Belleville and Government sts. **Amenities:** Complimentary bikes; free Wi-Fi in lobby. *In room:* A/C, TV, fridge, hair dryer, kitchen/kitchenette (in some units).

Expensive

Abigail's Hotel ★★   Located in a residential neighborhood just east of downtown, Abigail's began life in the 1920s as a luxury apartment house before being converted to a boutique hotel. If you like small, personalized bed-and-breakfast hotels, you'll enjoy this impeccably maintained property. In the original building, some of the 16 rooms are bright and sunny and beautifully furnished, with pedestal sinks and goose-down duvets. Others feature soaker tubs and double-sided fireplaces, so you can relax in the tub by the light of the fire. The six Celebration Suites in the Coach House are even more luxurious. Recent renovations added Italian-marble bathrooms, new furniture, and a new spa.

906 McClure St., Victoria, BC V8V 3E7. ✆ **800/561-6565** or 250/388-5363. Fax 250/388-7787. www. abigailshotel.com. 23 units. C$139–C$450 double. Rates include full breakfast. AE, MC, V. Free parking. Bus: 1 to Cook and McClure sts. **Amenities:** Concierge. *In room:* A/C, TV, hair dryer, free Wi-Fi, fireplace (in some rooms), Jacuzzi (in some rooms).

Isabella's Guest Suites ★ (Finds)   Two suites located above Willy's bakery provide affordable, fun, and surprisingly stylish accommodations in the heart of the city. The front suite is a large studio with a bed/sitting room that opens into a dining room and full kitchen. Bright colors and cheerful accents, upscale rustic furniture, high ceilings, large windows, and plenty of space make this a great home base for exploring Victoria. The second unit, a one-bedroom suite, overlooks the alley and patio of Il Terrazzo restaurant. The living room is painted in bright red, which goes surprisingly well with the wood floors and funky furniture. Both units have king-size beds and are nonsmoking. Breakfast is included and served at the bakery.

537 Johnson St., Victoria, BC V8W 1M2. ✆ **250/812-9216.** Fax 250/381-8415. www.isabellasbb.com. 2 units. C$150–C$195 double. Rates include continental breakfast. MC, V. Free parking. Bus: 5. *In room:* A/C, TV, hair dryer, kitchen.

Swans Suite Hotel ★★ (Kids)   In 1988, this heritage building was turned into a hotel, restaurant, brewpub, and nightclub. Located near the Johnson Street Bridge, it's just minutes from Bastion Square, Chinatown, and downtown. The suites are large and many are split-level, featuring open lofts and huge exposed beams. All come with fully equipped kitchens, dining areas, living rooms, queen-size beds, and original artwork. The two-bedroom suites are like little town houses; they're great for families, accommodating up to six comfortably. Swan's Brewpub is one of the most popular in the city and features nightly live entertainment. The one potential drawback to this otherwise fine hotel is that a homeless shelter is located across the street.

506 Pandora St., Victoria, BC V8W 1N6. ✆ **800/668-7926** or 250/361-3310. Fax 250/361-3491. www. swanshotel.com. 30 units. C$179–C$199 studio; C$219–C$359 suite. Children 12 and under stay free in parent's room. AE, DC, DISC, MC, V. Parking C$9. Bus: 23 or 24 to Pandora Ave. **Amenities:** Restaurant; brewpub; room service. *In room:* TV, hair dryer, kitchen, free Wi-Fi.

Inexpensive

Ocean Island Backpackers Inn ★ (Value)   All sorts of travelers make their way to this inexpensive, centrally located hostel (an alternative to the Hostelling International network), from families with children to on-the-go seniors and young adults with global wanderlust. The big, comfy lounge/common area always has all kinds of stuff going on, including live music and open-mic evenings. You can buy cheap meals and snacks, use the kitchen, or kick back with a beer or glass of wine. In addition to the dorm rooms, there are 60 private rooms, in various configurations, including some with their own bathrooms. The staff here goes out of its way to help guests make the most of their time in Victoria and on Vancouver Island.

791 Pandora Ave., Victoria, BC V8W 1N9. ✆ **888/888-4180** or 250/385-1788. Fax 250/385-1780. www.oceanisland.com. 50 units. C$21–C$27 dorm bed; C$27–C$75 private room (some with private bathroom). MC, V. Parking C$5. Bus: 70 to Pandora Ave. and Douglas St. **Amenities:** Restaurant; lounge. *In room:* TV (in some rooms), Wi-Fi (C$3/hr.).

OUTSIDE THE CENTRAL AREA

Expensive

Brentwood Bay Lodge & Spa ★★★ (Finds) Located on a pristine inlet about 20 minutes north of downtown Victoria, this contemporary timber-and-glass lodge offers the best of everything, including a fabulous spa, boat shuttle to Butchart Gardens, and all manner of eco-adventures, including kayaking, scuba diving, fishing, and boat trips through the surrounding waters. The rooms are beautifully outfitted with handcrafted furnishings, gas fireplaces, luxurious bathrooms with soaker tubs and body massage showers, balconies, and king-size beds fitted with the highest-quality Italian linens. The SeaGrille dining room and pub offers fine seasonal menus and great pub food. The hotel has its own marina and is a licensed PADI (Professional Association of Diving Instructors) dive center.

849 Verdier Ave., on Brentwood Bay, Victoria, BC V8M 1C5. ✆ **888/544-2079** or 250/544-2079. Fax 250/544-2069. www.brentwoodbaylodge.com. 33 units. C$179–C$419 double; C$369–C$699 suite. Rates include continental breakfast. AE, DC, MC, V. Free parking. Take Pat Bay Hwy. north to Keating Crossroads, turn left (west) to Saanich Rd., turn right (south) to Verdier Ave. **Amenities:** Restaurant; pub; concierge; Jacuzzi; heated outdoor pool; room service; spa. *In room:* A/C, TV/DVD, hair dryer, minibar, free Wi-Fi, fireplace, Jacuzzi (in suites).

Inexpensive

University of Victoria Housing, Food, and Conference Services (Value) One of the best deals going is found at the University of Victoria, when classes aren't in session and summer visitors are welcomed. All rooms have single or twin beds and basic furnishings; bathrooms, pay phones, and TV lounges are on every floor. Linens, towels, and soap are provided. The suites are an extremely good value—each has four bedrooms, a kitchen, a living room, and 1½ bathrooms. For C$5 extra per day, you can make use of the many on-campus athletic facilities. Each of the 28 buildings has a coin laundry. The disadvantage is that the U. Vic. campus is a painfully long way from everywhere—the city center is about a 20-minute drive away.

P.O. Box 1700, Sinclair at Finerty Rd., Victoria, BC V8W 2Y2. ✆ **250/721-8395.** Fax 250/721-8930. www.hfcs.uvic.ca. 898 units. May–Aug C$45 single; C$55 double; C$150 suite (sleeps 4 people). Rates for single and double rooms include continental breakfast and taxes. MC, V. Parking C$6. Closed Sept–Apr. Bus: 4 or 14 to University of Victoria. **Amenities:** Access to athletic facilities; indoor pool. *In room:* Free Wi-Fi.

4 WHERE TO DINE

Victoria has jumped on the foodie bandwagon and offers a cornucopia of culinary styles from around the world. It's not as savvy and sophisticated as Vancouver, and never will be, but with more than 700 restaurants in the area, something is available for every taste and wallet.

The touristy restaurants along Wharf Street serve mediocre food for folks they know they'll never have to see again, so avoid them. The canny visitor knows to head inland (even a block is enough), where the proportion of tourists to locals drops sharply and the quality jumps by leaps and bounds.

Victoria is not the kind of late-night, show-off, see-and-be-seen dining city that Vancouver is. Most restaurants in Victoria close at 10pm. Reservations are strongly recommended for prime sunset seating during summer, especially on Friday and Saturday. No provincial tax is added to restaurant meals in British Columbia, just the **6% goods and services tax (GST).**

Note: Because Victoria is so compact, most of the restaurants listed in this chapter are in downtown or Old Town and no more than a 10-minute walk from most hotels. Thus, in this chapter, I've listed public transit information only for those spots that are a bit farther out.

THE INNER HARBOUR
Expensive
The Blue Crab Bar and Grill ★★★ SEAFOOD   One of Victoria's best bets for seafood, the Blue Crab combines excellent fresh ingredients and a fairly uncomplicated preparation. It sits right on the Inner Harbour and has a wonderful view across the water. The Crab sources most of its ingredients locally, and it's a member of OceanWise, a group dedicated to sustainable fishing practices. For lunch you can tuck in to Pacific seafood chowder or a grilled arctic char sandwich; at dinner, try the fresh oysters, a Cortes Island clam and mussel pot, fresh halibut with pasta, or the signature hot pot of local seafood prepared with ginger and lemon-grass broth. The award-winning wine list features midrange and top-end vintages, drawn mostly from B.C., Washington, and California. The service is deft and obliging.

In the Coast Hotel, 146 Kingston St. ℂ **250/480-1999.** www.bluecrab.ca. Reservations recommended. Main courses lunch C$12–C$21, dinner C$15–C$35. AE, DC, MC, V. Daily 6:30am–10pm (dinner from 5pm).

Moderate
Canoe ★ PUB GRUB/PACIFIC NORTHWEST   What was once a Victorian power station is now one of Victoria's loveliest and liveliest brewpub restaurants, with an outdoor patio overlooking the harbor toward the Johnson Street Bridge and an industrial-inspired interior with massive masonry walls and heavy timber crossbeams. Canoe is popular because it has something tasty for every palate, all made with local ingredients whenever possible. The kitchen offers intriguing variations on standard pub fare and bar snacks, including thin-crust pizzas, classic burgers, and their signature pot pie. Head upstairs for finer fare such as premium top sirloin steak, seafood curry, or the day's fresh fish. The beer is excellent; the award-winning wine list is small but select.

450 Swift St. ℂ **250/361-1940.** www.canoebrewpub.com. Reservations recommended for weekend dinner and Sun brunch. Main courses C$13–C$23; pub fare and bar snacks C$9–C$17; lunch special C$12. AE, MC, V. Sun–Wed 11:30am–11pm; Thurs 11:30am–midnight; Fri–Sat 11:30am–1am.

DOWNTOWN & OLD TOWN
Expensive
Brasserie L'Ecole ★★ FRENCH   In the overheated world of food fashion, it's so refreshing to find simple French bistro fare deftly prepared and served at amazingly reasonable prices. Honesty is what's on offer at this warm, comfortable restaurant. L'Ecole's menu changes daily, depending entirely on what comes in fresh from Victoria's hinterland farms. Preparation is simple, no big reductions or complicated jus, just shellfish,

local fish, meats with red-wine sauces, and fresh vegetables with vinaigrettes. The wine list is small, but has good wine to match the excellent food. Very satisfying in every way.

1715 Government St. © **250/475-6260.** www.lecole.ca. Reservations recommended. Main courses C$22–C$24. AE, MC, V. Tues–Sat 5:30–11pm.

Café Brio ★★★ PACIFIC NORTHWEST/ITALIAN   Café Brio is one of Victoria's best and buzziest spots for casual but top-flight dining. The Tuscan-influenced cuisine strongly reflects the seasons, fresh local meats and produce, and Pacific seafood. The menu changes daily, but appetizers always include locally harvested oysters, a wonderful house-made paprika sausage, and a delicious charcuterie plate (the chef makes all his charcuterie on the premises). For entrees, choose from handmade pasta (such as fresh herb-ricotta agnolotti) or roasted or poached wild fish. The wine list is excellent, with an impressive selection of B.C. and international reds and whites. The service is deft, friendly, and knowledgeable, and the kitchen stays open as long as guests keep ordering.

944 Fort St. © **250/383-0009.** www.cafe-brio.com. Reservations recommended. Main courses C$14–C$49. AE, MC, V. Daily 5:30–9:30pm.

Camille's ★★★ PACIFIC NORTHWEST   The most romantic of Victoria's restaurants, Camille's is also one of the very best. Tucked away in two rooms beneath the old Law Chambers, its decor contrasts white linen with century-old exposed brick, stained-glass lamps, and candlelight. Chef and owner David Mincey was one of the founders of a Vancouver Island farm cooperative that brings local farmers together with local restaurants, so you're usually dining on foods found within a 100-mile radius of the restaurant. The ever-changing menu displays Mincey's love for cheeky invention and the seasonal bounty of Vancouver Island. To sample a bit of everything, try the five-course tasting menu, a fantastic bargain at C$50, or C$75 with wine pairings. The reasonable and extensive wine list comes with liner notes that are amusing and informative. A meal here is a quiet, memorable occasion.

45 Bastion Sq. © **250/381-3433.** Reservations recommended. Main courses C$22–C$37. AE, MC, V. Tues–Sun 5:30–10pm.

Il Terrazzo Ristorante ★★ ITALIAN   This charming spot in a converted heritage building off Waddington Alley is always a top contender for Victoria's best Italian restaurant. You can be assured of a good meal here. The northern Italian cooking includes wood-oven-roasted meats, fish, and pizzas, as well as homemade pastas. An emphasis on fresh produce and local seafood sets the tone for the menu, with appetizers such as artichokes stuffed with salmon and crabmeat drizzled with a light lemon-cream sauce, and entrees like salmon crusted with almond and black pepper and baked in the wood-burning oven, or a fabulous rack of lamb. The mood is bustling and upbeat, complete with an atmospheric courtyard furnished with flowers, marble tables, wrought-iron chairs, and heaters. The wine list is enormous, with some 1,200 vintages.

555 Johnson St. (off Waddington Alley). © **250/361-0028.** www.ilterrazzo.com. Reservations recommended. Main courses C$15–C$37. AE, MC, V. Mon–Sat 11:30am–3pm and 5–10pm; Sun 5–10pm.

Moderate

The Tapa Bar (Finds) TAPAS   The perfect meal for the commitment-shy, tapas are small and flavorful plates that you combine together to make a meal. Tapas to be sampled in this warm and welcoming spot include fried calamari, hearts of palm, and grilled portobello mushrooms. However, don't pass up on the *gambas al ajillo*—shrimp in a rich broth of garlic.

(Moments) Taking Afternoon Tea

Far from a simple cup of hot water with a Lipton tea bag beside it, a proper afternoon tea is both a meal and a ritual.

Any number of places in Victoria serve afternoon tea; some refer to it as high tea. Both come with sandwiches, berries, and tarts, but high tea usually includes some more substantial savory fare such as a meat-and-vegetable-filled turnover. Though the caloric intake can be hefty, it's really more about the ritual than the potential weight gain. For that reason, you don't want to go to any old teahouse. Note that in summer it's a good idea to book *at least* a week ahead.

If you want, and can afford, the best experience, head to the **Fairmont Empress** ★★★, 721 Government St. (© **250/384-8111;** p. 109), where tea is served in the Tea Lobby, a busy and beautifully ornate room at the front of the hotel, for C$49 to C$60. Reservations are essential and a "smart casual" dress code is in effect (no torn jeans, short shorts, or flip-flops).

More affordable, less crowded, and just as historic is tea on the lawn of **Point Ellice House,** 2616 Pleasant St. (© **250/380-6506;** www.pointellicehouse.ca), where the cream of Victoria society used to gather in the early 1900s. Afternoon tea costs C$23 and includes a half-hour tour of the mansion and gardens, plus the opportunity to play a game of croquet. Phone ahead for reservations and Christmas hours.

If you want your tea in a historic garden setting, head over to **Abkhazi Garden,** 1964 Fairfield Rd. (© **250/598-8096;** by car or bus no. 1 from downtown), where tea is served daily in the small, modernist house built by Russian Prince and Princess Abkhazi.

Set in impeccably maintained gardens, "Afternoon Tea at the Gardens" at the **Butchart Gardens Dining Room Restaurant** ★★★, 800 Benvenuto Ave. (© **250/652-8222;** www.butchartgardens.com; p. 117), is a memorable experience. You can savor this fine tradition for C$27 per person. Reservations recommended.

What the **White Heather Tea Room** ★★, 1885 Oak Bay Rd. (© **250/595-8020**), lacks in old-time atmosphere it makes up for with the sheer quality and value of the tea, and the charm of proprietress and tea mistress Agnes. For those feeling not so peckish, try the Wee Tea at C$14; for those a little hungrier, the Not So Wee Tea at C$18. If you feel like going the whole hog, try the Big Muckle Great Tea for Two at C$42. Call for reservations.

620 Trounce Alley. © **250/383-0013.** www.tapabar.ca. Tapas plates C$7–C$15. AE, MC, V. Mon–Thurs 11:30am–11pm; Fri–Sat 11:30am–midnight; Sun noon–10pm.

Zambri's ★ (Finds) ITALIAN   This little deli-restaurant in a strip mall off Yates Street has earned numerous accolades for its honest and fresh Italian cuisine served in an unpretentious, no-nonsense style. The lunch menu, served cafeteria-style, includes daily pasta specials and a handful of entrees such as fresh rockfish or salmon. In the evenings, the atmosphere is slightly more formal, with table service and a regularly changing a la carte menu. Menu items veer from penne with sausage and tomato to pasta with chicken liver pâté or peas and Gorgonzola. Many diners come for the three-course dinner (C$40–C$45), though this is not served every night (call ahead).

110-911 Yates St. ✆ **250/360-1171.** www.zambris.ca. Reservations not accepted. Lunch C$8–C$14; dinner main courses C$22–C$25. MC, V. Tues–Sat 11:30am–2:30pm and 5–9pm.

Inexpensive

J&J Wonton Noodle House ★ (Finds) CHINESE   This place doesn't go overboard on the atmosphere, but it's perfectly pleasant, and more importantly, you won't find better noodles anywhere in Victoria. The kitchen is glassed in so you can watch the chefs spinning out noodles. Lunch specials—which feature different fresh seafood every day—are good and cheap, so expect a line of locals at the door. If you miss the specials, noodle soups, wontons, and other dishes are also quick, delicious, and inexpensive. Dinner is pricier.

1012 Fort St. ✆ **250/383-0680.** www.jjnoodlehouse.com. Main courses C$11–C$20; lunch specials C$7–C$15. MC, V. Tues–Sat 11am–2pm and 4:30–8:30pm. Bus: 5.

rebar (Kids) VEGETARIAN   Even if you're not hungry, it's worth dropping in here for a juice blend—say grapefruit, banana, melon, and pear with bee pollen or blue-green algae for added oomph. If you're hungry, rejoice: rebar is the city's premier purveyor of vegetarian comfort food. Disturbingly wholesome as that may sound, rebar is not only tasty, but also fun, and a great spot to take the kids for brunch or breakfast. The room—in the basement of an 1890s heritage building—is bright and funky, the service is friendly and casual, and the food tends toward the simple and wholesome. The menu features quesadillas, omelets, and crisp salads. Juices are still the crown jewels, with more than 80 blends on the menu.

50 Bastion Sq. ✆ **250/361-9223.** www.rebarmodernfood.com. Main courses C$10–C$18. AE, MC, V. Mon–Thurs 8:30am–9pm; Fri–Sat 8:30am–10pm; Sun 8:30am–3:30pm. Reduced hours in the winter.

---

5 EXPLORING VICTORIA

Victoria's top draws are its waterfront—the beautiful view created by the Fairmont Empress and the Provincial Legislature Buildings on the edge of the Inner Harbour—and its historic Old Town. Two must-see attractions are the Butchart Gardens, about a 20-minute drive from downtown, and the Royal B.C. Museum on the Inner Harbour.

So attractive is this small capital city, though, that folks sometimes forget what a beautiful and wild part of the world it's set in. If you have time, step out of town and see some nature: sail out to see killer whales, beachcomb for crabs, kayak along the ocean shorelines, or hike into the hills for fabulous views and scenery. Pacific Rim National Park, a wild and wonderful wonderland on the west coast of Vancouver Island, is covered in chapter 8.

SEEING THE SIGHTS

The Top Attractions

British Columbia Aviation Museum ★   Located adjacent to Victoria International Airport, this small hangar is crammed with a score of original, rebuilt, and replica airplanes. The collection ranges from the first Canadian-designed craft ever to fly (a bizarre kitelike contraption) to slightly more modern water bombers and helicopters. Thursdays you can watch the all-volunteer crew in the restoration hangar working to bring these old aircraft back to life.

1910 Norseman Rd., Sidney. © 250/655-3300. www.bcam.net. Admission C$7 adults, C$5 seniors, free for children 12 and under. Summer daily 10am–4pm; winter daily 11am–3pm. Closed Dec 25, Jan 1. Bus: Airport.

Butchart Gardens ★★★ These internationally acclaimed gardens were created after Robert Butchart exhausted the limestone quarry near his Tod Inlet home, about 22km (14 miles) from Victoria. His wife, Jenny, gradually landscaped the deserted eyesore into the resplendent Sunken Garden, opening it for public display in 1904. Over the years, a Rose Garden, Italian Garden, and Japanese Garden were added. The gardens—still in the family—now display more than a million plants throughout the year. You'll be amazed at the gardeners' painstaking care and the beauty of the plantings.

On summer evenings, the gardens are illuminated with a variety of softly colored lights. June through September, musical entertainment is provided free Monday through Saturday evenings. You can even watch **fireworks displays** ★★★ on Saturdays in July and August. A very good lunch, dinner, and afternoon tea are offered in the Dining Room Restaurant in the historic residence; afternoon and high teas are also served in the Italian Garden (reservations recommended). Allow 2 to 3 hours; in peak summer months you'll encounter less congestion in the garden if you come very early or after 3pm. Admission prices vary according to season.

800 Benvenuto Ave., Brentwood Bay. © **866/652-4422** or 250/652-4422; dining reservations 250/652-8222. www.butchartgardens.com. Admission C$15–C$28 adults, C$7.75–C$14 youths 13–17, C$2–C$3 children 5–12, free for children 4 and under. Daily 9am–sundown (call or visit website for seasonal closing times); visitors can remain in gardens for 1 hr. after gate closes. Bus: 75; C$4.50 round-trip. Take Blanshard St. (Hwy. 17) north toward the ferry terminal in Saanich, then turn left on Keating Crossroads, which leads directly to the gardens—about 20 min. from downtown Victoria; it's impossible to miss if you follow the trail of billboards.

Craigdarroch Castle ★ Located in the highlands above Oak Bay, Robert Dunsmuir's home, built to cement his status and please his socially ambitious wife in the 1880s, is a stunner. The four-story, 39-room Highland-style castle is topped with stone turrets and chimneys, and filled with opulent Victorian splendor: detailed woodwork, Persian carpets, stained-glass windows, paintings, and sculptures. The nonprofit society that runs Craigdarroch does an excellent job showcasing the castle. You're provided with a self-tour booklet; several volunteer docents are happy to provide further information. The castle also hosts many events throughout the year, including theater performances, concerts, and dinner tours. Allow 30 minutes to 1 hour for castle tour.

1050 Joan Crescent (off Fort St.). © **250/592-5323.** www.craigdarrochcastle.com. Admission C$12 adults, C$11 seniors, C$3.75 children 5–12, free for children 4 and under. June 15 to Labour Day daily 9am–7pm; day after Labour Day to June 14 daily 10am–4:30pm. Closed Dec 25–26 and Jan 1. Bus: 11 to Joan Crescent. Take Fort St. out of downtown, just past Cook, and turn right on Joan Crescent.

Fort Rodd Hill & Fisgard Lighthouse Perched on an outcrop of volcanic rock, the **Fisgard Lighthouse** has guided ships toward Victoria's sheltered harbor since 1873. The light no longer has a keeper (the beacon has long been automated), but the site itself has been restored to its 1873 appearance. Two floors of exhibits in the light keeper's house recount stories of the lighthouse, its keepers, and the terrible shipwrecks that gave this coastline its ominous moniker "the graveyard of the Pacific."

Adjoining the lighthouse, **Fort Rodd Hill** is a preserved 1890s coastal artillery fort sporting camouflaged searchlights, underground magazines, and its original guns. Audiovisual exhibits bring the fort to life with the voices and faces of the men who served at the outpost. Displays of artifacts, room re-creations, and historic film footage add to the experience. Allow 1 to 2 hours.

603 Fort Rodd Hill Rd. (℃) **250/478-5849.** www.fortroddhill.com. Admission C$4 adults, C$3.50 seniors, C$2 children 6–16, free for children 5 and under, C$10 families. Feb 15–Oct daily 10am–5:30pm; Nov–Feb 14 daily 9am–4:30pm. Head north on Douglas St. until it turns into Hwy. 1. Stay on Hwy. 1 for 5km (3 miles), then take the Colwood exit (exit 10). Follow Hwy. 1A for 2km (1¼ miles), then turn left at the 3rd traffic light onto Ocean Blvd.; follow the signs to the site.

Maritime Museum of British Columbia

Housed in the former provincial courthouse, this museum is dedicated to recalling B.C.'s rich maritime heritage. The displays do a good job of illustrating maritime history, from the early explorers to the grand ocean liners. An impressive collection of ship models and paraphernalia—uniforms, weapons, gear—is complemented by photographs and journals. The museum also shows films. Allow 1 hour.

28 Bastion Sq. (℃) **250/385-4222.** www.mmbc.bc.ca. Admission C$10 adults, C$8 seniors and students, C$5 children 6–11, free for children 5 and under, C$25 families. Sept 16–June 14 daily 9:30am–4:30pm; June 15–Sept 15 daily 9:30am–5pm. Closed Dec 25. Bus: 5 to View St.

Miniature World (Kids)

It sounds cheesy—hundreds of dolls, miniatures, and scenes from old fairy tales, but Miniature World, inside the Fairmont Empress (the entrance is around the corner), is actually kinda cool, and kids love it. You walk in, and you're plunged into darkness, except for a moon, some planets, and a tiny spaceship flying up to rendezvous with an orbiting mother ship. This is the most up-to-date display. Farther in are re-creations of battle scenes, a miniature Canadian Pacific Railway running all the way across a miniature Canada, Victorian dollhouses, and a three-ring circus and midway. Better yet, most of these displays do something: The train moves at the punch of a button, and the circus rides whirl around and light up as simulated darkness falls. Allow about 30 minutes to see it all.

649 Humboldt St. (℃) **250/385-9731.** www.miniatureworld.com. Admission C$12 adults, C$9 youths, C$7 children 4–12, free for children 3 and under. Summer daily 8:30am–9pm; fall/winter daily 9am–5pm; spring daily 9am–7pm. Bus: 5, 27, 28, or 30.

Pacific Undersea Gardens

Those with some knowledge of Vancouver Island's marine environment will tell you that many of the creatures on display here are not indigenous to these waters, but your kids might enjoy a visit—or they might not, since the place is dark and kind of scary for little ones. One of the star attractions is a remarkably photogenic octopus (reputedly the largest in captivity). Injured seals and orphaned seal pups are cared for in holding pens alongside the observatory as part of a provincial marine-mammal rescue program. Allow 1 hour.

490 Belleville St. (℃) **250/382-5717.** www.pacificunderseagardens.com. Admission C$9.75 adults, C$8.75 seniors, C$7.75 youths 12–17, C$5.75 children 5–11, free for children 4 and under. Sept–Mar daily 10am–5pm; Apr–May daily 10am–6pm; June–Aug daily 9am–8pm. Bus: 5, 27, 28, or 30.

Provincial Legislature Buildings (Parliament Buildings) ★★

Built between 1893 and 1898 at a cost of nearly C$1 million, the Provincial Legislature Buildings (which some diehard Anglophiles insist on calling "the Parliament buildings") are one of the most noteworthy landmarks on Victoria's Inner Harbour. The 40-minute tour can

come across like an eighth-grade civics lesson, but it's worth it to see the fine mosaics,
marble, woodwork, and stained glass.

501 Belleville St. *℃* **250/387-3046.** www.leg.bc.ca. Free admission. Victoria Day (late May) to Labour Day Mon–Thurs 9am–5pm, Fri–Sun 9am–7pm; Sept to late May Mon–Fri 9am–5pm. Tours offered every 20–30 min. in summer; in winter call ahead for the public tour schedules as times vary due to school-group bookings. Bus: 5, 27, 28, or 30.

Royal B.C. Museum ★★★ (**Kids**)   One of North America's best regional museums, the Royal B.C. has a mandate to present the land and the people of coastal British Columbia. The second-floor **Natural History Gallery** showcases the coastal flora, fauna, and geography from the Ice Age to the present; it includes dioramas of a temperate rainforest, a seacoast, and a life-size woolly mastodon. The third-floor **Modern History Gallery** presents the recent past, including historically faithful re-creations of Victoria's downtown and Chinatown. On the same floor, the **First Peoples Gallery** ★★★ is an incredible showpiece of First Nations art and culture with rare artifacts used in day-to-day Native life, a full-size re-creation of a longhouse, and a hauntingly wonderful gallery with totem poles, masks, and artifacts. The museum also has an **IMAX theater** showing an ever-changing variety of large-screen movies. On the way out (or in), be sure to stop by **Thunderbird Park,** beside the museum, where a cedar longhouse houses a workshop where Native carvers work on new totem poles. To see and experience everything takes at least 2 hours.

675 Belleville St. *℃* **888/447-7977** or 250/356-7226. www.royalbcmuseum.bc.ca. Admission C$15 adults; C$9.50 seniors, students, and youths; free for children 5 and under; C$38 families. IMAX C$11 adults; C$9.50 students, C$8.75 seniors and children 6–18; C$5 children 5 and under. Museum daily 9am–5pm (June–Sept Fri–Sat 9am–10pm); IMAX daily 9am–8pm. Closed Dec 25 and Jan 1. Bus: 5, 28, or 30.

Victoria Butterfly Gardens ★ (**Kids**)   This is a great spot for kids, nature buffs, or anyone who just likes butterflies. An ID chart allows you to identify the hundreds of exotic butterflies fluttering through this lush tropical greenhouse. Species range from the tiny Central American Julia (a brilliant orange butterfly about 3 in. across) to the Southeast Asian Giant Atlas Moth (mottled brown and red, with a wingspan approaching a foot). You'll also see tropical birds, fish, and exotic plants, including an orchid collection. Allow 1 hour.

1461 Benvenuto Ave. (P.O. Box 190), Brentwood Bay. *℃* **877/722-0272** or 250/652-3822. www.butterfly gardens.com. Admission C$12 adults, seniors, and students; C$6.50 children 3–12; free for children 2 and under. Daily Feb 10am–4pm; Mar–Apr and Nov–Dec 9:30am–4:30pm; May–Oct 9am–5pm. Closed Jan. Bus: 75.

Parks & Gardens

With the mildest climate in Canada, Victoria's gardens are in bloom year-round. In addition to the world-renowned **Butchart Gardens** ★★★ (see above), the **Abkhazi Garden** ★, 1964 Fairfield Rd. (*℃* **250/598-8096;** www.abkhazi.com), and the gardens at **Hatley Park National Historic Site** ★, Royal Roads University, 200 Sooke Rd., Colwood (*℃* **866/241-0674** or 250/391-2666; www.hatleypark.ca), several city parks attract strollers and picnickers. The 61-hectare (151-acre), 128-year-old **Beacon Hill Park** ★ stretches from Southgate Street to Dallas Road between Douglas and Cook streets. In 1882, the Hudson's Bay Company gave this property to the city. Stands of indigenous Garry oaks (found only on Vancouver, Hornby, and Salt Spring islands) and manicured lawns are interspersed with floral gardens and ponds. Hike up Beacon Hill to get a clear view of the Strait of Georgia, Haro Strait, and Washington's Olympic Mountains. The children's farm, aviary, tennis courts, lawn-bowling green, putting green, cricket pitch, wading pool, and playground make this a wonderful place to spend a few hours with the family. The **Trans-Canada Highway's "Mile 0" marker** stands at the edge of the park on Dallas Road.

Just outside downtown, **Mount Douglas Park** has great views of the area, several hiking trails, and—down at the waterline—a picnic/play area with a trail leading to a good walking beach.

About 45 minutes southwest of town, **East Sooke Park** ★ is a 1,400-hectare (3,459-acre) microcosm of the West Coast wilderness: jagged seacoast, Native petroglyphs, and hiking trails up to a 270m (886-ft.) hilltop. Access is via the Old Island Highway and East Sooke Road.

ORGANIZED TOURS
Bus Tours
Gray Line of Victoria, 4196 Glanford Ave. (© **800/663-8390** or 250/388-6539; www.grayline.com), conducts a number of tours of Victoria and Butchart Gardens. The 1½-hour "Grand City Tour" costs C$28 for adults and C$18 for children ages 5 to 11. There are daily departures throughout the year, usually at noon and 2pm. For other tours, check the website.

Specialty Tours
Victoria Harbour Ferries, 1234 Wharf St. (© **250/708-0201;** www.victoriaharbourferry.com), offers a terrific 45-minute **harbor tour** ★ for C$20 adults, C$18 seniors, and C$10 for children under 12. Harbor tours depart from seven stops around the Inner Harbour every 15 or 20 minutes daily 10am to 4pm (longer hours May–Sept). If you wish to stop for food or a stroll, you can get a token good for reboarding at any time during the same day. A 50-minute **Gorge Tour** ★ takes you to the gorge opposite the Johnson Street Bridge, where tidal falls reverse with each change of the tide. The price is the same as for the harbor tour; June through September, gorge tours depart from the dock in front of the Fairmont Empress every half-hour 9am to 8:15pm; at other times the tours operate less frequently, depending on the weather. The ferries are 12-person, fully enclosed boats, and every seat is a window seat.

To get a bird's-eye view of Victoria, take a 30-minute tour with **Harbour Air Seaplanes,** 1234 Wharf St. (© **800/665-0212** or 250/384-2215; www.harbour-air.com). Rates are C$99 per person. For a romantic evening, try the "Fly and Dine" to Butchart Gardens deal; C$229 per person includes the flight to the gardens, admission, dinner, and a limousine ride back to Victoria.

Fresh Air Tours Ltd. (© **877/868-7790**) offers year-round scenic sightseeing mini-coach and cycling tours to Victoria's highlights, wineries, Butchart Gardens, the town of Sidney, Salt Spring Island, and seasonal tours such as the Halloween pumpkin patch and Christmas lights. The company provides complimentary hotel pickup and drop-off; on cycling tours, bicycles, helmets, and support van are provided.

Walking Tours
Victoria Bobby Walking Tours (© **250/995-0233;** www.walkvictoria.com) offers a leisurely story-filled walk around Old Town. Tours depart at 11am daily, May through September 15, from the Visitor Centre on the Inner Harbour; cost is C$15 per person.

Discover the Past (© **250/384-6698;** www.discoverthepast.com) organizes interesting walks year-round. In the summer, **Ghostly Walks** explores Victoria's haunted Old

Info Centre nightly at 7:30pm from May through October, Saturdays at 7:30pm from November through February, and Fridays and Saturdays at 7:30pm in March and April. The cost is C$12 adults, C$10 seniors and students, C$8 children 6 to 10, and C$30 for families. Check the website for other walks.

The name says it all for **Walkabout Historical Tours** (© 250/592-9255; www. walkabouts.ca). Charming guides lead tours of the Fairmont Empress, Victoria's Chinatown, Antique Row, and Old Town Victoria, or will help you with your own itinerary. The Empress Tour costs C$10 and begins at 10am daily in the Empress Tea Lobby. Other tours have different prices and starting points.

The **Victoria Heritage Foundation,** No. 1 Centennial Sq. (© 250/383-4546), offers the excellent free pamphlet *James Bay Heritage Walking Tour.* The well-researched pamphlet (also available at the Visitor Info Centre) describes a self-guided walking tour through the historic James Bay neighborhood.

---

6 OUTDOOR ACTIVITIES

BEACHES   The most popular beach is Oak Bay's **Willows Beach,** at Beach and Dalhousie roads along the esplanade. The park, playground, and snack bar make it a great place to spend the day building a sand castle. **Gyro Beach Park,** Beach Road on Cadboro Bay, is another good spot for winding down. At the **Ross Bay Beaches,** below Beacon Hill Park, you can stroll or bike along the promenade at the water's edge.

For a taste of the wild and rocky west coast, hike the oceanside trails in beautiful **East Sooke Regional Park** ★. Take Hwy. 14A west, turn south on Gillespie Road, and then take East Sooke Road.

Two inland lakes give you the option of swimming in freshwater. **Elk and Beaver Lake Regional Park,** on Patricia Bay Road, is 11km (6¾ miles) north of downtown Victoria; to the west is **Thetis Lake,** about 10km (6¼ miles; Hwy. 1 to exit 10 or 1A onto Old Island Hwy. 14, turn right at Six Mile Pub and follow the signs), where locals shed all their clothes but none of their civility.

BIKING   Biking is one of the best ways to get around Victoria. The 13km (8-mile) **Scenic Marine Drive bike path** ★★ begins at Dallas Road and Douglas Street, at the base of Beacon Hill Park. The paved path follows the walkway along the beaches before winding up through the residential district on Beach Drive. It eventually turns left and heads south toward downtown Victoria on Oak Bay Avenue. The **Inner Harbour pedestrian path** has a bike lane for cyclists who want to take a leisurely ride around the entire city seawall. The new **Galloping Goose Trail** (part of the Trans-Canada Trail) runs from Victoria west through Colwood and Sooke all the way up to Leechtown. If you don't want to bike the whole thing, you can park at numerous places along the way, as well as several places where the trail intersects with public transit. Contact **B.C. Transit** (© 250/382-6161; www.bctransit.com) to find out which bus routes take bikes. Bikes and child trailers are available at **Cycle B.C. Rentals,** 707 Douglas St. (May–Oct; © 250/380-2453; www.cyclebc.ca). Rentals run C$7 per hour and C$24 per day; helmets and locks are included.

BIRDING   The **Victoria Natural History Society** (www.vicnhs.bc.ca) runs regular weekend birding excursions. Their **event line** (© 250/479-2054) lists upcoming outings and gives contact numbers. **Goldstream Provincial Park** and the village of **Malahat—** both off Hwy. 1 about 40 minutes north of Victoria—are filled with dozens of varieties of migratory and local birds, including eagles. **Elk and Beaver Lake Regional Park,** off Hwy. 17, has some rare species such as the rose-breasted grosbeak and Hutton's vireo. Ospreys also nest there. **Cowichan Bay,** off Hwy. 1, is the perfect place to observe ospreys, bald eagles, great egrets, and purple martins.

BOATING, CANOEING & KAYAKING   Ocean River Sports, 1824 Store St. (✆ 800/ 909-4233 or 250/381-4233; www.oceanriver.com), can equip you with everything from a single or double kayak or a canoe to life jackets, tents, and dry-storage camping gear. Rental costs for a single kayak range from C$25 for 2 hours to C$40 per day. Multiday and weekly rates are also available. The company also offers numerous **guided tours** ★ of the Gulf Islands and the coast. For beginners, try the guided 5½-hour Explorer Tour of the coast around Victoria or Sooke for C$115. They also offer a guided 3-day/2-night trip to the nearby Gulf Islands for C$635.

Rowboats, kayaks, and canoes are available for hourly or daily rental from **Great Pacific Adventures,** 811 Wharf St. (✆ 877/733-6722 or 250/386-2277; www.greatpacific adventures.com).

Blackfish Wilderness Expeditions (✆ 250/216-2389; www.blackfishwilderness. com) offers a number of interesting kayak-based tours such as the kayak/boat/hike combo, where you boat to the protected waters of the Discovery Islands, hike one of the islands, and kayak to see the pods of resident killer whales that roam the waters around Victoria. Day tours start at C$70 per person.

DIVING   The coastline of **Pacific Rim National Park** is known as "the graveyard of the Pacific." Submerged in the water are dozens of 19th- and 20th-century shipwrecks and the marine life that has taken up residence in them. Underwater interpretive trails help identify what you see in the artificial reefs. If you want to take a look for yourself, contact the **Ogden Point Dive Centre,** 199 Dallas Rd. (✆ 888/701-1177 or 250/380-9119; www.divevictoria.com), which offers a 2-day Race Rocks and Shipwreck Tour package that starts at C$299 per person, including all equipment and transportation. The **Saanich Inlet,** about a 20-minute drive north of Victoria, is a pristine fjord considered one of the top cold-water diving areas in the world (glass sponges are a rarity found only here). Classes and underwater scuba adventures can be arranged through **Brentwood Bay Lodge & Spa** (p. 112), Canada's only luxury PADI (Professional Association of Diving Instructors) dive resort.

FISHING   Saltwater fishing's the thing out here, but unless you know the area, it's best to take a guide. **Adam's Fishing Charters** (✆ 250/370-2326; www.adamsfishingcharters. com) is located on the Inner Harbour down below the Visitor Info Centre. Chartering a boat and guide starts at C$95 per hour per boat, with a minimum of 5 hours.

To fish, you need a saltwater fishing license. Licenses (including the salmon surcharge) for nonresidents cost C$7.50 for 1 day, C$20 for 3 days, and C$33 for 5 days. Tackle shops sell licenses, have details on current restrictions, and often carry copies of the *B.C. Tidal Waters Sport Fishing Guide* and *B.C. Sport Fishing Regulations Synopsis for Non-Tidal Waters.* Independent anglers should also pick up the *B.C. Fishing Directory and Atlas.* **Robinson's Sporting Goods Ltd.,** 1307 Broad St. (✆ 250/385-3429), is a reliable source for information, recommendations, lures, licenses, and gear. For the latest fishing hot spots and recommendations on tackle and lures, check out **www.sportfishingbc. com.** You'll find official fishing information at the Fisheries and Oceans Canada website, **www.pac.dfo-mpo.gc.ca.**

GOLFING Victoria's Scottish heritage doesn't stop at the tartan shops. The greens here are as beautiful as those at St. Andrews. The **Cedar Hill Municipal Golf Course,** 1400 Derby Rd. (✆ **250/475-7151;** www.golfcedarhill.com), the busiest course in Canada, is an 18-hole, par-67 public course 3km (1¾ miles) from downtown Victoria. It's open on a first-come, first-served basis; daytime weekday greens fees are C$40 to C$45 and twilight fees (after 3pm) are C$25 to C$30. Golf clubs can be rented for C$15. The **Cordova Bay Golf Course,** 5333 Cordova Bay Rd. (✆ **250/658-4444;** www.cordovabaygolf.com), is northeast of the downtown area. Designed by Bill Robinson, the par-71, 18-hole course features 66 sand traps and some tight fairways. Greens fees are C$46 to C$60 depending on day and season; twilight fees range from C$39 to C$59.

The newest star of Vancouver Island golf courses, and the most expensive to play, is the 18-hole, 6,595m (7,212-yd.), par-72 course designed by Jack Nicklaus and his son for **Westin Bear Mountain Golf Resort & Spa,** 1999 Country Club Way (✆ **888/533-2327** or 250/391-7160 for tee time bookings). Golf carts (included with fee) and collared shirts (blue jeans not permitted) are mandatory on this upscale, mountaintop course that features breathtaking views and a spectacular 19th hole for recreational betting. Nonmember greens fees, depending on when you reserve and the time you play, range from C$65 to C$145.

You can call **A-1 Last Minute Golf Hot Line** at ✆ **800/684-6344** for substantial discounts and short-notice tee times.

HIKING **Goldstream Provincial Park** (30 min. west of downtown along Hwy. 1) is a tranquil site for a short hike through towering cedars and past clear, rushing waters.

The hour-long hike up **Mount Work** provides excellent views of the Saanich Peninsula and a good view of Finlayson Arm. The trail head is a 30- to 45-minute drive. Take Hwy. 17 north to Saanich, then take Hwy. 17A (W. Saanich Rd.) to Wallace Drive, turn right on Willis Point Drive, and right again on Ross-Durrance Road, looking for the parking lot on the right. Signs are posted along the way. Equally good, though more of a scramble, is the hour-plus climb up **Mount Finlayson** in Gowland-Tod Provincial Park (take Hwy. 1 west, get off at the Millstream Rd. exit, and follow Millstream Rd. north to the very end).

The very popular **Sooke Potholes** trail wanders up beside a river to an abandoned mountain lodge. Take Hwy. 1A west to Colwood, then Hwy. 14A (Sooke Rd.). At Sooke, turn north on Sooke River Road, and follow it to the park.

For a taste of the wild and rocky west coast, hike the oceanside trails in beautiful **East Sooke Regional Park** ★★. Take Hwy. 14A west, turn south on Gillespie Road, and then take East Sooke Road.

For serious backpacking, go 104km (65 miles) west of Victoria on Hwy. 14A to Port Renfrew and the challenging **West Coast Trail** ★★★ (p. 182), extending 77km (48 miles) from Port Renfrew to Bamfield in a portion of **Pacific Rim National Park** ★★★ (p. 181). The trail was originally a lifesaving trail for shipwrecked sailors. Plan a 7-day trek for the entire route; reservations are required, so call ✆ **604/663-6000.** The trail is rugged and often wet, but the scenery changes from old-growth forest to magnificent secluded sand beaches, making it worth every step. You may even spot a few whales along the way.

Island Adventure Tours (✆ **866/812-7103** or 250/812-7103; www.islandadventure tours.com) has a number of options for folks wanting to explore the outdoors. The 6-hour guided **rainforest walks** cost C$95 or a full-day hike including transportation and lunch. For the deluxe Juan de Fuca experience, sign up for a 3-day, fully catered backpacking trip along the rugged West Coast Trail for C$499.

For something less strenuous but still scenic, try the **Swan Lake Christmas Hill Nature Sanctuary,** 3873 Swan Lake Rd. (© **250/479-0211;** www.swanlake.bc.ca). A floating boardwalk winds its way through this 40-hectare (99-acre) wetland past resident swans; the adjacent Nature House supplies feeding grain on request.

WATERSPORTS   The **Crystal Pool & Fitness Centre,** 2275 Quadra St. (© **250/361-0732**), is Victoria's main aquatic facility. The 50m (164-ft.) lap pool; children's pool; diving pool; sauna; whirlpool; and steam, weight, and aerobics rooms are open Monday through Thursday 5:30 to 11pm, Friday 5:30am to 10:30pm, Saturday 6am to 6pm, and Sunday 8:30am to 4pm. Drop-in admission is C$4.75 for adults, C$3.75 for seniors and students, C$2.50 for children 6 to 12, and free for children 5 and under. **Beaver Lake** in Elk and Beaver Lake Regional Park (see "Birding," above) has lifeguards on duty as well as picnicking facilities along the shore.

Surfing has recently taken off on the island. The best surf is along the west coast at **China, French,** and **Mystic beaches** ★. To get there, take Blanshard Street north from downtown, turn left onto Hwy. 1 (Trans-Canada Hwy.), then after about 10km (6¼ miles), take the turnoff onto Hwy. 14A (Sooke Rd.). Follow Hwy. 14A north along the coast. The beaches are well signposted.

Windsurfers skim along outside the Inner Harbour and on Elk Lake when the breezes are right. Though French Beach, off Sooke Road on the way to Sooke Harbour, has no specific facilities, it is a popular local windsurfing spot.

WHALE-WATCHING   The waters surrounding the southern tip of Vancouver Island teem with orcas (killer whales), harbor seals, sea lions, harbor and Dall porpoises, and bald eagles. All whale-watching companies offer basically the same tour; the main difference comes in the equipment they use: Some use a 12-person Zodiac, where the jolting ride is almost as exciting as seeing the whales, whereas others take a larger, more leisurely craft. Both offer excellent platforms for seeing whales. In high season (June to Labour Day), most companies offer several trips a day. Always ask if the outfitter is a "responsible whale-watcher"—that is, doesn't go too close to disturb or harass the whales.

Seafun Safaris Whale Watching, 950 Wharf St. (© **877/360-1233** or 250/360-1200; www.seafun.com), is just one of many outfits offering whale-watching tours in Zodiacs and covered boats. Adults and kids will learn a lot from the naturalist guides, who explain the behavior and nature of the orcas, gray whales, sea lions, porpoises, cormorants, eagles, and harbor seals encountered along the way. Fares for the Zodiac tour are C$109 for adults and C$79 for children.

Other reputable companies include **Prince of Whales,** 812 Wharf St. (© **888/383-4884** or 250/383-4884; www.princeofwhales.com), just below the Visitor Info Centre, and **Orca Spirit Adventures** (© **888/672-ORCA** [6722] or 250/383-8411; www.orcaspirit.com), which departs from the Coast Harbourside Hotel dock.

7 VICTORIA SHOPPING

Victoria has dozens of specialty shops, and because the city is built on a pedestrian scale, you can easily wander from place to place seeking out whatever treasure you're after. Nearly all of the areas listed below are within a short walk of the Fairmont Empress (or in it); for those shops located more than 6 blocks from the hotel, bus information is provided. Stores in Victoria are generally open Monday through Saturday from 10am to 6pm; some, but not many, are open on Sundays during the summer.

Explorers beware: The brick-paved **Government Street promenade,** from the Inner Harbour 5 blocks north to Yates Street, is a jungle of cheap souvenir shops. There are gems in here, but to find these riches, you'll have to pass T-shirt stores, knickknack emporiums, and countless maple-syrup bottles.

SHOPPING A TO Z

ANTIQUES Victoria has long had a deserved reputation for antiques—particularly those of British origin. In addition to those listed below, check out **Romanoff & Company Antiques,** 837 Fort St. (© 250/480-1543); and for furniture fans, **Charles Baird Antiques,** 1044A Fort St. (© 250/384-8809).

The farthest from downtown, **Faith Grant's Connoisseur Shop Ltd.,** 1156 Fort St. (© 250/383-0121; www.faithgrantantiques.com; bus: 10 to Fort and Cook sts.), is also the best. The 16 rooms of this 1862 heritage building contain everything from Georgian writing desks to English flatware, not to mention fine ceramics, prints, and paintings. Furniture is especially strong here.

Vanity Fair Antiques & Collectibles, 1044 Fort St. (© 250/380-7274; www.vanity fairantiques.com; bus: 10 to Blanshard or Cook St.), is fun to browse, with crystal, glassware, furniture, and lots more.

ART Soaring white walls and huge arched windows make the **Fran Willis Gallery,** 1619 Store St. (© 250/381-3422; www.franwillis.com; bus: 5 to Douglas and Fisgard), one of Victoria's most beautiful gallery spaces. The collection is strong in contemporary oils, mixed media, and bronzes, almost all by B.C. and Alberta artists.

Winchester Galleries, 1010 Broad St. (© 250/386-2773; www.winchestergalleries ltd.com), a slightly daring gallery, features contemporary oil paintings. Unlike elsewhere in town, very few wildlife paintings ever make it onto the walls.

BOOKS All bookstores should look as good as **Munro's Books,** 1108 Government St. (© 888/243-2464 or 250/382-2464; www.munrobooks.com), a mile-high ceiling in a 1909 heritage building, complete with heavy brass lamps and murals on the walls. The store stocks more than 35,000 titles, including an excellent selection about Victoria and books by local authors. The staff is friendly and very good at unearthing obscure titles.

Committed to protecting Canada's endangered species and environment, the **Western Canada Wilderness Committee (WCWC) store,** 651 Johnson St. (© 250/388-9292; www.wildernesscommittee.org), raises funds for the cause. Choose from beautiful gift cards, posters, and souvenir T-shirts or mugs.

DEPARTMENT STORE & SHOPPING MALL The Bay Centre, between Government and Douglas sts., off Fort and View sts. (© 250/389-2228; www.thebaycentre.ca), is named after its new anchor store, Hudson's Bay Company (© 250/385-1311). The rest of the complex houses a full shopping mall disguised as a block of heritage buildings.

FASHION **Breeze,** 1150 Government St. (© 250/383-8871), a high-energy store for women, carries a number of trendy lines, such as Mexx, Powerline, and Mac+Jac. Shoes by Nine West and Steve Madden, plus stylish accessories, complete the look.

Still Life, 551 Johnson St. (© 250/386-5655), originally known for its vintage clothes, has updated and moved to a contemporary style that includes fashions from Diesel, Workwear, and Toronto designer Damzels-in-this-Dress.

W. & J. Wilson's Clothiers, 1221 Government St. (📞 **250/383-7177**), Canada's oldest family-run clothing store, has been owned/managed by the Wilsons since 1862. Look for sensible casuals or elegant cashmeres and leathers from British, Scottish, and other European designers.

Victoria may be laid-back, but a man still needs a power suit, and **British Importers,** 1125 Government St. (📞 **250/386-1496**), is the place to get it. Designer labels include Calvin Klein and Hugo Boss. Ties and leather jackets are also for sale.

FIRST NATIONS ARTS & CRAFTS   Natives from the nearby Cowichan band are famous for their warm, durable sweaters knit with bold motifs from hand-spun raw wool. In addition to these beautiful knits, craftspeople create soft leather moccasins, moose-hide boots, ceremonial masks, sculptures carved from argillite or soapstone, baskets, bearskin rugs, and jewelry. The **Quw'utsun' Cultural and Conference Centre** (p. 158) also has a large gift shop where you can watch artisans at work.

Alcheringa Gallery, 665 Fort St. (📞 **250/383-8224;** www.alcheringa-gallery.com), began as a shop handling imports from the Antipodes, but it has evolved into one of Victoria's truly great stores for aboriginal art connoisseurs. All the coastal tribes are represented in Alcheringa's collection, along with pieces from Papua New Guinea. The presentation is museum quality, with prices to match.

Beautiful and expensive First Nations artwork is sold in **Art of Man Gallery,** 721 Government St. (📞 **250/383-3800;** www.artofmangallery.com), located off the Tea Lobby in the Fairmont Empress hotel. You'll find high-quality works by some of the best-known artists in British Columbia.

Hill's Native Art, 1008 Government St. (📞 **250/385-3911;** www.hillsnativeart.com), is the store for established artists from up and down the B.C. coast, which means the quality is high, and so are the prices (although you can find good-quality work here for under C$300). Of course, you don't stay in business for 50 years without pleasing your drop-in customers, so Hill's has its share of dream catchers and other knickknacks.

FOOD & WINE   All those old-fashioned English sweets you love but can never find in North America (such as horehound drops and lemon sherbets) are sold at the **English Sweet Shop,** 738 Yates St. (📞 **800/848-1533** or 250/382-3325; www.englishsweets.com). They also sell English marmalade, lemon curd, jam, chutneys, tea and biscuits—you get the picture. There's a smaller version, the **British Candy Shoppe,** 2 blocks away at 638 Yates St. (📞 **250/382-2634**).

It's worth coming to **Murchie's,** 1110 Government St. (📞 **250/383-3112;** www.murchies.com), just to suck up the coffee smell or sniff the many specialty teas, including the custom-made blend served at the Fairmont Empress' afternoon tea.

Rogers' Chocolates, 913 Government St. (📞 **800/663-2220** or 250/881-8771; www.rogerschocolates.com), bills itself as "quite possibly the best chocolates in the world," and with original Tiffany glass, old-fashioned counters, and free samples, this 100-year-old shrine could possibly live up to the claim.

Before setting up shop at **Silk Road Aromatherapy and Tea Company,** 1624 Government St. (📞 **250/704-2688;** www.silkroadtea.com; bus: 5 to Douglas and Fisgard sts.), the two Victoria women who run this store first trained to become tea masters in China and Taiwan. Their Victoria store on the edge of Chinatown sells a wide variety of teas, including premium loose blends and tea paraphernalia such as teapots, mugs, and kettles; they offer a full line of aromatherapy products as well. The latest addition is the spa, which offers a range of treatments at very reasonable prices.

The Wine Barrel, 644 Broughton St. ((© 250/388-0606; www.thewinebarrel.com), sells more than 300 B.C. VQA (Vintner Quality Alliance) wines and wine accessories. It's known for carrying the largest selection of B.C. ice wines in Victoria.

JEWELRY High-quality, handcrafted Canadian jewelry is sold in **Artina's,** 1002 Government St. ((© 250/386-7000; www.artinas.com).

At **Jade Victoria,** 911 Government St. ((© 250/384-5233), you'll find jewelry made from British Columbia jade, which is mined in northern Vancouver Island, then crafted in Victoria and China into necklaces, bracelets, and other items.

The Patch, 719 Yates St. ((© 250/384-7070), the Island's largest provider of body jewelry, has studs, rings, and other bright baubles for your nose, navel, or nipple, much of it quite creative and reasonably priced.

OUTDOOR CLOTHES & EQUIPMENT Ocean River Sports, 1824 Store St. ((© 250/381-4233; www.oceanriver.com), is the place to go to arrange a sea kayak tour—they'll be happy to rent (or sell) you a boat and all the gear. This is also a good spot for outdoor clothing and camping musts, such as solar-heated showers or espresso machines.

Pacific Trekking, 1305 Government St. ((© 250/388-7088) is an excellent source for rain and hiking gear, as well as good for advice on local hiking trails.

Walkers Shoes, 1012 Broad St. ((© 250/381-8608), specializes in the finest European walking shoes for men and women.

PUBLIC MARKETS Market Square, 560 Johnson St. ((© 250/386-2441), was constructed from the original warehouses and shipping offices built in the 1800s. This pleasant and innovative heritage reconstruction features small shops and restaurants surrounding a central courtyard, often the site of live performances in summer.

---

8 VICTORIA AFTER DARK

Monday Magazine, a weekly tabloid published on Thursdays, is the place to start. Its listings section provides comprehensive coverage of what's happening in town and is particularly good for the club scene. If you can't find *Monday* in cafes or record shops, visit it online at **www.mondaymag.com.**

For information on theater, concerts, and arts events, contact the **Tourism Victoria Visitor Centre,** 812 Wharf St. ((© 800/663-3883 or 250/953-2033; www.tourism victoria.com). You can also buy tickets for Victoria's venues from the Visitor Centre, but only in person.

Whatever you decide to do with your Victoria evenings, chances are that your destination will be close at hand: One of the great virtues of Victoria's size is that nearly all of its attractions are no more than a 10-minute walk from the Fairmont Empress, right in the heart of the city, and easily reached by taking bus no. 5 to the Empress Hotel/Convention Centre. For those few nightlife spots a little farther out, bus information is provided.

THE PERFORMING ARTS

The **Royal Theatre,** 805 Broughton St., and the **McPherson Playhouse,** 3 Centennial Sq., share a common box office ((© 888/717-6121 or 250/386-6121; www.rmts.bc.ca). The **Royal**—built in the early 1900s and renovated in the 1970s—hosts concerts by the Victoria Symphony and performances by the Pacific Opera Victoria, as well as touring dance and theater companies. The **McPherson**—built in 1914 as the first Pantages Vaudeville Theatre—is home to smaller stage plays and performances by the Victoria Operatic Society.

THEATER Performing in an intimate playhouse that was once a church, the **Belfry Theatre Society ★★**, 1291 Gladstone Ave. (© **250/385-6815;** www.belfry.bc.ca; bus no. 22 to Fernwood St.), is an acclaimed theatrical group that stages four productions (usually dramatic works by contemporary Canadian playwrights) October through April, and one show in August. Tickets are C$21 to C$36.

The **Intrepid Theatre Company,** 2-1609 Blanshard St. (© **250/383-2663;** www. intrepidtheatre.com), runs two yearly theater festivals. In spring it's the **Uno Festival of Solo Performance ★★**, a unique event of strictly one-person performances. Come summer, Intrepid puts on the **Victoria Fringe Festival ★★**. Even if you're not a theater fan—*especially* if you're not—don't miss the Fringe. More than 50 performers or small companies from around the world put on amazingly inventive plays. The festival runs from late August to early September.

Theatre Inconnu, 1923 Fernwood Rd. (© **250/360-0234;** www.theatreinconnu. com), is Victoria's oldest alternative theater group. The quality is excellent, and tickets are inexpensive. They stage a two-man adaptation of Charles Dickens's *A Christmas Carol* every year.

The **Langham Court Theatre,** 805 Langham Court (© **250/384-2142;** www.langham courttheatre.bc.ca), performs works produced by the Victoria Theatre Guild, a local amateur society dedicated to presenting a wide range of dramatic and comedic works. From downtown, take bus no. 14 or 11 to Fort and Moss streets.

OPERA The **Pacific Opera Victoria ★★**, 1815 Blanshard St. (© **250/385-0222;** www.pov.bc.ca), presents three productions annually from October to April. Performances are normally at the McPherson Playhouse and Royal Theatre. Tickets cost C$30 to C$110.

The **Victoria Operatic Society,** 10-744 Fairview Rd. (© **250/381-1021;** www.vos. bc.ca), presents Broadway musicals and other popular fare at the McPherson Playhouse. Tickets cost C$18 to C$45.

ORCHESTRAL & CHORAL MUSIC The well-respected **Victoria Symphony Orchestra,** 610-620 View St. (© **250/385-9771;** www.victoriasymphony.bc.ca), kicks off its season on the first Sunday of August with Symphony Splash, a free concert performed on a barge in the Inner Harbour. Regular performances begin in September and last through May. The Orchestra performs at the Royal Theatre or the University Farquhar Auditorium. Tickets are C$14 to C$60 for most concerts.

DANCE Dance recitals and full-scale performances by local and international dance troupes such as DanceWorks and the Scottish Dance Society are scheduled throughout the year. Call the **Visitor Centre** at © **250/953-2033** to find out who's performing when you're in town.

COMEDY & SPOKEN WORD **Mocambo,** 1028 Blanshard St. (© **250/384-4468**), a coffeehouse near the public library, hosts a range of spoken-word events through the week (multimedia fusion demos, philosopher's cafes, argument for the joy of it, slam poetry), then lets loose on Saturdays with improv comedy. There is no cover.

MUSIC FESTIVALS **Folkfest** (📞 250/388-4728; www.icafolkfest.com) is a free multicultural celebration of song, food, and crafts. It takes place late June through early July on Ship Point.

Every day at noon from early July to late August, **Summer in the Square** (📞 250/361-0388), a popular festival in downtown's Centennial Square, offers free music. Each day features a different band and musical style. The festival's showstoppers are the Concerts Under the Stars held each Sunday from 7 to 9:30pm; the series features some 15 local bands over its 6-week run.

The Jazz Society runs a hotline listing jazz events throughout the year. Its raison d'être, however, is **JazzFest International** (📞 888/671-2112 or 250/388-4423; www.jazzvictoria.ca), held from late June to early July. The more progressive of Victoria's two summer jazz fests, this one offers a range of styles from Cuban, salsa, and world beat to fusion and acid jazz. This organization also puts on the excellent **Blues Bash** on Labour Day weekend on an outdoor stage in Victoria's Inner Harbour.

LIVE MUSIC **Swans Pub** (see "Bars & Pubs," below) presents a live band every night.

Hermann's Jazz Club, 753 View St. (📞 250/388-9166; www.hermannsjazz.com; cover C$5–C$10), cultivates a community-center feel, which is definitely and defiantly *not* chic. Still, the reasonable cover charge gets you in for some good old-time jazz and Dixieland. Open Thursday through Saturday at 8pm, Sunday at 4:30pm.

Lucky Bar, 517 Yates St. (📞 250/382-5825; www.luckybar.ca; cover C$5–C$20), is a long, low, cavernous space with a pleasantly grungy feel to it. DJs spin house and trance on the weekends, with bands often showing up earlier in the week.

Steamers, 570 Yates St. (📞 250/381-4340; cover free to C$5), is one of the best places to catch live music (7 nights a week) on the cheap. Once a strip bar, this long, narrow downtown spot got a new interior and was reborn as the city's premium blues bar. "Blues" here isn't taken too literally: Acts often stray into the realms of zydeco, Celtic, and world beat. Mondays present an open-stage acoustic jam (no cover).

DANCE CLUBS Most places are open Monday through Saturday until 2am, and Sunday until midnight. Drinks run from C$4 to C$8.

Opened in 2004, **Red Jacket,** 751 View St. (📞 250/384-2582), quickly became *the* hoppin' hot spot thanks to Caramel @ The Red Jacket, a Friday night bash featuring some of Victoria's finest urban DJ talent.

Groove the night away under an old-fashioned disco ball at **Sugar,** 858 Yates St. (📞 250/920-9950; www.sugarnightclub.ca; cover Fri–Sat C$3–C$6). Open Thursday through Saturday only; lineups start at 10pm, so come early. DJs spin mostly hip-hop, house, and Top 40 tunes.

LOUNGES, BARS & PUBS

LOUNGES **The Bengal Lounge,** in the Fairmont Empress, 721 Government St. (📞 250/384-8111), is one of the last outposts of the old empire—a Raffles or a Harry's Bar—except the martinis are ice-cold and jazz plays in the background (and on weekends, live in the foreground). Lately it's attracted the young and elegant lounge-lizard crowd.

Med Grill@Mosaic, 1063 Fort St. (📞 250/381-3417), is a bistro by day, but this cool, contemporary space turns into a martini spot at night (happy hour nightly 9–10pm), when DJs spin mellow sounds. Everything's reasonably priced and pretty.

VICTORIA

6

VICTORIA AFTER DARK

The Reef, 533 Yates St. (© **250/388-5375;** www.thereefrestaurant.com), is a Caribbean restaurant that transforms into a funky reggae lounge when the sun has faded away. Features include great martinis and good tunes, and a DJ now and again.

Bars & Pubs

BARS & PUBS **Big Bad John's,** in the Strathcona Hotel, 919 Douglas St. (© **250/383-7137**), is Victoria's first, favorite, and only hillbilly bar. It's a low, dark warren of a place, with a crowd of drunk and happy rowdies.

If it's a nice night, head for **Canoe,** 450 Swift St. (© **250/361-1940;** www.canoebrew pub.com), and its fabulous outdoor patio overlooking the Upper Harbour. The beer is brewed on the premises, and the food is fun and hearty.

Eating anywhere on Wharf Street would be a foolish newbie move, but drinking? That's another story. **Darcy's Wharf Street Pub,** 1127 Wharf St. (© **250/380-1322;** www.darcyspub.ca), is a large, bright, harborfront pub featuring a range of fine brews, pool tables, occasional live bands, and a lovely view of the sunset. The crowd is young and lively.

One of the best brewpubs in town, **Spinnakers,** 308 Catherine St. (© **250/386-2739;** www.spinnakers.com; bus: 24 to Songhees Rd.), did it first and did it well. Overlooking Victoria Harbour on the west side of the Songhees Point Development, Spinnakers' view of the harbor and Legislature is fabulous. The brewed-on-the-premises ales, lagers, and stouts are uniformly excellent, and the pub grub is always good. An onsite bakery sells various beer breads. The weekends often feature a band. There are also dartboards and pool tables.

The Sticky Wicket, 919 Douglas St. (© **250/383-7137**), is yet another pub in the Strathcona Hotel (see Big Bad John's, above)—but the Wicket is a standout. The beautiful wood interior spent many years in Dublin before being shipped here to Victoria. Elevators can whip you from deepest Dublin up three floors to the outdoor patio balcony, complete with beach volleyball.

Few drinking spots are more intriguing—or more enjoyable—than **Swans Brewpub,** in Swans Hotel, 506 Pandora Ave. (© **250/361-3310**). The intrigue comes from the founding owner's vast Pacific Northwest and First Nations art collection. The enjoyment comes from the room itself, on the ground floor of a beautifully converted 1913 feed warehouse across from the Johnson Street Bridge. The beer here is brewed on-site and delicious. There's live entertainment every night.

GAY & LESBIAN BARS Victoria's entertainment options for the gay and lesbian community are few. A good resource for local contacts can be found online at **www.gay victoria.ca.**

Hush, 1325 Government St. (© **250/385-0566;** C$5 cover on weekends), is a straight-friendly space (crowd is about 50/50) featuring top-end touring DJs spinning house, trance, and disco house. It's open Wednesday to Sunday.

Prism Lounge, 642 Johnson St. (entrance on Broad St.; © **250/388-0505;** www. prismlounge.com), has drag shows, karaoke, techno, Top 40—something different every night.

7

Southern Vancouver Island & the Gulf Islands

Stretching more than 450km (280 miles) from Victoria to the northwest tip of Cape Scott, Vancouver Island is one of the most fascinating destinations in Canada, a mountainous bulwark of deep-green forests, rocky fjords, and wave-battered headlands. For an area so easily accessible by car, the range of wildlife here is surprising: Bald eagles float above the shorelines, seals and sea lions slumber on rocky islets, and porpoises and orca whales cavort in narrow passes between islands.

The British Columbia capital, Victoria, is the ideal place to begin exploring the entire island; see chapter 6 for complete coverage of the city.

Duncan, the "City of Totem Poles" in the Cowichan Valley north of Victoria, reveals another facet of Vancouver Island culture. This lush green valley is the ancestral home of the Cowichan tribe, famed for its hand-knit sweaters; it also houses some of the island's best wineries and organic farms, making it a gastronomical hub.

Nestled just off the island's east coast lie the Gulf Islands. The fact that they are only reached by a confusing network of ferries just enhances their sense of remoteness and mystery. Part arty, counterculture enclave, part trophy-home exurb, and part old-fashioned farm and orchard territory, the Gulf Islands are full of contradictions and charm. The largest, Salt Spring Island, is a haven for artists who are attracted to its mild climate and pastoral landscapes.

Running down the spine of Vancouver Island is a lofty chain of mountains that functionally divides the island into west and east. In the west, which receives the full brunt of Pacific storms, vast rainforests grow along inaccessible, steep-sided fjords. Paved roads provide access in only a few places, and boat charters, ferries, and float-planes are the preferred means of transport.

The east side of Vancouver Island, and in particular the area from Nanaimo southward, is home to the vast majority of the island's population of 750,000. The climate here is drier and warmer than on the storm-tossed west coast, and agriculture is a major industry. Tourism is also key to the local economy: The southeast portion of Vancouver Island has the warmest median temperatures in all of Canada, and tourists and retirees flood the area in search of rain-free summer days.

While the Gulf Islands and the southern portions of Vancouver Island were long ago colonized by European settlers, the original First Nations peoples are very much a part of cultural and political life in the area. Historically, the Pacific coast of British Columbia was one of the greatest centers of art and culture in Native America, and this past is beautifully preserved in many museums and in several villages. Modern-day First Nations artists are very active, and nearly every town has galleries and workshops filled with their exquisite carvings, paintings, and sculpture.

This chapter covers the southern portion of Vancouver Island, along with the Gulf Islands. For the area from Nanaimo to Courtenay/Comox and including the West Coast Trail and Pacific Rim National Park, see chapter 8, "Central Vancouver Island." In chapter 9, "Northern Vancouver Island," we discuss the portion of the island from the town of Campbell River northward, including Strathcona Provincial Park.

1 ESSENTIALS

GETTING THERE

BY PLANE **Victoria** is the island's major air hub, with jet, commuter-plane, and float-plane service from Vancouver and Seattle. See chapter 6 for details.

Both standard commuter aircraft and floatplanes provide regularly scheduled service to a number of other island communities from both Victoria and Vancouver. All of the southern Gulf Islands, as well as many towns, can be reached by scheduled harbor-to-harbor floatplane service, either from Vancouver International's seaplane terminal or from downtown Vancouver's Coal Harbour terminal. In fact, it's easy to arrange a chartered floatplane for almost any destination along coastal Vancouver Island. Since float-planes don't require airport facilities, even the most remote fishing camp can be as accessible as a major city.

Commercial airline service is provided by **Air Canada** (© 888/247-2262; www.air canada.com), **Horizon Air** (© 800/252-7522; www.alaskaair.com), **Pacific Coastal** (© 800/663-2872; www.pacific-coastal.com), and **WestJet** (© 877/952-4638; www. westjet.com).

Commuter seaplane companies that serve Vancouver Island include **Harbour Air Seaplanes** (© 800/665-0212 or 604/688-1277; www.harbour-air.com), **Tofino Air** (© 866/486-3247 for Tofino base, 888/436-7776 for Sechelt base, or 800/665-2359 for Gabriola base; www.tofinoair.ca), and West Coast Air (© 800/347-2222 or 604/606-6800; http://westcoastair.com).

BY FERRY **BC Ferries** (© 888/BCFERRY [223-3779] or 250/386-3431; www.bc ferries.com) operates an extensive year-round network that links Vancouver Island, the Gulf Islands, and the mainland. Major routes include the crossing from Tsawwassen to Swartz Bay and to Nanaimo, and from Horseshoe Bay (northwest of Vancouver) to Nanaimo. In summer, reserve in advance. If you're taking a car, beware: Ticket prices add up quickly.

Washington State Ferries (© 888/808-7977 in Washington, 206/464-6400 in the rest of the U.S., or 250/381-1551 in Canada; www.wsdot.wa.gov/ferries) has daily service from Anacortes, in Washington, to Sidney, on Vancouver Island. One-way fares for a car and driver are around US$75 in high season.

The year-round passenger ferries run by **Victoria Clipper** (© 800/888-2535 or 206/448-5000; www.victoriaclipper.com) depart from Seattle's Pier 69; adult round-trip tickets range from US$134 to US$155.

From Port Angeles, Washington, the year-round (except for a 2-week maintenance break in Jan) Black Ball Transport's car ferry **MV *Coho*** (© 360/457-4491 in Port Angeles, or 250/386-2202 in Victoria; www.cohoferry.com) offers service to Victoria for US$15 per adult foot passenger, US$53 per vehicle. Also from Port Angeles, from mid-May to the end of September, foot passengers and bicyclists can pay US$25 round-trip to hop on the ***Victoria Express*** (© 800/633-1589 or 360/452-8088 in the U.S., or 250/361-9144 in Victoria; www.victoriaexpress.com).

In summer only, **Victoria/San Juan Cruises**' daily *Victoria Star 2* (© 800/443-4552; www.whales.com) passenger ferry travels between Bellingham and Victoria via the San Juan Islands. One-way adult fare is US$59.

BY BUS One of the easiest ways to get to Vancouver Island destinations is by bus. Conveniently, the bus will start its journey from a city center (such as Vancouver), take you directly to the ferry dock and onto the ferry, and then deposit you in another city center (Victoria or Nanaimo). A lot of the hassle of ferry travel is minimized, and the costs are usually lower than other alternatives. (If you're traveling to Vancouver on VIA Rail or Amtrak, bus connections are easy—the bus and train share the same terminal.)

Pacific Coast Lines (© **800/661-1725** or 604/662-8074; www.pacificcoach.com) offers bus service via BC Ferries from Vancouver to Victoria. The one-way fare is C$43 for adults. **Greyhound Canada** (© **800/661-8747** or 604/482-8747; www.greyhound. ca) provides seven daily trips between Vancouver and Nanaimo. Fare is C$22 one-way.

VISITOR INFORMATION

For general information on Vancouver Island, contact **Tourism Vancouver Island,** Ste. 501, 65 Front St., Nanaimo, BC V9R 5H9 (© **250/754-3500;** fax 250/754-3599; www.vancouverisland.travel). Also check out **www.vancouverisland.com**.

GETTING AROUND

While Vancouver Island has an admirable system of public transport, getting to remote sights and destinations is difficult without your own vehicle.

BY FERRY **BC Ferries** (© **888/BCFERRY** [223-3779] or 250/386-3431; www.bc ferries.com) routes link Vancouver Island ports to many offshore islands, including the southern Gulf Islands of Denman, Gabriola, Galiano, Hornby, Kuper, Mayne, the Penders, Salt Spring, Saturna, and Thetis. None of these islands has public transport, so once there, you'll need to hoof it, hitch it, hire a taxi, or arrange for bike rentals. Most innkeepers will pick you up from the ferry if you've reserved in advance.

BY TRAIN Another charming way to get around Vancouver Island is on **VIA Rail**'s **E&N Railiner,** also known as the *Malahat* (© **888/VIA-RAIL** [842-7245] or 250/383-4324; www.viarail.ca), which makes a daily round-trip run from Victoria to Courtenay in period passenger cars. The *Malahat* passes through some of the most beautiful landscapes on the east coast of Vancouver Island, taking about 4½ hours each way. Your ticket allows you to get on and off as many times as you'd like: You can stop at Duncan, Chemainus, Nanaimo, Parksville, or Qualicum Beach and catch the return train back, or take the next day's train north. Prices are very reasonable, especially with 7-day advance purchase. A round-trip between Victoria and Courtenay can cost as little as C$59. *Note:* The *Malahat* has no baggage car, and checked-baggage service is not available.

BY BUS **Island Coach Lines** (© **250/388-5248,** or book through Greyhound © **800/661-8747;** www.greyhound.ca) runs buses between Victoria and Nanaimo with stops at smaller centers along Hwy. 1 (see "By Car," below).

BY CAR The southern half of Vancouver Island is well served by paved highways. The trunk road between Victoria and Nanaimo is **Hwy. 1,** the Trans-Canada. This busy route alternates between four-lane expressway and congested two-lane highway, and requires some patience and vigilance, especially during the summer months. North of Nanaimo, the major road is **Hwy. 19,** which is now almost all four-lane expressway, a particular improvement being the new 128km (80-mile) **Inland Highway** section between Parksville and Campbell River. The older sections of 19, all closer to the island's east coast, are now labeled 19A. North of Campbell River, a long, unimproved section of Hwy. 19

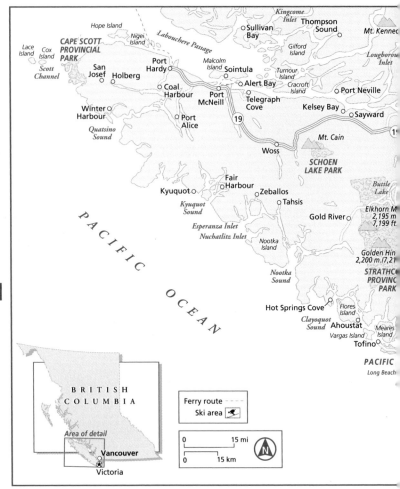

continues all the way to Port Hardy. The other major paved road system on the island, **Hwy. 4,** connects Parksville with Port Alberni and on to Ucluelet and Tofino, on the rugged west coast. This road is mostly two-lane, and portions of it are extremely winding and hilly. Access to gasoline and car services is no problem, even in more remote north Vancouver Island.

Rental cars are readily available. Agencies include **Avis** (© **800/879-2847** in Canada, 800/331-1212 in the U.S.; www.avis.com), **Budget** (© **800/268-8900** in Canada, 800/527-0700 in the U.S.; www.budget.com), and **National** (© **877/222-9058** in Canada and the U.S.; www.nationalcar.com).

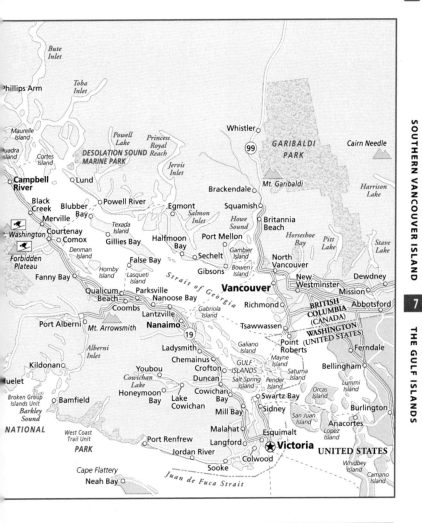

2 THE GULF ISLANDS ★★

The Gulf Islands are a collection of several dozen mountainous islands that sprawl across the Strait of Georgia between the British Columbia mainland and Vancouver Island. While only a handful of the islands are served by regularly scheduled ferries, this entire area is popular with boaters, cyclists, kayakers, and sailboat enthusiasts. Lying in the rain shadow of Washington State's Olympic Mountains, the Gulf Islands have the most temperate climate in all of Canada, without the heavy rainfall that characterizes much of coastal British Columbia. In fact, the climate here is officially listed as semi-Mediterranean!

> **Tips**   **A Note for Families**
>
> If you're traveling with kids, the Gulf Islands are a fairly inhospitable place to secure accommodations. Nearly all B&Bs have listed minimum ages for guests (usually 12 or 16), and there are only a few standard motels or cottage resorts where families are welcome. Note that for all accommodations, it's mandatory to make reservations well in advance, as the ferry system doesn't exactly make it easy to just drive on to the next town to find a place to stay.
>
> One option for families is to rent a cottage or private home. **Gulf Island Vacation Rentals,** 5402 Wilson Rd., Pender Island, BC V0N 2M1 (© **877/662-3414;** www.gulfislandvacationrentals.com), is a clearinghouse of private homes, bed-and-breakfast rooms, and cottages available for rental on the Gulf Islands.

The Gulf Islands are the northern extension of Washington's San Juan Islands, and they share those islands' farming and seafaring past. Agriculture, especially sheep raising, is still a major industry. The past few decades, however, have seen radical changes in traditional island life: The sheer beauty of the land- and seascapes, the balmy climate, and the relaxed lifestyle have brought a major influx of new residents. These islands were a major destination for Vietnam War–era draft evaders, many of whom set up homes, farms, and businesses here. The islands quickly developed a reputation as a countercultural hippie enclave, a reputation they still maintain. As one generation's radicals gray and become the islands' retirees, younger generations of free spirits have come to grow organic vegetables, explore an artistic urge, and hang out in the coffee shops.

Paralleling this youthful influx is another kind of land rush. Moguls, celebrities, and other wealthy refugees from urban centers have moved to the islands in droves. The quality of facilities has shot up: The islands now boast fine restaurants, elegant inns, and a multitude of galleries. In fact, the Gulf Islands are noted across Canada as a major center for crafts and arts.

The population influx is having some unexpected consequences. Groundwater is a precious commodity on these arid islands, and some inns will ask guests to monitor their water use. Adding to the problem is that saltwater aquifers underlie parts of the islands: Corrosive salt water doesn't do anyone much good.

Despite the one-direction migration, the Gulf Islands remain a charming destination. The islands are still underdeveloped, and some of the best restaurants and lodgings are tucked away in forests down long roads. There's little in the way of organized activities: no water slides, theme parks, and few major resorts; just incredible scenery, great biking and kayaking, lovely inns, and fine dining.

Gulf Islands National Park Reserve, 2220 Harbour Rd., Sidney, BC V8L 2P6 (© **250/654-4000;** www.pc.gc.ca), protects 34 sq. km (13 sq. miles) of the islands' unique marine ecosystem on 15 islands and more than 50 islets, plus 26 sq. km (10 sq. miles) of marine areas. A large portion of the reserve is on smaller Gulf Islands, such as Prevost, Portland, D'Arcy, and Tumbo, which have no BC Ferries service and can be reached only by kayak, canoe, water taxi, or private boat. Land on Mayne and North and South Pender islands is included in the park, though it is Saturna—the most remote and undeveloped of the islands served by BC Ferries—that has the most parkland acreage.

Getting There

BY FERRY   BC Ferries (℡ **888/BCFERRY** [223-3779] in North America, or 250/386-3431; www.bcferries.com) operates four different runs to the southern Gulf Islands, from Tsawwassen on the British Columbia mainland, and from Swartz Bay, Crofton, and Nanaimo on Vancouver Island. The system was designed primarily to get commuters to their jobs on the mainland or in Victoria. Getting exactly where you want to be, exactly when you want to be there, is anything but straightforward (and not always possible). Be aware that the ferries are not particularly large; to ensure that you make the one you want, arrive at least 15 minutes early (30 min. on summer weekends). You can make reservations on the routes from Tsawwassen, but not on the other runs.

Ticket pricing is confusing. There are separate fares for drivers, passengers, and vehicles, plus fees for bikes, kayaks, and canoes on most runs. Tickets from Vancouver Island (Chemainus, Crofton, Nanaimo, or Swartz Bay) are calculated as return fares; that is, when you buy a ticket and depart from one of these ports, you don't have to buy an additional ticket if you are returning to the same port. However, all fares via Tsawwassen are one-way: You pay going and coming. To make it more puzzling, outward-bound fares from Tsawwassen are more expensive than the same journey back to the mainland. Sample peak-season fares: a car and two passengers from Swartz Bay to Salt Spring Island, C$53; a single foot passenger, C$9.

If you are planning to visit several islands, consider purchasing a 4- or 7-day **SailPass** (www.bcferries.com/sailpass) from BC Ferries, which can reduce both fares and confusion. The SailPass is a one-price ticket that allows you to travel along 20 ferry routes in southern B.C., including those routes servicing the Gulf Islands (except for travel along the Inside Passage routes or to the Queen Charlottes). The ticket includes passage for a vehicle plus two adults (more adults can be added to the ticket by paying more). A 4-day ticket is C$189, and a 7-day ticket is C$229, which, given normal use, will represent a savings of about one-third over regular fares. The only hitch is that you need to pre-purchase the SailPass—you can't buy one at the ferry terminal. They can be ordered from the BC Ferry website above (allow a week for delivery) or purchased the same day from a number of regional tourist information centers; see the website for a full list of locations.

BY PLANE   A number of commuter airlines offer regular floatplane service from either Vancouver Harbour or Vancouver International Airport. One-way tickets to the islands usually cost C$85 to C$95 per person, not a bad fare when you consider the time and hassle involved in taking a ferry. However, floatplanes are small and seats sell out quickly,

---

ⓘ Tips   Make Saturna Your First Stop

If you're planning to make a circuit of the five southern Gulf Islands, consider starting with Saturna Island. Saturna is far easier to reach by ferry from Swartz Bay on Vancouver Island than it is from its sister Gulf Islands (to get to Saturna from Tsawwassen on the mainland requires a change of ferries). In fact, there's not even scheduled service between Saturna and Salt Spring Island. However, for reasons unknown, once on Saturna it's not difficult to continue on to other islands.

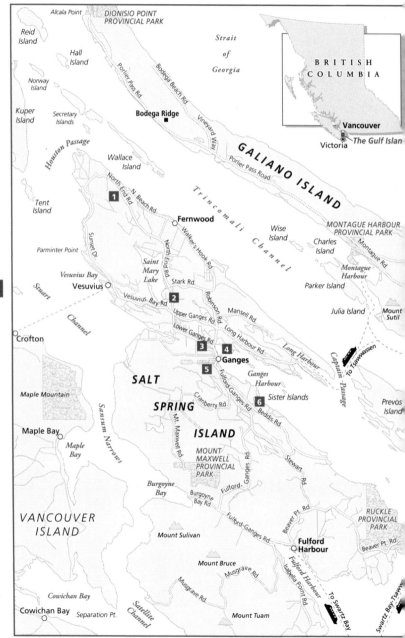

Alcala Point

Reid
Island

DIONISIO POINT
PROVINCIAL PARK

Hall
Island

Strait
of
Georgia

BRITISH
COLUMBIA

Norway
Island

Porlier Pass Rd.

Bodega Beach Rd.

Kuper
Island

Secretary
Islands

■ **Bodega Ridge**

Vineyard Way

Vancouver

Victoria   The Gulf Islan

Houston Passage

Wallace
Island

G A L I A N O   I S L A N D

Tent
Island

North End Rd.

N. Beach Rd.

Fernwood

Porlier Pass Road

Trincomali Channel

Wise
Island

Charles
Island

MONTAGUE HARBOUR
PROVINCIAL PARK

Parminter Point

Sunset Dr.

Walker's Hook Rd.

North End Rd.

Saint
Mary
Lake

Stark Rd.

Montague
Rd.

Montague
Harbour

Vesuvius Bay

Vesuvius

Vesuvius Bay Rd.

Upper Ganges Rd.

Robinson Rd.

Mansell Rd.

Parker Island

Julia Island

Mount
Sutil

Stuart

Lower Ganges Rd.

Long Harbour Rd.

Long Harbour

Captain Passage

To Tsawwassen

○ **Crofton**

Channel

Ganges

Ganges
Harbour

Prevost
Island

SALT

Fulford-Ganges Rd.

Maple Mountain

Sansum Narrows

SPRING

Cranberry Rd.

Beddis Rd.

Sister Islands

Maple Bay

Maple
Bay

ISLAND

MOUNT
MAXWELL
PROVINCIAL
PARK

Mt. Maxwell Rd.

Fulford- Ganges Rd.

Stewart Rd.

RUCKLE
PROVINCIAL
PARK

VANCOUVER
ISLAND

Burgoyne
Bay

Burgoyne
Bay Rd.

Fulford-Ganges Rd.

Beaver Pt. Rd.

Fulford
Harbour

Beaver Pt. Rd.

Mount Sulivan

Mount Bruce

Musgrave Rd.

Fulford Harbour

Isabella Point Rd.

To Swartz Bay

Cowichan Bay

Cowichan Bay

Separation Pt.

Satellite
Channel

Musgrave Rd.

Mount Tuam

Swartz Bay Tsaww

1 **2** **3** **4** **5** **6**

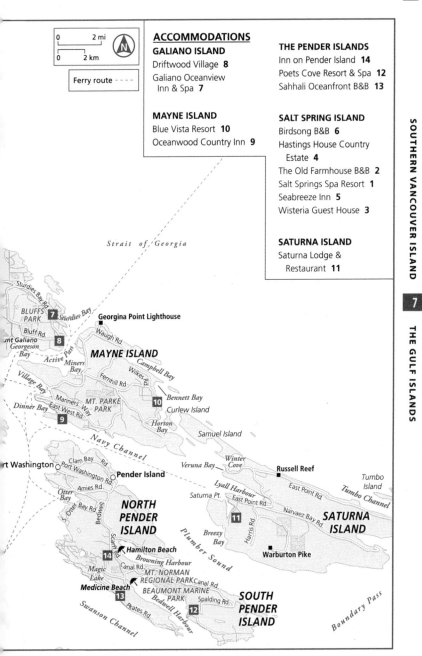

ACCOMMODATIONS

GALIANO ISLAND
Driftwood Village **8**
Galiano Oceanview
 Inn & Spa **7**

MAYNE ISLAND
Blue Vista Resort **10**
Oceanwood Country Inn **9**

THE PENDER ISLANDS
Inn on Pender Island **14**
Poets Cove Resort & Spa **12**
Sahhali Oceanfront B&B **13**

SALT SPRING ISLAND
Birdsong B&B **6**
Hastings House Country
 Estate **4**
The Old Farmhouse B&B **2**
Salt Springs Spa Resort **1**
Seabreeze Inn **5**
Wisteria Guest House **3**

SATURNA ISLAND
Saturna Lodge &
 Restaurant **11**

so reserve ahead of time. Call **Harbour Air Seaplanes** (© 800/665-0212 or 604/688-1277; www.harbour-air.com), or **Seair Seaplanes** (© 800/447-3247 or 604/273-8900; www.seairseaplanes.com).

Visitor Information

For general information on the Gulf Islands, contact **Tourism Vancouver Island,** Ste. 501, 65 Front St., Nanaimo, BC V9R 5H9 (© **250/754-3500;** fax 250/754-3599; www.vancouverisland.travel). Another good comprehensive resource is **www.gulfislands.com**.

Getting Around

Most innkeepers will pick up guests at the ferry or floatplane terminals, if given sufficient notice. There's also taxi service on most islands. Most taxis will quote you a fixed price for a journey when you phone to reserve the trip. Be sure to confirm the price when you're picked up.

BY BICYCLE   Winding country roads and bucolic landscapes make the Gulf Islands a favorite destination for cyclists. Although the islands' road networks aren't exactly large—and roads are quite steep and narrow—it can be great fun to bike the back roads, jump a ferry, and peddle to an outlying pub for lunch. Bikes can be taken onboard BC Ferries for a small surcharge. Note, though, that the narrow roads really fill up in summer, making them more idyllic for cycling other times of the year. Several parks have designated mountain-bike trails. Rentals are available on most islands.

BY KAYAK   The Gulf Islands' lengthy and rugged coastline, plus their proximity to other more remote island groups, make them a good base for kayaking trips. Most of the islands have kayak outfitters; however, not all of them will offer rentals separate from guided tours. If you're an experienced kayaker and just want to rent a kayak, call ahead to inquire. Kayaks and canoes can be taken on the ferries for a small fee.

SALT SPRING ISLAND

The largest of the Gulf Islands, Salt Spring is—to the outside world—a bucolic getaway filled with artists, sheep pastures, and cozy B&Bs. While this image is mostly true, Salt Spring is also a busy cultural crossroads: Movie stars, retirees, high-tech telecommuters, and hippie farmers all rub shoulders here. The hilly terrain and deep forests afford equal privacy for all lifestyles, and that's the way the residents like it.

Salt Spring is divided geographically into three distinct lobes. In fact, the island looks as if it were once three separate islands that somehow got pushed together. Most of the population lives in the area around Ganges and Vesuvius; the rugged lower third of the island is the least developed. Although Salt Spring's configuration makes for a lot of coastline, there are very few beaches, as the underlying granite forms headlands that drop straight into the sea.

GETTING THERE   Salt Spring Island is served by three different routes on **BC Ferries** (© **888/BCFERRY** [223-3779] or 250/381-5452; www.bcferries.com). From Tsawwassen on the mainland, ferries depart two to four times a day for Long Harbour, on the island's northeast coast. If you're on Vancouver Island, you can choose the Crofton–Vesuvius Bay run or the Swartz Bay (Victoria) to Fulford Harbour crossing.

Regular floatplane service operates from Vancouver International Airport and Vancouver's Inner Harbour seaplane terminal to Ganges Harbour. See "Essentials" (p. 132) for contact information.

VISITOR INFORMATION   The **Salt Spring Chamber of Commerce** operates a visitor center at 121 Lower Ganges Rd., Salt Spring Island, BC V8K 2T1 (© **250/537-5252;** www.saltspringtourism.com).

GETTING AROUND   If you don't have a car, you will need to rely on a bike or call **Silver Shadow Taxi** (© 250/537-3030). **Gulf Islands Water Taxi** (© **250/537-2510;** http://members.unet.ca/~watertaxi) offers scheduled speedboat service between Salt Spring, Mayne, and Galiano islands on Saturdays during July and August, plus Pender and Saturna islands on all school days during the rest of the year (the water taxi serves as the "school bus" for island students). There are morning and late afternoon scheduled services for commuters and students; charters are also available. The taxi leaves from Government Dock in Ganges Harbour. Fares are C$15 from any one point to another, or C$25 for a round-trip. Reservations are recommended; bikes are transported free of charge.

Exploring the Island

With a year-round population of 10,000 residents, Salt Spring is served by three ferries, making it by far the easiest of the Gulf Islands to visit. Not coincidentally, Salt Spring also has the most facilities for visitors. The center of island life is **Ganges,** a little village with gas stations, grocery stores, and banks, all overlooking a busy pleasure-boat harbor. You can easily spend an hour to most of a day poking around the art galleries, boutiques, and coffee shops here.

In fact, the island is famed across Canada as an artists' colony, and many people visit expressly to see the studios of local artists and craftspeople. Stop by the visitor center for the **Studio Tour Map** (or download a copy from www.saltspringstudiotour.com), which pinpoints over 30 island artists—glass blowers, painters, ceramists, weavers, carvers, and sculptors, many of whom are available for visits.

Pegasus Gallery, Mouat's Mall, 1-104 Fulford-Ganges Rd. (© **800/668-6131** or 250/537-2421; www.pegasusgallery.ca), displays a mix of contemporary Canadian painting and sculpture as well as Native carving and basketry. On Fridays from 5 to 9pm, a dozen Ganges galleries remain open late for the **Gallery Walk.** From mid-May to mid-September, **ArtCraft** (© **250/537-0899;** www.artcraftgallery.ca) features the work of more than 250 local artists at Mahon Hall, just north of Ganges at Park Drive and Lower Ganges Road (WinterCraft is the holiday version of this market, held in Dec).

Not to be missed is **Market in the Park** ★ (www.saltspringmarket.com), held April through October, Saturdays from 8am to 4pm, on the waterfront's Centennial Park. The market brings together a lively mix of craftspeople, farmers, musicians, and bakers. It's great fun, and a good chance to shop for local products.

BIKING   Although Salt Spring has the best network of paved roads, it's not the best island for cycling. With ferries unleashing cars throughout the day, there's a lot more traffic here than you'd expect. However, these same ferries—plus the **Gulf Islands Water Taxi** (see "Getting Around," above)—make Salt Spring a convenient base for cyclists. For rentals (starting at C$25 a day), contact **Salt Spring Adventure Co.,** at the Saltspring Marina in Ganges Harbour (© **877/537-2764** or 250/537-2764; www.saltspring adventures.com).

HIKING   **Ruckle Provincial Park** (www.env.gov.bc.ca/bcparks), on the southeast corner of the island, is the largest provincial park in the Gulf Islands; its entrance is 10km (6¼ miles) from the Fulford Harbour ferry terminal on Beaver Point Road. Eight kilometers (5 miles) of trails wind through forests to rocky headlands where the tide-pool exploring is excellent; some trails are designated for mountain bikes. Ruckle Park is also the only public campground on Salt Spring.

KAYAKING **Island Escapades,** 163 Fulford-Ganges Rd. (© **888/529-2567** or 250/537-2553; www.islandescapades.com), offers a 2-hour introduction to kayaking on the placid waters of Cusheon Lake, for C$50, with guided 3-hour ocean tours for C$65. **Salt Spring Adventure Co.** (see "Biking," above) offers kayak rentals in addition to instruction and guided tours. A 2-hour double kayak rental is C$50. **Sea Otter Kayaking,** 149 Lower Ganges Rd. (© **877/537-5678;** www.seaotterkayaking.com), offers a number of guided day-trips (C$115 including lunch) and also multiday expeditions to more remote islands.

Where to Stay

Ruckle Provincial Park, off Beaver Point Road (© **250/391-2300;** www.env.gov.bc.ca/bcparks), has 78 campsites for C$15.

Birdsong Bed and Breakfast ★★ This friendly and beautifully furnished B&B offers spectacular harbor views, epic breakfasts, and a relaxed make-yourself-at-home vibe—pretty much exactly what you're looking for in an ideal island getaway. Each of the three large guest rooms is decorated with an artful blend of antique and modern, all with private baths and individual balconies (or patio). Extras include high-end bedding and fireplaces (in two rooms). This expansive property sits amid extensive gardens and 139 sq. m (1,500 sq. ft.) of decks (plus hot tub), so there's always a new view and hidden nook to explore. If you want more room or privacy, there's also a two-bedroom cottage with full kitchen (breakfast is not included with the cottage, but is available for C$20 per person). Birdsong is just 10 minutes south of Ganges. Convenient—but just far enough away to make this superlative B&B seem a world away. Minimum stay requirements may apply.

153 Rourke Rd., Salt Spring Island, BC V8K 2E6. © **250/537-4608.** http://birdsongbedandbreakfast.com. 4 units. C$135–C$155 double; C$155 cottage. Low-season rates available. MC, V. *In room:* TV (upon request), CD player, hair dryer, no phone, Wi-Fi.

Hastings House Country House Hotel ★★ Idyllic only begins to describe this idealized English manor, with an incredible 9-hectare (22-acre) setting with marvelous harbor views and a sculpture garden, vegetable gardens and orchards that provide their bounty for the excellent restaurant (see "Where to Dine," below), and beautifully furnished guest rooms that wear their past grandly. In the 1930s, an English couple built a replica of a 16th-century Sussex manor house on the site of an old farm and trading post. When this beautifully situated property was converted into a luxurious resort, spa, and restaurant, nearly all of the historic structures were transformed into elegant accommodations that combine vintage integrity with modern luxury. For instance, the manor house now serves as the restaurant, with two guest suites on the second floor, while the handsome old barn contains five suites plus a spa. Other rooms are in the old farmhouse and the original trading post; if you prefer new construction, ask for the Hillside Suites.

160 Upper Ganges Rd., Salt Spring Island, BC V8K 2S2. © **800/661-9255** or 250/537-2362. Fax 250/537-5333. www.hastingshouse.com. 18 units. From C$275 double, including breakfast and afternoon tea. Extra person C$75 per night. Weekly cottage rental available. 2-day, spa, and gourmet packages available. AE, MC, V. Closed Nov–April. Children 16 and over welcome. **Amenities:** Restaurant; complimentary bikes; golf course nearby; spa. *In room:* TV, CD player, fridge, hair dryer, Wi-Fi, robes.

Old Farmhouse B&B ★★ One of the best-loved accommodations in the Gulf Islands, the Old Farmhouse combines top-quality lodgings and great multi-course breakfasts. This Victorian-era homestead was built in 1894 amid 1.2 hectares (3 acres) of meadows and orchards—in fact, the enormous 500-year-old arbutus tree in the front yard may be the world's largest. The bedrooms are in a stylistically harmonious guesthouse adjoining the original farmhouse. Each room has a balcony or patio; the decor incorporates just the right country touches—floral wallpaper, wainscoted walls—without lapsing into Laura Ashley excess. The farm's old chicken house has been transformed into the charming Chateau de Poulet, a cozy one-bedroom suite with a king-size bed. The extensive meadows are perfect for lolling with a book or playing a game of croquet.

1077 N. End Rd., Salt Spring Island, BC V8K 1L9. ✆ **250/537-4113.** Fax 250/537-4969. www.bbcanada.com/oldfarmhouse. 5 units. C$195. Rates include full breakfast. MC, V. Call to inquire about children and pets. Closed Oct–May. **Amenities:** Jacuzzi; Wi-Fi. *In room:* Hair dryer, no phone.

Salt Springs Spa Resort Salt Spring's notorious saltwater aquifers are put to good use at this ocean-side spa and chalet resort on the north end of the island. The center offers a variety of traditional Ayurvedic and modern holistic body, beauty, and fitness therapies including facials, massage, aromatherapy, and mineral baths utilizing the spa's salt spring water. Even if you're not into the spa scene, Salt Springs Spa Resort is worth considering for its knotty-pine chalets, which face the busy waters of Trincomali Channel and overlook Wallace Island. Each rustic-looking unit has a full kitchen, wood-burning fireplace, porch with gas grill, and two tubs: a therapeutic tub with jetted mineral water and a soaker tub.

1460 N. Beach Rd., Salt Spring Island, BC V8K 1J4. ✆ **800/665-0039** or 250/537-4111. Fax 250/537-2939. www.saltspringresort.com. 13 chalets. Late June to Aug C$199–C$299 double; Sept–Oct, Mar to late June, and Dec 21–31 C$135–C$219 double; Nov–Feb except winter holidays C$109–C$199 double. 2- and 3-bedroom suites available. Extra person C$20 per night. 2-night minimum stay in summer. Packages available. AE, MC, V. Free parking. **Amenities:** Free bikes; golf course nearby; free rowboats. *In room:* Hair dryer, no phone, Wi-Fi.

Seabreeze Inne ⓥ**alue** ⓚ**ids** An alternative to Salt Spring's expensive B&Bs, the Seabreeze is a well-maintained motel just south of Ganges. All rooms are clean and nicely furnished; some have electric fireplaces and kitchens. Guests share a large patio with grapevine-covered arbors, picnic tables, and gas barbecues.

101 Bittancourt Rd., Salt Spring Island, BC V8K 2K2. ✆ **800/434-4112** or 250/537-4145. Fax 250/537-4323. www.seabreezeinne.com. 29 units. July to mid-Sept C$105–C$155 double; shoulder and off-season rates available. Extra person C$15. Rates include continental breakfast. Minimum stays may apply. Senior discounts and weekly rates available. AE, MC, V. Dogs accepted by approval; add C$10 per day. **Amenities:** Golf course nearby; hot tub; play area. *In room:* TV, fridge, Wi-Fi.

Wisteria Guest House ★★ ⓕ**inds** This rambling inn, tucked off a side street in Ganges, was once a small nursing home. There's little evidence of its institutional past, however, as the new owners have done a sensational job of updating the rooms, adding new features, and injecting lots of color and energy into the operation. In the main guesthouse, there are two sets of rooms that share adjacent bathrooms. These inexpensive rooms are perfect for friends or families traveling together, functioning like a small apartment. The two additional guest rooms, two studios with private entrances, and the stand-alone cottage all have private bathrooms. All rooms are spacious, beautifully decorated, and absolutely shipshape, and there's a comfortable central lounge and dining area where you'll enjoy a fantastic breakfast—one of the owners was formerly the pastry chef at the New York Westin Hotel.

268 Park Dr., Salt Spring Island, BC V8K 2S1. ℂ **888/537-5899** or 250/537-5899. Fax 250/537-5644. www. wisteriaguesthouse.com. 9 units. From C$99 guest-room double with shared bathroom; from C$119 guest-room double en suite bathroom; from C$129 studio double with kitchenette or self-contained cottage. Breakfast included in rates. AE, MC, V. Children and pets welcome in cottage and studios. **Amenities:** Common room w/TV, beverage service, fridge, and microwave. *In room:* Hair dryer, no phone, Wi-Fi.

Where to Dine

Calvin's Bistro ★ CANADIAN   If you ask a local where to eat in Ganges, chances are the answer will be Calvin's, a friendly, bustling restaurant with good prices and flavorful food. Ingredients are fresh and local, like the island lamb available in multiple preparations. Wild fish is often available on the broad menu that ranges from traditional schnitzel to Northwest bouillabaisse, a tangy tomato broth rich with salmon, mussels, clams, and halibut. In good weather, deck seating overlooks the marina. The charmingly energetic Swiss owners will make you feel very welcome—if you want stuffy, formal service, this isn't your restaurant.

133 Lower Ganges Rd. ℂ **250/538-5551.** Reservations recommended. Dinner main courses C$16–C$28. MC, V. Tues–Sat 11:30am–2pm and 5pm to closing.

Hastings House ★★ CONTEMPORARY CANADIAN   Easily the most elegant culinary experience on the island, the rose-trellis-covered dining room at Hastings House combines old-world sophistication with the freshest of ingredients. Daily changing menus incorporate local produce and fish; many of the herbs and vegetables are grown on the grounds. The evening begins with cocktails served by the fireplace. The four-course meal includes an appetizer (perhaps ahi sashimi and prosciutto salad with onion marmalade), a small seafood course (such as gingered scallops with citrus cream), and a choice of four main dishes: Salt Spring lamb is nearly always featured, as is local salmon, Dungeness crab, or other seasonal fish. An a la carte menu is also available.

160 Upper Ganges Rd. ℂ **250/537-2362.** www.hastingshouse.com. Reservations required. Prix-fixe 4-course dinner C$110. AE, MC, V. Summer (mid-June to mid-Oct) seating at 7:30pm; spring and fall (Mar to mid-June and mid-Oct to Nov) seating at 7pm. Closed Nov–Mar.

House Piccolo ★ CONTINENTAL   Located in a heritage home in Ganges, House Piccolo offers excellent food and a good wine list in moderately formal surroundings. The Finnish origins of the chef are reflected in the northern European accents on the unusual menu, particularly the fish specials that feature the best of the local catch. You might see salmon chowder Finlandia; local black cod drizzled with red wine, honey, and balsamic vinegar reduction; or roasted venison with rowan- and juniper-berry-scented demi glace.

108 Hereford Ave. ℂ **250/537-1844.** www.housepiccolo.com. Reservations recommended. Main courses C$23–C$37. AE, DC, MC, V. Daily 5–9pm.

Moby's Marine Pub PUB   This airy pub offers the island's best entertainment (live music most weekends, plus karaoke on Fri evenings) and is a great spot for a burger and a pint of local beer. Located just east of Ganges, the dining room overlooks the harbor; in summer, a lively cocktail scene develops on the sunny waterfront deck. The menu offers the usual pub grub with twists—lamb burgers, local seafood fajitas.

24 Upper Ganges Rd. ℂ **250/537-5559.** Reservations not accepted. Main courses C$8–C$16. MC, V. Sun–Thurs 10am–midnight; Fri–Sat 10am–1am.

Oystercatcher Seafood Bar & Grill CANADIAN   If you're looking for a relaxing spot for a drink and some tempting eats, consider the Oystercatcher. Above Shipstone's Pub (with outdoor seating on the waterfront), this smartly atmospheric bar and grill features a menu that spans the gulf between pub fare and fine dining: You can get a burger or a plate of fresh shucked oysters, fish and chips, or fire-grilled local lamb rack with three-mustard sauce. The same menu is available on both levels. Service is youthful and friendly, and the barman pours a number of local brews and wines.

104 Manson Rd. (℃ **250/537-5041.** Reservations accepted. Main courses C$12–C$38. MC, V. Daily 11:30am–11pm.

GALIANO ISLAND

Galiano is an elongated string bean of an island stretched along the Gulf Islands' eastern flank. Though Galiano looks, on the map, like just a long, skinny sand spit, it is in fact the crest of an underground mountain range, with rocky, cliff-faced shorelines and dense forests.

Galiano is the closest Gulf Island to Vancouver, and many of the properties here are second homes of the city's elite. The rural yet genteel feel of the island is perfect for a romantic getaway or a relaxing break from the hassles of urban life. However, don't come to Galiano looking for high-octane nightlife or boutique shopping. There isn't much of a town on the island, just a few shops and galleries at Sturdies Bay. However, there are a number of notable and unique eateries and excellent inns and B&Bs.

GETTING THERE BC Ferries serves Sturdies Bay from both Tsawwassen and Swartz Bay. Floatplanes serve Galiano Island from the docks at Montague Harbour. **Harbour Air Seaplanes** and **Seair Seaplanes** are your best options here. For contact information, see p. 132.

VISITOR INFORMATION Contact **Galiano Island Chamber of Commerce** (℃ **866/539-2233;** www.galianoisland.com). A seasonal information booth sits at the top of the ferry dock ramp.

Exploring the Island

Galiano is perhaps the most physically striking of the Gulf Islands, particularly the mountainous southern shores. Mount Sutil, Mount Galiano, and the exposed cliffs above Georgeson Bay (simply called the Bluffs) rise above sheep-filled meadows, shadowy forests, and fern-lined ravines. **Active Pass,** the narrow strait that separates Galiano from Mayne Island, is another scenic high spot: All the ferry and much of the pleasure-craft traffic between Vancouver and Victoria negotiates this turbulent, cliff-lined passage. Watch the bustle of the boats and ferries from **Bellhouse Provincial Park,** a picnicking area at the end of Jack Road, or head to **Montague Harbour Provincial Park,** a beautiful preserve of beach and forest.

Like Salt Spring Island, Galiano is also a center for artists and craftspeople. **Island's Edge Art Gallery,** no. 4 at 33 Manzanita St. (℃ **250/539-9934**), displays the work of many Gulf Island painters and sculptors. Just up the road on Sturdies Bay Road, also check out **Art and Soul Craft Gallery** (℃ **250/539-2944**).

BIKING The farther north you go on Galiano, the more remote, making this area a favorite among cyclists. While you won't have to worry too much about traffic on the 30km-long (19-mile) paved road that runs up the island's west side, there are enough steep ascents to keep your attention focused. Mountain bikers can follow unmaintained logging roads that skirt the eastern shores. Contact **Galiano Bicycle Rental,** 36 Burrill Rd. (℃ **250/539-9906;** www.galianoisland.com/galianobicycle), for rentals. A full day's rental is C$30.

HIKING   Several short hikes lead to Active Pass overlooks, including the trail to the top of 330m (1,083-ft.) Mount Galiano and the cliff-edge path in Bluffs Park. Bodega Ridge is a park about two-thirds of the way up the island, with old-growth forest, wildflowers, and views of the distant Olympic and Cascade mountain ranges.

KAYAKING   Home to otters, seals, and bald eagles, the gentle waters of Montague Harbour are a perfect kayaking destination. In addition to rentals, **Gulf Island Kayaking** (② **250/539-2442;** www.seakayak.ca) offers a variety of guided part- and whole-day trips, including a 3-hour sunset paddle for C$55. If you want to really get away, consider a custom multiday kayaking/camping trip.

Where to Stay

The only campground is at **Montague Harbour Provincial Marine Park** (② **250/539-2115** for reservations, or 250/391-2300 for information; www.env.gov.bc.ca/bcparks) with 40 sites (15 walk-in and 25 drive-in; a portion of each takes reservations) for C$19. The camp offers beach access, but no showers or flush toilets.

Driftwood Village (Kids) (Finds)   This venerable choice is perfect as a comfortable retreat for couples or in summer as a laid-back vacation with the kids and pets in tow. The cottages, of differing vintages and styles, are scattered around an 8-hectare (2-acre) garden complete with ponds, flowers, and fruit trees. Most have fireplaces and decks with views onto Sturdies Bay, and all are decorated with a sense of eclectic artfulness that will instantly bring back youthful memories of idealized lakeside holidays.

205 Bluff Rd. E., Galiano Island, BC V0N 1P0. ② **866/502-5457** or 250/539-5457. Fax 250/539-5058. www.driftwoodcottages.com. 10 units. C$129 studio doubles and 1-bedroom cottages; C$160 1- or 2-bedroom luxury double cottages. Off-season and shoulder-season rates available. Extra person C$20. Rates include ferry pickup. MC, V. Pets accepted for C$10 per night. **Amenities:** Jacuzzi; badminton court. *In room:* TV or TV/VCR, full kitchen, no phone.

Galiano Oceanfront Inn & Spa ★★   Formerly the Galiano Lodge and one of the original accommodations on Galiano Island, the inn—with an unrestricted vista onto the harbor, the busy boat traffic on Active Passage, and the lighthouse on Mayne Island—is now a top destination in the Gulf Islands. Unique in the islands, the Galiano Inn is just a 5-minute stroll from the ferry dock, so guests can leave the car on the mainland. Each of the large, very plush rooms has a fireplace, a patio or balcony with stunning water views, and soaker or spa therapy tubs in addition to glass-walled showers. One room is wheelchair accessible. The deluxe Villa suites have large terraces, outdoor wood-burning fireplaces, outdoor baths, and outdoor grills in addition to upscale full kitchens. The **eat** restaurant, with notable regional cuisine (see review below), is in a separate, even more stunning building filled with Northwest Native art; **Madrona del Mar Spa,** a complete beauty and wellness center, shares the waterfront building.

134 Madrona Dr., Galiano Island, BC V0N 1P0. ② **877/530-3939** or 250/539-3388. Fax 250/539-3338. www.galianoinn.com. 20 units. C$249–C$299 double, includes full breakfast; C$425 Villa suite, breakfast not included. MC, V. Free parking. **Amenities:** Restaurant; lounge; golf course nearby; outdoor Jacuzzi; room service; kayak/boat rentals nearby; gardens; wine shop. *In room:* TV/DVD, CD player, fridge, hair dryer, minibar, Wi-Fi, robes.

Where to Dine

The convivial **Daystar Market Café** (② **250/539-2800**) is just north of Sturdies Bay at the intersection of Georgeson Bay and Porlier Pass roads. Part of an organic- and health-food store, it serves mostly vegetarian meals for lunch and dinner daily. **Montague Café,** at the Montague Harbour Marina (© **250/539-5733**), offers light dining right on the water. **Hummingbird Pub,** 47 Sturdies Bay Rd. (© **250/539-5472**), is a friendly, woodsy spot for beer and a burger.

eat ★★ CONTEMPORARY CANADIAN   This gorgeous dining room in the Galiano Oceanfront Inn has one of the best views in the Gulf Islands, overlooking the harbor and ferry traffic on Active Pass: A nine-sided post-and-beam room with glass walls lets you take it all in. The small, focused menu, featuring wild salmon, local crab, and island lamb, is enhanced with seasonal fish, shellfish, and produce bought directly from farmers and fishers, who just may deliver their goods to the pier outside the dining room. Much thought goes into the wine list, which is full of unusual choices from local micro-wineries (there are over 25 on the islands). The goal—amply reached—is to wed island wines and regional ingredients into a unique expression of Gulf Islands cuisine. In summer months, lunch and dinner are served on the patio, which is flanked by a wood-fired pizza oven.

134 Madrona Dr. © **250/539-3388.** www.galianoinn.com. Reservations suggested. Main courses C$18–C$30. MC, V. Dinner daily from 5:30pm; lunch served July to Labour Day only. Call for hours.

MAYNE ISLAND

Bucolic Mayne Island is a medley of rock-lined bays, forested hills, and pastureland. Mayne was once a center of Gulf Island agriculture, noted for its apple and tomato production. Many of the island's early farmhouses remain, and a rural, lived-in quality is one of Mayne's most endearing features.

GETTING THERE   **BC Ferries** serves Mayne Island with regularly scheduled runs from both Tsawwassen and Swartz Bay. **Harbour Air, Tofino Air,** and **Seair Seaplanes** all offer floatplane service between Mayne and Vancouver. For contact information, see p. 132.

VISITOR INFORMATION   Contact the **Mayne Island Community Chamber of Commerce,** Box 2, Mayne Island, BC V0N 2J0 (no phone; www.mayneislandchamber.ca).

Exploring the Island

Miner's Bay is by default the commercial center of the island, though in most locales this somewhat aimless collection of homes and businesses wouldn't really qualify as a village. It's this understated approach to life that provides Mayne Island with its substantial charm. Don't let the rural patina fool you: Some of the lodgings and restaurants are world-class, and even though organized activities are few, it's hard to be bored on such a lovely island.

Mayne doesn't boast the provincial parks and public lands that the other Gulf Islands do, though there are several beach-access sites that provide opportunities for swimming in warm weather and beachcombing during other times of the year. **Bennett Bay,** on the northeast coast, is the best swimming beach. **Campbell Bay,** just northwest, is another favorite pebble beach. **Dinner Bay Park** is lovely for a picnic.

On a sunny day, the grounds of the **Georgina Point Lighthouse** offer dramatic views. Located on the island's northern tip, this lighthouse juts into Active Pass and overlooks the southern shores of Galiano Island, less than a mile away.

Mayne Island is home to a number of artists; the widely available map of the island lists more than 20 studios that are open to visitors.

BIKING   Mayne is one of the best islands for cyclists. The rolling hills provide plenty of challenges, yet the terrain is considerably less mountainous than that of the other islands. For rentals, contact **Mayne Island Kayaking,** below.

HIKING   The roads on Mayne are usually quiet enough that they can also serve as paths for hikers. Those looking for more solitude should consider **Mount Parke Regional Park,** off Fernhill Road in the center of the island. The park's best views reward those who take the 1-hour hike to Halliday Viewpoint.

KAYAKING   Mayne Island Kayaking (© **250/539-0439;** www.kayakmayneisland. com), at Seal Beach in Miner's Bay, rents kayaks starting at C$28 for 2 hours, or C$48 for a full day. The company will drop off kayaks at any of six launching points on the island, and, if you get stranded, will even pick up kayaks (and too-weary kayakers) from other destinations.

Where to Stay

Blue Vista Resort (Kids)   This venerable resort is that rare Gulf Island lodging: a place where kids and pets are welcome. On the warm eastern side of Mayne Island—close to beaches, kayaking, and hiking—the comfortable, unfussy cabins are a great value and come with full kitchen, deck, and barbecue; some have a fireplace. You have a choice of studio, one-, and two-bedroom cabins; one-bedroom units have ramps for wheelchair access. Blue Vista is also a great location for an active holiday, with sea-kayak rentals and tours into the new Gulf Islands National Park Reserve, plus bike rentals.

563 Arbutus Dr., Mayne Island, BC V0N 2J0. © **877/535-2424** or 250/539-2463. www.bluevistaresort. com. 9 units. C$85–C$99 studio; C$105–C$125 1-bedroom cottage; C$105–C$150 2-bedroom cottage. Extra person C$10. Off-season and weekly rates available. MC, V. Pets accepted in 2 cottages for C$10 per night. **Amenities:** Ferry pickup. *In room:* TV, kitchen, no phone.

Oceanwood Country Inn ★★   This luxury property is one of the best places to stay in the Gulf Islands. A gem of understated elegance, it has an excellent restaurant, attentive staff, spacious rooms with sumptuous furnishings, and just the right blend of comfortable formality and relaxed hospitality. All but one of the rooms have magnificent views of Navy Channel and Saturna Island. The original inn's rooms are smaller and less expensive, yet still comfortable and beautifully outfitted; two have balconies. The rooms in the newer wing are large, with private decks, two-person tubs, and fireplaces. The Wisteria Suite is a three-tiered unit with two bathrooms, multiple decks, and an outdoor soaker tub.

The inn's public rooms are equally impressive. Facing the gardens are a comfortable living room and library, separated by a double-sided fireplace. The dining room is one of the most sophisticated places to eat on the Gulf Islands (see below).

630 Dinner Bay Rd., Mayne Island, BC V0N 2J0. © **250/539-5074.** Fax 250/539-3002. www.oceanwood. com. 12 units. Mid-June to mid-Sept C$179–C$349; mid-Sept to mid-Dec and early Jan to mid-June C$139–C$259. Extra person C$25. Rates include full breakfast and afternoon tea. MC, V. **Amenities:** Restaurant; bar; free bikes; golf course nearby; Jacuzzi; sauna; Wi-Fi. *In room:* Hair dryer, no phone.

Where to Dine

Manna Bakery Café, on Fernhill Road in Miner's Bay's tiny strip mall (© **250/539-2323**), is the place to go for a cappuccino and fresh-baked cinnamon roll. Just above the marina in Miner's Bay, the **Springwater Lodge** (© **250/539-5521**) is a comfortably ramshackle pub/restaurant with great views; try the fish and chips.

Oceanwood Country Inn ★★ CONTEMPORARY CANADIAN   Refined yet robust, the cuisine at Oceanwood is one of the Gulf Islands' best expressions of up-to-date, full-flavored cooking. The chef unites the rich bounty of Northwest fish, meat, game, and produce in a daily-changing tableau of impressive tastes and textures. Try spring nettle soup with hazelnut–goat cheese mousse, or maple-glazed sea scallops on wild mushroom risotto. The dining room overlooks a lily pond and garden; the decor is handsome but unfussy.

630 Dinner Bay Rd. ℂ **250/539-5074.** www.oceanwood.com. Reservations required. 4-course prix-fixe menu C$55. MC, V. Daily, most sittings 6–8pm. Call for hours mid-Oct to late Mar.

THE PENDER ISLANDS

The Penders consist of North and South Pender islands, separated by a very narrow channel that's spanned by a one-lane bridge. North Pender is much more developed, though that's all relative out in the Gulf Islands. It has a rather startling housing development on its southwest side, a 1970s suburb plopped down on an otherwise rural island. Neither of the Penders seems to share the long-standing farming background of the other Gulf Islands, so except where it's developed, forests are thick and all-encompassing. The Penders do have some lovely beaches and public parks with good hiking trails. Toss in a handful of local artists, and you have the recipe for a tranquil island retreat.

GETTING THERE **BC Ferries** serves Pender Island with regularly scheduled runs from both Tsawwassen and Swartz Bay. The commuter airlines mentioned in previous sections also offer floatplane service to and from Vancouver. For more information, see p. 132.

VISITOR INFORMATION The **Pender Island Visitor Info Centre,** 2332 Otter Bay Rd. (ℂ/fax **250/629-6541**), is open from May 15 to September 2. Or check out the chamber of commerce website at www.penderislandchamber.com.

Exploring the Islands

Mount Norman Regional Park, which encompasses the northwest corner of South Pender Island, features hiking trails through old-growth forest to wilderness beaches and ridge-top vistas. Access to trails is just across the Pender Island bridge.

The extensive network of roads makes these islands good destinations for cyclists. Rentals are available at **Otter Bay Marina,** 2311 McKinnon Rd. (ℂ **250/629-3579**), where you'll also find **Mouat Point Kayaks** (ℂ **250/629-6939**). If beachcombing or sunning are more your style, try **Hamilton Beach** on the east side of North Pender, or **Medicine Beach** and the beaches along **Beaumont Marine Park,** both of which flank Bedwell Harbour.

Where to Stay

Inn on Pender Island (Kids) (Value) The Inn on Pender Island is the name given to an enterprising complex at the center of North Pender. Nine large, unfussy units are housed in a modern motel building. Pets and kids are welcome. These basic rooms are a real deal in the otherwise expensive Gulf Islands. Also part of the complex are three log cabins. Each has a kitchenette and deck; two have hot tubs. These, too, are a great value when you consider the sky's-the-limit prices of comparable lodgings. Likewise, the restaurant is a just-fine place to eat, with good Northwest cuisine.

4709 Canal Rd., N. Pender Island, BC V0N 2M0. ℂ **800/550-0172** or 250/629-3353. Fax 250/629-3167. www.innonpender.com. 12 units. C$89–C$99 lodge double; C$159 cabin. Children stay free in parent's room (C$10 per night if use of a cot is required). MC, V. Small pets allowed for C$2. **Amenities:** Restaurant; Jacuzzi. *In room:* TV/VCR, fridge, kitchenette (in cabins only).

Poets Cove Resort and Spa ★★★ This very impressive resort opened in 2004 on the former Bedwell Harbour Resort site, which served for many years as a rustic boating lodge and the Canadian Customs office for U.S. and Canadian pleasure-boat traffic.

Poets Cove is a classy and sprawling complex that includes a 22-room Arts and Crafts–style lodge complete with the upscale Susurrus Spa, fitness center, ballroom, casual restaurant/pub, and fine-dining restaurant, plus 15 cottages and nine luxury-apartment-like villas (several boast three bedrooms) with full kitchens, fireplaces, balconies or decks, and—in addition to indoor soaker tubs—outdoor hot tubs in many. Kayak and charter boat rental is just out your front door, or simply enjoy one of the two swimming pools (one for adults only). Poets Cove sets the gold standard for marina resorts in southwest British Columbia; you can't go wrong here.

9801 Spalding Rd., S. Pender Island, BC V0N 2M3. $\copyright$ **888/512-7638** or 250/629-2100. Fax 250/629-2110. www.poetscove.com. 46 units. C$189–C$299 double lodge room; C$339–C$449 2-bedroom villa; C$419–C$529 3-bedroom villa; C$359–C$519 2-bedroom cottage; C$489–C$699 3-bedroom cottage. Extra person C$25. AE, MC, V. **Amenities:** Restaurant; bar; executive level rooms; health club; 2 pools; sports equipment rental; tennis court; market w/beer and wine sales; marina. *In room:* TV/DVD, fridge, hair dryer, robes, fireplace, soaker tubs, balcony or patio.

Sahhali Oceanfront Luxury B&B ★★ Views from this clifftop B&B are among the best in the Gulf Islands, taking in the San Juan Islands, Victoria, and the distant Olympic Mountains in a single wide-frame glance. In keeping with the extravagance of the view are the superlative comforts of this friendly B&B, complete with extras you expect only in high-end hotels. This architecturally significant structure was purpose-built as a B&B, with an expansive floor plan that makes the most of its aerie-like location. Each suite and the cottage have a wood-burning fireplace, private deck, and hot tub.

5915 Pirates Rd., Pender Island, BC V0N 2M2. $\copyright$ **888/724-4254** or 250/629-3756. www.sahhalibandb.com. 3 units. C$275–C$325 double, including breakfast; C$210–C$265 cottage, breakfast not included. Minimum stays may apply. AE, MC, V. **Amenities:** Rental bikes. *In room:* TV/DVD, fridge, hair dryer, full kitchen (cottage only), microwave, wet bar.

Where to Dine

Aurora ★★ PACIFIC NORTHWEST The swank dining room at Poets Cove Resort combines excellent food, a romantic setting, and terrific views—this is easily the most sophisticated place to eat on the Penders. Unsurprisingly, the menu features local fish and shellfish, including oysters on the half shell, wild salmon and halibut, and other seasonal fish specials. Local lamb is also a standout, and pan-seared arctic char is served with vanilla parsnip puree and braised spinach. One wall of the warmly formal dining room is dominated by a huge stone fireplace, and another by a bank of wine bottles, but you'll spend more time taking in the lovely view of the harbor and islands. Casual dining is also available in Syrens Lounge, which opens onto a voluminous patio.

In Poets Cove Resort and Spa, 9801 Spalding Rd. $\copyright$ **250/629-2100.** Reservations recommended. Main courses C$27–C$35. AE, MC, V. Mon–Fri 8am–2pm and 6–9pm; Sat 8–11am and 6–9pm; Sun 8am–1pm and 6–9pm.

Hope Bay Café ★★ NEW CANADIAN When the 1903 general store burned down a few years ago at Hope Bay, a tiny community perched above a rocky harbor, a group of island artists and merchants pooled resources to rebuild a new commercial center in this lovely waterfront spot. In the corner with the best views is the Hope Bay Café, a very pleasant, light-filled dining room whose informality veils some very serious and delicious cooking. It's a classic story: Big-city-trained chef (and his wife, a baker) comes to small community and cooks fantastic food. Get here before the crowds do. While the printed menu is small, and includes dishes such as pan-seared black cod with

sweet pea cream or pistachio-crusted halibut, the real attractions are the specials that vary
seasonally as local ingredients become available.

4301 Bedwell Harbour Rd. (Ⓒ **250/629-6668.** Main courses C$16–C$26. MC, V. Wed–Fri 11am–3pm and
5–8pm; Sat–Sun 10am–3pm and 5–8pm.

SATURNA ISLAND

The most remote of the southern Gulf Islands served by ferries, Saturna is both pristine
and, compared with its neighbors, mostly vacant (pop. 350). Whereas other islands are
best described as rural, Saturna is truly wild. It's not surprising that the new Gulf Islands
National Park Reserve has its largest presence on Saturna: About half the island is now
protected as reserve land.

Served by direct ferries from Swartz Bay and a few indirect sailings from Tsawwassen,
Saturna is hard to get to. It's easiest to ferry to Vancouver Island and then back out, or
over to Pender Island, which has direct sailings to Saturna. If you are planning to visit all
the Gulf Islands, start your journey on Saturna; it's easier to get away from Saturna by
ferry than it is to get to it.

Any visit to Saturna should include a stop at **Saturna Island Family Estate Winery**
(Ⓒ **877/918-3388** or 250/539-3521), a small, well-established winery in an extremely
dramatic setting. Perched between massive cliffs and the sea, the setting is reminiscent of
Corsica. The tasting room, open daily 11am to 4:30pm from May to October, is reached
by a precipitous single-track road with a 20% grade. The tasting room bistro also offers
soups and salads for lunch.

Its remoteness makes Saturna a favorite destination of outdoorsy types. The island
boasts nice beaches, including Russell Reef, Veruna Bay, and Shell Beach at **East Point
Park.** This park, with its still-active lighthouse, is a good spot to watch for orcas. Hikers
can drive to **Mount Warburton Pike ★** and follow the **Brown Ridge Nature Trail.**
Views from this craggy cliff-faced peak are astonishing, taking in southern Vancouver
Island, the San Juan Islands, and the Olympic Peninsula. Kayakers can explore the rocky
islets surrounding **Tumbo Island,** just offshore from Saturna's eastern peninsula. Facilities are few and far between, though in several cases, exemplary. For more information,
check out **www.saturnatourism.com**.

Where to Stay & Dine

At press time, the restaurant at the Saturna Lodge had closed, perhaps to open again
when the economy revives. In the meantime, lunch is available at the winery (above);
diners can also turn to the deli and cafe at the **Saturna General Store,** 101 Narvaez Bay
Rd. (Ⓒ **250/539-2936**), open Thursday through Saturday in summer, and the **Lighthouse Pub,** at the ferry terminal (Ⓒ **250/539-5725**), open daily in summer. Be sure to
inquire about current dining options when making reservations—and bring a picnic
hamper just in case.

Saturna Lodge ★   This well-established resort, which began its life as a 1940s boardinghouse, has been revamped into a very comfortable, upscale bed-and-breakfast. If your
idea of an island getaway is seclusion and genteel comfort, this is your lodging. Set amid
gardens, with views onto Boot Cove, the lodge has taken on a winery theme—each of
the charming guest rooms is named for a wine or grape varietal. The top of the line is the
Sauterne Room, a large suite with soaker tub, private deck, and king-size bed. Families
will like the suite of ground-floor rooms with private entrances, where a twin-bed room
and a queen room share a large bathroom. The attractive main-floor lounge overlooks the
gardens and has a fireplace, small library, and television.

130 Payne Rd., Saturna Island, BC V0N 2Y0. ℂ **866/539-2254** or 250/539-2254. Fax 250/539-2254. www. saturna.ca. 6 units. C$89–C$169 double. Rates include breakfast. Special packages available. MC, V. Closed Dec–Feb. No pets. **Amenities:** Guest lounge w/books, videos, and board games. *In room:* Hair dryer, no phone, Wi-Fi, robes.

3 WEST OF VICTORIA: SOOKE & BEYOND

Sooke: 30km (19 miles) W of Victoria

Following Hwy. 14 west from Victoria, the suburbs eventually thin; by the time you reach Sooke, the vistas open up to the south, where Washington's Olympic Mountains prop up the horizon. There are a number of reasons to explore this part of the island.

Hwy. 14 gives access to beaches and parks with good swimming and recreation, finally leading to Port Renfrew, a rough-and-ready deep-sea fishing village that's also the southern trail head for the famous West Coast Trail (see chapter 8). Day-trippers from Vancouver also come out to visit **Botanical Beach Provincial Park** ★, an area with spectacular tide-pool formations, unique geology, and one of the richest intertidal zones on the entire North American West Coast. About 4km (2½ miles) south of Port Renfrew, Botanical Beach is a ledge of sandstone that juts out into the churning waters of the Strait of Juan de Fuca. Over the millennia, tidal action has carved out pits and pools, in which you'll find sea urchins, clams, periwinkles, giant anemones, chitons, and sea stars. In spring and fall, watch for gray whales in the strait. Check local tide tables to maximize opportunities for wildlife-viewing and tide-pool exploration: A low tide of 1.2m (4 ft.) or less is best. Picnic facilities and toilets are available.

Ambitious backcountry drivers can make a loop journey from Hwy. 14. From Port Renfrew, a good logging road leads up the San Juan River valley, connecting to the southern shores of Cowichan Lake just west of Duncan. You can make this drive in 1 day, or divide the trip up by planning to spend the night camping at Cowichan Lake or at one of Duncan's moderately priced hotels.

The civilized reason to make the journey west from Victoria is the superlative Sooke Harbour House, one of the most renowned small inns in all of Canada.

IN & AROUND SOOKE

The little town of Sooke doesn't offer a lot to divert the visitor, but there are a number of recreation areas nearby that warrant a stop. **Sooke Potholes Provincial Park** preserves a curious geologic formation. The Sooke River flows down a series of rock ledges, pooling in waist-deep swimming holes before dropping in waterfalls to another series of pools and waterfalls. In July and August, the normally chilly river water warms up. The trails that link the pools are nice for a casual hike. There are more trails in adjacent **Sooke Mount Provincial Park.** To reach these parks, drive west on Route 14 almost to the town of Sooke; turn right on Sooke River Road. Fifteen kilometers (9⅓ miles) west of Sooke is **French Beach Park,** a sand-and-gravel beach that's one of the best places to watch for gray whales. The park has 69 campsites.

Where to Stay

Markham House B&B and Honeysuckle Cottage ★★ On the outskirts of Sooke, nestled in the woods, sits this admirably well-executed Tudor-style home on 4 hectares (10 acres) of landscaped grounds. The rooms are outfitted with antiques, featherbeds, and duvets. The cottage has its own kitchenette, wood stove, and hot tub. The main house features an elegant parlor with fireplace, plus a hot tub. Breakfasts are sumptuous and healthy. Outside, you can sit by the trout pond, play bocce, or practice your golf swing on the minifairway and green. Of course, you may also want to head out to the water or explore the region's parks, and your gracious hosts will help you make plans.

1775 Connie Rd., Sooke, BC V9Z 1C8. ℂ **888/256-6888** or 250/642-7542. Fax 250/642-7538. www.markhamhouse.com. 4 units. July–Sept and mid-Dec to Jan 3 C$120–C$250 double; Oct to mid-Dec and Jan 4–June C$105–C$185 double. Rates include full breakfast, turndown service, and afternoon tea on day of arrival. AE, DC, DISC, MC, V. From Victoria, take Hwy. 1 north, then exit 14 to Veteran's Memorial Pkwy. (Hwy. 14 S.) toward Sooke. Turn right on Hwy. 14 W. (Sooke Rd.) to Connie Rd. Approx. 25km (16 miles) from Victoria. Pets allowed in cottage. Children 16 and older welcome. **Amenities:** Golf course nearby; Jacuzzi; pool, badminton; croquet; gazebo. *In room:* TV/VCR/DVD, Wi-Fi, robes, fireplace.

Point-No-Point Resort ★   Get away from it all in your own little cabin on the ocean, with 16 hectares (40 acres) of wilderness around you, a wide, rugged beach in front of you, and nothing to do but laze the day away in your hot tub. This resort has been welcoming guests since 1952. All cabins have fireplaces and kitchens; newer ones have hot tubs and decks, and two are wheelchair accessible. Lunch and dinner are available in the sunny dining room; its tables are conveniently equipped with binoculars, so you won't miss a bald eagle as you eat. The food is exceptional: Think grilled wild salmon with fava beans, or duck confit with apricots and ginger.

1505 West Coast Hwy. (Hwy. 14), Sooke, BC V0S 1N0. ℂ **250/646-2020.** Fax 250/646-2294. www.pointnopointresort.com. 25 units. C$165–C$260 cabin double. 2- or 3-night minimum stay on weekends and holidays. Off-season rates available. Summer fishing packages available. AE, MC, V. Free parking. 64km (40 miles) west of Victoria. Pets allowed for C$10 per night and C$100 refundable dog deposit. No children in cabins with hot tubs. **Amenities:** Restaurant/teahouse; rooms for those w/limited mobility. *In room:* Kitchen, no phone.

Sooke Harbour House ★★★   This inn at the foot of a beautiful pebble-and-sand spit, 30km (19 miles) west of Victoria, has earned an international reputation for the warmth of its welcome, the quality of its food and lodging, and the drama of its vistas. Each individually decorated suite boasts a fireplace, bathrobes, antiques, fresh flowers, and views of the water—most have unusual nooks and corners that make them unique. The three top-floor rooms, very spacious suites with 6m (20-ft.) cathedral ceilings and beautiful furnishings, are perfect for romantic getaways. All but one of the rooms have decks overlooking the inn's splendid gardens and onto Sooke Harbour, where otters swim and dive, and many have Jacuzzis with a waterfront view. Massages and spa treatments can be arranged by appointment. The entire inn is absolutely filled with art—in fact, the quantity of art in Sooke Harbour House's common spaces makes it one of the largest public art collections on Vancouver Island. The extensive gardens, which grow many of the herbs and flowers that appear on your dinner table, are also fascinating; the gardener leads tours each morning. Sooke Harbour House has one of the best restaurants in Canada (see "Where to Dine," below).

1528 Whiffen Spit Rd., Sooke, BC V9Z 0T4. ℂ **800/889-9688** or 250/642-3421. Fax 250/642-6988. www.sookeharbourhouse.com. 28 units. July–Sept C$399–C$639 double; Jan 2–Mar C$259–C$479; Apr–June C$289–C$489 double; Oct–Dec 22 C$285–C$505; Dec 23–Jan 1 C$309–C$489. Rates include breakfast. Children 5 and under stay free in parent's room. AE, MC, V. Free parking. Take the Island Hwy. (Hwy. 1) to the Sooke/Colwood turnoff (junction Hwy. 14). Follow Hwy. 14 to Sooke. About 1.6km (1 mile) past the town's 3rd traffic light, turn left onto Whiffen Spit Rd. Pets allowed for C$40 per night for first pet, additional C$20 nightly for each additional pet. **Amenities:** Restaurant; babysitting; bike rentals; concierge; room service; spa services; garden tours; art gallery; 2 rooms for those w/limited mobility. *In room:* Fridge, hair dryer, Jacuzzi, steam shower.

7

(Moments) Hiking the Juan de Fuca Marine Trail

This long-distance hiking trail links China Beach Park, just past the town of Jordan River, to Botanical Beach Provincial Park, near Port Renfrew, along a stretch of near-wilderness coastline. Similar to the famed West Coast Trail but less extreme, the rugged 47km (29-mile) trail offers scenic beauty, spectacular hiking, wildlife-viewing, and roaring surf in its course along the Pacific coastline of the Strait of Juan de Fuca. Most of the trail is designed for strenuous day or multiday hiking. Unlike the West Coast Trail, it can be easily broken down into daylong segments between trail heads accessed along Hwy. 14: China Beach, Sombrio Beach, Parkinson Creek, and Botanical Beach. Plan on 3 days to hike the entire length; campsites are regularly spaced along the trail.

Conditions are always changing, so obtain up-to-date information before proceeding by checking the trail-head information shelters. If you're camping, keep a tide chart handy and refer to trail-head postings about points that will be impassable at high tide. Wear proper footwear—the trail gets very muddy—and appropriate clothing, plus rain gear if you're going to camp. And leave a plan of your trip (including which trail you're hiking), with arrival and departure times, with a friend or relative. Also, don't leave a car full of valuables in the trail-head parking lots—break-ins are common.

For information on Juan de Fuca Marine Park, contact **BC Parks,** South Vancouver Island District, 2930 Trans-Canada Hwy., Victoria, BC V9E 1K3 (☎ **250/391-2300;** www.env.gov.bc.ca/bcparks).

Where to Dine

On a long summer's evening, consider driving to beautiful and remote **Point-No-Point Resort** (see above) 64km (40 miles) west of Victoria, with its intimate dining room and savory regional specialties. Reservations are a must; main courses are C$22 to C$36.

17 Mile House PUB   For inexpensive but reliable fare, the 17 Mile House has the most character in the area. Built in the late 1800s, this establishment became a regional hub in the 1920s when it installed the only phone around. Today, you can sup on a nice salad, burger, or one of many pasta, meat, or seafood entrees while admiring the old wood, brick, and tile interior. You might tap out a tune on the pub's 150-year-old piano or settle for a game of billiards; Saturdays feature live music.

5126 Sooke Rd. ☎ 250/642-5942. www.17milehouse.com. Main courses C$8–C$24. Sun–Thurs 11am–11pm; Fri–Sat 11am–midnight. MC, V. On Sooke Rd. (Hwy. 14) btw. Connie Rd. and Gillespie Rd. Victoria bus 61.

Sooke Harbour House ★★★ NORTHWEST COAST   Acclaimed as one of the best restaurants in Canada, Sooke Harbour House treats you to a sensual culinary experience using almost all local ingredients, with an emphasis on the tastes of the Pacific Northwest and the produce of the inn's own gardens. The restaurant is situated at the rear of the inn, a rambling white house on a bluff, and offers a quiet atmosphere with spectacular views. The four-course prix-fixe menu may include such choices as duck confit with balsamic syrup and roasted shallot sauce, roasted garlic polenta and oxeye daisy and apple salad, smoked salmon with nasturtium-leaf puree, or rack of lamb marinated with coriander and juniper berry and served with quince sage syrup. With advance notice, the kitchen will prepare a seven- to nine-course gastronomic tasting menu for C$120. If you're ready for a splurge, the sommelier will pick a by-the-glass pairing for each dish from a wine list that's one of *Wine Spectator*'s "best in the world." The dining room is also open Sundays for a la carte lunch.

1528 Whiffen Spit Rd. (𝄢 **250/642-3421.** www.sookeharbourhouse.com. Reservations required. Prix-fixe 4-course menu C$75. Sun lunch main courses C$13–C$15. AE, MC, V. Daily 5–9pm (may close Tues–Wed in midwinter; call to confirm). Take the Island Hwy. to the Sooke/Colwood turnoff (junction Hwy. 14). Continue on Hwy. 14 to Sooke. Approx. 1.5km (1 mile) past the town's 3rd traffic light, turn left onto Whiffen Spit Rd.

4 NORTH OF VICTORIA: GOLDSTREAM PROVINCIAL PARK ★

North of Victoria, the Island Highway climbs up over the high mountain ridge called the Malahat, shedding the suburbs as it climbs. Goldstream Provincial Park is a tranquil arboreal setting that overflowed with prospectors during the 1860s gold-rush days, hence its name. Today, its natural beauty attracts hikers, campers, and birders who stop to spend a few hours or days in the beautiful temperate rainforest.

Hiking trails take you past abandoned mine shafts and tunnels as well as stands of Douglas fir, lodgepole pine, red cedar, indigenous yew, and arbutus trees. The **Gold Mine Trail** leads to Niagara Creek and the abandoned mine. The **Goldstream Trail** goes to the salmon-spawning areas (you might also catch sight of mink and river otters racing along this path).

Three species of salmon make **annual salmon runs** up the Goldstream River during the months of October, November, December, and February. Visitors can easily observe this natural wonder along the riverbanks. Goldstream is also a major attraction for bird-watchers, as numerous bald eagles winter here each year. January is the best month for spotting these majestic creatures.

For information on all provincial parks on the South Island, contact **BC Parks** (𝄢 **250/391-2300;** www.env.gov.bc.ca/bcparks). Goldstream Park's **Freeman King Visitor Centre** (𝄢 **250/478-9414**) offers guided walks and talks, plus programs geared toward kids throughout the year. It's open daily from 9:30am to 6pm; there is a C$3 per day vehicle fee. Take Hwy. 1 about 20 minutes north of Victoria.

WHERE TO STAY

The Aerie Resort and Spa ★★ It's safe to say, there's nothing else on Vancouver Island like this Relais & Châteaux member, which is designed to accommodate the most discriminating—even extravagant—tastes. The Aerie is a Mediterranean-style villa resort with opulent rooms and suites, dining rooms, and spa facilities scattered amid 14 hectares (35 acres) of gardens and fir forest. Austrian-born owner Maria Schuster dreamed of transporting the style and grandeur of private estates along the French and Italian Riviera to the Pacific Northwest. The result is a series of neo-Palladian villas boasting sumptuous furnishings and top-of-the-line designer decor. King suites have balconies, fireplaces, and Jacuzzi or soaker tubs; others are two stories. Suites in the unparalleled Villa Cielo development are in a newer building even higher up the mountain, making it more private and attractive to celebrities. Facilities include a helipad, a spa offering a variety of treatments, and an outdoor wedding chapel. Most guests also sample the excellent cuisine in the dining room (see below).

600 Ebedora Lane, P.O. Box 108, Malahat, BC V0R 2L0. ✆ **800/518-1933** or 250/743-7115. Fax 250/743-4766. 29 units. From C$195 double; from C$259 suites. Rates include a full breakfast. Packages available. AE, DC, MC, V. Free parking. Take Hwy. 1 north to the Spectacle Lake turnoff; take the 1st right and follow the winding driveway up. **Amenities:** Restaurant; lounge; concierge; indoor pool; room service; full-service spa; tennis court. *In room:* A/C, TV (VCRs available), fridge, hair dryer, minibar, Wi-Fi.

WHERE TO DINE

The Peak Dining Room at the Aerie ★★ FRENCH/NORTHWEST The dining room of this villa boasts panoramic views, a gold-leaf ceiling, chandeliers, and faux-marble columns. If you like formal service and innovative cuisine, there are few better restaurants in western Canada. Consider, for example, lime-scented papaya and Dungeness crab terrine with white gazpacho, or poached halibut with quince and grapefruit bouillon and rhubarb foam. If you like this kind of cutting-edge cuisine, consider the five-course Discovery Tasting Menu (C$85), where the chef's imagination really takes flight. An excellent selection of brandies and coffee drinks will take you over the peak and down the far side.

600 Ebedora Lane, Malahat. ✆ **250/743-7115.** Reservations required. Main courses C$35–C$42. AE, DC, MC, V. Daily 11am–2pm and 5:30–9pm. Free parking. Take Hwy. 1 to the Spectacle Lake turnoff; take the 1st right and follow the winding driveway.

Six Mile Pub PUB The Six Mile was popular with sailors when the Esquimalt Naval Base opened nearby in 1864, then became the hub for provincial bootleggers during Prohibition. With a lively bar and intimate dining rooms, it still has broad appeal. You can enjoy the ambience of the fireside room, which has an oak bar with stained glass, or the beautiful scenery from the patio. The food is seasoned with fresh herbs from the garden. Start with one of the house brews; then move on to a juicy prime rib or tasty veggie burger.

494 Island Hwy., View Royal. ✆ **250/474-3663.** www.sixmilepub.com. Main courses C$7–C$16. AE, DC, MC, V. Mon–Thurs 11am–midnight; Fri–Sat 11am–1am; Sun 10am–11pm. At the View Royal/Colwood exit off Island Hwy., approx. 10km (6¼ miles) north of Victoria.

5 DUNCAN & THE COWICHAN VALLEY

Duncan: 57km (35 miles) N of Victoria

The Cowichan Valley is one of the richest agricultural areas on Vancouver Island. The Cowichan Indians have lived in the valley for millennia, and today the band's reservation spreads immediately to the south of the town of Duncan. European settlers, drawn by the valley's deep soil and warm temperatures, established farms here in the 1870s. Although the orchards and sheep pastures of yore remain, the valley's providential location also makes it one of the few sites in western British Columbia for vineyards, a new and booming crop.

For visitors, the town of Duncan, at the center of the valley, may seem a pretty low-key place, but its centrality to excellent recreation and cultural sights makes it a comfortable hub for exploring this part of Vancouver Island. Cowichan Lake is a popular summertime getaway, with swimming beaches and boating. Maple Bay and Cowichan

Bay are marina-dominated harbor towns with good pubs and restaurants, plus enchanting views. And don't forget those wineries: Cowichan Valley is home to several good ones, most with tasting rooms open to the public.

ESSENTIALS

GETTING THERE   Duncan is 57km (35 miles) north of Victoria on Hwy. 1. It's also a stop on the **E&N Railiner.** For information, contact **VIA Rail** (© 888/VIA-RAIL [842-7245] or 250/383-4324; www.viarail.ca). **Vancouver Island Coach Lines** (© **250/388-5248,** or book through Greyhound © **800/661-8747;** www.greyhound. ca) offers bus transport from Victoria to Duncan. A one-way fare from Victoria to Duncan is C$18.

VISITOR INFORMATION   The **Duncan Visitor Information Centre,** 381A Trans-Canada Hwy. (© **250/746-4636**), is open from April 15 to October 15. Online, go to **www.city.duncan.bc.ca.** For year-round information on the entire valley, contact the **Cowichan Tourism Association,** 25 Canada Ave., Duncan (© **888/303-3337;** www. cowichan.bc.ca).

EXPLORING THE AREA
Duncan: The City of Totem Poles

Duncan is a welcoming city of 5,300, with a mix of First Nations peoples and descendants of European settlers. Congested Hwy. 1 runs to the east of the old town center, and you'll miss Duncan's old-fashioned charm if you don't get off the main drag (follow signs for Old Town Duncan).

Downtown Duncan still bustles with stationers, dress shops, bakeries, haberdasheries, cafes, candy shops—it's the quintessential small and friendly Canadian town. The main reason to make a detour downtown is to see the city's impressive collection of modern **totem poles.** The First Nations peoples of this region are famed for their carving skills. However, most historic totem poles are now in museums or are rotting in front of abandoned villages, and for a long time few First Nations artists had any reason to keep the old skills and traditions alive. In the 1980s, the mayor of Duncan began an ambitious project of commissioning local First Nations artists to carve new totem poles, which were then erected around the city. Today, with more than 80 totem poles rising above the downtown area, Duncan's public art is one of the world's largest collections of modern totem carving, a wonderful assemblage that represents the continuation of an ancient art form unique to the Northwest coast.

The totem poles are scattered around the city, mostly in the pedestrian-friendly downtown area: Simply follow the yellow shoe-prints on the pavement. You can also take a free guided tour, which starts from in front of the Cowichan Valley Museum, at the E&N Railway station, Station Street and Canada Avenue. The tours are given from May to mid-September, Tuesday through Saturday, from 10am to 4pm. Reserve for groups of five or more by calling the **Duncan Business Improvement Area Society** (© **250/715-1700**).

The B.C. Forest Discovery Centre (Kids)   This 41-hectare (101-acre) site explores the history of the logging industry. Over the years, the focus of the exhibits has shifted from an unreflective paean to tree cutting to a more thoughtful examination of sustainable forestry practices, woodland ecosystems, and the role (sometimes surprising) of wood products in our lives. No matter what you may think of logging as a practice, the history of forestry in British Columbia is fascinating, and this museum does a good job of presenting both the high and low points. Kids will love the vintage steam train, which circles the grounds on narrow-gauge rails.

2892 Drinkwater Rd., 2km (1¼ miles) north of Duncan on Hwy. 1 (near Somenos Lake). *©* **250/715-1113.** www.bcforestmuseum.com. Admission C$14 adults, C$12 seniors and students 13–18, C$9 children 5–12. June to Labour Day daily 10am–5pm; mid-Apr to May and Labour Day to mid-Oct Thurs–Mon 10am–4pm.

Quw'utsun' Cultural Centre ★ The Cowichan (Quw'utsun') people were the original inhabitants of this valley, and the tribe's cultural history and traditional way of life are the focus of Quw'utsun' Centre, on the southern edge of downtown Duncan ("Quw'utsun'" means "warming your back in the sun"). The parklike enclosure along the Cowichan River contains several modern longhouse structures flanked by totem poles. Join a guided tour of the village, or take a seat in the theater to watch the excellent presentation *The Great Deeds,* a retelling of Cowichan myth and history. At the building devoted to traditional carving, you can talk to carvers as they work, and even take up a chisel yourself.

The Cowichan tribes are famous for their bulky sweaters, knit with bold motifs from hand-spun raw wool. The gallery at Quw'utsun' is the best place in the valley to buy these sweaters (expect to pay around C$250), as well as carvings, prints, jewelry, and books. In summer, the cafe serves traditional foods. Thursday through Saturday in July and August, there's a midday alder-planked salmon barbecue feast with drumming and storytelling. Call ahead for details.

200 Cowichan Way. *©* **877/746-8119** or 250/746-8119. www.quwutsun.ca. Admission C$15 adults, C$12 seniors and students 13–17, C$8 children 12 and under and First Nations individuals. Daily Apr–Sept 10am–5pm.

Cowichan Bay

This small but busy port town edges along the mouth of the Cowichan River. Many visitors come to walk the boardwalks and admire the boats amid the sounds, smells, and sights of a working harborside village, just 7km (4⅓ miles) southeast of Duncan. The **Cowichan Bay Maritime Centre,** 1761 Cowichan Bay Rd. (*©* **250/746-4955;** www.classicboats.org), tells the story of the clash of Native and European cultures in the Cowichan Valley. It also serves as a workshop for the building of wooden boats. Hours are daily from 9am to dusk between April and October, with admission by donation. Be sure to stop at **Hilary's Cheese Company** and **True Grain Bread,** sharing space at 1725 Cowichan Bay Rd. (*©* **250/746-7664**). This outlet for local farm cheeses and artisanal and organic bread makes a perfect stop for outfitting a picnic.

KAYAKING **Cowichan Bay Kayak and Paddlesports,** 1765 Cowichan Bay Rd. (*©* **888/749-2333** or 250/748-2333; www.cowichanbaykayak.com), offers kayak rentals and guided tours from the docks on Cowichan Bay. A 3-hour paddle around the Cowichan River estuary with a stop at Genoa Bay is C$49. A 2-hour single kayak rental is C$25.

WHALE-WATCHING **Ocean Ecoventures,** 1745 Cowichan Bay Rd. (*©* **866/748-5333** or 250/748-3800; www.oceanecoventures.com), offers year-round, 3- to 4-hour whale-watching trips on 7m (23-ft.) rigid-hull inflatable boats. You're almost guaranteed to see orcas, and chances are good that you'll also see gray whales, harbor and Dall porpoises, sea lions, and bald eagles. Trips are C$109 adults and C$79 children 12 and under.

Maple Bay & Genoa Bay

Maple Bay is a lovely harbor town 7km (4⅓ miles) northeast of Duncan. Take Tzouhalem Road east to Maple Bay Road; then head northeast. Although not a major destination, it's worth the short drive just to take in the view—a placid bay of water beneath steep-sloped mountains. Ponder the vista at the **Brigantine Inn** ★, on Beaumont Avenue (© **250/746-5422**), a friendly pub with local brews and a bayside deck. If you're into **diving,** Maple Bay is worth exploring—it's said to have been one of Jacques Cousteau's favorite dive spots.

Genoa Bay is directly south of Maple Bay. This tiny harbor is actually on Cowichan Bay, though the mountainous terrain mandates that overland transport make a circuitous route around Mount Tzouhalem. Again, the point of the journey is the charm of the location. Enjoy a drink or a meal at the **Genoa Bay Cafe** (see "Where to Dine," below), a floating restaurant in the midst of extraordinary visual wonder.

Cowichan Valley Vineyards

The warm summers and mild winters of the Cowichan Valley make this one of the few areas in western British Columbia where wine grapes flourish. Pinot noir, pinot gris, Marechal Foch, and Gewürztraminer are popular varietals. The following wineries welcome guests, and most will arrange tours with sufficient notice. For more information, see **www.wineislands.ca**.

Blue Grouse Vineyards and Winery, 4365 Blue Grouse Rd., south of Duncan, off Lakeside Road near Koksilah Road (© **250/743-3834;** www.bluegrousevineyards.com), is open for tastings from 11am to 5pm Wednesday through Sunday from April to September, Wednesday through Saturday October through December, and Saturdays only January through March.

Cherry Point Vineyards, 840 Cherry Point Rd., near Telegraph Road southeast of Cowichan Bay in eastern Cobble Hill (© **250/743-1272;** www.cherrypointvineyards. com), is one of the most prominent Cowichan Valley wineries, with national awards to prove it. The tasting room is open daily from 10am to 5pm; with a bistro open for lunch May through September.

Zanatta Winery and Vineyards, 5039 Marshall Rd., south of Duncan near Glenora (© **250/748-2338;** www.zanatta.ca), is open April through early October, Wednesday through Sunday from noon to 4:30pm. It's open the same hours the rest of October through December, but on weekends only. Its restaurant, Vinoteca, is open Wednesday through Sunday, noon to 3pm, from April through early October, weekends only November to December.

Another twist on the local scene is **Merridale Cider,** 1230 Merridale Rd., Cobble Hill, west of Hwy. 1 (© **800/998-9908** or 250/743-4293; www.merridalecider.com), which produces both apple and pear cider. Tastings are available daily 10:30am to 5:30pm. In addition, meals are available at **La Pommeraie Bistro** Monday through Sunday from 11:30am to 4pm.

Cowichan Lake, Cowichan River & the Backcountry

Cowichan Lake, 28km (17 miles) west of Duncan on Hwy. 18, is a long, narrow lake nestled between mountain slopes. With an area population of about 3,000, the lake is one of the primary summer playgrounds for valley residents. A number of provincial parks provide access to swimming beaches, boat landings, and campsites; **Gordon Provincial Park,** on the lake's south shore, is the most convenient for Duncan-based travelers.

Backcountry explorers can follow the roads along both sides of 30km-long (19-mile) Cowichan Lake to access remote areas of Vancouver Island's wilderness west coast. Well-maintained forestry roads from Cayuse and Honeymoon Bay, on the south side of the lake, lead to **Port Renfrew,** one of the starting points of Pacific Rim National Park's famed West Coast Trail (see "West of Victoria: Sooke & Beyond," earlier in this chapter, as well as chapter 8, "Central Vancouver Island"). From here, paved roads connect to Sooke and Victoria. From the west end of Cowichan Lake, gravel roads lead to **Nitinat Lake,** renowned for its windsurfing, and **Carmanah/Walbran Provincial Park,** a vast preserve of misty old-growth forests.

The Cowichan River flows east out of Cowichan Lake. The **Cowichan River Trail,** which passes through fern glades and forests, provides excellent access to the beautiful jade-green waters. The 20km (12-mile) hiking trail begins just east of Cowichan Lake (follow signs from Hwy. 18 for Skutz Falls Trailhead) and follows the river to Glenora, southeast of Duncan. The river is popular for steelhead and trout fishing, as well as kayaking. Some canyon rapids are considered too dangerous for passage; ask locally before setting out.

WHERE TO STAY
In & Around Duncan

Best Western Cowichan Valley Inn ★ This is Duncan's most comfortable full-service lodging, conveniently located for visiting the B.C. Forest Discovery Centre. Its handsomely furnished guest rooms come with numerous amenities. A wheelchair-accessible room is available. The hotel's restaurant, Choices, is one of the best family restaurants in Duncan, and the hotel's beer-and-wine shop is one of the best places in town to purchase local wines.

6474 Trans-Canada Hwy., Duncan, BC V9L 6C6. (*) **800/927-6199** or 250/748-2722. Fax 250/748-2207. www.cowichanvalleyinn.com. 42 units. C$161–C$191 double. Extra person C$10. Senior and AAA discounts available. AE, DC, DISC, MC, V. Free parking. Located 2km (1¼ miles) north of Duncan. Pets allowed with approval. Children 17 and under stay free in parent's room. **Amenities:** Restaurant; pub; exercise room; golf course nearby; outdoor pool; beer-and-wine store; volleyball court. *In room:* A/C, TV, fridge, hair dryer, Wi-Fi.

Fairburn Farm Culinary Retreat & Guesthouse ★ (Finds) If you dream of an idealized back-to-the-land farm vacation with a focus on exploring regional cuisine and wines, then this is your destination. Picturesque Fairburn Farm consists of a beautifully preserved farmhouse with handsome guestrooms and a cottage, with 53 working hectares (131 acres) plus forested areas with trails. In addition to cooking classes with guest chefs and special events, Fairburn Farm also offers dinner service to overnight guests on Thursday, Friday, and Saturday evenings. From late June through August, a 6-course Sunday lunch is served on the veranda; the C$85 price includes local wines. The focus of a stay at Fairburn Farm may be mushroom-hunting expeditions, bread-making forums, tours of local farms, vineyards, cideries, cheese-making operations, and trips to the Duncan farmers' market—one of the best in B.C.—to buy the freshest and most flavorful ingredients for dinner. Call ahead to find out what's on the calendar during your stay, as events are timed to the cycles of the seasons and harvest.

3310 Jackson Rd., Duncan, BC V9L 6N7. (*) **250/746-4637.** Fax 250/746-4317. www.fairburnfarm.bc.ca. 5 units. June–Sept C$165–C$190 guesthouse double; C$950 cottage per week (does not include breakfast). Lower off-season rates. Rates include breakfast. Extra person C$20. MC, V. Free parking. Closed Oct 15–Nov 15. **Amenities:** Common room. *In room:* No phone, Wi-Fi.

Travelodge Silver Bridge Inn   Its reasonably priced, well-maintained rooms make the Silver Bridge a good choice. One-bedroom suites have full kitchens; the honeymoon suite boasts a gas fireplace and double Jacuzzi. Located next to the Cowichan River, the motel is within walking distance of the Quw'utsun' Cultural Centre. The pub, with an attractive shaded deck, is in a converted century-old house.

140 Trans-Canada Hwy., Duncan, BC V9L 3P7. (☎) **888/858-2200** or 250/748-4311. Fax 250/748-1774. www.travelodgeduncan.com. 34 units. C$149–C$219 double. Extra person C$10. AAA, senior, weekly, group, and corporate rates available. AE, DC, MC, V. Free parking. Pets allowed for C$10 per night. **Amenities:** Restaurant; pub; golf course nearby; room service. *In room:* A/C, TV, fridge, hair dryer, Wi-Fi, microwave.

In Cowichan Bay

Dream Weaver B&B ★   This handsome Victorianesque structure with wraparound porch is newly constructed as a B&B, offering large, stylish units with expansive views across the bay. The location—right above the harbor—couldn't be better. The top-of-the-line room is also top-of-the-house: The very spacious Magnolia Suite encompasses the entire attic floor, complete with dormers and quirky ceiling angles, fireplace, soaker tub, and picture window. Each suite has its own character, and is decorated with rich colors and fabrics—plus a dash of knowing restraint. All rooms have private bathrooms; two rooms have two-person Jacuzzi tubs.

1682 Botwood Lane, Cowichan Bay, BC V0R 1N0. (☎) **888/748-7689** or 250/748-7688. www.dream weaverbedandbreakfast.com. C$116–C$170. Lower off-season rates. Extra person C$25. MC, V. Free parking. *In room:* A/C, TV/DVD, CD player, fridge, Wi-Fi, fireplace.

Oceanfront Grand Resort and Marina ★★   This newly renovated hotel sits immediately above the marina in Cowichan Bay, with incredible views of the harbor and the peaks of Salt Spring Island. You have a choice of one- or two-bedroom units, all with oceanfront views, full kitchens, and separate living rooms. While regular rooms are perfectly nice and very large, the premium rooms resemble very swank apartments, with luxury linens, fine furniture, and marble floors. Apart from the lovely guest rooms, the Grand provides top-notch services and amenities. Fitness and pool facilities are comprehensive and beautifully maintained. The resort also offers fine dining, with Vancouver Island's largest Sunday brunch, with a 120-item buffet (C$20 adult, half price for children 10 and under). Best of all, you're just steps from the marina, where you can rent a kayak, charter a sailboat, or have a drink and watch the tides.

1681 Cowichan Bay Rd., Cowichan Bay, BC V0R 1N0. (☎) **800/663-7898** or 250/715-1000. Fax 250/715-1001. www.thegrandresort.com. 56 units. C$99–C$249 double. Extra person C$10. MC, V. Free parking. **Amenities:** Waterfront restaurant and lounge; wine-tasting room; complimentary guest computer in lobby; health club; Jacuzzi; indoor pool; sauna; wine and liquor shop; Wi-Fi. *In room:* 2 TVs, hair dryer, kitchenette.

WHERE TO DINE

For a truly charming experience, consider lunching at a Cowichan Valley vineyard (for winery contact information, see above). **Vinoteca,** at Zanatta Winery, offers Italian-style farm lunches April through early October, Wednesday to Sunday noon to 3pm. **The Bistro at Cherry Point Vineyards** serves very tempting salads, sandwiches, and light entrees, and is open daily 11:30am to 3pm May through September. **La Pommeraie Bistro** at Merridale Ciderworks offers very satisfying country cuisine daily 11:30am to 4pm.

Bistro 161 ★ BISTRO A haven for contemporary fine dining, Bistro 161 is in a renovated home, with patio seating in good weather. The husband-and-wife chef-owners come from an international background, and the tempting menu offers a selection of well-prepared dishes from around the world: French cassoulet, East Indian duck biryani, homey stuffed chicken, plus a selection of pasta and local seafood. The wine list features a number of local vintages. The pace can seem leisurely (nearly everything is house-made and cooked to order), but the quality is very high.

161 Kenneth St. 𝓒 250/746-6466. www.bistro161.com. Reservations recommended. Main courses C$17–C$28. MC, V. Mon–Sat 11am–3pm and 5–9pm.

Craig Street Brew Pub ★ BREWPUB Wine and cider aren't the only delectable liquids to flow in the Cowichan Valley. This attractive brewpub in downtown Duncan serves up house-brewed lagers, ales, and porters, plus a selection of regional guest pours, local wines, and cocktails. The antique back bar adds old-world character, and the wood-beamed interior is cozy (the fireplace adds warmth in winter); in summer there's a rooftop deck. The menu offers pub favorites such as thin-crust pizza, burgers, panini sandwiches, and salads, but with main course specials that will make you push your tankard aside and take notice: pork tenderloin with orange-ginger glaze, or saffron halibut with red pepper aioli.

25 Craig St. 𝓒 250/737-2337. www.craigstreet.ca. Reservations not accepted. Main courses C$8–C$18. MC, V. Mon–Wed 11am–11pm; Thurs–Sat 11am–midnight; Sun 11am–10pm.

Just Jakes BURGERS/LIGHT DINING This laid-back, funky restaurant is a cross between a fern bar and a soda fountain, and the staff is young and engaging. The menu offers a wide selection of burgers, salads, steaks, and pasta: pleasantly passé food that perfectly mirrors Duncan's attractively slow-paced downtown.

45 Craig St. 𝓒 250/746-5622. www.justjakes.ca. Reservations recommended. Main courses C$6–C$22. AE, MC, V. Mon–Thurs 11am–9pm; Fri–Sat 11am–11pm; Sun 10am–8pm.

In Cowichan Bay

Masthead Restaurant ★★ PACIFIC NORTHWEST The waterfront building that now houses the Masthead was the town's original hotel. Its handsome dining room is perched above the marina and offers wonderful views of the bay (in summer, the deck doubles as an outdoor dining area). The Masthead is one of the top regional, seasonal dining experiences in the Cowichan Valley. Locally caught wild salmon comes with hazelnut risotto, and pan-roasted venison is served with sautéed corn and chanterelle mushrooms. The daily changing three-course table d'hôte menu at C$33 is an excellent value. The dining room sparkles with crystal and candlelight, the mood deepened with black glass tabletops. The wine list is a work of love (with multiple pages of "geek" wines) and the choice of Scotch whisky prodigious.

1705 Cowichan Bay Rd., Cowichan Bay. 𝓒 250/748-3714. www.themastheadrestaurant.com. Reservations recommended. Main courses C$20–C$33. MC, V. Daily from 5pm.

Rock Cod Café SEAFOOD Rock Cod Café has the best fish and chips in the area. From the deck, you can watch the fish coming in off the boats. The chalkboard menu is crammed with whatever else is fresh. Since the cafe has a liquor license—something most British fish-and-chip shops can't boast—you can turn a humble meal into an afternoon's worth of pleasure.

4-1759 Cowichan Bay Rd., Cowichan Bay. 𝓒 250/746-1550. Reservations recommended in summer. Main courses C$6–C$17. MC, V. Daily 11am–9pm.

In Maple Bay

Grapevine on the Bay Café ★ SEAFOOD   Sitting above the water on Maple Bay, the Grapevine has a stellar view and a cozy, slightly funky vibe—you'll find it easy to relax and enjoy top quality seafood and local specialties. The menu offers a large selection of appetizers—in fact, a series of small plates is an excellent strategy for exploring the chef's many strengths. Local pan-fried oysters are served with spicy "wicked mayo," and salt-and-pepper tiger prawns come with a delicious peri-peri dip. Main courses include a one-two punch of local beef braised in local ale, and wondrously creamy Quw'utsun' seafood pie, with house smoked salmon, fresh seafood, and chunks of vegetable. Local mussels are a house specialty, and the gold standard is Belgian-style *moules et frites*—a hearty dish to savor as you sit on the outdoor deck on a long summer's evening, enjoying fresh squeezed cocktails or a locally brewed beer.

6701 Beaumont Ave. ⓒ **250/746-0797.** Reservations recommended. Main courses C$17–C$27. MC, V. Wed–Sun 7:30am–9pm.

In Genoa Bay

The Genoa Bay Cafe ★ PACIFIC NORTHWEST   One of the most delightful dining experiences in the Duncan area is found at the relaxed yet stylish Genoa Bay Cafe. From the dining room or the deck, you can follow the to-ing and fro-ing of pleasure boats and see towering forested bluffs reflected in the waters of the bay. Local roast leg of lamb served with mango chutney glaze is the house specialty, but it's given a close run by the slow-roasted ribs with apple-cranberry barbecue sauce. What makes dining at the Genoa Bay Cafe so satisfying—besides the dramatic scenery; the montage of docks, sailboats, and yachts in the adjacent marina; and the welcoming, friendly service—is the perfect blend of contemporary, imaginative cuisine and hearty home cooking.

5100 Genoa Bay Rd., Genoa Bay Marina, Genoa Bay. ⓒ **250/746-7621.** Reservations recommended. Main courses C$16–C$38. MC, V. Nov–Mar Thurs 5:30–9pm, Fri–Sun 11:30am–2:30pm and 5:30–8:30pm; Apr and Oct Wed–Sun 11:30am–2:30pm and 5:30–8:30pm; May–Sept daily 11:30am–2:30pm and 5:30–9pm. Call to confirm off-season hours.

6 EN ROUTE TO NANAIMO

CHEMAINUS: THE CITY OF MURALS

Settled in the 1850s by European farmers, Chemainus quickly became a major timber-milling and -shipment point, due to the town's Horseshoe Bay, the oldest deepwater port on the Canadian West Coast. Prosperity saw the building of handsome homes and a solid commercial district. By the mid–20th century, the sawmills here were among the largest in the world, fed by the seemingly unending supply of wood from Vancouver Island's vast old-growth forests.

When the mills closed in 1983, the town slid into decline. Economic prospects for Chemainus seemed dim until someone had the bright idea of hiring an artist to paint a mural depicting the town's history. Tourists took notice, and soon mural painting became the raison d'être of this town of only slightly more than 3,500 residents. Chemainus claims to be Canada's largest permanent outdoor art gallery. Much of downtown is now covered with murals, most dealing with area history and local events.

Stop by the **Chemainus Visitor Info Centre,** 9758 Chemainus Rd. (ⓒ **250/246-3944**), open from May to early September, for a walking-tour map of the murals, or go to www.muraltown.com for an online map. Across the street from the visitor center in Heritage Park is an informational kiosk where you can join a horse-drawn wagon tour of the murals from Chemainus Tours (✆ **250/246-5055;** www.chemainustours.com) for C$12 for adults, C$5 for kids. Or simply follow the yellow shoe-prints painted on the sidewalks.

Much of the town is quiet and pedestrian-oriented, making it a pleasant place for a stroll and a good spot for lunch. **Old Town Chemainus,** along Willow and Maple streets, is filled with Victorian cottages converted into shops and cafes. The **Chemainus Theatre,** 9737 Chemainus Rd. (✆ **800/565-7738** or 250/246-9820; http://chemainus theatrefestival.ca), is a late-19th-century opera house that now serves as a popular dinner theater. The season runs February through December; call ahead to reserve.

Where to Stay & Dine

There aren't lots of choices for fine dining in Chemainus. **Willow Street Café,** 9749 Willow St. (✆ **250/246-2434**), is a hip eatery serving up sandwiches, wraps, and salads; the deck is the best people-watching perch in town; open daily from 9am to 5pm. **Kudo's Japanese Restaurant,** 9875 Maple St. (✆ **250/246-1046**), serves sushi and other Japanese cuisine and is open for lunch and dinner daily.

Bird Song Cottage Bed & Breakfast ★ Filled with Victorian bric-a-brac and unusual objets d'art, Bird Song is an enchanting, English-style garden cottage. The exterior continues the theme, with a wraparound porch and turreted veranda, burbling fountains, and loads of architectural gingerbread. There is one guest room in the cottage, beautifully outfitted with quality linens and fresh flowers, with two more guest rooms in **Castlebury Cottage,** a separate structure behind the cottage that's designed as a small, whimsical, European-style castle that offers private, luxurious, and fully modern accommodations with TV/VCR, kitchen, fridge, coffeemaker, and other amenities. The upstairs Camelot suite has a fireplace, canopy bed, and two-person marble soaker tub. The style is thoroughly baroque, with lots of ornate flourishes and rough frescoed walls. The downstairs Sonnet suite is smaller but similarly appointed.

9909 Maple St., Chemainus, BC V0R 1K1. ✆ **250/246-9910.** Fax 250/246-2909. www.birdsongcottage. com. Birdsong Cottage: C$115 double. Extra person C$35. Rates include breakfast and evening tea. Castlebury Cottage: 2 units. May–Sept Camelot suite C$240, Sonnet suite C$140; Oct–Apr Camelot suite C$220, Sonnet suite C$120. Rates include breakfast basket. 2-night minimum on holiday weekends. Weekly rates available. MC, V. *In room:* TV, hair dryer.

CEDAR & YELLOW POINT

South of Nanaimo, a forested peninsula juts out into the waters of the Georgia Strait. The land is rural and mostly undeveloped. The little community of Cedar is as close as the area comes to a town; this wouldn't qualify as much of a destination if it weren't for the fact that one of Vancouver Island's most popular lodges and one of its best restaurants are located here. It's a short drive from Nanaimo, and a detour through the forests and farmland makes for a pleasant break from Hwy. 1.

Where to Stay

Yellow Point Lodge ★★ Value Beloved Yellow Point Lodge, a family-oriented resort and activity-focused summer camp established in the 1930s, is located on 73 hectares (180 acres) of forested waterfront, with over 2.5km (1½ miles) of rocky beach and secluded coves. The three-story log-and-stone building has an enormous lobby, a huge fireplace, and a dining room where guests share communal meals, all with wondrous views of the southern Gulf Islands. Inside the lodge are a number of comfortable hotel-like rooms, and scattered around the woods are cabins and cottages in a wide range of styles from rustic beach cabins that share communal wash houses to more luxurious one-, two-, and three-bedroom cottages with fireplaces. If this unique blend of summer camp and recreation resort appeals to you, be sure to reserve well ahead—the lodge is a summer tradition for people of all incomes.

3700 Yellow Point Rd., Ladysmith, BC V9G 1E8. © **250/245-7422.** Fax 250/245-7411. www.yellowpoint lodge.com. 53 units, 27 with private bathroom, most with shower only. C$137–C$212 double. Rates include all meals. AE, MC, V. Children must be 14 or older. **Amenities:** Licensed dining room; ferry, bus, train, or airport shuttle available for small fee; free bikes; golf course nearby; Jacuzzi; outdoor saltwater pool; sauna; tennis courts; free canoes and kayaks; volleyball and badminton courts. *In room:* Fridge (in some cabins), no phone.

Where to Dine

The Crow & Gate ★ (Finds) PUB   This Tudor-style pub on a 4-hectare (10-acre) farm is a friendly haven of English style, with low ceilings, handcrafted beams, and gleaming brass accents complemented by a brick fireplace and leaded-glass windows. The menu offers British standards like ploughman's lunch, steak and kidney pie, cold pork pie, Scotch eggs, and—every Wednesday and Saturday evening—roast beef and Yorkshire pudding. In summer, sit out on the flower-decked patio. Sorry, no minors.

2313 Yellow Point Rd. © **250/722-3731.** www.crowandgate.com. Reservations recommended. Main courses C$8–C$24. MC, V. Daily 11am–11pm; closes early when not busy and on some holidays (call ahead). Take the old Island Hwy. (Hwy. 19) north past Cassidy, or exit Island Hwy. 1 at Hwy. 19 to Cedar and Harmac. Cross the Nanaimo River, then turn right on Cedar Rd., which leads onto Yellow Point Rd. Continue for 1.6km (1 mile).

The Mahle House ★ PACIFIC NORTHWEST   The Mahle (pronounced "Molly") House is located in a tiny country town, in a salmon-pink heritage home overlooking a park. From this unlikely address, it has developed a huge reputation for excellent regional cuisine emphasizing locally grown, mostly organic produce and meats. On the weekly changing menu you might choose free-range chicken breast stuffed with Dungeness crab and served with lemon-grass sauce, or Chinook salmon, scallops, and porcupine prawns with saffron aioli and lemon oil. The award-wining wine list is extensive. The restaurant also offers "adventure" nights, when it's chef's choice: a Wednesday five-course dinner for C$40, a Thursday evening five-course tapas dinner for C$30 per person, and a three-course Sunday "country dinner" for C$30.

2104 Hemer Rd (at Cedar and Hemer rds.) © **250/722-3621.** www.mahlehouse.ca. Reservations recommended. Main courses C$18–C$34. AE, MC, V. Wed–Sun from 5pm. Closed Dec 21–29 and Jan 1–15.

Central Vancouver Island

Central Vancouver Island's major population center is Nanaimo, the arrival point for visitors taking ferries from the mainland and the site of a major 19th-century coal-mining operation. The city has moved away from its dependence upon resource extraction and is now sparkling with redevelopment, taking advantage of its scenic location—overlooking a bay full of islands, the choppy waters of Georgia Strait, and the glaciated peaks of the mainland.

In sharp contrast to the serenity of the island's east coast, the wild, raging beauty of the Pacific Ocean on Vancouver Island's west coast entices photographers, hikers, kayakers, and divers to explore Pacific Rim National Park, Long Beach, and the neighboring towns of Ucluelet, Tofino, and Bamfield. Thousands of visitors arrive between March and May to see Pacific gray whales pass close to shore as they migrate north to their summer feeding grounds. More than 200 shipwrecks have occurred off the shores in the past 2 centuries, luring even more travelers to this eerily beautiful underwater world. And the park's world-famous West Coast Trail beckons intrepid backpackers to brave the 5- to 7-day hike over the rugged rescue trail—established after the survivors of a shipwreck in the early 1900s died from exposure because there was no land-access route for the rescuers.

On east-central Vancouver Island, the towns of Parksville, Qualicum Beach, Courtenay, and Comox are famous for their warm, sandy beaches and numerous golf courses.

Note: See the "Vancouver Island" map (p. 60) to locate areas covered in this chapter.

1 ESSENTIALS

GETTING THERE

BY PLANE See chapter 6 for details on flights to **Victoria,** the main air hub for all of Vancouver Island.

Nanaimo and Comox/Courtenay have regular air service. **Air Canada Jazz** (*©* **888/247-2262;** www.aircanada.com) offers service to Vancouver from Nanaimo. **Pacific Coastal Airlines** (*©* **800/663-2872;** www.pacific-coastal.com) and Air Canada connector **Central Mountain Air** fly to/from Comox and Vancouver, while **WestJet** (*©* **877/952-4638;** www.westjet.com) provides Comox with nonstop service to/from Edmonton and Calgary.

Smaller towns in central Vancouver Island can be reached via floatplane, either from Vancouver International's seaplane terminal or from downtown Vancouver's Coal Harbour terminal.

Commuter seaplane companies include **Harbour Air Seaplanes** (© 800/665-0212 or 604/688-1277; www.harbour-air.com), **Tofino Air** (© 866/486-3247 for Tofino base, 888/436-7776 for Sechelt base, or 800/665-2359 for Gabriola base; www.tofinoair. ca), and **West Coast Air** (© 800/347-2222 or 604/606-6800; www.westcoastair.com).

BY FERRY **BC Ferries** (© 888/223-3779 or 250/386-3431; www.bcferries.com) links Vancouver Island, the Gulf Islands, and the mainland. Major routes include the crossing from Tsawwassen to Swartz Bay and to Nanaimo, and from Horseshoe Bay (northwest of Vancouver) to Nanaimo. In summer, reserve in advance. Sample fares are included in the regional sections that follow.

BY BUS One of the easiest ways to get to and from Vancouver Island destinations is by bus. **Greyhound Canada** (© 800/661-8747 or 604/482-8747; www.greyhound.ca) provides six daily trips between Vancouver and Nanaimo. Fare is C$17 one-way.

VISITOR INFORMATION

For information on central Vancouver Island, contact **Tourism Vancouver Island,** Ste. 501, 65 Front St., Nanaimo (© **250/754-3500;** www.vancouverisland.travel). Also check out **www.vancouverisland.com**.

GETTING AROUND

While Vancouver Island has an admirable system of public transport, getting to remote sights and destinations is difficult without your own vehicle.

BY FERRY **BC Ferries** (© 888/223-3779 or 250/386-3431; www.bcferries.com) routes link Vancouver Island ports to many offshore islands.

BY TRAIN A scenic way to travel is on **VIA Rail**'s **E&N Railiner,** the *Malahat* (© **888/VIA-RAIL** [842-7245] or 250/383-4324; www.viarail.ca), which runs from Victoria to Courtenay. See p. 133 for details.

BY BUS **Vancouver Island Coach** (© **250/388-5248,** or book through **Greyhound Canada** © **800/661-8747** or 604/482-8747; www.greyhound.ca) operates regular daily service between Victoria and Tofino. The 6-hour trip, departing Victoria at 7:30am and arriving in Tofino at 2:20pm, costs C$65. The bus also stops in Nanaimo and can pick up passengers arriving from Vancouver on the ferry. The **Tofino Bus** (© **866/986-3466;** www.tofinobus.com) also offers bus service from Victoria and Vancouver to Tofino. A one-way ticket from Victoria to Tofino is C$64.

BY CAR The southern half of Vancouver Island is well served by paved highways. The trunk road between Victoria and Nanaimo is **Hwy. 1,** the Trans-Canada, which requires some patience, especially during the busy summer months. North of Nanaimo, the major road is **Hwy. 19,** a new four-lane expressway that runs 128km (80 miles) to Campbell River. The older sections of 19, all closer to the island's east coast, are now labeled 19A. The other major paved road system on the island, **Hwy. 4,** connects Parksville with Port Alberni and on to Ucluelet and Tofino, on the rugged west coast. This road is mostly two-lane, and portions of it are extremely winding and hilly.

Rental cars are readily available. Agencies include **Avis** (© 800/879-2847 in Canada, 800/331-1212 in the U.S.; www.avis.com), **Budget** (© 800/268-8900 in Canada, 800/527-0700 in the U.S.; www.budget.com), and **National** (© 877/222-9058 in Canada and the U.S.; www.nationalcar.com).

CENTRAL VANCOUVER ISLAND

8

ESSENTIALS

2 NANAIMO & GABRIOLA ISLAND

Nanaimo: 113km (70 miles) N of Victoria

For over a century, Vancouver Island's second-largest city (pop. 79,000) was the center of vast coal-mining operations, without much in the way of cultural niceties. In the last 30 years, however, Nanaimo has undergone quite a change. With its redeveloped waterfront, scenic surroundings, good restaurants and lodging, and a location central to many other Vancouver Island destinations, downtown Nanaimo makes a pleasant stop for a few days. Note, however, that Nanaimo is a fairly sprawling city, complete with lots of suburban strip malls and plenty of traffic, so it may not hold the same charm as the island's less populous destinations.

Just a 20-minute ferry ride from Nanaimo Harbour is Gabriola Island, though it feels a world away. Gabriola makes a marvelous day trip, providing a little of everything—sandy beaches, galleries, petroglyph sites, tide pools, and a sense of wooded serenity.

ESSENTIALS

Getting There

BY PLANE   Regular service between Vancouver and Nanaimo Airport, 24km (15 miles) south of the city, is offered by **Air Canada Jazz** (✆ 888/247-2262; www.aircanada.com).

Harbour Air Seaplanes (✆ 800/665-0212 or 604/688-1277; www.harbour-air.com) and **West Coast Air** (✆ 800/347-2222 or 604/606-6800; www.westcoastair.com) offer floatplane flights from downtown Vancouver to Nanaimo Harbour; West Coast Air also has flights to Nanaimo from Vancouver International Airport's floatplane base.

BY CAR   Nanaimo is 113km (70 miles) from Victoria via Hwy. 1, the Trans-Canada Highway. At Nanaimo, Hwy. 1 crosses the Georgia Strait via the Horseshoe Bay ferry. North of Nanaimo, the main trunk road becomes Hwy. 19. It's 161km (100 miles) from Nanaimo to Campbell River, 206km (128 miles) to Tofino.

BY FERRY   **BC Ferries** (✆ 888/223-3779 or 250/386-3431; www.bcferries.com) operates two major runs to Nanaimo. The crossing from Horseshoe Bay in West Vancouver to Nanaimo's Departure Bay terminal is one of the busiest in the system; expect delays, especially at rush hour and summer weekends. New PacifiCat Ferries cut the normal 1½-hour crossing down to just over an hour. The Tsawwassen ferry arrives and departs at Nanaimo's Duke Point terminal, just south of town off Hwy. 1. Tickets for both ferries are C$14 per passenger and C$60 per car, with slightly lower midweek and low-season prices.

BY TRAIN   The **E&N Railiner** operates daily service between Victoria and Courtenay. For information, contact **VIA Rail** (✆ 888/VIA-RAIL [842-7245] or 250/383-4324; www.viarail.ca).

BY BUS   **Greyhound Canada** (✆ 800/661-8747 or 604/482-8747; www.greyhound.ca) provides seven daily trips between Vancouver and Nanaimo. Non-Greyhound buses continue both north and south from Nanaimo, though you can use Greyhound to book seats.

Visitor Information

Contact **Tourism Nanaimo,** Beban House, 2290 Bowen Rd., Nanaimo, BC V9T 3K7 (✆ 800/663-7337 or 250/756-0106; www.tourismnanaimo.com). In summer, an **info center** operates out of the Bastion, at Pioneer Waterfront Plaza.

(**Moments**)   **Only in Nanaimo: The World Championship Bathtub Race**

From its beginnings in 1967, Nanaimo's signature summer draw has grown into a weeklong series of events that shows off the city's good-natured spirit. In the early days, fewer than half of the original racing vessels—old claw-foot tubs fitted with engines—completed the crossing of 58km (36-mile) Georgia Strait from Nanaimo Harbour to Vancouver's Fisherman's Cove. These days, most contestants race in specially designed tubs that look like single-person speedboats. The race is the climax of late July's **Marine Festival,** which includes a street fair, parade, and traditional "Sacrifice to the Bathtub Gods." For information, go to www.bath tubbing.com.

Getting Around

Nanaimo Regional Transit System (© 250/390-4531; www.rdn.bc.ca) provides public transport in the Nanaimo area. Fares are C$2.25 for adults and C$2 for seniors and youths. For a cab, call **AC Taxi** (© 800/753-1231 or 250/753-1231) or **Swiftsure Taxi** (© 250/753-8911).

The **BC Ferries** route to Gabriola Island leaves from behind the Harbour Park Shopping Centre on Front Street (note that this is not the same dock as either the Tsawwassen- or Horseshoe Bay–bound ferries), roughly every hour between 7am and 11pm. In summer, the round-trip fare is C$9 per person, plus C$24 for a car. You can bring your bike free of charge.

EXPLORING NANAIMO

Nanaimo's steep-faced waterfront has been restructured with tiers of walkways, banks of flowers, marina boardwalks, and floating restaurants. Called **Pioneer Waterfront Plaza,** the area fills on Fridays with the local farmers' market. The **Bastion,** a white fortified tower, rises above the harbor as a relic of the 1850s when this area was the site of a Hudson's Bay Company trading post (it now holds a summer tourist information center).

Nanaimo's busy natural port has ferry links to Vancouver, Horseshoe Bay, and to Tsawwassen to the south, as well as to lovely **Gabriola Island** and to **Newcastle Island,** a car-free provincial park on the harbor's northern flank. Throughout the day, floatplanes buzz in and out of the boat basin, shuttling commuters back and forth to Vancouver. If you're up for a walk, the **Harbourside Walkway** stretches 4km (2½ miles) from the heart of the city all the way to Departure Bay.

The old downtown, just behind the Bastion and centered on Commercial, Front, and Bastion streets, is a series of pleasant winding streets behind the harbor. **Artisan's Studio,** 70 Bastion St. (© 250/753-6151), is a co-op gallery that displays the work of local artists and craftspeople.

Another good stroll is the **Old City Quarter,** an uptown section of the city center that was severed from the harborfront area when the Island Highway cut through downtown. Now reached from the harbor by walking up the Bastion Street overpass, the 3-block area has been redeveloped into housing, boutiques, and fine restaurants.

Nanaimo District Museum   Nanaimo's regional museum is a worthwhile introduction to the area's past, first as a home for the Snunéymuxw (the name from which

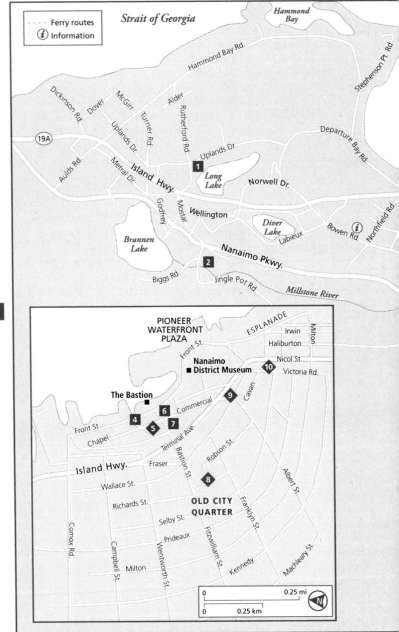

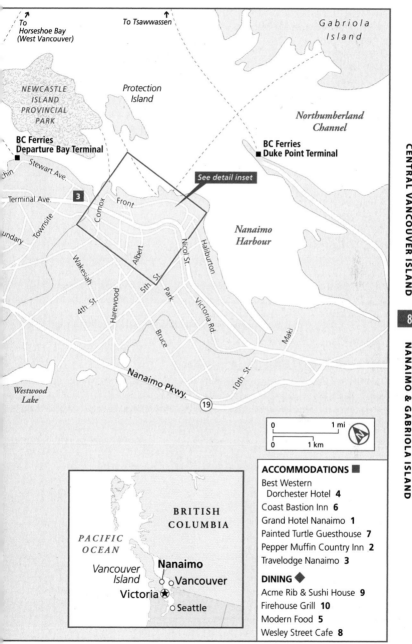

To Horseshoe Bay (West Vancouver)

To Tsawwassen

Gabriola Island

NEWCASTLE ISLAND PROVINCIAL PARK

Protection Island

Northumberland Channel

BC Ferries Departure Bay Terminal

BC Ferries Duke Point Terminal

Stewart Ave.

chin

Terminal Ave.

3

Comox

Front

See detail inset

Nanaimo Harbour

Townsite

undary

Wakesiah

Albert

Nicol St.

Haliburton

Victoria Rd.

Maki

5th St.

4th St.

Harewood

Park

Bruce

10th St.

Nanaimo Pkwy.

19

Westwood Lake

0   1 mi
0   1 km

PACIFIC OCEAN

BRITISH COLUMBIA

Vancouver Island

Nanaimo

Vancouver

Victoria

Seattle

ACCOMMODATIONS ■

Best Western Dorchester Hotel **4**
Coast Bastion Inn **6**
Grand Hotel Nanaimo **1**
Painted Turtle Guesthouse **7**
Pepper Muffin Country Inn **2**
Travelodge Nanaimo **3**

DINING ◆

Acme Rib & Sushi House **9**
Firehouse Grill **10**
Modern Food **5**
Wesley Street Cafe **8**

Nanaimo derives) people and then as a coal-mining boomtown. The museum relocated to the new and adjacent Vancouver Island Conference Centre in 2008. The expanded exhibit gallery portrays the unique aspects of Nanaimo's location, character, and natural history, featuring the Snunéymuxw First Nation, "colorful" citizens, and the coal mining, industrial, and social development of the community. Be sure to visit the Bastion, the last free-standing, original wooden HBC bastion in North America.

100 Museum Way. (☎ 250/753-1821. www.nanaimomuseum.ca. Admission C$2 adults, C$1.75 seniors, C75¢ children 6–12. Late May to Labour Day daily 10am–5pm; day after Labour Day to late May Tues–Sat 10am–5pm. From Front St., head up Museum Way, then left on Gordon St., and left again on Cameron Rd.

FERRYING TO NEWCASTLE ISLAND

Just outside Nanaimo harbor, **Newcastle Island Provincial Park** ((☎ 250/391-2300 for BC Parks, South Vancouver Island District) is an ideal destination for hikers, cyclists, and campers. The island was home to two Salish Indian villages before British settlers discovered coal here in 1849. The Canadian-Pacific Steamship Company purchased the island in 1931, creating a resort with a dance pavilion, teahouse, and floating hotel. The 300-hectare (741-acre) island has now largely returned to its natural state. It now attracts outdoorsy types with its many trails; selected walks range from 2 to 4km (1.3–2.5 miles). The popular **Mallard Lake Trail** leads through the wooded interior toward a freshwater lake; the **Shoreline Trail** runs across steep cliffs, onto sand and gravel beaches suitable for swimming, and up to a great eagle-spotting perch. The park maintains 18 **campsites,** with toilets, wood, fire pits, and water. Rate is C$14.

From April to Canadian Thanksgiving (mid-Oct), **Nanaimo Harbour Ferries** ((☎ 877/297-8526) offers ferry service to Newcastle Island from the wharf at the peninsula tip of **Maffeo-Sutton Park** (just north of downtown), operating daily between 10am and early evening. The round-trip fare for the 10-minute crossing is C$8 for adults and C$6 for children 12 and younger.

EXPLORING GABRIOLA ISLAND

Much of Gabriola (pop. 4,000) is reached along North Road and South Road, two country lanes that provide a loop route around the island. A third road, Taylor Bay Road, departs from the ferry dock to access Gabriola's rocky northern reaches. It takes about half an hour to drive from one end of the island to the other.

The main commercial center is just up the hill from the ferry terminal and is often referred to as **Folklife Village.** Stop by **Gabriola Artworks,** 575 North Rd. ((☎ 250/247-7412; www.gabriolaartworks.com), an excellent gallery of local arts and crafts.

Sandwell Provincial Park is one of Gabriola's nicest beaches and picnic areas, with paths leading through old-growth forests and to views of the Entrance Island lighthouse. Turn off North Road onto Barrett Road and follow the signs.

At the southern end of Gabriola is Silva Bay, a marina resort featuring an excellent restaurant and pub. Just south of Silva Bay is **Drumbeg Provincial Park,** which has a good swimming beach.

Gabriola Island and the area around Nanaimo are rich in prehistoric **petroglyph rock carvings.** On the South Road, near the United Church (about 10km/6¼ miles from the ferry terminal), a short path leads to a mix of fantastical creatures and abstract shapes scratched in sandstone. Park in the church lot and follow the signs. *Note:* The Snunéymuxw regard these petroglyphs as sacred and frown on people taking pictures or rubbings of them.

Taylor Bay Road leads to more parks and beaches on the north end of the island.
Gabriola Sands Provincial Park protects two of the island's best beaches, at Taylor Bay and Pilot Bay. Toward the end of the road (now called Berry Point Rd.) is the **Surf Lodge,** 885 Berry Point Rd. (📞 **250/247-9231**), with a pub and restaurant overlooking the Georgia Strait.

OUTDOOR PURSUITS

BUNGEE JUMPING **Wild Play Element Park,** 35 Nanaimo River Rd. (📞 **888/668-7874** or 250/753-5867; www.wildplayparks.com; follow signs from Nanaimo Lakes exit off Hwy. 1, south of Nanaimo), has North America's first legal bridge jump, which sends you over the Nanaimo River for C$100. For another adrenaline rush at this recreation hot spot (which also includes sky diving, paintball, a swinging bridge obstacle course, and a high-elevation swing), consider a ride on the zip-line (C$60), which launches daredevils, attached to a steel cable by a climbing harness, across a wooded canyon at speeds near 100kmph (62 mph).

DIVING ★★ While all of the waters off Vancouver Island are known for their superior diving opportunities, those around Nanaimo benefit from the efforts of the Nanaimo Dive Association, which is working to make Nanaimo a world-class diving destination. Rather unique are three artificial reefs formed by the sinking of decommissioned cargo ships just off the Nanaimo coastline. The HMCS *Saskatchewan* and the HMCS *Cape Breton* together form a reef 228m (748 ft.) in length. A third boat, the rescue tug *Rivtow Lion,* lies in shallow water just off Newport Island and is used for training. One of the single best dives in the Northwest is at **Dodds Narrows,** between Vancouver Island and Mudge Island. It boasts outstanding visibility, a high concentration of wildlife, and dramatic rock formations. Other area dives include **Snake Island Wall,** with a drop-off that seems to extend into the abyss.

With an office right on the waterfront, **Sundown Diving,** 22 Esplanade (📞 **250/753-1880;** www.sundowndiving.com), offers diving instruction, equipment rentals, and boat charters to most of the top diving spots in the Nanaimo area. Another local outfitter, **Mamro Adventures,** 1–5765 Turner Rd., Ste. 203 (📞 **250/756-8872;** www.mamro.com), can accommodate six passengers on trips of 1 to 10 days. Popular excursions include Port Hardy, famed for its dense marine-mammal population, and the Gulf Islands, Sunshine Coast, and Georgia Strait.

WHERE TO STAY
In Nanaimo

Best Western Dorchester Hotel ★ For the price, quality, and excellent downtown location, the Dorchester is hard to top. The hotel stands on the most venerable spot in Nanaimo: the site of the Hudson's Bay Company trading post in the 1850s, and then of the city's old opera house. Reminders of the opera-house days remain: The handsome chandeliers are all original, as are the ornate columns flanking the dining room. Guest rooms are comfortably furnished, though not exactly spacious. Pay a bit extra for a bayside room—the view is fantastic. Check the hotel website for seasonal Internet rates not available elsewhere. Rooms for those with disabilities are available.

70 Church St., Nanaimo, BC V9R 5H4. 📞 **800/661-2449** or 250/754-6835. Fax 250/754-2638. www.dorchesternanaimo.com. 70 units. C$131–C$175 double. Extra person C$10 per night. Senior, AAA, and Internet discounts, and corporate and off-season rates available. AE, DC, DISC, MC, V. Limited free parking. Pets accommodated for C$15 per night. **Amenities:** Restaurant; lounge; rooms for those w/limited mobility. *In room:* A/C, TV, hair dryer, Wi-Fi.

Coast Bastion Inn ★ At this modern high-rise hotel at the heart of downtown, every room boasts a waterfront view, and the Harbourside Walkway scene is just seconds away. It's worth the splurge for a superior room, with upgraded amenities and views from two sides. Two wheelchair-accessible rooms are available. The hotel connects to the Port Theatre complex.

11 Bastion St., Nanaimo, BC V9R 6E4. (℃ **800/663-1144** or 250/753-6601. Fax 250/753-4155. www.coast hotels.com. 177 units. High season C$143–C$240 double. Extra person C$10. Senior and AAA discounts, theater packages, and off-season rates available. AE, DC, DISC, MC, V. Valet parking C$10; self-parking C$6.50. Pets allowed for C$10 per day. **Amenities:** Restaurant; lounge; babysitting; exercise room; Jacuzzi; room service; sauna; rooms for those w/limited mobility. In room: A/C, TV, hair dryer, Wi-Fi.

Grand Hotel Nanaimo ★ The Grand Hotel is the area's most luxurious lodging. Rooms range from 56-sq.-m (603-sq.-ft.) suites with two TVs, a fireplace, kitchenette, and king-size bed to simpler but still very comfortable standard rooms. Deluxe rooms have jetted tubs and fireplaces; many rooms have balconies. There are two wheelchair-accessible units. The public areas are handsome, particularly the lobby with its soaring ceilings and chandelier. The Grand Hotel is about a 10-minute drive northwest of the city center.

4898 Rutherford Rd., Nanaimo, BC V9T 4Z4. (℃ **877/414-7263** or 250/758-3000. Fax 250/729-2808. www. thegrandhotelnanaimo.ca. 72 units. C$175–C$350 double. Extra person C$15 per day. Senior and AAA discounts available. AE, DC, DISC, MC, V. **Amenities:** Restaurant; lounge; golf course nearby; exercise room; indoor pool; room service; rooms for those w/limited mobility. In room: A/C, TV, hair dryer, Wi-Fi.

Painted Turtle Guesthouse (Finds) A European-style hostel with a real sense of style, the Painted Turtle is a revamped vintage hotel in the very center of downtown Nanaimo's shopping and nightlife. This is a fun place to spend a night or two, as it's filled with youthful energy, though guests here are by no means limited to the young. Travelers of all ages find this a pleasant place to stay, as it has a variety of room types, from four-bed dorm rooms to doubles, and two-, three-, and four bedroom options for groups. In true hostel fashion, the bathrooms are down the hall, but they are clean and well furnished. All linens and towels are provided; there's even a concierge desk and booking service to help you plan local excursions. The entire facility is well-maintained and nicely decorated, and the owners are very friendly and will do their best to ensure you have a great stay.

121 Bastion St., Nanaimo, BC V9R 3A2. (℃ **866/309-4432** or 250/753-4432. www.paintedturtle.ca. 20 rooms. C$25 dorm single; C$76 double. Discounts for Hostelling International members. **Amenities:** Great room w/fireplace, games, common area, and library; full self-catering kitchen; storage for bikes, skis, snowboards, luggage. In room: No phone, Wi-Fi.

Pepper Muffin Country Inn ★ (Kids) This country B&B on 2.4 hectares (6 acres) offers a rural getaway just minutes from downtown. A stream plays host to beaver, otter, and trout, and local crags are home to pileated woodpeckers and turkey buzzards. Although newly constructed as an inn, the building was designed with quirky angles and rooflines, and is tastefully furnished with antiques. Each guest room has a private entrance, balcony, and a private en suite bathroom. Bike trails and lakes are accessible nearby.

3718 Jingle Pot Rd., Nanaimo, BC V9R 6X4. (℃ **866/956-0473** or 250/756-0473. Fax 250/756-0421. www. peppermuffin.com. 3 units. C$89–C$149 double. Rates include breakfast. AE, MC, V. **Amenities:** Outdoor hot tub. In room: TV/VCR, hair dryer, Wi-Fi.

Travelodge Nanaimo   A midprice motel with a great location, this Travelodge is just a few blocks from the Vancouver ferry, and a short walk to downtown. All of the clean, comfortable rooms have balconies or patios. Some rooms have kitchens. The front desk can help you arrange activities around Nanaimo.

96 Terminal Ave. N., Nanaimo, BC V9S 4J2. ℂ **800/667-0598** or 250/754-6355. Fax 250/754-1301. www. travelodgenanaimo.com. 78 units. June–Sept C$100–C$119 double; lower off-season rates. Extra person C$6. Rates include continental breakfast. Senior and AAA discounts available. AE, DISC, MC, V. Free parking. Pets allowed for C$15 per night. **Amenities:** Exercise room; sauna. *In room:* A/C, TV, hair dryer, Wi-Fi.

WHERE TO DINE

In central Nanaimo there are several casual spots worth knowing about. **Tina's Diner,** 187 Commercial St. (ℂ **205/753-5333;** www.tinasdiner.com), is a classic '50s diner with big eggy breakfasts and sandwiches for lunch. **McClean's Specialty Foods,** 426 Fitzwilliam St. (ℂ **250/754-0100;** www.mcleansfoods.com), offers over 100 varieties of cheese, including many from Vancouver Island, plus other picnic comestibles. **Mon Petit Choux,** 101–120 Commercial St. (ℂ **250/753-6057;** www.monpetitchoux.ca), is a quintessential French bakery with excellent breads and pastries, plus an espresso bar. Light meals are available for breakfast and lunch.

Acme Rib and Sushi House INTERNATIONAL   In an arrowhead-shaped building on downtown Nanaimo's busiest corner, the Acme offers five pages' worth of menu choices, everything from sushi to traditional seafood, from BBQ to steaks. At this chic cocktail bar and '90s-retro dining room, sashimi and sushi rolls are particularly good, while more mainstream steaks and seafood, like fresh oysters and pan-seared snapper with grapefruit vinaigrette, are memorable. This is a great place to bring a group of people with differing food tastes, which is exactly how it's done in Nanaimo. The Acme is one of the top hangouts for the city's young urban hipsters.

14 Commercial St. ℂ **250/753-0042.** Reservations recommended. Main courses C$8–C$28. MC, V. Sun–Thurs 11am–11pm; Sat–Sun 11am–midnight.

Firehouse Grill ★ SUSHI/BARBECUE   Half sushi bar, half southern BBQ joint, the Firehouse Grill doesn't follow the rules, particularly since it also offers debonair good looks in the city's century-old fire hall. The dining room is dramatic—7.5m (25-ft.)

ⓘ Tips   Two Popular Pubs

In summer, for a pint of ale and a burger in a marvelous location, take the 10-minute Protection Connection ferry ride to the **Dinghy Dock Floating Marine Pub,** on Protection Island (ℂ **250/753-2373**). It's exactly what its name says—a floating pub—and boasts spectacular sunset views of Nanaimo and the Vancouver Island mountains. The ferry leaves on the hour from the Commercial Inlet boat basin, below Pioneer Waterfront Plaza.

You'll get a wonderful view of the harbor from the **Lighthouse Bistro and Pub,** off Harbourside Walkway at 50 Anchor Way (ℂ **250/754-3212**). Open daily from 11am to midnight and until 1am in summer (the restaurant closes earlier), this floating pub is adjacent to the city's floatplane base—watch these boats take off just beside your table.

ceilings, redbrick walls, towering windows, modern art, and stark white chairs and fixtures. The large menu provides even more theatrics. There are two pages of sushi rolls, nigiri, maki, and sashimi, including the signature Firehouse Roll with prawns, Dungeness crab, and amberjack (hamachi). Then there's the rest of the menu, which features excellent grilled ribs, steaks, and Southern-style jambalaya and whole Dungeness crab poached in Cajun stock. Don't spend too much time pondering what links these two cuisines; just mix and match from both halves of the menu, grab a cocktail, and enjoy yourself.

7 Victoria Rd. ⟨Ⓒ 250/741-8858. Reservations recommended. Tapas C$1.50–C$15; main courses C$11–C$24. MC, V. Daily 11am–midnight.

Modern Cafe ★ CONTEMPORARY CANADIAN   This chic, arty cafe is a good spot to have a quiet meal, or meet friends for late-night dessert and coffee. One menu is devoted to tapas, like almond-crusted baked brie with cranberry apple compote and West Coast fish cakes in creamy chipotle sauce, while another features "hand helds" or sandwiches. Main dishes feature local meats and vegetables—the Veggie Stack, a tower of portobello mushrooms, mashed yams, tomatoes, and won tons, is a nice break from rich meat dishes. With contemporary art on the redbrick walls, Modern Food's setting exudes a level of casual sophistication unusual for Nanaimo.

221 Commercial St. ⟨Ⓒ 250/754-5022. Main courses C$12–C$19. MC, V. Sun–Mon 11am–11pm; Thurs–Sat 11am–midnight.

Wesley Street Café ★★ CONTEMPORARY CANADIAN   Nanaimo's premier fine-dining restaurant serves the city's most up-to-date food in a comfortably formal Old Town Quarter dining room. Chef Jeff Massey pairs European preparations with regional Northwest flavors, as in herb-crusted albacore tuna with grand fir-infused rhubarb glaze, and porcini mushroom and roast garlic stuffed chicken. Monday through Thursday, the cafe offers three-course dinners for an unbelievable C$25, and on Friday and Saturday, four-course dinners for $45. The huge wine list features many B.C. selections.

321 Wesley St. ⟨Ⓒ 250/753-6057. www.wesleycafe.com. Reservations required. Main courses C$18–C$28. AE, MC, V. Tues–Sat 11:30am–2pm and 5:30–9pm.

3 PARKSVILLE & QUALICUM BEACH

37km (23 miles) N of Nanaimo

These twin resort towns near the most popular beaches on Vancouver Island now market themselves as the tourist region of Oceanside. Spending a week here is a family tradition for many residents of British Columbia. With miles of sand and six golf courses, it's the perfect base for a relaxing vacation. Parksville (pop. 10,500) and Qualicum Beach (pop. 7,500) are also good stopping-off points for travelers making the trip to or from Victoria and Tofino.

ESSENTIALS

GETTING THERE   **Island Coach Lines** (⟨Ⓒ 250/388-5248,** or book through Greyhound ⟨Ⓒ 800/661-8747;** www.greyhound.ca) offers bus transport from Nanaimo to the Parksville and Qualicum area along the Hwy. 1/Hwy. 19 corridor; one-way fare from Victoria to Parksville is C$32. **VIA Rail**'s **E&N Railiner,** or the *Malahat* (⟨Ⓒ 888/VIA-RAIL** [842-7245] or 250/383-4324; www.viarail.ca), stops in both towns on its daily trip from Victoria to Courtenay. **KD Air** (⟨Ⓒ 800/665-4244,** 604/688-9957, or

port for C$245 round-trip. Otherwise, the closest available air service is at Nanaimo or
Comox.

VISITOR INFORMATION   For information on Qualicum Beach and Parksville, contact the **Oceanside Tourism Association** (© **250/248-6300;** www.visitparksvillequalicum
beach.com). For information once you're there, go to the **Qualicum Beach Visitor
Information Centre,** 2711 W. Island Hwy., Qualicum Beach (© **250/752-9532;** www.
qualicum.bc.ca), or the **Parksville Visitor Info Centre,** 1275 E. Island Hwy. (© **250/
248-3613**).

EXPLORING THE AREA

While Qualicum Beach and Parksville share similar beaches and are all but connected by
country-club developments and marinas, there are differences. Parksville has several large
resorts and beachfront hotels, and is more of a developed strip without much of a town
center. In contrast, Qualicum Beach has more of a town center with shopping and
cafes—but this part of town is a few miles inland, away from the beach.

In Qualicum Beach, you can access the beach from many points along Hwy. 19A, the
old Island Highway. Likewise, in Parksville, the beach is accessible downtown from the
old Island Highway, near the junction of Hwy. 4A, and at the adjacent Parksville Community Beach and Playground. However, the best beaches are preserved in **Rathtrevor
Beach Provincial Park,** just east of Parksville's town center. The 348-hectare (860-acre)
park offers trails, bird-watching sites, and a campground.

Note: If you're looking for miles of broad, white-sand strands lapped by azure water,
you might be surprised. The sea is quite shallow here, with a very gentle slope. When the
tide goes out, it exposes hundreds of acres of gray-sand flats. When the tide is in, the
beach disappears beneath the shallow waters. There are benefits to this: The summer sun
bakes the sand while the tide is out, so when the tide comes back in, the shallow water
is warmed by the sand, thus making the water agreeable for swimming.

When you're not on the beach, one particularly good place to stop in Qualicum Beach
is the **Old School House,** 122 Fern Rd. W. (© **250/752-6133;** www.theoldschool
house.org), which now houses galleries, studios, and a gift shop.

There's no better place for a garden stroll than the **Milner Gardens and Woodland,**
2179 W. Highland Hwy. (© **250/752-6153;** www.mala.ca/milnergardens), a heritage
garden recently opened to the public. Comprising 24 hectares (59 acres) of old-growth,
Douglas-fir forest and 4 hectares (10 acres) of planted gardens, the Milner Gardens are
part of a 1930s estate, which also includes a historic home where Queen Elizabeth II
once stayed. Given to the local university in 1996, the estate was gradually turned into a
destination garden by a small army of horticulture students and local volunteers. Plantings include an artist's garden and many unusual rhododendrons, at their most colorful
in late spring. Paths thread through the forests, and garden tours are available. Afternoon
tea is served in the Milner house. Open 10am to 5pm daily from May through Labour
Day, and Thursday through Sunday in April and Labour Day through mid-October
(Canadian Thanksgiving); C$10 adults, C$6 students 12 and older.

Horne Lake Caves Provincial Park

West of Qualicum Beach, **Horne Lake Caves Provincial Park** (© **250/954-4600** for
Strathcona Park District) offers access to a lakeside park area, with camping and canoeing, and a system of caves on the slopes of the Beaufort Range (bring at least two sources

of light, and, in summer, rent a helmet from the park office). From mid-June to Labour Day, the park offers guided tours, like the family-oriented Riverbend Cave Interpretive Program. The park is located 26km (16 miles) west of Qualicum Beach, off exit 75 from Hwy. 19 or 19A. For more adventure, contact **Island Pacific Adventures/Horne Lake Adventures** (© **250/757-8687;** www.hornelake.com) to reserve space on its 3-hour Wet and Wild Expedition (C$54), which features climbing and splashing through part of the cave system; children must be 12 years of age or older.

WHERE TO STAY

Campsites at **Rathtrevor Beach Provincial Park** (© **800/689-9025** for reservations, or 250/248-9449 in the off season), open year-round, go for C$15 to C$24.

Casa Grande Inn   The handsome Casa Grande Inn is one of Qualicum Beach's top choices for its comfortably furnished rooms and selection of room types. It's also one of the newer lodgings along this stretch of the beach. You have a choice of standard hotel-type units, rooms with kitchenettes and that can sleep up to four, or one-bedroom suites with full kitchens. All rooms have balconies. The beach is just across the road, and shopping is just a 10-minute drive away.

3080 W. Island Hwy., Qualicum Beach, BC V9K 2C5. © **888/720-2272** or 250/752-4400. Fax 250/752-4401. www.casagrandeinn.com. 17 units. C$110–C$150 double; C$140–C$175 suite. Lower off-season rates. AE, MC, V. Free parking. *In room:* A/C, TV, fridge, hair dryer, Wi-Fi.

Pacific Shores Resort and Spa ★   Pacific Shores is a large timeshare development perched above a half-mile of waterfront in a grove of arbutus and fir trees—this marvelous location, plus a wide range of room types, make this a good lodging choice for a relaxing getaway. Accommodations include basic hotel-style units or large suites with up to two bedrooms, a kitchen, fireplaces, a balcony, and two bathrooms, one with a jetted tub; it's a good idea to call and discuss the various unit configurations with the reservations staff. Families are welcome, and minimum stays of a week are preferred in summer. But you usually will also have the option to rent a hotel-style room for shorter stays. Several rooms offer wheelchair access. Trails lead across the property, which includes its own fish hatchery. Most impressive are the extensive 6-hectare (15-acre) gardens—if you see a plant you like, you may be able to purchase a cutting from the nursery (U.S. citizens can bring home up to a dozen plants from Canada, with some restrictions). The Aqua-terre Spa offers a full selection of spa and massage treatments. The Landing West Coast Grill offers regional fine dining plus two saltwater aquariums as walls—reportedly, the largest private aquarium in B.C.

1–1600 Stroulger Rd., Nanoose Bay, BC V9P 9B7. © **866/986-2222** or 250/468-7121. Fax 250/468-2001. www.pacific-shores.com. 132 units. C$110–C$175 hotel room; C$165–C$235 1-bedroom condo; C$315–345 2-bedroom condo; C$500 3-bedroom condo. AE, DISC, MC, V. Free parking. **Amenities:** Restaurant; lounge; on-site babysitting; health club w/full weight room; Jacuzzis; picnic and barbecue area; large indoor pool w/"ozonated" water; sauna; complimentary use of kayaks and canoes; outdoor children's play area; convenience store and deli; rooms for those w/limited mobility. *In room:* TV/VCR, fridge (hotel rooms), kitchen (condos), Wi-Fi, fireplace.

Quality Resort Bayside (Value)   Perched right above the sands in central Parksville, this resort offers lots of amenities at moderate prices. Half of the rooms face the beach, and the other half look onto the mountains of Vancouver Island; all are comfortably furnished and have balconies. Heron's offers West Coast cuisine, with summer seating on the deck. The bar features darts, pool, and satellite sports broadcasts.

240 Dogwood St., Parksville, BC V9P 2H5. © **800/663-4232** or 250/248-8333. Fax 250/248-4689. www. **179**
qualityresortparksville.com. 59 units. Oct–Mar C$99–C$119 double; Apr–June C$109–C$139 double;
July–Sept C$129–C$179 double. Extra person C$15. AE, DC, DISC, MC, V. Free parking. Pets allowed for
C$15. **Amenities:** Oceanview restaurant; bar; golf course nearby; health club w/squash courts; Jacuzzi;
indoor pool; room service. *In room:* A/C, TV, hair dryer, Wi-Fi.

Tigh-Na-Mara Resort Hotel ★★★ (Kids) This time-honored log-cabin resort just
keeps getting better. Established in the 1940s on a forested waterfront beach, Tigh-Na-
Mara has expanded over the years with an ever-widening variety of accommodations
choices (all log built), including studio and one-bedroom lodge rooms, plus one- and
two-bedroom cottages. The recently built ocean-side condo units all have stunning sea
views as well as balconies or patios. All have fireplaces and full bathrooms, and almost all
have a kitchen. The cottages are comfortably lived-in and homey, while the condos are
new and lavish. Families will especially appreciate the lengthy list of supervised child-
friendly activities (many of them free); the restaurant in the log-and-stone lodge serves
an eclectic version of Northwest cuisine. The new and impressive **Grotto Spa** ★★ is the
largest in the province and offers a mineral pool, body and massage treatments, plus a
full line of aesthetic spa services. The spa also offers the spa-client-only Treetop Tapas and
Grill, where friends and couples wine and dine in bathrobes after their treatments.

1155 Resort Dr., Parksville, BC V9P 2E5. © **800/663-7373** or 250/248-2072. Fax 250/248-4140. www.
tigh-na-mara.com. 192 units. July–Aug C$199–C$359 double. Rates vary throughout the year. Extra person C$10–C$20. 2 night minimum stays apply in midsummer and on holidays. MC, V. Free parking. Pets
allowed in cottages Sept–June, add C$30 per stay. **Amenities:** Restaurant; bar; babysitting; bike rental;
children's programs; concierge; golf courses nearby; fitness facilities; indoor pool; sauna; full spa facilities;
unlit tennis court; paddle boats; basketball; children's outdoor playground; table tennis. *In room:* TV w/
on-demand movies, fridge, Wi-Fi, gas or wood-burning fireplace.

WHERE TO DINE

Beach House Café INTERNATIONAL The flavors of Asia and Austria mingle at
this popular beachside restaurant. An outstanding choice is the Madras shrimp and fruit
coconut-milk curry, also available as a vegetarian dish by request. On the European side
of the menu, the Jagerschnitzel (veal medallions with wild-mushroom sauce) is a standout. The dining room is comfortable, filled with sun and views.

2775 W. Island Hwy., Qualicum Beach. © **250/752-9626.** Reservations suggested. Main courses C$10–
C$22. MC, V. Daily 11am–2:30pm and 5–10pm.

Kalvas Restaurant SEAFOOD Kalvas is the locals' special-occasion restaurant, a
rustic-looking lodge with a bustling dining room. The specialties are steaks and seafood
prepared in traditional supper-club style: sole amandine, New York steak, steamed
Dungeness crab served with drawn butter, and nine preparations of Fanny Bay oysters.

180 Molliet St., Parksville. © **250/248-6933.** Reservations recommended. Main courses C$12–C$60. MC,
V. Sun–Fri 5–10pm; Sat 5–11pm.

Lefty's Fresh Foods INTERNATIONAL Originally a vegetarian eatery, Lefty's has
added healthy chicken and meat dishes. The emphasis is on modern comfort food: salads,
sandwiches, burgers, pasta, stir-fries, and focaccia pizzas. In addition to the original
Qualicum Beach location, there's now also a Lefty's in Parksville.

710 Memorial St., Qualicum Beach, and 101–280 E. Island Hwy., Parksville. © **250/752-7530** (Qualicum)
and 250/954-3886 (Parksville). www.leftys.tv. Main courses C$8–C$20. AE, DC, MC, V. Thurs–Sat 8am–
10pm (to 9pm off season); Sun–Wed 8am–8pm.

Shady Rest Waterfront Pub & Restaurant CANADIAN   Both the restaurant and the pub here have outdoor seating, and both serve the same Qualicum Beach–style comfort food. The appetizer menu is extensive, and entrees range from stir-fries to burgers, plus the freshest local seafood.

3109 W. Island Hwy., Qualicum Beach. © **250/752-9111.** Reservations recommended for the restaurant. Main courses C$10–C$18. MC, V. Restaurant daily 8am–9pm; pub-food service Sun–Thurs 11am–9pm, Fri–Sat 11am–10pm. Pub until 1am most nights.

4 EN ROUTE TO VANCOUVER ISLAND'S WEST COAST

From Parksville, Hwy. 4 cuts due west, climbing up over the mountainous spine of Vancouver Island before dropping into Port Alberni, at the head of the Pacific's Alberni Inlet. From here, you can join the mail boats **MV _Lady Rose_** ★ and **MV _Frances Barkley_** ★ as they ply the inlet's narrow waters, delivering mail, supplies, and passengers to isolated communities. Bamfield, the southern terminus of the mail-boat run, is one of the two departure points for the West Coast Trail. Mail boats from Port Alberni also negotiate the waters of Barkley Sound and the Broken Group Islands before arriving at Ucluelet, a gentrifying fishing port.

THE DRIVE TO PORT ALBERNI

West of Parksville is the **North Island Wildlife Recovery Centre,** 1240 Leffler Rd., Errington (© **250/248-8534;** www.niwra.org), which takes in injured and orphaned wildlife, with the goal of returning them to the wild. Guided tours of the center are available March through October. The tour includes the Museum of Nature, with hands-on exhibits and a nature walk through a waterfall; the Eagle Flight cage (Canada's largest), where eagles can be viewed through one-way glass; an extensive public viewing area that houses the non-releasable wildlife; and a nature trail around the center's release pond, showing B.C.'s flora. In addition, the "Wildlife Learning Centre" offers live animal presentations. It's open mid-March through October, daily from 9am to 5pm; admission is C$5 adult, C$3 children. Take a left from Hwy. 4 onto Bellevue Road; turn right onto Ruffels Road and then left onto Leffler Road.

Just 3km (1¾ miles) west of the junction with Hwy. 19, turn south to **Englishman's Falls Provincial Park.** Easy trails lead to both the upper and lower falls. Picnic tables and a basic campground are available.

Below the cliffs of 1,818m (5,965-ft.) Mount Arrowsmith, Hwy. 4 passes along the shores of **Cameron Lake.** The western end of the lake is preserved as **MacMillan Provincial Park,** with a magnificent stand of old-growth forest called Cathedral Grove.

Finally, you'll reach **Port Alberni,** a hardworking town of nearly 20,000. The busy port is home to a number of fishing charters and boat-tour companies, as well as the mail boats that offer day trips to Bamfield and Ucluelet. If you need a hotel, consider the **Hospitality Inn,** 3835 Redford St. (© **877/723-8111** or 250/723-8111; www.hospitalityinn portalberni.com), with doubles from C$145; or the **Best Western Barclay Hotel,** 4277 Stamp Ave. (© **800/563-6590** or 250/724-7171; www.bestwesternbarclay.com), with rooms from C$139 in high season.

Lady Rose Marine Services (© 800/663-7192 Apr–Sept, or 250/723-8313; www. ladyrosemarine.com) operates two packet freighters that deliver mail and supplies to communities along the Alberni Inlet and Barkley Sound. The boats take sightseers to the wild outback of Vancouver Island, for a fascinating glimpse into the daily life of remote fishing and logging communities. You'll likely spot bald eagles, bears, orcas, and porpoises. Year-round, the freighters depart from north Harbour Quay at 8am on Tuesday, Thursday, and Saturday. They head to Bamfield via Kildonan, with an hour-long layover before returning to Port Alberni at 5pm. From the first Friday in July to the first Friday in September, there's an additional 8am Friday sailing from Port Alberni to Bamfield. The company also operates from Sechart (see the box on p. 187).

June through September, freighters depart on Monday, Wednesday, and Friday at 8am for Ucluelet via Sechart near the Broken Group Islands, arriving back in Port Alberni at 7pm. The freighters also convey kayakers bound for the Broken Group Islands. Lady Rose Marine Services drops off kayakers at Sechart, on a spur of Vancouver Island across from the islands themselves; kayakers then make the crossing on their own (Oct–May the freighters will drop kayakers at the islands with advance notice). From the first Sunday in July to the first Sunday in September, there's an extra 8am Sunday sailing to Bamfield via Sechart.

Round-trip fares are double the one-way fare. One-way fare to Bamfield is C$29. One-way fare to Ucluelet is C$36. You can go to Kildonan for C$25 each way, or to Sechart for C$33. Children 8 to 15 pay half the adult fare. Bring windproof jackets and hats, as the weather can change dramatically during the course of the trip. Reservations are required.

5 THE WEST COAST TRAIL ★ & PACIFIC RIM NATIONAL PARK ★

The west coast of Vancouver Island is a magnificent area of old-growth forests, stunning fjords (or "sounds" in local parlance), rocky coasts, and sandy beaches. And although **Pacific Rim National Park** (www.pc.gc.ca) was established in 1971, it wasn't until 1993 that the area really exploded into the greater consciousness. That was when thousands of environmentalists from around the world gathered to protest the clear-cutting of old-growth forests in Clayoquot Sound. When footage of the protests ran on the evening news, people who saw the landscape for the first time were moved to come experience it firsthand. Tourism in the area has never looked back.

Three units make up the park. Along the southwest coast is a strip of land that contains the 75km (47-mile) **West Coast Trail,** which runs between Port Renfrew (covered in chapter 7) and Bamfield (see above). Though considered one of the world's great hikes, the grueling 5- to 7-day journey—with frequent dangerous river crossings and rocky scrambles—is not for the inexperienced. **Broken Group Islands** is a wilderness archipelago in the mouth of Barkley Sound, and a popular diving and kayaking spot (p. 187). **Long Beach** fronts onto the Pacific between Ucluelet and Tofino. Long Beach is more than 30km (19 miles) long, broken here and there by rocky headlands and bordered by tremendous groves of cedar and Sitka spruce. Park entry is C$7.80 adults, C$6.80 seniors, C$3.90 youths, and C$20 families.

The town of **Ucluelet** (pronounced "You-*clue*-let," meaning "safe harbor") sits on the southern end of the Long Beach peninsula, on the edge of Barkley Sound. Though it has a winter population of only 1,900, thousands of visitors arrive between March and May to see the Pacific gray whales.

At the far northern tip of the peninsula, **Tofino** (pop. 1,600) borders beautiful Clayoquot Sound. Hikers and beachcombers come to Tofino simply for the scenery. Others use it as a base from which to explore the sound—it's the center of the local eco-tourism business. No small number of travelers arrive here with eating in mind: This remote town is noted for its excellent restaurants.

ESSENTIALS

Getting There

BY PLANE   Orca Airways (© 888/359-6722 or 604/270-6722; www.flyorcaair.com) offers year-round flights between Vancouver International Airport and Tofino.

BY CAR   Tofino, Ucluelet, and Long Beach all lie near the end of Hwy. 4 on the west coast of Vancouver Island. From Nanaimo, take the Island Highway (Hwy. 19) north for 52km (32 miles). Just before the town of Parksville is a turnoff for Hwy. 4, which leads to the mid-island town of Port Alberni (38km/24 miles) and then to the coastal towns of Tofino (135km/84 miles west of Port Alberni) and Ucluelet (103km/64 miles west). The road is paved but very winding after Port Alberni.

BY FERRY   A 4½-hour ride aboard the **Lady Rose Marine Services** (© 800/663-7192 Apr–Sept, or 250/723-8313; www.ladyrosemarine.com) MV *Lady Rose* takes you from Port Alberni to Ucluelet. See p. 181 for more information.

BY BUS   Greyhound Vancouver Island Coach (© 250/388-5248) operates regular daily service between Victoria and Tofino. The 6-hour trip, departing Victoria at 7:30am and arriving in Tofino at 2:35pm, costs C$65. The bus also stops in Nanaimo and can pick up passengers arriving from Vancouver on the ferry. The **Tofino Bus** (© 866/986-3466;** www.tofinobus.com) also offers daily bus service from Victoria and Vancouver to Tofino. A one-way ticket from Victoria to Tofino is C$64.

Visitor Information

The **Pacific Rim Visitor Centre,** located just north of the Ucluelet junction with Hwy. 4 (© 250/726-4600; www.pacificrimvisitor.ca), is a clearinghouse of information on the west coast of Vancouver Island. It's open all year. From October through March, it's open Tuesday to Saturday 10am to 4pm; through mid-June, it's open the same days but till 5pm. From mid-June through September, it's open daily 9am to 7pm.

THE HIKE OF A LIFETIME: THE WEST COAST TRAIL

The rugged West Coast Trail has gained a reputation as one of the world's greatest extreme hiking adventures. Each year, about 9,000 people tackle the entire challenging 75km (47-mile) route, and thousands more hike the very accessible 11km (6¾-mile) **oceanfront stretch** at the northern trail head near Bamfield. Imperative for the full hike are a topographic map and tidal table, stamina for rock climbing as well as hiking, and advanced wilderness-survival and minimum-impact camping knowledge. Go with at least two companions, pack weatherproof gear, and bring 15m (50 ft.) of climbing rope per person. Only 52 people per day are allowed to enter the main trail (26 from Port Renfrew, 26 from Bamfield), and registration with the park office is mandatory. Most people make the hike in 5 to 7 days.

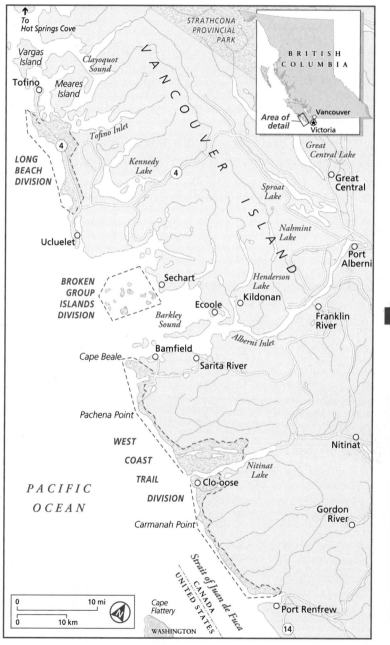

To Hot Springs Cove

STRATHCONA PROVINCIAL PARK

Vargas Island

Clayoquot Sound

Tofino

Meares Island

VANCOUVER ISLAND

Tofino Inlet

LONG BEACH DIVISION

Kennedy Lake

4

4

Ucluelet

BROKEN GROUP ISLANDS DIVISION

Sechart

Barkley Sound

Ecoole

Kildonan

Henderson Lake

Sproat Lake

Nahmint Lake

Great Central Lake

Great Central

Port Alberni

Franklin River

Bamfield

Cape Beale

Sarita River

Alberni Inlet

Pachena Point

WEST COAST TRAIL DIVISION

PACIFIC OCEAN

Clo-oose

Nitinat Lake

Nitinat

Carmanah Point

Gordon River

Cape Flattery

Strait of Juan de Fuca

CANADA
UNITED STATES

WASHINGTON

Port Renfrew

14

0   10 mi
0   10 km

N

Area of detail

BRITISH COLUMBIA

Vancouver

Victoria

The West Coast Trail land is temperate coastal rainforest dominated by old-growth spruce, hemlock, and cedar. The topography ranges from sandy beaches to rocky headlands and wide sandstone ledges. Caves, arches, tidal pools, and waterfalls add variety to the shoreline.

If you hike the trail from May 1 through June 14 or September 16 to September 30, which the park service considers shoulder season, you no longer need reservations. Simply show up at one of the trail **information centers** at Gordon River in the south or Pachena Bay in the north, attend the orientation session, and set off. You will need reservations if you intend to hike the trail in high season, from June 15 through September 15. Call **Super Natural BC** (© 800/435-5622 or 250/387-1642) after April 1 to schedule your entry reservation for the coming high season. In summer, you can also contact the **parks service** (© 250/728-3234 or 250/647-5434; www.pc.gc.ca) for information. Make your reservations as early as possible. There's a C$25 booking fee and C$128 trail-use fee. If you want to try your luck, there are 10 daily first-come, first-served wait-list openings at each trail head information center. The park service says you'll probably wait 1 to 3 days for an opening.

UCLUELET

When fishing was the premier industry on the coast, a constant flow of ships frequented Ucluelet's processing and packing plants. With the boom in eco-tourism, however, the town is scrambling to reinvent itself. It now offers a few fine B&Bs and cabin resorts but has yet to catch up to Tofino. Ucluelet is cheaper though, just as close to Long Beach, and more likely to have vacancies in the high season.

Fishing, kayaking, and whale-watching are the main attractions. For custom fishing charters, contact **Roanne Sea Adventures,** in the boat basin (© 250/726-4494; www. roanne.ca). To combine lodging with your fishing expedition, check out **Island West Resort,** 1990 Bay St. (© 250/726-7515; www.islandwestresort.com), or, for more luxury, Oak Bay Marine Group's **Canadian Princess Resort** (see below).

Subtidal Adventures, 1950 Peninsula Rd., in the West Ucluelet Mall (© 877/444-1134 or 250/726-7336; www.subtidaladventures.com), offers whale-watching trips, kayaking expeditions, and a sunset cruise into the Broken Group Islands (C$89 adult). **Aquamarine Adventures,** Small Craft Harbour Floathouse 200, near the base of Hemlock Street (© 866/726-7727 or 250/726-7727; www.westcoastwhales.com), operates whale-watching tours (C$79–C$89) using 12-seater Sundancers, rigid-hulled inflatable vessels that allow for maximum maneuverability. **Majestic Ocean Kayaking,** 1167 Helen Rd. (© 800/889-7644 or 250/726-2868; www.oceankayaking.com), offers 3-hour kayak trips around Ucluelet harbor (C$60 adults) and more adventurous day-trips to the Broken Group Islands (C$235 adults).

(**Moments**) **Diving the Graveyard of the Pacific**

The waters off the park's West Coast Trail are known throughout the world as "the graveyard of the Pacific." Hundreds of 19th- and 20th-century shipwrecks silently attest to the hazards of sailing without an experienced guide in these unforgiving waters. Underwater interpretive trails narrate the history of the area—rated among the world's best by the Cousteau Society. Follow the links at **www.3routes.com** for an index of diving outfitters that serve Vancouver Island dive sites.

The 3km (1.9-mile) **Wild Pacific Trail** takes you out to the Amphitrite Lighthouse, a prime whale-watching spot.

Where to Stay

Ucluelet has a number of newish condo developments with cookie-cutter accommodations, but for something more unique, reserve at one of the following.

Black Rock Resort ★★   New, and stunningly situated on a rocky promontory above the pounding Pacific, the Black Rock Resort is *the* place to stay in Ucluelet if you're looking for upscale, fashion-forward design. Rooms feature large, beautifully furnished rooms with incredible vistas: From your floor-to-ceiling windows or balcony, watch for whales, or just relax and watch the waves blasting against the rocks. (*Note:* Lower priced rooms have forest views.) You have a choice of room types: large studio-style hotel rooms or one- and two-bedroom suites, all decorated with somewhat chilly contemporary decor (nothing to distract from the view). All units have gas fireplaces, kitchenettes, and particularly elegant bathrooms, with "rain" showerheads, heated floors, and two-person soaker tubs. The resort's spa, called Drift, offers an extensive range of rejuvenating and restorative treatments. The restaurant, Fetch, offers marvelous regional fine dining (see below).

Marine Drive (P.O. Box 310 596), Ucluelet, BC V0R 3A0. ✆ **877/762-5011** or 250/726-4800. Fax 250/726-2430. www.blackrockresort.com. 133 units. From C$315 double; C$385–C$465 suite. Lower off-season rates. **Amenities:** Restaurant; lounge; free airport transfers; room service; spa. *In room:* TV/DVD, CD player, kitchenette, Wi-Fi, balcony, gas fireplace.

Canadian Princess Resort   If you're coming to Ucluelet to fish—or even if you're not—the Canadian Princess Resort is an enjoyable and high-spirited place to stay. You can lodge either on land in standard hotel-style rooms or in traditional bunk-roomed cabins onboard the *Canadian Princess,* a former survey ship permanently moored adjacent to the hotel in Ucluelet's central Boat Basin. Hotel accommodations are very comfortable, while the ship cabins are authentically snug, with the toilet and shower down the hall. Also aboard the ship are a fine-dining restaurant and two lounges, all with charming maritime decor. The resort focuses on fishing trips out into the Pacific—each day, cabin cruisers set out on guided fishing trips; gear is provided.

1943 Peninsula Rd., Ucluelet, BC V0R 3A0. ✆ **800/663-7090** or 250/726-7771. Fax 250/726-7121. www.canadianprincess.com. 76 units. C$89–C$215 double. Guided fishing packages with 2 fishing trips and 2 nights' stay begin at C$479 in high season. AE, MC, V. Closed late Sept to late Apr. **Amenities:** Restaurant; 2 lounges. *In room (hotel):* TV, hair dryer.

A Snug Harbour Inn ★   A beautiful cliff-top B&B, A Snug Harbour Inn even overlooks its own little bay. Guests can make use of several large decks (one with a hot tub) and a monstrous telescope to watch the sea lions on the reef just offshore. The inn is luxurious—the rooms are spacious, with queen- or king-size beds, opulent bathrooms, and jetted tubs. The heart-shaped tub with a waterfall may be a bit over-the-top, but who's complaining? Owner Skip Rowland had the inn built by a shipwright, and the craftsmanship is evident, with wonderful woodwork and fine nautical joinery. The cottage features two luxury rooms, each with a king-size bed, jetted tub, fireplace, heated floors, and balcony. One room is wheelchair accessible; the other is pet friendly.

460 Marine Dr., Box 367, Ucluelet, BC V0R 3A0. ✆ **888/936-5222** or 250/726-2686. www.awesomeview.com. 6 units. June–Sept C$270–C$355 double; Nov–Feb C$190–C$225 double; Oct and Mar–May C$215–C$280 double. Rates include breakfast. DC, MC, V. Children 16 and older welcome. **Amenities:** Deck w/Jacuzzi; great room w/kitchen, fireplace, and guest fridge. *In room:* TV/DVD, hair dryer, fireplace, Jacuzzi, private deck.

Terrace Beach Resort ★ This oceanfront assemblage of cottages, cabins, lofts, and suites, set along boardwalks and decks amid magnificent old-growth spruce and firs, feels like an old-time fishing village, huddled before the waves. Except that at the Terrace Beach Resort, all the accommodations are modern and top-notch. Five different kinds of accommodations are offered, from oceanfront cabins to two-story loft units and suites, nearly all with balconies and most with views over the surging surf. Each of the units is individually decorated, and most have private hot tubs, full kitchens (no ovens, but a gas barbecue on the deck), dining areas, and large four-piece bathrooms. Some of the cabins are truly commodious, with four stories, sleeping up to eight, and with room for six in the hot tub! Have a look at the website; then call the resort to discuss which of the units fits your needs—there are many choices, all of them very pleasant.

1002 Peninsula Rd. (Box 96), Ucluelet, BC V0R 3A0. © **250/726-2901.** Fax.250/726-2900. www.terrace beachresort.ca. 20 units. C$99–C$189 suites; C$189–C$349 lofts; C$349–C$369 cabins. Extra person C$10. Children 12 and under stay free in parent's room. 2-night minimum stay during high season. MC, V. Pets $20 per stay. **Amenities:** Wi-Fi. *In room:* TV/VCR, CD player, hair dryer, kitchen, fireplace, Jacuzzi and/or jetted tub, gas barbecue.

Where to Dine

Fine dining is only just beginning to have a presence in Ucluelet, as urban refugees with a flair for cooking try to make a go of coastal living. Overlooking the harbor is **Eagle's Nest Marine Pub,** 140 Bay St. (© **250/726-7515**), open Monday to Saturday 10am to midnight and Sunday 10am to 10pm, with traditional pub grub. The **Stewart Room Restaurant** on the Canadian Princess, 1943 Peninsula (© **250/726-7771**), offers seafood and fine dining aboard a 71m (233-ft.) moored ship.

Fetch ★★ CONTEMPORARY CANADIAN Not only does this restaurant have an eye-popping view of the surging Pacific and trendsetting decor, but it also has Andrew Springett, former chef at the Wickaninnish Inn. He brings all his skills and magic to this stunning new restaurant. As much as possible, all ingredients are sourced locally, and that's good news, as the waters off Ucluelet are abundant with excellent quality fish and shellfish, and Vancouver Island has myriad small farms and ranches. Springett is a master at combining vibrant flavors and textures, such as parsnips and apples with crispy duck confit, and curried Dungeness crab with mango and fennel. Service is excellent, and every bite is a revelation. If you're in the mood for a drink and a snack, the lounge menu at Float will also provide great pleasure.

Marine Dr. © **250/726-4800.** www.blackrockresort.com. Reservations required. Main courses C$26–C$30. AE, MC, V. Daily 7:30am–9pm.

TOFINO

Once the center of massive environmental protests that drew the world's attention, Tofino is now a rather schizophrenic town—part eco-tourism outfitters, activists, and serious granolas; part former loggers and fishermen; and part Tla-o-qui-aht and Ahousaht peoples, who live mostly outside the town. Conflict was common in the early years, but recently all parties seem to have learned to get along.

The reason for Tofino's popularity is not hard to fathom. Tofino offers incredible marine vistas at the end of a thin finger of land, battered by the Pacific to the west and lapped by Tofino Sound on the east. The town is notched with tiny bays and inlets, with a multitude of islands, many of them very mountainous, just off the coast. Farther east, the jagged, snowcapped peaks of Strathcona Park fill the horizon.

Broken Group Islands

Lying off the coast of Ucluelet in Barkley Sound are the Broken Group Islands, an archipelago of about 300 islands and islets that are part of Pacific Rim National Park. Due to the relatively calm waters, abundant wildlife, and dramatic seascapes, these islands are popular destinations for experienced sea kayakers and ocean canoeists. Divers can explore historic shipwrecks as well as reefs teeming with marine life. The underwater drop-offs shelter large populations of feather stars, rockfish, and wolf eels that grow as long as 2m (6^1/$_2$ ft.) and occasionally poke their heads out of their caves.

Access to the Broken Group Islands is limited. In Ucluelet, you'll find a number of operators who can arrange a trip, including **Majestic Ocean Kayaking** (see above), with fully guided 4-day trips to the islands beginning at C$999. You can also pass through the islands on a packet freighter from Port Alberni (see "MV *Lady Rose* & MV *Frances Barkley*," on p. 181).

Sechart is also the site of the **Sechart Whaling Station Lodge,** an operation of **Lady Rose Marine Services** (© 800/663-7192 Apr–Sept, or 250/723-8313; www.ladyrosemarine.com). It primarily serves the needs of kayakers, though it's open to anyone who wants a unique wilderness experience. Rates are C$140 per person or C$210 for two people sharing the same room, including three family-style meals a day. The only ways to get to the lodge are via the packet freighters, a **Toquart Connector Water Taxi** (© 250/720-7358) from Bamfield, or your own vessel. Kayak rentals are available. For reservations, contact Lady Rose Marine Services (above).

Tofino is becoming more crowded and subject to a particular brand of gentrification. On the beaches south of town, luxury inns serve the rarified demands of upscale travelers attracted to the area's scenery. There are more fine-dining restaurants and boutiques here than can possibly be justified by the town's size. Dining is as big a draw as sea kayaking for many Tofino visitors.

With all the bustle, it can be difficult at times to find solitude in what's actually still an amazingly beautiful and wild place. Accordingly, more people decide to avoid the crowds and visit Tofino in winter, to watch dramatic storms roll in from the Pacific.

Outdoor Pursuits

FISHING   Sportfishing for salmon, steelhead, rainbow trout, Dolly Varden char, halibut, cod, and snapper is excellent off the west coast of Vancouver Island. **Clayoquot Ventures** (© 888/534-7422 or 250/725-2700; www.tofinofishing.com) organizes fishing charters throughout the Clayoquot Sound area. Deep-sea, and both saltwater and freshwater fly-fishing, excursions are offered. The company supplies all the gear, a guide, and a boat. Prices start at a minimum of C$110 per hour, with a minimum of 5 hours. A day-long fishing trip for 3 adults on an 8m (26-ft.) boat costs C$995. A nonresident saltwater or freshwater license is available at tackle shops, which also carry *BC Tidal Waters Sport Fishing Guide, BC Sport Fishing Regulations Synopsis for Non-Tidal Waters,* and the *BC Fishing Directory and Atlas.*

HIKING In and around **Long Beach,** numerous marked trails 1 to 3.5km (.6–2.2 miles) long take you through the thick, temperate rainforest edging the shore. The **Gold Mine Trail** (about 3.5km/2.2 miles long) near Florencia Bay still has a few artifacts from the days when a gold-mining operation flourished here. The partially boardwalked **South Beach Trail** (less than 1.5km/.9 mile long) leads through the moss-draped rainforest onto small, quiet coves like Lismer Beach and South Beach, where you can see abundant life in the rocky tidal pools. The 1km (.6-mile) **Schooner Beach Trail,** just south of Tofino, passes through mature rainforest before dropping onto scenic Schooner Beach, at the northern end of the park's Long Beach. The **Big Cedar Trail,** on Meares Island, is a 3km (1.9-mile) boardwalked path that was built to showcase the old-growth forest. Maintained by the Tla-o-qui-aht band, the trail has a long staircase leading up to the Hanging Garden Tree, which is said to be between 1,000 and 1,500 years old. Many Tofino outfitters offer tours and boat transportation to the trail.

Nearer to town, the paths in the 5-hectare (12-acre) **Tofino Botanical Gardens,** 1084 Pacific Rim Hwy. (✆ **250/725-1220;** www.tbgf.org), meander past theme gardens and old-growth forest and wind down to Tofino Inlet. Admission is C$10 for adults, C$6 for students, and free for children under 12. Open daily from 9am to dusk.

KAYAKING Perhaps the quintessential Clayoquot experience, and certainly one of the most fun, is to slip into a kayak and paddle out into the sound. For beginners, half-day tours to Meares Island (usually with the chance to do a little hiking) are an especially good bet. For rentals, lessons, and tours, try **Pacific Kayak,** 606 Campbell St., at Jamie's Whaling Station (✆ **250/725-3232;** www.tofino-bc.com/pacifickayak). The **Tofino Sea-Kayaking Company,** 320 Main St., Tofino (✆ **800/863-4664** or 250/725-4222; www.tofino-kayaking.com), offers kayaking packages ranging from 4-hour paddles around Meares Island (from C$74 per person) to weeklong paddling and camping expeditions. Instruction by experienced guides makes even your first kayaking experience a comfortable, safe, and enjoyable one.

Guides from the Nuu-chah-nulth First Nation also give tours on oceangoing canoes. **Tla-ook Cultural Adventures** (✆ **877/942-2663** or 250/725-2656; www.tlaook.com) offers paddle trips with commentary by First Nations guides to Meares Island (C$64 per person) and other Clayoquot Sound destinations. Daylong paddle excursions explore traditional hunting and fishing grounds and end with a salmon feast (C$140 per person).

SURFING The big, lashing waves that the Pacific delivers to Long Beach have become popular with surfers. A number of businesses have sprung up to address their needs, including **Pacific Surf School,** 440 Campbell St. (✆ **888/777-9961** or 250/725-2155; www.pacificsurfschool.com), which offers lessons and camps for beginners, plus rentals and gear sales. A 3-hour group lesson is C$79; private lessons are also available. **Live to Surf Inc.,** 1180 Pacific Rim Hwy. (✆ **250/725-4464;** www.livetosurf.com), is Tofino's oldest surf shop, since 1984. It also has the largest selection of new and used boards, and offers lessons and advice on local beaches.

WHALE-WATCHING, NATURE TOURS & BIRDING A number of outfitters conduct tours through this region inhabited by gray whales, bald eagles, porpoises, bears, orcas, seals, and sea lions. In addition, **Hot Springs Cove,** accessible only by water, is a natural hot spring 67km (42 miles) north of Tofino. Take a water taxi, sail, canoe, or kayak up to Clayoquot Sound to enjoy swimming in the steaming pools and bracing waterfalls. A number of kayak outfitters and boat charters offer trips to the springs.

March to October, **Jamie's Whaling Station,** 606 Campbell St., Tofino, BC V0R 2Z0 (✆ **800/667-9913** or 250/725-3919; www.jamies.com), uses a 20m (66-ft.) power cruiser as well as a fleet of Zodiacs for tours to watch the gray whales. In addition to whale-watching and hot springs expeditions, **Seaside Adventures** (© 888/332-4252 or 250/725-2292; www.seaside-adventures.com) offers bear-watching trips from May through September. Fares for both companies' expeditions generally run between C$80 and C$100 per person for a 2- or 3-hour tour.

March to November, **Remote Passages,** Meares Landing, 71 Wharf St. (© 800/666-9833 or 250/725-3330; www.remotepassages.com), runs daily 2½-hour whale-watching tours in Clayoquot Sound on Zodiac boats, costing C$84 for adults and C$69 for children under 12. The company also conducts a 7-hour whale-watching/hot springs trip at C$110 for adults and C$95 for children under 12. Reservations are recommended.

For bird-watchers, the protected waters of Clayoquot Sound and the beaches of Pacific Rim National Park offer fantastic birding opportunities. **Just Birding** (© 250/725-2520; www.justbirding.com) offers a range of bird-watching adventures, from walking tours of the beaches to paddle trips to bald eagle habitat to boat tours for offshore pelagic birding. Guided trips begin at C$79 per person.

Rainy-Day Activities: Shopping, Storm-Watching & More

When you'd rather be indoors, snuggle up with a book at the **Wildside Booksellers and Espresso Bar,** 320 Main St. (© 250/745-4222), or get a massage or salt glow at the **Ancient Cedars Spa** at the Wickaninnish Inn (© 250/725-3100).

Or, check out the galleries. The **Eagle Aerie Gallery,** 350 Campbell St. (© 250/725-3235), constructed in the style of a First Nations longhouse, features the innovative work of Tsimshian artist Roy Henry Vickers. The **House of Himwitsa,** 300 Main St. (© 250/725-2017; www.himwitsa.com), is also First Nations owned/operated. The quality and craftsmanship of the shop's artwork, masks, baskets, totems, gold and silver jewelry, and apparel are excellent. The **Reflecting Spirit Gallery,** 441 Campbell St. (© 250/725-4229), offers medicine wheels, rocks, and crystals, as well as a great selection of Native art, carvings, wood crafts, and pottery.

Watching the winter storms from big windows has become very popular in Tofino. For a slight twist on this, try the outdoor storm-watching tours offered by the **Long Beach Nature Tour Co. ★** (© 250/726-7099; www.oceansedge.bc.ca). Owner Bill McIntyre, former chief naturalist of Pacific Rim National Park, can explain how storms work and the best locations to get close to them without getting swept away.

Where to Stay

There are easily 100 or more places to stay in Tofino; mid-March through October, the **Long Beach Visitor Information Centre,** about 1.5km (1 mile) from the Hwy. 4 junction to Tofino (© 250/725-3414; www.tourismtofino.com), is open daily 10am to 6pm, and keeps a helpful list of vacancies. Stop here before driving into town if you don't have reservations.

Best Western Tin-Wis Resort (Kids) The Tla-o-qui-aht First Nations band runs this large, hotel-like lodge on MacKenzie Beach. All rooms are spacious, with oceanfront views. Although the Tin-Wis is less deluxe than some of the neighboring beachfront lodges, it's also a good deal less expensive while offering perfectly comfortable rooms and fine amenities. Options include queen loft units and deluxe king rooms with fireplaces, kitchenettes, and Jacuzzi tubs. Most units have sofa beds, making them a good choice for families. The Calm Waters restaurant features contemporary Pacific Northwest cuisine with a focus on local First Nations ingredients.

1119 Pacific Rim Hwy. (Box 380), Tofino, BC V0R 2Z0. ✆ **800/661-9995** or 250/725-4445. Fax 250/725-4447. www.tinwis.com. 85 units. C$242–C$262 double. Substantially lower off-season rates. Senior, AAA, and group discounts available. AE, DC, DISC, MC, V. **Amenities:** Restaurant; lounge; well-equipped exercise room; large Jacuzzi. *In room:* TV, fridge, hair dryer, Wi-Fi.

The Clayoquot Wilderness Resort ★★ (Finds)

This upscale resort company offers an interesting twist on luxury accommodations. The Bedwell River Outpost features safari-style luxury tent accommodations located a short boat or plane ride from Tofino on the Bedwell River. Twenty canvas platform tents, beautifully furnished with Adirondack-style furniture, Oriental rugs, antiques, and other comforts, serve as guest rooms and suites, while dining tents, a lounge tent, and even a massage tent offer visitors a taste of upscale camping. The heart of the outpost is the ranch-style log cookhouse, with a towering double-sided fieldstone fireplace in the open-kitchen attended by chef Timothy May. A range of activities such as horseback riding, sailing, kayaking, and fishing is included in the package. After a full day's adventure, retreat to the three spa-treatment tents for a massage or a revitalizing soak in a wood-fired hot tub. Most packages also include return airfare from Vancouver.

P.O. Box 130, Tofino, BC V0R 2Z0. ✆ **888/333-5405** in North America or 250/725-2688. Fax 250/726-8558. www.wildretreat.com. 20 tents. Mid-May to late Sept. 3-day packages from C$4,750 per person double occupancy. Includes all activities, meals, and transport. AE, MC, V. **Amenities:** Restaurant; bar; Jacuzzi; sauna; watersports equipment; Wi-Fi. *In room:* No phone.

The Inn at Tough City ★

This is possibly Tofino's nicest small inn and certainly the quirkiest (by the way, Tough City was an early nickname for Tofino). Built from salvaged and recycled material, it's filled with antiques, stained glass, and bric-a-brac. The rooms are all unique, with cheerful jewel-toned walls and a dollop of thrift-store chic; several feature soaker tubs, fireplaces, or both. Some rooms have balconies. The on-site restaurant, Tough City Sushi, features seafood and sushi and is open for dinner year-round, lunch in summer season only.

350 Main St. (P.O. Box 8), Tofino, BC V0R 2Z0. ✆ **877/725-2021** or 250/725-2021. Fax 250/725-2088. www.toughcity.com. 8 units. Mid-May to mid-Oct C$169–C$229 double. Shoulder and off-season discounts. AE, MC, V. Pets C$10 per night. **Amenities:** Restaurant. *In room:* TV, hair dryer, Wi-Fi.

Long Beach Lodge Resort ★★

A contender for the title of Tofino's most upscale lodge is this extremely handsome log-and-stone resort perched above the waves on Cox Bay. The great room, filled with fine furniture and flanked by a huge granite fireplace and massive windows overlooking Cox Bay, is the heart of the lodge, serving as dining room, cocktail lounge, and a comfortable living room for snoozing, reading, and watching surfers. Accommodations include lodge rooms (with less expensive rooms facing the forest, not the Pacific) and free-standing duplex cottages. All feature marvelous fir furniture, slate-floored bathrooms with soaker tubs and separate showers, bathrobes, and loads of rich decor (including original artwork); some rooms have fireplaces and balconies/patios. The cottages are 93-sq.-m (1,001-sq.-ft.) dwellings with all the above, plus private hot tubs, a large sitting area with overstuffed couches and chairs, washer and dryer, and a full kitchen.

1441 Pacific Rim Hwy. (Box 897), Tofino, BC V0R 2Z0. ✆ **877/844-7873** or 250/725-2442. Fax 250/725-2402. www.longbeachlodgeresort.com. 60 units. Late June to Oct 1 C$309–C$439 double, C$549 cottage. 3-night minimum cottage stay in high season. Lower shoulder and off-season rates; packages available. Extra person C$30. AE, DC, MC, V. Pets allowed in some cottages. **Amenities:** Restaurant; exercise room; beautifully furnished lodge great room w/fireplace. *In room:* TV/DVD, CD player, fridge, hair dryer.

Middle Beach Lodge ★★ This beautiful lodge/resort complex is on a headland overlooking the ocean just south of Tofino. The rustic look was accomplished by using largely recycled beams and salvaged lumber, and as a result the lodge exudes a sense of venerability and history, despite its recent construction. Accommodations are in a variety of structures: a "beach house" with standard hotel rooms, two lodges (one family oriented, one adults only) with a mix of suites and guest rooms, and oceanfront cabins, some of which can sleep seven. Although most of the suites and cabins have decks, soaker or Jacuzzi tubs, gas fireplaces, CD players, and kitchenettes, it's a good idea to phone the lodge to discuss specific room features, as there are many subtle variations. All guests have access to two lofty common rooms overlooking the ocean. These are good spots to pour a coffee or something stronger and look out over the waves crashing in.

400 Mackenzie Beach Rd. (P.O. Box 100), Tofino, BC V0R 2Z0. ✆ **866/725-2900** or 250/725-2900. Fax 250/725-2901. www.middlebeach.com. 45 units, 19 cabins. C$140–C$200 double; C$245–C$360 suite; C$255–C$460 cabin. 2-night minimum stay required. Shoulder and off-season rates available. Rates include complimentary continental breakfast. AE, MC, V. **Amenities:** Restaurant; exercise room. *In room:* TV/VCR (suites and cabins only), fridge, kitchenette, no phone.

Red Crow Guest House ★ While the Wickaninnish and other coastal lodges show you the wild, stormy west-facing side of Tofino, the Red Crow displays the kinder, subtler beauty on the peninsula's east side. By the sheltered waters of Jensen Bay (excellent for viewing eagles, seals, and shorebirds), this pleasant Cape Cod–style home sits in 2.8 secluded hectares (7 acres) of old-growth forest. Two rooms are in the lower level of the house (with private entrances), opening out onto a fabulous view of the bay—perhaps best seen from the inn's outdoor hot tub. Rooms here are large and pleasant, with queen- or king-size beds and 1920s-style furnishings. In addition, there's a charming two-bedroom garden cottage with full kitchen. Guests have free use of bikes, and canoes are available for exploring offshore islands.

1084 Pacific Rim Hwy. (Box 37), Tofino, BC V0R 2Z0. ✆ **250/725-2275.** Fax 250/725-3214. www.tofinoredcrow.com. 2 rooms, 1 cottage. C$195 suite double; cottage $235 double. Shoulder and off-season rates available. Extra person C$25. V only. *In room:* CD player, fridge, hair dryer, no phone, Wi-Fi.

The Tides Inn on Duffin Cove This comfy B&B offers a friendly welcome and spectacular views of Duffin Cove, an easy stroll from the village center. All rooms have en suite bathrooms, private entrances, and decks or balconies, and one has a fireplace. For families or friends traveling together, there's also a two-bedroom, two-bathroom suite with a wet bar, pool table, and large shared living room. At the bottom of the yard, past the hot tub, a wooden stairway leads down to a semiprivate beach.

160 Arnet Rd. (Box 325), Tofino, BC V0R 2Z0. ✆ **250/725-3765.** Fax 250/725-3325. www.tidesinntofino.com. 3 units. June 15–Sept 30 C$155–C$165. Lower shoulder and off-season rates. Rates include full breakfast. 2-night minimum stay. MC, V. Children 12 and over welcome. **Amenities:** Jacuzzi; deck. *In room:* TV/VCR, fridge, hair dryer, no phone.

Whalers on the Point Guesthouse This woodsy but modern hostel is one way to save money in an increasingly expensive town. Located downtown, with views of Clayoquot Sound, it offers both shared and private rooms; wheelchair-accessible rooms are available. The hostel offers discounted activities, arranged through local outfitters.

81 West St. (Box 296), Tofino, BC V0R 2Z0. ✆ **250/725-3443.** Fax 250/725-3463. www.tofinohostel.com. 55 beds. May–Sept C$30–C$32 dorm single, C$85–C$100 private double; Oct–Apr C$24–C$29 dorm single, C$50–C$65 private double. Hostelling International member, multiday, and family discounts available. MC, V. **Amenities:** Kitchen; Internet kiosk; sauna; Wi-Fi; TV room. *In room:* No phone.

The Wickaninnish Inn ★★★ No matter which room you book at this beautiful inn of cedar, stone, and glass, you'll wake to a magnificent view of the untamed Pacific. The Wick, as it's affectionately known, is on a rocky promontory, surrounded by an old-growth spruce and cedar rainforest and the sprawling sands of Chesterman Beach. Perennially ranked as one of the top inns in North America, the Wick succeeds by blurring the distinction between outdoors and indoors through art, furnishings, architecture, and building materials. Rustic driftwood furniture, richly printed textiles, and local artwork highlight the rooms, each of which features a private balcony, oceanfront view, fireplace, down duvet, soaker tub and stone-lined shower, and luxurious bath amenities. Winter storm-watching packages have become so popular that the inn is nearly as busy in winter as it is in summer. The Pointe Restaurant (see "Where to Dine," below) is one of the top dining rooms in western Canada. The staff can arrange whale-watching, golfing, fishing, and diving packages. Affiliated with Aveda, the inn's Ancient Cedars Spa offers a host of packages and beauty and relaxation treatments.

Osprey Lane at Chesterman Beach, P.O. Box 250, Tofino, BC V0R 2Z0. ✆ **800/333-4604** in North America, or 250/725-3100. Fax 250/725-3110. www.wickinn.com. 75 units. From C$500 double. Special packages available year-round. Reduced shoulder and off-season rates. AE, DC, MC, V. Drive 5km (3 miles) south of Tofino toward Chesterman Beach to Osprey Lane. **Amenities:** Restaurant; bar; babysitting; spa; beach access; walking trail; shuttle service; rooms for those w/limited mobility. *In room:* A/C, TV, CD player, hair dryer, minibar, Wi-Fi, fireplace.

Camping

The 94 campsites on the bluff at **Green Point** are maintained by Pacific Rim National Park (✆ **250/726-7721**). The grounds are full every day in July and August, and the average wait for a site is 1 to 2 days. Leave your name at the ranger station when you arrive to be placed on the list. You're rewarded for your patience with a magnificent ocean view, pit toilets, fire pits, pumped well water, and free firewood (no showers or hookups). Sites are C$18 to C$24. The campground is closed October to March.

The **Bella Pacifica Resort & Campground,** 3.5km (2 miles) south of Tofino on the Pacific Rim Highway (P.O. Box 413), Tofino, BC V0R 2Z0 (✆ **250/725-3400;** www.bellapacifica.com), is privately owned and has 165 campsites from which you can walk to Mackenzie Beach or take the resort's private nature trails to Templar Beach. Flush toilets, hot showers, water, laundry, ice, fire pits, firewood, and full and partial hookups are available. Rates are C$24 to C$48 per two-person campsite. Reserve at least a month in advance for a summer weekend; open mid-February to mid-November.

Where to Dine

For a cup of java and a snack, it's hard to beat the **Caffé Vincenté,** 441 Campbell St. (✆ **250/725-2599**), a touch of urban hip near the entrance to town. See the Inn at Tough City under "Where to Stay," above, for a description of **Tough City Sushi** ★.

The Common Loaf Bake Shop BAKERY/CAFE Locally famous as the gathering place for granolas and lefty rabble-rousers back when they amassed in Tofino to take their stand, the Loaf has since expanded, which just goes to show you can make money selling idealism along with your muffins. Located at the "far" end of town, the Common Loaf does baked goods really well: muffins, cookies, whole-grain breads, and sticky cinnamon buns. It also serves soups, curry, and pizza for lunch.

180 First St. ✆ **250/725-3915.** Reservations not accepted. Main courses C$4–C$12. No credit cards. Summer daily 8am–9pm; winter daily 8am–6pm.

The Pointe Restaurant ★★ PACIFIC NORTHWEST   The famed restaurant at the Wickaninnish Inn is perched on the water's edge at Chesterman Beach, where a 240-degree view of the roaring Pacific is the backdrop to an exceptional dining experience that can only be described as pure Pacific Northwest. The menu focuses on farm-fresh, organic Vancouver Island ingredients, such as quail, lamb, and rabbit, and the bounty of the very waters overlooked by the restaurant, including Dungeness crab, spotted prawns, halibut, and salmon. Grilled octopus is served with baby shrimp and pancetta vinaigrette, while chestnut-honey glazed duck breast comes with fresh porcini pasta. Service is top-notch and the wine list wins top awards from *Wine Spectator.*

The Wickaninnish Inn, Osprey Lane at Chesterman Beach. ✆ **250/725-3100.** Reservations required. Main courses C$29–C$52; 4-course gastronomic menu C$80. AE, MC, V. Daily 8am–9:30pm.

The RainCoast Cafe SEAFOOD/ASIAN FUSION   This cozy restaurant, just off the main street, has developed a deserved reputation for some of the best—and best value—seafood and vegetarian dishes in town. In addition to tempting main courses, there are a number of small plates, which you can assemble into a meal, many featuring local shrimp, oysters, and clams in innovative preparations. Many courses reflect an Asian influence: Local mussels are served with fresh thyme, orange zest, and white wine cream, while fresh wild Chinook salmon comes with maple miso wasabi glaze.

120 Fourth St. ✆ **250/725-2215.** Main courses C$18–C$33. AE, MC, V. Daily 5–9:30pm.

The Schooner ★ PACIFIC NORTHWEST   This big red barn of a building looks like the sort of place that serves up family-style crab suppers—and so it did until a few years ago. However, after a major menu and decor makeover, the Schooner is now one of Tofino's top fine-dining choices. As you'd expect, local fish and shellfish in hearty yet sophisticated preparations dominate the menu. The signature dish is Halibut Bowden Bay, in which local halibut is stuffed with crab, shrimp, and brie and served with an apple brandy peppercorn sauce. Starters include clams in chardonnay and fresh spot prawns in sambal butter. Breakfasts here are legendary—smoked salmon eggs Benedict will kick-start your vacation. In good weather, dine on the deck with views across Tofino Inlet to myriad offshore islands.

331 Campbell St. ✆ **250/725-3444.** Reservations suggested. Main courses C$27–C$39. MC, V. Daily 9–11:30am, noon–3pm, and 5–9:30pm.

Shelter ★★ CONTEMPORARY CANADIAN   You don't come to this landlocked restaurant for the view, but rather for the cooking, which is remarkable in its bright flavors and textures. Shelter, which buys most of its fish and fresh ingredients directly from producers—right off the boat and right off the land—is one of the best of Tofino's new crop of restaurants. Their signature bouillabaisse is stuffed with local fish and shellfish and simmered in a fire-roasted tomato broth; a delicate halibut filet surmounts a bed of spot-prawn risotto. Local white wines dominate the wine list, chosen to highlight the delicate flavors of fish and seafood. Just as there's no ocean view in the narrow, fireplace-warmed dining room, there also are no kitschy totem poles or wooden seagulls in fishing nets. Instead, a single, heraldic surfboard, emblematic of the youthful energy of Shelter's cooking style, dominates the dining room.

601 Campbell St. ✆ **250/725-3353.** www.shelterrestaurant.com. Reservations recommended. Main courses C$16–C$30. MC, V. Daily 5–10pm.

SOBO INTERNATIONAL   This friendly, ambitious restaurant with "fresh food from here and there" got its start as a catering wagon in the Tofino Botanical Gardens, where it was discovered and written up by visiting journalists from the likes of the *New York Times.* It's since moved downtown and during the day, SOBO serves tasty but informal dishes such as smoked seafood chowder, wood-fired pizzas, soba noodle salad, and fish tacos. The evening, however, unveils a more formal dinner service with a creative approach: House-made pappardelle noodles are topped with duck ragu, and roast quail comes glazed with chili and honey.

311 Neill St. ⓒ **250/725-2341.** www.sobo.ca. Reservations recommended on weekends. Main courses C$20–C$24. MC, V. Daily 11am–5pm and 5:30–9:30pm.

6 DENMAN & HORNBY ISLANDS

From Qualicum Beach, follow Hwy. 19A, the "old highway" north, passing forests and viewpoints that look onto Denman and Hornby Islands in the Georgia Strait. Along the way, you'll pass through several small communities, including **Fanny Bay.** The area around Fanny Bay is Vancouver Island's most renowned oyster farming area; ask for Fanny Bay oysters by name at local restaurants. Just north of Fanny Bay is Buckley Bay, the ferry terminus for Denman and Hornby Islands.

"Flower children" were attracted to rural **Hornby** (pop. 1,300) and **Denman** (pop. 1,200) during the 1960s and 1970s. They started organic farms and thriving art communities on these remote islands off the coast of Vancouver Island. Both islands have maintained their bohemian charm, and they mostly deserve their reputation as colonies of "alternative" lifestyles; if you're looking for a laid-back place for a quiet family vacation, these islands are close to perfect. Hornby Island's beaches and provincial parks are another excellent reason to make the journey; and Helliwell Provincial Park features a hiking path along the edge of spectacular ocean-fronting cliffs. The gentle waters around and between these islands are famed for sea kayaking. For more information on Hornby and Denman Islands, go to www.hornbyisland.com and www.denmanisland.com.

GETTING THERE Local **BC Ferries** (ⓒ **250/386-3431**) operate year-round between Buckley Bay and Denman Island; the 18 daily ferry trips take 10 minutes each way, and round-trip tickets cost C$7.90 per passenger and C$19 per vehicle. To reach Hornby Island, you'll need first to cross to Denman; the ferry to Hornby leaves from Denman's southern shore. A dozen ferries daily make the 10-minute crossing between the two islands, with the same fares as above.

The islands are great for two-wheel exploration. Ferry passengers can bring bikes on the ferry for free; bike rentals are widely available.

EXPLORING THE ISLANDS

Denman Island offers a pleasant mix of beaches, art galleries, and opportunities to picnic and relax. Just up the hill from the ferry landing is **Denman Village,** for which the word quaint might have been invented. The old-fashioned **Denman Island General Store** (ⓒ **250/335-2293**), with a cafe, bike rentals, gasoline, and a liquor store, is the primary gathering point on the island. Worth exploring in the village is the **Denman Island Craft Shop** (ⓒ **250/335-0881**), which represents over 70 island craftspeople; also check out the summer-only **Denman Island Art Gallery** (no phone) and the **Island Time Bakery** (ⓒ **250/335-3319**), with excellent pizza. Denman also has a number of sandy beaches, including **Bayle Point,** which also has a spectacular view of the Chrome Island are an inspiration to many of the local artisans. The beaches at Fillongley are pleasant for beachcombing or swimming in summer. While driving the back roads, watch for farm stands with local produce and signs for **open studios.** Potters, jewelers, painters, and sculptors open their doors so visitors can view their work during the summer months.

Hornby Island is, if possible, even more laid-back, decentralized, and alternative than Denman. The commercial center of the island, which is basically the **Hornby Island Co-op** general store, at the corner of Central and Shields roads (© 250/335-1121), with groceries, liquor, deli, and gasoline, is on the opposite side of the island from the ferry landing. Next to the Co-op is **Island Potters** (© 250/335-1153), which offers both paintings and pottery from area artists. An intriguing addition to Hornby Island is **Carbrea Vineyard and Winery,** 1885 Central Rd. (© 250/335-1240), a small, family-owned winery with a tasting room where you can sample estate Pinot noir, Pinot gris, Gewürztraminer, and an unusual fortified wine made with blackberries. The tasting room is open noon to 6pm Wednesday through Sunday in summer and 1 to 5pm weekends only in spring and fall. Call ahead to confirm hours. Gardeners will love **Old Rose Nursery,** 1020 Central Rd. (© 250/335-2603), a long-established nursery that specializes in heritage and English roses. The display garden, with over 1,000 mature rose plants, is open to the public from late May through July, but it is at its peak in mid- to late June. Phone ahead for hours.

Tribune Bay Provincial Park on Hornby is one of the finest white-sand beaches on the Canadian west coast; during low tides in summer, the sun bakes the sand, which then warms the incoming tides, making the water perfect for swimming. Hornby is also a great destination for birding. The Heliwell Bluffs in **Heliwell Bay Provincial Park** are home to thousands of nesting birds in the high cliffs along the coast; walking trails edge along the cliffs, making this a dramatically scenic hike.

KAYAKING

The calm waters here, flecked with islands and home to abundant sea and bird life, are some of the most renowned for kayaking in all B.C. On Denman, **Denman Hornby Canoes and Kayaks,** 4005 East Rd. (© 250/335-0079; www.denmanpaddling.ca), has rentals and half- and full-day guided excursions. One of their most popular trips is to Sandy Island, a favorite destination of sea kayakers off the northern tip of Denman Island. Called Tree Island by locals, the island is accessible only by boat or, at low tide, by foot. With a mere 33 hectares (81 acres), the small island is essentially a broad sand spit peppered with trees; in summer, the shallow water gets beautifully warm for swimming.

On Hornby, arrange guided tours or rent kayaks from **Hornby Ocean Kayaks** (© 250/335-0448; www.hornbyisland.com/Kayaking), near the Central Road school building.

ACCOMMODATIONS & DINING

Lodging is limited on these two islands, so be sure to have a reservation in place before heading across on the ferry to spend the night.

On Denman Island

There aren't many places to eat on Denman. **Café on the Rock,** in the general store in Denman Village (© 250/335-2999), is open for three meals daily, and serves light entrees, vegetarian meals, and home-made desserts; it also serves alcohol The **Kaleidoscope**

8

Market, in Denman Village (© **250/335-0451**), has a deli. The only public campground is at **Fillongley Provincial Park** (www.env.gov.bc.ca/bcparks), where sites are C$19. For reservations, contact Discover Camping (© **800/689-9025;** www.discover camping.ca).

Denman Island Guest House and Hostel   This turn-of-the-century farmhouse-cum-inn has a laid-back island atmosphere and rustic guest rooms with a shared bathroom. There are both dorm-style hostel rooms and traditional rooms, all filled with funky old furniture and a pleasant Summer of Love atmosphere. On the main floor is a licensed coffeehouse, and the hot tub in the backyard is a great place to soak up the easygoing island vibe.

3806 Denman Rd., Denman Island, BC V0R 1T0. © **250/335-2688.** 5 units. C$24 dorm single; C$50 private double. MC, V. **Amenities:** Coffee shop; bike rentals; hot tub; Wi-Fi. *In room:* No phone.

Hawthorn House Bed & Breakfast **Kids**   Children are welcome at this restored 1904 heritage house, which is tastefully decorated with Canadiana and surrounded by beautiful gardens with ocean and mountain views. The sitting room features a stone fireplace. All rooms have private or en suite bathrooms; the largest of the rooms is actually a small cottage, with its own entrance. Fruit and vegetables come from the organic garden, and the fresh-every-morning eggs come from a farm just down the road. Also on the premises are a hot tub and a friendly dog, and bikes are available for rent.

3375 Kirk Rd., Denman Island, BC V0R 1T0. © **250/335-0905.** Fax 250/335-0905. 3 units. C$95–C$110 double. Additional person C$20. Rates include full breakfast. AE, MC, V. Children welcome. **Amenities:** Hot tub. *In room:* A/C, TV/DVD, Wi-Fi.

On Hornby Island

With 114 campsites, **Tribune Bay Campground,** 5200 Shields Rd. (© **250/335-2359**), is the largest on Hornby. It's adjacent to Tribune Bay Provincial Park, with its sandy beaches, and within walking distance of the Co-op grocery store. Sites are C$32.

Hornby Island Resort   Make reservations well in advance for accommodations at this popular waterfront resort located next to the ferry terminal. The two-bedroom rustic cottages come with full kitchens and bathrooms; the lodge rooms have private bathrooms. The campsites are well maintained, and campground facilities include hot showers and a laundry. There's a playground on the beach, overlooked by the Thatch Pub, which is open daily in summer for drinks and light meals plus live music Thursday to Saturday. The licensed Wheelhouse Restaurant is open daily in summer for lunch and dinner, with a full-on barbecue taking over the deck on weekends. The Wheelhouse closes from early October through mid-May, but the Thatch Pub is open at least part of the week year-round; call ahead if you're planning a winter visit to inquire about its schedule.

4305 Shingle Spit Rd., Hornby Island, BC V0R 1Z0. © **250/335-0136.** Fax 250/335-9136. 2 lodge rooms, 2 cottages, 8 campsites. C$110 double lodge room; C$135 cottages per night (2-night minimum on weekends in May, June, and Sept), or $800 per week July to Labour Day; C$25–C$35 campsites. Off-season and weekly rates available. MC, V. **Amenities:** Restaurant; pub; tennis court; Wi-Fi; playground; beach volleyball; horseshoe pitch. *In room:* TV, no phone.

Sea Breeze Lodge ★   This well-loved resort offers comfortable waterfront cottages, with a choice of studio, one, or two bedrooms, all with private baths and some with full kitchens and fireplaces. The 5-hectare (12-acre) property is beautifully situated above a secluded stretch of beach. The cottages have been around a while, and have a pleasant, lived-in quality that more than makes up for the slightly faded gentility of the furnishings.

The lodge dining room is the best place to eat on the islands, though it is only open season-ally. From late June through Labour Day, all cottages come with American Plan meals (all meals are included in the room rate); the dining room is open at lunch and dinner to non-guests with reservations. The restaurant is open weekends only from Easter weekend through late June, and from Labour Day through Canadian Thanksgiving (early Oct). During high season, preference is given to weeklong reservations, though some per-day openings are usually available. Rates drop substantially in the off season, when there is no American Plan. The prices are rather complex; check the website or call the lodge to discuss what accommodations options may be available during your visit.

Big Tree 3-2, Hornby Island, BC V0R 1Z0. ✆ **888/516-2321** or 250/335-2321. www.seabreezelodge.com. 16 cottages. C$150–C$165 per adult per day, or C$950–C$1,025 per adult per week, including 3 meals daily. Discounted rates for children. Lower off-season rates. MC, V. **Amenities:** Restaurant; hot tub; sauna; grass tennis court; Wi-Fi; playground; dock. *In room:* No phone.

7 COURTENAY & COMOX

62km (39 miles) N of Qualicum Beach

Facing each other across the Courtenay Estuary, Comox (pop. 12,500) and Courtenay (pop. 20,000) are twin towns that provide a bit of urban polish to a region rich in out-door recreation. Because they're north of the Victoria-to-Tofino circuit that defines much of the tourism on Vancouver Island, these towns are refreshingly untouristy. Comox has a working harbor with a fishing fleet; Courtenay, a lumber-milling center, has an old downtown core where the shops have largely transformed into boutiques, but which still seems homey. Which isn't to say that these towns lack sophistication: You'll find excellent lodging and restaurants, as well as the new and opulent Crown Isle Golf Resort. Depend on the pace of change to quicken even further: The Comox Valley is the one of the fastest-growing regions of Vancouver Island.

Courtenay and Comox are also stepping-off points for adventures in the Beaufort Mountains, just to the west. From Mount Washington Alpine Resort, trails lead into the southeast corner of Strathcona Provincial Park. There are also adventures to be had at sea level: The shallow Courtenay Estuary is home to abundant wildlife, particularly birds and sea mammals, and is a popular destination for sea kayakers.

ESSENTIALS
Getting There
BY PLANE **Comox Valley Regional Airport,** north of Comox, welcomes daily flights from Vancouver, Calgary, and Edmonton. The airport is served by **Pacific Coastal Airlines** (✆ **800/663-2872;** www.pacific-coastal.com) and **WestJet** (✆ **877/952-4638;** www.westjet.com).

BY FERRY **BC Ferries** (✆ **888/BC-FERRY** [223-3779] in B.C., or 250/386-3431; www.bcferries.com) crosses from Powell River on the mainland to Little River, just north of Comox. The one-way fare is C$12 per passenger and C$38 per vehicle. Nanaimo's Duke Point and Departure Bay are the closest terminals with connections to the Vancouver area. If you'd like to see the Sunshine Coast on your way to Comox/Courtenay—and stay overnight to make it possible and worthwhile—cross from Horseshoe Bay to Lang-dale in Gibsons, then drive along Hwy. 101 to Earl's Cove in Sechelt, crossing again to Saltery Bay, finally ferrying from Westview in Powell River to Comox.

BY TRAIN & BUS Courtenay, which is 90 minutes north of Nanaimo on Hwy. 19, is also the terminus for **VIA Rail's E&N Railiner,** or *Malahat* (*©* 888/VIA-RAIL [842-7245] or 250/383-4324; www.viarail.ca), which offers daily service from Victoria. **Vancouver Island Coach Lines** (*©* **250/388-5248,** or book through Greyhound *©* **800/661-8747;** www.greyhound.ca) offers bus transport from Nanaimo to the Comox and Courtenay area along the Hwy. 19 corridor. One-way fare from Victoria to Courtenay is C$45.

Visitor Information

Contact the **Comox Valley Visitor Info Centre,** 2040 Cliffe Ave., Courtenay (*©* **888/357-4471** or 250/334-3234; www.discovercomoxvalley.com).

EXPLORING THE AREA

Hwy. 19A becomes Cliffe Avenue as it enters Courtenay. It then crosses the Courtenay River and continues north toward Campbell River, bypassing the old town centers of both Courtenay and Comox. This is a comparative blessing, as it allows these commercial districts to quietly gentrify without four lanes of traffic shooting past. The new Inland Hwy. 19 bypasses the towns altogether; the Comox Valley Parkway exit will take you from the highway over to Cliffe Avenue.

Courtenay

Courtenay's town center revolves around Fourth, Fifth, and Sixth streets just west of the Courtenay River. It's a pleasant place for a stroll, with a number of boutiques, art galleries, and housewares shops to browse. It's also the heart of Courtenay's dining and coffee shop culture.

Stop by the **Comox Valley Art Gallery,** Duncan Avenue at Sixth Street (*©* **250/334-2983**), a public contemporary exhibition space for local and regional artists. The gallery shop carries the work of more than 100 artists. The **Artisans Courtyard,** 180B Fifth St. (*©* **250/338-6564**), is a co-op with more than 60 members. Next door is the **Potter's Place,** 180A Fifth St. (*©* **250/334-4613**), which offers the works of 29 potters, ranging from porcelain to raku.

The **Courtenay District Museum & Paleontology Centre,** 207 Fourth St. (*©* **250/334-0686;** www.courtenaymuseum.ca), tells the story of the region's First Nations peoples with a good collection of masks, basketry, and carvings. The museum's highlight is a 12m (39-ft.) cast skeleton of an elasmosaur, a Cretaceous-era marine reptile. (The Comox Valley was once covered by a tropical sea, and the area now yields a wealth of marine fossils.) With four departures daily June through August, the museum leads

---

ⓘ Tips Special Events

The **Filberg Festival** attracts over 140 artists and craftspeople from across the province. It takes place at Filberg Park, with some events in the lodge and others in tents and booths. The festival includes musical entertainment and theater. It's held the first weekend of August; admission is C$10 adults, 13 and under free. Tickets can be purchased at **www.sidwilliamstheatre.com** or by calling *©* **866/898-8499** or 250/338-2420, ext. 3. For information, contact the park or the festival coordinator (*©* **250/334-9242;** www.filbergfestival.com).

3-hour **fossil tours** of its paleontology lab and to a local fossil dig for C$25 adults, C$20 seniors and students, C$15 children 4 to 12, or C$75 per family. Call ahead for reservations; tours also run on Saturdays in April and May. Admission to the museum alone is by donation. Summer hours are Monday to Saturday 10am to 5pm and Sunday noon to 4pm. Winter hours are Tuesday to Saturday 10am to 5pm.

Comox

The old center of Comox is small, with just a few shops and cafes to tempt travelers. What's definitely worth exploring, however, is the **marina area** in Comox Harbour. Walkways offer views of the boats and the bay; rising above it all are the jagged peaks of Strathcona Park. Another excellent place for a stroll is **Filberg Heritage Lodge and Park,** 61 Filberg Rd. (© **250/334-9242;** www.filberg.com). A full 3.6 hectares (9 acres) of lawn and forest, plus a petting zoo, surround a handsome Arts and Crafts–style home. Once a private residence, the lodge is now open for tours from 11am to 5pm on Easter weekend plus weekends in May and September, and daily from July to Labour Day.

Parks & Beaches

Continue past the marina on Comox Road to **Gooseneck Park,** a local favorite. **Saratoga Beach** and **Miracle Beach Provincial Park** are about a half-hour drive north of Courtenay on Hwy. 19. **Seal Bay Regional Nature Park and Forest,** 24km (15 miles) north of Courtenay off Hwy. 19, is a 714-hectare (1,764-acre) preserve laced with hiking and mountain-biking trails. Hours are from 6:30am to 11pm.

OUTDOOR PURSUITS

KAYAKING   With the Courtenay Estuary and Hornby, Tree, and Denman islands an easy paddle away, sea kayaking is very popular. **Comox Valley Kayaks,** 2020 Cliffe Ave., Courtenay (© **888/545-5595** or 250/334-2628; www.comoxvalleykayaks.com), offers rentals, lessons, and tours. Rentals start at C$20 for 4 hours.

SKIING   **Mount Washington Alpine Resort** ★ (© **888/231-1499,** 250/338-1386, or 250/338-1515 for snow report; www.mtwashington.bc.ca) is a 5-hour drive from Victoria and open year-round (for hiking or skiing, depending on the season). The summit reaches 1,588m (5,210 ft.), and the mountain averages 860 centimeters (339 in.) of snow per year. A 505m (1,657-ft.) vertical drop and 60 groomed runs are served by eight lifts and a beginners' tow. Fifty-five kilometers (34 miles) of Nordic track-set and skating trails connect to Strathcona Provincial Park. The resort has seen a massive surge in development, and now has accommodations for 4,000 guests and seven restaurants and pubs. Lift rates are C$62 for adults, C$50 for seniors and students, and C$33 for kids 7 to 12. Take the Strathcona Parkway 37km (23 miles) to Mount Washington, or use turnoff 130 from Inland Hwy. 19.

WHERE TO STAY

The **Travelodge Courtenay,** 2605 Island Hwy. (© **800/795-9486** or 250/334-4491; www.travelodgecourtenay.com), offers extras at a relatively modest cost. The motel's clean, unfussy rooms start at C$94 double.

Best Western Westerly Hotel   The Westerly presents a rather off-putting visage: The three-story slant-fronted wall of glass that encases the lobby probably seemed like a stylish idea when the hotel was first built . . . But once you get past the exterior, you'll discover that the guest rooms are spacious and nicely furnished, with a full complement of extras like an indoor pool and health club. Ask for rooms in the back wing, as they are newer and offer balconies, some overlooking the river. Unfortunately, these rooms are also closest to the steel bridge that links Courtenay and Comox, and these rooms can sometimes be noisy. In most ways, however, this central location is a plus, as the Westerly is within easy walking distance of Courtenay's vibrant downtown area, and also near the shopping centers along Cliffe Avenue.

1590 Cliffe Ave., Courtenay, BC V9N 2K4. (C) **800/668-7797** or 250/338-7741. Fax 250/338-5442. www. bestwestern.com. 108 units. C$115–C$174 double. Extra person C$20. Off-season and senior rates available. Ski and golf packages available. AE, MC, V. Pets accepted. **Amenities:** Restaurant; pub; lounge; exercise room; Jacuzzi; indoor pool; limited room service; sauna; liquor store. *In room:* A/C, TV w/pay movies, hair dryer, Wi-Fi.

Greystone Manor B&B ★ (Finds)   For many guests, the high point of a stay here is a chance to wander the lush .6-hectare (1½-acre) gardens. The charming innkeepers claim that gardening wasn't even a particular passion in their lives until they bought this property. But a passion it has now become: Every year, they put in more than 3,500 bedding plants. The house itself is a handsome 1918 Tudor-style Craftsman. Guests share a magnificent wood-paneled sitting room with loads of unpainted moldings, a grand piano, and comfy couches.

4014 Haas Rd., Courtenay, BC V9N 9T4. (C) **866/338-1422** or 250/338-1422. www.greystonemanorbb. com. 3 units. C$105 double. Rates include full breakfast. MC, V. Children 13 or older accepted. *In room:* Hair dryer, no phone.

Kingfisher Oceanside Resort and Spa ★★   Located 7km (4⅓ miles) south of Courtenay, this long-established resort has modernized with an added bank of beachfront suites and a classy spa. The older motel units are large, nicely furnished rooms with balconies or patios, most with views of the pool and the Strait of Georgia. The newer one-bedroom suites are splendid, each with a full kitchen, two TVs, a fireplace, and a balcony that juts out over the beach; most suites have a two-person whirlpool tub in addition to a full bathroom with heated tile floors. Our favorite is no. 401, on the end of the building, with banks of windows on two sides. Two rooms are available for people with disabilities.

The **Kingfisher restaurant** is one of the best places to eat in Courtenay. The spa offers a wide selection of treatments and body work. Trained technicians offer thalassotherapy baths and wraps, massage, reiki, and facials. Guests also have access to a steam cave. *Note:* Smoking is not permitted on the premises.

4330 Island Hwy. S, Courtenay, BC V9N 9R9. (C) **800/663-7929** or 250/338-1323. Fax 250/338-0058. www. kingfisherspa.com. 64 units. From C$170 double oceanview room; C$220 suite. Extra person C$25. Golf, ski, spa packages available. Senior discounts available. AE, DC, DISC, MC, V. Free parking. Pets allowed in some rooms, add C$25. **Amenities:** Restaurant; oceanview fitness room; golf course nearby; hot tub; outdoor heated pool; full-service spa; tennis court; shuttle service; 2 rooms for those w/limited mobility. *In room:* TV (suites have TV/DVD), fridge, hair dryer, Wi-Fi.

Old House Village Hotel and Spa ★★   These new timeshare suites sit on a riverside parcel of land that previously was a spacious garden estate around the Old House Restaurant (see below). Too bad the gardens had to go, but at least these suites are topnotch. Each of the large studio, one-, or two-bedroom suites has a full kitchen with all appliances (including washer and dryer), and all have balconies or patios to view the vernal setting. The living room decor evokes the woodsy Northwest, with a stone-faced fireplace and soft earth-tone colors and fabrics. One penthouse unit is extra large, with a loft bedroom. Newly opened is Oh Spa, with an extensive menu of beauty, rejuvenating, and revitalizing treatments.

1800 Riverside Lane, Courtenay, BC V9N 8C7. (*C*) **888/703-0202** or 250/703-0202. Fax 250/703-0209. www.oldhousevillage.com. 79 suites. C$119–C$289 double. Extra person C$20. AE, MC, V. Free parking. **Amenities:** Restaurant; bar; exercise room; 2 Jacuzzis; pool; infrared sauna; spa. *In room:* A/C, 2 TVs, full kitchen, Wi-Fi, fireplace.

The Villas at Crown Isle Resort ★★ (**Value**) For the money, these golf resort villas and guest rooms are an incredible deal, and you don't have to be a golfer to make the most of the facilities. Located at Crown Isle Golf Resort, they overlook the first fairway and are just yards from the spectacular clubhouse. The villas are truly large and filled with luxury touches: Many have gourmet kitchens, Jacuzzis, fireplaces, VCRs, and balconies. Another building has "Fairway Rooms," which are well-appointed hotel-style rooms with balconies, some with kitchenettes. Guests have access to the state-of-the-art fitness equipment in the resort clubhouse, and, of course, there's that par 72, 18-hole golf course.

399 Clubhouse Dr., Courtenay, BC V9N 9G3. (*C*) **888/338-8439** or 250/703-5050. Fax 250/703-5051. www. crownisle.com. 90 units. From C$159 Fairway Room; from C$259 1-bedroom villa; from C$319 2-bedroom villa. Lower shoulder and off-season rates. Extra person C$15. Golf and ski packages available. AE, MC, V. Free parking. **Amenities:** 2 restaurants; bar; golf course; health club; room service; spa. *In room:* A/C, TV, hair dryer.

WHERE TO DINE

Atlas Café ★ (**Value**) INTERNATIONAL This cafe serves up affordable, flavorful variations on world cuisine. The globe-trotting menu hops from Asia and the Mediterranean to Mexico and the Pacific Northwest. Happily, many of the dishes are vegetarian. Portions are large, so this is a good destination for a hungry group with different tastes. Although some of the meat dishes passed C$20, the majority of dishes are between C$12 and C$17. The decor is quite sophisticated—the bar is an aquamarine jewel box and the dining room boudoir red. The only downside: The wine list is limited, especially considering B.C.'s burgeoning wine culture.

250 Sixth St., Courtenay. (*C*) **250/338-9838.** www.atlascafe.ca. Reservations accepted for parties of 6 or more only. Main courses C$9–C$26. MC, V. Mon 8:30am–3:30pm; Tues–Sat 8:30am–10pm; Sun 8:30am–9pm.

The Black Fin Pub PUB On the short walk from downtown Comox to the marina, you'll pass this hospitable pub overlooking the harbor. The menu is large and, for a pub, quite interesting; some of the dishes feature Asian flavors. Entrees range from schnitzel to curry chicken, though with waterfront views, you might find local pan-fried oysters, grilled wild salmon, and halibut fish and chips hard to resist. The usual burgers and sandwiches are also in abundance. Sunday brunch is served until 2pm, and there's an afternoon tea on Monday and Thursday.

132 Port Augusta St., Comox. (*C*) **250/339-5030.** Reservations accepted for parties of 4 or more in early evening. Main courses C$11–C$28. AE, MC, V. Food service Sun–Thurs 11am–10pm; Fri–Sat 11am–10:30pm. Hours may be extended in summer.

Kingfisher Oceanside Restaurant ★ SEAFOOD/CONTINENTAL The dining room at this resort brings together waterfront views with high-quality cuisine. If you're staying at the Kingfisher to partake of the spa services, you'll be pleased with the spa menu, which features low-fat, low-calorie entrees such as tandoori-rubbed wild salmon.

On the regular menu, one popular entree is cedar plank–baked salmon with sage and blackberry chutney. Also offered are steaks, schnitzels, and lamb dishes. Bimonthly in summer (once a month in winter), the restaurant serves a grand Friday-evening seafood buffet with an incredible selection of local fish and seafood (C$45).

4330 Island Hwy. S., 7km (4¹/₃ miles) south of Courtenay. ✆ **250/338-1323.** www.kingfisherspa.com. Reservations advised. Main courses C$12–C$35. AE, DC, DISC, MC, V. Daily 7–10:30am, 11am–2pm, and 5–9pm.

Old House Restaurant ★ CONTEMPORARY CANADIAN   Right on the banks of the Courtenay River, the very charming and atmospheric Old House Restaurant is in a rambling 1930s heritage home (with four fireplaces and rough-hewn timbers) that looks like it belongs in England's Cotswolds. The menu, however, is anything but quaint, featuring zippy international and West Coast dishes. One section of the menu is dedicated to "sharing," with foods like crispy barbecued duck tacos with mango chile chutney to pass with drinks. Main courses offer globe-trotting preparations of local seafood and meat: Pan-seared halibut with creamy Moroccan curry is a delicious match of flavors. The patio is a wonderful place for a drink.

1760 Riverside Lane, Courtenay. ✆ **250/338-5406.** www.oldhouserestaurant.ca. Reservations recommended. Main courses C$16–C$36. AE, MC, V. Sun–Thurs 11am–9pm; Fri–Sat 11am–9:30pm.

Toscanos ITALIAN   Toscanos is a cheerful restaurant located between downtown Comox and Comox Harbor, with a million-dollar view of the bay and distant Beaufort Mountains. The dining room is rather minimalist, lacking the rustic clutter that passes for decor in many Italian restaurants. The menu is divided between pasta dishes and chicken, veal, and seafood entrees. Desserts include classics such as tiramisu and profiteroles.

140 Port Augusta, Comox. ✆ **250/890-7575.** www.toscanos.ca. Reservations recommended. Main courses C$13–C$24. MC, V. Mon–Sat 11am–2pm and 5–9pm. Closed on major holidays.

Northern Vancouver Island

In this chapter, we cover the portion of Vancouver Island from the town of Campbell River—the "Salmon-Fishing Capital of the World"—northward. West of Campbell River lies Strathcona Provincial Park, the oldest provincial park in British Columbia and the largest on Vancouver Island.

The waters along the island's northeast coast near Port McNeill are home to both resident and transient orca whales; the latter move annually from Johnstone Strait to the open Pacific. In this vicinity are also two tiny unique communities: the First Nations town of Alert Bay on Cormorant Island, and Telegraph Cove, a boardwalk community on pilings above the rocky shore.

The Island Highway's final port of call, Port Hardy is the starting point for the Inside Passage ferry cruise up the northern coast. It carries passengers bound for Prince Rupert, where it meets the ferries to the Queen Charlotte Islands and to Alaska, and links to the Yellowhead Highway and VIA Rail's *Skeena* run (see chapter 11 for complete coverage of these destinations).

Note: See the "Vancouver Island" map (p. 60) to locate areas covered in this chapter.

1 ESSENTIALS

GETTING THERE

BY PLANE   See chapter 6 for information on Vancouver Island's major air hub, **Victoria.** The **Campbell River and District Regional Airport,** located south of Campbell River off Jubilee Parkway, has regularly scheduled flights on commuter planes to and from Vancouver on **Pacific Coastal Airlines** (© 800/663-2872; www.pacific-coastal.com). Pacific Coastal Airlines is the only scheduled air carrier with flights to/from Port Hardy and Vancouver.

BY FERRY   **BC Ferries** (© 888/BC-FERRY [223-2779] or 250/386-3431; www.bcferries.com) operates a route linking Powell River to Comox, not too far south of Campbell River, but reaching Powell River from other points on the mainland requires taking two other ferries—a daunting and costly prospect if your destination is Campbell River and points north (see p. 204 for details). Nanaimo's Duke Point and Departure Bay are the closest terminals with connections to the Vancouver area. Port Hardy also connects with Prince Rupert via a 15-hour journey that winds through the Inland Passage. Sample fares are included in the regional sections that follow.

BY BUS   **Greyhound Canada** (© 800/661-8747 or 604/482-8747; www.greyhound.ca) offers three daily trips between Nanaimo and Campbell River (C$32 one-way) Only one bus daily goes all the way to Port Hardy. These buses are operated by **Vancouver Island Coach Lines** (© 250/388-5248), but you can book through Greyhound.

For general information on Vancouver Island, contact **Tourism Vancouver Island,** Ste. 501, 65 Front St., Nanaimo (© **250/754-3500;** fax 250/754-3599; www.vancouverisland. travel). Also check out **www.vancouverisland.com**.

GETTING AROUND

While Vancouver Island has an admirable system of public transport, getting to remote sights and destinations is difficult without your own vehicle.

BY FERRY **BC Ferries** (© **888/BC-FERRY** [223-3779] in B.C., or 250/386-3431; www.bcferries.com) links Vancouver Island ports to many offshore islands, including Quadra, Alert Bay, and Sointula. None of these islands has public transport, so once there you'll need to hoof it, hitch it, hire a taxi, or arrange for bike rentals. Most innkeepers will pick you up if you've reserved in advance.

BY BUS See "Getting There," above, for information on **Vancouver Island Coach Lines.**

BY CAR North of Nanaimo, the major road on Vancouver Island is **Hwy. 19,** a particular improvement being the new 128km (80-mile) four-lane expressway between Parksville and Campbell River. The older sections of 19, all closer to the island's east coast, are now labeled 19A. North of Campbell River, a long, two-lane section of Hwy. 19 continues all the way to Port Hardy. Access to gasoline is no problem, even in more remote northern areas, but don't head out on a long stretch of unpaved road without filling up.

Rental cars are readily available. Agencies include **Avis** (© **800/879-2847** in Canada, 800/331-1212 in the U.S.; www.avis.com), **Budget** (© **800/268-8900** in Canada, 800/527-0700 in the U.S.; www.budget.com), and **National** (© **877/222-9058** in Canada and the U.S.; www.nationalcar.com).

2 CAMPBELL RIVER & QUADRA ISLAND

Campbell River: 45km (28 miles) N of Courtenay; 266km (165 miles) N of Victoria

Busy and utilitarian, Campbell River (pop. 33,000) gives the impression of a town that works for a living. For years, it has been known as the "Salmon-Fishing Capital of the World," but it is also home to a large pulp and paper mill. Between Quadra Island and Campbell River, the broad Strait of Georgia squeezes down to a narrow 1.6km-wide (1-mile) channel called Discovery Passage. All of the salmon that enter the Strait of Juan de Fuca near Victoria to spawn in northerly rivers funnel down into this tight churning waterway with 4m (13-ft.) tides. Historically, vast hauls of incredibly large fish have been pulled from these waters; fishing lodges have lined these shores for decades. However, salmon numbers at Campbell River have fallen drastically in recent years, and the days of pulling 60-pound chinooks from the turbulent waters are largely over. Today, you're as likely to take a wildlife-viewing trip on the sound as go fishing for salmon—and if you do fish, there are numerous restrictions.

Salmon or no salmon, there are plenty of other attractions in and around Campbell River. The city has an excellent museum with a world-class collection of Native artifacts heading the list, and hiking on Quadra Island and in Strathcona Provincial Park appeals

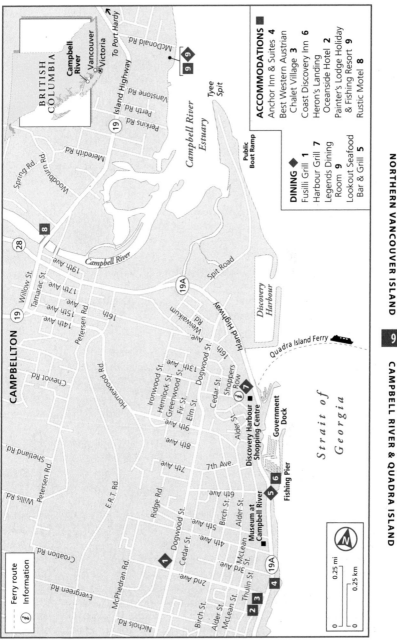

BRITISH COLUMBIA

Campbell River

Vancouver

Victoria

To Port Hardy

McDonald Rd.

Island Highway

Vanstone Rd.

Perth Rd.

Perkins Rd.

(19)

Meredith Rd.

Spring Rd.

Woodburn Rd.

Campbell River Estuary

Tyee Spit

Public Boat Ramp

Campbell River

(28)

19th Ave.

Spit Road

Willow St.

Tamarac St.

17th Ave.

(19)

14th Ave.

15th Ave.

16th

Petersen Rd.

CAMPBELLTON

Cheviot Rd.

Homewood Rd.

Ironwood St.

Hemlock St.

Greenwood St.

Fir St.

Elm St.

Cedar St.

Alder St.

13th Ave.

Dogwood St.

16th

Weiwaikum Rd.

Island Highway

(19A)

Discovery Harbour

Spit Road

Quadra Island Ferry

Shetland Rd.

Petersen Rd.

Willis Rd.

E.R.T. Rd.

Ridge Rd.

9th Ave.

8th Ave.

7th Ave.

7th Ave.

Shoppers Row

Discovery Harbour Shopping Centre

Government Dock

Fishing Pier

Strait of Georgia

Croation Rd.

McPhedran Rd.

Evergreen Rd.

Nichols Rd.

Dogwood St.

Cedar St.

2nd Ave.

Thulin St.

Birch St.

Alder St.

McLean St.

4th Ave.

5th Ave.

6th Ave.

Birch St.

Alder St.

McLean St.

3rd Ave.

(19A)

Museum at Campbell River

Fishing Pier

ACCOMMODATIONS

Anchor Inn & Suites **4**
Best Western Austrian
Chalet Village **3**
Coast Discovery Inn **6**
Heron's Landing
Oceanside Hotel **2**
Painter's Lodge Holiday
& Fishing Resort **9**
Rustic Motel **8**

DINING ◆

Fusilli Grill **1**
Harbour Grill **7**
Legends Dining
Room **9**
Lookout Seafood
Bar & Grill **5**

Ferry route

ⓘ Information

0   0.25 mi

0   0.25 km

N

to outdoorsy types. Also, the historic Kwakwaka'wakw Cultural Centre has reopened on Quadra Island, which holds a fascinating collection of repatriated First Nations potlatch masks and totems. To reach Quadra Island, take the 10-minute ferry from downtown Campbell River to Quathiaski Cove, on Quadra Island. Trips depart on the hour from about 6am to 10pm (no Sun 7am sailing). Round-trip fares are C$8 per adult passenger, C$19 per vehicle; you can bring a bike for free.

ESSENTIALS

GETTING THERE **By Plane** The **Campbell River and District Regional Airport,** south of Campbell River off Jubilee Parkway, has regular flights on commuter planes from Vancouver on **Pacific Coastal Airlines** (© 800/663-2872; www.pacific-coastal. com).

By Car On the four-lane Inland Highway (Hwy. 19), Campbell River is 45km (28 miles) north of Courtenay and 266km (165 miles) north of Victoria. Campbell River is the end of this newly improved stretch of roadway. The old Island Highway, Hwy. 19A, also runs into the center of Campbell River, right along the water as you approach town.

By Bus **Vancouver Island Coach Lines** (© 250/388-5248, or book through Greyhound © 800/661-8747; www.greyhound.ca) offers bus transport from Victoria and Nanaimo to Campbell River. One-way fare from Nanaimo to Campbell River is C$32. (Nanaimo is the closest ferry service to the Vancouver area.)

VISITOR INFORMATION The **Campbell River Visitor Info Centre,** 1235 Shoppers Row (© 877/286-5705 or 250/830-0411; www.visitorcentre.ca or www.campbellriver. travel), is open daily in July and August, and Monday through Saturday the rest of the year.

EXPLORING CAMPBELL RIVER

Downtown Campbell River won't win any awards for quaintness. Busy Island Highway whizzes through town, and the commercial district is dominated by strip malls. The surrounding area offers excellent recreation, however, and lodging is relatively inexpensive, so the city makes a good launching pad for exploration.

The Museum at Campbell River ★ **Kids** Campbell River's captivating museum is worth seeking out for the carvings and artifacts from local First Nations tribes; the contemporary carved masks are especially fine. Also compelling is the sound-and-light presentation *The Treasures of Siwidi,* which uses traditional masks to retell an ancient Native myth. You can see a replica of a pioneer-era cabin, tools from the early days of logging, and exhibits on the salmon fishing industry. The gift shop is a great place to buy Native art and jewelry.

470 Island Hwy. © 250/287-3103. www.crmuseum.ca. Admission C$6 adults, C$4 seniors and students, C$15 families; free for children 5 and under. Mid-May to Sept daily 10am–5pm; Oct to mid-May Tues–Sun noon–5pm.

OUTDOOR PURSUITS

DIVING The decommissioned **HMCS *Columbia*** was sunk in 1996 near the sea-life-rich waters of Seymour Narrows off the Quadra Island's west coast. For information on diving to this artificial reef and on other diving sites (with enticing names like Row and Be Damned, Whisky Point, Copper Cliffs, and Steep Island) in the Campbell River area, contact **Beaver Aquatics** (© 250/287-7652; www.connected.bc.ca/~baquatics).

FISHING ★ The coho salmon in these waters weigh up to 9-kilograms (20 lb.), and even these are dwarfed by the tyee—14-kilogram-plus (31-lb.-plus) chinook (king) salmon. But fishing isn't what it once was in Campbell River. Some salmon runs are now catch-and-release only, and others are open for limited catches; many fishing trips are now billed more as wildlife adventures than hunting-and-gathering expeditions.

To fish here, you need nonresident saltwater and freshwater licenses, available at outdoor-recreation stores throughout Campbell River, including **Painter's Lodge Holiday & Fishing Resort,** 1625 McDonald Rd. (© **250/286-1102;** www.painterslodge.com). The staff at the lodge can also provide information on guided boats and fishing rules.

If you'd like to get out onto the waters and fish, be sure to call ahead and talk to an outfitter or the tourist center to find out what fish are running during your visit and if the seasons have opened. Because of plummeting numbers of salmon and of recent treaties with the United States, the coming years will see more restricted fishing seasons in the waters off Vancouver Island. Don't be disappointed if there's no salmon fishing when you visit or if the salmon you hook is catch-and-release only, though. For one thing, there are other fish in the sea: Not all types of salmon are as threatened as the coho and tyee; or, you can also consider fishing for halibut and other bottom fish. And if you really just want to get out on the water and have an adventure, consider a wildlife-viewing boat tour, offered by many fishing outfitters.

There are dozens of fishing guides in the Campbell River area, with a range of services that extends from basic to pure extravagance. Expect to pay around C$100 per hour for 4 to 5 hours of fishing with a no-frills outfitter. A flashier trip on a luxury cruiser can cost more than C$120 per hour. The most famous guides are associated with the Painter's Lodge and its sister property, April Point Lodge on Quadra Island (see "Where to Stay," below). A few smaller fishing-guide operations include **Coastal Wilderness Adventures** (© **866/640-1173** or 250/287-3427; www.coastwild.com) and **CR Fishing Village,** 260 Island Hwy. (© **250/287-3630;** www.fishingvillage.bc.ca).

You can also check out the Info Centre's directory of fishing guides by following the links at www.campbellriverchamber.ca. Most hotels in Campbell River also offer fishing/lodging packages; ask when you reserve.

HIKING For day hikes, drive to Strathcona Provincial Park (later in this chapter), or explore Quadra Island's Mount Seymour or Morte Lake parks. For a pleasant hike closer to Campbell River, drive west 6km (3¾ miles) on Hwy. 28 to **Elk Falls Provincial Park.** Easy 1- to 2-hour hikes lead to a fish hatchery and let you explore a stream with beaver ponds. From the park, you can also join the **Canyon View Trail,** a loop hike that follows the banks of the Campbell River.

WILDLIFE TOURS **Eagle Eye Adventures** (© **250/286-0809** or 250/890-0464; www.eagleeyeadventures.com) offers a range of excursions via Zodiac and floatplane. A popular 4-hour trip takes you up a series of sea rapids, with the chance to see bears, eagles, orcas, and sea lions. Excursions cost C$109 for adults, C$79 for children under 13. Check the company's website for other options. **Painter's Lodge** (see "Fishing," above) also offers wildlife-watching trips.

CAMPING

The 122 campsites at **Elk Falls Provincial Park** (© **250/954-4600**) go for C$14 in summer (see also "Hiking," above).

NORTHERN VANCOUVER ISLAND

9

CAMPBELL RIVER & QUADRA ISLAND

Anchor Inn & Suites ★ Each spacious room here has a balcony and ocean view. Best of all, because the Anchor Inn is on the ocean side of busy Island Highway, you won't have to look over the traffic to see the water. In addition to the standard rooms and suites, the Anchor Inn offers five styles of theme suites—Arabian, African, Arctic, English, and Western—that feature extras such as Jacuzzi tubs. (Western suites are the best choice if you have kids, as they have bunk beds hidden in a "jail cell.") And even if you're not up to an exotic hotel room, you'll like the fact that all the rooms are recently renovated and have balconies.

261 Island Hwy., Campbell River, BC V9W 2B3. ℂ **800/663-7227** or 250/286-1131. Fax 250/287-4055. www.anchorinn.ca. 76 units. C$129 double; C$249–C$289 theme room double. Extra person C$10. Theme, honeymoon, golf, and fishing packages available. AE, MC, V. Free parking. **Amenities:** 2 restaurants; lounge; exercise room; Jacuzzi; indoor pool. *In room:* TV w/pay movies, fridge, hair dryer, Wi-Fi.

Best Western Austrian Chalet Village Overlooking Discovery Passage, this recently renovated oceanfront hotel offers a choice of regular or housekeeping units (with kitchenettes); some rooms are in loft chalets. Most units have a fridge, and some have VCRs. The staff can arrange whale-watching, fishing, or golfing trips.

462 S. Island Hwy., Campbell River, BC V9W 1A5. ℂ **800/667-7207** or 250/923-4231. Fax 250/923-2840. www.bwcampbellriver.com. 59 units. May–Sept from C$145 double, from C$175 kitchenette unit, loft chalet, or minisuite. Lower off-season rates. Extra person C$10. Senior and AAA discounts available. Children 13 and under free. AE, DC, DISC, MC, V. Pets allowed in smoking rooms only for C$5 per night. **Amenities:** Restaurant and pub adjacent; exercise room; Jacuzzi; indoor pool; sauna; courtyard w/BBQs; miniature putting green; table tennis. *In room:* TV, fridge, hair dryer, balcony or patio.

Coast Discovery Inn Part of the sprawling Discovery Harbour Marina and Shopping Centre, the Coast is right in the thick of downtown and offers dramatic views from its upper stories. The accommodations are spacious and nicely furnished. Superior rooms offer ocean views, bathrobes, and upgraded toiletries. One wheelchair-accessible unit is available.

975 Shoppers Row, Campbell River, BC V9W 2C4. ℂ **800/663-1144** or 250/287-7155. Fax 250/287-2213. www.coasthotels.com. 88 units. From C$133 double. Extra person C$10. Family plan, senior, and AAA discounts, and corporate rates available. AE, DC, DISC, MC, V. Pets allowed for C$20 per night. **Amenities:** Restaurant; pub; exercise room; Jacuzzi; room service; 1 room for those w/limited mobility. *In room:* TV w/pay movies and Nintendo, hair dryer, Wi-Fi.

Heron's Landing Oceanside Hotel ★ This hotel on the southern edge of town offers large and nicely furnished rooms at moderate prices. Accommodations range from standard hotel rooms to two-bedroom suites. The suites all come with large bedrooms, kitchens, sitting rooms, and dining areas; handsome furnishings abound, including leather couches, fine carpeting, feather duvets, and hand-painted armoires. Kitchens are fully equipped with china, utensils, and appliances. Most units have balconies and views of Discovery Passage. The hotel itself—wrapped in carved-wooden-rail balconies lined by flower boxes—is resplendent in the Bavarian style so favored in Canada.

492 S. Island Hwy., Campbell River, BC V9W 1A5. ℂ **888/923-2849** or 250/923-2848. Fax 250/923-2849. www.heronslandinghotel.com. 23 units. C$99–C$145 double; C$125–C$175 1-bedroom suite; C$175–C$300 2-bedroom suite. Extra person C$15. Off-season rates available. Fishing charters arranged. AE, DC, MC, V. Free parking. Dogs allowed, add C$25 per night. **Amenities:** Restaurant; bar next door; babysitting; golf course nearby. *In room:* TV, fridge, kitchen, hair dryer, Wi-Fi.

Painter's Lodge Holiday & Fishing Resort ★★ This resort has been a favorite fishing hideaway for film stars such as John Wayne, Bob Hope, and Goldie Hawn. Built in 1924 on an awe-inspiring wooded point overlooking the Discovery Passage, the lodge retains a rustic grandeur, with spacious rooms and suites decorated in natural wood and pastels. Four secluded, self-contained cottages are also available for rent. Guests can enjoy all three meals and cocktails in **Legends Dining Room** (see "Where to Dine," below), Tyee Pub, and Fireside Lounge. Amenities include guided fishing trips and jogging and hiking trails around the grounds. Painter's Lodge is also well equipped for business conferences. Wheelchair-accessible rooms are available.

1625 McDonald Rd., Box 460, Campbell River, BC V9W 5C1. ⓒ **800/663-7090** or 250/286-1102. Fax 250/286-0158. www.painterslodge.com. 94 units. C$175–C$319 double; C$239–C$299 cottage. Extra person C$15. Off-season discounts available. AE, MC, V. Closed Nov–Mar. **Amenities:** Restaurant; pub; lounge; babysitting; bike and scooter rentals; children's center; exercise room; Jacuzzi; heated outdoor pool; 2 unlit tennis courts; kayak rentals. *In room:* TV, hair dryer, Wi-Fi.

Rustic Motel Ⓥⓐⓛⓤⓔ Located on .8 hectares (2 acres) of parkland beside the river, the Rustic offers moderately priced rooms with everything you'll need for a comfortable stay (some have full kitchens). There are also three two-bedroom suites and a three-bedroom cabin (all with kitchen). In summer, the Rustic is decked out with baskets of flowers.

2140 N. Island Hwy., Campbell River, BC V9W 2G7. ⓒ **800/567-2007** or 250/286-6295. Fax 250/286-9692. www.rusticmotel.com. 41 units. C$90–C$100 double. Extra person C$10. Kitchen C$10 extra. Rates include continental breakfast. AE, DC, MC, V. Free parking. Pets allowed for C$5 per night. **Amenities:** Jacuzzi; sauna; barbecue. *In room:* A/C, TV, fridge, hair dryer, Wi-Fi, microwave.

WHERE TO DINE

In addition to the restaurants listed below, try **Koto,** 80 10th Ave. (ⓒ **250/286-1422**), an excellent sushi bar, open Tuesday through Friday from 11am to 2pm and Tuesday through Saturday from 5:30 to 9pm.

Fusilli Grill ITALIAN A good, casual Italian restaurant located in the suburbs southwest of downtown, Fusilli Grill makes almost all of its own pasta and utilizes local produce, meats, and seafood as much as possible. Lunch features a variety of sandwiches on fresh-baked focaccia. At dinner, there's a choice of pasta, steak, fish, and chicken dishes, plus a few Mexican and Asian options for variety.

4–220 Dogwood St. ⓒ **250/830-0090.** www.fusilligrill.bc.ca. Reservations recommended. Main courses C$11–C$24. AE, DC, MC, V. Mon 4:30–9:30pm; Tues–Fri 11am–9:30pm; Sat–Sun 4:30–9:30pm.

Harbour Grill ★ CONTINENTAL/SEAFOOD Owned by the proprietors of the respected but now defunct Le Chateaubriand, Harbour Grill still features much of that restaurant's same quality menu in an attractive location, complete with views of Discovery Passage. The dinner menu features many worthy relics of mid-20th-century fine dining. Yes, you can actually order a real chateaubriand here, an arm-size roast of beef tenderloin drizzled with béarnaise and topped with asparagus. Other classics of Kennedy-era cuisine include duck with orange sauce and veal Oscar. In summer, fresh seafood receives more contemporary preparations. The Harbour Grill isn't exactly a food museum—for one thing, the new location is too bright and modern—it's more like time-travel cuisine, and great fun at that.

112–1334 Island Hwy., in the Discovery Harbour Mall. ⓒ **250/287-4143.** www.harbourgrill.com. Reservations recommended. Main courses C$20–C$32. AE, DC, MC, V. Daily from 5:30pm.

Legends Dining Room ★ INTERNATIONAL The dining room at Painter's Lodge is flanked entirely by windows, affording every table a view of busy Discovery Passage and the free speedboat taxi that runs between the hotel and April Point Lodge on Quadra Island. If you're having dinner here, consider hopping that water taxi for a pre-dinner cocktail at April Point. Return with salt spray in your hair, ready for a great meal at Legends. Start with the excellent smoked salmon–stuffed mushroom caps. The entrees have regional flair—try the Cuban-style pork chops, marinated in rum and tandoori spices and served with apple and sun-dried cranberry chutney. As you'd expect at a fishing resort, fish and seafood are menu favorites.

At Painter's Lodge, 1625 McDonald Rd. (✆ **250/286-1102.** Reservations recommended. Main courses C$14–C$37. AE, DC, MC, V. Daily 7am–10pm. Closed Nov–Mar.

The Lookout Seafood Bar & Grill CANADIAN A pleasant dining room and patio that overlooks Discovery Pass and Quadra Island, the Lookout offers a range of burgers, fish and chips, and sandwiches during the day. The dinner offerings expand to include steak, pasta, and seafood dishes—unsurprisingly, salmon is the specialty. If you're just looking for a light meal, try the tapas menu.

921 Island Hwy. (✆ **250/286-6812.** www.lookoutseafoodgrill.ca. Reservations recommended in summer. Dinner main courses C$8–C$30. AE, MC, V. Mon–Sat 11am–10pm; Sun 10am–9pm.

QUADRA ISLAND

Quadra Island sits right across Discovery Channel from Campbell River, and a visit to the island should definitely be part of your itinerary when you're in the area. The main reason to make the ferry crossing is to visit the excellent **Nuyumbalees Cultural Centre** ★★ (formerly the Kwakiutl Museum and Cultural Center), Wei Wai Road in Cape Mudge Village (✆ **250/285-3733;** http://nuyumbalees.com). It has one of the world's best collections of artifacts, ceremonial masks, and tribal costumes once used by the Cape Mudge Band in elaborate potlatch ceremonies conducted to celebrate births, deaths, tribal unity, the installment of a new chief, marriages, and other important occasions. Bands and villages spent months, even years, planning feasts and performances, carving totem poles, and amassing literally tons of gifts for their guests. The Canadian government outlawed the potlatch in 1922 as part of an enforced-assimilation policy, then lifted the ban in 1951. During the time potlatches were outlawed, the artifacts in the Kwakiutl Museum were removed to museums and private collections in eastern Canada and England, where they were preserved and cataloged. The collection was repatriated to the Cape Mudge Band beginning in 1979; the current cultural center and museum was built in the early 1990s.

The *Ah-Wa-Qwa-Dzas* (a place to relax and tell stories) is across the street from the cultural center and serves as a venue for salmon barbecues, storytelling, and traditional dance performances. The museum's gift gallery has a good selection of artwork, prints, and carvings of many talented local artists, as well as books and cards, jewelry, and clothing. Behind the museum is **K'Ik'Ik G'Illas,** or "The House of Eagles," a longhouse-like structure used to teach carving, dancing, and other traditional ways of life. Ask at the museum to tour the building, which has two carved house posts and an especially impressive totem pole in addition to colorful carvings and wall murals. In the lobby of the museum, you can make petroglyph rubbings from fiberglass castings of ancient stone carvings. Across from the museum is a park where a series of petroglyphs document a few of the island's ancient legends.

The cultural center is open Tuesday to Saturday from 10am to 4pm from May through September. Admission is C$15 for adults, C$5 for children under 12, and C$10 for seniors. Family admission is C$30.

Where to Stay

April Point Lodge & Fishing Resort ★   Secluded April Point Lodge, world famous for its saltwater fishing charters, has magnificent views of the Discovery Passage. This luxury fishing resort along with Painter's Lodge, just across the channel, are under the same ownership; there's free boat-taxi service between the two properties for registered guests, which makes it easy to go from Campbell River for drinks or dinner, or to use the pool, tennis courts, and Jacuzzis at Painter's Lodge. Guesthouses are tastefully furnished, with hot tubs, fireplaces, and kitchens. The lodge suites are also nicely appointed. The new Aveda Concept Spa provides luxury pampering in a Japanese-style structure overlooking the water. Facilities include helicopter access and seaplane service to Vancouver, as well as a marina.

April Point Rd., Quadra Island, c/o Box 1, Campbell River, BC V9W 4Z9. © **800/663-7090** or 250/285-2222. www.aprilpoint.com. 56 units. C$179–C$239 lodge; C$239–C$355 cabin or guesthouse. Extra person C$15 in lodge, C$25 in guesthouse. AE, MC, V. Closed mid-Oct to early Apr. **Amenities:** Restaurant (see "Where to Dine," below); sushi bar; lounge; babysitting; bike and scooter rentals; spa; kayak rentals. *In room:* TV, hair dryer, Wi-Fi.

Tsa-Kwa-Luten Lodge ★   Owned by the Laichwiltach Cape Mudge Band, this modern luxury resort is designed to resemble a Native Big House. Overlooking the Discovery Passage, it offers both lodge suites and waterfront cabins. The cabins contain full kitchens; some have fireplaces and hot tubs. Some suites have lofts, Jacuzzis, or fireplaces. All units are beautifully decorated with contemporary Native art. Accommodations for travelers with disabilities are available. The staff can arrange fishing trips and heli-fishing charters. Open mid-April to mid-October.

Lighthouse Rd., Box 460, Quathiaski Cove, Quadra Island, BC V0P 1N0. © **800/665-7745** or 250/598-3366. Fax 250/285-2532. www.capemudgeresort.com. 34 units. C$105–C$145 double; C$149–C$279 cottage and guesthouse. Lower shoulder-season rates. Meal plans available. AE, DC, MC, V. Free parking. Children 11 and under stay free in parent's room. **Amenities:** Restaurant (see "Where to Dine," below); lounge; bike rentals; exercise room; Jacuzzi; sauna; lit tennis courts nearby. *In room:* Hair dryer.

Where to Dine

April Point Lodge & Fishing Resort NORTHWEST/SUSHI   The lodge restaurant features Northwest cuisine and floor-to-ceiling windows offering lovely views. To start, try pan-seared Fanny Bay oysters with chile-and-lime crème fraîche, or choose from the menu of the adjoining sushi bar. For an entree, opt for a daily seafood special or, if you're not in the mood for fish, filet mignon with crisp latkes and caramelized red-onion glaze is an excellent choice.

900 April Point Rd. © **800/663-7090** or 250/285-2222. www.aprilpoint.com. Reservations recommended. Main courses C$15–C$40. AE, DC, MC, V. Daily 7am–9pm. Closed mid Oct to early-Apr.

Tsa-Kwa-Luten Lodge SEAFOOD   The restaurant features fresh seafood and steaks prepared with Continental finesse and an eye toward Native traditions. Standouts include pepper-crusted venison tenderloin with rosemary jus, and cedar plank–baked salmon accompanied by seasonal fruit salsa.

1 Lighthouse Rd. & 800/665-7745 or 250/598-3366. www.capemudgeresort.com. Reservations recommended. Main courses C$14–C$32. AE, DC, MC, V. Daily 7am–9pm. Closed mid-Oct to mid-April.

3 STRATHCONA PROVINCIAL PARK ★

38km (24 miles) W of Campbell River

British Columbia's oldest provincial park, and the largest on Vancouver Island at 250,000 hectares (617,763 acres), **Strathcona Park** is located west of Campbell River and Courtenay. Mountain peaks, many glaciated or mantled with snow, dominate the park, and lakes and alpine meadows dot the landscape. Roosevelt elk, Vancouver Island marmot and wolf, and black-tailed deer have evolved into distinct species, due to Vancouver Island's separation from the mainland. **Buttle Lake** provides good fishing for cutthroat and rainbow trout and Dolly Varden.

Summers in Strathcona are usually pleasantly warm; evenings can be cool. Winters are fairly mild except at higher elevations, where heavy snowfall is common. Snow remains year-round on the mountain peaks and may linger into July at higher elevations. Rain can be expected at any time of year.

ESSENTIALS

GETTING THERE   Campbell River and Courtenay are the primary access points for the park. Hwy. 28 passes through the northern section of the park and provides access to Buttle Lake, 48km (30 miles) west of Campbell River. There are two access routes to the Forbidden Plateau area from Courtenay. To reach Paradise Meadows from Courtenay and Hwy. 19, follow signs to Mount Washington Resort via the Strathcona Parkway. Twenty-five kilometers (16 miles) up the parkway, you'll come to the resort's Nordic Lodge road on the left. Turn onto this road and go another 1.6km (1 mile) to the Paradise Meadows parking lot. To reach Forbidden Plateau, follow the signs on the Forbidden Plateau road from Hwy. 19 and Courtenay. It's 19km (12 miles) to the former Forbidden Plateau ski area (now closed) and the trail head.

VISITOR INFORMATION   Contact the **BC Parks District Manager,** Box 1479, Parksville (© **250/954-4600;** www.env.gov.bc.ca/bcparks).

SEEING THE HIGHLIGHTS

The Buttle Lake area (off Hwy. 28) and the Forbidden Plateau area (accessed through Courtenay) both have something to offer visitors. Just outside the park boundaries, **Strathcona Park Lodge** (see "Where to Stay," below) offers lodging, dining, and a variety of activities. The rest of the park is largely undeveloped and requires hiking or backpacking into the alpine wilderness to see and enjoy much of its scenic splendor.

A paved road joins **Hwy. 28** (the Gold River Hwy.) near the outlet of **Buttle Lake** and winds its way southward, hugging the shoreline. Along this scenic road are numerous cataracts and creeks that rush and tumble into the lake.

Some of the more prominent peaks include Mount McBride, Marble Peak, Mount Phillips, and Mount Myra. **Elkhorn Mountain,** at 2,192m (7,192 ft.), is the second-highest mountain in the park. Elkhorn, along with Mount Flannigan and Kings Peak, can be seen from Hwy. 28. The highest point on Vancouver Island at 2,200m (7,218 ft.), the **Golden Hinde** stands almost in the center of the park to the west of Buttle Lake.

A second area of the park, **Forbidden Plateau,** is accessed by gravel road from Courtenay. Those who hike into the plateau are rewarded with an area of subalpine beauty and views that extend from the surrounding glaciers and mountains to farmlands and forest.

(Fun Facts) Forbidden Plateau: What's in a Name?

The Forbidden Plateau is a high-elevation lake basin that stretches between the snow-clad peaks of Mount Albert Edward and Mount Washington within the boundaries of Strathcona Provincial Park. As its name suggests, this area is the subject of curious legends and stories, many of them rather creepy. According to one legend, the Native Comox people sent their women and children to the plateau to protect them from raids by other coastal tribes. Once, when warriors from the Cowichan tribe were about to attack the Comox, the women and children fled to the Forbidden Plateau for protection. After the raid, the Comox men climbed up to the plateau to fetch their wives and families, only to discover that they had all vanished without a trace. However, the plateau was covered in snow that was tinted a mysterious pink color. According to the story, the women and children had been killed by evil spirits and the snow had been stained by their blood. The entire plateau became taboo due to the feared presence of malevolent spirits, and when British settlers came to this area in the 19th century, they could find no Native scouts to guide them through these highlands. Stories of mysterious events continued as prospectors and frontiersmen began to settle on the Forbidden Plateau, including a series of unexplained deaths. Adding to the sense of menace, the Forbidden Plateau was the epicenter of a 7.3 level earthquake in 1946, the strongest on-land earthquake ever recorded in Canada. A ski area once operated near the Forbidden Plateau, though the structures were repeatedly damaged by unexplained fires and the resort ceased operation in 1990s—the abandoned lifts and lodges only add to the general haunted atmosphere.

Whatever you make of evil spirit legends, there is a scientific explanation for the pink-colored snow, a phenomenon that has been noted by many visitors to the plateau. It turns out that pink snow can be caused by a snow-dwelling algae called *Chlamydomonas nivalis*. As sunlight becomes stronger in spring, the algae develop a pink-colored outer surface to protect against ultraviolet rays, giving a rosy cast to their snowy home.

The 440m (1,444-ft.) **Della Falls,** one of the 10 highest waterfalls in the world (and the highest in Canada), is located in the southern section of the park, and is reached by a rugged multiday hike (see "Hiking," below).

HIKING

FROM THE BUTTLE LAKE AREA   The 3km (1.9-mile) **Upper Myra Falls Trail** starts just past the Westmin mine operation. This 2-hour hike leads through old-growth forests and past waterfalls. The 6.6km (4.1-mile) **Marble Meadows Trail** starts at Phillips Creek Marine Campsite on Buttle Lake. It features alpine meadows and limestone formations; allow 6 hours round-trip. The 900m (2,953-ft.) **Lady Falls Trail,** which begins at the Hwy. 28 viewing platform, takes about 20 minutes and leads to a picturesque waterfall.

FROM THE PARADISE MEADOWS TRAIL HEAD (MOUNT WASHINGTON) The 2.2km (1.4-mile) **Paradise Meadows Loop Trail** is an easy walk through subalpine meadows, taking about 45 minutes. The 14km (8.7 mile) **Helen McKenzie–Kwai Lake–Croteau Lake Loop Trail** takes 6 hours and offers access to beautiful lakes and mountain vistas. There's designated camping at Kwai Lake. From Lake Helen McKenzie, the trail follows forested slopes over rougher terrain before rising to a rolling subalpine area to Circlet Lake, which offers designated camping. Allow 4 hours.

FROM FORBIDDEN PLATEAU The 5km (3.1-mile), 2-hour **Mount Becher Summit Trail** starts at the former ski lodge and goes up one of the runs to the trail head near the T-bar. It provides excellent views of the valley and the Strait of Georgia.

OTHER TRAILS IN STRATHCONA PARK The **Della Falls Trail** is 32km (20 miles) round-trip. It starts at the west end of Great Central Lake (btw. Port Alberni and Tofino on Hwy. 4) and follows the old railway grade up the Drinkwater Valley. You must take a boat across the lake to get to the trail head. At **Ark Resort,** 11000 Great Central Lake Rd. (© **250/723-2657;** www.arkresort.com), you can take a high-speed water taxi or rent a motorboat or canoe. The whole trip will take 3 to 6 days. The trail passes historic railroad logging sites and accesses Love Lake and Della Lake. Some unbridged river crossings can be hazardous.

CAMPING

Buttle Lake, with 85 sites, and **Ralph River,** with 76 sites, are both located on Buttle Lake, accessible via Hwy. 28 (the Gold River Hwy.) west of Campbell River. Sites go for C$14. The campgrounds have water, toilets, and firewood.

WHERE TO STAY

Strathcona Park Lodge ★★ This rustic lodge, north of Strathcona Park along upper Campbell Lake, has something to offer everyone who loves the outdoors—from families to Golden Agers. Lodge activities include climbing and rappelling, canoeing, fishing, and swimming. The package options offered by the lodge are numerous, so call to discuss your interests. The popular Adventure Unlimited package includes lodging, meals, and activities (climbing, kayaking, orienteering, hiking, and more) for 4 (C$840) or 7 days (C$1,595) per person, based on double occupancy. The lodge is also a lovely place to just hang out and is a good base for exploring the park. All accommodations are sparely yet comfortably furnished. Some chalet units have shared bathrooms; all other rooms have private bathrooms. The lakefront cabins with kitchens are the most charming, though you must reserve well in advance. From mid-March through mid-November, the Whale Room serves three buffet-style meals daily, with guests sitting at long communal tables, while the Canoe Club Café offers more traditional restaurant-style meals.

40km (25 miles) west of Campbell River on Hwy. 28. Mailing address: Box 2160, Campbell River, BC V9W 5C5. © **250/286-3122.** Fax 250/286-6010. www.strathcona.bc.ca. 39 units. From C$80 chalet double with shared bathroom; from C$139 double with private bathroom; C$175–C$440 cabin. 2- or 3-night minimum stays in cabins. Off-season discounts available. MC, V. **Amenities:** 2 restaurants; babysitting; children's programs; exercise room; sauna; canoe and kayak rentals. *In room:* No phone.

4 WEST TO GOLD RIVER & NOOTKA SOUND

Hwy. 28 continues past Strathcona Park another 9km (5⅔ miles) to **Gold River** (pop. 2,049), a logging port and mill town just to the east of the Muchalet Inlet, and the only major northwestern island community accessible by paved road. The wild coastline

around the **Nootka Sound,** to the west of Gold River, was the site of the first European **215**
settlement in the northwest, founded by British Captain James Cook in 1778. The tiny
coastal communities here are almost completely isolated from roads, and rely on the **MV**
Uchuck III for public transport and movement of goods. Passengers are welcome to join
the MV *Uchuck III* as it goes between Gold River, Nootka Sound, and Kyuquot Sound.

Late September through early May, the Tahsis Inlet day trip leaves on Tuesdays at 9am,
traveling into Nootka Sound and up the Tahsis Inlet between Vancouver and Nootka
islands to the village of Tahsis. The 9-hour round-trip costs C$60 for adults, C$55 for
seniors, and C$30 for children 6 to 12.

From early June to mid-September, the MV *Uchuck III* runs a day trip on Wednesdays
(early June through Labour Day) and Saturdays (late June through mid-Sept) from Gold
River to Friendly Cove, or Yuquot, the ancestral home of the Mowachaht people. The
return trip runs 6 to 7½ hours and costs C$70 for adults, C$65 for seniors, and C$35
for kids. It was Friendly Cove where Captain Cook first made contact with the Native
peoples of Vancouver Island and established a trading fort.

On Thursdays year-round, the boat departs for Kyuquot Sound, to the north. This
2-day trip goes up the Tahsis and Esperanza inlets to the open sea and eventually the
village of Kyuquot, where passengers stay overnight before returning the following day.
The cost, which includes lodging, is C$465 for two. A similar trip departs Mondays for
Zeballos, a former gold-mining town and good wildlife-viewing spot just a way from
Tahsis. This trip costs C$375 for two, including lodging.

For more information on other trips (including a twice yearly trip btw. Gold River and
Victoria), or to make reservations, contact **Nootka Sound Service Ltd.** (© **250/283-
2515** or 250/283-2325; www.mvuchuck.com). The MV *Uchuck III* will also take kayakers to various destinations on its routes; inquire for details.

If you need accommodations in Gold River, contact the **Tourist Info Centre**
(© **250/283-2202;** www.goldriver.ca) or try the **Ridgeview Motor Inn,** 395 Donner
Ct. (© **800/989-3393** or 250/283-2277; www.ridgeview-inn.com), where doubles
range from C$90 to C$135 in high summer season.

5 TELEGRAPH COVE, PORT MCNEILL, ALERT BAY & PORT HARDY

Port McNeill: 198km (123 miles) N of Campbell River

It's a winding 198km (123-mile) drive through forested mountains along the Island
Highway (Hwy. 19) from Campbell River to **Port McNeill,** on northern Vancouver
Island. But the majestic scenery, crystal-clear lakes, and unique wilderness along the way
make it worthwhile.

The highway rejoins the coast along **Johnstone Strait,** home to a number of orca
(killer whale) pods, which migrate annually from the Queen Charlotte Strait south to
these salmon-rich waters. Whale-watching trips out of Port McNeill and Telegraph Cove
are the principal recreational activities; this is one of the most noted whale-watching areas
in British Columbia.

Also worth a visit is the island community of **Alert Bay,** a traditional First Nations
townsite festooned with totem poles and carvings. The museum houses a famous collection of ceremonial masks and other artifacts.

NORTHERN VANCOUVER ISLAND

9

TELEGRAPH COVE & PORT HARDY AREA

The Island Highway's terminus, **Port Hardy,** is 52km (32 miles) north of Port McNeill. Although it's a remote community of only 5,470, Port Hardy is the starting point for two adventures along the rugged Pacific coast: the Inside Passage ferry cruise (see chapter 11) to Prince Rupert and the Discovery Coast ferry cruise to Bella Bella, with road access to the B.C. interior (see chapter 11).

ESSENTIALS

GETTING THERE There are three principal ways to get to Vancouver Island's north-ernmost towns and islands: by car, bus, and plane. You can also reach Port Hardy from the north via the Inside Passage ferry from Prince Rupert (see chapter 11).

By Plane **Pacific Coastal Airlines** (© 800/663-2872; www.pacific-coastal.com) flies daily from Vancouver to Port Hardy Airport.

By Car Telegraph Cove is 198km (123 miles) north of Campbell River along the Island Highway (Hwy. 19). Port McNeill is another 9km (5⅔ miles) north. Port Hardy is 238km (148 miles) north of Campbell River.

By Bus **Vancouver Island Coach Lines** (© 250/388-5248, or book through Grey-hound © 800/661-8747; www.greyhound.ca) offers bus transport from Victoria and Nanaimo to Port Hardy and other towns in northern Vancouver Island. One-way fare from Nanaimo to Port Hardy is C$63.

VISITOR INFORMATION The **Port McNeill Visitor Info Centre,** 351 Shelley Crescent (© 250/956-3131; www.portmcneill.net), is open year-round on weekdays and daily in summer from 10am to 6pm. The **Alert Bay Visitor Info Centre,** 116 Fir St. (© 250/974-5213; www.alertbay.ca), is open in summer daily from 9am to 6pm, and the rest of the year Monday through Friday from 9am to 5pm. The **Port Hardy Visitor Info Centre,** 7250 Market St. (© 250/949-7622; www.ph-chamber.bc.ca), is open June through September daily from 8:30am to 7pm, and October through May Monday through Friday from 8:30am to 5pm.

TELEGRAPH COVE

Telegraph Cove (pop. 20), 22km (14 driving miles) southeast of Port McNeill—by way of the Island Highway and then a stretch of paved and gravel road—has an unusual story. The town's handful of permanent residents lives in one of the few remaining elevated-boardwalk villages on Vancouver Island, overlooking Johnstone Strait. This postcard-perfect fishing village's buildings are perched on stilts over the water, making it an entertaining destination for a stroll.

First a sawmill and fishing port, then an army camp, now a resort, Telegraph Cove bustles in summer. The town is largely dominated by comfortably rustic **Telegraph Cove Resort,** which offers many historic boardwalk homes as rental units. With a good restaurant, busy boat basin, and wonderful bay and island views, the resort village is a longtime family favorite.

Whale-Watching & Other Outdoor Pursuits

Telegraph Cove is right on the Johnstone Strait, a narrow passage that serves as the summer home to hundreds of orcas as well as dolphins, porpoises, and seals. Bald eagles also patrol the waterway, and more unusual birds pass through the area, an important stop on the Pacific Flyway.

Seventeen kilometers (11 miles) south of Telegraph Cove, the **Robson Bight Ecological Reserve** ★★ provides fascinating whale-watching. Orcas regularly beach themselves in the shallow waters of the pebbly "rubbing beaches" to remove the barnacles from their tummies. Boat tours are not allowed to enter the reserve itself, but you can watch from nearby areas. **Stubbs Island Whale-Watching,** at the end of the Telegraph Cove boardwalk (✆ **800/665-3066** or 250/928-3185; www.stubbs-island.com), offers tours from May through early October in boats equipped with hydrophones, so you can hear the whales' underwater communication. In high season, these 3½-hour cruises cost from C$84 to C$94 for adults.

From May to mid-October, **Tide Rip Tours,** 28 Boardwalk (✆ **888/643-9319** or 250/339-5320; www.tiderip.com), offers daylong boat excursions to watch grizzly bears for C$288. Other wildlife-viewing trips are available.

For kayaking tours, contact **Telegraph Cove Sea Kayaking** (✆ **888/756-0099** or 250/756-0094; www.tckayaks.com), which offers guided day trips out onto Telegraph Cove (C$165 per person) or Johnstone Strait (C$350 per person), where you might kayak with orcas. Kayak rentals are also available.

Where to Stay & Dine

Although both of the following establishments have mailing addresses in Port McNeill, they are located in or near Telegraph Cove.

Hidden Cove Lodge   Built years before a road reached this isolated harbor, Hidden Cove was meant to be approached by boat, and it still saves its best face for those who arrive this way. The handsome lodge, with a cathedral-ceilinged great room, is nestled beside a secluded cove. The guest rooms are clean and simply decorated, all with private bathrooms. Three self-contained cabins have efficiency kitchens and decks. Hidden Cove's easygoing, unaffected atmosphere belies the fact that it attracts the rich and famous. The restaurant, open to non-guests by reservation only, serves quality international dishes. Whale-watching, birding, heli-fishing, kayaking, and hiking tours can be arranged.

Lewis Point, 1 Hidden Cove Rd., Box 258, Port McNeill, BC V0N 2R0. ✆/fax **250/956-3916.** www.bcbb only.com/1263.php. 8 lodge rooms, 3 cottages. C$170 lodge double, includes breakfast; C$199 1-bedroom cottage; C$299 2-bedroom cottage. Extra person C$25. 2-night minimum stay. Off-season rates available. MC, V. Free parking. Take the Island Hwy. (Hwy. 19) to turnoff for Telegraph Cove/Beaver Cove; turn right and follow signs. The lodge is 6.5km (4 miles) from Telegraph Cove. **Amenities:** Restaurant; golf course nearby. *In room:* No phone.

Telegraph Cove Resorts   Most of the accommodations offered by Telegraph Cove Resorts are refurbished homes from the early 20th century, scattered along the boardwalk. They range from small rooms in a former fishermen's boardinghouse to three-bedroom homes that sleep up to nine. All have bathrooms and kitchens, but no phones or TVs. There are also hotel-style rooms (no kitchens) at the Wastell Manor, a large home built in 1912. Although none of the historic properties are exactly fancy, they are clean and make for a unique experience—it really is like staying in a historic logging camp. On Sunday, the resort encourages guests to join the afternoon potluck. Amenities include moorage and fishing charters. In addition, 121 campsites are a short walk from the boardwalk. Open May through October 15, the campground provides hot showers, laundry, toilets, fire pits, and water. Sites are C$25 to C$30.

Box 1, Telegraph Cove, BC V0N 3J0. ✆ **800/200-HOOK** (4665) or 250/928-3131. Fax 250/928-3105. www. telegraphcoveresort.com. 24 units. Mid-June to Sept C$110–C$300 cabin, C$165–C$195 suite; Oct 1 to mid-Oct and May 1–June 14 C$85–C$170 cabin, C$100–C$150 suite. Extra person C$10. Packages available. MC, V. Closed mid-Oct to Apr. Located 26km (16 miles) south of Port McNeill. Pets allowed in some cabins for C$5 per night. **Amenities:** Restaurant; pub; kayak rentals. *In room:* No phone.

Port McNeill (pop. 3,000) is a logging and mill town—not particularly quaint—that serves as an access point for whale-watching and other wildlife tours, numerous outdoor-recreation opportunities, and the ferry to Alert Bay. Alert Bay (pop. 1,000) is a fascinating destination for anyone interested in First Nations culture. It has a world-renowned collection of totem carvings and wall murals, as well as historic buildings.

During the second week of June, the Nimpkish Reserve hosts **June Sports & Indian Celebrations** (✆ **250/974-5556,** the 'Namgis First Nation office) on the soccer field in Alert Bay. Traditional tests of strength and agility are demonstrated by the island's tribal members.

BC Ferries (✆ **888/BC-FERRY** [223-3779] or 250/386-3431; www.bcferries.com) runs daily service between Port McNeill and Alert Bay. The crossing takes about 45 minutes; peak fares are C$9.20 per passenger, C$22 per vehicle. If you're going to Alert Bay mostly to visit the U'mista Cultural Centre, you can easily leave your vehicle at Port McNeill. It's about a half-hour walk from the ferry dock to the center.

Exploring Alert Bay

Alert Bay has a rich First Nations heritage that can be seen in its proudly preserved architecture and artifacts. It has been a Kwakwaka'wakw (Kwagiulth) village for thousands of years. The integration of Scottish immigrants into the area during the 19th and 20th centuries is clearly depicted in the design of the **Anglican Church** on Front Street (✆ **250/974-5401**). The cedar building was erected in 1881; its stained-glass window designs reflect a fusion of Kwakwaka'wakw and Scottish motifs. It's open in summer Monday through Saturday from 8am to 5pm.

Walk a mile from the ferry terminal along Front Street to the island's two most interesting attractions: a 53m (174-ft.) **totem pole**—the world's highest—stands next to the **Big House,** the tribal community center. The cedar totem pole features 22 figures of bears, orcas, and ravens. The Big House is usually closed to the public, but visitors are welcome to enter the grounds to get a closer look at the building, which is covered with traditional painted figures. In July and August, the **T'sasala Cultural Group** (✆ **250/974-5475;** www.tsasala.org) presents dance performances in the Big House, usually at 1pm on Thursday, Friday, and Saturday. The cost is C$15 for adults and C$6 for children under 12.

A few yards down the road from the Big House is the **U'Mista Cultural Centre** ★★, Front Street (✆ **250/974-5403;** www.umista.org), which displays carved masks, cedar baskets, copper jewelry, and other potlatch artifacts. The potlatch was traditionally a highly important ceremony for the Kwagiulth: While dancers and singers clad in elaborate masks and robes performed and sang, villagers would engage in ritual gift-giving, exchanging ceremonial objects, totems, shields, and other hand-carved artifacts created especially for the ritual. However, in the 1880s, the Canadian government outlawed the ceremony as part of an effort to "civilize" the Kwagiulth, and, in 1921, its officers confiscated the entirety of the band's potlatch treasures and regalia, which was sent to museums in eastern Canada and sold to private collectors.

By the 1970s and 1980s, pressures from Native groups and changes in government perspectives resulted in the partial repatriation of potlatch ceremonial artifacts to the Kwagiulth, who established the U'Mista Cultural Centre to exhibit this wondrous collection. Admission is C$8 for adults, C$7 for seniors and students, and C$1 for children 12 and under. The museum is open in summer daily from 9am to 5pm, and in winter Monday through Friday from 9am to 5pm.

Whale-Watching & Other Outdoor Pursuits

Orcas, dolphins, and eagles all gather along Johnstone Strait to snack on fish that converge at this narrows between Vancouver Island and a series of tightly clustered islands.

From Port McNeill, **Mackay Whale Watching Ltd.,** 1514 Broughton Blvd. (✆ **877/663-6722** or 250/956-9865; www.whaletime.com), offers daily tours to Johnstone Strait on a 17m (56-ft.) passenger cruiser with hydrophone. A 4- to 5-hour trip costs C$105.

Seasmoke Tours/Sea Orca Expeditions (✆ **800/668-6722** in B.C., or 250/974-5225; www.seaorca.com) offers whale-watching sailing trips from Alert Bay from June to September. You can also arrange to be picked up from the **Alder Bay Resort** on Vancouver Island (✆ **250/956-4117;** www.alderbayresort.com), convenient if you don't want to make the ferry crossing to Alert Bay. Excursions aboard a 13m (43-ft.), hydrophone-equipped sailboat include tea and scones. Five-hour tours cost C$95. Seasmoke also offers tour/lodging packages at two bungalows on Alert Bay.

Where to Stay & Dine

If you can't get into the recommended Telegraph Cove–area resorts and don't want to continue on to Port Hardy or Campbell River, try Port McNeill's 62-unit **Haida-Way Motor Inn,** 1817 Campbell Way (✆ **800/956-3373** or 250/956-3373; www.pmhotels.com), which rents rooms for C$105 in high season and offers on-premises restaurants and pubs. Just across the road is the new **Black Bear Resort,** 1812 Campbell Way (✆ **866/956-4900** or 250/956-4900; www.blackbearresort.net), which has rooms starting at C$140 double, which includes complimentary continental breakfast.

Oceanview Camping & Trailer Park, Alder Road, Alert Bay (✆ **250/974-5213;** fax 250/974-5470), has a great view of the Johnstone Strait and nature trails that fan out from the 23 sites. Rates are C$14 to C$18. Full hookups, flush toilets, hot showers, a free boat launch, and boat tours make this a great deal. The 'Namgis Nation runs the **Gwakawe Campground,** Alert Bay (✆ **250/974-5274**), where C$13 gets you a beachfront site and access to showers, laundry, water, and firewood.

In Alert Bay, the **Old Customs House Restaurant,** 19 Fir St. (✆ **250/974-2282;** http://alert-bay.com/customs), has a menu of burgers, pasta, and fish and chips; it's open for three meals daily. There are also three bed-and-breakfast rooms upstairs, going for C$50 to C$75 double.

Nimpkish Hotel ★ This vintage waterfront hotel in Alert Bay has recently undergone a top-to-bottom makeover to emerge as the most comfortable and gracious place to stay for miles around. Many of the rooms have wonderful water views and balconies; all are furnished with the kind of low-key elegance that you don't expect on a remote island. The pub, with its large deck that extends over the water, is a perfect spot for a sundowner drink.

318 Fir St., Alert Bay, BC V0N 1A0. ✆ **888/646-7547** or 250/974-5716. www.nimpkishhotel.com. 9 units. C$100–C$185 double. Rates include continental breakfast. Low-season rates available. MC, V. **Amenities:** Pub; sunroom. *In room:* TV, fridge, Wi-Fi, fireplace.

PORT HARDY

Port Hardy is the final stop on the Island Highway. This sizable community is slowly moving away from a resource-based economy: Fishing, forestry, and mining have waned—though not disappeared—and the town is gradually developing an economy based on tourism.

A principal reason to venture here is the ferry to **Prince Rupert**—in fact, the ferry is a mainstay of the local tourism industry. The night before the 15-hour Inside Passage ferry runs, the town is booked up and reservations are needed at most restaurants. Port Hardy is also the point of departure for the Discovery Coast ferry cruise (see chapter 11).

People also visit for diving and excellent halibut and salmon fishing. Sportfishing is very good here, as the runs of salmon in local rivers continue to be strong and are therefore open to more fishing than at threatened runs elsewhere. The **Port Hardy Museum,** 7110 Market St. (© **250/949-8143**), holds relics from early Danish settlers, plus a collection of stone tools from about 8,000 B.C. found just east of town. Admission is by donation. The gift shop is one of the few places in town where you can find local carving and artwork. Hours are from mid-May to mid-October Tuesday through Saturday from 11:30am to 5:30pm, and from mid-October to mid-May Wednesday through Saturday from noon to 5pm.

Outdoor Pursuits

DIVING ★   Diving is excellent in the Port Hardy area. **North Island Diving and Kayaking,** 8625 Shipley St. (© **250/902-0565;** www.odysseykayaking.com), is a full-service dive service, with rentals, instruction, and guided dives. Guided kayak trips and rental kayaks are also available. For more information on diving in the region, follow the links at **www.3routes.com**.

FISHING   From Port Hardy, you can arrange day charter trips with local outfitters. **Catala Charters and Lodge** (© **800/515-5511** or 250/949-7560; www.catalacharters. net) offers guided 4-hour fishing trips for up to four people for C$500. **Codfather Charters** (© **250/949-6696;** www.codfathercharters.com) offers year-round multiday fishing charters and accommodations in a waterfront lodge.

To simply rent a boat, contact **Hardy Bay Boat Rental,** Quarterdeck Marina at 6555 Hardy Bay Rd. (© **250/949-7048** or 250/949-0155; www.hardybayfishing.com). Rates start at C$22 per hour or C$190 per day.

Port Hardy is the stepping-off point for trips to remote **fishing camps,** many with long pedigrees and well-to-do clientele. One of the only camps directly accessed from Port Hardy is **Duval Point Lodge** (© **250/949-6667;** www.duvalpointlodge.com), which offers multiday packages from its base camp about 8km (5 miles) north of town (accessed by boat). Guests receive a short training session; groups are then given their own boat and pointed to the channel. From here on, you keep your own schedule and run expeditions as you see fit. Guests stay in two, two-story floating lodges, each with four bedrooms, a mix of private and shared bathrooms, and a full kitchen. The outfitter provides rod and reel, bait, boat, cleaning area, and freezers. Guests do their own cooking. Guides are available, though part of the fun here is the satisfaction of running your own boat and interacting with other guests. The lodge also has two land-based log cabins, each with three bedrooms. Anyone who comes in their own boat can stay in these cabins; rates start at C$570 for 4 midweek nights. Boat/lodging packages start at C$970 for 4 nights/5 days of fishing and accommodations. The lodge is closed October through May. Duval Point is not for those looking for five-star comforts and pampering. But if you want access to excellent fishing and adventure with congenial hospitality, it's a great value.

If you are looking for creature comforts, one of the area's most famous and upscale fishing lodges is **Nimmo Bay Resort** (© **800/837-HELI** [4354] or 250/956-4000; www.nimmobay.com), a full-service floating resort where 3 days/3 nights at the lodge and fishing with transportation by helicopter will run you around C$7,250 per person. Access is by floatplane or boat.

KAYAKING **North Island Diving and Kayaking,** 8625 Shipley St. (℃ **888/792-3366** or 250/902-0565; www.odysseykayaking.com), gives guided day trips to islands in the protected waters of Beaver Harbour near Port Hardy starting at C$99. Rates include lunch and transportation. Kayak rentals are also available.

Hiking Cape Scott

Cape Scott Provincial Park is a 21,870-hectare (54,042-acre) coastal wilderness at the northwest tip of Vancouver Island. Cape Scott is true wilderness, preserving magnificent areas of coastal British Columbia, with little development other than trails. But for visitors looking to experience primal forests and miles of wild beaches, the park is a magical destination. The trail head for all park trails, in the extreme southeast corner of the park, is reached by a 67km (42-mile) part-paved, part-gravel road from Port Hardy. From there, follow signs for Winter Harbour or Holberg, and follow signs for the park from Holberg.

The park is characterized by 64km (40 miles) of spectacular ocean frontage, including about 23km (14 miles) of wide, sandy beaches, running from Nissen Bight in the north to San Josef Bay in the south and interspersed with rocky promontories and headlands. **Nels Bight,** midway between the eastern boundary of the park near Nissen Bight and the Cape Scott Lighthouse, is a 3km-long (1¾-mile), white-sand beach; it's considered the most impressive of the nine beaches in the park. **Hansen Lagoon** is a stopping place for Canada geese and a variety of waterfowl traveling the Pacific Flyway. Deer, elk, black bear, otter, cougars, and wolves are in evidence in the forested and open uplands, and seals and sea lions inhabit offshore islands.

The easiest and most popular hike in the park is the 2.5km (1.6-mile) one-way from the trail head to **San Josef Bay.** The trail leads through forest along the San Josef River, reaching the beach in about 45 minutes. Once at the beach, you can explore the ruins of the Henry Ohlsen home and post office, a relic of the Danish settlements of the early 1900s. The first section of beach is wide and white, flanked by rocky cliffs, and makes a great spot for a picnic. San Josef Bay is also a good place to explore by kayak; surfers ride the high waves here as well.

For long-distance hikers, the highlight of the park is the 24km (15-mile) one-way trail out to the **Cape Scott Lighthouse** at the very northern tip of Vancouver Island. Most hikers manage it in 3 days, with 2 nights spent at Nels Bight campground—which means you won't be carrying your gear on the final leg to Cape Scott. Nels Bight is a spectacular coastline of sand and rocky beaches, and is a popular place to camp; fresh water is available.

There is no best time to visit the park, although midsummer is generally preferred, as the trails are less muddy. Facilities in the park are minimal. Be sure to wear waterproof boots, and if you're spending the night, be prepared for sudden changes of weather any time of year. For more information, contact **BC Parks District Manager** (℃ **250/954-4600;** www.env.gov.bc.ca/bcparks).

Where to Stay & Dine

Port Hardy has several well-worn hotel complexes. The lodgings recommended below are significantly more attractive than most of the alternatives, so reserve well in advance, especially on days when the ferries run. Likewise, most restaurants in Port Hardy are very basic. The hotel restaurant suggested below isn't fancy, but it's better than the alternatives.

The **Wildwoods Campsite,** Forestry Road (📞 **250/949-6753;** www.wildwoods campsite.com), is off the road to the ferry terminal. The 60 sites offer fire pits, hot showers, toilets, beach access, and moorage for C$15 to C$20. Tenters will like the wooded sites at **Quatse River Campground,** 5050 Hardy Rd. (📞 **250/949-2395;** www.quatse campground.com), with 62 sites at C$20 to C$25.

Glen Lyon Inn   This attractive hotel and restaurant development sits right above the Hardy Bay marina, above the mouth of the Glen Lyon River. All rooms have views of the harbor, the to-ing and fro-ing of boat traffic, and the wooded hills beyond. Rooms are recently renovated; most have balconies, fridge, and microwave, while suites have fireplaces, two-person jetted tubs, and stereos. The restaurant and pub, **Malone's,** is probably the tops for dining in Port Hardy.

6435 Hardy Bay Rd., Port Hardy, BC V0N 2P0. 📞 **877/949-7115** or 250/949-7115. Fax 250/949-7415. www.glenlyoninn.com. C$110–C$160 double; C$145–C$195 suite. Extra person C$10. AE, DC, MC, V. **Amenities:** Restaurant; pub; exercise room; marina. *In room:* A/C, TV, fridge and microwave (most rooms), hair dryer, Wi-Fi.

Oceanview B&B   Perched on a bluff overlooking Port Hardy Bay, Oceanview is a comfortably furnished, spotless modern home. A large room with two queen-size beds and a bathroom overlooks the cul-de-sac and gardens; the other spacious units offer views of the bay. Free coffee, tea, and hot cocoa are served in the evening. The hostess offers a friendly welcome and advice on local travel.

7735 Cedar Place, Box 1837, Port Hardy, BC V0N 2P0. 📞/fax **250/949-8302.** www.island.net/~oceanvue. 3 units, 2 with shared bathroom. C$100–C$120 double. Extra person C$15. Rates include continental breakfast. No credit cards. Children must be 12 or older. *In room:* TV, hair dryer, no phone, Wi-Fi.

10

The Sunshine Coast & Whistler

One of British Columbia's most scenic drives and the province's most celebrated year-round recreation center are both just north of Vancouver, making great destinations for a weekend away or a short road trip. The Sunshine Coast Highway is the name given to Hwy. 101 as it skirts the islands, fjords, and peninsulas of the mainland's Strait of Georgia coast. The scenery is spectacular, and the fishing and logging communities along the route offer friendly hospitality. No small part of the charm of this drive is the ferry rides: To reach road's end at Lund, you'll need to take two ferries, both offering jaw-dropping vistas of glaciered peaks floating above deep-blue waters. To make this route into a full loop trip, catch a third ferry from Powell River across the Strait of Georgia to Comox, and begin your exploration of Vancouver Island (see chapters 7, 8, and 9).

The road to Whistler is equally spectacular, as it follows fjordlike Howe Sound, flanked by cliffs and towering peaks. But there's more to do here than gawk at the landscape: Whistler is Canada's premier skiing destination in winter (it hosted the ski events for the 2010 Winter Olympics) and a golf, hiking, and white-water rafting mecca in summer. Accommodations, dining, and recreational facilities are first-class, and the well-planned lodging developments have yet to overwhelm the natural beauty of the valley.

1 THE SUNSHINE COAST

Powell River: 142km (88 miles) N of Vancouver

It's a travel writer's truism that the "getting there" part of a trip is half the fun. In the case of the Sunshine Coast—that strip of wildly scenic waterfront real estate north of Vancouver, along the mainland Strait of Georgia coast—the "getting there" is practically the entire reason for making the journey. But what a journey!

Backed up against the high peaks of the glaciated Coastal Mountain range, overlooking the tempestuous waters of the Strait of Georgia and on to the rolling mountains of Vancouver Island, this maritime-intensive trip involves two ferry rides and a lovely meandering drive between slumbering fishing villages. It eventually terminates at Lund, the end of the road for the Pacific Coast's Hwy. 101.

Powell River is the only town of any size along this route. Long a major lumber-milling center, Powell River is beginning to focus on tourism as a supplement to its resource-based economy. Diving in the sea-life-rich waters of the Georgia Strait is a particularly popular activity along the Sunshine Coast.

Getting There

BY CAR & FERRY   Getting to Powell River and the Sunshine Coast requires taking a couple of ferries. From West Vancouver's Horseshoe Bay **BC Ferries** (© **888/BC-FERRY** [223-3779] or 250/386-3431; www.bcferries.bc.ca) terminal, ferries embark for Langdale, a 40-minute crossing. Driving north along Hwy. 101, the road hugs the coast along the Sechelt Peninsula, terminating 81km (50 miles) later at Earls Cove, where another ferry departs for a 50-minute crossing to Saltery Bay. The fare for each ferry is C$12 per passenger, C$39 per car in peak season. From Saltery Bay, Powell River is another 31km (19 miles). Lund, the terminus of Hwy. 101, is another 28km (17 miles).

You can also cross to Comox/Courtenay, on central Vancouver Island, from Powell River. This popular 75-minute crossing makes for a scenic loop tour of British Columbia's rugged coast and islands. The fare is C$12 per passenger, C$39 per vehicle in peak season. (See chapter 8 for coverage of Comox and Courtenay.)

BY BUS   **Malaspina Coach Lines** (© **877/227-8287**) offers service from Vancouver to Powell River via Hwy. 101 and the Sechelt Peninsula.

BY PLANE   **Pacific Coastal Airlines** (© **800/663-2872** or 604/273-8666; www.pacificcoastal.com) flies from Vancouver to Powell River.

VISITOR INFORMATION   Contact the **Powell River Visitors Bureau,** 4690 Marine Ave. (© **877/817-8669;** www.discoverpowellriver.com).

EXPLORING THE AREA

Although Powell River is only 142km (88 miles) north of Vancouver, it feels light-years removed from the urban sprawl. It's probably because of the ferries: Commuting from the Sunshine Coast—the name given to the rocky, mountain-edged coastline that lies in the rain shadow of Vancouver Island—wouldn't make sense if you worked in Vancouver's financial district.

Hwy. 101 is a very scenic route, with soaring 3,048m (10,000-ft.) peaks to the east and the swelling blue waters of the Strait of Georgia to the west. The first town north of the Horseshoe Bay–Langdale Ferry is **Gibsons** (pop. 3,732), a bucolic seaside community that served as the setting for the 1980s TV series *The Beachcombers*. Much of the action took place in **Molly's Reach Restaurant,** 647 School Rd. (© **604/886-9710**), which has evolved from a film set of a restaurant into a real eatery with fine home-style cooking. Wander along the Gibsons Seawalk, which leads from the Government Wharf to Gibsons Marina, and watch fishing boats unload their catch. **Roberts Creek Provincial Park,** 9km (5⅔ miles) north of town, has a great tide-pool area that's perfect for picnicking.

Twenty-eight kilometers (17 miles) north of Gibsons is **Sechelt** (pop. 7,545), an arty little town on a sandy finger of land—all that connects the Sechelt Peninsula to mainland British Columbia. The town is a delightful clutter of galleries and cafes. The **Sechelt Indian Nation** is headquartered here; the imposing House of Hewhiwus contains a cultural center, museum, and gift shop. A couple of miles north of Sechelt is **Porpoise Bay Provincial Park,** with a nice beach and riverside trail.

Continue north along Hwy. 101, past the turning to Madiera Park and Pender Harbour, and admire views of Vancouver Island. Drive past the Earls Cove ferry terminal to **Skookumchuk Narrows Provincial Park.** All of the seawater that lies behind 40km-long (25-mile) Sechelt Peninsula—which includes three major ocean inlets—churns

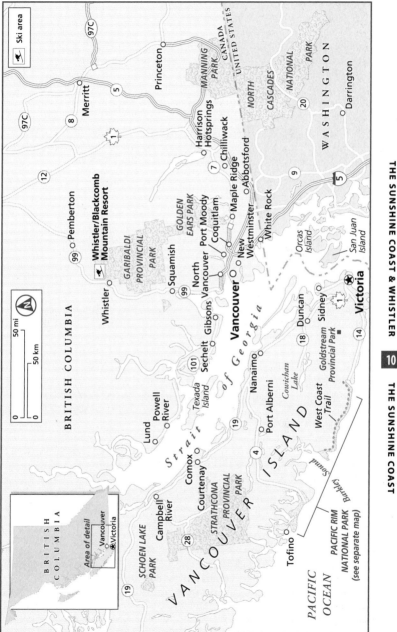

back and forth through this passage in an amazing display of tidal fury. It's about an hour's walk to the park's viewing area. Tides are so fierce, causing boiling whirlpools and eddies, that they actually roar.

Powell River (pop. 13,300) is dominated by one of the world's largest pulp and paper mills. That said, the town sits on a lovely location, and if you're feeling adventurous, it's a major center for diving and kayaking.

The old portion of town is called the **Homesite,** a company town that grew up alongside the original lumber mill near the harbor. The only designated National Historic Region in British Columbia, the Homesite contains more than 30 commercial buildings and about 400 residential buildings, all in late Victorian style. Ask at the visitor center for the heritage walking-tour brochure. The **Powell River Historic Museum,** 4800 Marine Dr. (© **604/485-2222;** www.powellrivermuseum.ca), has one of the largest archives of historical photos in the province, along with artifacts from the Native Sechelt. It's open year-round Monday through Friday from 9am to 4:30pm, plus the same hours on weekends from June to Labour Day. Admission is C$2 adult.

From Powell River, many travelers take the ferry over to Comox/Courtenay on Vancouver Island and continue the loop back south. However, Powell River isn't the end of the road. That honor goes to tiny **Lund,** 28km (17 miles) north on Hwy. 101. The main reason to make the trip is to say you did it, and to pop into the century-old Lund Hotel for a drink or a meal.

OUTDOOR PURSUITS

CANOEING & KAYAKING   The Sunshine Coast, with its fjord-notched coastline, myriad islands, and protected waters, makes for excellent kayaking. The **Desolation Sound** area, north of Lund, is especially popular. The **Powell Forest Canoe Route,** a 4- to 8-day backcountry paddle, links four lakes in an 81km (50-mile) circuit. **Powell River Sea Kayaks** (© **866/617-4444** or 604/483-2160; www.bcseakayak.com) has its office 30km (19 miles) north of Powell River on Okeover Inlet, and offers rentals and tours to adjacent Desolation Sound.

DIVING   The center for diving along the Sunshine Coast, Powell River boasts visibility of over 30m (98 ft.) in winter, lots of sea life, and varied terrain. Area dive spots include five shipwrecks and several boats sunk as artificial reefs. **Alpha Dive Services,** 7050 Field St. (© **604/485-6939;** www.divepowellriver.com), is one of the area's leading outfitters, with a shop in Powell River and diving operations in Okeover Inlet and Desolation Sound.

WHERE TO STAY & DINE

In Sechelt

Four Winds B&B ★   It's hard to imagine a more compelling site: a thrust of bare rock stretching out into the Strait of Georgia, backed up against a grove of fir and spruce. This modern home is lined with picture windows, all the better to capture the astonishing view of islands and sea, frequently visited by whales, herons, and seals. Guest rooms are beautifully decorated and have a hot tub or Jacuzzi; the suite has a balcony. Most notably, one of the owners is a licensed massage therapist, and will schedule sessions utilizing craniosacral therapy, and neuromuscular and hot-stone techniques.

5482 Hill Rd., Sechelt, BC V0N 3A8. © **800/543-2989,** 604/885-3144, or 604/740-1905. Fax 604/885-3182. www.fourwindsbeachhouse.com. 3 units. C$139–C$219 double. Rates include full breakfast. MC, V. **Amenities:** Golf course nearby; hot tub; Jacuzzi; spa treatments. *In room:* A/C, TV/DVD/VCR, fridge, hair dryer, Wi-Fi.

Rockwater Secret Cove Resort ★★   "Glamping" isn't exactly an attractive word, but it's been invented to describe the pleasures of "glamour camping," which attain a very high level at Rockwater Secret Cove Resort. Canvas wall tents stand on platforms above a thrust of rock jutting out into the sea. Forget memories of dusty scouting trips: The Tenthouse Suites have the amenities of a luxury hotel room—king-size beds with fine linens, hydrotherapy tubs for two, propane fireplaces, rainforest showers, heated slate floors, and private verandas overlooking the Straight of Georgia. In season, the resort also offers massage treatments in the "spa without walls"—private outdoor platforms with spacious views. If tents aren't your thing, the resort also offers more conventional lodging, a choice of cabins and lodge rooms and suites, all beautifully furnished. The resort also offers a wide selection of recreational opportunities, from sailing to mountain biking to naturalist-led hikes.

5356 Ole's Cove Rd., Halfmoon Bay, BC V0N 1Y2. ℂ **877/296-4593** or 604/885-7038. Fax 604/885-7036. www.rockwatersecretcoveresort.com. 15 tenthouse suites, 14 rooms and suites, 11 cabins. Tenthouse suites C$219–C$449 double (low–high season rates); rooms and suites C$135–C$279 double; cabins C$149–259 double. Extra person C$25. MC, V. **Amenities:** Restaurant; lounge; heated pool; recreation room; spa treatment facilities; barbecue pit; dock; sun decks. *In room:* TV (rooms, suites, cabins), fridge, hair dryer, Wi-Fi, robes.

In Madeira Park

Painted Boat Resort Spa & Marina ★   This beautifully located timeshare development offers families or friends traveling together the opportunity to rent elegantly furnished two-bedroom suites right on the rocky coast of Malespina Strait. The entire complex is newly built, and interiors are right out of a design magazine, with full kitchens, granite countertops, stainless steel appliances, stone fireplaces, two bathrooms, and abundant windows and French doors leading out onto decks and patios where gorgeous waterfront vistas await. All very nice, but it's the abundant facilities at Painted Boat that really make it stand out. The marina offers kayak tours and rentals, the fitness facilities are top-notch, and in summer there's an infinity pool. For relaxation and pampering, the resort offers a spa with treatments rooms and an outdoor spa garden. Best of all, **The Restaurant at Painted Boat ★★** (ℂ **604/883-3000**) is the best place to eat for miles around, with a menu rich with local fish and seafood.

12849 Lagoon Rd., Madeira Park, BC V0N 2H0. ℂ **866/902-3955** or 604/883-2456. Fax 604/883-2122. www.paintedboat.com. From C$240 double. Extra person 17 and older C$50; ages 6–16 C$30. **Amenities:** Restaurant; lounge; health club; Jacuzzi; seasonal infinity pool; spa; kayak rentals. *In room:* TV/DVD, full kitchen, Wi-Fi, fireplace, gas grill, deck or patio.

In Powell River

Beach Gardens Resort ★   Long popular with divers and kayakers, the Beach Gardens—just south of Powell River—has 48 brand-new rooms, all with incredible views overlooking Malaspina Strait. Several banks of perfectly comfortable older rooms, also with views and some with full kitchens, rent at a discount. Amenities include a marina, pub, and beer-and-wine store.

7074 Westminster Ave., Powell River, BC V8A 1C5. ℂ **800/663-7070** or 604/485-6267. Fax 604/485-2343. www.beachgardens.com. 68 units. C$99–C$145 double. AE, MC, V. Free parking. Pets allowed. **Amenities:** Waterfront restaurant; pub; marina w/fishing and diving charters; moorage. *In room:* A/C, TV, hair dryer, Wi-Fi, private deck overlooking Malaspina Strait.

Desolation Sound Resort ★★   Twenty minutes north of Powell River on Okeover Inlet near Lund is Desolation Sound Resort, which offers luxury and a wilderness experience rolled into one. Accommodations are in extremely attractive chalets perched on high pilings above a steeply sloping shoreline. These log structures, built by local craftspeople, come in various configurations and sleep up to eight. Spaces are fully modern and beautifully maintained, with cedar interiors, full kitchens, hardwood floors, and tasteful decor—some units have private hot tubs, and all have decks (with gas grills) overlooking the water. Chartered boating, kayaking, or diving trips can be arranged; guests are free to use resort canoes and kayaks.

2694 Dawson Rd., Okeover Inlet, Powell River, BC V8A 4Z3. (✆ **800/399-3592** or 604/483-3592. Fax 604/483-7942. www.desolationresort.com. 12 units. July–Sept and winter holidays C$149–C$289 double, C$229–C$424 chalet; May–June C$129–C$259 double, C$259–C$399 chalet; Oct–Apr C$109–C$199 double, C$199–C$314 chalet. Extra person C$25 per night. Discounts for stays over 3 nights. Packages available. AE, MC, V. Pets allowed in off season for additional charge. **Amenities:** Free use of kayaks and canoes; powerboat rentals and charter cruises can be arranged. *In room:* Kitchen, no phone.

2 WHISTLER: NORTH AMERICA'S PREMIER SKI RESORT ★

120km (75 miles) N of Vancouver

The premier ski resort in North America, according to *Ski, Snow Country,* and *Condé Nast Traveler* magazines, the **Whistler/Blackcomb** complex boasts more vertical feet, more lifts, and more ski terrain than any other ski resort in North America. And it isn't all just downhill skiing: There's also backcountry, cross-country, snowboarding, snowmobiling, heli-skiing, and sleigh riding. In summer, there's mountain biking, rafting, hiking, golfing, and horseback riding. And then there's **Whistler** itself, a full-service resort town with a year-round population of 10,000 plus 125 hotels and lodgings.

The towns north of Whistler, **Pemberton** and **Mount Currie,** are refreshment stops for cyclists and hikers and gateways to the icy alpine waters of **Birkenhead Lake Provincial Park** and the majestic **Cayoosh Valley,** which winds through the glacier-topped mountains to the Cariboo town of Lillooet (see chapter 12 for more on this town).

The area got the ultimate seal of approval from the International Olympic Committee when Whistler landed the opportunity to stage many of the alpine events for the 2010 Winter Games. So come test yourself on the same slopes that Olympic champions have skied on.

ESSENTIALS

Getting There

BY CAR   Whistler is about a 2-hour drive from Vancouver along Hwy. 99, also called the **Sea-to-Sky Highway** ★. The drive is spectacular, winding along the edge of Howe Sound before climbing up through the mountains.

Parking at the mountain is free for day skiers; there are large parking lots along Fitzsimmons Creek between Whistler Village and Upper Village. However, most hotels will charge a fee for overnight parking.

BY BUS   **Whistler Express,** 8695 Barnard St., Vancouver (✆ **604/266-5386** in Vancouver, or 604/905-0041 in Whistler; www.perimeterbus.com), operates door-to-door bus service from Vancouver International Airport to over 25 lodgings in Whistler. With

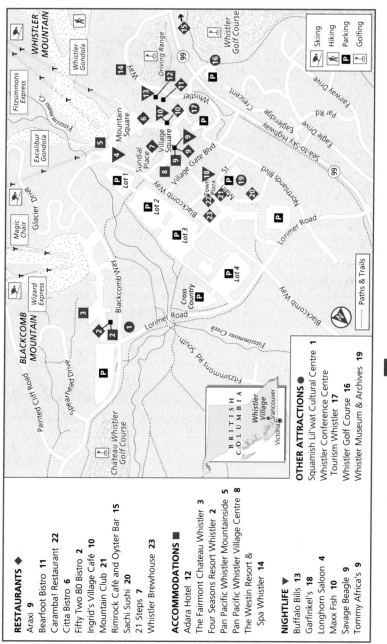

RESTAURANTS ◆

Araxi **9**
Bearfoot Bistro **11**
Caramba! Restaurant **22**
Citta Bistro **6**
Fifty Two 80 Bistro **2**
Ingrid's Village Café **10**
Mountain Club **21**
Rimrock Café and Oyster Bar **15**
Sachi Sushi **20**
21 Steps **7**
Whistler Brewhouse **23**

ACCOMMODATIONS ■

Adara Hotel **12**
The Fairmont Chateau Whistler **3**
Four Seasons Resort Whistler **2**
Pan Pacific Whistler Mountainside **5**
Pan Pacific Whistler Village Centre **8**
The Westin Resort &
Spa Whistler **14**

NIGHTLIFE ▼

Buffalo Bills **13**
Garfinkel's **18**
Longhorn Saloon **4**
Maxx Fish **10**
Savage Beagle **9**
Tommy Africa's **9**

OTHER ATTRACTIONS ●

Squamish Lil'wat Cultural Centre **1**
Whistler Conference Centre
Tourism Whistler **17**
Whistler Golf Course **16**
Whistler Museum & Archives **19**

advance reservations, some buses will pick up passengers at downtown Vancouver hotels. Buses depart seven times daily in the summer and 12 times in winter. The trip typically takes 3 hours, though weather and construction on the Sea-to-Sky Highway may delay the bus; one-way fares are C$49 to C$59 for adults and C$25 to C$35 for children. Kids under 5 ride free. Reservations are required year-round. **Greyhound,** Pacific Central Station, 1150 Station St., Vancouver (© **604/662-8051** in Vancouver, or 604/482-8747 in Whistler; www.greyhound.ca), operates service from the Vancouver Bus Depot to the Whistler bus depot at 2029 London Lane. The trip takes about 2½ hours; one-way fares are C$21 for adults and C$16 for children ages 5 to 12. **Pacific Coach Lines** (© **800/661-1725** or 604/662-7575; www.pacificcoach.com) operates one-way and return bus service from Vancouver International Airport and Vancouver hotels to Whistler area hotels for C$37 each way. **Snowbus** (© **604/685-7669;** www.snowbus.ca) offers service to/from Whistler and Vancouver area suburbs (Richmond, Burnaby, North Vancouver) and other neighborhood locations in addition to downtown Vancouver and the airport. On Friday and weekend morning departures, riders have the option of hot breakfasts; free movies are offered during the journey. Also available from the website is a C$20 SnowCard (free to B.C. residents), which offers discounts on Snowbus transportation and lift ticket packages, as well as discounts at Vancouver and Whistler area restaurants, recreational clothing stores, and ski and board shops. One-way fare between Vancouver and Whistler is C$23. Snowbus operates daily, though only during ski season.

BY TRAIN The **Whistler Sea to Sky Climb,** a new route from Rocky Mountaineer Vacations (© **877/460-3200** or 604/606-7245; www.whistlermountaineer.com), offers service between Vancouver and Whistler along the highly scenic Sea-to-Sky corridor. There's one train in each direction daily, departing 8:30am from North Vancouver Station, arriving at Whistler Station at 11:30am. The train returns in the afternoon, departing Whistler Station at 2:30pm and arriving at North Vancouver Station at 6pm. Currently, the train operates mid-May to late September only. The least expensive fair is C$129 adults, C$90 children 2 to 11 one-way; or C$219 adults, C$153 children round-trip.

Visitor Information

The **Whistler Visitor Info Centre,** easy to find on the Village Bus Loop at 4230 Gateway Dr., Whistler, BC V0N 1B4 (© **877/991-9988** or 604/935-3357; www.whistler. com), is open daily 9am to 5pm. **Tourism Whistler** is at the Whistler Conference Centre at 4010 Whistler Way, Whistler, BC V0N 1B0, open daily 9am to 5pm (© **800/944-7853;** www.tourismwhistler.com). Both offices can assist you with event tickets, reservations for recreation, and last-minute accommodations bookings.

Getting Around

Be sure to pick up a map when you get to Whistler and study it—the curving streets are made for pedestrians but defy easy negotiation by drivers, particularly in the winter darkness. **Whistler Village** is at the base of the ski runs at Whistler Peak. **Upper Village,** at the base of Blackcomb ski runs, is just across Fiztsimmons Creek from Whistler Village. As development continues, the distinction between these two "villages" is disappearing, though Whistler Village is the center for most independent restaurants, shopping, and the youthful nightlife scene. Upper Village, centered on the Four Seasons and Fairmont Chateau Whistler hotels, is quieter and more upscale. However, both villages are compact, and signed trails and paths link together shops, lodgings, and restaurants in the central resort area. The walk between the two village resort areas takes about 10 minutes.

Many smaller inns, B&Bs, restaurants, and services are located outside the nucleus of Whistler Village and Upper Village. **Creekside** is a large development east (downhill) from Whistler Village (there are lifts onto Whistler Mountain from Creekside—in fact, this was the original lift base for the resort), while the shores of **Alta Lake** are ringed with residential areas and golf courses.

BY BUS   The year-round Whistler and Valley Express (WAVE) **public bus system** (© 604/932-4020) offers 14 routes in the Whistler area. Buses have both bike and ski racks. Most routes cross paths at the Gondola Transit Exchange off Blackcomb Way, near the base of the Whistler Mountain lifts. One-way fares are C$2 for adults and C$1.50 for seniors and students. For a route map, go to www.busonline.ca.

BY TAXI   The village's taxis operate round-the-clock. Taxi tours, golf-course transfers, and airport transport are also offered by **Airport Limousine Service** (© 604/273-1331), **Whistler Taxi** (© 604/938-3333), and **Sea to Sky Taxi** (© 604/932-3333).

BY CAR   Rental cars are available from **Avis** in the Cascade Lodge, 4315 Northlands Blvd. (© **800/TRY-AVIS** [879-2847] or 604/932-1236).

Special Events

Downhill ski competitions are held December to May, including the **TELUS Winter Classic** (Jan), and the **TELUS World Ski & Snowboard Festival** (Apr). In August, mountain bikers compete in **Crankworx.**

The **Whistler Summit Concert Series** (© 604/932-3434) is held during August weekends. The mountains provide a stunning backdrop for the on-mountain concerts.

The second weekend in September ushers in the **Whistler Jazz & Blues Festival** (© 604/932-2394), featuring live performances in the village squares and the surrounding clubs. **Cornucopia** (© 604/932-3434) is Whistler's premier wine-and-food festival. Held in November, the opening gala showcases top wineries from the Pacific region plus lots of food events and tastings from local chefs.

HITTING THE SLOPES

Whistler/Blackcomb Resort   The **Whistler/Blackcomb Mountains,** 4545 Blackcomb Way, Whistler, BC V0N 1B4 (© **866/218-9690** or 604/932-3434, snow report 604/687-1032; www.whistlerblackcomb.com), are jointly operated by Intrawest, so your pass gives access to both ski areas. You can book nearly all accommodations and activities in Whistler from their website.

From its base in Whistler Village, **Whistler Mountain** has 1,530m (5,020 ft.) of vertical and over 100 marked runs that are serviced by a total of 20 lifts. From its base in Upper Village, **Blackcomb Mountain** has 1,610m (5,282 ft.) of vertical and over 100 marked runs that are served by a total of 17 lifts. Both mountains also have bowls and glade skiing, with Blackcomb offering glacier skiing well into August. Together, the two mountains comprise the largest ski resort in North America, offering over 3,378 skiable hectares (8,100 acres)—1,214 hectares (3,000 acres) more than the largest U.S. resort.

During winter, lift tickets for 2 days of skiing on both mountains range from C$125 to C$178 for adults, C$106 to C$152 for seniors, and C$65 to C$92 for children 7 to 12. Lifts are open 8:30am to 3:30pm (to 4:30pm mid-Mar to season closing, depending on weather and conditions). Whistler/Blackcomb offers ski lessons and guides for all levels and interests. Phone **Guest Relations** at © 604/932-3434 for details. Ski, snowboard, and boot rentals are available from the resort, and can be booked online. In addition, dozens of independent shops provide equipment rentals. **Affinity Sports**

From Peak to Peak

Intrawest, the corporation behind Whistler/Blackcomb Resort, has built a record-defying gondola that links together the peaks of Whistler (elev. 2,182m/7,159 ft.) and Blackcomb (elev. 2,284m/7,493 ft.) mountains. The **Peak to Peak Gondola** has the longest free-span lift in the world at 3km (1³/₄ miles) and a total length of 4.4km (2³/₄ miles). The Peak to Peak Gondola is also the highest detachable lift in the world, at 436m (1,430 ft.) above the valley floor. The gondola includes 28 cars carrying up to 29 passengers each, with cars leaving approximately every 54 seconds; it is capable of carrying 2,050 people per hour each way. The cars take 11 minutes to travel from peak to peak. Clearly, the new gondola offers skiers greater flexibility for skiing the highest runs of both mountains (during ski season, use of the gondola is included in the cost of lift tickets) and offers summer visitors one of the most attention-grabbing gondola rides in the world. From late June through mid-October, a day ticket to the gondola is C$42 adult, C$35 seniors and youths 13 to 18, and C$19 children 7 to 12.

(www.affinityrentals.com) has seven locations in the Whistler area, with online reservations available. **Summit Ski** (☏ **604/938-6225** or 604/932-6225; www.summitsport.com) has three locations in Whistler and rents high-performance and regular skis, snowboards, cross-country skis, and snowshoes.

BACKCOUNTRY SKIING The **Spearhead Traverse,** which starts at Whistler and finishes at Blackcomb, is a well-marked backcountry route that has become extremely popular. **Garibaldi Provincial Park** (☏ **604/898-3678**) maintains marked backcountry trails at **Diamond Head, Singing Pass,** and **Cheakamus Lake.** These are ungroomed and unpatrolled trails, and you have to be self-reliant—you should be at least an intermediate skier, bring appropriate clothing and avalanche gear, and know how to use it. There are several access points along Hwy. 99 between Squamish and Whistler.

CROSS-COUNTRY SKIING The 32km (20 miles) of easy-to-very-difficult marked trails at Lost Lake start at the Lorimer Road bridge over Fitzsimmons Creek, just west of Upper Village. Passes are C$18 per day. The Lost Lake trails link to the Nicklaus North Golf Course, with cross-country ski trails leading through the undulating golf course grounds along the shores of Green Lake. The **Valley Trail System** in the village becomes a well-marked cross-country ski trail during winter.

A 1-hour cross-country lesson runs about C$39 and is available from Cross Country Connection (☏ **604/905-0071**; www.crosscountryconnection.bc.ca), also at the trail head. They also offer Nordic ski rentals, though customers having lessons have dibs on rentals. The website also has a downloadable map of the trail system.

New in 2010 is **Whistler Olympic Park** and **Callaghan Country** (☏ **877/764-2455** or 604-964-2455; www.whistlerolympicpark.com), developed for the cross-country, biathlon, Nordic combined and ski jumping events for the Vancouver 2010 Olympic and Paralympic Winter Games. Located 10km (6¼ miles) southwest of Whistler, these two areas combine to offer 70km (43 miles) of cross-country ski trails and 10km (6¼ miles) for snowshoeing. A cross-country day pass is C$20 adults; lessons and tours are also available.

HELI-SKIING & BOARDING   Forget lift lines and crowds. Ride a helicopter to the crest of a Coast Range peak and experience the ultimate in powder skiing. If you're a confident intermediate-to-advanced skier in good shape, consider joining a heli-ski trip. **Whistler Heli-Skiing** (ℂ **888/HELISKI** [435-4754] or 604/932-4105; www.whistler heliskiing.com) offers a three-run day, with 1,400 to 2,300m (4,593–7,546 ft.) of vertical helicopter lift, which costs C$795 per person. **Coast Range Heli-Skiing** (ℂ **800/701-8744** or 604/894-1144; www.coastrangeheliskiing.com) offers a four-run day, with 1,800 to 4,000m (5,906–13,123 ft.) of vertical helicopter lift, which costs C$880 per person. Both trips include a guide and lunch.

SNOWCAT SKIING & BOARDING   Lifts and choppers aren't the only way up a mountain. **Powder Mountain Catskiing** (ℂ **877/PWDRFIX** [793-7347] or 604/932-0169; www.powdermountaincatskiing.com) uses snowcats to climb up into a private skiing area south of Whistler where skiers and boarders will find 1,740 skiable hectares (4,300 acres) on two mountains. The price, C$499 per person, pays for a full day of skiing, usually six to ten runs down 2,100 to 3,000 vertical meters (6,890–9,942 ft.) of untracked powder, plus transport to/from Whistler, breakfast, lunch, and guides.

OTHER WINTER PURSUITS

DOG SLEDDING   Explore the old-growth forests of the Soo Valley Wildlife Preserve while mushing a team of eager Huskies. Soo Valley Quest offers a choice of dog-sledding trips, and if the weather and terrain permit, you may even get to drive the dogs yourself. A 2½-hour Woof Pack tour costs C$280 for two people sharing a sled; book through the central booking agency ℂ **888/403-4727;** www.whistlerblackcomb.com.

ICE CLIMBING   Climb a frozen waterfall with **Coast Mountain Guides** (ℂ **604/932-7711;** www.coastmountainguides.com). Guides provide all equipment; beginners welcome. Climbs start at C$347 per person.

SLEIGH RIDING   For an old-fashioned horse-drawn sleigh ride, contact **Blackcomb Horsedrawn Sleigh Rides,** 103–4338 Main St., Whistler, BC V0N 1B4 (ℂ **604/932-7631;** www.blackcombsleighrides.com). Giant Percheron horses lead the way, and comfortable sleighs with padded seats and cozy blankets keep you warm. A number of tours are available, starting with basic half-hour rides for C$55 for adults, and C$35 for children 3 to 12. Longer rides and dinner sleigh-ride combos are also available.

SNOWMOBILING   The year-round ATV/snowmobile tours offered by **Canadian Snowmobile Adventures Ltd.,** Carleton Lodge (ℂ **604/938-1616;** www.canadian snowmobile.com), are a unique way to take to the Whistler Mountain trails. Exploring the Fitzsimmons Creek watershed, a 2-hour tour costs C$125 for a driver and C$99 for a passenger. If you're up for more adventure, consider a nighttime snowmobile tour to a remote mountain cabin, where a fondue dinner awaits, for C$225 driver, C$189 passenger.

SNOWSHOEING   Snowshoeing makes a great family outing; kids really enjoy the experience of walking on snow. Most ski rental outfits also offer snowshoe rentals, so you won't have to look far to find a pair. If you want to just rent the snowshoes and find your own way around, rentals are typically C$15 per day. **Outdoor Adventures@Whistler,** P.O. Box 1054, Whistler, BC V0N 1B0 (ℂ **604/932-0647;** www.adventureswhistler. com), has guided tours for novices at C$79 for 1½ hours.

BIKING Whistler is world famous for its mountain biking. While many gonzo riders come from around the world to test themselves on the many technical trails, others come to enjoy the gentler pleasures of simply biking through the forest.

Some of the best mountain-bike trails in the village are in Whistler and Blackcomb mountains' **Bike Park** (✆ **866/218-9690** or 604/904-8134; www.whistlerbike.com), which offers more than 200km (124 miles) of lift-serviced trails and mountain pathways with more than 1,490m (4,888 ft.) of vertical drop. The park has three access lifts and two jump areas; the trail system is labeled from green circle to blue square to black diamond. High season per-day lift tickets and park admission are C$51 adults, C$45 seniors and youths 13 to 18, and C$28 children 7 to 12. There's also the **Air Dome,** a 780-sq.-m (8,396-sq.-ft.) covered indoor mountain bike training facility with a huge foam pit, ramps, and a quarter pipe and half pipe. A 3-hour pass is C$16. If you're not ready for daredevil riding on the mountain, the 30km (19-mile) paved **Valley Trail** is a pedestrian/bicycle route linking parks, neighborhoods, and playgrounds around Whistler Village. For other biking trails, check out the comprehensive Whistler biking website at www.whistlermountainbike.com.

In summer, nearly every ski shop switches gears and offers bike rentals. You'll have absolutely no problem finding a bike to rent in Whistler Village. If you want to call ahead and reserve a bike, try **Whistler Bike Co.,** 4205 Village Square (✆ **604/938-9511;** www.bikeco.ca). Prices range from C$33 per half-day for a commuting-style bike to C$45 to C$85 per half-day for a high-end mountain bike.

CANOEING & KAYAKING The 2-hour River of Golden Dreams Kayak & Canoe Tour offered by **Whistler Outdoor Experience,** P.O. Box 151, Whistler, BC V0N 1B0 (✆ **604/932-3389;** www.whistleroutdoor.com), is a great way to get acquainted with an exhilarating stretch of slow-moving glacial water that runs between Green Lake and Alta Lake behind the village of Whistler. Packages range from C$54 per person unguided to C$84 per person with a guide. **Outdoor Adventures Whistler** (✆ **604/932-0647;** www.adventureswhistler.com) leads canoe trips down the Lillooet River. A guided, 3-hour sunset cruise in six-person canoes is C$99 for adults, C$49 kids ages 4 to 12.

GOLF Robert Trent Jones, Jr.'s, **Fairmont Chateau Whistler Golf Club,** at the base of Blackcomb Mountain (✆ **604/938-2092,** or pro shop 604/938-2095), is an 18-hole, par-72 course. The 6,067m (6,635-yd.), par-72 signature course was selected in 1993 as Canada's best new golf course by *Golf Digest* magazine. Greens fees are C$79 to C$195 in high season. A multiple-award-winning golf course, **Nicklaus North at Whistler** (✆ **604/938-9898**) is a 5-minute drive north of the village on the shores of Green Lake. The 6,317m (6,908-yd.), par-71 course's mountain views are spectacular. Greens fees are C$75 to C$175. The 6,105m (6,676-yd.) **Whistler Golf Club** (✆ **800/376-1777** or 604/932-4544), designed by Arnold Palmer, features nine lakes, two creeks, and magnificent vistas. In addition to the 18-hole, par-72 course, the club offers a driving range, putting green, sand bunker, and pitching area. Greens fees are C$79 to C$159.

HIKING There are numerous easy hiking trails in and around Whistler. (Just remember—never hike alone, and bring plenty of water with you.) You can take ski lifts up to Whistler and Blackcomb mountains' trails during summer, but you have a number of other choices as well. The **Lost Lake Trail** starts at the northern end of the Day Skier Parking Lot at Blackcomb. The 30km (19 miles) of marked trails that wind around creeks, beaver dams, blueberry patches, and lush cedar groves are ideal for biking, cross-country skiing, or just strolling and picnicking.

The **Valley Trail System** is a well-marked paved trail connecting parts of Whistler. The trail starts on the west side of Hwy. 99 adjacent to the Whistler Golf Course and winds through quiet residential areas, as well as golf courses and parks. Garibaldi Provincial Park's **Singing Pass Trail** is a 4-hour hike of moderate difficulty. The fun way to experience this trail is to take the Whistler Mountain gondola to the top and walk down the well-marked path that ends in the village.

The Whistler Village Gondola (Whistler Base) and Wizard Express-Solar Coaster Express (Blackcomb Base) are open in summer and provide access to the Peak to Peak Gondola (see above) as well as miles of alpine hiking trails, including the Peak Interpretive Walk; guided hikes are available.

Nairn Falls Provincial Park is about 33km (21 miles) north of Whistler on Hwy. 99. It features a 1.5km-long (1-mile) trail leading you to a stupendous view of the icy-cold Green River as it plunges 60m (197 ft.) over a rocky cliff into a narrow gorge on its way downstream. On Hwy. 99 north of Mount Currie, **Joffre Lakes Provincial Park** is an intermediate-level hike leading past several brilliant-blue glacial lakes up to the very foot of a glacier. The **Ancient Cedars** area of Cougar Mountain is an awe-inspiring grove of towering cedars and Douglas firs. Some of the trees are over 1,000 years old and measure 2.5m (8 ft.) in diameter.

HORSEBACK RIDING **Adventure Ranch** near Pemberton (© **604/894-5200;** www. adventureranch.net) leads 2-hour horseback tours for C$69 from its Lillooet River–side ranch, 30 minutes from Whistler.

JET BOATING **Whistler River Adventures** (© **604/932-3532;** www.whistlerriver. com) takes guests up the Lillooet River from near Pemberton. The tour surges past large rapids, spectacular glacier peaks, and traditional Native fishing camps. Deer, bear, osprey, and spawning salmon are frequently seen. This 3-hour-long trip is C$109; kids 5 to 15 get a C$10 discount.

RAFTING **Whistler River Adventures** (see "Jet Boating," above) offers five different day trips on local rivers, ranging from a placid all-generation paddle to a roaring white-water adventure. Four-hour paddle trips on the Cheakamus River are gentle enough for families (C$89 adults, C$69 kids ages 10–16, and C$54 kids ages 5–9), while the 8-hour round-trip Elaho-Squamish River white-water trip is for those seeking an adrenaline high (C$159 adults, C$149 kids 10–16). All trips include equipment and ground transport. The 8-hour trip includes a salmon barbecue lunch.

ZIP-LINING One of Whistler's most popular year-round thrills is the steel zip-line rides offered by **Ziptrek Ecotours** (© **866/935-0001** or 604/935-0001; www.ziptrek. com). Zip-lining involves gliding along a suspended steel cable using a pulley and climbing harness at speeds up to 89kmph (55 mph). Guided tours include the Bear Tour that links five zip-lines that range in height and length from 24 to 610m (79–2,001 ft.), spanning 11 hectares (27 acres) in the valley between Whistler and Blackcomb Mountains, an area of untouched coastal temperate rainforest. The adrenaline-pumping Eagle tour extends 1,828 meters (5,997 ft.) and drops 20 stories to end in Whistler Village itself. Tickets are C$99 (Bear Tour) and $119 (Eagle Tour) adults, C$79 and C$99, respectively, for seniors and youths 6 to 14. For those not up to zip-lining, Ziptrek also offers **TreeTrek,** a network of suspended boardwalks, aerial stairways, and bridges at heights of over 182m (597 ft.) in the tree canopy. Tickets are C$39 adults and C$29 seniors and youth 14 and under.

EXPLORING THE TOWN

SEEING THE SIGHTS   The **Squamish Lil'wat Cultural Centre** (✆ 866/441-7522 or 604/898-1822; www.slcc.ca) is an architecturally stunning showcase of soaring glass and stone, designed to celebrate the joint history and living cultures of the Squamish and Lil'wat Nations. The facility includes both indoor and outdoor space, anchored by the monumental Great Hall with traditional artifacts and 66m (217-ft.) glass plank walls revealing spectacular mountain and forest views. The center also features a gallery of Squamish and Lil'wat sacred cultural treasures and icons, plus a shop for First Nations art. Outdoors is a Squamish longhouse, which was the traditional dwelling of the Squamish people, and a replica Lil'wat "ístken" or "Pit House," which was the traditional dwelling of the Lil'wat people. The center is open daily 9:30am to 5pm, and admission is C$18 adult, C$14 seniors and students, C$11 youths 13 to 18, and C$8 kids 6 to 12.

To learn more about Whistler's heritage, flora, and fauna, visit the **Whistler Museum & Archives Society,** 4329 Main St., off Northlands Boulevard (✆ 604/932-2019; www. whistlermuseum.com). June to Labour Day, the museum is open daily 10am to 4pm; call ahead for winter opening hours. Admission is C$5 for adults, C$4 seniors and students, and C$3 youths 7 to 18.

The **Path Gallery,** 4338 Main St. (✆ 604/932-7570), is devoted to Northwest Coast Native art, including totem poles, carved masks, and prints. **Gallery Row** in the Hilton Whistler Resort consists of three galleries: the **Whistler Village Art Gallery** (✆ 604/938-3001), the **Black Tusk Gallery** (✆ 604/905-5540), and the **Adele Campbell Gallery** (✆ 604/938-0887). Their collections include fine art, sculpture, and glass.

SHOPPING   **Whistler Village,** and the area surrounding the **Blackcomb Mountain lift,** brim with clothing, jewelry, craft, specialty, gift, and equipment shops open daily 10am to 6pm. You'll have absolutely no problem finding interesting places to shop in Whistler—both quality and prices are high.

SPAS   Spas are definitely a growth industry in Whistler. Nearly all the large hotels now feature spas, and a number of independent spas line the streets of Whistler Village. The **Vida Wellness Spa** at Chateau Whistler Resort (✆ 604/938-2086) is considered one of

---

(Kids) Activities for Kids

At the base of Blackcomb Mountain, the **Adventure Zone** offers a kid-centric collection of activities in a circus-like atmosphere. Activities include horseback riding, minigolf, bungee trampolines, flying trapeze, wall-climbing, gondola rides, spinning human gyroscopes, zip-lining, luge rides, and more. A five-adventure pass costs C$42; see www.whistlerblackcomb.com for more information.

Based at Blackcomb Mountain, the **Dave Murray Summer Ski Camp,** P.O. Box 98, Whistler, BC V0N 1B0 (✆ 604/932-5765; www.skiandsnowboard.com), is North America's longest-running summer ski camp. Five-day junior programs cost about C$1,195 with full board and lodging, or C$1,025 without lodging mid-June to mid-July.

---

the best in Whistler. Open daily 8am to 9pm, it offers massage therapy, aromatherapy, skin care, body wraps, and steam baths. Another noteworthy hotel spa is the Westin Resort's **Avello Spa,** 400–4090 Whistler Way (© **877/935-7111** or 604/935-3444; www.whistlerspa.com), which offers a host of spa services as well as holistic and hydrotherapy treatments. **The Spa at Four Seasons Resort** (© **604/966-2620**) has 15 treatment rooms, a Vichy shower, yoga and fitness classes, and a vast assortment of luxurious treatments from mineral scrubs to wildflower baths. **Solarice Wellness Centre and Spa,** with locations at 4308 Main St. (© **866/368-0888** or 604/966-0888), and 4230 Gateway Dr. (© **888/935-1222** or 604/935-2222; www.solarice.com), is a highly atmospheric day spa with exotic-themed treatment rooms and a wide selection of beauty and relaxation treatments. The therapists at **Whistler Physiotherapy** (© **604/932-4001** or 604/938-9001; www.whistlerphysio.com) have a lot of experience with the typical ski, board, and hiking injuries. There are three locations: 339–4370 Lorimer Rd., at Marketplace; 202–2011 Innsbruck Dr., next to Boston Pizza in Creekside; and 4433 Sundial Place in Whistler Village.

WHERE TO STAY

For a first-time visitor, figuring out lodging at Whistler can be rather intimidating. One of the easiest ways to book rooms, buy ski passes, and plan activities is to visit the official Whistler Blackcomb Resort website at **www.whistlerblackcomb.com**. Most hotels and condo developments are represented at this one-stop shopping and information site.

Lodgings in Whistler are very high quality, and the price of rooms is equally high. The hotels listed below offer superlative rooms with lots of extras. However, the smaller inns offer great value and excellent accommodations, often with services and options that can, for many travelers, make them a more attractive option than the larger hotels. At these smaller, owner-operated inns, rates typically include features that are sometimes available for an extra fee at hotels. These inns are located outside of the central villages and usually offer a quieter lodging experience than the hotels in Whistler Village.

In addition to the hotels and inns below, Whistler is absolutely loaded with condo developments. To reserve one of these units—which can range from studios, to one- to five-bedroom fully furnished condos, to town houses and chalets, with prices from around C$175 to C$1,500 a night—many travelers find the easiest thing to do is simply decide on a price point and call one of the central booking agencies, such as **Whistler Superior Properties** (© **877/535-8282** or 604/932-3510; www.whistlersuperior.com) or **Whistler Canada.net** (© **888/905-0434** or 604/905-0434; www.whistlercanada.net); **Whistler Accommodations** (© **866/905-4607** or 604/905-4607; www.whistleraccommodation. com) focuses on condos and hotels in the Upper Village.

One other excellent booking service is **Allura Direct** (© **866/4-ALLURA** [425-5872] or 604/707-6700; www.alluradirect.com), through which owners of rental properties in Whistler rent directly to the public (and you escape the 10% local hotel tax, though 5% provincial GST is still levied). The website has an excellent search engine, and offers lots of information and photos of numerous properties located throughout Whistler. Though owners are screened—we encountered no problems and got a fabulous deal on a one-bedroom condo—quality can vary, so we recommend you do your homework and book only with those owners who accept credit cards.

Reservations for peak winter periods should be made by September at the latest.

Adara Hotel ★★   Rustic naturalism meets contemporary color and modern Scandinavian style at this chic boutique hotel. The hip design takes the woodsy look so prevalent in Whistler hotels and sets it on its ear, with super-magnified wood-grain laminate, faux fur throws, and photo transfers of logs on glass shower walls. It's fun to look at, but more importantly, it's comfortable. Rooms and suites feature spa-like bathrooms with large showers and rain shower heads, CD and iPod players, luxurious bedding, "floating" fireplaces, artful design details, and views of Whistler, Whistler Village, or the mountains. Some rooms have full kitchens.

4122 Whistler Green, Whistler, BC V0N 1B4. ℭ **866/502-3272** or 604/905-4009. Fax 604/905-4665. www.adarahotel.com. 41 units. Late Dec to mid-Apr C$389–C$439 double, from C$539 suite; mid-Apr to Nov C$129–C$149 double, from C$179 suite. **Amenities:** Hot tub; outdoor heated pool; Wi-Fi. *In room:* A/C, flatscreen TV, CD and iPod player, fridge, hair dryer, fireplace.

Fairmont Chateau Whistler ★★★   Perennially rated the top ski resort hotel in North America by reader surveys in such magazines as *Condé Nast Traveler,* the Fairmont re-creates the look of a feudal castle at the foot of Blackcomb Mountain, but with every modern comfort added. Massive wooden beams support an airy peaked roof in the lobby, while in the hillside Mallard Bar, double-sided stone fireplaces cast a cozy glow on the couches and leather armchairs. Rooms and suites are very comfortable and beautifully furnished, and feature duvets, bathrobes, and soaker tubs (some offer stunning views of the slopes). Fairmont Gold service guests can have breakfast or relax après-ski in a private lounge with the feel of a Victorian library. All guests can use the heated outdoor pool and Jacuzzis, which look out over the base of the ski hill. The hotel's **Vida Wellness Spa** ★ is among the best in town. The Fairmont pays attention to the needs of skiers, with a recreation concierge, ski storage next to the slopes, and ski valets to help make pre- and après-ski as expeditious and pleasant as possible.

4599 Chateau Blvd., Whistler, BC V0N 1B4. ℭ **800/606-8244** or 604/938-8000. Fax 604/938-2058. www.fairmont.com/whistler. 550 units. Winter C$399–C$669 double, C$499–C$1,809 suite; summer C$119–C$379 double, C$275–C$1,409 suite. AE, MC, V. Underground valet parking C$25. Pets are welcome. **Amenities:** 4 restaurants; bar; babysitting; children's programs; concierge; concierge-level rooms; health club; 18-hole golf course; Jacuzzi; heated indoor/outdoor pool; room service; outstanding spa facility; 2 tennis courts; secure ski and bike storage; rooms for those w/limited mobility. *In room:* A/C, TV w/movie channels, hair dryer, minibar, Wi-Fi.

Four Seasons Resort Whistler ★★★   The Four Seasons Resort Whistler is a très chic, très elegant monument to refinement. Easily the most refined and elegant of Whistler's hotels, the Four Seasons is monumental in scale—the expansive stone, glass, and timber lobby is like a modern-day hunting lodge—while maintaining the atmosphere of a very intimate and sophisticated boutique hotel—a rare achievement. The Four Season's urbane good taste extends to the large guest rooms, decorated in wood and cool earth tones and beautifully furnished with rich fabrics and leather furniture. All rooms have a balcony, fireplace, and very large, amenity-filled bathrooms with soaker tubs. The standard room is a very spacious 46 sq. m (495 sq. ft.), and superior and deluxe level rooms are truly large. A separate wing of the hotel contains private residences—139 to 344-sq.-m (1,496–3,703-sq.-ft.) apartments with two to four bedrooms. With 15 treatment rooms, the exquisite **Spa at the Four Seasons Resort** ★ is Whistler's largest, and a heated outdoor pool and three whirlpool baths fill half the hotel courtyard.

4591 Blackcomb Way, Whistler, BC V0N 1B4. ℭ **888/935-2460** or 604/935-3400. Fax 604/935-3455. www.fourseasons.com/whistler. 273 units. Mid-June to mid-Sept and Nov 27–Dec 19 C$305–C$670 double;

mid-Sept to late Nov and mid-Apr to mid-June C$265–C$435 double; Dec 20–Jan 1 C$1,025–C$1,775 double; Jan 2 to mid-April C$405–C$920 double. AE, DC, DISC, MC, V. Underground valet parking C$28, self-park C$23. **Amenities:** Restaurant; lounge; concierge; health club; Jacuzzis; heated outdoor pool; room service; superlative spa; ski and bike storage; rooms for those w/limited mobility. *In room:* A/C, TV/DVD, CD player, hair dryer, minibar, Wi-Fi.

Pan Pacific Whistler Mountainside ★★   The Pan Pacific's slightly older and more family-oriented Mountainside all-suite property has a lot going for it, with top-notch furnishings, kitchenettes, and loads of amenities. Comfortable as the rooms are, however, the true advantage to the Pan Pacific Mountainside is its location at the foot of the Whistler Mountain gondola. Not only can you ski right to your hotel, but thanks to a large heated outdoor pool and Jacuzzi deck, you can sit at the end of the day sipping a glass of wine, gazing up at the snowy slopes, and marvel at the ameliorative effects of warm water on aching muscles. With sofa beds and fold-down Murphy beds, the studio suites are fine for couples, while the one- and two-bedroom suites allow more space for larger groups or families with kids.

4320 Sundial Crescent, Whistler, BC V0N 1B4. ⓒ **888/905-9995** or 604/905-2999. Fax 604/905-2995. www.panpacific.com. 121 units. Jan 1 to late Apr C$199–C$849 studio, C$299–C$1,049 1-bedroom, C$599–C$1,499 2-bedroom; late Apr to late Nov C$129–C$329 studio, C$169–C$429 1-bedroom, C$229–C$529 2-bedroom; late Nov–Dec 31 C$199–C$849 studio, C$299–C$1,049 1-bedroom, C$399–C$1,499 2-bedroom. AE, DC, MC, V. Underground valet parking C$20. **Amenities:** Restaurant; pub; concierge; fitness center w/whirlpool and steam room; Jacuzzi; heated outdoor pool; room service; ski, bike, and bag storage; rooms for those w/limited mobility. *In room:* A/C, TV w/pay movie channels, fridge, hair dryer, Wi-Fi, stove w/oven, microwave, dishwasher, pay Nintendo.

The Pan Pacific Whistler Village Centre ★★★   The Pan Pacific chain has two handsome properties in Whistler, both just steps off Blackcomb Way in Whistler Village. The all-suite Pan Pacific Whistler Village Centre is an imposing structure with curious gables and a dormered roofline, underscoring the fact that this is anything but an anonymous corporate hotel. All in all, suites in the Village Centre are more like apartments than hotel rooms; it's also more couples-oriented than its family-friendly sister property. All one-, two-, and three-bedroom suites have a balcony, fireplace, flatscreen TV, full kitchen with granite counters, soaker tub, bathrobes, handsome furniture, and floor-to-ceiling windows to let in the amazing mountain vistas. The penthouse suites are truly magnificent, with cathedral ceilings, massive stone fireplaces, multiple balconies, and loads of room—the Blackcomb Suite has 156 sq. m (1,679 sq. ft.)! The Village Centre has a fitness center with sauna, massage therapy and spa treatment rooms, a lap pool, and two hot tubs. Rates include a full breakfast buffet and afternoon/evening hors d'oeuvres in the Pacific Lounge, a guest-only facility with an outdoor patio.

4299 Blackcomb Way, Whistler, BC V0N 1B4. ⓒ **888/966-5575** or 604/966-5500. Fax 604/966-5501. www.panpacific.com. 83 units. Jan 1 to late Apr C$249–C$999 1-bedroom, C$499–C$1,399 2-bedroom, C$1,299–C$2,799 3-bedroom penthouse; late Apr to late Nov C$179–C$429 1-bedroom, C$249–C$529 2-bedroom, C$699–C$999 3-bedroom penthouse; late Nov–Dec 31 C$249–C$999 1-bedroom, C$349–C$1,399 2-bedroom, C$799–C$2,799 3-bedroom penthouse. AE, DC, DISC, MC, V. Underground valet parking C$20. **Amenities:** Restaurant; pub; concierge; fitness center; Jacuzzi; heated outdoor pool; room service; sauna; ski, bike, and golf bag storage; rooms for those w/limited mobility. *In room:* A/C, TV w/pay movie channels and Web TV, fridge, hair dryer, Wi-Fi, stovetop, microwave convection oven, dishwasher, pay Nintendo.

The Westin Resort and Spa Whistler ★★★   Talk about location: The all-suite Westin Resort snapped up the best piece of property in town and squeezed itself onto the mountainside at the bottom of the Whistler gondola. It's central to all the restaurants and nightspots in Whistler Village, yet slightly apart from the crowds. The two-towered hotel is built in the style of an enormous mountain chalet with cedar timbers and lots of local granite and basalt finishings. All 419 suites received an update in 2007 and offer full kitchens, soaker tubs, slate-lined showers, and an elegant and restful decor; there are even "workout" suites with an array of fitness equipment. The beds, Westin's signature Heavenly Beds, are indeed divine. If you're here to ski, expect little luxuries including a ski valet service and (no more cold toes!) a boot-warming service. That is certainly one of the reasons why the Westin has already grabbed several top awards; the hotel's **Avello Spa ★** is extremely well-appointed for après-ski pampering and the indoor/outdoor pool, hot tubs, steam baths, and sauna will warm up ski-weary limbs.

4090 Whistler Way, Whistler, BC V0N 1B4. ✆ **888/634-5577** or 604/905-5000. Fax 604/905-5589. www. westinwhistler.com. 419 units. Mid-Apr to late Nov C$179–C$489 junior suite, C$269–C$599 1-bedroom suite; C$429–C$1,049 2-bedroom suite; late Nov to mid-Apr C$209–C$589 junior suite, C$319–C$689 1-bedroom suite, C$539–C$1,519 2-bedroom suite. Children 17 and under stay free in parent's room. AE, DC, DISC, MC, V. Parking C$32. **Amenities:** Restaurant; bar; babysitting; bike rental; children's program; concierge; health club; indoor and outdoor Jacuzzi; indoor and outdoor pool; room service; sauna; spa. *In room:* A/C, TV w/pay movies, hair dryer, fully appointed kitchen, Wi-Fi.

Outside the Village

Alpine Chalet Whistler ★★   This cozy alpine-style lodge sits in a quiet location near Alta Lake and the Whistler Golf Club. The entire inn is designed to provide luxurious lodgings, privacy, and a welcoming sense of camaraderie in the comfortable, fireplace-dominated guest lounge. There are three room types: alpine rooms, comfortable lodge rooms that will suit the needs of most skiers and travelers; chalets, which are larger and feature fireplaces and other extras; and the master suite, the largest and most opulent room, with a fireplace, cathedral ceiling, Jacuzzi, and large private balcony. All rooms have balconies or terraces, fine linens, bathrobes, and other upscale amenities you'd expect at a classy hotel. Evening meals are available by reservation.

3012 Alpine Crescent, Whistler, BC V0N 1B3. ✆ **800/736-9967** or 604/935-3003. Fax 604/935-3008. www.whistlerinn.com. 8 units. Early Jan to Apr C$189–C$269; mid-Dec to early Jan C$259–C$399; May to mid-Dec C$149–C$229. Rates include full breakfast. MC, V. Free parking. **Amenities:** Guest lounge; 8-person hot tub; steam room; heated ski lockers. *In room:* A/C, TV/DVD, hair dryer, Wi-Fi, heated floor.

Cedar Springs Bed & Breakfast Lodge ★ (Kids)   The no-children policy at many Whistler inns can be a real challenge for families, but the Cedar Springs provides an excellent solution. Guests at this large and charming lodge a mile north of Whistler Village have a choice of king-, queen-, or twin-size beds in comfortably modern yet understated surroundings. Two family suites, with two queen-size and two twin beds, are just the ticket for families. What's more, the lodge is just next door to a park, biking paths, and a sports center with swimming pool. Cedar Springs also offers excellent accommodations for couples and solo travelers. The large honeymoon suite boasts a fireplace and balcony. Most rooms feature handmade pine furniture; all have bathrooms with heated tile floors. The guest sitting room has a TV, VCR, fireplace, and video library. A sauna and hot tub on the sun deck overlooking the gardens add to the pampering after a day of play. A gourmet breakfast is served by the fireplace in the dining room, and guests are welcome to enjoy afternoon tea. Lodge owners Jackie and Jeorn offer lots of extras such as complimentary shuttle service to ski lifts, heated ski gear storage, bike rentals, and free Wi-Fi.

8106 Cedar Springs Rd., Whistler, BC V0N 1B8. ✆ **800/727-7547** or 604/938-8007. Fax 604/938-8023. www.whistlerinns.com/cedarsprings. 8 units. High winter season C$175–C$285 double; spring, summer, fall C$95–C$169 double. Rates include full breakfast and afternoon tea. MC, V. Free parking; 2-minute walk to public transport. Take Hwy. 99 north toward Pemberton 4km (2¹/₂ miles) past Whistler Village. Turn left onto Alpine Way, go a block to Rainbow Dr., and turn left; go a block to Camino St. and turn left. The lodge is a block down at the corner of Camino and Cedar Springs Rd. **Amenities:** Jacuzzi; sauna; guest lounge w/TV/VCR/DVD; secure ski and heated gear storage. *In room:* Hair dryer, no phone, Wi-Fi.

Chalet Luise B&B Inn ★★

This homey inn is just outside of Whistler Village, so park the car and walk to dining, shopping, and recreation. Chalet Luise is a very charming small inn with an equally charming hostess. The inn has just the right Bavarian touch to create a festive, holiday-card atmosphere. The guest rooms are bright and cheerful, and come with pine furniture and high-quality linens; some have fireplaces and balconies. At the back is a gazebo with hot tub; the large guest lounge has a TV, fireplace, and a self-service coffee bar with a microwave for guest use. There are a number of decks, all lovingly festooned with flowerpots in summer. All rooms have private bathrooms. Breakfast is a buffet of fresh baked goods plus a hot main course. Room rates are complex; check the website for current rates and minimum-stay requirements.

7461 Ambassador Crescent, Whistler, BC V0N 1B7. © **800/665-1998** or 604/932-4187. Fax 604/938-1531. www.chaletluise.com. 8 units. C$139–C$175 double. Rates include full breakfast. MC, V. Free parking. **Amenities:** Hot tub; sauna; bike storage. *In room:* Hair dryer, Wi-Fi.

Durlacher Hof Pension Inn ★★ (Finds)

This lovely inn boasts both an authentic Austrian feel and a sociable atmosphere. Both are the result of the exceptional care and service shown by owners Peter and Erika Durlacher. Guests are greeted by name at the entryway, provided with slippers, and then given a tour of the three-story chalet-style property. The rooms vary in size from comfortable to quite spacious and come with goose-down duvets and fine linens, private bathrooms (some with jetted tubs) with deluxe toiletries, and incredible mountain views from private balconies. Better still is the downstairs lounge, with a welcoming fireplace and complimentary après-ski appetizers baked by Erika; likewise, breakfasts are substantial and lovingly prepared. Peter and Erica are fonts of knowledge about local restaurants and recreation; they will happily arrange tours and outings.

7055 Nesters Rd., Whistler, BC V0N 1B7. © **877/932-1924** or 604/932-1924. Fax 604/938-1980. www.durlacherhof.com. 8 units. Mid-Dec to Mar 31 C$139–C$499 double; mid-June to Sept 30 C$109–C$299 double. Discounted rates for spring and fall. Extra person C$35. Rates include full breakfast and afternoon tea. MC, V. Free parking. Take Hwy. 99 about 1km (²/₃ mile) north of Whistler Village to Nester's Rd. Turn left and the inn is immediately on the right. **Amenities:** Jacuzzi; sauna; 1 room for those w/limited mobility. *In room:* TV, hair dryer, no phone, Wi-Fi.

Edgewater Lodge (Finds)

This lodge has probably the most unique location of any lodging in Whistler. It sits on a jut of land that thrusts into Green Lake, a quiet 3km (1¾ miles) north of Whistler Village. From each room, there are gum-swallowing vistas across the lake to Wedge Mountain and the ski slopes on Whistler and Blackcomb. The intimate lodge offers personal and professional service. Half the rooms are standard hotel-style bedrooms; the other half are one-bedroom suites with a sofa bed in the sitting room. All share a large lobby guest area with couches and a huge fireplace. The Edgewater is also noteworthy for its fine Northwest cuisine dining room.

The lodge is very convenient to all-season recreation—in summer, you can fish and boat in Green Lake, or test your drive on the adjacent Nicklaus North Golf Course. Come winter, in addition to downhill skiing, ice-skating and cross-country skiing are right out the front door—the valley's major Nordic ski trail runs right by the property.

8841 Hwy. 99, Box 369, Whistler, BC V0N 1B0. © **888/870-9065** or 604/932-0688. Fax 604/932-0686. www.edgewater-lodge.com. 12 units. High season C$195–C$335 double; low season from C$119–C$225 double. 2-night minimum stay required on weekends. Rates include breakfast. AE, MC, V. Free parking. **Amenities:** Restaurant; lounge; Jacuzzi. *In room:* TV, hair dryer, Wi-Fi.

Hostelling International Whistler (Value)

One of the few inexpensive spots in Whistler, the hostel also happens to have one of the nicest locations: on the south edge of Alta Lake, with a dining room, deck, and lawn looking over the lake to Whistler Mountain. Inside, the hostel is extremely pleasant; there's a lounge with a wood-burning stove, a common kitchen, a piano, Ping-Pong tables, and a sauna, as well as a drying room for ski gear and storage for bikes, boards, and skis. In the summer, guests have use of a barbecue, canoe, and rowboat. As with all hostels, most rooms and facilities are shared. Beds at the hostel book up very early. Book by September at the latest for the winter ski season.

5678 Alta Lake Rd., Whistler, BC V0N 1B5. © **604/932-5492.** Fax 604/932-4687. www.hihostels.ca. 25 beds in 1- to 6-bed dorms. C$30–C$33 IYHA members; C$33–C$36 nonmembers. Family and group memberships available. MC, V. Free parking. **Amenities:** Bike rental; sauna; canoe and kayak rental; fireplace; Wi-Fi.

Inn at Clifftop Lane ★★

This large home, built as a B&B, sits above the Whistler Village on a quiet side street just south of Whistler Creekside, and offers large and beautifully furnished rooms. The inn strikes that perfect balance between the hominess of a B&B and the formality of a small boutique hotel. Each of the guest rooms is spacious, with an easy chair and living area, plus a bathroom with a jetted tub and bathrobes. The home is filled with books and decorated with antiques and folk art collected during the owners' travels, lending a cheerful élan to the breakfast rooms and guest lounge. Outdoors, steps lead through the forest to a hot tub and a private deck. This is a great choice for travelers seeking understated comfort and elegance with friendly, professional service.

2828 Clifftop Lane, Whistler, BC V0N 1B2. © **888/281-2929** or 604/938-1229. Fax 604/938-9880. www. innatclifftop.com. 5 units. Summer from C$119–C$139; winter from C$145–C$259. Ski packages available. Rates include full breakfast. AE, MC, V. Free parking. **Amenities:** Lounge; hot tub; library. *In room:* TV, hair dryer, Wi-Fi, robes, jetted tub.

WHERE TO DINE

Whistler overflows with dining choices: Whistler Village alone has over 90 restaurants. You'll have no trouble finding high-quality, reasonably priced food. **Ingrid's Village Café,** just off the Village Square at 4305 Skiers Approach (© **604/932-7000**), is a locals' favorite for simple, homelike food, for both quality and price. A large bowl of Ingrid's clam chowder costs just C$5, while a veggie burger comes in at C$6.50. It's open daily 8am to 6pm.

The **Citta Bistro,** in the Whistler Village Square (© **604/932-4177**), has a great patio and serves thin-crust pizzas such as the Californian Herb, topped with spiced chicken breast, sun-dried tomatoes, fresh pesto, and mozzarella, as well as gourmet burgers such as the Citta Extraordinaire, topped with bacon, cheddar, and garlic mushrooms. Main courses are C$7 to C$14; it's open daily 11am to 1am. The **Whistler Brewhouse,** 4355 Blackcomb Way (© **604/905-2739**), is a great spot for a microbrew ale, a plate of wood-fired pizza or rotisserie chicken (C$15–C$23), and a seat on the patio; open daily 11:30am to midnight, until 1am on weekends. **Sachi Sushi,** 4359 Main St. (© **604/935-5649**), is the best of Whistler's many sushi restaurants—the udon noodles and hot pots are excellent as well. Sushi rolls cost from C$8 to C$17; open Monday to Thursday 11am to 10pm, Friday and Saturday 11am to 11pm, and Sunday 11:30am to 9pm.

Araxi Restaurant & Bar ★★★ CONTEMPORARY CANADIAN   Frequently awarded for its wine list, as well as voted best restaurant in Whistler, this is one of the resort's top places to dine. Outside, the heated patio seats 80 people, while inside, the artwork, antiques, and terra-cotta tiles provide a subtle Mediterranean ambience that serves as a theater for the presentation of extraordinary food. Diners have a choice of a la carte items or a four-course tasting menu, which changes monthly, for C$68. The kitchen makes the most of local ingredients such as house-smoked trout, Pemberton cheese and lamb, and Howe Sound oysters. Chef James Walt has a deft hand, producing dishes that are inventive yet tradition-based and full of flavor: Boudin blanc sausage is fashioned from squab and foie gras, and presented with Jerusalem artichoke puree; delicate lamb meat rilletts come with a single, perfect pumpkin ravioli. Don't hesitate to ask for a suggestion when contemplating the nearly encyclopedic wine list—the wine staff here is exceedingly friendly and knowledgeable.

4222 Village Sq. ℂ **604/932-4540.** www.araxi.com. Main courses C$29–C$45. AE, MC, V. Mid-May to Oct daily 11am–3pm and 5–11pm.

Bearfoot Bistro ★★★ PACIFIC NORTHWEST   One of the very best in Whistler, Barefoot Bistro has created an enormous following for its regional, seasonal cuisine. The emphasis is on innovation, new flavors, and unusual preparations—in short, this is a cutting-edge restaurant for serious gastronomes. In the dining room, choose either three or five courses from the admirably broad menu, with selections such as lobster with Meyer lemon fava-bean risotto, popcorn-crusted lingcod with littleneck clam corn chowder, or braised pork belly with Dungeness crab grapefruit salad. There's nothing ordinary about the food, or the wine list, which has earned awards from *Wine Spectator* magazine. A number of specialty tasting menus are also available. Appetizers and more casual meals are available in the fireside room and the cozy Champagne Bar.

4121 Village Green. ℂ **604/932-3433.** www.bearfootbistro.com. Reservations required on weekends. 3-course menu C$39–C$98 (low–high season); 5-course menu C$98–C$148. AE, MC, V. Daily 5–10pm.

Caramba! Restaurant MEDITERRANEAN   The room is bright and filled with the pleasant buzz of nattering diners. The kitchen is open, and the smells wafting out hint tantalizingly of fennel, artichoke, and pasta. Caramba! is casual dining, but its Mediterranean-influenced menu offers fresh ingredients, prepared with a great deal of pizzazz. Try the pasta, free-range chicken, or roasted pork loin from the wood-fired rotisserie. Better still, if you're feeling especially good about your dining companions, order a pizza or two; a plate of grilled calamari; some hot spinach, cheese, and artichoke-and-shallot dips; and a plate of sliced prosciutto and bullfighters toast (savory toasted Spanish bread with herbs).

12–4314 Main St., Town Plaza. ℂ **604/938-1879.** Main courses C$11–C$22. AE, MC, V. Daily 11:30am–10:30pm.

Fifty Two 80 Bistro & Bar ★ SEAFOOD/CANADIAN   The suave dining room at the upscale Four Seasons Resort Whistler celebrates "fire and ice"—fire from the stone fireplace and dramatic backlit onyx panels and ice from the display of fresh fish and shellfish that greets diners. The design may be high-concept, but the food is more easygoing and hearty. For appetizers, the Pacific Northwest chowder, brimming with local seafood, is a great choice. Fresh lobster, prime Canadian steaks, spit-roasted meats, and fresh fish entrees round out the menu. Combine the a la carte selections into three- or four-course dinners for a great value on sublimely prepared food.

4591 Blackcomb Way (in the Four Seasons Whistler Resort). ℂ **604/935-3400.** Reservations required. Main courses C$18–C$46. AE, DC, DISC, MC, V. Daily 7am–10pm.

Mountain Club ★ CONTEMPORARY CANADIAN The dining room is chic, with feints toward woodsy decor, but the food at Mountain Club is at once casual and serious. Most of the menu is served small-plates style, and even the main courses are available in half portions, so this is a good destination if you want a light meal or wish to sample a number of dishes. For a hearty side dish, the truffled vegetables are a real pleasure; the Asian-style prawn dumplings are served in a delicate lemon-grass broth; beef tenderloin is served with tangy blue cheese bread pudding. A lot of care goes into the food, but the ambiance is anything but fussy, as the restaurant's ironic design provides a youthful, high-spirited vibe.

#40 4314 Main St. ⓒ **604/932-6009.** www.themountainclub.ca. Main dishes C$15–C$28. MC, V. Mon–Sat 5pm–1am; Sun 5pm–midnight.

Rimrock Cafe and Oyster Bar ★★ SEAFOOD Upstairs in a long, narrow room with a high ceiling and a massive stone fireplace at one end, Rimrock is very much like a Viking mead hall of old. It's not the atmosphere, however, that causes people to hop in a cab and make the C$5 journey out from Whistler Village. What draws folks in is the food. The first order of business should be a plate of oysters. Chef Rolf Gunther serves them up half a dozen ways, from raw with champagne to cooked "in hell" (broiled with fresh chiles). For my money, though, the signature Rimrock oyster is still the best: broiled with béchamel sauce and smoked salmon. Other appetizers are lightly seared ahi tuna or Quebec foie gras with apple raspberry salad. Main dishes are focused on seafood and game. Look for lobster and scallops with toasted almond butter and crispy leeks or grilled Arctic caribou with porcini cream and orange cranberry relish. The accompanying wine list has a number of fine vintages from B.C., California, New Zealand, and Australia.

2117 Whistler Rd. ⓒ **877/932-5589** or 604/932-5565. www.rimrockwhistler.com. Main courses C$24–C$40. AE, MC, V. Daily 11:30am–11:30pm.

21 Steps INTERNATIONAL/TAPAS The steps in question lead up to a second-floor dining room overlooking the central plaza of Whistler Village—a great vantage point for enjoying well-priced, made-from-scratch food while you people-watch. The menu is divided into a selection of small and large plates, though servings are generous—a couple of small plates should appease the standard appetite. The cooking borrows a little from Asia, a little from Italy, but everything is prepared with gusto. My favorite is garlic chile prawns, scattered with scallions, peanuts, and crispy wontons. Combine that small plate with bite-size bacon-wrapped slices of filet mignon, served with horseradish aioli, and you've got a fine meal, though it would mean missing out on the perfectly cooked roast chicken, served with forest mushroom pan gravy. On the third floor is a

---

Ⓜ **Moments** **Après-Ski**

"Après-ski" refers to that delicious hour after a hard day on the slopes, when you sit back with a cold drink, nurse the sore spots, and savor the glow that comes from a day well skied. On the Blackcomb side, **Merlin's Bar,** at the base (ⓒ **604/938-7735**), is the most obvious spot, but hidden away inside the Chateau Whistler Resort is something better: the **Mallard Bar** (ⓒ **604/938-8000**), one of the most civilized après-ski bars on the planet.

smaller, more intimate space called the Attic that serves as a lounge, though full dinner service is available as well.

4433 Sundial Place (Whistler Village Square). ℂ **604/966-2121.** www.21steps.ca. Main courses C$14–C$32. AE, MC, V. Daily 6pm–midnight.

WHISTLER AFTER DARK

For a town of just 10,000, Whistler has a more-than-respectable nightlife scene. You'll find concert listings in the *Pique,* a free local paper available at cafes and food stores. **Tommy Africa's,** 4216 Gateway Dr. (ℂ **604/932-6090**), and the dark and cavernous **Maxx Fish,** in Whistler Village Square below the Amsterdam Cafe (ℂ **604/932-1904**), cater to the 18- to 22-year-old crowd; you'll find lots of beat and not much light. The crowd at **Garfinkel's,** at the entrance to Village North (ℂ **604/932-2323**), is similar, though the cutoff age can reach as high as 26 or 27. **Buffalo Bills,** across from the Whistler Gondola (ℂ **604/932-6613**), and the **Longhorn,** 4284 Mountain Sq. (ℂ **604/932-5999**), cater to the 30-something crowd. Bills has a pool table, a video ski machine, and a smallish dance floor. The Longhorn usually has live music or entertainment on the weekends, when it's jammed with partiers.

11

Northern British Columbia

When you're talking about the "north" in Canada, you have to be careful. Although the following destinations are certainly northerly—at least a day's very long drive from Vancouver, or by a 15-hour ferry trip from Vancouver Island—most of this chapter's towns and sights are geographically in British Columbia's midsection. By the time you reach Prince George or Prince Rupert, however, you'll feel the palpable sense of being in the north: The days are long in summer and short in winter, and the spruce forestlands have a primordial character. First Nations peoples make up a greater percentage of the population here than in more southerly areas, and Native communities and heritage sites are common.

One of the most dramatic ways to reach northern British Columbia is by ferry. The BC Ferries Inside Passage route operates between Port Hardy, on Vancouver Island, and Prince Rupert, on the mainland; this full-day ferry run passes through mystical land- and seascapes, with excellent wildlife-viewing opportunities. From Prince Rupert—a fishing town with an excellent Native arts museum—you can catch another ferry to the Queen Charlotte Islands, which lie truly on the backside of beyond. Part of these islands is preserved as Gwaii Haanas National Park Reserve, a refuge of rare flora and fauna, and the ancient homeland of the Haida people.

Inland from Prince Rupert, the Yellowhead Highway (Hwy. 16) follows the mighty Skeena and Bulkley rivers past First Nations villages and isolated ranches, finally reaching Prince George, the largest city in northern British Columbia. Prince George is also a transportation gateway. Whether you're coming west from Edmonton, east from Prince Rupert, north from Vancouver, or south from Alaska, you'll pass through this city at the junction of the Fraser and Nechako rivers.

From Hwy. 16, there are two options for travelers who wish to explore realms even farther north. The famed 2,280km (1,417-mile) Alaska Highway—the only overland route to the 49th state—begins at Dawson Creek. More than 960km (597 miles) of the route wind across northern British Columbia, through black-spruce forest and over the Continental Divide. The Alaska Highway exercises an irresistible attraction to die-hard road-trippers, many of them retirees with RVs. Another route north, the Stewart-Cassiar Highway, also labeled Hwy. 37, leaves the Yellowhead Highway west of the Hazeltons, cutting behind the towering Coast Mountains to eventually join the Alaska Highway in the Yukon.

Frigid weather and short days make winter travel difficult in northern British Columbia; rather, explore this beautiful wilderness landscape under the glow of the summer's midnight sun.

1 THE INSIDE PASSAGE ★ & DISCOVERY COAST

The ferry cruise along British Columbia's Inside Passage combines the best scenic elements of Norway's rocky fjords, Chile's Patagonian range, and Nova Scotia's wild coastline. While many people experience the Inside Passage as part of an expensive Alaska cruise, you can see the same scenery for far less money on a BC ferry.

BC Ferries (© 888/BC-FERRY [223-3779] or 250/386-3431; www.bcferries.com) operates the **Inside Passage ferry** between Port Hardy (see chapter 9) and Prince Rupert (on the mainland, see below), with stops at the small Discovery Coast communities of Bella Coola, Ocean Falls, Shearwater, McLoughlin Bay (Bella Bella), and Klemtu. These stopovers became so popular that in 1994, the company added the **Discovery Coast ferry** to its schedule, which is dedicated to serving these remote villages. The ferry system also connects Prince Rupert to the remote **Queen Charlotte Islands,** the ancestral home of the Haida tribe (see later in this chapter).

For information on the region, go to the **Northern BC Tourism Association** website at www.hellobc.com/nbc or contact **Tourism Prince Rupert** at 110 1st Ave W., Prince Rupert, BC V8J 1A8 (© 800/667-1994 or 250/624-5637; www.tourismprince rupert.com).

THE INSIDE PASSAGE ★

Fifteen hours may seem like a long time to be on a ferry. But you'll never get bored as the MV *Northern Adventure* ★ noses its way through an incredibly scenic series of channels and calm inlets, flanked by green forested islands. Whales, porpoises, salmon, bald eagles, and sea lions line the route past the mostly uninhabited coastline. This 491km (305-mile) BC Ferries run between Port Hardy and Prince Rupert follows the same route as expensive Alaska-bound cruise ships, but at a fraction of the cost.

The ferry from Port Hardy initially crosses a couple hours' worth of open sea—where waters can be rough—before ducking behind Calvert Island. Except for a brief patch of open sea in the Milbanke Sound north of Bella Bella, the rest of the trip follows a narrow, protected channel between the mainland and a series of islands.

The actual Inside Passage begins north of Bella Bella, as the ferry ducks behind mountainous Princess Royal and Pitt islands. The passage between these islands and the mainland is very narrow—often less than a mile wide. The scenery is extraordinarily dramatic: Black cliffs drop thousands of feet directly into the channel, notched with hanging glacial valleys and fringed with forests. Powerful waterfalls shoot from dizzying heights into the sea. Eagles float along thermal drafts, and porpoises cavort in the ferry's wake. Even in poor conditions (the weather is very unpredictable here), this is an amazing trip.

Mid-May through September, the 117m (384-ft.) *Northern Adventure* ferry crosses every other day, leaving Port Hardy (or southbound, Prince Rupert) at 7:30am and arriving in Prince Rupert (or, Port Hardy) at 10:30pm. In midsummer, with the north's long days, the trip is made almost entirely in daylight. The ferry carries up to 600 crew and passengers and 101 vehicles. You can wander around the ferry and lounge on inside and outside deck seating. On board you'll find a cafeteria, snack bar, playroom, and gift shop. Midsummer one-way fares between Prince Rupert and Port Hardy are C$170 per adult car passenger or walk-on, C$390 for a normal-size vehicle. A car with two passengers adds up to C$730; fuel surcharges are sometimes added. Reservations are mandatory. The ship's cabins rent for between C$75 and C$85 for day use. Ferry service to/from Prince Rupert and Port Hardy continues at least once weekly the rest of the year, with somewhat lower fares; service, however, runs overnight, not during the day, as in summer. See the BC Ferries website for dates and prices. In summer, the ferry leaves both Prince Rupert and Port Hardy at 7:30am, so under normal circumstances, you'll arrive at your destination at 10:30pm—thus you probably won't need a cabin to sleep in. You should, however, make lodging reservations at your destination in advance; by the time the ship docks and you wait to drive your car off, it can be close to midnight.

At Prince Rupert, you can also catch an **Alaska Marine Highway ferry** (*©* **800/642-0066;** www.dot.state.ak.us/amhs), which stops here on its run between Bellingham, Washington, and Skagway, Alaska. Passenger fare from Prince Rupert to Skagway is US$171 per adult; a car and two adult passengers costs US$730. The trip can range anywhere from 30 to 50 hours, depending on the number of stops.

THE DISCOVERY COAST PASSAGE

Also departing from Port Hardy, the Discovery Coast's *Queen of Chilliwack* connects small, mostly First Nations communities along the fjords and islands of the northern coast, including Namu, Bella Bella, Shearwater, Ocean Falls, and Klemtu. The most popular part of this run is the summer-only service to Bella Coola, which links to Hwy. 20, a paved and gravel road that's a day's drive from Williams Lake, in central British Columbia's Fraser Valley (see "Williams Lake" in chapter 12).

In summer, a direct ferry runs on Thursday to Bella Coola, a Tuesday circular run goes north to McLoughlin Bay and Shearwater before returning to Port Hardy via Bella Coola, and a Saturday circular run goes to the above ports as well as Klemtu and Ocean Falls before returning via Bella Coola (there's a map on the BC Ferries website to help you make sense of the different routings). The Tuesday and Saturday departures require a night on the boat. In high season, fares between Port Hardy and Bella Coola are C$170 per adult passenger and C$340 for a car. Note that there is no reason to take a car to any of these destinations except for Bella Coola, as there is otherwise no road system to drive on.

For sleeping, you might snag one of 110 extra-wide reclining seats. Otherwise, BC Ferries recommends bringing a tent or cot, which you can set up on the leeward side of the boat. You can rent pillows and blankets for C$5; lockers and showers are available. Pets are allowed on board, but must remain in vehicles on the car deck; owners can descend to those decks to tend to their pets' needs.

---

2 PRINCE RUPERT

491km (305 miles) N of Port Hardy; 756km (470 miles) W of Prince George

British Columbia's most northerly coastal city, Prince Rupert (pop. 17,000) is a city in transition. For years a major fishing and timber port, it is now turning to tourism to bolster its economy. Although scarcely a fancy place, Prince Rupert has much to offer travelers. Eco-tourism has taken off, sportfishing is excellent in local rivers and in the protected waters of Chatham Sound, and the town is a convenient hub for exploring yet more distant sights of the Pacific Northwest. From here, ferries go north to Alaska, west to the Queen Charlotte Islands, and south to Vancouver Island and Bellingham, Washington.

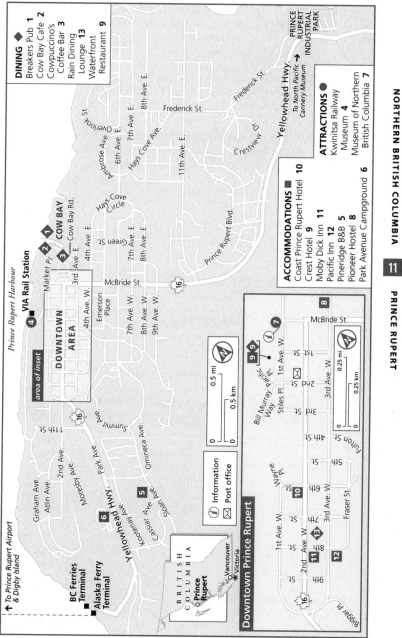

DINING ◆
Breakers Pub **1**
Cow Bay Cafe **2**
Cowpuccino's
  Coffee Bar **3**
Rain Dining
  Lounge **13**
Waterfront
  Restaurant **9**

ATTRACTIONS ●
Kwinitsa Railway
  Museum **4**
Museum of Northern
  British Columbia **7**

ACCOMMODATIONS ■
Coast Prince Rupert Hotel **10**
Crest Hotel **9**
Moby Dick Inn **11**
Pacific Inn **12**
Pineridge B&B **5**
Pioneer Hostel **8**
Park Avenue Campground **6**

PRINCE
RUPERT
INDUSTRIAL
PARK

Yellowhead Hwy.
To North Pacific
Cannery Museum →

Prince Rupert Harbour

VIA Rail Station

COW BAY

area of inset

DOWNTOWN
AREA

Downtown Prince Rupert

BRITISH
COLUMBIA
Prince
Rupert
Vancouver
Victoria

ⓘ Information
✉ Post office

0   0.5 mi
0   0.5 km

0   0.25 mi
0   0.25 km

To Prince Rupert Airport
& Digby Island →

BC Ferries
Terminal

Alaska Ferry
Terminal

Bill Murray Way · Pacific Ave.

McBride St.

Frederick St.

Crestview Dr.

Prince Rupert Blvd.

Prince Rupert exudes a hardworking, good-natured vigor, and the population is a well-integrated mix of First Nations and European-heritage Canadians. You'll experience the palpable sense of being on the northern edge of the world, which gives the city—situated on a series of rock ledges above the broad expanse of the Pacific—a sense of purpose and vitality.

ESSENTIALS

GETTING THERE   By Ferry   For information on BC Ferries service from Port Hardy and Alaska Marine Highway service between southeast Alaska and Washington, see "The Inside Passage," above. For information on BC Ferries service to the Queen Charlotte Islands, see later in this chapter.

By Train   A **VIA Rail** (© 888/VIA-RAIL [842-7245]; www.viarail.ca) train, the *Skeena,* operates between Prince Rupert and Prince George 4 days weekly (3 in winter). One-way fares start at C$68 in summer season. The train follows the same route as the Yellowhead Highway along the scenic Skeena River valley. At Prince George, travelers can continue on to Jasper, with connections to the mainline VIA Rail line between Vancouver and Toronto.

By Plane   Air Canada Jazz (© 888/247-2262; www.flyjazz.ca) provides service between Vancouver and Prince Rupert. **Hawkair** (© 800/487-1216; www.hawkair.ca) also offers daily service from Vancouver.

Both these airlines fly into Prince Rupert's Digby Island airport, which is indeed on an island. Upon collecting their luggage, arriving passengers board a bus that meets every scheduled flight and transports all passengers to the ferry terminal. Once there, the entire bus boards the ferry and crosses to Prince Rupert. The bus deposits the passengers at the Highliner Plaza Hotel (815 1st Ave. W.). Taxis are available. The bus/ferry fare from the airport to Prince Rupert is included in your airline ticket so there's no fee assessed for the service while you're traveling. The entire voyage takes roughly 35 minutes. While this process may sound complex, in fact it's as simple as collecting your luggage and getting on the bus. The driver takes care of the rest.

To catch a flight from Digby Island, the process works in reverse. Meet the airport bus at the Highliner Plaza Hotel. Once loaded, it then proceeds across the ferry to the airport. Call the airport bus at © 250/622-2222 to find out what time the bus leaves for your flight.

By Car   Prince Rupert is the terminus of the Yellowhead Highway, Canada's most northerly transcontinental roadway. Between Prince Rupert and Prince George, the route is 756km (470 miles) of extraordinary scenery. For car rentals, call **National** (© 800/CAR-RENT [227-7368] or 250/624-5318; www.nationalcar.com). If you are planning on renting a car while in Prince Rupert, reserve well in advance, as the cars get snapped up fast, especially on days when trains or ferries arrive.

(Tips)   **Special Events**

During the second week in June, Prince Rupert hosts **Seafest** (© 250/624-9118), which features a fishing derby, parades, games, food booths, bathtub races, and the annual blessing of the fleet.

By Bus   Greyhound Canada (© **800/661-8747** or 604/482-8747; www.greyhound. ca) serves Prince Rupert and Prince George with two buses daily each way in summer. The one-way fare is about C$120.

VISITOR INFORMATION   The **Prince Rupert Visitor Info Centre,** Ste. 215, Cow Bay Road (© **800/667-1994** in Canada, or 250/624-5637; www.tourismprincerupert. com), is on the waterfront in the Atlin Terminal building, about 2km (1¼ miles) from Hwy. 16. The center is open year-round, Monday through Saturday from 8am to 4pm, Monday through Friday from 5:30 to 9pm, and Sunday from 8 to 11am and 5:30 to 9pm (all day in summer).

EXPLORING THE AREA

Prince Rupert gets more than 18 hours of sunlight a day in summer. And despite its far-north location, this coastal city enjoys a mild climate most of the year. Mountain biking, cross-country skiing, fishing, kayaking, hiking, and camping are just a few of the region's popular activities.

Northern British Columbia's rich First Nations (Native Canadian) heritage has been preserved in Prince Rupert's museums and archaeological sites. But you don't need to visit a museum to get a sense of the community's history. Relics of the city's early days are apparent in its old storefronts, miners' shacks, and churches. Built on a series of rocky escarpments, the city rises ledge by ledge, starting at the harbor with the train station and the **Kwinitsa Railway Museum** (© **250/627-1915** or 250/627-3207). This area is overlooked by the old commercial center, with several blocks of turn-of-the-20th-century storefronts still busy with commerce. **Studio 9 Gallery,** 515 Third Ave. W. (© **250/624-2366**), offers a selection of local, regional, and First Nations art. **Java dot Cup,** 516 Third St. (© **250/622-2822**), is a lively and youthful coffeehouse and Internet cafe. The downtown area is overlooked by the historic residential area, which is dominated by massive stone churches.

The bustling **Cow Bay** district on the north waterfront, with galleries, restaurants, and the visitor center in the Atlin Terminal building, is Prince Rupert's major center for tourist activity. Just south of Atlin Terminal is Prince Rupert's cruise-ship dock, which serves a number of cruise lines.

Museum of Northern British Columbia ★

This museum displays artifacts of the Tsimshian, Nisga'a, and Haida First Nations, who have inhabited this area for more than 10,000 years. There are also artifacts and photographs from Prince Rupert's 19th-century European settlement. In summer, the museum sponsors a number of special programs, including walking tours of Prince Rupert. The gift shop is one of the best places in town to buy Native art. Also sponsored by the museum is the **Carving Shed,** a working studio located a block away on Market Place. There's no sign for the Carving Shed, but you'll recognize it as the long wooden building with a totem pole at the front door. If the door is open, that means that visitors are welcome. Be discreet while the carvers concentrate. There is no admission, but tips are welcome.

100 First Ave. © **250/624-3207.** Fax 250/627-8009. www.museumofnorthernbc.com. Admission C$5 adults, C$2 students, C$1 children 6–11, C$10 families. Summer Mon–Sat 9am–8pm, Sun 9am–5pm; winter Mon–Sat 9am–5pm.

North Pacific Historic Fishing Village ★★

Salmon canning was one of the region's original industries, back when the salmon run up the Skeena River was one of the greatest in North America. The province's oldest working salmon-cannery village, built on the waterfront of Inverness Passage in 1889, was home to hundreds of First Nations, Japanese, Chinese, and European workers and their families. Every summer, fishing fleets dropped off their catches at the cannery, where the salmon was packed and shipped out to world markets. This company-owned community reached its apex from 1910 to 1950, when the workforce numbered 400 and the community grew to about 1,200; the cannery has been closed since 1968.

Now a National Historic Site, the North Pacific Cannery Village Museum complex includes the cannery building, various administration buildings and residences, the company store, a hotel, and a dining hall—a total of over 25 structures linked by a long boardwalk (the land is so steep here that most of the houses were built on wharves). Workers were segregated by race: the Chinese, Japanese, and First Nations workers had their own micro-neighborhoods along the boardwalk, all overseen by the European bosses. Guided tours of the cannery complex, offered on the hour, provide a very interesting glimpse into a forgotten way of life.

The **boardinghouse** now operates as the historically authentic B&B, the **Waterfront Inn,** which is rustic but clean and cheerful with small rooms and squeaky floors—a very unique experience. Doubles cost from C$45. The **Cannery Café** is open during museum hours.

20km (12 miles) south of Prince Rupert in Port Edward. Mailing address: Box 1104, Prince Edward, BC V0V 1G0. ☏ **250/628-3538.** Admission C$12 adults, C$9 seniors, C$6 students 5–18, free for children 4 and under. July and Aug daily 11am–5pm (Thurs till 8pm); May, June, and Sept daily noon–5pm. Closed Oct–Apr. Take the Port Edward turnoff on Hwy. 16 and drive 5km (3 miles) past Port Edward on Skeena Dr.

ARCHAEOLOGICAL, WILDLIFE & ADVENTURE TOURS

Prince Rupert is at the center of an amazingly scenic area, but unless you have your own boat, you'll find it hard to get around. A good option is to sign on with a local tour operator. One of the most unusual excursions is the **Pike Island Archaeological Tour,** operated by the Metlakatla band of the Tsimshian First Nation. Tiny Pike Island (Laxspa'aws) is 9km (5⅔ miles) from Prince Rupert in Venn Passage, and is at the center of a rich archaeological area that was once one of the most densely populated regions in pre-Contact Native America. The island has three village sites that were abandoned 18 to 20 centuries ago. Although none have been excavated, guides point out the house depressions in the forest floor and discuss the midden deposits, the shellfish and bone piles that were essentially the garbage pits of these prehistoric people. Tours are offered daily from May to Labour Day, starting at 11:30am and returning to Prince Rupert at 4pm; they cost C$65 adults, C$49 children 5 to 12. The trails on the island are not difficult, but are not wheelchair accessible. The Pike Island tours are offered by **Seashore Charters** (☏ **800/667-4393** or 250/624-5645; www.seashorecharters.com), which has an office at Atlin Terminal. Seashore Charters offer a variety of other tours, including whale-watching.

One of Prince Rupert's most unique adventures takes you to Canada's only wildlife preserve dedicated to the grizzly bear. Access to the **Khutzeymateen Grizzly Bear Preserve,** northwest of Prince Rupert, is highly restricted, and a very limited number of outfitters can offer trips to this pristine wilderness, home to abundant numbers of *Ursus horribilis.* There's no other access to the preserve, and humans are forbidden to actually land. The most affordable option is **Palmerville Adventures** (☏ **888/580-2234** or 250/624-8243; www.palmerville.bc.ca), which offers trips to the preserve on jet boats.

Their half-day trip combines an air flight (either by seaplane or helicopter, depending on the size of the group) plus a journey into the preserve on a covered jet boat, with rates starting at C$425 per person. Although **Prince Rupert Adventure Tours** (✆ 800/201-8377 or 250/627-9166; www.adventuretours.net) is not one of the two outfitters that are allowed into the Khutzeymateen preserve itself, this outfitter does offer affordable day trips to the area near the wilderness area. Of course the grizzlies don't recognize boundaries, so the chances of viewing bears, as well as other wildlife such as eagles, seals, and mountain goats, is good. A 6-hour trip, including a sack lunch, is offered May through July and costs C$180 for adults. This outfitter also offers a variety of whale- and wildlife-watching tours, kayak drop-off and pickup, plus the popular, 1½- to 2-hour Kaien Island Circle Tours trip, which circumnavigates Prince Rupert's Kaien Island. The trip visits the city's busy docks and the seaplane terminal, and circles the island to view wildlife and such phenomena as reversing tidal rapids. The cost is C$55. Tours are offered May through September and leave from Atlin Terminal at Cow Bay.

For a historical 2-hour walking tour of the city, contact **Heritage Walking Tour** (✆ **250/624-3207** or 250/624-5637). It leaves daily May through August from the Museum of Northern British Columbia (see above) and is free with museum admission. A self-guided walking-tour booklet is also available for C$2.

OTHER OUTDOOR PURSUITS

FISHING   Prince Rupert is famed for its excellent sportfishing. There are dozens of charter operators based in town. The **Visitor Info Centre,** in Cow Bay (✆ **800/667-1994** in Canada, or 250/624-5637; www.tourismprincerupert.com), or **Seashore Charters** (✆ **800/667-4393** or 250/624-5645) can steer you to the one that best serves your needs.

Fishing charters can range in length from a half-day to a weeklong trip, and range in facilities from rough-and-ready boats to luxury cruisers. Expect a guided trip to cost from C$500 per person per day. Long-established companies include **Frohlich's Fish Guiding** (✆ **250/627-8443**) and **Predator Fishing Charters** (✆ **250/627-1993**; www.citytel.net/~predator), which also provides charters for diving.

HIKING   **Far West Sports,** 212 Third Ave. W. (✆ **250/624-2568**), is one of the best sources of information about hiking and mountain-biking trails. The area experiences annual as well as seasonal changes in trail conditions, and some hiking and backcountry ski areas are too challenging for beginners.

There are a number of good hiking options right in Prince Rupert. One trail follows Hays Creek from McBride Street down to the harbor. Just 6.4km (4 miles) east on Hwy. 16 is a trail head for three more wilderness hikes. The 4km (2.5-mile) loop **Butze Rapids Trail** winds through wetlands to Grassy Bay and to Butze Rapids, a series of tidal cataracts. The sometimes-steep trail to the **Tall Trees** grove of old-growth cedars and to the viewpoint on **Mount Oldfield** requires more stamina. Check with the visitor center or the **North Coast Forest District Office,** 125 Market Place (✆ **250/624-7460**; www.for. gov.bc.ca/dnc), for more information.

KAYAKING & CANOEING   The waters surrounding Prince Rupert are tricky, and rough tidal swells and strong currents are common. **Skeena Kayaking** (✆ **250/624-5246**) offers kayak trips along the Skeena River and to the Kutzmateen Grizzly Bear Sanctuary. A 4-hour kayak rental is C$45.

The **Pioneer Hostel,** 167 Third Ave. E. (*C* **888/794-9998** or 250/624-2334; www. pioneerhostel.com), is in a historic rooming house within easy walking distance of both downtown and Cow Bay. Pioneer Hostel is well-run and clean, with accommodations from C$22 to C$60 a person.

A mile from the ferry terminal, **Park Avenue Campground,** 1750 Park Ave. (*C* **800/667-1994** or 250/624-5861; www.princerupertrv.com), has 77 full-hookup and 10 unserviced sites, plus open areas for tent camping. Facilities include laundry, showers, toilets, playground, and phones. Reserve in advance in summer. Rates range from C$20 for tenters to C$32 for RVs.

Coast Prince Rupert Hotel   Right downtown, the six-story Coast offers views of the harbor and mountains from just about every spacious room. Rooms are well maintained and feature standard business travel furnishings. The hotel's one suite is a good deal at C$185, with a king-size bed and a separate corner sitting room with a kitchen. Three meals daily are offered at Charlie's, just off the lobby, while drinks are available at the Rupert Pub. There's dancing 3 nights a week at Bogart's.

118 Sixth St., Prince Rupert, BC V8J 3L7. *C* **800/663-1144** or 250/624-6711. Fax 250/624-3288. www. coasthotels.com. 92 units. C$129 double. Extra person C$10. Family plan, corporate and off-season rates, and senior and AAA discounts available. AE, DC, DISC, MC, V. **Amenities:** Restaurant; lounge; night club; guest passes to full-service health club; room service; beer-and-wine store. *In room:* A/C, TV, fridge (on request), hair dryer, Wi-Fi.

Crest Hotel ★   The Crest offers the best views in town, good dining, and beautifully furnished, though not expansive, rooms. Situated on the bluff's edge overlooking Tuck Inlet, Metlakatla Pass, and the harbor, this is one of the finest hotels in northern British Columbia. The rooms feature quality furniture, feather duvets, and a relaxed stylishness. Standard rooms come with either two doubles or one queen-size bed; suites feature king-size beds. The wood-paneled lobby and common rooms are opulent, and it's hard to imagine more impressive views anywhere than from the jutting outdoor hot tub and the well-equipped fitness room. The staff will happily set you up with fishing charters and wildlife-viewing trips. The Waterfront Restaurant is the best in town (see "Where to Dine," below), and Charley's Lounge, with a heated deck, has the city's best year-round view from a bar stool.

222 First Ave. W., Prince Rupert, BC V8J 1A8. *C* **800/663-8150** or 250/624-6711. Fax 250/627-7666. www. cresthotel.bc.ca. 102 units. C$129–C$169 double; C$209–C$279 suite. AE, MC, V. Free parking. Small pets allowed for C$10. **Amenities:** Restaurant; coffee shop; bar; exercise room; Jacuzzi; room service; sauna. *In room:* TV, hair dryer, Wi-Fi.

Moby Dick Inn (**Value**)   Well established and comfortable, the Moby Dick is a clean, unfussy choice—it's all the hotel most travelers will need while in Prince Rupert. It has a central location between downtown and the ferry docks. Rooms are nicely outfitted, and some of them have harbor views. Wheelchair-accessible units are available.

935 Second Ave. W., Prince Rupert, BC V8J 1H8. *C* **800/663-0822** or 250/624-6961. Fax 250/624-3760. www.mobydickinn.com. 63 units. C$79–C$105 double. Children 11 and under stay free in parent's room. AE, DC, DISC, MC, V. Small pets allowed. **Amenities:** Restaurant; bar; Jacuzzi; room service; sauna; rooms for those w/limited mobility. *In room:* TV, fridge, hair dryer, Wi-Fi.

Pacific Inn ★   Recently renovated, this motor lodge is a good value for its large, clean, and attractive rooms in a convenient location, midway between downtown and the ferry docks. The owners take pride in the place, and it shows. The front desk will arrange local tours and activities.

909 Third Ave. W., Prince Rupert, BC V8J 1M9. ☎ **888/663-1999** or 250/627-1711. Fax 250/627-4212. www.pacificinn.bc.ca. 77 units. C$105–C$115 double. Rates include continental breakfast. Off-season rates and senior discounts available. AE, MC, V. Pets allowed for C$10. **Amenities:** Restaurant. *In room:* TV, fridge (on request), hair dryer, Wi-Fi.

Pineridge B&B ★★   This very attractive B&B sits above the town, between downtown and the ferry terminals, and offers the largest and most sophisticated rooms in Prince Rupert. The uncluttered bedrooms are furnished with quality art (the owners are also gallery owners) and feature soothing colors, handsome pine furniture, and nice touches such as bathrobes and down duvets. Guests share a large sitting room with a TV, fridge, couches, a library, phone, and games. The traditional European breakfast is a highlight of the stay. The entire house is tastefully decorated with clean-lined, modern furnishings and local art and crafts. The friendly hosts will help you plan activities and arrange charters.

1714 Sloan Ave., Prince Rupert, BC V8J 3Z9. ☎ **888/733-6733** or 250/627-4419. Fax 250/624-2366. www. pineridge.bc.ca. 3 units. C$99 double. Rates include full breakfast. MC, V. Closed Oct–Mar. Follow signs to ferry terminal, turn left (or from ferry turn right) onto Smithers St., go 2 blocks, and turn right onto Sloan Ave. Not suitable for children. *In room:* Hair dryer, phone (on request), Wi-Fi, robes.

WHERE TO DINE

Cowpuccino's Coffee Bar, 25 Cow Bay Rd. (☎ **250/627-1395**), is a friendly, slightly funky coffee shop with good homemade muffins at breakfast and desserts in the evening.

Breakers Pub ★ PUB   Breakers is a popular pub with a harbor view and well-prepared international food. The offerings range from salads and wraps to pasta, pizza, and grilled local fish. This is a hopping social spot, with a new game room and dance floor; the young and prosperous of Prince Rupert gather here to get happy with a microbrew or two.

117 George Hills Way (on the Cow Bay Wharf). ☎ 250/624-5990. www.breakerspub.ca. Reservations not needed. Main courses C$8–C$24. AE, DC, MC, V. Mon–Thurs 11:30am–midnight; Fri–Sat 11:30am–1am; Sun noon–midnight.

Cow Bay Café ★ PACIFIC NORTHWEST   This homey place is like a little Vancouver street cafe plunked down on the edge of a dock. The casual, slightly hippie atmosphere feels refreshing so far north, and is nicely matched by the menu, which features lots of vegetarian options. Choices include salads, pastas, soups, and sandwiches; at night, fresh fish is prepared with zest. Order dessert when you order the rest of your meal, because popular items often sell out by the end of the evening.

205 Cow Bay Rd. ☎ **250/627-1212.** Reservations recommended. Main courses C$11–C$26. AE, MC, V. Tues noon–2:30pm; Wed–Sat noon–2:30pm and 6–8:30pm.

Rain Dining Lounge INTERNATIONAL/TAPAS   Swank cocktails and tapas-like small plates have arrived in Prince Rupert. This rather smart restaurant serves notably good martinis plus a very tempting selection of tapas and small plates for sharing. Though you can order such meaty dishes as beef Wellington and fiery Burmese lamb curry, the temptation here is the excellent selection of dishes featuring local seafood and fish. Pan-seared scallops are served with vegetable tempura and rich vanilla-bean saffron cream, and smoked halibut brandade is topped with curry oil and slices of fried bread.

The menu is large and ambitious, good reading material while you sip on something delicious from the 100-strong cocktail list.

737 Second Ave. © **250/627-8272.** www.raindl.com. Reservations recommended. Main courses C$7–C$20. MC, V. Mon–Sat 5pm–2am; Sun 11am–2pm.

Waterfront Restaurant ★★ PACIFIC NORTHWEST   Easily Prince Rupert's most sophisticated restaurant, the Waterfront is flanked by banks of windows that overlook the busy harbor. The white-linen-and-crystal elegance of the dining room is matched by the inventiveness of the cuisine. Understandably, much of the menu is devoted to local seafood; Fisherman's Chowder features cream and thyme broth spiked with salmon, halibut, and shrimp. Pan-fried halibut cheeks are topped with three-mustard and caper berry sauce. "Casual plates" feature smaller portions, salads, and tempting appetizers such as seared sea scallops with mango salsa. The wine list features a number of impressive B.C. vintages.

In the Crest Hotel, 222 First Ave. W. © **250/624-6771.** www.cresthotel.bc.ca. Reservations suggested. Main courses C$13–C$40. AE, DC, MC, V. Daily 6:30am–10pm.

3 THE QUEEN CHARLOTTE ISLANDS

The misty and mysterious Queen Charlotte Islands were the muse for 19th-century painter Emily Carr, who documented her impressions of the towering totem poles and longhouses at the abandoned village of Ninstints, on Anthony Island. The islands still lure artists, writers, and photographers wishing to experience their haunting beauty.

The Queen Charlottes—also called by their Native name, Haida Gwaii—are the homeland of the Haida people. Sometimes referred to as the Vikings of the Pacific, the Haida were mighty seafarers, and during raiding forays, ranged as far south along the Pacific Coast as Oregon. The Haida were also excellent artists, carvers of both totems and argillite, a slatelike rock that they transformed into tiny totemic sculptures and pendants. The Haida today make up about half of the islands' population of 6,000.

The Queen Charlottes have a reputation as the "Canadian Galapagos," as these islands—ranging between 51 and 136km (32–85 miles) from the mainland—have evolved their own endemic species and subspecies of flora and fauna. The Canadian government preserved the southern portion of Moresby Island as **Gwaii Haanas National Park Reserve and Haida Heritage Site** ★. UNESCO followed suit by naming the islands a World Heritage Site.

The islands are primordial and beautiful, but visiting them requires some planning. In fact, if you're reading this in Prince Rupert and thinking about a spur-of-the-moment trip to the Charlottes, you may want to reconsider. Lodging on the islands is limited, and reservations are necessary year-round. The most interesting areas—the abandoned Haida villages—are accessible only by boat, and the Gwaii Haanas National Park limits the number of people who can access the archaeological sites each day. There are only 125km (78 miles) of paved roads, and none of them even come close to the park or the islands' wild western coastline. In short, simply showing up on the Queen Charlottes is not a good idea. The best way to visit is by arranging, in advance, to join a guide or outfitter on a kayaking, flightseeing, sailing, or boating excursion.

ESSENTIALS

GETTING THERE   By Ferry   BC Ferries (© **888/BC-FERRY** [223-3779] in B.C., or 250/386-3431; www.bcferries.bc.ca) crosses between Prince Rupert and Skidegate, on northerly Graham Island. The 6½- to 7-hour crossing can be quite rough; take precautions if you're prone to seasickness. Ferries run daily in summer; call ahead to reserve. The one-way high-season tickets are C$39 for a passenger and C$140 for most passenger vehicles.

By Plane   Air Canada Jazz (© **888/247-2262**; www.flyjazz.ca) provides daily flights from Vancouver to Sandspit Airport on northern Moresby Island. **Pacific Coastal Airlines** (© **800/663-2872** or 604/273-8666; www.pacific-coastal.com) provides daily service from Vancouver's South Terminal to Masset during the summer and service three times a week during the shoulder and winter season. **North Pacific Seaplanes** (© **800/689-4234** or 250/627-1341; www.northpacificseaplanes.com), based in Prince Rupert, offers floatplane service to Masset, Sandspit/Queen Charlotte City.

VISITOR INFORMATION   The Queen Charlotte Islands Visitor Info Centre, 3220 Wharf St., Queen Charlotte (© **250/559-8316**; www.qcinfo.ca), is open May through September daily from 8am to 8pm. The info center now offers a booking and reservation service.

GETTING AROUND   In the Queen Charlotte Islands, the island-to-island Skidegate–Alliford Bay ferry operates 12 daily sailings between the main islands. The fare is C$6 each way or C$14 per vehicle. With so few roads on the islands, it's fair to ask if it even makes sense to take a car on a short trip. **Budget** (© **250/637-5688**) has a bureau at the Sandspit airport; **Rustic Car Rentals** (© **250/559-4641**) has a bureau at the BC Ferry terminal. Some lodgings also offer car rentals.

EXPLORING THE ISLANDS

Most visitors come to the Charlottes to view its abundant and unusual wildlife, and to visit the ancient Haida villages. In both cases, you'll need to either have your own boat or arrange for a guide to get you from the islands' small settlements to the even more remote areas. The islands provide superlative wilderness adventures—camping, hiking, diving, sailing, kayaking, and fishing—although due to their isolation and sometimes extreme weather, you'll need to plan ahead before setting out.

　　Graham Island is the more populous of the two major islands. **Queen Charlotte City** is a fishing and logging town with a population of about 1,200, sitting above the scenic waters of Beaverskin Bay. QCC, as the village is sometimes dubbed, has the majority of lodgings and facilities for travelers, as well as the administrative headquarters for **Gwaii Haanas National Park Reserve** (see below).

　　Skidegate Village (pronounced "*Skid*-a-gut"), just east of the Skidegate ferry terminal, is home to the **Haida Heritage Centre at Kaay 'Ilnagaay** (© **250/559-4643**; www. haidaheritagecentre.com), which includes the Haida Gwaii Museum, which houses the world's largest collection of argillite carvings, made from the slatelike stone found only in the Queen Charlottes. The newly expanded facility encompasses 149 sq. m (16,000 sq. ft.) and displays historic totem poles, contemporary and historic Haida art, and extensive photo archives. Admission is C$12 for adults, C$9 students 13 to 18, and C$5 for children 6 to 12. The museum is open daily mid-June to mid-September 10am to 6pm, the same hours but Monday through Saturday May to mid-June, and Tuesday through Saturday 11am to 5pm from mid-September through April (closed Dec 25–Jan 5). Next to the museum is the longhouse-style office of the **Haida Gwaii Watchmen,** the Native guardians of the islands' Haida villages and heritage sites. Ask here for information on visiting these sites.

Heading north from Skidegate on Hwy. 16, **Tlell** is an old agricultural community and now somewhat of an artists' colony; watch for signs pointing to studios. Past the logging town of Port Clements, the highway ends at **Masset,** the island's largest town with a population pushing 1,500. **Old Massett,** just north of Masset, is one of the largest Haida settlements on the island, and a good place to shop for carvings and jewelry. Just north of the Masset town center, trails lead through the **Delkatla Wildlife Sanctuary,** one of the first southerly landfalls on the Pacific Flyway.

From Masset, continue north and then east on Tow Hill Road to **Naikoon Provincial Park,** where whales can be spotted from the beaches and peregrine falcons fly overhead. The **Agate Beach Campground** (✆ 250/847-7320) is a popular place to camp (C$14).

On **Moresby Island,** the principal center of population is **Sandspit** (pop. 460). In summer, Parks Canada operates an information center for visitors headed to the wilderness **Gwaii Haanas National Park Reserve and Haida Heritage Site** ★. There are no roads or shore facilities in the park, and access is by boat or floatplane only. Although there are many amazing sights in this part of the Queen Charlottes, you'll need to be committed to the journey to get here: The distances are great and the costs high. If you're a dedicated wildlife watcher, it may be worth it to see the rare fauna and flora. Perhaps the most famous site in the park is **SGang Gwaay 'Ilnagaay,** or **Ninstints,** on Anthony Island, an ancient Native village revered as sacred ground by the modern-day Haida. Centuries-old totem poles and longhouses proudly stand in testimony to the culture's 10,000-year heritage.

If you are contemplating traveling on your own to Gwaii Haanas, you have a fair number of hurdles to clear, in addition to arranging for a boat. Only a limited number of people are allowed to enter Gwaii Haanas per day, and these are apportioned between those on organized tours and those traveling independently. (Six standby places are also available daily on a first-come, first-served basis.) You must make a reservation and register your trip with park authorities, and also attend a mandatory orientation session before entering the park. Call **Super Natural British Columbia** at ✆ 800/435-5622 to reserve a spot; reservations are C$15. Entry to the park is C$20 per day. The **Haida Gwaii Watchmen** (✆ 250/559-8225) manage access to SGang Gwaay 'Ilnagaay and other ancient villages in the park, and watchmen members there will explain the history and cultural significance of the sites you may visit. For more information, contact **Gwaii Haanas National Park Reserve,** Box 37, Queen Charlotte City, BC V0T 1S0 (✆ 250/559-8818; www.pc.gc.ca/pn-np/bc/gwaiihaanas), or the **Queen Charlotte Islands Visitor Info Centre** (✆ 250/559-8316; www.qcinfo.ca).

TOURS & EXCURSIONS TO GWAII HAANAS NATIONAL PARK RESERVE

By far the easiest and most convenient way of visiting Gwaii Haanas is by joining a guided tour. Outfitters must be registered with park officials; the list of authorized tour operators is the best place to start shopping for expeditions into the park. Note that the park entry fee of C$20 per day may or may not be included in the cost of tour packages, so ask when booking.

Many outfitters, such as **Butterfly Tours Great Expeditions** (© 604/740-7018; www.butterflytours.bc.ca)—alternately booked through **Great Expeditions** (© 800/663-3364 or 604/257-2040; www.greatexpeditions.com)—offer kayaking packages that suit every age and experience level; Butterfly's 8-day tours start at C$2,480. Longtime sea-kayak outfitter **Ecosummer Expeditions** (© 800/465-8884 or 250/674-0102; www.ecosummer.com) offers 10-day trips to Gwaii Haanas, with prices starting at C$2,425. **Pacific Rim Paddling Company** (© 250/384-6103; www.pacificrimpaddling.com) has 7-day kayak trips to the park, with prices from C$2,095.

Sailing into Gwaii Haanas is another popular option, and most sailboat operators also have kayaks aboard for guests' use. **Bluewater Adventures** (© 888/877-1770 or 604/980-3800; www.bluewateradventures.ca) offers 8-day tours starting at C$4,200. **Ocean Light II Adventures** (© 604/328-5339; www.oceanlight2.bc.ca) offers 8-day Haida Gwaii sailings on a 22m (72-ft.) boat for C$3,500.

Inland Air Charters (© 888/551-4222 or 250/559-4222; www.inlandair.bc.ca) offers sightseeing seaplane flights to Hot Springs Island and SGang Gwaay 'Ilnagaay. The latter trip includes a landing at Rose Bay and a 20-minute boat ride to the ancient village, plus a guided tour. You need to charter the entire plane, at a cost of C$3,420, but the cost can be divided by up to five passengers; check the website, as weight restrictions may apply.

Diving charters around the islands, but not in Gwaii Haanas, can be arranged through **Emerald Sea Sail and Scuba** (© 250/635-5818; www.qcislands.net/emeraldsea).

Fishing

Langara Fishing Adventures (© 800/668-7544 or 604/232-5532; www.langara.com) offers fishing packages with accommodations at two of the most exclusive lodges in western Canada. Geared toward those who want to be pampered, the outfitter picks up guests at Vancouver Airport and delivers them to Langara Island, just north of Graham Island. There are two lodges: the slightly more rustic Langara Fishing Lodge and the utterly upscale and opulent Langara Island Lodge. At both, rooms are luxurious, and the dining room serves expertly prepared Pacific Northwest dishes. Packages include air transport from Vancouver, lodging, meals, boats, tackle, weather gear, and freezing or canning of your catch. Guided fishing trips cost extra, as do whale-watching and heli-touring. Also available are fishing trips to even more remote fishing lodges in the Queen Charlottes. At Langara Fishing Lodge, rates start at C$3,895 for a 4-day trip; at Langara Island Lodge, 4 days cost from C$4,495. Packages are offered April to October.

For something more low-key, **Naden Lodge,** 1496 Kelkatla St., Masset (© 800/771-8933 or 250/626-3322; www.nadenlodge.bc.ca), offers B&B accommodations and guided fishing trips from a lovely location right above Masset's boat basin. Numerous charter operators can be found in Masset, Queen Charlotte, and Skidegate. Contact the **Queen Charlotte Islands Visitor Info Centre** (© 250/559-8316; www.qcinfo.ca) for suggestions.

WHERE TO STAY & DINE

Food on these remote islands is pretty perfunctory. Stop in at the **Mile Zero Pub,** Collison Avenue at Main Street, Masset (© 250/626-3210), for a pint and a fish tale or two. The **Golden Pam,** 2062 Collison Ave., Masset (© 250/626-3672), serves hearty portions of seafood, steaks, pasta dishes, sandwiches, and salads. **Oceana,** at 3119 Third Ave. in Queen Charlotte City (© 250/559-8683), offers both Chinese and Continental cuisine, and is open for lunch and dinner.

Dorothy & Mike's Guest House The atmosphere here is serene: A large deck overlooks the Skidegate Inlet, while gardens surround the house. The warm, cozy guest rooms are filled with local art and antiques; one suite comes with a full kitchen, and all three have private entrances. All guests have access to a common area with an entertainment center and reading library. The inn is within walking distance of the ocean, restaurants, and shopping.

3127 Second Ave. (Box 595), Queen Charlotte City, BC V0T 1S0. ✆ **250/559-8439.** Fax 250/559-8439. www.qcislands.net/doromike. 9 units, 2 with shared bathroom. May–Sept C$70 double with shared bathroom, C$20–C$125 double with private bathroom. Rates include breakfast. Off-season rates available. No credit cards. Drive 3.5km (2 miles) away from the Skidegate ferry terminal on Second Ave. *In room:* TV.

Premier Creek Lodging Great for the budget-conscious, this heritage lodge dates back to 1910. Many rooms have great views over gardens to Bearskin Bay. There's a range of accommodations, from small, single units with shared bathrooms to suites with kitchens. There's also a full-fledged hostel in a separate building (C$25).

3101 Third Ave. (Box 268), Queen Charlotte City, BC V0T 1S0. ✆ **888/322-3388** or 250/559-8415. Fax 250/559-8198. 14 units. C$35–C$90 double. AE, MC, V. **Amenities:** Fridge; bike rentals, microwave. *In room:* TV, kitchen (some units only), Wi-Fi.

Sea Raven Motel The largest lodging in the Queen Charlottes, the Sea Raven is a comfortable motel with many room types, ranging from simple single units to deluxe accommodations with decks; many have ocean views. A few units sport kitchenettes. The rooms are simply furnished, but very clean.

3301 Third Ave. (Box 519), Queen Charlotte City, BC V0T 1S0. ✆ **800/665-9606** or 250/559-4423. Fax 250/559-8617. www.searaven.com. 39 units. C$75–C$95 double. AE, DC, MC, V. Limited street parking available. Pets allowed for C$10. **Amenities:** Restaurant. *In room:* TV, kitchenette (7 rooms only), Wi-Fi.

Spruce Point Lodging This rustic inn, overlooking the Hecate Strait, features rooms with private entrances as well as excellent views. Each unit has a fridge and a choice of either private shower or tub. Some rooms have full kitchen facilities, and all have complimentary tea and coffee service. Your friendly hosts can arrange kayaking packages to the surrounding islands.

609 Sixth Ave., Queen Charlotte City (on Graham Island), BC V0T 1S0. ✆ **250/559-8234.** www.qcislands. net/sprpoint. 7 units. C$85. MC, V. Drive about 15 min. west on the main road away from the Skidegate ferry terminal, then turn left at Sam & Shirley's Grocery (the corner store). *In room:* TV, fridge.

---

4 THE YELLOWHEAD HIGHWAY: FROM PRINCE RUPERT TO PRINCE GEORGE

It's a long 756km (470 miles) from Prince Rupert to Prince George. Even though it's possible to make the journey in 1 long day, it's far more pleasant to take it slowly, enjoy the scenery, and stop at some of the cultural sights along the way.

The route initially follows the glacier-carved Skeena River valley inland, through the industrial city of **Terrace** and to the **Hazeltons,** twin towns with a lovely river setting and an excellent First Nations cultural center. **Smithers,** cradled in a rich agricultural valley, is another scenic spot, and the most pleasant place along the route to spend a night. Between Burns Lake and Fort Fraser is a series of long, thin lakes, famed for trout angling and rustic fishing resorts.

GETTING THERE **By Car** Terrace is 152km (94 miles) east of Prince Rupert on the Yellowhead Highway (Hwy. 16). From Terrace to Prince George, it's another 571km (355 miles).

By Train VIA Rail (✆ **888/VIA-RAIL** [842-7245]; www.viarail.ca) operates four-times-weekly service between Prince George and Prince Rupert, with stops including Smithers, New Hazelton, and Terrace. The train follows the same route as the Yellowhead Highway.

By Bus Greyhound Canada (✆ **800/661-8747** or 604/482-8747; www.greyhound. ca) travels between Prince Rupert and Prince George. One-way fare from Prince Rupert to Terrace is about C$26.

VISITOR INFORMATION **Kermodei Tourism,** 4511 Keith Ave. (✆ **877/635-4944** or 250/635-4944; http://kermodeitourism.ca), provides extensive information on the area.

TERRACE

The Yellowhead Highway (Hwy. 16) follows the lush Skeena River valley from Prince Rupert, on the coast of the Inside Passage, to the province's interior. It's the gateway to the land-based return route from the Inside Passage ferry cruise. The long, winding valley is home to a diverse community of fishers, loggers, and aluminum and paper-mill workers in Terrace, and is the ancestral home of the Gitxsan, Haisla, Tsimshian, and Nisga'a First Nations.

If you want to understand glacial geology, this drive will provide instant illumination. It's easy to picture the steep-sided valley choked with a bulldozer of ice, grinding the walls into sheer cliffs. Streams drop thousands of feet in a series of waterfalls. There are many small picnic areas along this route; plan on stopping beside the Skeena to admire the astonishing view.

Terrace is an industrial town of about 14,000 and has only just begun to develop itself for tourism. Stop by the store at the **House of Sim-oi-Ghets,** off Hwy. 16 (✆ **250/638-1629;** www.kitsumkalum.bc.ca/hos.html), a cedar longhouse owned by the Kitsumkalum tribal band of the Tsimshian Nation. It offers jewelry, carvings, bead and leather work, and moccasins.

Where to Stay & Dine

Best Western Terrace Inn Overlooking the surrounding mountains, this hotel's well-appointed rooms feature little touches not normally found in the backcountry. A few deluxe accommodations sport Jacuzzi tubs. Facilities include a piano bar and lounge, plus a pub with live entertainment. Lava-bed tours are available upon request.

4553 Greig Ave., Terrace, BC V8G 1M7. ✆ **800/488-1898** or 250/635-0083. Fax 250/635-0092. www. bestwestern.com/ca/terraceinn. 62 units. C$114–C$125 double. Group, corporate, senior, and weekend discounts available. AE, DC, DISC, MC, V. Free parking. Small pets accepted for C$10. **Amenities:** Restaurant; bar; lounge; well-equipped exercise room; Jacuzzi; room service. *In room:* A/C, TV, hair dryer, Wi-Fi.

Coast Inn of the West This comfortable hotel in downtown Terrace offers pleasant rooms in the heart of the town. Facilities include a lounge that provides evening entertainment, a gift shop, and a restaurant open for three meals daily.

4620 Lakelse Ave., Terrace, BC V8G 1R1. ✆ **800/663-1144** or 250/638-8141. Fax 250/638-8999. www. coasthotels.com. 58 units. C$95–C$139 double. Senior and AAA rates available. AE, DC, DISC, MC, V. **Amenities:** Restaurant; bar; lounge; room service. *In room:* A/C, TV, hair dryer, Wi-Fi.

Forty kilometers (25 miles) northwest of town, the **Khutzeymateen Grizzly Bear Preserve** is the province's first official sanctuary of its kind. You must be part of an authorized group or accompanied by a ranger to observe these amazing creatures (see "Archaeological, Wildlife & Adventure Tours," earlier in this chapter).

North America's rarest subspecies of black bear, the **kermodei,** also makes its home in the valley. The kermodei is unique, a nonalbino black bear born with white fur. Its teddy-bear face and round ears are endearing, but the kermodei is even larger than the impressive Queen Charlotte Islands black bear.

Also north of Terrace, at the **Nisga'a Memorial Lava Beds Provincial Park,** vegetation has only recently begun to reappear on the lava plain created by a volcanic eruption and subsequent lava flow in 1750, which consumed this area and nearly all of its inhabitants.

The route to the park's near-lunar landscape begins in Terrace at the intersection of the Yellowhead Highway (Hwy. 16) and Kalum Lake Drive (Nisga'a Hwy.). Follow the paved highway north along the Kalum River past Kalum Lake. Just past Rosswood is **Lava Lake** (where the park boundary begins). While there are a number of short interpretive trails to volcanic curiosities along the parkway, the primary hiking trail is the 3km (1.9-mile) **Volcanic Cone Trail,** which leads through old-growth forest to a volcanic crater. To protect the site, it is required that you hire a local guide; reservations are mandatory. There are scheduled 4-hour guided hikes at 10am Monday through Saturday from June 15 through Labour Day; the cost is C$30 adults. Call to schedule at the park office ©️ **250/638-8490.** Hikes depart from the **Nisga'a Visitor Centre** (©️ **250/638-9589;** www.env.gov.bc.ca/bcparks).

Continuing on Nisga'a Highway, the road picks its way across the lava flow. As you approach the Nass River, the road forks: To the left is the visitor center and to the right is the town of **New Aiyansh,** the valley's largest Nisga'a village, with basic facilities for travelers. The entire trip is 120km (75 miles); allow at least 2 hours each way.

The Nass River valley is the homeland of the Nisga'a indigenous peoples. In 1998, the Nisga'a and the Canadian federal government concluded an agreement that gives the Nisga'a tribe full title to about 2,000 sq. km (772 sq. miles) of land, a cash settlement, and powers of self-government.

Maps also show an unpaved road linking New Aiyansh with Hwy. 37 to the east. Called the Cranberry Connector by locals, it's a heavily rutted and pot-holed logging road that is perfectly passable but very slow going. If your destination is Stewart or Dease Lake, then it's worth inching your way across this shortcut (it will take about 2 hr. to make the 77km/48-mile journey to Cranberry Junction on Hwy. 37). If you are heading back toward the Hazeltons, however, you're better off returning to Terrace and driving at highway speed up Hwy. 16.

In winter, **Shames Mountain,** 35km (22 miles) west of town (©️ **877/898-4754** or 250/635-3773; www.shamesmountain.com), is known for its small crowds and huge quantities of snow. Open mid-December to mid-April, it has one double chair and one T-bar lift, along with 28 groomed trails. Lift tickets are C$42 for adults, C$32 for seniors and youths 13 to 18, and C$23 for children 7 to 12. Facilities include a rental and repair shop, store, cafeteria, and pub.

Seventy-five kilometers (47 miles) west of Terrace (48km/30 miles west of the Hazeltons) is the junction of Hwy. 16 and the Stewart-Cassair Highway (also labeled as Hwy. 37), one of two roads leading to the far north of British Columbia, eventually joining the famed Alaska Highway in the Yukon. This route is not as popular as the Alaska Highway, which begins farther east in Dawson Creek, though the scenery is more spectacular and the road conditions about the same. The route is now mostly paved, though there are a few gravel sections. Thus, expect delays due to road construction. To put it mildly, the winters up here are hard on the roads. It's a total of 718km (446 miles) between the Yellowhead Highway and the junction of the Alaska Highway near Watson Lake, in the Yukon.

Even if you don't want to drive all the way to the Yukon or Alaska, you should consider a side trip to the twin communities of **Stewart**, B.C., and **Hyder**, Alaska, 153km (95 miles) north on the Stewart-Cassair Highway to Meziadin Junction, then 64km (40 miles) west on Hwy. 37A. What a drive! These two, boundary-straddling villages lie at the head of the Portland Canal, a very long and narrow fjord—in fact the world's fourth longest. The setting—the two ports huddle below high-flying peaks and massive glaciers—is alone worth the drive.

From Meziadin Junction, Hwy. 37A immediately arches up to cross the mighty glacier-choked Coast Mountains, before plunging precipitously down to sea level at Stewart. You'll want to stop at the Bear Glacier Rest Area, where massive **Bear Glacier**—glowing an eerie, aqua blue—descends into Strohn Lake, frequently bobbing with icebergs. Watch mountain goats and bears along this stretch of road.

Stewart (pop. 900) is Canada's most northerly ice-free port, and is now a major copper-mining center. The tidy little town contrasts vividly with Hyder (pop. 70), Stewart's grubby Alaskan cousin: One feels like it's an outpost of an empire, the other feels like it's the end of the road. Facilities are basic but serviceable; the best place to stay is the **King Edward Hotel and Motel,** in Stewart, on Fifth Avenue (© **800/663-2126** in B.C., or 250/636-2244; www.kingedwardhotel.com), which has double rooms for C$69 to C$119.

THE HAZELTONS

The Skeena and Bulkley rivers join at the Hazeltons (pop. 2,000). Straddling two river canyons and set below the rugged Rocher de Boule mountains, the Hazeltons are actually three separate towns: **Hazelton** itself, **South Hazelton,** and **New Hazelton,** all located along an 8km (5-mile) stretch. The junction of these two mighty rivers was home to the Gitxsan and Wet'suwet'en peoples, for whom the rivers provided both transport and a wealth of salmon. In the 1860s, it became the upriver terminus for riverboat traffic on the Skeena, and Hazelton became a commercial hub for miners, ranchers, and other frontier settlers farther inland.

The old town center of Hazelton, though small, still has the feel of a pioneer settlement. And you can get a sense of the Gitxsan culture by visiting **'Ksan Historical Village ★★**, off Hwy. 62 (© **877/842-5518** or 250/842-5544; www.ksan.org), a re-creation of a traditional village. Some of the vividly painted longhouses serve as studios, where you can watch artists carve masks and hammer silver jewelry. If possible, plan your visit to coincide with a performance by the **'Ksan Performing Arts Group,** a troupe of singers and dancers who entertain visitors with music, masks, costumes, and pageantry. The shop here is a great source for Native art and gifts, and the Wilp Tokx, or the House of Eating, is a good place to try Native cooking. There's a C$2 admission for entrance to a small museum and the grounds themselves. To see the interior of the longhouses, you'll need to join a guided tour, which costs C$10 for adults, C$8.50 for seniors and students. If you take the tour, you don't have to pay the grounds fee. 'Ksan is open from April through September daily from 9am to 5pm. The rest of the year, only the museum and shop are open, Monday through Friday from 9:30am to 4:30pm.

There aren't many lodging choices, but the **28 Inn,** 4545 Yellowhead Hwy. 16, New Hazelton (✆ **877/842-2828** or 250/842-6006; www.28inn.com), with a dining room and pub, is clearly the best, with rooms going for C$74 double. The area's best dining room is the **Hummingbird Restaurant,** 2720 Hwy. 62 (✆ **250/842-5628**), which serves German specialties. It's open nightly for dinner, weekdays for lunch, and Sunday for brunch.

The **'Ksan Historical Village** (see above) and **Seeley Lake Provincial Park,** 9.5km (6 miles) west of New Hazelton (✆ **250/847-7320**), have campgrounds. For advance information on the area, call the **Hazeltons Travel Info Centre** (✆ **250/842-6071** in summer, 250/842-6571 Oct–May). The summer-only **visitor center** is at the junction of highways 16 and 62 (Main St.).

SMITHERS & THE BULKLEY VALLEY

Smithers (pop. 6,200) is located in a stunningly beautiful valley that truly resembles the northern Alps. Flanked on three sides by vast ranges of glaciated peaks, it is cut through by the fast-flowing Bulkley River. The heart of Smithers occupies the old commercial strip on **Main Street,** which is perpendicular to the current fast-food and motel haven that is Hwy. 16. This attractive area is lined with Bavarian-theme storefronts that offer outdoor gear, gifts, and local crafts. But what Smithers really has to offer is found in its gorgeous mountain backdrop. With 2,621m (8,599-ft.) **Hudson Bay Mountain** rising directly behind the town, snowcapped ranges ringing the valley, and the area's fast-flowing rivers and streams, you'll feel the urge to get outdoors.

Driftwood Canyon Provincial Park, 11km (6¾ miles) northeast of Smithers, preserves fossil-bearing formations laid down 50 million years ago. Considered one of the world's richest fossil beds, the park has interpretive trails leading through a section of exposed creek bed, which was carved by an ice-age glacier. To get here, drive 3km (1¾ miles) east of Smithers and turn east on Babine Lake Road.

Regional information can be obtained from the **Smithers Visitor Info Centre,** 1411 Court St. (✆ **800/542-6673** or 250/847-3337; www.tourismsmithers.com). Hours are 9am to 8pm Monday to Saturday mid-May to October 1.

Outdoor Pursuits

FISHING The Bulkley River has excellent fishing for steelhead, chinook, and coho salmon, though restrictions apply. The best fishing areas on the Bulkley are from the confluence of the Morice River south of Smithers to the town of Telkwa.

HIKING The 9km (5.6-mile) **Perimeter Trail** is a good place to jog; especially along the Bulkley River in Riverside Park. Two excellent hikes are on **Hudson Bay Mountain.** Three kilometers (1¾ miles) west of Smithers, take Kathlyn Lake Road 10km (6¼ miles) to the trail head. It's an easy .8km (.5-mile) stroll to view the impressive **Twin Falls.** From the same trail head, climb up to Glacier Gulch to get close to the toe of **Kathlyn Glacier.** This strenuous hike is just under 6.4km (4 miles) one-way, but allow at least 3 hours to make the climb.

Follow Hudson Bay Mountain Road west out of Smithers for 10km (6¼ miles) to **Smithers Community Forest,** with an extensive trail system. The easy 4km (2.5-mile) Interpretive Nature Trail makes a loop through the forest. For more rugged hiking, **Babine Mountains Recreation Area** protects 32,400 hectares (80,062 acres) of subalpine meadows, lakes, and craggy peaks. This roadless area is accessible only on foot, but many sights are within the range of day hikers. The **Silver King Basin Trail** passes through subalpine forest before reaching an alpine meadow that explodes with wildflowers in July. To reach the Babine Mountains, go 3km (1¾ miles) east of Smithers and take Babine Lake Road.

Where to Stay

The well-maintained **Aspen Motor Inn,** 4268 Hwy. 16 (© **800/663-7676** or 250/847-4551; www.hiway16.com/aspen), offers an on-site restaurant and large rooms from C$80. **Riverside Park Municipal Campsite,** 1600 Main St. N. (© **250/847-1600**), has 40 sites starting at C$14 with dry toilets, fire pits, and water.

Hudson Bay Lodge The largest and most comfortable hotel in Smithers, this is a popular stop for the tour-bus crowds making their way to and from the Prince Rupert ferries. The crowds notwithstanding, the facilities here are high quality. The lodge has three restaurants, including the fine-dining **Pepper Jack's Grill,** which offers well-prepared steak and seafood.

3251 Hwy. 16 E. (Box 3636), Smithers, BC V0J 2N0. © **800/663-5040** or 250/847-4581. Fax 250/847-4878. www.hudsonbaylodge.com. 96 units. From C$125 double. AE, DC, MC, V. **Amenities:** 2 restaurants; pub w/dining service; Jacuzzi; liquor store. In room: A/C, TV w/pay movies, hair dryer, Wi-Fi.

Stork Nest Inn ⟨**Value**⟩ The Stork Nest does more than most Smithers lodgings to look Bavarian, with gables, flowers, and a corbeled roofline. Though the rooms aren't the largest in the province, they are clean, pleasant, and nicely furnished. The honeymoon suite features a Jacuzzi, and wheelchair-accessible rooms are available.

1485 Main St. (Box 2049), Smithers, BC V0J 2N0. © **250/847-3831.** Fax 250/847-3852. www.storknestinn. com. 23 units. C$95–C$105 double. Rates include full breakfast. AE, MC, V. Free parking. **Amenities:** Sauna; rooms for those w/limited mobility. In room: A/C, TV, fridge, hair dryer (on request), Wi-Fi.

Where to Dine

The **Alpenhorn Pub and Bistro,** 1261 Main St. (© **250/847-5366**), is a pleasant, sports-bar type of pub with gourmet burgers, pastas, sandwiches, and ribs. It's open daily from 11am to midnight.

THE LAKES DISTRICT

Between Smithers and Prince George lies a vast basin filled with glacier-gouged lakes, dense forests, and rolling mountains. There are over 300 lakes, whose combined shorelines add up to more than 4,800km (2,983 miles). Not surprisingly, sportfishing is the main draw here, and rustic fishing lodges are scattered along the lakeshores.

But this isn't an easy place to plan a casual visit. Many of the lodges are fly-in or boat-in, and offer only weeklong fishing packages. Most are very rustic indeed. If this is what you're looking for, contact the Burns Lake Chamber of Commerce (see below), which can connect you with the lodge or outfitter that suits your needs.

If you have a day to spare and want to explore the region, there's a paved loop starting in Burns Lake that explores the shores of four of the lakes. Take Hwy. 35 south from Burns Lake, past Tchesinkut Lake to Northbank on François Lake. From here, take the free half-hour ferry across François Lake and continue south to Ootsa Lake. Here, the road turns west, eventually returning to François Lake, Hwy. 16 at Houston, and then back east to Burns Lake.

Burns Lake is nominally the center of the Lakes District, and if you end up here needing a place to stay, try the **Burns Lake Motor Inn,** on Hwy. 16 W. (© **800/663-2968** or 250/692-7545). For information on the region, contact the **Burns Lake Visitor Centre,** 540 Yellowhead Hwy. (© **250/692-3773**), open in July and August daily and year-round at varying times; call for hours.

At Vanderhoof, 133km (83 miles) east of Burns Lake, take Hwy. 27 north 59km (37 miles) to **Fort St. James National Historic Site ★** (© **250/996-7191**), one of the most interesting historic sites in northern British Columbia. Fort St. James was the earliest non-Native settlement in the province, a fur-trading fort established in 1806. In summer, costumed docents act out the roles of traders, craftsmen, and explorers. The park is open daily mid-May through September from 9am to 5pm. Summer admission is C$7.80 for adults, C$6.55 for seniors, C$3.90 for youths 6 to 16, and C$20 for families. Free audio-guided tours of the grounds are available in winter; call ahead to request one.

---

5 PRINCE GEORGE

396km (246 miles) W of Jasper, Alberta; 756km (470 miles) E of Prince Rupert

The largest city in northern British Columbia, Prince George (pop. 82,000) makes a natural base for exploring the sights and recreational opportunities of the province's north-central region, which is filled with forested mountains, lakes, and mighty rivers.

There has been settlement at the junction of the Fraser and Nechako rivers for millennia; the two river systems were as much a transportation corridor for the early First Nations people as for the European settlers who came later. A trading post was established in the early 1800s; the Grand Trunk Railroad, which passed through here in 1914, put Prince George on the map.

What makes the city's economic heart beat is lumber—and lots of it. Prince George is at the center of vast softwood forests, and three major mills here turn trees into pulp, and pulp into paper. The economic boom that these mills introduced has brought a relative degree of sophistication to the lumber town—there's a civic art gallery, good restaurants, and the University of Northern British Columbia.

ESSENTIALS

GETTING THERE By Plane Air Canada Jazz (© 888/247-2262; www.flyjazz.ca) provides daily service to Prince George to/from Vancouver. **WestJet** (© 888/937-8538; www.westjet.com) also serves Prince George, offering economical flights to the rest of Canada.

By Train The *Skeena* run on **VIA Rail** (© 800/561-8630; www.viarail.ca), which operates between Prince Rupert and Jasper, stops overnight in Prince George. Connections to the main VIA Vancouver-Toronto line are available at Jasper. Although the Rocky Mountaineer's Fraser Discovery Route excursion train passes through Prince George, it doesn't stop and isn't an option for travelers bound for northern B.C.

By Bus Greyhound Canada (© 800/661-8747 or 604/482-8747; www.greyhound.ca) serves Prince George with daily buses from Vancouver. Fares begin at C$83. Greyhound also offers daily buses between Prince Rupert and Jasper along the Yellowhead Highway.

By Car Prince George is about a third of the way across the province on the east-west Yellowhead Highway (Hwy. 16). South from Prince George, Hwy. 97 drops through the

Cariboo District on its way to Kelowna (712km/442 miles) and Vancouver (via Hwy. 1, 808km/502 miles). From Prince George, you can also follow Hwy. 97 north to join the Alaska Highway at Dawson Creek (421km/262 miles).

VISITOR INFORMATION Contact the **Prince George Visitor Info Centre,** 1300 First Ave. (© **800/668-7646** or 250/562-3700; www.tourismpg.com). It's open daily from 9am to 6pm.

GETTING AROUND The local bus system is operated by **Prince George Transit** (© 250/563-0011). For a cab, call **Emerald Taxi** (© 250/563-3333) or **Prince George Taxi Holdings** (© 250/564-4444).

Car-rental agencies include **Avis** (© 800/272-5871 in Canada, 800/230-4898 in the U.S.; www.avis.com), **Budget** (© 800/268-8900 in Canada, 800/527-0700 in the U.S.; www.budget.com), **Hertz** (© 800/263-0600 or 250/963-7454; www.hertz.com), **National** (© 800/CAR-RENT [227-7368] in Canada and the U.S.; www.nationalcar. com), and **Thrifty** (© 800/THRIFTY [847-4389] or 250/963-8711; www.thrifty.com).

EXPLORING THE AREA

Downtown Prince George is located on a spur of land at the confluence of the Fraser and Nechako rivers. The old commercial district at first seems a bit forlorn, but a stroll around the city center—concentrated along Third Avenue and George Street—reveals a down-and-dirty charm that's reminiscent of towns in the Yukon or Northwest Territories. And the prevalence of tattoo parlors, pawnshops, and old-fashioned coffee shops enhances the impression of a rough-and-ready frontier community.

The **Two Rivers Gallery** (© **888/221-1155** or 250/614-7800; www.tworiversart gallery.com) occupies a stylish space in the Civic Centre Plaza, at Patricia Boulevard and Dominion Street. This architecturally innovative, C$5-million structure showcases the work of local and regional artists. There's also a sculpture garden, gift shop, and cafe. Hours are Monday through Saturday from 10am to 5pm, Sunday from noon to 5pm. Admission is C$5 for adults, C$4 for seniors and students, and C$2 for children 5 to 12. After viewing the gallery, cross Patricia Street and wander the trails in **Connaught Hill Park.** From the top of the hill are good views of the Fraser River and downtown.

The **Prince George Native Art Gallery,** 1600 Third Ave. (© **250/614-7726;** www. pgnfc.com), is part of the local First Nations community center. At this sales gallery, you can view birch-bark biting art, cedar-wood carvings, beadwork, and limited-edition prints by regional Native artists. The gallery is a good place to pick up gifts and curios of your trip. It's open Tuesday through Friday from 9am to 5pm and Saturday from 10am to 4pm, with extended summer hours possible.

There are more than 120 parks within the city limits, many of them linked by the Heritage River Trails system. The best is 36-hectare (89-acre) **Fort George Park,** on the site of the original fur-trading post. On the grounds are a First Nations burial ground, a miniature railway, a one-room schoolhouse, and the **Exploration Place** (© **250/562-1612;** www.theexplorationplace.com), a kid-focused science and nature museum. Adults will enjoy the history gallery, which details the customs of the region's Native Carrier people, and moves on to tell the story of the fur-trading and logging past. There are also numerous interactive science exhibits; an Internet cafe; and a SimEx theater, in which viewers' seats move in tandem with motions in films. Admission is C$8.95 for adults, C$6.95 for seniors and students, C$5.95 for children 2 to 12, or C$21 per family; there are also combo tickets that include admission to SimEx films. It's open daily 10am to 5pm from mid-May through mid-October, the same hours Wednesday through Sunday the rest of the year. The park is on the Fraser River end of 20th Avenue; from downtown, take Queensway Street south, then turn east on 20th Avenue.

The **Heritage River Trails** take you on an 11km (6.8-mile) circuit covering the historic sights of town. The loop starts at Fort George Park, goes along the Fraser River, passes through Cottonwood Island Park and along the Nechako River to the Cameron Street bridge, and leads through town and back to Fort George Park.

WHERE TO STAY

If you're looking for a bed-and-breakfast, try the **Prince George B&B Hot Line** (✆ **877/562-2626** or 250/562-2222; www.princegeorgebnb.com).

Coast Inn of the North ★   One of the best of British Columbia's Coast hotel chain is right in the thick of things in downtown Prince George. The guest rooms are nicely furnished; the corner suites are large, with king-size beds, a balcony, and lots of light and space (some suites have Jacuzzis). Among the numerous facilities is an indoor pool. Small pets are allowed in the guest rooms.

770 Brunswick St., Prince George, BC V2L 2C2. ✆ **800/663-1144** or 250/563-0121. Fax 250/563-1948. www.coasthotels.com. 155 units. C$140–C$175 double. Extra person C$10. Family plan, corporate and off-season rates, and senior and AAA discounts available. AE, MC, V. Free parking with engine heater plug-ins. **Amenities:** 3 restaurants; pub; dance club; exercise room; Jacuzzis; indoor pool; room service; saunas. *In room:* A/C, TV, hair dryer, minibar, Wi-Fi.

Four Points by Sheraton Prince George ★★   The newest hotel in Prince George, the sleek new Four Points has lots going for it in addition to its relative youth. The rooms are large and very nicely furnished, and the hotel is located just west of the old downtown area. The staff goes out of its way to make you feel welcome, and the pool and exercise room are particularly tip-top. If you're here on business, the suites offer lots of room and amenities for road warriors.

1790 Hwy. 97 S., Prince George, BC V2L 5L3. ✆ **800/368-7764** or 250/564-7100. Fax 250/564-7199. 74 units. From C$139 double; from C$170 suite. AE, MC, V. Free parking. **Amenities:** Restaurant; exercise room; pool. *In room:* A/C, TV, fridge, hair dryer, Wi-Fi, microwave.

Goldcap Travelodge (Value)   If you're looking for value, it's hard to beat the large, clean, unfussy rooms at the Travelodge, right downtown. Kitchen units with microwaves and fridges are available for a small extra fee. An on-site family restaurant is open for three meals daily.

1458 Seventh Ave., Prince George, BC V2L 3P3. ✆ **800/663-8239** or 250/563-0666. Fax 250/563-5775. www.travelodgeprincegeorge.com. 77 units. C$90–C$125 double. Kitchens available for C$10. Off-season rates and senior discounts available. AE, MC, V. Free parking. Pets accepted. **Amenities:** Restaurant; sauna. *In room:* A/C, TV, fridge, microwave.

Ramada Hotel (Downtown Prince George) ★   The grandest of hotels in Prince George, the Ramada offers a variety of top-notch rooms—from standard to presidential— right in the center of the city. The Tower Suites, with a selection of large business and specialty suites that offer free breakfast and high-end toiletries, were refurbished in 2007. Some units have Jacuzzis; all have heated bathroom floors.

444 George St., Prince George, BC V2L 1R6. ✆ **800/830-8833** or 250/563-0055. Fax 250/563-6042. www.ramadaprincegeorge.com. 193 units. C$105–C$169 double. Extra person C$20. Senior discounts available. AE, DC, DISC, MC, V. Free secure, covered parking. Valet parking available. **Amenities:** Restaurant; bar; exercise room; Jacuzzi; large indoor pool; room service; rooms for those w/limited mobility. *In room:* A/C, TV w/pay movies, Wi-Fi.

Kids Family Fun

The **Ol' Sawmill Bluegrass Jamboree** (📞 250/564-8573), held 26km (16 miles) up North Nechako Road in mid-August, is a musical event for the whole family, with weekend camping, music workshops, arts and crafts, play areas for the kids, and many talented bluegrass performers.

Sandman Inn   Along Hwy. 97 west of downtown, the inn offers large, comfortable guest rooms including one- and two-bedroom suites. Kitchenettes and wheelchair-accessible units are available. A 24-hour Denny's restaurant is on-site. For a comfortable room that avoids downtown, this is a good choice.

1650 Central St., Prince George, BC V2M 3C2. 📞 800/SANDMAN (726-3626) or 250/563-8131. Fax 250/563-8613. www.sandmanhotels.com. 144 units. C$124–C$174 double. Senior and AAA discounts available. AE, DC, DISC, MC, V. Small pets allowed for C$5 per day. **Amenities:** Restaurant; indoor pool; room service; sauna; rooms for those w/limited mobility. *In room:* A/C, TV, hair dryer, Wi-Fi.

WHERE TO DINE

For a light meal, head to **Javva Mugga Mocha,** 304 George St. (📞 250/562-3338), a fun hangout for espresso drinks, sandwiches, and baked goods. **Cimo Mediterranean Grill,** 601 Victoria St. (📞 250/564-7975), is a good spot for hand-made pasta.

North 45 ★ CONTEMPORARY CANADIAN   This bustling dining room serves pasta, seafood, and local meats in innovative, Mediterranean-influenced preparations that seem refreshing in northern B.C. The appetizers are tempting, and a couple of these—perhaps bruschetta topped with shrimp, scallops, and tomatoes, and a beef carpaccio with truffle oil, capers, and wild mushrooms—could make a meal. But don't miss out on pasta dishes such as smoked salmon, chives, and lemon cream sauce with tagliolini. The steaks are just fine, mind you, but a real standout for meat eaters is grilled duck breast with figs. Then again, the selection of entree salads might be what you're looking for after a few days of travel in the carnivorous north.

1493 3rd Ave. 📞 250/564-5400. Reservations suggested. Main courses C$14–C$35. MC, V. Mon–Fri 11:30am–2pm and 5–9pm; Sat 5–9pm.

Ric's Grill STEAKHOUSE   This chic dining room serves an expanded steak and chop menu that mixes old-fashioned meat and potatoes with imaginative New Canadian cuisine. Ric's also features an impressive selection of fish and shellfish dishes, plus pasta, chicken, and salads. It's a stylish and friendly spot for dinner.

547 George St. 📞 250/614-9096. Reservations suggested. Main courses C$14–C$40. AE, MC, V. Sun–Tues 4:30–10pm; Wed–Thurs 11:30am–10pm; Fri 11:30am–11pm; Sat 4:30–11pm; Sun 4:30–10pm.

Waddling Duck Restaurant ★ PUB   The Waddling Duck looks like an old English pub, complete with exposed beams, stone walls, and a huge fireplace, but the food is up-to-date and sure to please. Entrees include burgers, pizza, steaks, fresh fish, and imaginative dishes like pork loin stuffed with prosciutto, apple, and Stilton cheese. The Waddling Duck also offers a number of vegetarian options; at lunch, try the C$10 all-you-can-eat buffet. Service is very friendly and professional.

1157 Fifth Ave. 📞 250/561-5550. Reservations not needed. Main courses C$10–C$23. MC, V. Daily 11am–10pm.

6 THE ALASKA HIGHWAY

Constructed as a military freight road during World War II to link Alaska to the Lower 48, the Alaska Highway—also known as the Alcan Highway, and Hwy. 97 in British Columbia—has become something of a pilgrimage route for recent retirees.

Strictly speaking, the Alaska Highway starts at Mile 1 marker in **Dawson Creek,** on the eastern edge of British Columbia, and travels north and west for 2,242km (1,393 miles) to **Delta Junction,** in Alaska, passing through the Yukon along the way. The **Richardson Highway** (Alaska Rte. 4) covers the additional 158km (98 miles) from Delta Junction to **Fairbanks.**

Popular wisdom states that if you drive straight out, it takes 3 days between Dawson Creek and Fairbanks. However, this is a very *long* winding road, and RV traffic is heavy. If you try to keep yourself to a 3-day schedule, you'll have a miserable time.

WHAT TO EXPECT

Summer is the only opportunity to repair the road, so construction crews really go to it; you can count on lengthy delays and some very rugged detours. Visitor centers along the way get notifications of daily construction schedules and conditions, so stop for updates, or follow the links to "Road Conditions" from the website **www.themilepost.com.** You can also call © **867/456-7623** for 24-hour highway information.

Although there's gas at most of the communities that appear on the road map, most close up early in the evening, and gas prices can be substantially higher than in, say, Edmonton or Calgary. You'll find 24-hour gas stations and plenty of motel rooms in the towns of Dawson City, Fort St. John, Fort Nelson, Watson Lake, and Whitehorse.

Try to be patient when driving the Alaska Highway. In high season, the entire route, from Edmonton to Fairbanks, is one long caravan of RVs. Many people have their car in tow, a boat on the roof, and several bicycles chained to the spare tire. Thus encumbered, they lumber up the highway; loath (or unable) to pass one another. These convoys of RVs stretch on forever, the slowest of the party setting the pace for all.

DRIVING THE ALASKA HIGHWAY

This overview of the Alaska Highway is not meant to serve as a detailed guide for drivers. For that, you should purchase the annual *Alaska Milepost* (www.themilepost.com), which offers exhaustive, mile-by-mile coverage of the trip (and of other road trips into the Arctic of Alaska and Canada).

The route begins (or ends) at **Dawson Creek,** in British Columbia. Depending on where you join the journey, Dawson Creek is a long 590km (367-mile) drive from Edmonton or a comparatively short 406km (252 miles) from Prince George on Hwy. 97. Dawson Creek is a natural place to break up the journey, with ample tourist facilities. If you want to call ahead to ensure a room, try the **Ramada Limited Dawson Creek,** 1748 Alaska Ave. (© **800/663-2749** or 250/782-8595).

From Dawson Creek, the Alaska Highway soon crosses the Peace River and passes through **Fort St. John,** in the heart of British Columbia's far-north ranch country. The highway continues north, parallel to the Rockies. First the ranches thin, and then the forests thin. Moose are often seen from the road.

From Fort St. John to **Fort Nelson,** you'll find gas stations and cafes every 65 to 80km (40–50 miles), though lodging options are pretty dubious. Fort Nelson is thick with motels and gas stations; because it's hours from any other major service center, this is a good place to spend the night. Try the **Fort Nelson Travelodge Hotel,** 4711 50th Ave. S. (© **888/515-6375** or 250/774-3911).

At Fort Nelson, the Alaska Highway turns west and heads into the Rockies; from here, too, graveled **Liard Highway** (B.C. Hwy. 77; Northern Territories Hwy. 7) continues north to Fort Liard and Fort Simpson, the gateway to **Nahanni National Park,** a very worthy side trip.

From Fort Nelson, the Alaska Highway through the Rockies is mostly narrow and winding—and likely to be under construction. Once over the Continental Divide, the Alaska Highway follows tributaries of the Liard River through **Stone Mountain** and **Muncho Lake** provincial parks. Rustic lodges are scattered along the road. The lovely log **Northern Rockies Lodge** ★, at Muncho Lake (© **800/663-5269** or 250/776-3481; www.northern-rockies-lodge.com), offers lakeside lodge rooms, log cabins, and campsites.

At the town of **Liard River,** stop and stretch your legs or go for a soak in the two deep-forest soaking pools at **Liard Hot Springs.** The boardwalk out into the mineral-water marsh is pleasant even if you don't have time for a dip.

As you get closer to **Watson Lake** in the Yukon, you'll notice that mom-and-pop gas stations along the road will advertise that they have cheaper gas than at Watson Lake. Believe them, and fill up: Watson Lake is an unappealing town whose extortionately priced gas is probably its only memorable feature. The truth in advertising award goes to **A Nice Motel** (© **867/536-7222**), a very nicely furnished lodging that's easy to miss behind the local Petro Canada gas station at 609 Frank Trail, where you sign in for the motel. Don't worry—the rooms are easily the best in Watson Lake.

The long road between Watson Lake and **Whitehorse** travels through forests and rolling hills to Teslin and Atlin lakes, where the landscape becomes more mountainous and the gray clouds of the Gulf of Alaska's weather systems hang menacingly on the horizon. Whitehorse is the largest town along the route of the Alaska Highway, and unless you're in a great hurry, plan to spend at least a day here.

Hope for good weather as you leave Whitehorse; the trip past **Kluane National Park** is one the most beautiful parts of the entire route. Tucked into the southwestern corner of the Yukon, a 2-hour drive from Whitehorse, these 22,015 sq. km (8,500 sq. miles) of glaciers, marshes, mountains, and sand dunes are unsettled and virtually untouched—and designated as a **UNESCO World Heritage Site.** Bordering on Alaska in the west, Kluane contains **Mount Logan** and **Mount St. Elias,** respectively the second- and third-highest peaks in North America. (Denali is the highest.)

Because Kluane is largely undeveloped, casual exploration is limited to a few day-hiking trails and aerial sightseeing trips. The vast expanse of ice and rock in the heart of the wilderness is well beyond striking range of the average outdoor enthusiast. The area's white-water rapids are world-class but, likewise, not for the uninitiated. For more information on recreation in Kluane, see the website at **www.pc.gc.ca/eng/pn-np/yt/kluane/index.aspx**.

After Kluane, the Alaska Highway edges by Kluane Lake before passing Beaver Creek and crossing over into Alaska. From the border to Fairbanks is another 481km (299 miles).

12

The Cariboo Country & the Thompson River Valley

South of Prince George along Hwy. 97 and beyond into British Columbia's interior, the Canadian Wild West hasn't changed much in the past century. This is Cariboo Country, a vast landscape that changes from alpine meadows and thick forests to rolling prairies and arid canyons before it encounters the gigantic glacial peaks of the Coast Mountains. The Cariboo's history is synonymous with the word *gold*.

From Vancouver, the Sea-to-Sky Highway (Hwy. 99) passes through Whistler and the Cayoosh Valley, eventually descending into the town of Lillooet, which was Mile 0 of the Old Cariboo Highway during the gold-rush days of the 1860s. Prospectors and settlers made their way north up what's now called the Cariboo Gold Rush Trail (Hwy. 99 and Hwy. 97).

Hwy. 97 follows the gold-rush trail through the towns of 70 Mile House, 100 Mile House, 108 Mile House, and 150 Mile House. The towns were named after the mile-marking roadhouses patronized by prospectors and settlers headed north to the gold fields.

The gold-rich town of Barkerville sprang up in the 1860s after a British prospector named Billy Barker struck it rich on Williams Creek. Completely restored, the town brings the rough gold-rush days to life. The streets are only 5.5m (18 ft.) wide, thanks to a drunken surveyor. Nowadays, you can try your hand at panning for the shiny gold flakes and nuggets that still lie deep within Williams Creek.

Gold isn't the only thing that attracts thousands of visitors to this area. Cross-country skiers and snowmobilers take to the creek-side paths in winter; canoeists head a few miles north of Barkerville to a 120km (75-mile) circular route called Bowron Lakes.

From Williams Lake, back-roads enthusiasts can also drive Hwy. 20 west to the Pacific coastal community of Bella Coola, which in the early days of European exploration was one of the most important First Nations communities on the coast. From Bella Coola, you can catch the Discovery Coast ferry to Port Hardy on the northern tip of Vancouver Island (see chapter 11).

Due east, on the opposite side of Cariboo Country, the Thompson River valley's arid lowlands attract fishers and boaters to the shores of the lower Thompson River and the Shuswap Lakes. Heading north from this dry terrain, you'll reach a majestic 1.3-million-hectare (3.2-million-acre) forested mountain wilderness formed by glaciers and volcanoes—Wells Gray Provincial Park.

1 CARIBOO COUNTRY ESSENTIALS

GETTING THERE

Whether you travel by train or by car, the trip from Whistler to Cariboo Country is a visually exhilarating experience.

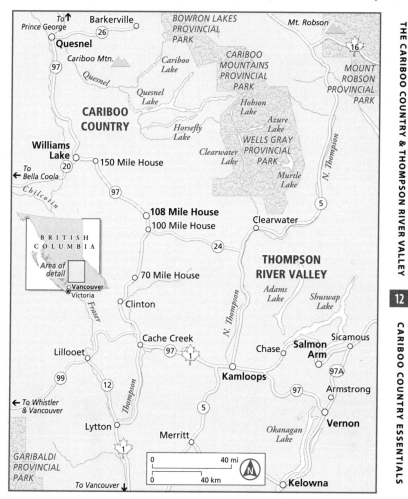

BY CAR   The shortest and most scenic route from Vancouver is along Hwy. 99 (the Sea-to-Sky Hwy.) past Whistler to Lillooet, continuing to Hwy. 97 and turning north to 100 Mile House and points north. From Vancouver to Quesnel, it's 600km (373 miles). If you want to bypass the dramatic but slow Hwy. 99 and head straight up to the central Cariboo district, you can take the Hwy. 1 expressway east from Vancouver, then jump onto Hwy. 97 at Merritt.

BY TRAIN   For decades, **BC Rail** operated the *Cariboo Prospector,* which linked Vancouver to Prince George with stops in other towns in the Cariboo Country. In 2002, however, BC Rail discontinued passenger service along this route. **Rocky Mountaineer**

Vacations (© 877/460-3200 or 604/606-7245), which operates the very successful excursion train service between Vancouver and Banff and Jasper in the Canadian Rockies, in 2006 began service along this route with its **Fraser Discovery Route** excursion trains. For information, go to **www.rockymountaineer.com**. The train departs from Whistler, with an overnight stop in Quesnel before continuing on to Jasper, where the train will link with other Rocky Mountaineer Vacations trains.

BY BUS **Greyhound Canada** (© 800/661-8747; www.greyhound.ca) travels from Vancouver through the Cariboo to Prince George via highways 1 and 97, passing through Kamloops, 100 Mile House, Williams Lake, and Quesnel. Note that these routes do not pass through Lillooet, which has no bus service.

BY PLANE **Central Mountain Air** (© 888/865-8585; www.flycma.com) offers daily service between Quesnel and Vancouver. It also offers daily flights between Williams Lake and Vancouver. **Pacific Coastal Air** (© 800/663-2872 or 604/273-8666; www. pacific-coastal.com) links Vancouver to Anahim Lake, Bella Coola, and Williams Lake.

VISITOR INFORMATION

Contact the **Cariboo Chilcotin Coast Tourist Association,** 118A N. First Ave., Williams Lake, BC V2G 1Y8 (© 800/663-5885 or 250/392-2226; www.landwithoutlimits.com).

2 EN ROUTE TO 100 MILE HOUSE

There's nothing subtle about the physical setting of **Lillooet** (pop. 2,058). To the west, the soaring glaciated peaks of the Coast Mountains dominate the sky. To the east rise the steep desert walls of the Fountain Range, stained with rusty red and ocher. Cleaving the two mountain ranges is the massive and roaring Fraser River. From the peaks of the Coast Range to the riverbed is a drop of nearly 2,700m (8,858 ft.)—all of this making for an incredibly dramatic backdrop to the town.

In 1858, a trail was cut from the Fraser Valley goldfields in the south to the town of Lillooet, later established as Mile 0 of the 1860s **Cariboo Gold Rush Trail.** At the big bend on Main Street, a cairn marks MILE 0 of the original Cariboo Wagon Road.

From Lillooet, Hwy. 99 heads north along the Fraser River Canyon, affording many dramatic vistas before turning east to its junction with Hwy. 97. Thirty kilometers (19 miles) north on Hwy. 97 is **Clinton,** the self-avowed "guest-ranch capital of British Columbia." This is certainly handsome ranch country, with broad cattle- and horse-filled valleys rolling between dry mountain walls.

Hat Creek Ranch Now a provincial heritage site, Hat Creek Ranch was built in 1861 and served as a stagecoach inn for miners. This open-air museum of frontier life has more than 20 period buildings, including a blacksmith shop, barn, and stable. There's also a good exhibit on the culture of the region's First Nations Shuswap tribe. In summer, concessionaires operate horse-drawn wagon and horseback rides, plus a ranch-house restaurant. You can stroll the grounds year-round; however, regular visitor services and guided tours are offered only from mid-May to the end of September.

At junction of Hwy. 99 and Hwy. 97. © 800/782-0922 or 250/457-9722. www.hatcreekranch.com. Admission C$9 adults, C$8 seniors, C$6 children 6–12, C$20 families. May–Sept 30 daily 9am–5pm (July–Aug until 6pm).

Big Bar Guest Ranch (Kids)   A longtime favorite for horse-focused family vacations, the Big Bar is a comfortable destination with lots of recreational and lodging options. Summer activities include riding and pack trips, or you can canoe, fish, pan for gold, bike, and go for hayrides. In winter, the ranch remains open for cross-country skiing, snowshoeing, snowmobiling, and ice fishing. The centerpiece of the property is the hand-hewn log Harrison House, built in the early 1900s, which now serves as guest lounge, with a huge stone fireplace, and game area with pool and foosball tables. The Big Bar is the quintessential old-fashioned guest ranch—not a New Age lifestyle resort—where lots of attention is spent on the quality of the horses and the wranglers. Guests will enjoy the family-style meals after a hearty day of horseback riding or hiking. In addition to 10 comfortable, no-fuss lodge rooms in the main lodge, there are 4 quite comfortable one-bedroom log cabins, each with a sleeping loft and fold-out couch, sleeping up to eight, with full kitchens and fireplaces. In addition, other lodging options include tepees, a six-bedroom lodge, and campsites. If you're looking for an Old West adventure, not just an opportunity to dress up in a Stetson and denim, then this might be the guest ranch for you.

54km (34 miles) northwest of Clinton off Hwy. 97. Mailing address: P.O. Box 27, Jesmond, BC V0K 1K0. ℭ 250/459-2333. Fax 250/459-2400. www.bigbarranch.com. 16 units, 4 cabins. C$240 double occupancy in lodge rooms, including 3 meals daily; C$189 double occupancy in cabin, meals not included; C$75 per person tepee, including meals. Extra person in cabin C$40 per person. C$81 child in lodge rooms. C$25 campground site for 2 tents or 1 RV. MC, V. **Amenities:** Dining room; fireside lounge; hot tub; playground; trail rides; fishing pond. *In room:* No phone.

Cariboo Lodge Resort ★   There's been a log lodge on this site for well over a century—the original was built to serve frontier trappers and miners. Times have changed, and so has the Cariboo Lodge. This modern log lodge and motel offers stylish, fully modern guest rooms plus an Old West pub (complete with stuffed heads) and restaurant; the resort makes a perfect base for exploring central British Columbia. The proprietors will organize horseback rides, rafting and mountain-biking tours, and cross-country ski trips. Rooms are large and nicely furnished—without the Old West clutter you'd normally expect in such a place.

1414 Cariboo Hwy., Box 459, Clinton, BC V0K 1K0. ℭ 877/459-7992 or 250/459-7992. www.cariboo lodgebc.com. 20 units. From C$74 double. MC, V. **Amenities:** Restaurant; pub; liquor store. *In room:* A/C, TV, fridge, microwave.

Echo Valley Ranch and Spa ★ (Finds)   East meets West at this remarkable resort, which is both amazingly sumptuous and rather mannered. Occupying a scenic plateau with views over the Fraser River valley, Echo Valley Ranch combines features of a traditional guest ranch—horseback riding and hiking—with Thai and European spa facilities. Guest rooms are in two central lodges—three-story log buildings straight out of *House Beautiful*—or in individual cabins. Even more astonishing is the Baan Thai building, a massive four-story log structure that's half American West, half Thai palace, which contains VIP lodging, conference rooms, and Thai spa treatment space. Guest rooms are very comfortable, and meals are served family-style in the main lodge. Recreation opportunities include horseback riding, hiking, rafting, mountain biking, pack trips, and gold panning. Spa facilities include an indoor pool and Jacuzzi, plus a full selection of therapeutic, aesthetic, and hydrotherapy treatments featuring standard therapies plus Thai stretching and massage. This isn't your typical guest ranch, but if you're looking for upscale spa facilities plus horseback riding, this is the place for you. Check the website for 3- to 14-day spa and recreation packages.

50km (31 miles) northeast of Clinton. Mailing address: P.O. Box 16, Jesmond, BC V0K 1K0. ✆ **800/253-8831** or 250/459-2386. www.evranch.com. 20 units. June–Sept from C$299 per person based on double occupancy, 3-day minimum stay; Oct–May C$220 per person based on double occupancy, 3-day minimum stay. Nightly stays sometimes available; contact ranch 2 weeks before proposed arrival dates. Rates include all meals and access to all ranch facilities; horseback riding and guided activities are extra. Packages available. MC, V. Special kids weeks; otherwise children 13 and older only. **Amenities:** Restaurant; lounge; exercise room; Jacuzzi; indoor pool; sauna; spa. *In room:* Fridge, hair dryer, robes.

3 100 MILE HOUSE & THE SOUTH CARIBOO DISTRICT

100 Mile House: 174km (108 miles) N of Lillooet; 320km (199 miles) S of Prince George

Named for the roadhouse inn that marked the 100th mile north of Lillooet in the days of the Cariboo gold rush, 100 Mile House (pop. 1,978) is an attractive ranching community at the heart of a vast recreational paradise. There are thousands of lakes in the valleys that ring the town, making canoeing, fishing, and boating popular activities. In winter, the gently rolling landscape, combined with heavy snowfalls, make 100 Mile House a major cross-country ski destination.

Thirteen kilometers (8 miles) north is 108 Mile House, another frontier-era community now famed for its golf course and **108 Mile House Heritage Site** (✆ 250/791-5288). This collection of ranch buildings includes an enormous log barn built to stable 200 Clydesdales, the horsepower that drove the stagecoaches.

For information on this region, contact the **South Cariboo Visitor Info Centre,** 422 Hwy. 97 S., 100 Mile House (✆ **250/395-5353;** www.southcariboo.com).

FISHING & WATERSPORTS

100 Mile House is a pleasant enough little town, but it's the outdoor recreation in the surrounding South Cariboo Lakes District that brings most people here. There are dozens of lakes, nearly all with rustic fishing resorts as well as provincial parks offering campgrounds and public boat launches. Be sure to pick up the *Cariboo-Chilcotin Fishing Guide* at the visitor center. For tackle, licenses, and advice, head to **Donex Pharmacy,** 145 Birch St. (✆ **250/395-4004**).

One lake-filled area lies southeast of 100 Mile House along Hwy. 24, which connects Hwy. 97 with Hwy. 5 at Little Fort, on the Thompson River. This scenic drive climbs up along a high plateau between the watersheds of the Fraser and Thompson rivers. The road leads to so many excellent fishing lakes that it's often referred to as the "Fishing Highway."

On Sheridan Lake, the **Loon Bay Resort,** 40km (25 miles) southeast of 100 Mile House (✆ **250/593-4431;** www.loonbayresort.com), rents tackle, canoes, and motorboats; sells licenses; and maintains cabins (from C$70 double) and campsites.

Perhaps the most beautiful of all these lakes is **Lac des Roches,** 88km (55 miles) east of 100 Mile House. The handsome **Lac Des Roches Resort** (✆ **250/593-4141;** www.lacdesroches.com) offers boat rentals, campsites (C$15), and lakeside cabins (from C$89 double).

Northeast of 100 Mile House is another lake-filled valley. **Canim Lake** is the most developed, with good swimming beaches. The venerable **Ponderosa Resort** (☎ 250/397-2243; www.ponderosaresort.com) offers boat rentals, guided fishing, and horseback riding. Motel-style rooms are C$95, cabins are C$105 to C$120, and campsites are around C$25. At **Canim Beach Provincial Park,** 45km (28 miles) from 100 Mile House, campsites are C$14.

If you're looking for a wilderness canoeing experience, **Moose Valley Provincial Park** preserves a series of small glacial lakes that are linked by short portage trails. The most popular route begins at Marks Lake and links with 11 other lakes, making for a leisurely 2-day loop paddle. For more information, contact **BC Parks,** Cariboo District (☎ 250/398-4414; www.env.gov.bc.ca/bcparks).

OTHER OUTDOOR PURSUITS

CROSS-COUNTRY SKIING   In February, the town hosts the **Cariboo Marathon,** a 50km (31-mile) race that draws more than 1,000 contestants. There's an extensive public trail system with 200km (124 miles) of groomed trails in the area, with some parts lit at night. Many resorts and guest ranches also have groomed trails.

GOLF   The region's finest course is undoubtedly at **108 Ranch Resort,** in 108 Mile House (☎ 800/667-5233 or 250/791-5211; www.108resort.bcresorts.com). The 18-hole championship course has undulating fairways and fast putting greens. The resort offers a driving range, a pro shop, and lessons.

WHERE TO STAY & DINE

The shipshape **Red Coach Inn,** 170 Hwy. 97 N., 100 Mile House (☎ 800/663-8422 or 250/395-2266), offers rooms from C$67 to C$99, just a short walk from downtown.

Hills Health & Guest Ranch   This spa and guest ranch offers a full complement of beauty and health treatments as well as activities such as horseback riding, mountain biking, hayrides, downhill skiing on the ranch's own ski area, and cross-country skiing on 167km (more than 100 miles) of private trails. Popular activities include breakfast horseback rides, line-dancing lessons, and lake canoeing. The spa has a variety of offerings, including massage, facials, and reflexology. Also popular are 6- to 30-day weight-loss and physical therapy programs guided by professional nutritionists and therapists. Within the vast spa building are hydrotherapy pools, an aerobics gym, dry saunas, and 16 treatment rooms. The guest rooms are rather basic, featuring ranch-style natural pine decor; also available are three-bedroom chalets with kitchens. The lodge restaurant serves a unique blend of cowboy favorites and spa cuisine, specializing in fondue and hot-rock cooking. All programs, therapies, and activities can be customized to form your own personalized package vacation—this is an ambitious resort, with over 100 employees.

Hwy. 97; Box 26, 108 Mile Ranch, BC V0K 2Z0. ☎ 250/791-5225. Fax 250/791-6384. www.spabc.com. 46 units. From C$129 per person, based on double occupancy. 2-night minimum. All-inclusive packages available. AE, DISC, MC, V. **Amenities:** 2 restaurants; lounge; bike rentals; exercise room; nearby golf course; indoor pool; full-service spa; ski rentals. In room: A/C, TV, Wi-Fi.

108 Resort and Conference Centre ★   This upscale hotel and resort centers on its fantastic golf course, although even if you're not a duffer, there's a lot to like here. Other activities here include horseback riding, mountain biking, and canoeing. In winter, the golf course is transformed into a vast undulating cross-country center. Guest rooms are large and beautifully furnished, all with balconies that overlook either the golf course or a small lake. Golf, cross-country-skiing, and horseback-riding packages are available. The on-site clubhouse restaurant offers good Northwest cuisine.

13km (8 miles) north of 100 Mile House, 4618 Telqua Dr., Box 2, 108 Mile Ranch, BC V0K 2Z0. © **800/667-5233** or 250/791-5211. Fax 250/791-6537. www.108resort.bcresorts.com. 62 units and 11 campsites. C$119–C$135 double. Extra person C$20. Off-season rates and packages available. AE, MC, V. **Amenities:** Restaurant; bar; bike rentals; Jacuzzi; indoor pool; sauna; canoe rentals; stables. *In room:* A/C, TV, hair dryer, kitchenette (some rooms), Wi-Fi.

Ramada Limited (Value) The area's newest hotel, the Ramada has large, well-furnished rooms in a variety of configurations and styles. In addition to standard hotel rooms there are king-size-bed suites with Jacuzzi tubs, fireplaces, and balconies, and family suites with full kitchens and an extra sofa bed. Small pets are allowed in some of the guest rooms. All in all, it's a good value.

917 Alder Rd. (Hwy. 97), 100 Mile House, BC V0K 2E0. © **877/395-2777** or 250/395-2777. Fax 250/395-2037. www.ramada.com. 36 units. From C$102 double; from C$180 suite. AE, MC, V. *In room:* A/C, TV, fridge, hair dryer.

4 WILLIAMS LAKE

90km (56 miles) N of 100 Mile House; 539km (334 miles) N of Vancouver

Unabashedly a ranch town, Williams Lake (pop. 12,000) is known across the West for its large, hell's-a-poppin' rodeo, the **Williams Lake Stampede,** held the first weekend of July. It's also the gateway to the Chilcotin, the coastal mountainous area to the west. As the trade center for a large agricultural area, the little lakeside town bustles with activity.

The downtown area is west of the Hwy. 97 strip, centered on Oliver Street. The **Cariboo Friendship Society Native Arts and Crafts Shop,** 99 S. Third Ave. (© **250/398-6831**), sells the work of local Native artists. The building that houses the shop was constructed to resemble a Shuswap pit-house dwelling. The old train depot has been in part converted into **Station House Gallery,** 1 MacKenzie Ave. N. (© **250/392-6113**), with local arts and crafts.

The **Museum of the Cariboo Chilcotin,** 113 N. Fourth Ave. (© **250/392-7404;** www.cowboy-museum.com), is the only museum in B.C. to focus on ranching and rodeo, honoring both the cowboys of the past and those of the present. The museum is home to the B.C. Cowboy Hall of Fame and also features an exhibit on ranching women, Native arrowheads, and a replica blacksmith shop. It's open Monday through Saturday from 10am to 4pm from June through August, and 11am to 4pm Tuesday through Saturday the rest of the year. Admission is C$2 adult.

For information, contact the **Williams Lake Visitor Centre,** 1660 S. Broadway (© **250/392-5025;** www.williamslakechamber.com).

OUTDOOR PURSUITS

Red Shreds Bike and Board Shop, 95 S. First Ave. (© **250/398-7873;** www.redshreds.com), offers a bounty of information on local hiking, mountain biking, and kayaking; bike and kayak rentals; and a number of specialty trail maps.

FISHING There are more than 8,000 lakes in the area, and as many streams and rivers. Stop by **Harry's Sporting Supply,** 615 Oliver St. (© **250/398-5959**), to find out where the fish are biting.

(Moments) The Williams Lake Stampede

The **Williams Lake Stampede** is one of Canada's top rodeos, and is the only British Columbia rodeo on the Canadian Professional Rodeo Association circuit. Begun in the 1920s, the Stampede has grown into a 4-day festival held over the July 1 long weekend. Rodeo cowboys from across Canada and the western United States gather here to compete for prizes in excess of C$80,000.

What makes the Stampede so popular is that in addition to the usual rodeo events—barrel racing, bareback and saddle bronc riding, calf roping, bull riding—there are a number of unusual competitions that provide lots of laughs and action. The Ranch Challenge pits real working cowboys from area ranches in a pouch-passing pony express race, a hilarious wild cow-milking contest, and a cattle-penning contest. There are also chariot races with two-horse teams and a chuck-wagon race with four-horse teams. In a variation on British sheepdog trials, the Top Dog Competition pits a cowboy and his ranch dog against three unruly cows. The dog puts the cows through a course of barrels, then into a pen; the fastest dog wins.

Other Old West events, such as barn dances, a parade, midway rides, and grandstand entertainment, add to the fun. Because the Stampede is very popular, accommodations go fast—make plans well ahead.

For more information, contact the Williams Lake Stampede, P.O. Box 4076, Williams Lake, BC V2G 2V2 (© **250/392-6585;** www.williamslakestampede.com). All reserved seats cost C$17; general seating is C$15 adults and C$10 seniors and children under 12.

WHITE-WATER RAFTING   The Chilko-Chilcotin-Fraser river system that runs from the Coast Mountains east is a major rafting destination, though not for the faint of heart or the unguided novice. Inquire at **Red Shreds** (see above) for information and rentals. **Chilko River Expeditions,** P.O. Box 4723, Williams Lake, BC V2G 2V7 (© **250/398-6711;** www.chilkoriver.com), leads a variety of trips on the three rivers, including a 1-day trip on the Chilcotin for C$125 adults.

WHERE TO STAY

Coast Fraser Inn   The Fraser Inn overlooks Williams Lake from its hillside perch north of town along Hwy. 97. Large and modern, it offers a level of facilities not usually found in small ranch towns. Most rooms have great views.

285 Donald Rd., Williams Lake, BC V2G 4K4. © **888/452-6789,** 888/331-8863 in the U.S., or 250/398-7055. Fax 250/398-8269. www.coasthotels.com. 79 units. From C$119 double. Extra person C$10. AE, MC, V. Pets accepted. **Amenities:** Restaurants; bar; exercise room; Jacuzzi; sauna; beer-and-wine store. *In room:* A/C, TV, hair dryer, minibar, Wi-Fi.

Drummond Lodge   This motel just east of downtown has a lovely location right above the lake and is adjacent to public parkland. Standard rooms are clean and well-furnished while larger suitelike rooms have kitchenettes and balconies overlooking the extensive gardens.

1405 Hwy. 97 S., Williams Lake, BC V2G 2W3. © **800/667-4555** or 250/392-5334. Fax 250/392-1117. www.drummondlodge.com. 24 units. C$80–C$130. DC, MC, V. Pets C$7. **Amenities:** Barbecue; gardens. *In room:* A/C, TV, Wi-Fi.

Sandman Inn and Suites   Just 2 blocks from downtown Williams Lake, the Sandman has a newer wing of large one-bedroom suites, plus an older wing with regular motel units. You'll find the place clean, friendly, and close to everything you'll want to do in Williams Lake. A 24-hour Denny's restaurant shares the premises.

664 Oliver St., Williams Lake, BC V2G 1M6. ℭ **800/726-3626** or 250/392-6557. Fax 250/392-6242. www. sandman.ca. 59 units. C$104–C$179 double. Senior discounts offered. AE, MC, V. Small pets allowed for C$10 per day. **Amenities:** Restaurant; indoor pool; sauna. *In room:* A/C, TV, hair dryer, Wi-Fi.

WHERE TO DINE

Laughing Loon Neighborhood Pub PUB   Located just southeast of Williams Lake on Hwy. 97, this pleasant Victorian-style pub serves high-quality food in a handsome dining room or in a lush garden setting. The menu offers pub standards such as burgers and sandwiches, plus Greek specialties and local Cariboo-area beef steaks and fresh salmon from Bella Coola.

1730 S. Broadway (Hwy. 97). ℭ **250/398-5666.** Reservations not accepted. Main courses C$9–C$19. AE, MC, V. Sun–Fri 11:30am–10pm; Sat 11:30am–11pm.

5 WEST ON HWY. 20 TO BELLA COOLA

456km (283 miles) W of Williams Lake

Hwy. 20 cuts through a rugged land of lakes and mountains on its way to Bella Coola, a Native village on a Pacific inlet. This journey takes the adventurous driver from Williams Lake and the desert canyons of the Fraser River to glaciated peaks and finally to the shores of a narrow ocean fjord. It's an amazingly scenic trip, but be ready for lots of gravel roads and steep grades. There aren't a lot of facilities along the way, so start out with a full tank of gas. You can easily make this trip in a day, especially in summer, but leave plenty of time to stop and explore.

After climbing up out of the Fraser Canyon, Hwy. 20 winds along the **Chilcotin Plateau,** miles of spacious grasslands that are home to some of the largest ranches in North America. At Hanceville, the route drops onto the **Chilcotin River,** famed for its white-water rafting and kayaking. The **Chilcotin Hotel,** in Alexis Creek (ℭ **250/394-4214**), is a popular place to stop for a home-style meal. You can camp right on the river at **Bull Canyon Provincial Parks,** with 20 sites at C$14 apiece. The park is 10km (6¼ miles) west of Alexis Creek, 126km (78 miles) west of Williams Lake.

Just past Redstone, Hwy. 20 leaves the Chilcotin River and climbs up the valley. **Puntzi Lake** is home to a number of old-time fishing resorts. The **Putzi Lake Resort** (ℭ **250/481-1176;** www.puntzilake.com) has boat and tackle rentals, and rents campsites starting at C$15 and cabins or lodge rooms from C$50.

As Hwy. 20 presses closer to the Coast Mountains, the landscape is increasingly dotted with lakes and marshes. At the wee community of **Tatla Lake,** the pavement ends and the gravel begins. **Anahim Lake,** 328km (204 miles) west of Williams Lake and the largest settlement on the Chilcotin Plateau (pop. 522), is noted for its fishing and outdoor recreation. The **Escott Bay Resort** (ℭ **888/380-8802** or 250/742-3233; www.escottbay. com) offers cabins starting at C$75. The general store in Anahim Lake is over a century old, and its coffeepot is always on. The enormous glaciated peak that dominates the southern skyline is **Mount Waddington,** which at 4,016m (13,176 ft.) is the highest point in the Coast Mountains.

As you begin the final ascent up to 1,494m (4,902-ft.) **Heckman Pass,** note the Rainbow Range, 2,400m-plus (7,874-ft.-plus) peaks that are brilliantly colored by purple, red, and yellow mineralization.

Thirty kilometers (19 miles) from Anahim Lake, Hwy. 20 crests Heckman Pass, and then begins **"The Hill."** Bella Coola residents had long dreamed of a road connection to the rest of the province, and a succession of provincial governments promised to build one from the Chilcotin Plateau down to the Pacific. When years went by and nothing happened—civil engineers doubted that a safe road could be made down the steep western face of the Coast Mountains—the locals took matters in their own hands. In 1953, two men in bulldozers set out, one from Heckman Pass, the other from the end of the road at the base of the Coast Mountains. In just 3 months, the two bulldozers kissed blades at the middle of the mountain, and Hwy. 20 was born. You'll feel your heart in your mouth on a number of occasions as you corkscrew your way down the road. The most notorious portion is 10km (6¼ miles) of gravel switchbacks, with gradients up to 18%, which drop 1,405m (4,610 ft.).

This part of Hwy. 20 passes through **Tweedsmuir Provincial Park,** British Columbia's second-largest park at 1 million hectares (2.5 million acres). This vast wilderness park of soaring mountains, interlocking lakes, and abundant wildlife is accessible by long-distance hiking trails, floatplane, and canoe. In fact, the Eutsuk Lake–Whitesail Lake circuit provides more than 320km (199 miles) of canoeing waters with just one portage. For information, contact **BC Parks,** 281 First Ave. N., Williams Lake (© **250/398-4414**).

The town at the end of the road, **Bella Coola** (pop. 992), is a disorganized little burg in a green glacier-carved valley. Ancestral home to the Bella Coola tribe, Bella Coola once held a Hudson's Bay Company trading fort, then became a fishing center for Norwegian settlers. The waterfront is a busy place in summer, with fishing and pleasure boats coming and going.

Besides the lure of the end of the road, the main reason to drive to Bella Coola is to catch the **BC Ferries Discovery Coast** service (see chapter 11). This summer-only ferry connects Bella Coola with other even more isolated coastal communities. The ferry terminates at Port Hardy, on Vancouver Island, making this an increasingly popular loop trip. The journey lasts 12 to 14 hours. In high season, fares between Port Hardy and Bella Coola are C$170 per adult passenger and C$340 for a car.

WHERE TO STAY & DINE

There are basic campsites (pump your own water, pit toilets) at **Bailey Bridge Campsite** (© **250/982-2342**). See also the Bella Coola Motel, below.

Bella Coola Motel   Located right in the middle of downtown, this motel occupies the site of the old Hudson's Bay Company trading post on the waterfront. Guest rooms are spacious, and all include basic kitchens. RV and tent sites go for C$15 to C$19.

1224 Clayton St., Box 188, Bella Coola, BC V0T 1C0. ©/fax **250/799-5323.** www.bellacoolavalley.com. 10 units. C$90–C$110 double. Extra person C$10. Senior and AAA discounts available. AE, MC, V. Free parking. Pets conditionally accepted with deposit. **Amenities:** Bike, canoe, and scooter rentals; free airport shuttle *In room:* TV, kitchen.

Bella Coola Valley Inn   This is the closest lodging to the ferry terminal, and the inn offers standard motel-style units. Extras include a BC Ferries ticket agency, a popular restaurant, and a coffee shop with Wi-Fi.

441 MacKenzie St., Box 183, Bella Coola, BC V0T 1C0. © **888/799-5316** or 250/799-5316. Fax 250/799-5610. www.bellacoolavalleyinn.com. 20 units. C$115 double. Extra person C$10. AE, MC, V. **Amenities:** Restaurant; pub; airport and ferry shuttle service; sauna. *In room:* A/C, TV, fridge, Wi-Fi.

120km (75 miles) N of Williams Lake; 654km (406 miles) N of Vancouver; 101km (63 miles) S of Prince George

Like most other towns in the Cariboo District, Quesnel (pop. 8,500) was founded during the gold-rush years. Now mostly a logging center, Quesnel serves as gateway to the ghost town of Barkerville and to the canoe paddler's paradise, the Bowron Lakes. It also serves as the overnight stop on Rocky Mountaineer Vacations train tour line, the Frazer Discovery Route.

Quesnel is located on a jut of land at the confluence of the Fraser and Quesnel rivers. The small downtown is almost completely surrounded by these rivers. **Ceal Tingley Park,** on the Fraser side, is a pleasant place for a stroll, and it's one of the few spots where you can get right down to the huge and powerful Fraser. Directly across the street is a Hudson's Bay Company trading post built in 1882; it currently houses a restaurant.

The main commercial strip is **Reid Street,** a block east of Hwy. 97. A walk along Reid Street reveals the kinds of old-fashioned shops and services that have been gobbled up by behemoths like Wal-Mart in the United States.

Over on the Quesnel River side of downtown is **Le Bourdais Park,** which contains the visitor center and the **Quesnel and District Museum and Archives,** 405 Barlow Ave. (© 250/992-9580), which tells the story of the gold rush and has good exhibits on the Chinese who worked in the camps. It's open daily May to October; the rest of the year, Monday through Friday afternoons only.

A rodeo, river-raft races, and more than 100 other events attract thousands to Quesnel during the second week of July for **Bill Barker Days** (© 250/992-8716). For general information, contact the **Quesnel Visitor Info Centre,** in Le Bourdais Park, 703 Carson Ave. (© 866/783-7635 or 250/992-3522; www.northcariboo.com), open March through October.

WHERE TO STAY

Ten Mile Lake Provincial Park, 11km (6¾ miles) north of Quesnel off Hwy. 97 (© 250/398-4414), has 141 campsites from C$14. Open May through October, the park has flush toilets and showers.

Best Western Tower Inn   Right in the middle of downtown, though off the busy main thoroughfare, the Tower Inn offers clean, crisp guest rooms. Begbie's Bar and Bistro is a popular eatery and hangout.

500 Reid St., Quesnel, BC V2J 2M9. © 800/663-2009 or 250/992-2201. Fax 250/992-5201. www.bwtower inn.ca. 63 units. C$98–C$135 double. Extra person C$10. AE, MC, V. **Amenities:** Restaurant; bar; exercise room. *In room:* A/C, TV/VCR w/pay movies, fridge, hair dryer, Wi-Fi.

Ramada Limited (Kids)   This well-equipped hotel is in the center of Quesnel, and while that's not promising a lot, it's more interesting than staying at a freeway exit. Next door is the city government and civic center, with a fitness center and skating rink. For the price, the rooms are nicely furnished, and there's a pool area for the kids.

383 St. Laurent Ave., Quesnel, BC V2J 2E1. © 800/992-1581 or 250/992-5575. Fax 250/995-2254. www. ramada.ca. 46 units. C$73–C$99 double. Rates include continental breakfast. AE, MC, V. **Amenities:** Indoor pool; Jacuzzi. *In room:* A/C, TV, fridge, hair dryer, Wi-Fi.

Talisman Inn A well-maintained older motel close to downtown, the Talisman has large, light-filled rooms that overlook a grassy courtyard. Kitchen units and executive suites are available. Some rooms have Jacuzzis, and several are equipped for those with disabilities.

753 Front St., Quesnel, BC V2J 2L2. (C) **800/663-8090** or 250/992-7247. Fax 250/992-3126. www. talismaninn.bc.ca. 87 units. C$69–C$89 double; C$120 2-bedroom suite; C$149 executive suite. Extra person C$10. Rates include continental breakfast. Corporate and senior rates available. AE, DC, DISC, MC, V. Free parking. Pets allowed in some units. **Amenities:** Exercise room; rooms for those w/limited mobility. *In room:* A/C, TV w/pay movies, fridge, Wi-Fi.

WHERE TO DINE

Mr. Mike's Steakhouse & Bar CANADIAN Mr. Mike's is probably the hippest place in Quesnel, with a cocktail menu that would make a Yaletown club in Vancouver proud and their own brand of microbrewed beers. The dining room serves up eclectic fare that focuses on steaks, but includes grilled salmon and boutique burgers. A few Mexican- and Thai-influenced dishes also make their way onto the menu.

450 Reid St. (C) **250/992-8181.** Reservations recommended. Main courses C$8–C$32. AE, MC, V. Daily 10am–midnight.

River Rock Pub and Steakhouse PUB This pub overlooks the Moffat Bridge and the Fraser River, with an outdoor deck to frame the view. The menu is broad, ranging from burgers to steaks to East Indian specialties. Families are welcome, and you're sure to find something that will appeal to everyone.

290 Hoy St. (C) **250/991-0110.** Reservations not needed. Main courses C$7–C$19. MC, V. Daily 11:30am–10pm.

---

7 EAST TO BARKERVILLE ★ & BOWRON LAKES ★

Barkerville: 83km (52 miles) E of Quesnel

Barkerville is one of the premier tourist destinations in interior British Columbia, as well as one of the most intact ghost towns in Canada. However, what lures paddlers and campers to the Cariboo Mountains today isn't a flash of gold, but the splash of water at the Bowron Lakes. These are a chain of six major—and a number of smaller—interconnecting lakes that attract canoeists and kayakers who paddle and portage around the entire 115km (71-mile) circuit.

Follow the signs in Quesnel to Hwy. 26 E. The 87km (54-mile) drive to Barkerville takes you deep into the forests of the Cariboo Mountains, where moose and deer are often spotted from the road. The paved highway ends at Barkerville. Bowron Lakes is another 30km (19 miles) northeast on a gravel road.

EXPLORING BARKERVILLE: AN OLD WEST GHOST TOWN

The 1860 Cariboo gold rush was the reason thousands of miners made their way north from the played-out Fraser River gold deposits to Williams Creek, east of Quesnel. **Barkerville** ★ was founded on its shore after Billy Barker discovered one of the region's richest gold deposits in 1862. The town sprang up practically overnight; that year, it was reputedly the largest city west of Chicago and north of San Francisco. Many of the claims continued to produce well into the 1930s, but Barkerville's population moved on, leaving behind an intact ghost town that was designated a historic park in the 1950s.

The original 1869 **Anglican church** and 125 other buildings have been lovingly reconstructed or restored. The **Richland courthouse** stages trials from the town's past. From May to Labour Day, "townspeople" dress in period costumes. Visitors can pan for gold, dine in the Chinatown section, or take a stagecoach ride. In winter, the town becomes a haven for **cross-country skiers.** During the holidays, Barkerville hosts a special **Victorian Christmas** celebration.

Admission to the town is C$14 adults, C$13 seniors, C$8.50 teens 13 to 18, C$4.20 children 6 to 12, and C$31 families. Barkerville is open year-round, daily from dawn to dusk, with interpretive activities from mid-May through September. For information, contact **Barkerville Historic Town,** Box 19, Barkerville, BC V0K 1B0 (© **250/994-3332;** www.barkerville.ca).

Where to Stay & Dine

There are three campgrounds in **Barkerville Provincial Park,** Hwy. 26 (© **250/398-1414**), open year-round. Sites go for C$14 to C$18. **Lowhee Campground** is the best and closest to the park entrance, with both tent and RV sites, plus showers, flush toilets, pumped well water, and a sani-station.

The Wells Hotel Established in 1933, the 15 historic rooms at this restored hotel near Barkerville are filled with lovely antique furnishings. The hotel offers amenities that you'll truly appreciate after a day of hiking, canoeing, skiing, or gold panning: fine dining, a frothy cappuccino, and a soothing hot tub. Guest rooms are tastefully refurbished and decorated with antiques and local artwork. Some units have private bathrooms and/or fireplaces. Continental breakfast is included in all rates.

Pooley St. (Box 39), Wells, BC V0K 2R0. © **800/860-2299** in Canada, or 250/994-3427. Fax 250/994-3494. www.wellshotel.com. 15 units. From C$90 double. Lower winter rates. Rates include breakfast. AE, MC, V. **Amenities:** Restaurant; lounge; pub; bike rental; Jacuzzi. *In room:* Wi-Fi.

PADDLING BOWRON LAKES: A CANOEIST'S PARADISE

Thirty kilometers (19 miles) northeast of Barkerville over an unpaved road, there's access to a circle of lakes that attracts canoeists and kayakers from around the world. The 123,120-hectare (304,236-acre) **Bowron Lakes Provincial Park** is a majestic paddler's paradise set against a backdrop of glacial peaks.

The 7-day circular route is 120km (75 miles) of unbroken wilderness. It begins at Kibbee Creek and Kibbee Lake, flows into Indianpoint Lake, Isaac Lake, and the Isaac River, and continues to McCleary, Lanezi, Sandy, and Una lakes before entering the final stretch: Babcock Lake, Skoi Lake, the Spectacle Lakes, Swan Lake, and finally Bowron Lake. The long, narrow lakes afford visitors a close look at both shores. You'll catch sight of moose, mountain goats, beavers, black bears, and grizzly bears. Be prepared to portage for a total of 8.5km (5¼ miles) between some of the creeks that connect the lakes. The longest single portage is 3km (1¾ miles). You must pack everything in and out of the wilderness camps.

The number of canoes and people allowed to enter the park per day is restricted in summer. Permit bookings are handled by **Super Natural British Columbia** (© **800/435-5622** or 250/387-1642). Fees for a full circuit are C$60 per person per one-person canoe/kayak, or C$120 per two-person canoe/kayak. There's a reservation fee of C$18. After September 25, permits can be purchased at the **Bowron Lakes Park office,** at the start of the circuit (📞 **250/398-4414**). The park does not close in winter, but there are no rangers in the park after mid-October, so extreme caution must be used. For information on the park, contact the **District Manager,** 301-640 Borland St., Williams Lake (📞 **250/398-4414;** www.env.gov.bc.ca/bcparks).

You don't have to make the entire journey to enjoy this incredible setting. Open May through October, the **campground** at the park's entrance is a relaxing spot to camp, fish, boat, or simply observe the abundant flora and fauna.

Where to Stay

Bowron Lake Lodge & Resorts　This rustic resort provides all the creature comforts you could ask for in a wilderness setting. Guests can choose from comfortable lodge rooms, cabins, or campsites. There are 5km (3.1 miles) of trails, 610m (2,001 ft.) of private beach, and an airstrip. Views across the lake and onto the forested craggy peaks are extremely dramatic.

Bowron Lake, 672 Walkem St., Quesnel, BC V2J 2J7. 📞 **250/992-2733.** 16 units, 50 campsites. C$65–C$125 double; C$28 campsite. MC, V. Closed Nov–Apr. **Amenities:** Restaurant; lounge; bike, canoe, and motorboat rentals. *In room:* No phone.

8　THE THOMPSON RIVER VALLEY

Kamloops: 345km (214 miles) NE of Vancouver; 218km (135 miles) W of Revelstoke

From its juncture with the Fraser River at Lytton, the Thompson River cuts north, then east through an arid countryside grazed by cattle. **Kamloops,** a major trade center for this agricultural region, is increasingly a retirement center for refugees from the mists of the Pacific coast. In the South Thompson River valley, the **Shuswap Lakes** are popular with houseboaters. It's easy to rent a houseboat in **Salmon Arm** and navigate the 1,000km (621 miles) of waterways, landing at campsites and beaches along the way.

Rising up from the dry terrain of Kamloops, heading north along Hwy. 5, the road enters the cool forests of the High Country. High above the town of **Clearwater** is the pristine wilderness of **Wells Gray Provincial Park.**

KAMLOOPS & VICINITY

At the confluence of the north and south forks of the Thompson River, Kamloops (pop. 84,000) is the province's fifth-largest city. The forest-products industry is the city's primary economic force, although Kamloops is also a major service center for ranchers and farmers. For travelers, Kamloops makes a handy stopover between other destinations, though it isn't really a tourist town. Its greatest attraction is the all-season Sun Peaks Resort, in the mountains north of the city.

Essentials

GETTING THERE　You can fly into Kamloops on **Air Canada Jazz** (📞 **888/247-2262;** www.flyjazz.ca), which operates daily 50-minute flights from Vancouver, and rent a car at the airport from **Budget** (📞 **800/268-8900** in Canada, 800/527-0700 in the U.S.; www.budget.com), or **Hertz** (📞 **250/376-3022;** www.hertz.com).

Kamloops is a junction point for many provincial roads, including the Trans-Canada Highway and the Coquihalla toll road (Hwy. 5), the fastest route to/from Vancouver.

There are six daily **Greyhound Canada** (© **800/661-8747;** www.greyhound.ca) buses from Vancouver; the fare is C$56. **VIA Rail** (© **888/VIA-RAIL** [842-7245]; www. viarail.ca) passes through on the main transnational route. Kamloops is also the overnight stop for the Grand Canadian Railtour Company's luxury *Rocky Mountaineer* (© **800/665-7245**). For more information on this train, see p. 273.

VISITOR INFORMATION   Contact the **Kamloops Visitor Info Centre,** 1290 W. Trans-Canada Hwy., at exit 368 (© **800/662-1994** or 250/347-3377; www.adventure kamloops.com).

Exploring the Area

Kamloops is a sprawling city in a wide river valley flanked by high desert mountains. A major service center for agricultural industries, Kamloops isn't exactly a tourist town. The downtown core centered around **Victoria Street,** however, is a pleasant, tree-lined area. North of downtown along the Thompson is **Riverfront Park,** a lovely expanse of green in an otherwise arid landscape. The stern-wheeler *Wanda-Sue* (© 250/374-7447) plies the river waters, providing narrated sightseeing tours.

Kamloops Art Gallery   This is the only public art museum in the Thompson region and the largest in the province's interior, with a collection of more than 1,200 works by Canadian artists. The gallery also mounts changing exhibits of international works.

465 Victoria St. © 250/828-3543. www.kag.bc.ca. Admission C$3 adults and senior couples, C$2 seniors and students, C$5 families; "pay what you can" Thurs 5–9pm. Mon–Sat 10am–5pm (Thurs until 9pm); Sun noon–4pm.

Secwepemc Museum & Heritage Park ★   The Secwepemc (pronounced "*She-whep-m*," anglicized as Shuswap) people have lived along the Thompson River for thousands of years. This 4.8-hectare (12-acre) heritage park contains an actual archaeological site which was inhabited 2,400 to 1,200 years ago, plus reconstructions of traditional villages from five different eras. Also featured are displays of native plants and their traditional uses and a replica of a salmon-netting station.

355 Yellowhead Hwy. © 250/828-9801. www.secwepemc.org/museum. Admission C$6 adults, C$4 children 7–17 and seniors. June 15 to Labour Day Weekend daily 8am–4pm; Labour Day to June 14 Mon–Fri 8am–4pm.

ⓘTips   The Salmon Run & Other Special Events

One of nature's most amazing phenomena, the **Adams River Salmon Run** ★, takes place in late October. Every 4 years, 1.5 to 2 million sockeye salmon struggle upstream to spawn in the Adams River. Trails provide riverside-viewing, with trained staff ready to interpret the spectacle. From Kamloops, take the Trans-Canada Highway (Hwy. 1) to Squilax, about 10km (6¼ miles) east of Chase. Follow the signs north to Roderick Haig-Brown Provincial Park. The next expected run of sockeye is in 2010.

In January, the **Reino Keski-Salmi Loppet** (© 250/832-7740) attracts cross-country skiers from across North America to the Larch Hills Cross-Country Ski Hill, east of Kamloops in Salmon Arm.

Sun Peaks Resort ★, on Todd Mountain Road, Heffley Creek (℃ **800/807-3257** or 250/578-7232, 250/578-7232 for snow report; www.sunpeaksresort.com), is a major all-season resort and mountain community with some of the most complete sports and recreation facilities in British Columbia. Of course, in winter the focus is on downhill skiing. Sun Peaks offers great powder skiing on three different mountains, with 1,471 hectares (3,635 acres) of skiable terrain, making it Canada's third-largest ski area. The total vertical drop is 881m (2,890 ft.), with 121 runs serviced by a high-speed quad, fixed-grip quad, triple chair, double chair, T-bar, and beginner platter. Snowboarders have a choice of two half pipes, one with a super-large boarder-cross, and a terrain park with handrails, cars, a fun box, hips, quarter pipes, transfers, and fat gaps that were designed by Ecosign Mountain Planners and some of Canada's top amateur riders. Lift tickets are C$71 for adults, C$57 seniors and youths 13 to 18, and C$36 for children 6 to 12. Nordic skiers have 28km (17 miles) of groomed cross-country trails, and 12km (7½ miles) of backcountry runs. The resort also offers dog sledding, snowshoeing, and snowmobile trails.

In summer, the lifts continue to operate, providing mountain bikers and hikers access to the high country. Sun Peak's bike park offers 26 trails, dropping 595m (1,952 ft.) through varied terrain. The lifts run daily late June through Labour Day, and then Friday, Saturday, and Sunday through September. A day pass to the bike park and lifts costs C$38 adults, C$32 seniors and youths 13 to 18, and C$22 children 6 to 12. For hikers, a ride on the lifts up to alpine trails costs C$16 adults, C$14 seniors and youths 13 to 18, and C$12 children 6 to 12.

The Sun Peaks Resort Golf Course is another top summer draw. At 1,200m (3,937 ft.) above sea level, this 18-hole, Graham Cooke–designed course offers spectacular alpine vistas that are sure to challenge your concentration. And while golfers enjoy the course, other members of the family have the option of horseback riding, canoeing, fishing, or hiking, all of which can be easily arranged with the resort's Guest Services. The resort offers a wide variety of lodging options including nine hotels, a selection of condos, B&Bs, and one- to four-bedroom town homes and chalets. With a choice of over 20 dining and nightlife options, Sun Peaks offers a more lively social and gastronomic scene that most midsize Canadian cities.

GOLF **Aberdeen Hills Golf Links,** 1185 Links Way (℃ **250/828-1149** or 250/828-1143), is an 18-hole course with panoramic views. **The Dunes,** 652 Dunes Dr. (℃ **888/881-4653** or 250/579-3300), is a Graham Cooke–designed 18-hole championship course. **Kamloops Golf & Country Club,** 3125 Tranquille Rd. (℃ **250/376-8020**), is an 18-hole semi-private championship course. **Pineridge Golf Course,** 4725 E. Trans-Canada Hwy. (℃ **250/573-4333**), is an 18-hole course designed to be "the best short course ever built."

Rivershore Estates and Golf Links ★ (℃ **250/573-4622**) is an award-winning Robert Trent Jones, Sr., design and has been host to the Canadian National Championships. For family-friendly golf, **McArthur Island Golf Centre** (℃ **250/553-4211**) offers a 9-hole course, driving range, miniature golf, pro shop, and restaurant.

Where to Stay

In addition to the following downtown lodgings, you'll find a phalanx of easy-in, easy-out motels at Hwy. 1, exit 368, south and west of the city center.

(Moments) Houseboating on the Shuswap Lakes

From Kamloops, the South Thompson River valley extends east to the Shuswap Lakes, a series of waterways that is an extremely popular summer destination for family houseboating parties. With more than 1,000km (621 miles) of shoreline, these long, interconnected lakes provide good fishing, water-skiing, and other boating fun.

The best way to see the lakes is to rent a houseboat; after all, Shuswap is the "Houseboating Capital of Canada." Houseboats come equipped with staterooms, bathrooms, and kitchens. All you need to bring is your bedding and food. Reserve well in advance; by late spring, all boats are usually rented for the high season, from mid-June to Labour Day. Low-season rates are up to half off the prices below. Of the numerous rental operations along the Shuswap Lakes, the following are two of the largest.

Admiral House Boats, Sicamous Creek Marina (R.R. 1, Site 6, Comp 30), Sicamous (© **250/836-4611;** www.admiralhouseboats.com), rents houseboats from April to October. Super Admiral boats, which sleep up to 10, have three private staterooms and one and a half bathrooms. Rentals are available in 3-, 4-, and 7-day increments. In high season, a week on a Super Admiral houseboat goes for C$3,395.

Twin Anchors Houseboat Vacations (www.twinanchors.com) has two locations, one in Salmon Arm at 750 Marine Park Dr. (© **800/665-7782** or 250/832-2745), and the other in Sicamous at 101 Martin St. (© **800/663-4026** or 250/836-2450). It offers four types of boats, ranging from two- to four-stateroom models. A week on a two-stateroom CruiseCraft II that sleeps 15 and comes with hot tub costs C$5,940 per week. Rentals are available in 3-, 4-, and 7-day increments.

The main commercial center for the Shuswap Lakes is **Salmon Arm** (pop. 15,000), 108km (67 miles) east of Kamloops on Hwy. 1. Right on the downtown lakefront is the **Prestige Harbourfront Resort & Convention Centre** ★★. A towering castellated structure, the Harbourfront Resort has very stylish and comfortable guest rooms, and public areas are suitably grand. In high season, rates begin at C$200.

Coast Canadian Inn ★   Ideally located in downtown, the Coast Canadian is one of the top hotels in Kamloops, with spacious guest rooms and lots of extras, such as WebTV Internet access; superior rooms offer bathrobes and upgraded toiletries. The protected outdoor pool and hot tub area is heated for all-season use. The Pronto Restaurant is a popular spot for fine dining.

339 St. Paul St., Kamloops, BC V2C 2J5. © **800/663-1144** or 250/372-5201. Fax 250/372-9363. www.coasthotels.com. 94 units. C$129–C$205 double. Extra person $10. Family plan, corporate and off-season rates, and senior discounts available. AE, DC, MC, V. **Amenities:** Restaurant; pub; exercise room; Jacuzzi; outdoor pool; room service; sauna; beer-and-wine store. *In room:* A/C, TV w/pay movies and Nintendo, WebTV, hair dryer, Wi-Fi.

Plaza Heritage Hotel ★   The Plaza began its life as *the* downtown hotel in Kamloops. A masterful renovation of this 1920s luxury lodging allows it to once again reclaim
that title. The restoration preserves the vintage feel of the decor while adding luxury
touches such as fine furniture and spacious bathrooms. Each room is individually decorated—some in full Victoriana, others in equally stylish understatement. There are a
number of room types and bed configurations—ask the reservation clerk to specify a
room that will best serve your needs. The lobby restaurant offers fine dining, while the
lounge is a comfortable spot for a friendly brew.

405 Victoria St., Kamloops, BC V2C 2A9. ℂ **877/977-5292** or 250/377-8075. Fax 250/377-8076. www.
plazaheritagehotel.com. 67 units. From C$109–C$179 double. AE, MC, V. **Amenities:** Restaurant; coffee
shop; lounge; beer-and-wine store. *In room:* A/C, TV, hair dryer, Wi-Fi.

Scott's Inn–Downtown (Value)   A standard motel with clean, comfortable rooms and
many extra features, Scott's is located in a quiet residential neighborhood within easy
walking distance of downtown. Some units have kitchenettes. Save some money here
without taking a cut in quality.

551 11th Ave., Kamloops, BC V2C 3Y1. ℂ **800/665-3343** or 250/372-8221. Fax 250/372-9444. www.
scottsinn.kamloops.com. 51 units. C$71–C$81 double. Kitchen C$10 extra. Extra person C$6–C$10. Rates
include continental breakfast. Group, senior, corporate, and off-season discounts available. AE, MC, V.
Amenities: Restaurant; Jacuzzi; indoor pool. *In room:* A/C, TV w/pay movies, Wi-Fi.

Where to Dine

Brownstone Restaurant ★★ NEW CANADIAN   With the most up-to-date cuisine in Kamloops, the Brownstone also offers period elegance and gracious service in
downtown's historic Canadian Imperial Bank of Commerce building, built in 1904. The
food is very refined yet full flavored, with a choice of small plates or full dinner service.
Crab and chipotle profiterole with tomato onion jam, crispy duck thigh with blueberry
sauce, and rosemary-marinated and applewood-smoked rack of pork with apple chutney
and scalloped potatoes are exemplars of the blend of tradition and innovation that fuels
the kitchen. In addition to the gracious dining room, in summer there's dining on a
lovely outdoor patio.

118 Victoria St. ℂ **250/851-9939.** Reservations recommended. Main courses C$18–C$40. MC, V. Mid-
May to mid-Oct daily 5–10pm; the rest of the year Tues–Sun 5–10pm.

Chapters Viewpoint Restaurant INTERNATIONAL/MEXICAN   Perched on a
hill above Kamloops, Chapters offers a great view over the city; the terrace is the place to
be for summer drinks. The menu, which features steaks, prime rib, and classic Continental specialties, also includes a number of New Mexican dishes, including the local favorite steak ranchero, a red pepper–rubbed New York strip that's grilled and served with a
topping of cheese. You'll also find chile relleno and a selection of enchiladas.

In the Howard Johnson Panorama Inn & Suites, 610 Columbia St. ℂ **250/374-3224.** Reservations recommended. Main courses C$12–C$35. AE, DC, MC, V. Daily 7am–2:30pm and 5–10pm.

Ric's Mediterranean Grill ★ GRILL   Part of a western Canadian chain, Ric's is
always a solid choice for satisfying fine dining, and there's no better place to make your
acquaintance than here, one of the first locations. Out in Kamloops, nobody cares if you
mix cuisines, so you'll find a wide-ranging menu—among the tapas, selections such
as spicy Dungeness crab bruschetta; and from the dinner menu, chutney prawns and
scallops, Tequila lime barbecued ribs, or citrus-chile-glazed swordfish. The decor matches

the food; Ric's is a handsome place with warm wood furnishings and dramatic black and gold accents.

227 Victoria St. © **250/372-7771.** Main courses C$14–C$38. AE, MC, V. Mon–Thurs 11am–9:30pm; Fri 11am–10pm; Sat 4–10pm; Sun 4–9:30pm.

THE UPPER THOMPSON RIVER VALLEY

From Kamloops, the North Thompson River flows north into increasingly rugged terrain. The little town of **Clearwater** is the gateway to **Wells Gray Provincial Park,** the mountain wilderness park of choice for purist hikers and outdoor adventurers as the nearby Canadian Rockies become increasingly crowded and commercialized.

Although **Greyhound** offers bus service daily between Vancouver and Clearwater, you'll need a car to explore the best areas of the High Country. Clearwater is 103km (64 miles) north of Kamloops on Hwy. 5.

The **Clearwater–Wells Gray Info Centre,** 425 E. Yellowhead Hwy. 5 (© **250/674-2646;** www.clearwaterbcchamber.com), is at Hwy. 5 and Wells Gray Park Road. From October 16 to April 14, it's open Monday through Saturday from 9am to 5pm; April 15 to June 30 and September 1 to October 15, daily from 9am to 6pm; July 1 to August 31, daily from 8am to 8pm.

Exploring Wells Gray Provincial Park

Wells Gray Provincial Park (© **604/371-6400;** www.env.gov.bc.ca/bcparks) is British Columbia's third-largest park, encompassing more than 526,500 hectares (1.3 million acres) of mountains, rivers, lakes, volcanic formations, glaciers, forests, and alpine meadows. Wildlife abounds, including mule deer, moose, bears, beaver, timber wolves, mink, and golden eagles.

Wells Gray has something to offer everyone: birding and wildlife-viewing, hiking, boating, canoeing, and kayaking. Guide operations offer horseback riding, canoeing, rafting, fishing, and hiking. The history enthusiast can learn about the early homesteaders, trappers, and prospectors, or about the natural forces that produced Wells Gray's many volcanoes, mineral springs, and glaciers.

Most of Wells Gray is remote wilderness that can be viewed only after a vigorous hike or canoe excursion. In the southern quarter of the park, however, a road runs 34km (21 miles) from the park entrance to Clearwater Lake. Called simply the **Corridor,** it provides access to many of the park's features as well as its campgrounds and many of its trail heads.

Twice as tall as Niagara Falls, the park's **Helmcken Falls** is Canada's fourth-highest waterfall, and is an awesome sight easily reached by paved road. Boating, canoeing, kayaking, and fishing are popular pastimes on **Clearwater, Azure, Mahood,** and **Murtle lakes.** The wilderness campgrounds along these lakes make perfect destinations for overnight canoe or fishing trips.

Multiday hiking destinations include the area around Ray Farm Homestead, Rays Mineral Spring, and the thickly forested **Murtle River Trail** that leads to **Majerus Falls, Horseshoe Falls,** and **Pyramid Mountain,** a volcanic upgrowth that was shaped when it erupted beneath miles of glacial ice that covered the park millions of years ago.

Guided Tours & Excursions

Area accommodations make it easy to get out and explore the wilderness. Both **Trophy Mountain Buffalo Ranch** and **Helmcken Falls Lodge** (see "Where to Stay," below) and the **Wells Gray Guest Ranch,** Wells Gray Road (© **250/674-2792** or 250/674-2774; www.wellsgrayranch.com), offer a wide variety of recreational options, including horseback riding, canoeing, rafting, and hiking trips in summer, and dog sledding, cross-country snowshoeing, snowmobiling, and ice fishing in winter.

Interior Whitewater Expeditions (*✆* **800/661-7238** in Canada, or 250/674-3727; www.interiorwhitewater.bc.ca) offers half- to 5-day rafting and kayaking trips. Consider a 3-hour white-water screamer on the Clearwater River for C$95, or a more leisurely 3-hour float down the North Thompson for C$75.

Wells Gray Chalets & Wilderness Adventures (*✆* **888/SKI-TREK** [754-8735] or 250/587-6444; www.skihike.com) offers backcountry hut-to-hut hiking and cross-country ski trips. Ian Eakins and Tay Briggs run this family-owned company that maintains three chalets nestled deep in the park. Each sleeps up to 12 and is equipped with a kitchen, bedding, sauna, and propane lighting and heat. It's the best of both worlds: You can experience untrammeled wilderness and great rural hospitality. Two of the nicest people you could hope to have as guides, Ian and Tay are extremely knowledgeable about the wildlife and history of the park. They offer guided or self-catered hiking and cross-country ski packages as well as guided 3- and 6-day canoe trips that are custom-designed for families. Guided summer hikes are roughly C$140 to C$150 per person per day; guided winter cross-country ski trips are roughly C$180 per person per day.

Where to Stay

Most campers head to Wells Gray Provincial Park's **Spahats, Clearwater,** and **Dawson Falls campgrounds** ★ (*✆* **250/851-3000**), which offer fire pits, firewood, pumped well water, pit toilets, and boat launches. Each of the 88 sites goes for C$14 per night; check the sign outside the Clearwater visitor center to make sure the grounds aren't full before driving all the way up to the park.

12

Dutch Lake Motel and Campground
The nicest lodging in the town of Clearwater itself, the Dutch Lake Motel overlooks its namesake lake in a quiet setting away from the highway. All guest rooms have balconies; some have kitchenettes. Canoe rentals can be arranged.

333 Roy Rd. (R.R. 2, Box 5116), Clearwater, BC V0E 1N0. *✆* **877/674-3325** or 250/674-3325. Fax 250/674-2916. www.dutchlakemotel.com. 27 units. C$101–C$130 double; campsites C$26–C$30. Lower off-season rates. AE, MC, V. **Amenities:** Restaurant; bar; tennis courts. *In room:* A/C, TV, fridge, hair dryer, Wi-Fi.

Helmcken Falls Lodge ★
Established in the 1920s as a humble trappers' camp, this venerable property has grown into a handsome complex of buildings that includes a 1940s hand-hewn log lodge, which is now home to Wells Gray's best dining room. Accommodations are in a variety of structures, including two log buildings each with four hotel-style rooms, plus a two-story chalet building, and the original trapper's log cabin with two rustic guest rooms. Helmcken Falls Lodge is noted for its recreational activities. The lodge maintains its own horse herd and offers a variety of guided rides in the park, from 1 hour to overnight. Naturalist-led half- and full-day hikes and canoeing trips through the park are another specialty. Cross-country ski rentals are available in winter. The friendly staff can arrange a wide variety of other recreational opportunities with area outfitters; families are welcome. The lodge also overlooks a 9-hole golf course. Call ahead for dinner reservations in the atmospheric log dining room, with delicious home-cooked meals (open for breakfast and dinner; packed lunches available).

Wells Gray Park Rd., Box 239, Clearwater, BC V0E 1N0. *✆* **250/674-3657.** Fax 250/674-2971. www.helmckenfalls.com. 21 units. C$168–C$199 high-season double. Lower off-season rates. Rafting and kayaking packages available. AE, MC, V. Located 35km (22 miles) north of Clearwater. **Amenities:** Licensed restaurant. *In room:* No phone.

Nakiska Ranch ★★   Gorgeous log cabins, grazing cattle on acres of mowed meadows, and Wells Gray's majestic forests and mountains surround the main lodge of this working ranch. The six log one-bedroom cabins are the original log ranch buildings from the turn of the 20th century, but beautifully renovated and updated with full kitchens, spacious bathrooms, and lovely furnishings straight out of the pages of *House Beautiful*. Each of the cabins has a private patio with gas barbecue; three have fireplaces. In addition, there are two rooms each with two twin beds and private bathrooms in the main lodge. The lodge features a TV lounge with video library; phones and fax machine are also available. Families are welcome. A full Swiss-style breakfast is available for C$12 per person. Your hosts will arrange horseback rides and other recreation. Open in winter by reservation only.

Trout Creek Rd. (off Wells Gray Park Rd.), Clearwater, BC V0E 1N0. (℃ **250/674-3655.** Fax 250/674-3387. www.nakiskaranch.bc.ca. 8 units. Summer C$105 double, C$125–C$150 cabin; winter C$95 double, C$120–C$145 cabin. MC, V. Drive up Wells Gray Park Rd. for 30km (19 miles); it will take about 30 min. Turn right at the ranch sign onto Trout Creek Rd. The park entrance is a 10-min. drive from the ranch. Small pets accepted. **Amenities:** Lounge. *In room:* Fridge, kitchen (cabins only), hair dryer, no phone.

Trophy Mountain Buffalo Ranch and Campground   You can't miss the small buffalo herd grazing in a pasture as you drive up the Wells Gray Park Road. Beyond this pastoral setting stand a log lodge, campsites, and camping cabins. The lodge came into existence nearly a century ago out on the North Thompson River. The abandoned structure was taken apart log by hand-hewn log and reassembled in its present location. The lodge restaurant is fully licensed, and the lodge rooms are cozy and clean; all have private bathrooms. The rustic bunkhouses, tent sites, and RV sites are extremely well kept. Dishwashing sinks are set up on the deck of the shower house, where hot water flows liberally. Hiking and horseback-riding trails surround the ranch, and guided rides run to the cliffs overlooking the Clearwater River valley and to the base of a secluded waterfall (C$65 for a 3-hr. trip). This friendly, unfussy guest ranch is just the spot if you're looking for clean and simple accommodations with lots of Old West atmosphere. It's open May through October and December through March (depending on snow conditions).

R.R. 1 (P.O. Box 1768), Clearwater, BC V0E 1N0. (℃ **250/674-3095.** Fax 250/674-3131. www.buffaloranch. ca. 7 units, 15 campsites, 2 bunkhouses. C$85–C$105 double; C$18–C$22 campsite; C$35 bunkhouse. MC, V. Drive up Wells Gray Park Rd. for 20km (12 miles); it will take about 20 min. Turn left at the ranch sign. *In room:* No phone.

Where to Dine

The **Clearwater Country Inn,** 449 Yellowhead Hwy. E. (℃ **250/674-3121**), has good home-style cooking; it's open daily from 4am to 9pm. **Helmcken Falls Lodge** (℃ **250/674-3657**), described above, and the Black Horse Saloon at the **Wells Gray Guest Ranch,** Wells Gray Road (℃ **250/674-2774**), offer lunch and buffet-style dinners; reservations are required. The friendly **River Café,** 73 Old N. Thompson Hwy. (℃ **250/674-0088**), in Clearwater, offers salads, espresso drinks, and fresh-baked snacks.

13

The Okanagan Valley

Just south of the High Country on Hwy. 97, the arid Okanagan Valley, with its long chain of crystal-blue lakes, is the ideal destination for freshwater-sports enthusiasts, golfers, skiers, and wine lovers. Ranches and small towns have flourished here for more than a century; the region's fruit orchards and vineyards will make you feel as if you've been transported to the Spanish countryside. Summer visitors get the pick of the crop—at insider prices—from the many fruit stands that line Hwy. 97. Be sure to stop for a pint of cherries, homemade jams, and other goodies.

An Okanagan-region chardonnay won gold medals in 1994 at international competitions held in London and Paris. In 2000, several other Okanagan vintages picked up quite a number of medals at international competitions. And more than 100 other wineries produce vintages that are following right on their heels. Despite these coveted honors, the valley has only recently begun to receive international publicity. Most visitors are Canadian, and the valley isn't yet a major tour-bus destination. Get here before they do.

Many retirees have chosen the Okanagan Valley as their home for its relatively mild winters and dry, desert-like summers. It's also a favorite destination for younger visitors, drawn by boating, water-skiing, sportfishing, and windsurfing on 128km-long (80-mile) Okanagan Lake. The town of Kelowna in the central valley is the hub of the province's winemaking industry and the area's largest city.

1 ESSENTIALS

GETTING THERE

BY CAR The 387km (240-mile) drive from Vancouver via the Trans-Canada Highway (Hwy. 1) and Hwy. 3 rambles through rich delta farmlands and the forested mountains of Manning Provincial Park and the Similkameen River region before descending into the Okanagan Valley's antelope-brush and sagebrush desert. For a more direct route to Kelowna, take the Trans-Canada Highway to the Coquihalla Toll Highway, which eliminates more than an hour's driving time. The 203km (126-mile) route runs from Hope through Merritt over the Coquihalla Pass into Kamloops.

BY BUS **Greyhound Canada** (© 800/661-8747; www.greyhound.ca) runs daily buses from Vancouver to Penticton and Kelowna, with service continuing on to Banff and Calgary. The one-way fare to Penticton is C$67.

BY PLANE **Air Canada Jazz** (© 888/247-2262; www.aircanada.ca) and **WestJet** (© 888/937-8538; www.westjet.com) offer frequent daily commuter flights from Calgary and Vancouver to Penticton and Kelowna. **Horizon Air** (© 800/252-7522; www. alaskaair.com), a division of Alaska Air, provides service to and from Seattle and Kelowna.

Contact the **Thompson Okanagan Tourism Association,** 2280 Leckie Rd., Kelowna (✆ **250/860-5999;** www.totabc.com), which is open daily from 8am to 4:30pm. For information about the Okanagan wineries, contact **Penticton & Wine Country Chamber of Commerce,** 553 Railway St., Penticton (✆ **800/663-5052** or 250/493-4055; www.tourismpenticton.com). The friendly staff at its Wine Country Visitor Centre can help you with itineraries, restaurants, activities, and lodging. The center also has an excellent wine shop, filled with the best of B.C. wines and regional cheeses.

2 TOURING THE WINERIES

British Columbia has a long history of producing wines, ranging from fantastic to truly bad. In 1859, missionary Father Pandosy planted apple trees and vineyards and produced sacramental wines for the valley's mission. Other monastery wineries cropped up, but none worried about the quality of their bottlings. After all, the Canadian government had a reputation for subsidizing domestic industries, such as book publishing and cleric wineries, to promote entrepreneurial growth.

In the 1980s, the government threatened to pull its support of the industry unless it could produce an internationally competitive product. The vintners listened. Rootstock was imported from France and Germany, and European-trained master vintners were hired to oversee the development of the vines and the winemaking process. The climate and soil conditions turned out to be some of the best in the world for winemaking, and today, British Columbia wines are winning international gold medals. Competitively priced, in the range of C$10 to C$50, they represent some great bargains in well-balanced chardonnays, pinot blancs, and Gewürztraminers; full-bodied merlots, pinot noirs, and cabernets; and dessert ice wines that surpass the best muscat d'or.

The valley's more than 100 vineyards and wineries conduct free tours and tastings throughout the year. The **Okanagan Wine Festival** (✆ 250/861-6654; www.thewine festivals.com), an annual celebration of wine and food, is held in early October at area vineyards and restaurants; for many, the key event is a B.C.-wide tasting held at the Penticton convention center.

Contact local visitor centers for information, as new wineries continue to open and established ones reinvent themselves with new and ever more sophisticated facilities. Vineyard restaurants are particularly in the vanguard, and many tasting rooms now offer food in addition to wine, and some offer lodgings.

3 OSOYOOS

Just across the border from Washington State on Hwy. 97, **Osoyoos** (pop. 5,000) is a small agricultural town on Osoyoos Lake that's making a rapid transition to being a wine country resort destination in its own right. The steep and narrow mountain slopes that encase the entire Okanagan region are particularly high here, making this the driest and hottest area in all of Canada. All that heat makes great conditions for irrigated fruit crops, wineries, and sun worshipers seeking summer beachfront. Osoyoos Lake has miles of sandy beaches and the warmest lake water in Canada.

A dizzying profusion of boating and water recreation awaits on Osoyoos Lake. To rent jet-boats, power boats, Sea-doos, ski boats, pedal boats, aqua bikes, and pontoon boats, walk along the marinas on Hwy. 3, where you'll find a number of rental services.

If you're really not into the jet-boat scene, Osoyoos has one unique feature to interest you. The land in the Okanagan Valley between Osoyoos and Penticton's Skaha Lake is considered the northernmost extension of the Sonoran desert that begins in Mexico. These "pocket deserts"—as the thin strip of arid steppes are called locally—are highly endangered ecosystems, as a century's worth of irrigation has served to put almost all the desert into cultivation.

One area of the Osoyoos desert is preserved at the **Desert Center** (© 877/899-0897 or 250/495-2470; www.desert.org). This interpretive center features nature trails through antelope brush grasslands that are home to many endangered and threatened species such as the burrowing owl, the spadefoot toad, the northern rattler, and the pallid bat. The center is open mid-May to mid-September Wednesday through Monday 9:30am to 4:30pm, with hour-long tours at 10am, noon, and 2pm. The center is also open late April to mid-May and mid-September to early October, but with self-guided tours only. Admission is C$7 adult, C$6 seniors and students, C$5 children 6 to 12, and C$16 for a family. The Desert Center is about 2 miles north of Osoyoos on Hwy. 97, at 146th Street.

Nk'Mip Cellars, 1400 Rancher Creek Rd. (© **250/495-2985;** www.nkmipcellars. com), is a top Osoyoos-area winery, located at the Spirit Ridge Resort (see below). North America's first First Nations–owned and –operated winery, Nk'Mip Cellars (pronounced *In*-ka-meep) produces a full range of wines; particularly excellent are the pinot blanc, syrah, and a meritage blend. The tasting room is open daily 9am to 5pm.

Contact the **Osoyoos Visitor Info Centre** at 9912 Hwy. 3 (© **888/676-9667** or 250/495-3366; www.destinationosoyoos.com).

WHERE TO STAY & DINE

Spirit Ridge Vineyard Resort & Spa ★★ This luxury-level lodging overlooks Lake Osoyoos, the steep-sloped Okangan Valley, and miles of vineyards. Opened in 2007, Spirit Ridge brings a Santa Fe look to the Sonoran desert landscape. Lodgings are in one-bedroom suites, or one- or two-bedroom villas, each with full kitchen, dining and living room (with fireplace), and balcony. The resort offers a full-service spa plus the **Passatempo Restaurant,** with "wine country comfort food." Guests have private access to beaches on Osoyoos Lake; the 9-hole **Sonora Dunes Golf Course** (© **250/495-4653;** www.sonoradunes.com) and **Nk'Mip Cellars Winery** (© **250/495-2985;** www. nkmipcellars.com) **are adjacent.**

1200 Rancher Creek Rd., Osoyoos, BC V0H 1V6. © **877/313-9463** or 250/495-5445. Fax 250/495-5447. www.spiritridge.ca. 226 units. C$135–C$349 1-bedroom suite; C$175–C$349 1-bedroom villa; C$199–C$429 2-bedroom villa; C$199–C$429 3-bedroom suite. AE, MC, V. Free parking. **Amenities:** Restaurant; lounge; golf course; fitness center; hot tubs; outdoor pools w/water slide; spa; deli/market; meeting space; rooftop deck; cultural center; winery; beach access. *In room:* A/C, TV/DVD, hair dryer, full kitchen and dining room, Wi-Fi, fireplace.

4 OLIVER

52km (32 miles) S of Penticton

The absolute center of the Okanagan fruit-growing orchards is Oliver (pop. 4,300). What makes the area interesting to travelers, however, is its many wineries. Scarcely a tourist town, Oliver exists to serve the needs of local farmers, orchardists, and winemakers. It makes a reasonable stop if you're not obsessed with the resort and watersports lifestyle prevalent in the rest of the Okanagan Valley. For more information on the region, contact the **South Okanagan Visitor Info Centre,** 36205 93rd St. (℃ **250/498-6321;** www.sochamber.ca).

Many of the long-established wineries that put the region's name on the wine-producing map are within a short drive of Oliver. Especially proud of their location are the wineries along the "Golden Mile," situated on the slopes of the mountains west of Oliver along Road 8. **Festival of the Grape** (℃ **250/498-6321;** www.sochamber.ca) occurs in the first weekend of October, and is part of the larger Okanagan Wine Festival. Another notable winegrowing area is just north of Oliver, near the town of **Okanagan Falls.**

Notable Oliver-area wineries that welcome visitors include **Burrowing Owl Winery** ★, halfway between Osoyoos and Oliver at 100 Black Sage Rd. (℃ **877/498-0620** or 250/ 498-6202; www.bovwine.ca), which makes exceptional wines; its award-winning merlot is one of B.C.'s top wines. Their **Sonora Room** dining room is an equally excellent vineyard restaurant (closed in late fall), and the 10-bedroom **Guest House at Burrowing Owl** is a top boutique lodging (see below).

Gehringer Brothers Estate Winery, Road 8 between Osoyoos and Oliver (℃ **250/498-3537**), offers German-style wines, including Riesling, pinot gris, pinot noir, and pinot blanc, plus a notable ice wine. Try the crisp Ehrenfelser white wine, which carries intense flavors of apricot and almond. The tasting room is open June through mid-October daily; call for off-season hours.

Near Oliver, **Tinhorn Creek Vineyards,** Road 7 (℃ **888/846-4676;** www.tinhorn. com), is one of the top Okanagan wineries. Specialties include Gewürztraminer, pinot gris, chardonnay, pinot noir, cabernet franc, merlot, and ice wine.

The town of **Okanagan Falls** is 20km (12 miles) north of Oliver along Hwy. 97. Adjacent to a wilderness area and bird sanctuary overlooking Vaseaux Lake, **Blue Mountain Vineyards & Cellars,** 2385 Allendale Rd. (℃ **250/497-8244;** www.blue mountainwinery.com), operates a wine shop and tasting room by appointment only. **Blasted Church Vineyards** ★, 378 Parsons Rd. (℃ **250/497-1125;** www.blasted church.com), has impossible-to-miss wine labels, and delicious and affordable wines. One of my favorites.

WHERE TO STAY & DINE

Guest House at Burrowing Owl ★★ The top-echelon Burrowing Owl Winery offers 10 spectacular guest rooms in the midst of a vineyard. This newly constructed boutique inn has large and airy rooms, filled with light, fine art, native stone, and gracious good taste. Most rooms have king-size beds (two have two doubles), and all have balconies overlooking the grape vines and the nearby desert hills. Relax by the 25m (82-ft.) outdoor pool and patio, and definitely have dinner at the **Sonora Room** ★, the winery's excellent New Canadian restaurant.

100 Black Sage Rd. (R.R. 1, Comp 20, Site 52), Oliver, BC V0N 1T0. ℃ **877/498-0620** or 250/498-0620. www.bovwine.ca. 11 units. July 1 to mid-Oct C$325. 2-night minimum stay in high season. Lower off-season rates. AE, MC, V. Free parking. **Amenities:** Restaurant; guest lounge; hot tub; outdoor pool; wine shop and tasting bar. *In room:* A/C, flatscreen TV, fridge, Wi-Fi, fireplace.

5 PENTICTON

80km (50 miles) N of Oliver; 60km (37 miles) S of Kelowna; 396km (246 miles) W of Vancouver via the Coquihalla Hwy.

One of the belles of the Okanagan, Penticton (pop. 41,500) is a lovely midsize city with two entirely different lakefronts. Above the town is the toe-end of vast Okanagan Lake; to the south are the upper beaches of Lake Skaha. It's a lovely setting, and a peach of a place for a recreation-dominated holiday. "Peach" has additional significance here, as Penticton is also the center for apple, peach, cherry, and grape production. But there's a lot more to Penticton than agriculture: Facilities range from hostels to world-class resorts, and the restaurants are among the best in this part of British Columbia.

The **Penticton & Wine Country Chamber of Commerce** is at 553 Railway St. (© **800/663-5052** or 250/493-4055; www.tourismpenticton.com). It also houses the British Columbia Wine Information Centre and an excellent wine shop with all sorts of local vintages. It's open daily 9am to 6pm.

EXPLORING THE TOWN

It's hard to beat Penticton's location. With Okanagan Lake lapping at the northern edge of town, Lake Skaha's beaches forming the town's southern boundary, and the Okanagan River cutting between the two, Penticton has the feel of a real oasis. Hemmed in by lakes and desert valley walls, Penticton is pleasantly compact and in summer fairly hums with activity. As elsewhere in the Okanagan Valley, watersports are the main preoccupation, but Penticton also has an air of gentility that suggests there's a little more going on than just jet-skiing.

The old commercial center is along **Main Street** toward the north end of town; there's also a lot of activity along **Lakeshore Drive,** the boulevard that parallels the beachfront of Okanagan Lake. Lined with hotels and restaurants on one side, clogged with sun worshipers on the other, Lakeshore Drive is a very busy place in summer.

Right on the lakefront is the **SS** *Sicamous,* a stern-wheeler that plied the waters of Okanagan Lake from 1914 to 1935. Now preserved as a museum, it's beached in the sand, and currently houses a scale model of the historic Kettle Valley Railway. It's open in summer daily from 9am to 9pm, the rest of the year Monday through Friday from 9am to 4pm.

Even if you're not into sunbathing, a saunter along the **beachfront promenade** is called for. Beach volleyball, sand castles, and a drinks kiosk in the shape of a giant peach are just the beginning of what you'll encounter along this long, broad strand: It's prime people-watching territory.

At the eastern end of the beachfront is the **Art Gallery of the South Okanagan,** 199 Front St. (© **250/493-2928**), a showcase for local artists. The gift shop is a good spot to pick up a souvenir. Just beyond the gallery is the **Marina on Lake Okanagan** (© **250/770-2000**), where you can rent all manner of watercraft.

The beach along Skaha Lake is usually more laid-back than the Okanagan lakefront. The relatively more secluded nature of this beach, plus a large water park for the kids, makes it a good destination for families. **Skaha Lake Marina** (© **250/492-7368**) is at the east edge of the beach.

The two main wine-producing areas near Penticton are along the west lake slopes near Summerland, and north along the east slopes of Okanagan Lake near the community of Naramata, one of the first winegrowing regions in British Columbia.

To begin your explorations, follow Upper Bench Road from Penticton, which turns into Naramata Road and leads to **Naramata,** 14km (8¾ miles) north. **La Frenz Winery,** 740 Naramata Rd. (© **250/492-6690;** www.lafrenzwinery.com), makes excellent small-lot bottlings of semillon, viognier, and merlot.

Poplar Grove Winery ★, 1060 Poplar Grove Rd. (© **250/493-9463;** www.poplar grove.ca), produces a top-notch claret-style wine; try the cabernet franc if it's available—it's a wonderful wine that sells out every year. Poplar Grove is building a new winery and tasting room on the Naramata Bench; call ahead for hours and opening dates.

Hillside Estate, 1350 Naramata Rd. (© **250/493-6274;** www.hillsideestate.com), is open daily (call ahead in midwinter). From Easter weekend until the Okanagan Wine Festival in October, it operates the **Barrel Room Bistro,** a patio restaurant at the winery, open for lunch daily. It opens for dinner on weekends starting May 1, and opens nightly for dinners in mid-June.

Lake Breeze Vineyards, 930 Sammet Rd. (© **250/496-5659;** www.lakebreeze.ca), opens its tasting room weekends in April and daily from May 1 through October from 10am to 5pm. Its restaurant, **The Patio,** is open for lunch from May 1 to early October.

North of Penticton along Hwy. 97 near Summerville is the other wine-producing area. **Sumac Ridge Estate Winery,** 17403 Hwy. 97 (© **250/494-0451;** www.sumacridge.com), offers tastings daily; the Burgundy-style wines are excellent. Be sure to also try to their sparkling wines, which include both traditional and red (Shiraz-based) bubblies. Besides operating a shop and tasting room open daily year-round, the winery runs the fine **Cellar Door Bistro.**

Located 43km (27 miles) north of Penticton, the **Hainle Vineyards Estate Winery,** 5355 Trepanier Bench Rd. (© **250/767-2525;** www.hainle.com), was the first Okanagan winery to produce ice wine. The wine shop is open mid-April through October, and weekdays only the rest of the year, for tasting.

THE KETTLE VALLEY STEAM RAILWAY

The Kettle Valley Railway, which was completed in 1914 to link coastal communities to the burgeoning mining camps in Kettle River valley, became one of the Okanagan Valley's top draws after much of it was converted into a rails-to-trails pathway for hikers and mountain bikers called the Kettle Valley Rail Trail. Unfortunately, the massive forest fires of 2003 burned a number of the historic wooden trestles that bridged the route through steep Myra Canyon, closing it for 4 years. The trestles have been rebuilt, and in 2008 this part of the route reopened to hikers and bikers (see "Biking," below).

One section of the Kettle Valley Railway, however, is in use by original steam trains. The **Kettle Valley Railway Society,** 18404 Bathville Rd., Summerland (© **877/494-8424** in B.C., or 250/494-8422; www.kettlevalleyrail.org), offers a 2-hour journey on a 10km (6¼-mile) section of the original track west of Summerland, 16km (10 miles) north of Penticton. The first Thursday in July to Labour Day, the train runs Thursday through Monday at 10:30am and 1:30pm, departing from the Prairie Valley Station off Bathville Road; from mid-May to late June and from Labour Day to mid-October, the train runs at the same times Saturday through Monday only. In addition, on most Saturdays there's an afternoon train that involves a "train robbery" and barbecue. Check

OUTDOOR PURSUITS

BIKING   The best Okanagan Valley off-road bike trail is the Kettle Valley Rail Trail. The tracks and ties have been removed, making way for some incredibly scenic biking. The most picturesque and challenging section of the route is from Naramata, north of Penticton along the east side of Okanagan Lake. The rails-to-trails route climbs up steep switchbacks to Chute Lake and then across 17 trestles (recently rebuilt after burning in a forest fire) as it traverses Myra Canyon. The entire mountain bike route from Naramata to Westbridge in the Kettle River Valley is 175km (109 miles) and can take from 3 to 5 days. For more information on cycling the route, contact the visitor center above, or contact the **Bike Barn,** 300 W. Westminster (© **250/492-4140**), which has bike rentals and lots of friendly advice. Also check the website at www. spiritof2010trail.ca.

BOATING & WATERSPORTS   The Okanagan Valley's numerous local marinas offer full-service boat rentals. One of the most convenient, the **Marina on Okanagan Lake,** 291 Front St., Penticton (© **250/492-2628**), rents ski-boats, Tigersharks (similar to jet skis or Sea-Doos), fishing boats, and tackle.

A popular activity is renting a rubber raft from **Coyote Cruises** (© **205/492-2115**), in the blue building along the river at Riverside Drive, then floating from Okanagan Lake down to Skaha Lake, which takes about 2 hours. On a hot day, you'll be joined by hundreds of other people in rafts, inner tubes, and rubber dinghies; the water fight of your life is almost guaranteed.

SKIING   Cross-country and powder skiing are the Okanagan Valley's main winter attractions. Intermediate and expert downhill skiers frequent the **Apex Resort,** Green Mountain Road, Penticton (© **800/387-2739**, 250/492-2880, 250/292-8111, or 250/492-2929, ext. 2000, for snow report; www.apexresort.com), with 56 runs and 52km (32 miles) of cross-country ski trails. Day passes are C$60 adults, C$49 seniors and ages 13 to 18, and C$37 kids 12 and under. Facilities include an ice rink, snow golf, sleigh rides, casino nights, and racing competitions.

WHERE TO STAY

There are three major lodging areas: the northern lakefront on Okanagan Lake, the southern lakefront on Lake Skaha, and the Main Street strip that connects the two. Penticton has a lot of older motels, many of which have seen years of hard use.

Naramata Heritage Inn & Spa ★★   Built in 1908, the Naramata Inn served as a hotel, private residence, and girls' school before undergoing extensive and loving renovation as a classic wine-country inn. This inn is a half-hour northwest of Penticton on the quiet side of Lake Okanagan in the tiny community of Naramata. It offers very charming rooms (note that some are authentically small), restored to glow with period finery, but modern luxury—the linens are top-notch and the bathroom's heated tile floors are a nice touch on a cool morning. In addition to en suite bathrooms with showers, rooms also have a claw-foot tub in the bedroom for soaking and relaxing. The inn also offers a spa for upscale pampering, plus the best dining in the area. There are few places in the otherwise utilitarian Okanagan as unique as this.

3625 First St., Naramata, BC V0H 1N0 (19km/12 miles north of Penticton on the east side of Okanagan Lake). (C 866/617-1188 or 250/496-6808. www.naramatainn.com. 12 units. High season C$182–C$510 double. Rates include continental breakfast. Lower off-season rates. AE, MC, V. **Amenities:** Restaurant (see "Where to Dine," below); wine bar; limited room service; spa; Wi-Fi. In room: A/C, hair dryer.

Penticton Lakeside Resort Convention Centre & Casino

Set on the water's edge, the Penticton Lakeside Resort has its own stretch of sandy Lake Okanagan beachfront, where guests can sunbathe or stroll along the adjacent pier. The deluxe suites feature Jacuzzis, and the lakeside rooms are highly recommended for their view. All rooms and suites are smartly furnished with quality furniture; all rooms have balconies (some suites have two-person Jacuzzi tubs). The menus at the Hooded Merganser Restaurant and the Barking Parrot Bar & Patio feature locally grown ingredients. Other facilities include an extensive pool and health club facility, and a casino.

21 W. Lakeshore Dr., Penticton, BC V2A 7M5. (C 800/663-9400 or 250/493-8221. Fax 250/493-0607. www.rpbhotels.com. 204 units. C$226–C$273 double. Lower off-season rates. AE, DC, DISC, MC, V. Free parking. When you arrive in town, follow the signs to Main St. Lakeshore Dr. is at the north end of Main St. Pets accepted with C$20 fee. **Amenities:** Restaurant; lounge; babysitting; children's center; concierge; health club; Jacuzzi; indoor pool; room service; sauna; tennis courts; watersports equipment rental; volleyball court. In room: A/C, TV/VCR w/pay movies, hair dryer, Wi-Fi.

Ramada Inn & Suites ★

The newest hotel in the Penticton area, the Ramada isn't particularly near either lakefront but is a good choice if you have no patience with older and well-worn lodgings even though they may have a better location (however, the Ramada is adjacent to the Penticton Golf and Country Club). In exchange, you'll get large, nicely furnished rooms in a resort-like setting with good restaurants and a courtyard garden. If you want to step up from the standard rooms (which are perfectly nice, mind you), you'll find that the suites have options like stone-fronted fireplaces, Jacuzzi tubs, and full kitchens.

1050 Eckhardt Ave. W., Penticton, BC V2A 2C3. (C 800/665-4966 or 250/492-8926. www.pentictonramada. com. 125 units. C$119–C$219 double; C$169–C$274 suite. Additional person C$20. AE, DC, MC, V. Free parking. Pets accepted with C$10 fee. **Amenities:** 2 restaurants; pub and lounge; fitness center; hot tub; room service; outdoor heated pool; gas barbecues; playground. In room: A/C, TV, fridge, Wi-Fi, voice mail.

Waterfront Inn (Value)

This older, standard-issue motel is right across from a park with beach access to Lake Skaha. The rooms are clean and basic, but if you're here for the lakefront action, you'll enjoy the relative quiet of this location and the fact that you won't have to cross four lanes of traffic to get to the water.

3688 Parkview St., Penticton, BC V2A 6H1. (C 800/563-6006 or 250/492-8228. Fax 250/492-8228. www.waterfrontinn.net. 21 units. High season C$90–C$140 double. Kitchen C$10 extra. AE, DC, MC, V. Closed mid-Oct to Apr. **Amenities:** Splash pool; sauna; playground. In room: A/C, TV, fridge, Wi-Fi.

WHERE TO DINE

A number of Penticton-area vineyards now have restaurants; in fact, in good weather, these winery dining rooms are extremely charming places to eat, as most dining is alfresco (there are no bad views in the valley) and there's an explosion of local boutique and organic market produce available to young chefs. Of the wineries noted above, Sumac Ridge's **Cellar Door Bistro** ((C 250/494-0451) is open daily year-round (except late Dec and early Jan) for lunch and dinner. Hillside Estate operates the **Barrel Room Bistro,** 1350 Naramata Rd. ((C 250/493-6274; www.hillsideestate.com), which is open for lunch daily from Easter weekend through early October, and open for dinner on weekends starting May 1, and nightly for dinners in mid-June. Lake Breeze Vineyards operates

The Patio, 930 Sammet Rd. (✆ **250/496-5659;** www.lakebreeze.ca), open for lunch from May 1 to early October.

Granny Bogners CONTINENTAL   Granny Bogners, in a shake-sided heritage home in a quiet residential area, tops the list when it comes to locals' favorite special-occasion restaurant. The menu is slightly old-fashioned but reassuringly so and admirably prepared: Choices include chicken *cordon bleu,* filet mignon with béarnaise sauce, grilled salmon, veal medallions in port-and-mushroom sauce, and a number of German specialties. Despite the white linen and crystal, the dining room retains a kind of rustic nonchalance. In summer, dine out on the lovely garden patio.

302 W. Eckhardt Ave. ✆ **250/493-2711.** Reservations required. Main courses C$16–C$36. AE, MC, V. Tues–Sun 5:30–9:30pm.

Naramata Inn ★ PACIFIC NORTHWEST   Built in 1908, the Naramata Inn is resplendent in early-20th-century character. The Cobblestone Wine Bar serves some of the most sophisticated food in the Okanagan Valley, and with a very impressive wine list. Using only the freshest ingredients—many from its own garden—the Cobblestone offers a selection of tasting menus that focus on regional ingredients; wine pairings are available for each of the menus. Expect such refined dishes as seared deep sea scallop and kurobuta pork belly confit with parsnip ravioli, and double smoked bacon-wrapped quail breast with matsutake mushrooms. At lunch, expect soup, salads, and delicious hearth breads.

3625 First St., Naramata (19km/12 miles north of Penticton on the east side of Okanagan Lake). ✆ **250/496-5001.** www.naramatainn.com. Reservations required. 5-course menu C$70. MC, V. Apr–Oct daily 11:30am–10pm. Call for winter hours.

Theo's Greek Restaurant (Value) GREEK   Don't be surprised when previous visitors to Penticton immediately offer testimonials about Theo's, a popular place with excellent, flavorful cooking. The taverna-style dining room has whitewashed walls, a stone floor, and lush greenery. The menu features delectable calamari, succulent marinated lamb, and specialties like seared chicken livers and a standout moussaka. Even the requisite local salmon is wrapped in phyllo pastry with feta cheese and baked until flaky and golden.

687 Main St. ✆ **250/492-4019.** www.eatsquid.com. Reservations recommended. Main courses C$12–C$26. AE, DC, MC, V. Mon–Thurs 11am–10pm; Fri–Sat 11am–11pm; Sun 4–10pm.

Villa Rossa Ristorante ★ ITALIAN   Villa Rossa is one of the top Penticton options for traditional Italian cuisine. It has an attractive patio shaded by grapevines, just the spot on a warm evening. The menu is varied, with classic dishes such as *osso buco,* chicken Marsala, and pasta joining Canadian specialties such as steaks and salmon. Good wine list, too.

795 W. Westminster Ave. ✆ **250/490-9595.** www.thevillarosa.com. Reservations suggested. Main courses C$16–C$37. AE, MC, V. Mon–Fri 11:30am–2:30pm; daily 5–10pm.

Zia's Stonehouse Restaurant ★ CONTINENTAL   Located north of Penticton in Summerland, this restaurant is set inside a historic stone home that was built a century ago by an Italian immigrant. An appealing international menu is served inside the landmark building. Although the menu focuses on Mediterranean preparations of local meats and produce, there are also gestures toward Asian and American cuisine as well. Zia's, with its dedication to the memory of Italian aunts and their home-style cooking, is often selected by Okanagan locals as the area's most romantic restaurant.

14015 Rosedale Ave., Summerland. ✆ **250/494-1105.** www.ziasstonehouse.com. Reservations required. Main courses C$14–C$29. AE, DC, MC, V. Daily 11:30am–2:30pm and 5:30–10pm.

6 KELOWNA

395km (245 miles) E of Vancouver

Kelowna (pop. 106,700) is the largest city in the Okanagan, and one of the fastest-growing areas in Canada. You won't have to spend much time here to understand why: The city sits astride 128km-long (80-mile) Okanagan Lake at the center of a vast fruit-, wine-, and vegetable-growing area, with lots of sun and a resort lifestyle. This is about as close to California as it gets in Canada. Kelowna is especially popular with retirees, who stream here to escape the Pacific pall of Vancouver and the winter cold of Alberta. Predictably, watersports and golf are the main leisure activities, and it's hard to imagine a better outdoor-oriented family-vacation spot.

With plenty of marinas and a beautiful beachfront park that flanks downtown, you'll have no problem finding a place to get wet. In fact, Kelowna's only problem is its popularity. The greater Kelowna area now has a population of 162,000. Traffic is very heavy, particularly along Hwy. 97 as it inches right through the heart of the city.

ESSENTIALS

GETTING THERE   The Kelowna airport is north of the city on Hwy. 97. **Air Canada Jazz** (© **888/247-8747**) offers regular flights from Calgary and Vancouver. **Horizon Air** (© **800/547-9308;** www.alaskaair.com) offers service from Seattle. **WestJet** (© **888/937-8538;** www.westjet.com) operates flights from Vancouver, Victoria, Calgary, and Edmonton.

Greyhound Canada (© **800/661-8747**) travels between Vancouver and Kelowna daily. The adult fare is C$68. Three buses per day continue on to Calgary. The toll Coquihalla Highway (Hwy. 5) links Kelowna and the Okanagan to the Vancouver area. The 395km (245-mile) drive from Vancouver takes 4 hours. From Kelowna to Calgary, it's 623km (387 miles) over slower roads.

VISITOR INFORMATION   The **Kelowna Visitor Info Centre** is at 544 Harvey Ave. (© **800/663-4345** or 250/861-1515; www.tourismkelowna.com).

GETTING AROUND   The local bus service is operated by **Kelowna Regional Transit System** (© **250/860-8121**). A one-zone fare is C$2. For a taxi, call **Checkmate Cabs** (© **250/861-1111**).

EXPLORING THE CITY

Greater Kelowna is a big, sprawling place that has engulfed both sides of Okanagan Lake, but the sights of most interest are contained in a relatively small area. And that's good, because traffic in Kelowna can be vexing. Beware of the heavily traveled **Harvey Street** and the **Okanagan Lake Bridge;** the latter has been rebuilt but is still prone to jams.

Downtown is a pleasant retail area that retains a number of older buildings that now house shops, galleries, and cafes. The main commercial strip is **Bernard Street.** The showpiece of Kelowna is lovely **City Park,** which flanks downtown and the bridge's east side and has over half a mile of wide, sandy beach. At the north edge is a marina where you can rent boats and recreational equipment, or sign up to learn to water-ski and parasail. Here, too, is where you board the **MV *Fintry Queen,*** which offers boat tours of the lake (see below).

Continue north through the busy marina to **Waterfront Park,** with an island band shell and promenades along the lakefront and lagoons. The **Grand Okanagan Lakefront**

> **(Tips) Special Events**
>
> Kelowna gets its busy summer festival season off to a bang with the **Knox Mountain Hill Climb** (📞 **250/861-1990**), held for half a century on the second-to-last weekend in May. This motor-sport race involves both cars and motorcycles, and is the longest hill-climb race in North America. The **Okanagan Wine Festival** (📞 **250/861-6654;** www.owfs.com) is celebrated in late September and early October in wineries and restaurants throughout the area.

Resort towers above the park, and it's worth a stop to step inside the opulent lobby, or to enjoy a drink beside the pool.

The **Rotary Center for the Arts,** 421 Cawston Ave. (📞 **250/717-5304**), is a multi-purpose venue with a 330-seat performing arts theater, plus two art galleries and a number of open studios for artists and craftspeople. It's a fun place to wander, watching artists at work, and you may find a gift to buy or a piece to add to your collection. The center also contains a lunchtime cafe with soup and sandwiches.

B.C. Orchard Industry Museum This museum, housed in an old apple-packing plant, tells the story of the region's apple-and-soft-fruit industry, with archival photos, equipment, and a hands-on discovery corner. Sharing space with the Orchard Museum is the **Wine Museum** (📞 **250/868-0441**), with a few exhibits on the history of Okanagan wine production. The shop sells a good selection of regional vintages.

1304 Ellis St. 📞 **250/763-0433.** www.kelownamuseum.ca. Admission by donation. Mon–Sat 10am–5pm.

Kelowna Art Gallery Kelowna's 1,394-sq.-m (15,005-sq.-ft.) regional gallery hosts nearly 20 shows per year of work by regional, national, and international artists. The permanent collection is a good body of works by primarily British Columbian artists. The shop is a great place for unique handcrafted gifts.

1315 Water St. 📞 **250/762-2226.** www.galleries.bc.ca/kelowna. C$5 adults, C$4 seniors and students, C$10 families. Tues–Sat 10am–5pm (Thurs to 9pm); Sun 1–4pm.

Kelowna Museum This ambitious museum touches on the history of life in the Okanagan Valley. Starting out with local fossils, exhibits move through the prehistoric culture of the Native Okanagans and on to the lives of the farmers and ranchers. Eclectic only begins to describe the collection—radios, dolls, books—but everything is well curated, and you're sure to find something of interest.

470 Queensway Ave. 📞 **250/763-2417.** www.kelownamuseum.ca. Admission by donation. Mon–Sat 10am–5pm.

TOURING THE WINERIES

Just north of city center, **Calona Wines,** 1125 Richter St., Kelowna (📞 **250/762-3332;** www.calonavineyards.ca), offers tastings in western Canada's oldest and largest (since 1932) winery. Many antique winemaking machines are on display, alongside the state-of-the-art equipment the winery now uses.

North of Kelowna is **Gray Monk Estate Winery,** 1055 Camp Rd., Okanagan Centre (📞 **800/663-4205** or 250/766-3168; www.graymonk.com). Noted for its pinot noirs, Gray Monk has a patio lounge and gives winery tours daily. The tasting room is open

THE OKANAGAN VALLEY

13 KELOWNA

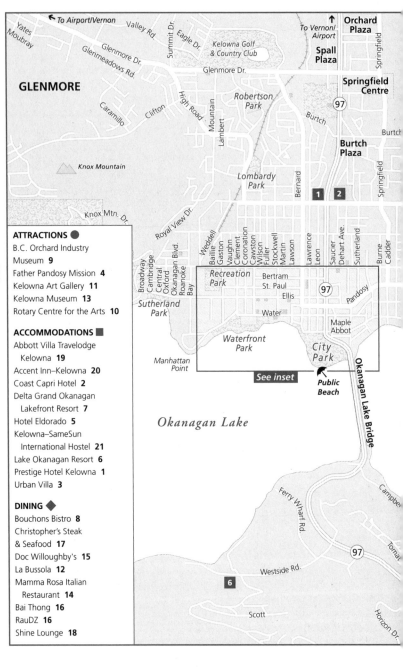

ATTRACTIONS ●

B.C. Orchard Industry
Museum **9**
Father Pandosy Mission **4**
Kelowna Art Gallery **11**
Kelowna Museum **13**
Rotary Centre for the Arts **10**

ACCOMMODATIONS ■

Abbott Villa Travelodge
Kelowna **19**
Accent Inn–Kelowna **20**
Coast Capri Hotel **2**
Delta Grand Okanagan
Lakefront Resort **7**
Hotel Eldorado **5**
Kelowna–SameSun
International Hostel **21**
Lake Okanagan Resort **6**
Prestige Hotel Kelowna **1**
Urban Villa **3**

DINING ◆

Bouchons Bistro **8**
Christopher's Steak
& Seafood **17**
Doc Willoughby's **15**
La Bussola **12**
Mamma Rosa Italian
Restaurant **14**
Bai Thong **16**
RauDZ **16**
Shine Lounge **18**

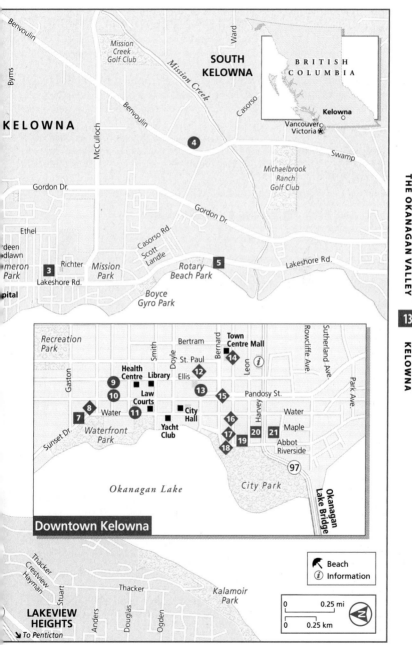

Downtown Kelowna

daily year-round. The winery's **Grapevine Restaurant** offers serious Continental cuisine in its lake-view dining room, which is open for lunch daily from Easter weekend through October; nightly dinner service begins on May 1.

South of Kelowna on the east side of the lake is **Cedar Creek Estate Winery,** 5445 Lakeshore Rd. (© **250/764-8866;** www.cedarcreek.bc.ca). Cedar Creek produces notable pinot noir, chardonnay, and meritage blends. **The Terrace Restaurant** is open for lunch daily.

Across Okanagan Lake from Kelowna is Westbank, home to **Mission Hill Wines,** 1730 Mission Hill Rd. (© **250/768-7611;** www.missionhillwinery.com), one of the most architecturally eye-catching wineries in the Okanagan. The tasting room is open daily, except for major winter holidays; check the website for tours.

An experience worth savoring even if you're not an oenophile is the **Quail's Gate Estate,** 3303 Boucherie Rd., Westbank (© **250/769-4451;** www.quailsgate.com), famous for its ice wines, marvelous chenin blanc, and rich merlot. The **Old Vines Patio Restaurant ★**, with marvelous views of vineyards and the lake, is open daily for lunch and dinner, save for a staff holiday the first 2 weeks in January.

ORGANIZED TOURS & EXCURSIONS

Built in 1948, the paddle-wheeler **MV *Fintry Queen,*** on the dock off Bernard Avenue (© **250/763-2780;** www.fintryqueen.com), was once a working ferry but is now a tour boat and restaurant. Call for details on sailings and special lunch and dinner cruises.

If you want to visit the wineries and leave the driving to someone else, contact **Okanagan Wine Country Tours** (© **866/689-9463** or 250/868-9463; www.okwine tours.com), which offers packages ranging from a 3-hour Afternoon Delight for C$75 to the Daytripper for C$145.

OUTDOOR PURSUITS

BIKING The Kettle Valley Railway's **Myra Canyon** route near Kelowna has reopened (many of the trestles burned during the Okanagan wildfires in 2003). Although the route is often accessed from Naramata (p. 299), bikers in Kelowna can reach the east side of the route by following Hwy. 33 south from Kelowna. Inquire at **Sports Rent,** 3000 Pandosy St. (© **250/861-5699**), for other mountain biking routes in the area, including bike parks at Apex Mountain Resort and Silver Star Mountain Resort.

GOLF The Okanagan's warm climate is good for more than just growing grapes and apricots. The valley also is home to 50 golf courses; for information, contact www.totabc. com/trellis/golf. The greens fees throughout the Okanagan Valley range from C$65 to C$175 and are a good value not only because of the beautiful locations, but also for the quality of service you'll find at each club.

Harvest Golf Club, 2725 Klo Rd. (© **250/862-3103**), is one of the finest courses in the Okanagan, a championship course in an orchard setting. The **Okanagan Golf Club ★**, off Hwy. 97 near the airport (© **800/898-2449** or 250/765-5955), has two 18-hole courses, the Jack Nicklaus–designed Bear Course and the Les Furber–designed Quail Course.

HIKING The closest trails to Kelowna are in **Knox Mountain Park,** immediately north of the city. From downtown, follow Ellis Street to its terminus, where there's a parking area and trail head. The most popular trail climbs up the cactus-clad mountainside to the summit, from which you'll enjoy magnificent views of the lake and orchards.

SKIING & SNOWBOARDING   One of British Columbia's largest ski areas and one of North America's snowboarding capitals, **Big White Ski Resort** ★, Parkinson Way, Kelowna (② **250/765-3101**, 250/765-SNOW [7669] for snow report, or 250/765-8888 for lodge reservations; www.bigwhite.com), is famed for its hip-deep champagne powder snow. The resort spreads over a broad mountain, featuring long, wide runs. Skiers here cruise open bowls and tree-lined glades. There's an annual average of 7.5m (25 ft.) of fluffy powder, so it's no wonder the resort's 118 named runs are so popular. There are 16 lifts, capable of carrying 28,000 skiers per hour. For snowboarders, there is a 150m-long (492-ft.) super pipe with 5.1m (17-ft.) transitional walls and a 120m (394-ft.) standard half pipe. The resort also offers more than 25km (16 miles) of groomed cross-country ski trails, a recreational racing program, and night skiing. Adult lift tickets are C$71. Big White is 55km (34 miles) southeast of Kelowna off Hwy. 33.

Only a 15-minute drive from Westbank, **Crystal Mountain Resorts Ltd.** (② **250/768-5189,** or 250/768-3753 for snow report; www.crystalresort.com) has a range of ski programs for all types of skiers, specializing in clinics for children, women, and seniors. The resort's 20 runs are 80% intermediate-to-novice grade and are serviced by one double chair and two T-bars. The runs are equipped for day and night skiing. There's also a half pipe for snowboarders. Lift tickets start at C$46 adults and C$38 children.

WATERSPORTS   The marina just north of City Park has a great many outfitters that can rent you a boat, jet ski, windsurfing board, or paddle boat. If you want to call ahead, try **Dockside Marine Centre** (② **250/765-3995;** www.docksidemarine.com), which offers a wide range of boats and watercraft. To try parasailing, call **Kelowna Parasail Adventures** (② **250/868-4838**), which offers flights for C$67.

WHERE TO STAY

Abbott Villa Travelodge Kelowna (Value)   For the money, this is one of the best places to stay in Kelowna, as it has one of the best locations downtown—right across from the City Park beaches. You'll be able to walk to the lakefront and to your favorite restaurants. The standard-issue motel units are clean and well maintained.

1627 Abbott St., Kelowna, BC V1Y 1A9. ② **800/663-2000** or 250/763-7771. Fax 250/762-2402. www.travelodge.com. 52 units. High season C$135–C$165 double. Kitchen C$10 extra. AE, MC, V. **Amenities:** Restaurant; Jacuzzi; heated outdoor pool; sauna. *In room:* A/C, TV, Wi-Fi.

Accent Inn–Kelowna   So you're heading into Kelowna on a summer weekend, and even though you're dreaming of a beachfront hotel, you didn't call 6 months ago to secure a room. Every place is absolutely booked and you're going to have to stay in a decent, basic motel, and you just hope it's clean, new, and functional. This is it.

1140 Harvey Ave., Kelowna, BC V1Y 6E7. ② **800/663-0298** or 250/862-8888. Fax 250/862-8884. www.accentinns.com. 101 units. High season C$139–C$169 double. Kitchen C$10 extra. MC, V. Pets accepted with C$15 fee. **Amenities:** Restaurant; exercise room; Jacuzzi; outdoor pool; sauna. *In room:* A/C, TV, Wi-Fi.

Coast Capri Hotel   Somewhat apart from the downtown area, the Coast Capri offers large, newly furbished rooms, most with balconies. You'll need to drive to the beaches from here, and the surrounding blocks are filled with strip malls, but if you can't get into one of the beachfront hotels yet still want high-quality lodgings, then this is your next-best choice. The **Vintage Dining Room** is a great old-fashioned steakhouse—probably the best place in town for an elegant dinner of prime rib or steak.

1171 Harvey Ave., Kelowna, BC V1Y 6E8. ② **800/663-1144** or 250/860-6060. Fax 250/762-3430. www.coasthotels.com. 185 units. High season C$185–C$205 double. AE, MC, V. **Amenities:** 2 restaurants; 2 bars; exercise room; Jacuzzi; heated outdoor pool. *In room:* A/C, TV, free Wi-Fi.

Delta Grand Okanagan Lakefront Resort & Conference Centre ★★★ (**Kids**)

This elegant lakeshore resort sits on 10 hectares (25 acres) of beach and parkland, but it's an easy walk to downtown restaurants and the arts district. The recently updated rooms are spacious and regally outfitted with opulent furniture and upholstery, with knockout views from every window. Suites offer Jacuzzi tubs and separate showers, and deluxe condos offer full kitchens—good for families. Grand Club rooms occupy the top two floors of the resort, and offer secured access and a private lounge (with complimentary breakfast). Two-bedroom units come with full kitchen, fireplace, three TVs, and washer and dryer. Even more fabulous are the Royal Private Villas, sumptuous guest units in their own building that are essentially luxury apartments, with access to a private infinity pool. This is an ideal location for visitors who want to feel pampered in sophisticated surroundings while maintaining easy access to the waterfront. The restaurant and lounge overlook the resort's private marina, where guests can moor their small boats. Motorized swans and boats sized for kids offer fun for children in a protected waterway. The state-of-the-art fitness room and spa offers a variety of wellness and aesthetic treatments.

1310 Water St., Kelowna, BC V1Y 9P3. (✆) **800/465-4651** or 250/763-4500. Fax 250/763-4565. www.delta hotels.com. 390 units. High season C$239–C$384 double; C$359–C$1,639 suites, condos, or luxury villas. Extra person C$15. Off-season discounts available. AE, DC, MC, V. **Amenities:** 3 restaurants; pub; lounge; concierge; health club w/spa; indoor and outdoor pool; room service; watersports equipment rentals; casino. *In room:* A/C, TV, hair dryer, minibar (on request), Wi-Fi.

Hotel Eldorado ★★   This is one of the most charming places to stay in Kelowna if you like historic inns. With a history dating back to 1926, the waterfront Eldorado has been fully restored and is now decorated with a unique mix of antiques; a wing with 30 new guest rooms and six luxury suites was added in 2005. All rooms are individually decorated, and there's a wide mix of floor plans and layouts, some with CD players and fridges. The third-floor guest rooms with views of the lake are the largest and quietest. Some rooms also feature lakeside balconies. On the premises are a boardwalk cafe, lounge, spa, and dining room. The staff can arrange boat moorage, boat rentals, and water-skiing lessons.

500 Cook Rd. (at Lakeshore Rd.), Kelowna, BC V1W 3G9. (✆) **866/608-7500** or 250/763-7500. Fax 250/861-4779. www.eldoradokelowna.com. 55 units. C$179–C$449 double. Lower off-season rates available. AE, DC, MC, V. From downtown, follow Pandosy Rd. south 1.5km (1 mile). Turn right on Cook Rd. **Amenities:** Fine-dining restaurant; bar; boardwalk cafe; fitness center; Jacuzzi; indoor pool; spa services; steam room; marina. *In room:* A/C, TV, hair dryer, Wi-Fi.

Kelowna-SameSun International Hostel   If you're on a budget, this new, centrally located backpackers' lodge is just the ticket. Newly built, it has most of the amenities of a hotel, except many of the guest rooms are dorm style. The huge communal kitchen, the common area filled with couches, and the vast back patio and barbecue area are where everyone hangs out; the bedrooms are clean and comfortable. The private rooms have en suite bathrooms and cable TV. Extras include free continental breakfast and parking. You'll be close to the beach as well as downtown eats and nightlife. There's a new generation of hip, upscale hostels out there, and this is one of the best.

245 Harvey Ave., Kelowna, BC V1Y 6C2. (✆) **877/562-2783** or 250/763-9814. Fax 250/763-9814. www. samesun.com. 88 beds. C$28 dorm single; $79 private double. MC, V. **Amenities:** Wi-Fi; kitchen; TV lounge; patio. *In room:* A/C, no phone.

Lake Okanagan Resort ★   The long, winding road that leads to this secluded hideaway is a sports-car driver's dream come true. And there are many more activities to keep

guests occupied once they arrive at this woodsy resort with its country-club atmosphere.
Located on 122 hectares (301 acres) of Okanagan Lake's hilly western shore, it offers
one-, two-, three-, and five-bedroom units, plus all the facilities you'd expect. Because the
resort is built on a hillside, every room has a terrific view.

2751 Westside Rd., Kelowna, BC V1Z 3T1. ☎ **800/663-3273** or 250/769-3511. Fax 250/769-6665. www.
lakeokanagan.com. 135 units. C$159–C$329 studio suite; C$299–C$329 1-bedroom suite. Off-season
discounts and packages available. AE, MC, V. Free parking. Drive 18km (11 miles) up Westside Rd. **Amenities:** 2 restaurants; 2 bars; summer children's camp; concierge; par-3 golf course; health club and spa;
Jacuzzis; 3 outdoor pools; tennis courts; watersports equipment rentals. *In room:* A/C, TV, hair dryer,
kitchen, Wi-Fi.

Prestige Hotel Kelowna   One of the closest hotels to the City Park beaches, the
Prestige Hotel is a cornerstone of downtown Kelowna. Rooms are nicely furnished, large,
and comfortable, with glass-fronted balconies; suites come with canopy beds, robes,
VCRs, and double Jacuzzis; several have themes, such as the medieval or Egyptian suites.

1675 Abbott St., Kelowna, BC V1Y 8S3. ☎ **87/PRESTIGE** (877/737-8443) or 250/860-7900. Fax 250/860-
7997. www.prestigeinn.com. 67 units. High season C$199–C$229 double; from C$259 suite. AE, DISC, MC,
V. **Amenities:** Restaurant; bar; concierge; exercise room; Jacuzzi; indoor pool; room service. *In room:* A/C,
TV w/pay movies, fridge, hair dryer, Wi-Fi, voice mail.

Urban Villa ★   Somewhere between a B&B inn and a small boutique hotel, the
Urban Villa is a very stylish lodging in a quiet residential neighborhood just a few minutes
south of downtown Kelowna. The entire inn is beautifully decorated with chic, modern
decor, and the rooms are large and sumptuous, with top-quality linens, fine furniture, and
handsome art—you'll spend time wondering how to reproduce the intense, saturated wall
colors in your own home. The large yard has lots of patio and garden space to enjoy the
outdoors, and the inn is just a few minutes' walk from the beach.

2735 Richter St., Kelowna, BC V1Y 2R4. ☎ **866/961-2220** or 250/862-2220. www.urbanvilla.ca. 7 units.
High season C$150–C$240 double. Rates include breakfast. Low-season rates available. MC, V. Free off-
street parking. **Amenities:** Lounge w/TV; 3 decks; fireplace; coffee/tea service. *In room:* A/C, TV, hair dryer,
Wi-Fi, robes.

Camping

Okanagan Lake Provincial Park (☎ **250/494-6500**), 11km (7 miles) north of Summerland and 44km (27 miles) south of Kelowna on Hwy. 97, has 168 campsites nestled
amid 10,000 imported trees. Sites go for C$22. Facilities include free hot showers, flush
toilets, a sani-station, and a boat launch.

Closer to Kelowna is **Bear Creek Provincial Park** (☎ **250/494-6500**), 9km (5⅔
miles) north of Hwy. 97 on Westside Road, about 3km (1¾ miles) west of the Okanagan
Lake Floating Bridge. The park has 80 sites for C$22 each.

WHERE TO DINE

For the kind of hearty cooking that fulfills gastronomic stereotypes, try **Mamma Rosa
Italian Restaurant,** 561 Lawrence Ave. (☎ **250/763-4114;** www.mammarosa.ca), a
third-generation Italian family restaurant that serves up affordable house-made pastas
and very good pizzas.

A number of Kelowna-area vineyards offer dining. **Grapevine Restaurant,** at Gray
Monk Estate Winery, 1055 Camp Rd., Okanagan Centre (☎ **800/663-4205** or
250/766-3168; www.graymonk.com), creates ambitious Continental dishes in a lovely
dining room with great lake views; the restaurant is open for lunch and dinner, March to

October. From its perch above vineyards and Okanagan Lake, the **Old Vines Patio Restaurant** ★, at Quail's Gate Estate, 3303 Boucherie Rd., West Kelowna (𝒞 **250/769-4451;** www.quailsgate.com), serves notable regional cooking; it's open daily for lunch and dinner, save for a staff holiday the first 2 weeks in January.

Bai Thong Thai Restaurant ★ THAI Bai Thong has an encyclopedic menu of house specialties, making this the best Thai restaurant in the Okanagan. Almost all dishes can be made vegetarian. Choose from red, green, or yellow curries, or from signature dishes like *goong pad num prick pao,* stir-fried shrimp with fresh vegetables in fiery Thai sauce.

1530 Water St. 𝒞 **250/763-8638.** Reservations not needed. Main courses C$12–C$18. MC, V. Mon–Fri 11:30am–2:30pm and 5–9:30pm; Sat–Sun 5–9:30pm.

Bouchons Bistro ★ FRENCH This Gallic transplant offers classic French bistro fare just a few blocks from the Okanagan lakefront. The dining room, with ocher walls, stained-glass panels, and handwritten menus, actually feels Parisian. The menu doesn't stray far from classic French cuisine, though dishes are prepared with the freshest and best of local products—the level of cooking at Bouchons will make you appreciate French cuisine once again. Cassoulet is a house specialty, and you can't go wrong with duck confit glazed with honey and spices. A recent game-meat-focused menu offered wonderful wild fowl consommé with foie gras wontons. There's also a five-course table d'hôte for C$39. The wine list is half French, half Okanagan vintages. In summer, there's alfresco dining in the garden-like patio.

1180 Sunset Dr. 𝒞 **250/763-6595.** www.bouchonsbistro.com. Reservations suggested. Main courses C$20–C$36. MC, V. Daily 5:30–10pm.

Christopher's Steak & Seafood STEAKHOUSE Christopher's is a local favorite for drinks and steaks in a dark, fern bar–like dining room. The decor and menu haven't changed much since the early years of the Reagan administration, but that's a plus if you're looking for Alberta beef served up in simple abundance. Pasta, chicken, and seafood are also offered.

242 Lawrence Ave. 𝒞 **250/861-3464.** www.christophersrestaurant.ca. Reservations recommended. Main courses C$14–C$45. AE, DC, MC, V. Sun–Thurs 4:30–10pm; Fri–Sat 4:30–11pm.

Doc Willoughby's Pub CANADIAN For a scene that's casual but on the edge of trendy, with a publike atmosphere but with better food, try Doc Willoughby's, in the heart of downtown. The building was once a pioneer drugstore (note the hammered-tin ceiling), but the interior has been done up in a strikingly contemporary design. This is a good spot for lunch, as the entire front of the restaurant opens to the street; you can watch the to-ing and fro-ing of tourists as you choose from salads, burgers, and sandwiches. At dinner, the eclectic menu offers lots of fish, chicken, and pasta dishes.

353 Bernard Ave. 𝒞 **250/868-8288.** Reservations not needed. Main courses C$14–C$30. AE, MC, V. Mon–Thurs 11:30am–11pm; Fri–Sat 11:30am–midnight; Sun 4:30–10pm.

La Bussola ITALIAN La Bussola is a solid and dependable traditional Italian restaurant with a big local reputation. All of your favorites are here—pasta al pesto, lasagna, chicken piccata—along with an especially large selection of veal specialties. The house signature dish is grilled chicken breast with a creamy white-vermouth sauce.

1451 Ellis St. 𝒞 **250/763-3110.** www.labussolarestaurant.com. Reservations recommended. Main courses C$14–C$36. AE, MC, V. Mon–Sat 5–10pm.

RauDZ Regional Table ★★ CONTEMPORARY CANADIAN   This is the hottest of dining spots in Kelowna, and the second solo venture (after multi-starred Fresco, in this same space) of chef/owner Rod Butters, who has worked at some of western Canada's top restaurants. The cooking focuses on fresh, relatively unfussy regional cuisine sourced from local farmers, ranchers, fishers, and food artisans. Start with a salmon "BLT" with crispy pancetta and fig-anise toasts and move on to duck meatloaf served with garlic-oil-roasted beets and turnips, or oat-crusted arctic char, with maple butter and potato, spinach, and bacon sauté. Service is top-notch; the wine list celebrates the vintages of the Okanagan Valley.

1560 Water St. ℂ **250/868-8805.** www.raudz.com. Reservations recommended. Main courses C$14–C$30. Daily 5–10pm.

Shine Lounge ★ TAPAS   This attractive, modern restaurant is an offshoot of the successful western Canadian Ric's Grill chain, and combines the buzz of a cocktail lounge with a large and wide-ranging international tapas menu. There's something here to please every appetite and taste. Highlights include an orange-and-ginger-glazed duck breast salad, a selection of sashimi, oysters on the half shell, sliders, flatbread pizza, crisp crab and shrimp sushi with pineapple and asparagus, satay—the list of delicious options is endless. The dining room is dark and sleek, with moody lighting, a perfect match for the varied and sophisticated food; in summer, there's an outdoor patio half a story above the street.

1585 Abbott St. ℂ **250/763-9463.** Reservations recommended. Tapas C$7–C$17. AE, MC, V. Tues–Sat 6–11pm.

Southeastern British Columbia & the Kootenay Valley

With the high-flying Rockies to the east and the rugged Purcell and Selkirk mountain ranges to the west, southeastern British Columbia has as much beauty and recreation to offer as anywhere else in the province. If you're looking to avoid the crowds at Banff and Jasper national parks on the Alberta side of the Rockies, try one of the smaller parks covered in this chapter.

Trenched by the mighty Kootenay and Columbia rivers, this region has a long history of mining, river transport, and ranching. More recently, the ranches have given way to golf courses, but development out in this rural area of British Columbia is still low-key. And while that means that you may not have the ultimate dining experience here, it also means that prices are lower across-the-board—and you won't have to compete with tour-bus hordes while you hike the trails.

In pre-Contact Native America and the early years of western exploration, the Kootenay Valley was a major transportation corridor. Due to a curious accident of geology, the headwaters of the vast Columbia River—which flows north from Columbia Lake for 275km (171 miles) before bending south and flowing to the

Pacific at Astoria, Oregon—are separated from the south-flowing Kootenay River by a low, 2km-wide (1¼-mile) berm of land called Canal Flats. The Kootenay River then zigzags down into the United States before flowing back north into Canada to join the Columbia at Castlegar, British Columbia.

Because a short portage was all that separated these two powerful rivers, Canal Flats was an important crossroads when canoes and riverboats were the primary means of transport. The fact that an easily breached ridge was all that separated two major rivers caught the imagination of an early entrepreneur, William Adolph Baillie-Grohman. In the 1880s, he conceived a plan to breach Canal Flats and divert much of the Kootenay's flow into the Columbia. Unsurprisingly, he ran into opposition from people living and working on the Columbia, and had to settle for building a canal and lock system between the two rivers. Only two ships ever passed through the canal, and today this curiosity is preserved as Canal Flats Provincial Park, 44km (27 miles) north of Cranbrook, with picnic tables and a boat launch on Columbia Lake.

1 REVELSTOKE

410km (255 miles) W of Calgary; 565km (351 miles) NE of Vancouver

Located on the Columbia River at the foot of Mount Revelstoke National Park, Revelstoke sits in a narrow fir-cloaked valley between the Selkirk and the Monashee mountains. It's a spectacular, big-as-all-outdoors setting, and unsurprisingly, Revelstoke makes the most of the outdoor-recreation opportunities on its doorstep. Winter is high season

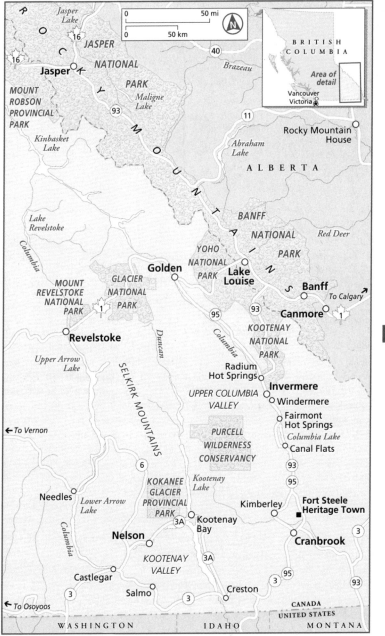

here, as the city is a major center for powder skiing and boarding, heli-skiing, and snow-mobiling. Summer activities include rafting, hiking, and horseback riding.

The town was established in the 1880s, when the Canadian Pacific Railway pushed through. Much of the handsome downtown core was built then; most restaurants and hotels are housed in century-old buildings. Revelstoke is a charming and beautiful desti-nation, and for years it's been surprisingly unheralded. But with the opening of a new destination ski resort just south of town, Revelstoke is suddenly poised for the big times.

ESSENTIALS

GETTING THERE Revelstoke is 192km (119 miles) from Kelowna on Hwy. 1. It's 565km (351 miles) northeast of Vancouver and 410km (255 miles) west of Calgary. **Greyhound Canada** (© 800/661-8747 or 403/260-0877; www.greyhound.ca) operates five buses daily from Vancouver, costing C$92. From Revelstoke to Calgary costs C$62 one-way.

VISITOR INFORMATION Contact the **Revelstoke Visitor Information Centre,** 204 Campbell St. (© 800/487-1493 or 250/837-5345; www.revelstokecc.bc.ca).

EXPLORING THE TOWN

Downtown Revelstoke (pop. 8,500) sits on a shelf of land above the confluence of the Columbia and Illecillewaet rivers. Founded in the 1880s, the town center retains a num-ber of original storefronts and is pleasant to explore. You'll see plenty of coffeehouses, galleries, and some standout architectural jewels, like the domed **Revelstoke Court-house,** 1123 Second St. W. **Grizzly Plaza,** near Victoria Road and Campbell Avenue, is lined with redbrick storefronts. It's the site of the Saturday farmers' market, as well as free live music from July to Labour Day, Monday through Saturday from 7 to 10pm.

Revelstoke Museum Located in the town's original post office, this small museum contains memorabilia from Revelstoke's pioneer mining and railroading days. Upstairs is the community art gallery, with works by local and regional artists.

315 W. First St. © **250/837-3067.** Admission by donation. Mid-May to Labour Day Mon–Fri 1–5pm; Labour Day to mid-May Mon, Wed, and Fri 1–4:30pm.

Revelstoke Railway Museum It's the railroad that really put Revelstoke on the map, and this noteworthy museum—built to resemble an original Canadian Pacific Railway shop—tells the story of western Canadian rail history. Its collection of antique rolling stock includes a beautifully restored CPR steam engine from the 1940s. Other exhibits focus on the building of the first transcontinental line across Canada and the communications systems that kept the trains running safely.

719 Track St. W., across from downtown on Victoria Rd. © **250/837-6060.** www.railwaymuseum.com. Admission C$8 adults, C$6 seniors, C$4 students, free for children 5 and under. July–Aug daily 9am–8pm; May–June and Sept–Oct daily 9am–5pm; Mar–Apr Thurs–Tues 9am–5pm; rest of year Fri–Tues 11am–4pm.

TOURING THE DAMS

The Columbia River has the steepest descent of any large river in North America, and in terms of volume, is the continent's third-largest river, making it irresistible to hydroelec-tric dam builders. Two of the many electricity-generating dams on the river are near Revelstoke, and both are open for tours. **Revelstoke Dam,** 4km (2½ miles) north of Revelstoke on Hwy. 23, is 470m (1,542 ft.) across and 175m (574 ft.) high. Self-guided tours of the visitor center explain how hydroelectricity is produced and how the dams impact the local ecosystem. An elevator shoots to the top of the dam, where you'll get a feeling for the immensity of this structure. The visitor center is open May to mid-June and mid-September to mid-October daily from 9am to 5pm, and mid-June to mid-September daily from 8am to 8pm. Admission is free.

A 140km (87-mile) drive up Hwy. 23 along the shores of Revelstoke Lake takes you to **Mica Dam,** the first large dam on the Columbia—and large it is, much larger than Revelstoke Dam. More than 792m (2,598 ft.) across and 200m (656 ft.) high, Mica Dam forms Kinbasket Lake, which stretches for more than 160km (99 miles) and contains 14.8 trillion cubic meters (523 trillion cubic ft.) of water. The visitor center is open mid-June to Labour Day daily from 10:30am to 4:30pm. Tours are offered at 11am and 1:30pm.

OUTDOOR PURSUITS

Revelstoke is surrounded by rugged mountains with extremely heavy snowfalls (almost 18m/59 ft. annually). The town is particularly known as a center for heli-skiing, a sport that employs helicopters to deposit expert skiers high on mountain ridges, far from lifts and ski areas.

BIKING   The mountains around Revelstoke are etched with old logging roads that have been converted into mountain-bike trails; ask at the visitor center for a map.

GOLF   **Revelstoke Golf Club** (© **800/991-4455** or 250/837-4276) is an 18-hole, par-72 championship course established in 1924, with narrow fairways lined with mammoth conifers and small lakes. The club—one of the oldest in British Columbia—has a driving range, clubhouse with lounge and restaurant, and pro shop. Greens fees are C$59 for 18 holes.

SKIING   **Revelstoke Mountain Resort** (6km/3¾ miles southeast of Revelstoke; © **866/922-8754** or 250/814-0087; www.revelstokemountainresort.com) is a new billion-dollar four-season resort that includes 21 lifts, 110 ski trails, 5,000 housing units, a pedestrian village, and an 18-hole golf course. The resort is home to the longest lift-serviced vertical in North America, with 1,713 vertical meters (5,620 vertical ft.) of skiing. An eight-person gondola and high-speed quads access the five bowls, terrain park, natural and man-made glades, and vast backcountry terrain that counts a whopping 208,413 hectares (515,000 acres). Located in the legendary Monashee and Selkirk Mountains along the Columbia River, the resort also differentiates itself by providing downhill, cat skiing, and heli-skiing all from the same base. Lift tickets are C$74 adults, C$57 seniors and children ages 13 to 18, and C$26 children 6 to 12.

Also now based out of the resort, the long-established **Selkirk Tangiers Heli-Skiing** (© **800/663-7080;** www.selkirk-tangiers.com) offers helicopter-assisted skiing and snowboarding trips to more than 200 approved areas in the Monashee and Selkirk mountains, with some runs up to 2,195m (7,201 ft.) in length. A 4-day package, with access to 13,000 vertical meters (42,651 vertical ft.) of powder, accommodations, and meals starts at C$3,820. For cat skiing, look no further than **Revelstoke Cat Skiing** (© **866/922-8754;** www.revelstokecatskiing.com), which offers snowcat access to untracked terrain in the powder-rich Selkirk Mountains. A day's package, including guides, unlimited vertical, and meals, is C$400.

Revelstoke is also one of the home bases of **CMH Heli-Skiing** (© **800/661-0252;** www.cmhski.com), a longtime purveyor of helicopter skiing to remote slopes and glaciers in the Monashee and Selkirk mountains. CMH offers 7- and 10-day trips to 12 locations; prices begin at C$6,685 for 1 week, including lodging, food, and transport from Calgary.

SNOWMOBILING A detailed brochure of snowmobiling trails is available from the visitor center; contact **Great Canadian Snowmobile Tours** (ⓒ **800/667-8865** or 250/837-6500; www.snowmobilerevelstoke.com) for guided trips.

WHITE-WATER RAFTING **Apex Rafting Company** (ⓒ **888/232-6666** or 250/837-6376; www.apexrafting.com) offers excursions down the Illecillewaet River's Albert Canyon. The trip provides thrills, but nothing too extreme. In summer, daily 4-hour trips cost C$85 for adults and C$69 for kids 16 and under.

WHERE TO STAY

Martha Creek Provincial Park, just north of Revelstoke on Hwy. 23 (ⓒ **250/825-3500**), sits on Lake Revelstoke and has 28 campsites that go for C$14 each.

Accommodations are also available at the four-season Revelstoke Mountain Resort, just south of Revelstoke. The **Nelson Lodge** offers 221 condo suites at the base of the lifts, high-end lodgings that include full kitchen, fireplace, and washer and dryer. Rates are from C$349 double in winter high season, and C$259 summer high season. Also at the resort is **Sandman Inn,** a hotel with rooms from C$124 in both winter and summer high seasons. You can make reservations for both through resort (**866/922-8754** or 250/814-0087; www.revelstokemountainresort.com).

Courthouse Inn Bed and Breakfast This inn is newly built but designed to fit in architecturally with its historic neighbors close to downtown. The comfortable guest rooms, with hardwood floors, quality furniture, and private baths, are decorated according to themes that reflect history (the Marie Antoinette room is the largest, with a four-poster king bed) or local sights and recreation. Guests share a living room with a fireplace and complimentary coffee, tea, and hot chocolate. The hosts are particularly friendly, offering a level of professional service you'd expect at a hotel.

312 Kootenay St., Revelstoke, BC V0E 2S0. ⓒ **877/837-3369** or 250/837-3369. www.courthouseinn revelstoke.com. 10 units. C$140–C$180 double. Rates include full breakfast. MC, V. **Amenities:** Complimentary passes to pool and health club; Wi-Fi. *In room:* A/C, hair dryer, no phone.

Glacier House Resort Just 5 minutes north from Revelstoke, across the Columbia River in a meadow overlooking the Monashee and Selkirk mountains, is this quiet alpine resort with outstanding amenities and a recreational focus. There are cozy, simply decorated rooms in the spacious lodge building, plus 10 free-standing log chalets that range from one to three bedrooms. Each chalet has a fireplace and deck, and some have TVs, hot tubs, and kitchenettes. In addition to a spa, indoor pool, and sauna, Glacier House also has a restaurant and bar; plus it operates an outfitting company to provide guided hiking, biking, and snowmobiling trips. This is a great destination for a family that wants a backcountry-style vacation without roughing it.

1870 Glacier Lane (Box 250), Revelstoke, BC V0E 2S0. ⓒ **877/837-9594** or 250/837-9594. Fax 250/837-9592. www.glacierhouse.com. 26 units. High season C$120–C$160 lodge room; C$160–C$275 chalet. MC, V. **Amenities:** Restaurant; pub w/pool tables; fitness center; Jacuzzi; indoor pool; sauna; sports equipment rentals. *In room:* TV (in all lodge rooms and larger chalets), hair dryer, fireplace.

The Hillcrest Hotel, A Coast Resort ★★ On the eastern edge of Revelstoke, this new hotel does its best to look like a grand mountain lodge, complete with turrets, balconies, log beams, stone walls, and a vast lobby dominated by a river-rock fireplace. The Hillcrest has the most complete facilities in Revelstoke, and its rooms are large and comfortable—many offer mountain views, and suites come with Jacuzzis. The only downside is that you'll need to drive to get to downtown Revelstoke.

3km (1³/₄ miles) east of Revelstoke on Hwy. 1 (Box 1979), Revelstoke, BC V0E 2S0. 📞 **250/837-3322.** Fax 250/837-3340. www.hillcresthotel.com. 75 units. C$159–C$219 double; C$239–C$349 suite. AE, MC, V. **Amenities:** Restaurant; lounge; exercise room; Jacuzzis; sauna. *In room:* A/C, TV, hair dryer, Wi-Fi.

Minto Manor B&B ★   If you enjoy historic homes and gracious B&Bs, the Minto should be your Revelstoke destination. This elegant 1905 Edwardian mansion is full of character and offers three spacious guest rooms, each with a private bathroom, antiques, and an ersatz Victorian decor. Guests share a TV lounge, sitting room, and a music room with two pianos. The house has numerous stained-glass windows and wraparound porches.

815 MacKenzie Ave. (P.O. Box 3089), Revelstoke, BC V0E 2S0. 📞 **877/833-9337** or 250/837-9337. Fax 250/837-9327. www.mintomanor.com. 3 units. C$95–C$145. AE, MC, V. **Amenities:** TV room; complimentary passes to Railway Museum and aquatic center. *In room:* No phone, Wi-Fi.

Mulvehill Creek Wilderness Inn and Bed & Breakfast ★★★ (Finds)   One of the best small lodgings in all of British Columbia, this inn sits in a clearing in the forest, just steps from Arrow Lake and a magnificent 90m (295-ft.) waterfall. The cedar shake–sided lodge has three queen rooms, one king room, and two units with twin beds, plus two fireplace suites (one with Jacuzzi and private deck). All rooms are beautifully decorated with locally made pine furniture and original folk art. The lounge is lined with bookcases; grab a novel and curl up by the fireplace. From the deck, look onto the organic garden, which supplies much of the produce served here. Your hosts will happily arrange cross-country skiing, snowshoeing, horseback-riding, biking, and fishing excursions. A couple of days at Mulvehill may well be the highlight of your trip to British Columbia, and if you're feeling romantic, there's even a wedding chapel. Children 16 and older only.

4200 Hwy. 23 S. (19km/12 miles south of Revelstoke), P.O. Box 1220, Revelstoke, BC V0E 2S0. 📞 **877/837-8649** or 250/837-8649. www.mulvehillcreek.com. 8 units. C$145–C$185 double; C$245 suite. Rates include Swiss-style breakfast. AE, MC, V. Children 16 and older only. **Amenities:** Jacuzzi; heated outdoor saltwater pool; free snowshoes, toboggans, and canoes; hiking trails; picnic areas; sun decks. *In room:* Hair dryer, no phone.

Regent Hotel ★   The finest lodging in downtown Revelstoke, the Regent is a refurbished heritage hotel facing historic Grizzly Plaza. The bedrooms are of varying sizes (some compact, some large) individually decorated with restrained good taste; some have private Jacuzzis. The One Twelve Restaurant offers fine dining (see "Where to Dine," below).

112 First St. E., Revelstoke, BC V0E 2S0. 📞 **888/245-5523** or 250/837-2107. Fax 250/837-9669. www.regenthotel.ca. 45 units. C$139–C$199 double. AE, MC, V. Pets accepted in limited rooms for C$15. **Amenities:** Restaurant; lounge; pub; complimentary mountain bikes; free aquatic center passes; outdoor hot tub; sauna. *In room:* A/C, TV, hair dryer.

SameSun Budget Lodge   Located on the edge of downtown, the hostel is in a spacious older home with oak floors and French doors. There's a large TV area, plus an outdoor patio and shared barbecue. There are tent sites in the large backyard.

400 Second St. W., Revelstoke, BC V0E 2S0. 📞 **877/562-2783** or 250/837-4050. Fax 250/837-6410. www.samesun.com. 90 beds. C$24 per person bunk; C$53 per person private room. MC, V. **Amenities:** Bike rentals; computer and Internet access; kitchen; TV lounge. *In room:* No phone.

WHERE TO DINE

One Twelve Restaurant WESTERN CANADIAN   This handsome restaurant is one of Revelstoke's best fine-dining options, with a good selection of steaks, seafood (about half the menu options), and Continental cuisine. Seared scallops are topped with lime caramel, and mustard-crusted leg of lamb is a house favorite. Good service, an intriguing wine list, woodsy but elegant decor, and a fireplace all enhance the experience.

In the Regent Hotel, 112 First St. E. © 250/837-2107. www.regenthotel.ca. Reservations suggested. Main courses C$14–C$42. AE, MC, V. Mon–Sat 11:30am–2pm and 5:30–9pm.

Woolsey Creek Café ★ NEW CANADIAN   The menu at this pleasant and informal restaurant blends French accents with North American favorites. Choose from a broad choice of salads and appetizers—you could easily make a meal of the small plates, such as duck confit rillettes, crab tartar, baked brie, and even nachos. Main courses emphasize regional and organic produce, meats, and fish; wild B.C. salmon comes with chardonnay cream sauce, and chicken breast is stuffed with local forest mushrooms and drizzled with basil cream. Pastas are especially good—my favorite is arugula penne with chorizo, goat cheese, pine nuts, and dried tomato pesto. Desserts are all made in-house. The knotty pine interior is divided into a bar and dining room, though the distinction disappears when the cafe is busy, which is often.

604 Second St. W. © 250/837-5500. Reservations recommended. Main courses C$15–C$26. MC, V. Daily 7am–10pm.

2 MOUNT REVELSTOKE NATIONAL PARK

Just west of Glacier National Park is Mount Revelstoke National Park, a glacier-clad collection of craggy peaks in the **Selkirk Range.** Comprising only 417 sq. km (161 sq. miles), Mount Revelstoke can't produce the kind of awe that its larger neighbor, Glacier National Park, can in good weather; it does, however, offer easier access to the high country and alpine meadows.

The park is flanked on the south by Hwy. 1, the Trans-Canada Highway. It has no services or campgrounds, but all tourist services are available in the neighboring town of Revelstoke (see above).

For information, contact **Mount Revelstoke National Park** (© 250/837-7500; www.pc.gc.ca/eng/pn-np/bc/revelstoke/index.aspx). Entry per day to the park costs C$7.80 for adults, C$6.80 for seniors, C$3.90 for children 6 to 16, and C$20 per family.

EXPLORING THE PARK

The most popular activity in the park is the drive up to the top of 1,829m (6,001-ft.) **Mount Revelstoke,** with great views of the Columbia River and the peaks of Glacier Park. To reach Mount Revelstoke, take the paved Meadows in the Sky Parkway north from the town of Revelstoke and follow it 23km (14 miles) to Balsam Lake. The parkway is closed to trailers and motorcoaches, as it is a very narrow mountain road with 16 steep switchbacks.

At **Balsam Lake,** at the Meadows in the Sky area, free shuttles operated by the parks department make the final ascent up to the top of Mount Revelstoke, but only after the road is clear of snow, usually from early July to late September. If the shuttle isn't running, you have a choice of several easy hiking trails around Balsam Lake that lead past rushing brooks through wildflower meadows. The **Eagle Knoll Trail** and the **Parapets** are two options that take under an hour. At the summit are longer trails, including the 6km (3.7-mile) **Eva Lake Trail.**

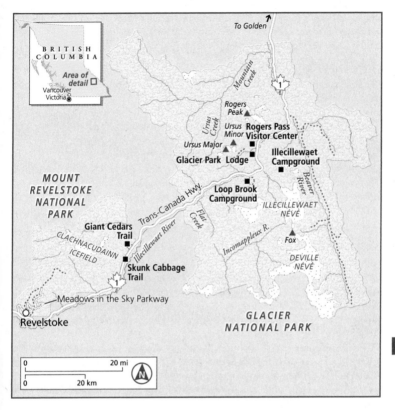

If you don't make the trip up to the Meadows in the Sky area, you can enjoy a short hike in the park from along Hwy. 1. The **Skunk Cabbage Trail** winds through a marsh that explodes with bright yellow and odoriferous flowers in early summer. Another popular hike is the **Giant Cedars Trail,** a short boardwalk out into a grove of old-growth cedars that are more than 1,000 years old.

3 GLACIER NATIONAL PARK

72km (45 miles) E of Revelstoke; 80km (50 miles) W of Golden

Located amid the highest peaks of the Selkirk Mountains, Canada's Glacier National Park amply lives up to its name. More than 400 glaciers repose here, with 14% of the park's 2,168 sq. km (837 sq. miles) lying under permanent snowpack. The reason that this high country is so covered with ice is the same reason that this is one of the more unpopulated places to visit in the mountain West: It snows and rains a lot here.

For information, contact **Glacier National Park** (© **250/837-7500;** www.pc.gc.ca/pn-np/bc/glacier/index.aspx). The visitor center is at Rogers Pass. There's no charge if you pass through the park on Hwy. 1 without stopping, but if you do stop to hike or picnic, the entry fee is C$7.80 for adults, C$6.80 for seniors, C$3.90 for children 6 to 16, and C$20 per family.

EXPLORING THE PARK

The primary attractions in the park are viewpoints onto craggy peaks and hiking trails leading to wildflower meadows and old-growth groves; heavy snow and rainfall lend a near-rainforest feel to the hikes. Spring hikers and cross-country skiers should beware of avalanche conditions, a serious problem in areas with high snowfall and steep slopes. Call the park information number (© **250/837-7500**) for weather updates.

Glacier Park is crossed by the Trans-Canada Highway and the Canadian Pacific Railway tracks. Each has had to build snowsheds to protect its transportation system from the effects of heavy snows and avalanches. **Park headquarters** are just east of 1,250m (4,101-ft.) Rogers Pass; stop here to watch videos and see the displays on natural and human history in the park. New exhibits focus on the role of the railroads in opening up this rugged area of Canada. You can sign up for ranger-led interpretive hikes here as well. On a typically gray and wet day, the visitor center may be the driest place to enjoy the park.

HIKING

Several easy trails leave from the park's Rogers Pass visitor center. **Abandoned Rails Trail** follows a rails-to-trails section of the old CPR track for a 1-hour round-trip journey along a gentle grade through a wildflower-studded basin. The **Balu Pass Trail** is a more strenuous 5km (3.1-mile) hike up to the base of the glaciers on 2,728m (8,950-ft.) Ursus Major.

The other important trail head is at **Illecillewaet Campground,** west of Rogers Pass along Hwy. 1. Seven major trails head up into the peaks from here, including the **Asulkan Valley Trail,** which follows a stream up a narrow valley to a hikers' hut. These trails require more exertion than the trails at Rogers Pass, and will take most of a day to complete.

Farther down the Illecillewaet Valley are two other popular routes. **Loop Brook Trail** is a 1-hour saunter through a riparian wetland. The .5km (.3-mile) **Rockgarden Trail** climbs up a valley wall of moss-and-lichen-covered boulders to a vista point onto 2,880m (9,449-ft.) Smart Peak. Stop at the **Hemlock Grove Picnic Area** and follow the boardwalk through the old-growth hemlock forest.

The longest hike in the park is the 42km (26-mile) **Beaver Valley Trail,** which follows the Beaver River on the eastern edge of the park. This trail takes 3 days, one-way, to complete. If you plan on backcountry camping, you'll need to register at the visitor center and purchase a C$9.80 wilderness pass.

WHERE TO STAY

Illecillewaet and **Loop Brook** campgrounds are just west of Rogers Pass off Hwy. 1 and along the Illecillewaet River. Both operate on a first-come, first-served basis. Facilities include flush toilets, kitchen shelters, firewood, and drinking water. Illecillewaet offers guided hikes and fireside programs as well. Rates at both campgrounds are C$22 per night.

Glacier Park Lodge This large complex is just below Rogers Pass, where Hwy. 1 edges over the Selkirk Range in Glacier National Park. The setting is spectacular: The glaciered faces of towering peaks crowd around a broad cirque blanketed with wildflowers and boulders, at the center of which sits this handsome lodge. One hundred thirty-nine kilometers (86 miles) of hiking and cross-country ski trails lead out into the wilderness (the hotel will prepare a picnic lunch for you on request). Guest rooms are comfortable and nicely furnished with extra-long beds; three of the suites are large enough to accommodate families.

Rogers Pass, BC V0E 2S0. © **800/528-1234** or 250/837-2126. Fax 250/837-2130. www.glacierparklodge. ca. 50 units. C$99–C$155 double; C$129–C$185 suite. AE, DISC, MC, V. **Amenities:** 2 restaurants; bar; Jacuzzi; heated outdoor pool; room service; sauna. *In room:* TV, Wi-Fi.

4 GOLDEN

134km (83 miles) W of Banff; 713km (443 miles) E of Vancouver

For more than a century, Golden (pop. 4,500) has been known primarily as a transport hub, first as a division point on the transcontinental Canadian Pacific Railway, next as the upstream steamboat terminus on the Columbia River, and then as a junction of two of Canada's busiest highway systems.

Nowadays, Golden is known for its outdoor recreation. The town sits in a breathtaking location in the trenchlike Columbia River valley, between the massive Rocky Mountains and the soaring Purcell Range, within a 90-minute drive of five major national parks. The fact that Golden is near—and not in—the parks is largely the reason for the area's recent phenomenal growth. Outfitters that offer heli-skiing, heli-hiking, and other recreation that isn't allowed in the national parks (for conservation reasons) choose to make Golden their base. And with park towns such as nearby Banff trying to limit further development, businesses and outfitters that want a Rocky Mountain hub find Golden a convenient and congenial center.

Golden won't win any awards for quaint charm, however. It's basically a functional little town with lots of motel rooms in a magnificent location.

Note that Golden and the other communities in this part of the Columbia Valley are in the Mountain Time zone, an hour earlier than the rest of British Columbia.

ESSENTIALS

GETTING THERE Golden is at the junction of Hwy. 1 (the Trans-Canada Hwy.) and Hwy. 95. The closest airport is in Calgary. **Greyhound Canada** (© **800/661-8747** or 403/260-0877; www.greyhound.ca) links Golden to Vancouver, Banff, and Calgary, and to Cranbrook to the south. The one-way fare from Golden to Vancouver is C$120; to Calgary, it's C$51.

VISITOR INFORMATION Contact the **Kicking Horse Country Visitor Info Centre,** 500 10th Ave. N. (© **800/622-4653** or 250/344-7125; www.tourismgolden.com).

GETTING AROUND If you need a rental car while in Golden, contact **National,** 915 11th Ave. (© **250/344-9899;** www.nationalcar.com).

EXPLORING THE AREA

You could spend several days in the Golden area without realizing that the town has an older downtown core. It's a block west of busy 10th Avenue, on **Main Street.** There's not much here—just a handful of shops and cafes—but it's a pleasant break from the commercial sprawl along highways 1 and 95.

The **Golden and District Museum,** 1302 11th Ave. (℃ **250/344-5169**), tells the story of Golden's rail history. It also has an old log schoolhouse and blacksmith's shop. It's open Monday through Friday from 10am to 6pm in May, June, and September, and daily in July and August. Admission is by donation.

OUTDOOR PURSUITS

FISHING   The Columbia River runs through town and offers fair fishing for rainbow trout and kokanee salmon. There's better fishing in the **Kinbasket Lake** section of the river, which begins just north of Golden.

GOLF   **Golden Golf & Country Club** (℃ **866/727-7222** or 250/344-2700; www. golfgolden.com) is an 18-hole championship course along the Columbia River. Bill Newis designed the front 9 holes; Les Furber took care of the back 9. The clubhouse includes a pro shop with equipment rentals. Greens fees are C$70 to C$80.

HELI-HIKING   Although based in Banff, **CMH Heli-Hiking** (℃ **800/661-0252** or 403/762-7100; www.cmhhike.com) offers a variety of helicopter-assisted hiking packages in the mountains west of Golden. Three-, 4-, or 6-day heli-hiking trips involve staying at remote high-country lodges accessible only by long hikes or by helicopter. Prices vary depending on time of year and individual lodge, but 3-day trips begin at C$2,490; rates include lodging, food, and helicopter transport.

Mid-June through September, **Purcell Helicopter Skiing** (℃ **877/435-4754** or 250/344-5410; www.purcellhelicopterskiing.com) offers heli-hiking day trips in the Purcell Mountains west of Golden. Guided day hikes go for C$350 to C$525, including lunch. Sightseeing tours start at C$105 per person. All trips are based on 4-passenger minimums.

HELI-SKIING ★   Banff-based **CMH Heli-Skiing** (see "Heli-Hiking," above) has eight high-country lodges in the mountain ranges near Golden. Prices vary greatly depending on the lodge and time of year, but start at C$6,685 all-inclusive for a week. Rates include lodging, food, helicopter transport, use of specialized powder skis, and ground transport from the nearest large airport (usually Calgary).

If you prefer more of a DIY approach to heli-skiing, **Purcell Helicopter Skiing** (see "Heli-Hiking," above) offers day trips to peaks in the Selkirk and Purcell ranges. Three-run (C$709) and five-run (C$849) packages are available, and include the helicopter ride, lunch, a guide, and instruction; you'll provide your own skis and lodging.

HORSEBACK RIDING   Located at Kicking Horse Mountain Resort, **Flying W Trail Rides** (℃ **250/344-0495;** www.flyingwtrailrides.com) offers 1-hour (C$34) and 2-hour (C$60) trail rides.

SKIING ★   **Kicking Horse Mountain Resort** (℃ **866/754-5425;** www.kickinghorse resort.com) has transformed the winter scene in Golden. Located 14km (8¾ miles) west of Golden, it features a 1,260m-long (4,134-ft.) vertical drop, a gondola lift that takes skiers up above elevations of 2,450m (8,038 ft.), and the Eagle's Eye, the highest-elevation restaurant in Canada. It has six lifts and over 1,113 hectares (2,750 acres) of skiable terrain. Lift tickets are C$73 a day. Several lodging options are now available at the resort, including five lodges, three-bedroom town houses, and resort homes. You can also spend a night at the Eagle's Eye Suites and wake up at the crest of the Selkirk Mountains (at C$1,995 per couple, the views won't provide the only unforgettable memory of this overnight stay).

WILDLIFE VIEWING   Visitors can get up close and personal with gray wolves at **Northern Lights Wildlife Wolf Centre,** 1745 Short Rd. (℃ **877/377-WOLF** [9653] or

Exploring the Columbia River Wetlands

South (upstream) from Golden are the Columbia River Wetlands, a 144km-long (89-mile) Wildlife Management Area that supports an incredible diversity of wildlife. More than 270 bird species have been seen in this stretch of river, marsh, and lake. The largest wetlands west of Manitoba, the Columbia River Wetlands are also a major breeding ground for the bald eagle, osprey, and great blue heron. Moose, elk, mink, and beaver make their homes here as well.

Wetlands Wildlife Safari (© 866/344-4931 or 250/344-4931; www.wetlandswildlife.ca) gives tours of the Columbia wetlands south (upstream) of Golden in sturdy, inflatable rubber rafts. A guided 3-hour excursion includes shuttles and snacks and costs C$69 for adults.

250/344-6798; www.northernlightswildlife.com). The center offers interpretive talks about wolves and their role in a healthy natural ecosystem. The wolves of Northern Lights, which live in a .5-hectare (1¼-acre) enclosure, have all been adopted from various facilities. Born and bred in captivity, these wolves are not candidates for release into the wild. Admission to the center, which includes a 20-minute introduction to the wolves, is C$10 adults, C$8 seniors and children ages 12 to 18, C$6 children ages 4 to 11, and C$30 for families. For an additional fee, the wolves are also available for custom photographic sessions. In July and August, the center is open daily 9am to 7pm; May, June, and September, it's open daily 10am to 6pm. The rest of the year, it's open daily noon to 5pm.

WHITE-WATER RAFTING   The **Kicking Horse River,** which enters the Columbia at Golden, is one of the most exciting white-water runs in Canada, with constant Class III and Class IV rapids as it tumbles down from the Continental Divide through Yoho. A trip down the Kicking Horse will be a highlight of your vacation in the Rockies. Rafting trips are usually offered from mid-May to mid-September.

Alpine Rafting (© 888/599-5299 or 250/344-6778; www.alpinerafting.com) offers the daylong Kicking Horse Challenge trip for C$149, including a barbecue steak lunch. A gentler, family-friendly 2-hour introduction to white water goes for C$65 for adults and C$30 for children 12 and under.

Glacier Raft Company (© 250/344-6521; www.glacierraft.com) offers a variety of options. The easygoing scenic float day trip goes to the gentle upper valley of the Kicking Horse; it's for those who want an introduction to rafting or who don't want the thrills of white water. Cost is C$65 for adults and C$40 for kids 14 and under. Two separate day trips explore the white-water sections of the Kicking Horse and cost C$109 to C$139. Deduct C$10 from the white-water trip rates if you take your trip on a weekday. All day trips include a steak barbecue lunch.

Wet 'n' Wild Adventures (© 800/668-9119 or 250/344-6546; www.wetnwild.bc.ca) offers Kicking Horse trips from Banff, Lake Louise, and Golden (the shuttle from Banff and Lake Louise costs C$16 round-trip). The standard day trip is C$99, including lunch. If you just want to shoot the rapids of the lower canyon, a half-day trip is available for C$69. For beginners, a morning introduction to white water is C$60 for adults and C$40 for children 12 and under, including lunch.

Alpine Meadows Lodge ★ This family-owned lodge enjoys a great location—high above Golden, looking across onto the face of the Rockies, yet only 10 minutes to skiing, golf, and tourist services. The lodge, which was constructed from timber felled on the property, has a central three-story great room, flanked by wraparound balconies and open staircases. A huge stone fireplace dominates the living area. The guest rooms are light-filled and airy, with simple, unfussy decor; all of them have Jacuzzi tubs in the bathrooms. In addition, a four-bedroom, two-bathroom chalet with full kitchen is also available for rent. Outdoor recreation is literally right out the door, with paths from the lodge leading to hiking trails in neighboring federal forestland. The staff is very helpful and will make it easy for you to get out into the wilderness or onto the fairways.

717 Elk Rd., Golden, BC V0A 1H0. ☏ **888/700-4477** or 250/344-5863. Fax 250/344-5853. www.alpine meadowslodge.com. 10 units, 1 chalet. C$99–C$129 double; C$350–C$425 chalet, with minimum stay requirements. Rates include breakfast. Golf, skiing, rafting, and flightseeing packages available. MC, V. **Amenities:** Lounge (offers TV and Internet access). *In room:* A/C, no phone.

Golden Rim Motor Inn (Value) Of the dozens of older motels in Golden, this is the pick of the litter. Standing above the precipitous Kicking Horse River valley, just .8km (½ mile) east of Golden, the Golden Rim boasts sweeping views of the Rockies and the Columbia Valley. It offers standard queen-size-bed motel rooms, with some kitchen and Jacuzzi units available.

1416 Golden View Rd., Golden, BC V0A 1H0. ☏ **877/311-2216** or 250/344-2216. Fax 250/344-6673. 81 units. C$79–C$125 double. AE, MC, V. **Amenities:** Restaurant; bar; Jacuzzi; indoor pool w/water slide; sauna. *In room:* A/C, TV, hair dryer, Wi-Fi.

Hillside Lodge & Chalets This stylish, European-style lodge with five stand-alone chalets sits on 24 forested hectares (59 acres) above the quiet Blaeberry River, 16km (10 miles) north of Golden. Guests stay in comfortable lodge rooms or delightful one- or two-bedroom chalets, the latter with wood stoves, kitchenettes, decks, and handcrafted furniture. All accommodations are recently built, so you'll find everything completely shipshape.

1740 Seward Frontage Rd., Golden, BC V0A 1H0. ☏ **250/344-7281.** Fax 250/344-7281. www.hillside chalets.com. 14 units. C$138–C$148 lodge double, includes full German-style breakfast; C$135–C$160 1-bedroom chalet (breakfast not included); C$230–C$260 2-bedroom chalet (breakfast not included). MC, V. **Amenities:** Dining room (guests only); lounge w/TV; exercise room; sauna. *In room:* Fridge, hair dryer, no phone.

Kapristo Lodge Homey, lodge-style Kapristo is an excellent choice for the recreation-oriented vacationer. It sits high above the Columbia Valley, with sweeping views of the Purcell Mountains from the large flagstone-and-planking patio. Guest rooms are comfortably furnished with down quilts and handsome furniture. What sets this apart from other lodges around Golden is its friendly informality and its owner's efforts to ensure that guests have a good time, whether rafting a river, riding horseback, or sunning on the deck.

1297 Campbell Rd., Golden, BC V0A 1H0. ☏ **250/344-6048.** Fax 250/344-6755. www.kapristolodge.com. 3 units. C$130–C$200 double. Extra person C$35. Rates include breakfast. MC, V. **Amenities:** Dining room (guests only); Jacuzzi; sauna. *In room:* No phone.

Prestige Mountainside Resort Golden ★ Easily the swankest place to stay in Golden itself, the Prestige Inn is recently built and well-appointed, with excellent facilities and a good family restaurant. Guest rooms are spacious, each with two phones and lots of extras. There are a variety of room types, including kitchenettes, themed suites, and large rooms in the Premier Wing that feature common foyers.

1049 Trans-Canada Hwy., Golden, BC V0A 1H0. (C) **877/737-8443** or 250/344-7990. Fax 250/344-7902. www.prestigeinn.com. 82 units. C$109–C$179 double; C$179–C$399 suite. AE, DISC, MC, V. **Amenities:** Restaurant; bar; concierge; exercise room; Jacuzzi; indoor pool; room service. *In room:* A/C, TV w/pay movies, hair dryer, kitchenette, Wi-Fi.

Vagabond Lodge ★★ Kicking Horse Mountain Resort offers a large and growing selection of lodging options, but one of the best is this handsome, small boutique-style hotel. The log-built Vagabond Lodge has beautifully appointed public areas, including a lobby filled with overstuffed chairs and couches, a hand-split log bar and dining area, and a central, pine-spindled staircase, all warmed by an enormous stone fireplace. The guest rooms are large and furnished with woodsy good taste, with such features as feather-rest mattresses and duvets, heated bathroom floors, and balconies (in six rooms). Breakfast is included in rates. The owners are very friendly and will do their best to ensure that you have a great stay. Highly recommended.

1581 Cache Close, Kicking Horse Mountain Resort, Golden, BC V0A 1H0. (C) **866/944-2622** or 250/344-2622. Fax 250/344-2668. www.vagabondlodge.ca. 10 units. C$135–C$295 double. Rates include breakfast (and lunch during ski season). MC, V. **Amenities:** No-host bar; concierge; hot tub; TV room; secure heated ski storage w/boot dryer; coffee and tea service. *In room:* Hair dryer, no phone, Wi-Fi, robes.

WHERE TO DINE

Cedar House ★ PACIFIC NORTHWEST Perched high above the Columbia Valley south of Golden, Cedar House has one of the best views in the region. The log lodge is divided into cozy dining areas and is flanked by decks, all the better to take in the vista. The exciting menu features seasonal specials and local meats and vegetables, all cooked in an open kitchen. Seared wild salmon with lemon balm and chile butter, and grilled pork tenderloin with fig, thyme, and sherry jus are standouts.

735 Hefti Rd., 10 min. south of Golden on Hwy. 95. (C) **250/344-4679.** www.cedarhousecafe.com. Reservations recommended. Main courses C$16–C$29. MC, V. Daily 5–10:30pm.

Corks Restaurant CONTEMPORARY CANADIAN The best choice for dining at the Kicking Horse Mountain Resort base is this friendly small restaurant (with a great patio in summer) in the Copper Horse Lodge. Though the dining room features crystal, linen, and candlelight, Corks is more of a casual bistro with a small, though varied menu. You could do far worse than settle for a salad, such as adobe-rubbed roast chicken salad with cucumber slaw, watermelon, and peach chutney, though that means you'd miss out on the excellent thin-crust pizzas and main courses such as wild Coho salmon with French lentil pilaf and orange fennel broth. The wine list has an intriguing selection of New World wines.

2 Cache Close, in the Copper Horse Lodge, Kicking Horse Mountain Resort. (C) **250/344-6201.** Reservations recommended. Main courses C$18–C$35. MC, V. Mon–Sat 4–10pm.

Eagle's Eye Restaurant ★★ NEW CANADIAN Canada's highest-elevation restaurant, the Eagle's Eye towers above the new Kicking Horse Resort. Diners take the ski gondola 1,200m (3,937 ft.) up to 2,410m (7,907 ft.) above sea level to reach this dining room with a 360-degree view of the nearby Rocky, Selkirk, and Purcell mountain ranges (with confirmed reservations, you'll ride the gondola up and back for free). With a panorama like this, the food needn't be good; it's excellent, however, with an emphasis on

Alberta lamb and beef, British Columbia salmon and oysters, and seasonal specials like pistachio-crusted halibut with truffled potatoes.

Kicking Horse Resort, west of Golden on Dyke Rd. ℂ **250/344-8626.** Reservations required. Main courses C$26–C$42. AE, MC, V. Summer daily 10am–10pm; off season Mon–Thurs 10am–3:30pm, Fri–Sun 10am–9pm. Closed mid-Oct to mid-Dec and mid-Apr to mid-May. Call to confirm spring opening and fall closing dates.

Eleven 22 Grill & Liquids INTERNATIONAL This intimate restaurant shows Golden's more youthful and alternative side. A converted house, Eleven 22 offers a number of small plates, pasta and risotto specialties, and a daily changing cannelloni selection. One favorite is *nasi goring*, Malaysian-style fried rice. You can also order up-to-date Canadian main courses such as a pork chop with candied fennel or roast duck breast with maple glaze, all concocted with local organic ingredients. For the quality and size of servings, prices are very reasonable.

1122 10th Ave. S. ℂ **250/344-2443.** www.eleven22.ca. Main courses C$11–C$23. MC, V. Daily 5–10pm.

Kicking Horse Grill INTERNATIONAL Housed in a historic log cabin near downtown, this bustling restaurant is a culinary League of Nations: The menu changes every season to reflect not only fresh ingredients, but also the international travels of the owners. Start with leek soup with lychees or a falafel salad; then move on to tandoori lamb chops or a grilled ahi tuna steak with lime noodles. If you're happy to remain gastronomically in Golden, there's a selection of steaks and chops (including an excellent pork chop with apple, pear, and cilantro marmalade finished with Belgian chocolate flakes). The dining room is a puzzling mix of white linen, crystal, and the Wild West.

1105 Ninth St. ℂ **250/344-2330.** www.thekickinghorsegrill.ca. Reservations recommended. Main courses C$18–C$30. AE, MC, V. Daily 5–10pm.

Whitetooth Grill ★ CONTEMPORARY CANADIAN This downtown Golden bistro is both casual and rather chic, with a friendly vibe that's as welcoming to families as it is to couples on a date. Considering the quality of the cooking, the Whitetooth is also a good value. Your evening meal might be as simple as a grilled tuna steak sandwich with wasabi aioli and cucumber-fennel slaw. It could also be homey, such as Savoy cabbage rolls stuffed with garbanzos and ratatouille, or full-on gourmet, such as elk-meat cassoulet. Whitetooth is a great spot for breakfast, because you can wake up to a choice of familiar classics or the more exotic—perhaps Hang'n'Tuff eggs Benedict, with avocado and Dungeness crab.

427 9th Ave N., ℂ **250/344-5120.** www.whitetoothbistro.com. Reservations not accepted. Main courses C$10–C$27. MC, V. Daily 9am–10pm.

5 THE KOOTENAY VALLEY: CRANBROOK & NELSON

Cranbrook: 80km (50 miles) N of the U.S.-Canada border

CRANBROOK

The largest city in southeastern British Columbia, Cranbrook (pop. 19,000) exists mostly as a trade center for loggers and agriculturists. The town itself has few tourist sights, but Cranbrook is central to a number of historic and recreational areas and offers ample numbers of hotel rooms. Its setting is spectacularly dramatic: a broad forested valley that looks onto the sky-piercing Canadian Rockies and back side of the U.S. Glacier National Park.

Essentials

GETTING THERE Cranbrook is near the junction of the north-south Hwy. 93/95 corridor and the east-west Hwy. 3. **Greyhound Canada** (© **800/661-8747;** www.greyhound.ca) operates buses that travel on both of these road systems. One-way service from Cranbrook to Golden costs C$38. **Air Canada Jazz** (© **888/247-2262;** www.flyjazz.ca) operates flights from Vancouver to the Cranbrook Airport, north of town.

VISITOR INFORMATION The **Cranbrook Visitor Info Centre** is at 2279 Cranbrook St. N. (© **800/222-6174** or 250/426-5914; www.cranbrookchamber.com). It's open daily 9am to 6pm.

Exploring the Area

It's worth getting off the grim Hwy. 95 strip to visit the pleasant downtown area around Baker Street. As you stroll the broad, tree-lined streets, you'll see a number of heritage brick storefronts and commercial buildings. Especially impressive is the grand, turreted 1909 **Imperial Bank** building at Baker and Eighth streets.

Canadian Museum of Rail Travel ★ Cranbrook was established as a rail division point, so it's fitting that the town is home to this fascinating museum that preserves a number of historic rail cars, including several "cars of state" designed for royalty. The Royal Alexandra Hall is a 279-sq.-m (3,003-sq.-ft.) oak-paneled dining room salvaged from Winnipeg's Royal Alexandra Hotel, a CPR hotel torn down in 1971. The ornate moldings, panels, and furniture were carefully numbered and stored for nearly 30 years before being reconstructed here. Other highlights include a complete set of 12 cars built in 1929 for the Canadian Pacific Railway's Trans-Canada Limited run. Rather like a traveling luxury hotel, the restored cars gleam with brass and inlaid walnut and mahogany. In summer, the Royal Alexandra Hall offers tea service.

57 Van Horne St. S. © 250/489-3918. www.trainsdeluxe.com. Admission (may vary according to which tours are taken) C$13 adults, C$11 seniors, C$6.50 teens 13–18, C$3 children 12 and under, C$32 families. Mid-Apr to mid-Oct daily 10am–6pm; mid-Oct to mid-Apr Tues–Sat 10am–5pm. Tours given on the half-hour.

Fort Steele Heritage Town ★ **Kids** During the 1864 gold rush, a cable ferry stretched across a narrow section of the Kootenay River, enabling prospectors to safely cross the turbulent waters. A small settlement sprang up, and after another mining boom—this time for silver, lead, and zinc—Fort Steele had more than 4,000 inhabitants. But when the railroad pushed through, it bypassed Fort Steele in favor of Cranbrook. Within 5 years, all but 150 of the citizens had left. In the 1960s, the crumbling ghost town was declared a heritage site. Today, more than 60 restored and reconstructed buildings grace the townsite, including a hotel, churches, saloons, and a courthouse and jail.

Tips **Special Events**

Sam Steele Days (© **250/426-4161**) celebrate the Wild West heritage of the Cranbrook area. This annual festival, held the third weekend of June, features an indoor rodeo, parade, barbecue, pancake breakfast, street dances, sports tournaments, and more.

In summer, living-history actors give demonstrations of period skills and occupations. There are also rides on a steam train, horse-drawn wagon, and a variety show at the Wild Horse Theatre. The International Hotel Restaurant serves Victorian fare.

16km (10 miles) northeast of Cranbrook on Hwy. 93/95. ℰ **250/426-7352**, or 250/426-7352 for recorded information. www.fortsteele.bc.ca. Admission to grounds July to Labour Day C$5, free children 5 and under. Rides and entertainment extra. Free evening admission for theater and restaurant patrons. May–June and Labour Day to mid-Oct daily 9:30am–5pm; July to Labour Day daily 9:30am–6:30pm. Evening entertainment and restaurant July to Labour Day Tues–Sun. The grounds remain open in winter with free entry, though without services.

Outdoor Pursuits

FISHING Eighteen area rivers, including the Elk River, St. Mary River, and Kootenay, are often rated among Canada's top fishing destinations. Trophy fish are taken all season long. For lake fishing, Moyie Lake, 30km (19 miles) south of Cranbrook, has a good stock of kokanee, rainbow, and bull trout.

GOLF The **St. Eugene Mission Golf Resort** (ℰ **877/417-3133** or 250/417-3417; www.steugene.ca) is an 18-hole, Les Furber–designed course with a links section. *Golf Digest* has rated the St. Eugene Mission course as one of the top three new courses in Canada. High-season greens fees are C$60 to C$81. The **Cranbrook Golf Club,** 2700 Second St. S. (ℰ **888/211-8855** or 250/426-6462), is a long-established 18-hole course with greens fees starting at C$49. The **Mission Hills Golf Course** (ℰ **250/489-3009**) has 18 holes and a par-3 rating, plus a clubhouse and restaurant. The course has recently added a full-length, all-grass practice facility, plus a 3-hole practice loop. Greens fees are C$24.

SKIING Ninety-three kilometers (58 miles) east of Cranbrook, on the western face of the Rockies, is one of the best skiing and snowboarding areas in British Columbia. **Fernie Alpine Resort,** Ski Area Road, Fernie (ℰ **250/423-4655;** www.skifernie.com), is a relatively unheralded resort that's popular with in-the-know snowboarders. Average snowfall is about 9m (30 ft.), with a vertical drop of 857m (2,812 ft.). There are 107 trails in five alpine bowls, with a total of more than 1,013 hectares (2,503 acres) of skiable terrain served by four quads, two triples, two T-bars, a Poma, and a handle tow with the capacity to handle 13,716 skiers per hour (but it's never *that* busy). Adult lift tickets are C$76. Amenities include lodging (ℰ **800/258-SNOW** [7669] for reservations), restaurants, rentals, and instruction. The resort, lodges, and lifts remain open in summer, with hiking, mountain biking, and horseback riding the main activities.

Twenty minutes west of Cranbrook is the **Kimberley Alpine Resort** (ℰ **800/258-7669** or 250/427-4881; www.skikimberley.com), a family-friendly ski resort with over 60% of its 80 runs rated beginning and intermediate. The slopes offer a vertical rise of 751m (2,464 ft.) with 729 hectares (1,801 acres) of skiable terrain serviced by five lifts, including a high-speed quad. There are a number of ski-in, ski-out accommodations here, including the new and very comfortable Mountain Spirit Resort and Spa (ℰ **877/432-6006,** or 250/432-6000; www.mountainspirit.ca).

Where to Stay

Fort Steele Resort & RV Park, 16km (10 miles) north of Cranbrook on Hwy. 95 (ℰ **250/426-5117**), has 300 sites costing from C$22 to C$28. It offers pull-throughs, a tenting area, hot showers, and a swimming pool.

Cedar Heights B&B This stylish, contemporary home is situated in a residential area just minutes from downtown Cranbrook. The rooms are beautifully furnished and have private entrances. Two lounges contain a fireplace, wet bar, fridge, coffee and tea service, and games. From the spacious deck, take in the view of the magnificent Rockies.

1200 13th St., Cranbrook, BC V1C 5V8. (C) **800/497-6014** or 250/426-0505. Fax 250/426-0045. www. bbcanada.com/cedarheights. 3 units. C$90–C$135 double. Extra person C$30. Rates include full breakfast. MC, V. Children must be 12 or older. **Amenities:** Jacuzzi. *In room:* A/C, TV/VCR, hair dryer.

Prestige Rocky Mountain Resort & Convention Centre ★★ By far the poshest place to stay in Cranbrook itself, the first-class Prestige resort features very large and stylish rooms with lots of extras; some rooms have kitchenettes. There's fine dining at Munro's, drinks and lighter meals at Chattanooga's Bar and Grill, and an espresso bar for your caffeine fix. Other perks include a spa offering aromatherapy and massage.

209 Van Horne St. S., Cranbrook, BC V1C 6R9. (C) **887/737-8443** or 250/417-0444. Fax 250/417-0400. www.prestigeinn.com. 109 units. C$159–C$249 double; from C$189–C$249 suite. Extra person C$20. Off-season rates and golf/ski packages available. AE, DISC, MC, V. **Amenities:** Restaurant; bar; full health club (fee); Jacuzzi; indoor pool; room service; spa. *In room:* A/C, TV w/pay movies, fridge, hair dryer, kitchenette (in some), Wi-Fi.

St. Eugene Mission Resort ★★ This extraordinary resort is both the newest and one of the oldest places to stay in the Cranbrook area. The resort hotel, along with a noted golf course, spa, casino, and First Nations cultural center, is on the grounds of a former residential school built for the education and acculturation of the local Kootenay Indian band in the late 19th century. The original mission school structure was renovated and now houses a number of unique guest accommodations; a brand-new adjacent lodge also features rooms and suites. The mission's historic barn is now the golf clubhouse and, in 2004, a health club was added. With financial backing from the Ktunaxa Kinbasket Tribal Council and the federal government, the transformation of the old mission has been accomplished with great attention to historic detail. Rooms are simply but elegantly appointed, and the views are magnificent, with miles of open links and pine forest and the Rockies rising to fill the sky.

7777 Mission Rd., Cranbrook, BC V1C 7E5. (C) **866/292-2020** or 250/420-2000. Fax 250/420-2001. www. steugene.ca. 125 units. C$132–C$199 double. Extra person C$20. Golf and ski packages available. Off-season rates available. AE, MC, V. **Amenities:** Restaurant; lounge; golf course; health club; outdoor pool; sauna; steam room; casino. *In room:* A/C, TV w/movie channels, hair dryer, Wi-Fi, robes.

Where to Dine

Allegra Mediterranean Cuisine ★★ MEDITERRANEAN The chef-owner of this excellent restaurant is from the Italy-fronting cantons of Switzerland, but the menu here spans the sunny foods of the entire Mediterranean basin. Certainly Italian foods are make their appearance—with marvelous pasta dishes such as fig and prosciutto-stuffed ravioli—but the flavors of southern France, Greece, North Africa, and beyond are also featured. Moroccan chicken tagine and pan-seared salmon with chipotle and maple syrup are just two facets of imaginative menu. The dining room is simple, even spartan, but you're here to savor the food, after all.

1225 Cranbrook St. N. (C) **250/426-8812.** Reservations suggested. Main courses C$14–C$24. MC, V. Wed–Sun 5–9pm.

Apollo Ristorante & Steak House GREEK/STEAKHOUSE Ask a local to recommend a restaurant, and Apollo is sure to be among the first choices. The menu covers not only traditional Greek dishes, but also a broad selection of pasta, steaks and prime rib, sandwiches, seafood, even pizza. With such a large dining room and ambitious menu, you might suspect that quality would suffer. But you'll be pleased with the hearty, slightly old-fashioned tastiness of the results.

1012 Cranbrook St. N. (*C*) **250/426-3721.** Main courses C$9–C$24. AE, MC, V. Daily 11am–10pm.

Heidi's Restaurant ★ CONTINENTAL   The menu at this pleasantly refined restaurant, with redbrick walls and potted plants, is dominated by the cuisines of Germany and Italy. Appetizers range from empanadas with cumin beef to classic escargots. Entrees include steaks from local beef, schnitzels, pastas, fresh fish, and specialties like osso buco and seared duck breast served with black-currant sauce, spaetzle, and red cabbage.

821C Baker St. (*C*) **250/426-7922.** Reservations recommended. Main courses C$13–C$28. AE, MC, V. Mon–Thurs 11am–2:30pm and 5–9pm; Fri–Sat 11:30am–2:30pm and 5–10pm; Sun 5–9pm.

NELSON ★★

102km (63 miles) N of the U.S.-Canada border

Nelson (pop. 10,000) is quite possibly the most pleasant and attractive town in the British Columbian interior. The late-19th-century commercial district is still intact, with an eclectic mix of old-fashioned businesses, coffeehouses, and fancy boutiques and galleries. Nelson also offers high-quality B&Bs, hotels, and restaurants, and the setting—along a shelf of land above the West Arm of Kootenay Lake—is splendid.

Nelson was born as a silver-mining town in the 1880s, and its veins proved productive and profitable. By 1900, Nelson was the third-largest city in the province, with an architecturally impressive core of Victorian and Queen Anne–style homes. Today, the gracious town center, coupled with convenient access to recreation in nearby lakes, mountains, and streams, has added to Nelson's newfound luster as an arts capital. Nelson claims to have more artists and craftspeople per capita than any other city in Canada. It certainly has an appealingly youthful, comfortably countercultural feel, and makes a great place to spend a day or two.

Essentials

GETTING THERE   Nelson is 102km (63 miles) north of the U.S.-Canada border, 242km (150 miles) north of Spokane, Washington, and 657km (408 miles) east of Vancouver. **Greyhound Canada** ((*C*) **800/661-8747;** www.greyhound.ca) operates daily service from Vancouver for C$115 one-way.

VISITOR INFORMATION   Contact the **Nelson Visitor Info Centre,** 225 Hall St. ((*C*) **250/352-3433;** www.discovernelson.com).

Exploring the Area

Nelson's main attractions are, in order, the city itself and what's just beyond. As an introduction to the town's wonderful Victorian architecture, stop by the visitor center for brochures on the driving and walking tours of Nelson's significant heritage buildings.

Not to be missed are the château-style **City Hall** (now Touchstones Nelson museum; see below), 502 Vernon St., and **Nelson Court House,** designed by F. M. Rattenbury, famed for his designs for the B.C. Parliament Buildings and the Empress Hotel, both of which continue to dominate Victoria. Note the three-story, turreted storefront at the corner of Baker and Ward streets, and the **Mara-Barnard building,** 421–431 Baker St., once the Royal Bank of Canada building, with elaborate brickwork and bay windows.

The story of Nelson's human history is told at the **Touchstones Nelson—Museum of Art and History,** 502 Vernon St. ((*C*) **250/352-9813**), which has a number of exhibits on the Native Ktunaxa and from the silver-mining days when Nelson was one of the richest towns in Canada. Two galleries are devoted to changing art exhibits. Hours are Tuesday through Saturday from 10am to 5pm (Thurs till 8pm), and Sunday noon to 4pm. Admission is C$10 for adults, C$6 for seniors and students, C$4 children 7 to 18, and C$25 families.

Nelson has a number of beautiful parks. **Gyro Park,** at Vernon and Park streets, features formal gardens, an outdoor pool, and panoramic views of Kootenay Lake and the Selkirk Mountains. **Lakeside Park,** which flanks Kootenay Lake near the base of the Nelson Bridge, offers swimming beaches, tennis courts, and a playground.

You can explore Nelson's lakefront on foot on the **Waterfront Pathway,** which winds along the shore from near the Prestige Resort to Lakeside Park. Or, in summer, hop on the restored **streetcar no. 23,** which runs from Lakeside Park to Hall Street, along the waterfront. At the turn of the 20th century, Nelson had a streetcar system and was the smallest city in Canada to boast such public transport. The system fell out of use in the 1940s, but a stretch of the track remains intact. The streetcar runs on weekends only from Easter weekend to mid-June. It operates daily from mid-June to Labour Day, after which it resumes weekend-only operations until Canadian Thanksgiving weekend. Tickets are C$3 for adults and C$2 for seniors and students.

Outdoor Pursuits

FISHING   Fishing is legendary in 200m-deep (656-ft.) Kootenay Lake, which has 500km (311 miles) of lakefront. For guided trips and advice, contact **Split Shot Charters** (© 877/368-FISH [3474]; www.split-shot.com).

GOLF   **Granite Pointe Golf Club,** 1123 Richards St. W. (© 250/352-5913; www.granitepointe.ca), is a hilly 18-hole, par-72 course with fantastic views of Kootenay Lake. Greens fees are C$54; rentals, a clubhouse with dining, and a driving range are available.

HIKING   Accessible right in town is a 9km (5.6-mile) rails-to-trails system on the old Burlington Northern line that follows the southern edge of the town along the flanks of Toad Mountain. You can join the path at a number of places; from downtown, follow Cedar Street south to find one entry point. The closest wilderness hiking is at **Kokanee Glacier Provincial Park,** 21km (13 miles) northeast of Nelson on Hwy. 3A, then 16km (10 miles) north on a gravel road.

KAYAKING   For rentals or a guided half-day tour (C$79), contact **Kootenay Kayak Co.,** 579 Baker St. (© 877/229-4959 or 250/229-4549; www.kootenaykayak.com).

MOUNTAIN BIKING   The visitor center has a free map of old logging roads and rail lines that are available for biking. The Burlington Northern rails-to-trails system (see "Hiking," above) is also open to mountain bikers. For rentals and trail conditions, contact **Gerick Cycle & Sports,** 702 Baker St. (© 800/665-4441; www.gericks.com).

SKIING   Sixteen kilometers (10 miles) south of Nelson off Hwy. 6 is the **Whitewater Ski Resort** (© 800/666-9420 or 250/354-4944; www.skiwhitewater.com), with some of British Columbia's best snow conditions. The ski area is in a natural snow-catching bowl below an escarpment of 2,490m (8,169-ft.) peaks. The average snowfall is 12m (39 ft.), and that snow falls as pure powder. The mountain consists of groomed runs, open bowls, glades, chutes, and tree skiing; 80% of the runs are rated either intermediate or advanced. There are two double chairs and a handle tow; the vertical drop is 390m (1,280 ft.). Lift tickets cost C$57. Facilities include a day lodge with rentals, dining, and drinks. The Nordic Centre has 18km (11 miles) of groomed cross-country ski trails.

If you're looking for backcountry skiing, the **Baldface Lodge** (© **250/352-0006;** www.baldface.net) is your ticket. A short helicopter ride takes you from Nelson to the backcountry lodge, where there are exquisite dining and accommodations, plus snowcat access to 14,568 hectares (35,998 acres) of powder snow terrain. The rates are very complex (see the website for precise costs), but count on spending around C$800 per day in peak season, including unlimited guided snowcat skiing, all meals, and lodging. In summer, the lodge is open July 15 to October 15 for hiking and mountain biking.

Where to Stay

Best Western Baker Street Inn
The Baker Street Inn stands at the end of the historic downtown area, within easy walking distance of both shopping and dining. Guest rooms are rather basic, but very clean and comfortable.

153 Baker St., Nelson, BC V1L 4H1. © **888/255-3525** or 250/352-3525. Fax 250/352-2995. www.bw bakerstreetinn.com. 70 units. C$149–C$259 double. Extra person C$10. AE, DISC, MC, V. **Amenities:** Restaurant; lounge; exercise room; Jacuzzi. *In room:* A/C, TV, fridge, hair dryer, Wi-Fi, microwave.

Cloudside Inn ★
This spacious B&B is perched on a hill just a block off Baker Street, with views of the lake and Kootenay Peak. The handsome painted lady–style Victorian has six rooms with a mix of private and shared bathrooms, plus a garden, patio, and deck. The third floor is a two-bedroom, self-contained apartment. Rates include full breakfast. The proprietors here offer the very epitome of friendly English-style B&B hospitality.

408 Victoria St., Nelson, BC V1L 4K5. © **800/596-2337** or 250/352-3226. www.cloudside.ca. 7 units. C$85–C$199 double; C$159–C$249 apt. Extra person C$15. Golf, spa, romance, and ski packages available. MC, V. Free off-street parking. **Amenities:** Lounge w/TV and Internet access; front and rear sun decks. *In room:* No phone, Wi-Fi.

Dancing Bear Inn (Value)
The Dancing Bear is a first-rate hostel right in the thick of things downtown. The atmosphere and furnishings are more like what you'd expect to find in a B&B—a grimy backpackers' flophouse this is definitely not. The furniture is locally made from pine, beds are made up with down duvets, and paintings by area artists grace the walls. This is not your everyday hostel, and even if you're not into the hostelling scene, you'll find it a great place to meet people.

171 Baker St., Nelson, BC V1L 4H1. © **250/352-7573.** Fax 250/352-9818. www.dancingbearinn.com. 35 beds. C$21–C$25 dorm bed; C$44–C$56 private unit. Family and group rates, seasonal packages, and discounts for Hostelling International members available. MC, V. **Amenities:** Computer w/Internet access; Wi-Fi; kitchen; common room w/TV/VCR. *In room:* No phone.

Hume Hotel
This beautifully preserved 1898 hotel has been renovated to accommodate modern ideas of comfort while maintaining its vintage charm. For an antique hotel, the rooms are good-size, environmentally friendly, and smartly furnished. You'll want to visit the Hume Hotel even if you're not staying here, just to check out the wonderful bars, nightclub, and lobby area.

422 Vernon St., Nelson, BC V1L 4E5. © **877/568-0888** or 250/352-5331. Fax 250/352-5214. www.hume hotel.com. 43 units. C$99–C$149 double. Extra person C$10. Rates include breakfast. Golf and ski packages available. AE, MC, V. **Amenities:** 2 restaurants; 2 bars; access to nearby health club; day spa; liquor store. *In room:* TV, Wi-Fi.

New Grand Hotel
Originally built in 1914, the Art Deco New Grand Hotel has been lovingly restored and updated as a hip and happening hotel and nightspot for the young at heart. The renovated rooms wear their age gracefully, without attempting to

match a period style. The decor is comfortably eclectic, with hardwood floors, Oriental rugs, contemporary art, and mid-century reproduction furniture. The result is simple, charming, and clutter free. If you're looking for inexpensive rooms, a number of double and triple rooms are available hostel-style, with shared bathrooms and a kitchen area. The hotel's Uptown Tavern is a popular bar and grill, while Louie's Steakhouse offers excellent prime beef and martinis.

616 Vernon St., Nelson, BC V1L 4G1. © **888/722-2258** or 250/352-7211. Fax 250/352-2445. www.new grandhotel.ca. 34 units. C$42–C$47 hostel rooms per person; C$72–C$107 double; C$111–C$131 suite. **Amenities:** Restaurant; bar. *In room:* A/C, TV.

Prestige Lakeside Resort & Convention Centre ★   Down on the lakeshore, the Prestige is Nelson's full-service resort, offering spacious, beautiful rooms with all the services you'd expect at a luxury hotel. All units have balconies, and a number of theme rooms (including African and prehistoric ones) will spice up a special occasion. Some rooms have kitchenettes. The Prestige chain has opened another lakeshore lodging, in many ways an adjunct to this large hotel. The **Prestige Lakeview Inn,** 1301 Front St., is a smaller boutique hotel with upscale, European-style rooms. Facilities, such as the restaurant and pool, are shared with the sister property; rates are parallel. To contact the Prestige Lakeview Inn directly, call © **250/352-3595.**

701 Lakeside Dr., Nelson, BC V1L 6G3. © **877/737-8443** or 250/352-7222. Fax 250/352-3966. www. prestigeinn.com. 101 units. C$119–C$259 double; C$239–C$650 themed room or suite. Extra person C$20. Off-season rates available. AE, DC, DISC, MC, V. **Amenities:** Restaurant; bar; coffee bar; concierge; exercise room; Jacuzzi; indoor pool; room service; spa. *In room:* A/C, TV w/pay movies, fridge, hair dryer, kitchenette (in some rooms), Wi-Fi.

Where to Dine

The restaurants at the **Prestige Lakeside Resort** and the **Hume Hotel** (see "Where to Stay," above) are good, and a wander down **Baker Street** will reveal dozens of cafes, coffeehouses, and inexpensive ethnic restaurants. Don't miss the **Dominion Café,** 334 Baker St. (© **250/352-1904**), an old diner offering sandwiches, light entrees, baked goods, and a friendly, relaxed atmosphere. A popular hangout, morning to night, is **Jigsaws Coffee Co.,** 503 Baker St. (© **250/352-5961**).

All Seasons Café ★★★ NORTHWEST   The All Seasons is reason enough to visit Nelson. Located in a handsome heritage home a block off busy Baker Street, it isn't easy to find, but if you want to eat at British Columbia's best restaurant east of Vancouver, then persevere. Menus, which change seasonally, feature local produce and meats. To start, try the outstanding "pan-kissed" king scallops with butternut puree and anise-scented salmon roe cream. Main courses include a number of vegetarian and fish options, plus meaty creations such as crispy-skin duck breast with caramelized pear, plum chutney, and watercress risotto; and roast rack of lamb with fig-pecan Stilton compound and port jus. The wine list has many Okanagan Valley selections, and the service is friendly and professional.

620 Herridge Lane. © **250/352-0101.** www.allseasonscafe.com. Reservations required. Main courses C$17–C$39. AE, MC, V. Daily 5–10pm; Sun brunch 10am–2:30pm.

Bibo ITALIAN   Bibo is a small but atmospheric restaurant and watering hole with a look that's half Old West and half Old World. But the food is straightforward comfort-style European, with house-made pasta and gnocchi, carpaccio with truffled Dijon mustard sauce, risotto, plus grilled fish and meats. An entire menu is devoted to charcuterie and cheeses—with its focus on great cheese, Bibo also serves a killer fondue.

Lunch is mostly soup, salads, and sandwiches. In summer, the deck is a quiet spot to relax with a drink.

518 Hall St. ✆ **250/352-2744.** Reservations suggested. Main courses C$12–C$23. MC, V. Mon–Sat 11am–11pm; Sun 10am–3pm. Call to confirm hours for winter lunch.

Fusion 301 ★ TAPAS In the heart of downtown's Baker Street district, Fusion offers a selection of small plates and "bigger things" in a numerous (40-plus) array of styles and flavors, all matched with excellent wine selections. During winter, the restaurant is confined to the snug dining room, but in summer the entire enterprise spills out onto the street, more than doubling the zone of tapas consumption. Start out with jumbo prawns stuffed with goat cheese, garlic, and herbs, or individual lamb chops with emerald mint sauce. The menu's larger dishes include wild B.C. salmon with wild mushroom ragout and portobello mushrooms stuffed with artichoke and Manchego cheese. Still hungry? Head back for decadent favorites like French Canadian poutine or Indian butter chicken.

301 Baker St. ✆ **250/352-3011.** Reservations not accepted. Tapas C$5–C$22. MC, V. Mon–Sat noon–10pm; Sun 10am–9pm.

---

6 THE UPPER COLUMBIA VALLEY: A GOLFING & RECREATIONAL PARADISE

Between Radium Hot Springs (p. 415) and Canal Flats, the Columbia Valley is broad and green, flanked by the towering peaks of the Rockies to the east and the Purcell Mountains to the west. Nestled in the valley are two lovely lakes, Windermere Lake and Columbia Lake, the latter considered the birthplace of the Columbia River. It's a stunningly dramatic landscape, and the entire valley is undergoing extensive development as an upscale resort area, mostly in the form of golf courses and country-club communities. You'll find no fewer than nine 18-hole and six 9-hole courses within 25 miles of each other, and other outdoor recreational activities—skiing, mountain biking, hiking, and rafting—have also developed as a major focus (the following golf courses are dependably open from May–Sept). The main towns in this part of the Columbia Valley are Invermere and Windermere; though they are on opposite sides of Lake Windermere, they're only 7km (4⅓ miles) apart.

PANORAMA MOUNTAIN VILLAGE & GREYWOLF GOLF COURSE

Panorama, 40km (25 miles) west of Invermere on Panorama Road (✆ **800/663-2929** or 250/342-6941; www.panoramaresort.com), is a major four-seasons resort and residential community. Besides golf and skiing, the recreation-oriented resort offers a host of other activities, including horseback riding, white-water rafting, ATV touring, tennis, hiking, and mountain biking.

The **Panorama Ski Resort** boasts one of the highest vertical drops in Canada, at 41,219m (3,999 ft.). There are over 120 named runs in 1,152 hectares (2,847 acres) of skiable terrain, with nine lifts including one high-speed quad. Fifty-five percent of the runs are intermediate or advanced, and a further 25% are rated expert. Adult day lift tickets are C$74. The resort is also home to the Bilodeau School of Skiing and Snowboarding and the Greywolf Nordic Ski Centre, with 20km (12 miles) of groomed trails.

The resort also offers heli-skiing packages in the Purcell Mountains behind the resort. A day-trip with three helicopter-assisted descents, including breakfast and lunch, is $690 per person.

In summer, the lifts open to mountain bikers, who find a real challenge in both the single-track trails with natural obstacles and the expert terrain with man-made stunts. The trails aren't for first-timers: 86% are rated intermediate to expert.

Greywolf Golf Course at Panorama (② **888/473-9965** or 250/341-4100; www.greywolfgolf.com) is considered one of B.C.'s top courses, and when it opened in 1999 Greywolf was named best new course of the year in Canada. The 6,529m (7,140-yd.) course has bent grass greens and fairways, and spectacular mountain vistas from every hole. Water comes into play on 14 of 18 holes. The "Cliffhanger" is the signature 16th hole—it requires a drive across a steep-sided gorge. Greens fees are C$99 to C$149 for 18 holes, depending on season.

Panorama offers many lodging options ranging from traditional hotel rooms, hostel accommodations, condominiums, and town houses to private home rentals. Double room rates range from C$80 to C$200; for information and reservations call ② **866/601-7383.** The resort has 11 restaurants and bars in the village, with three more choices on the slopes.

FAIRMONT HOT SPRINGS RESORT

People have been visiting the hot water springs at Fairmont for millennia, but the early Native people who came here to cure their aches and pains wouldn't recognize it now. The springs are now the center of **Fairmont Hot Springs Resort,** 16km (10 miles) south of Windermere on Hwy. 93/95 (② **800/663-4979** or 250/345-6000; www.fairmonthot springs.com). Fairmont is a four-season resort, with two famed golf courses, a number of large country-club developments, and a winter ski area, but for many families the big draw remains the hot springs. The mineral water here is rich in calcium, but contains no sulfur, the odiferous agent that fouls the air at most hot springs resorts.

The main attraction at the resort is the 297-sq.-m (3,200-sq.-ft.) lap pool filled with hot mineral water, plus a diving pool and several soaker pools. Amazingly, all the water in the pools is drained nightly and refilled with fresh water. At Fairmont, more than 5.7 million liters (1.5 million gal.) of 102°F (39°C) water flow out of the mountain and through the pools per day. Single entry to the pool complex is C$10 adults, C$9 seniors and youths aged 13 to 17, and C$8 for children 4 to 12. Massage, hydrotherapy, and other spa services are also available.

Fairmont boasts two 18-hole courses and a 9-hole course. **Mountainside Golf Course,** just below the hot springs off Fairway Drive (② **250/345-6514**), is a par-72 course. Mountainside's most famous hole is its 549m (600-yd.) 4th hole. **Riverside Golf Resort,** off Riverview Road (② **250/345-6346**), is a championship 18-hole course, with a driving range, full practice area, pro shop, and lessons available. The Riverside is unique in that it spans the Columbia River, and uses the mighty river as a natural water hazard. The Riverside course is 5,968m (6,527 yd.) in length and was named Canada's golf course of the year in 1998. Greens fees for both courses range from C$69 to C$80 for 18 holes. The par 3, 9-hole **Creekside Golf Course** (② **250/345-6660**) is great for learners and families, with rates ranging from C$15 to C$18.

Fairmont Hot Springs Ski Resort offers a half pipe and snowboard park, triple chair lift, and 13 runs for a full day of skiing enjoyment. Fairmont is not as large a ski area as others in the Columbia Valley—it has a vertical drop of 305m (1,000 ft.)—but it's a good place for families or beginners. Adult day lift tickets are C$44.

Accommodations at Fairmont Hot Springs Resort are in the rambling 140-room lodge. Summer high-season rates range between C$184 and C$339 for a double room.

14

The Radium Resort, 8100 Golf Course Rd., Radium Hot Springs (✆ **250/347-6266;** www.radiumresort.com), is a year-round destination with a resort community and ample recreational activities, but the focus is on its two golf courses. The **Resort Course** is the oldest is the Columbia Valley, built in 1957. This par-69 course offers incredible vistas and some equally dramatic elevation changes that present challenges to golfers used to flatter courses. Greens fees range from C$32 to C$59. The newer **Springs Course,** designed by Les Furber, follows the rugged natural contours of the land and is often ranked among the top courses in Canada. This par-72 course features four tee boxes per hole to allow for play from 4,721 to 6,188m (5,163–6,767 yd.). Greens fees are C$79 to C$110. The resort offers accommodations in standard hotel-style rooms or in condos, starting at C$99 for a double in high season.

Eagle Ranch Golf Resort, 9581 Eagle Ranch Trail, Invermere (✆ **877/877-3889** or 250/342-0562; www.eagleranchresort.com), is located on the bluffs above Lake Windermere and the Columbia Wetlands, and the layout weaves in natural features such as deep ravines and hoodoos. This 18-hole, 6,077m (6,646-yd.), par-72 championship golf course is both scenic and very challenging. Greens fees range from C$85 to C$130. The clubhouse restaurant, Saliken, is a destination in its own right. **Copper Point Golf Course,** 651 Hwy. 93/95, Invermere (✆ **877/418-4653** or 250/341-3392; www. copperpointgolf.com), offers two courses for a total of 36 holes of golf. The original par-70 **Copper Point Course,** with a length of 6,224m (6,807 yd.), lets the natural terrain of the Rockies do the work, as the layout follows the rise and fall of the foothills, with several dramatic elevation changes built into the course. Greens fees are C$95 to C$125. The new-in-2008 **Ridge at Copper Point Course** is, as you might guess, on a series of bluffs above the original course. The rugged terrain is a major factor in the play at this innovative par-62 Masters-style course. With 4,638m (5,072 yd.), the course is faster to play than most area courses yet still very demanding. Greens fees are C$75 to C$85.

Gateways to the Canadian Rockies: Calgary & Edmonton

Stretching from the Northwest Territories to the U.S. border of Montana in the south, flanked by the Rocky Mountains in the west and the province of Saskatchewan in the east, Alberta is a big, beautiful, empty chunk of North America. It has 3.2 million inhabitants, roughly half of whom live in and around Edmonton, the provincial capital, and Calgary, a former cow town grown large and wealthy with oil money.

Both Calgary and Edmonton serve as gateways to the famed Canadian Rockies that rise on their western horizons. Since both cities function as air hubs for the major national parks—there are no scheduled flights to destinations within the Canadian Rockies—and since both Calgary and Edmonton are on major east-west road systems, chances are good you'll spend some time here. (See chapter 16 for complete coverage of the Rockies.)

Culturally, Calgary and Edmonton are a beguiling mix of rural Canadian sincerity and big-city swagger and affluence. Both cities are models of modern civic pride and hospitality; in fact, an anonymous behavioral survey recently named Edmonton Canada's friendliest city.

Early settlers first came to Alberta for its wealth of furs; the Hudson's Bay Company established Edmonton House on the North Saskatchewan River in 1795. The Blackfoot, one of the West's most formidable Indian nations, maintained control of the prairies until the 1870s, when the Royal Canadian Mounted Police arrived to enforce the white man's version of law and order. The Mounties' Fort Calgary was established on the Bow River in 1875. Open-range cattle ranching prospered on the rich grasslands, and agriculture is still the basis of the rural economy. Vast oil reserves were discovered beneath the prairies in the 1960s, introducing a tremendous boom across the province.

Plan to take a day or two to explore these lively cities—more, if your itinerary will accommodate it. Calgary has excellent museums and one of the most exciting restaurant scenes in Canada. Edmonton, dominated by its university and its capital status, has a vital arts scene and—not to be dismissed lightly—one of the largest shopping malls–cum–entertainment palaces in the world.

1 CALGARY: HOME OF THE ANNUAL STAMPEDE ★★

128km (80 miles) E of Banff; 296km (184 miles) N of the U.S. border

Calgary dates only from the summer of 1875, when a detachment of the Northwest Mounted Police reached the confluence of the Bow and Elbow rivers. The solid log fort they built had attracted 600 settlers by the end of the year. Gradually, the lush prairie lands around the settlement drew tremendous beef herds, many of them from overgrazed U.S. ranches in the south. Calgary grew into a cattle metropolis and a large meatpacking center. When World War II ended, the placid city numbered barely 100,000.

The oil boom erupted in the late 1960s, and in a decade it transformed the pace and complexion of the city. In 1978 alone, C$1-billion worth of construction was added to the skyline, creating office high-rises, hotel blocks, walkways, and shopping centers so quickly even locals weren't sure what was around the corner. In the mid-1990s, the oil market heated up again, and Alberta's pro-business political climate tempted national companies to build their headquarters here. With world oil prices at all-time highs, Calgary continues to boom in the 21st century, and building cranes continue to dominate the skyline.

In February 1988, Calgary was the site of the Winter Olympics, giving it the opportunity to roll out the welcome mat on a truly international scale. The city outdid itself in hospitality, erecting a whole network of facilities, including the Canada Olympic Park, some 15 minutes west of downtown.

Calgary, with its population of one million, has an imposing skyline with dozens of business towers topping 40 stories. Despite this, the city doesn't seem urban. With its many parks and convivial populace, Calgary retains the atmosphere of a much smaller, friendlier town.

ESSENTIALS
Getting There
BY PLANE   **Calgary International Airport** (www.calgaryairport.com) lies 16km (10 miles) northeast of the city. The airport is served by **Air Canada** (© 800/372-9500), **Delta** (© 800/221-1212), **American Airlines** (© 800/433-7300), **United** (© 800/241-6522), **Continental** (© 800/525-0280), and **Northwest** (© 800/447-4747), among others. Air Canada runs an air shuttle service almost hourly to and from Edmonton. Cab fare to downtown hotels comes to around C$35.

BY TRAIN   The nearest **VIA Rail** station is in Edmonton (see "Edmonton: Capital of Alberta," later in this chapter). You can, however, take a scenic train ride to/from Vancouver/Calgary on the **Rocky Mountaineer,** operated by the **Great Rocky Mountaineer Railtours** (© 800/665-7245 or 604/606-7245; www.rockymountaineer.com). The lowest-priced tickets begin at C$679 for 2 days of daylight travel, which includes four meals and overnight accommodations in Kamloops; many other packages are available.

BY BUS   **Greyhound** buses (© 800/661-8747 or 403/260-0877; www.greyhound.ca) link Calgary with most other points in Canada, including Banff and Edmonton. Bus service is no longer offered between Calgary and the U.S. along Hwy. 2 and I-15. The depot is at 877 Greyhound Way SW, west of downtown near the corner of 9th Avenue SW and 16th Street SW.

BY CAR   From the U.S. border in the south, Hwy. 2 runs to Calgary and continues north to Edmonton (via Red Deer). From Vancouver in the west to Regina in the east, take the Trans-Canada Highway.

VISITOR INFORMATION   The downtown **Visitor Service Centre** is at the base of Calgary Tower at 101 9th Ave. SW (© 800/661-1678 or 403/750-2362; www.tourism calgary.com). There's also a tourist office at the airport. Direct written requests to **Tourism Calgary,** 200–238 11th Ave. SE, Calgary, AB T2G 0X8.

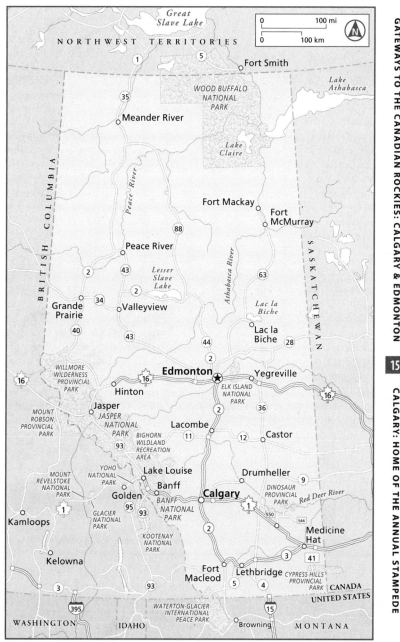

> **(Tips) A Word About Walking**
>
> The "Plus-15" system is a series of enclosed walkways, connecting downtown buildings, 4.5m (15 ft.) above street level. These walkways enable you to shop in living-room comfort, regardless of the weather. Watch for the little "+15" signs on the streets for access points.

CITY LAYOUT Central Calgary lies between the Bow River in the north and the Elbow River to the south. The two rivers meet at the eastern end of the city, forming **St. George's Island,** which houses a park and the zoo. South of the island stands Fort Calgary, birthplace of the city. The Bow River makes a bend north of downtown, and in this bend nestles **Prince's Island Park** and **Eau Claire Market.** The Canadian Pacific Railway tracks run between 9th and 10th avenues, and **Central Park** and **Stampede Park,** scene of Calgary's greatest annual festival, stretch south of the tracks. Northwest, across the Bow River, is the **University of Calgary**'s lovely campus. The airport is northeast of the city.

Calgary is divided into four quadrants: **northeast** (NE), **southeast** (SE), **northwest** (NW), and **southwest** (SW), with avenues running east-west and streets north-south. The north and south numbers begin at Centre Avenue, the east and west numbers at Centre Street—a recipe for confusion if ever there was one.

GETTING AROUND Calgary Transit System (*C* 403/276-1000; www.calgary transit.com) operates buses and a light-rail system called the C-Train. You can transfer from the light rail to buses on the same ticket. The ride costs C$2.50 for adults and C$1.50 for children; the C-Train is free (buses are not) in the downtown stretch between 10th Street and City Hall. Tickets are good for travel in only one direction.

Car-rental firms include **Avis,** 211 6th Ave. SW (*C* 403/269-6166); **Budget,** 140 6th Ave. SE (*C* 403/226-0000); and **Hertz,** 227 6th Ave. SW (*C* 403/221-1681). Each of these has a bureau at the airport.

To summon a taxi, call **Checker Cabs** *C* 403/299-9999), **Red Top Cabs** (*C* 403/974-4444), or **Yellow Cabs** *C* 403/974-1111).

(*Fast Facts*) Calgary

American Express The office at 605 5th Ave. SW (*C* 403/294-7100) is open Monday to Friday 9am to 5pm.

Area Code Calgary's area code is **403.**

Doctors If you need nonemergency medical attention, check the phone number for the closest branch of **Medicentre,** a group of walk-in clinics open daily 7am to midnight.

Drugstores Check the phone book for **Shoppers Drug Mart,** which has more than a dozen stores in Calgary, most open until midnight. The branch at the Chinook Centre, 6455 Macleod Trail S. (*C* 403/253-2424), is open 24 hours.

Emergency For medical, fire, or crime emergencies, dial *C* **911.**

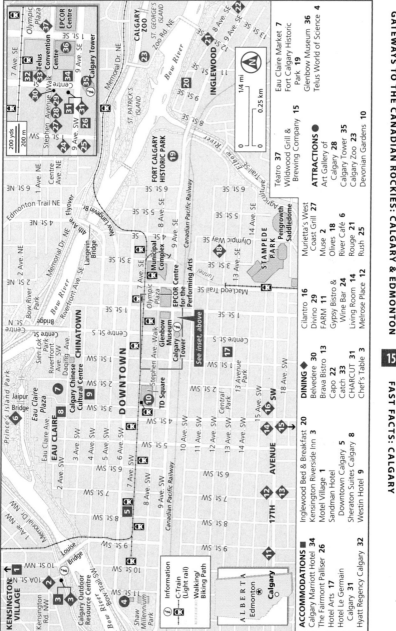

KENSINGTON VILLAGE

EAU CLAIRE

CHINATOWN

Calgary Chinese Cultural Centre 9

DOWNTOWN

17TH AVENUE SW

INGLEWOOD

CALGARY ZOO

FORT CALGARY HISTORIC PARK 19

STAMPEDE PARK

Pengrowth Saddledome 18

ACCOMMODATIONS ■
Calgary Marriott Hotel 34
The Fairmont Palliser 26
Hotel Arts 17
Hotel Le Germain Calgary 31
Hyatt Regency Calgary 32
Inglewood Bed & Breakfast 20
Kensington Riverside Inn 3
Motel Village 1
Sandman Hotel Downtown Calgary 5
Sheraton Suites Calgary 8
Westin Hotel 9

DINING ◆
Belvedere 30
Brava Bistro 13
Capo 22
Catch 33
CHARCUT 31
Chef's Table 3
Cilantro 16
Divino 29
FARM 11
Gypsy Bistro 24
Living Room 14
Melrose Place 12
Murrieta's West Coast Grill 27
Muse 2
Olives 18
River Café 6
Rouge 21
Rush 25
Téatro 37
Wildwood Grill & Brewing Company 15

ATTRACTIONS ●
Art Gallery of Calgary 28
Calgary Tower 35
Calgary Zoo 23
Devonian Gardens 10
Eau Claire Market 7
Fort Calgary Historic Park 19
Glenbow Museum 36
Telus World of Science 4

Information
C-Train (Light rail)
Walking/ Biking Path

200 yds
200 m

1/4 mi
0.25 km

ALBERTA
Calgary
Edmonton

Hospitals If you need medical care, try **Foothills Hospital,** 1403 29th St. NW
(© **403/670-1110**).

Newspapers Calgary's two dailies, the *Calgary Herald* (www.calgaryherald.com)
and the *Calgary Sun* (www.calgarysun.com), are both morning papers. *Ffwd* (www.
ffwdweekly.com) is a youth-oriented newsweekly and a good place to look for
information on the local music and arts scene.

Police The 24-hour number is © **403/266-1234.** Dial © **911** in emergencies.

Post Office The main post office is at 207 9th Ave. (© **403/974-2078**). Call
© **403/292-5434** to find other branches.

Time Calgary is on Mountain Time, the same as Edmonton and Denver, and it
observes daylight saving time.

EXPLORING THE CITY
The Top Attractions

Calgary Tower   Reaching 762 steps or 190m (623 ft.) into the sky, this Calgary
landmark is topped by an observation terrace offering unparalleled views of the city and
mountains and prairies beyond. The high-speed elevator whisks you to the top in just 63
seconds. A stairway from the terrace leads to the cocktail lounge, where you can enjoy
drinks and a panoramic vista. Photography from up here is fantastic. The **Sky 360 Restaurant** (© **403/532-7966**) is the near-mandatory revolving restaurant.

9th Ave. and Centre St. SW. © **403/266-7171.** www.calgarytower.com. Elevator ride C$13 adults, C$11
seniors, C$10 youths 13–17, C$5 children 4–12. Complimentary elevation to restaurant with purchase of
main course. June–Aug daily 9am–10pm (last lift 9:30pm); Sept–May daily 9am–9pm (last lift 8:30pm).
LRT: 1st St. E.

Calgary Zoo, Botanical Garden & Prehistoric Park ★ Kids   Calgary's large and
thoughtfully designed zoo resides on St. George's Island in the Bow River. The Calgary
Zoo comes as close to providing natural habitats for its denizens as is technically possible. You'll particularly want to see the troop of majestic lowland gorillas and the
African warthogs. The flora and fauna of western and northern Canada are on display
in the Botanical Garden, and there's an amazing year-round tropical butterfly enclosure as well. Adjoining the zoo is the Prehistoric Park, a three-dimensional textbook of
ancient dinosaur habitats populated by 22 amazingly realistic replicas—these imposing
reproductions will give dino-loving children something to think about. Call to inquire
about special summer events, such as Thursday Jazz Nights and free interpretive talks
called "Nature Tales."

1300 Zoo Rd. NE. © **403/232-9300.** www.calgaryzoo.ab.ca. Admission C$18 adults, C$16 seniors, C$12
youths 13–17, C$10 children 3–12. Labour Day to Apr 30 all rates reduced by C$2. Daily 9am–5pm. LRT:
Zoo station.

Canada Olympic Park Kids   This lasting memento of Calgary's role as host of the
1988 Winter Olympics stands in Olympic Park, which was the site for ski jumping, luge,
and bobsledding during the games. Exhibits include the world's largest collection of
Olympic souvenirs, such as the torch used to bring the flame from Greece, costumes and
equipment used by the athletes, superb photographs, and a gallery of all medal winners.
The reason that the park is still an exciting destination is the activities and lessons

(Moments) The Calgary Stampede

Each July, Calgary puts on the biggest, wildest, woolliest Western fling on Earth: the **Calgary Stampede.** To call the stampede a show would be a misnomer. The whole city participates by going mildly crazy for the occasion, donning Western gear, whooping, hollering, dancing, and generally behaving uproariously.

Many of the organized events spill out into the streets, but most take place in Stampede Park, a show, sports, and exhibition ground south of downtown that was built for just this purpose. Portions of the park become amusement areas, whirling, spinning, and rotating with the latest rides. Other parts are set aside especially for the kids, who romp through Kids' World and the Petting Zoo. Still other areas host livestock shows, a food fair, handicraft exhibitions, an art show, lectures, an international bazaar, a casino, lotteries, and entertainment on several stages.

The top attractions, though, are the **rodeo events,** the largest and most prestigious of their kind in North America. Cowboys from all over the world take part in such competitions as riding bucking broncos and bulls, roping calves, and wrestling steers for prize money topping C$2 million. At the world-famous **Chuckwagon Race,** you'll see old-time Western cook wagons thundering around the track in a fury of dust and pounding hooves. At night, the arena becomes a blaze of lights when the Stampede Grandstand takes over with precision-kicking dancers, clowns, bands, and spectacles.

Reserving accommodations well ahead is essential—as many months ahead of your arrival as you can possibly foresee. Some downtown watering holes even take reservations for space at the bar; that should give you an idea of how busy Calgary gets.

The same advice applies to reserving tickets for Stampede events. Tickets to the rodeo begin at C$23 but go up from there, depending on the event, the seats, and whether the event takes place in the afternoon or evening. For mail order bookings, contact the **Calgary Exhibition and Stampede,** P.O. Box 1060, Station M, Calgary, AB T2P 2K8 (© **800/661-1767;** fax 403/223-9736; www. calgarystampede.com).

available. In winter, both adults and children can take downhill and cross-country ski lessons, learn to ski jump or snowboard, or get an introduction to snow skating. More exciting are the opportunities to ride a bobsled down the Olympic track or to take a zip-line off the ski jump tower—harnessed onto a cable system, reaching speeds between 120 and 140kmph (75–87 mph), this will get the adrenaline pumping for road trip–weary teenagers (C$55). Other summer activities include a mountain-bike course, and chairlift rides up to the ski-jump tower.

88 Canada Olympic Park Rd. SW. © **403/247-5452.** www.winsportcanada.ca. Admission C$16 per person, C$48 per family; separate fees for activities and lessons. Summer daily 9am–9pm; off season Mon–Fri 9am–9pm, Sat–Sun 9am–5pm. Take Hwy. 1 west.

Eau Claire Market & Prince's Island Park   Eau Claire Market is part of a car-free pedestrian zone north of downtown on the banks of the Bow River that links to lovely Prince's Island Park, a bucolic island in the Bow River lined with paths, shaded by cottonwood trees, and populated by hordes of Canada geese. This is where much of downtown Calgary comes to eat, drink, shop, sunbathe, jog, and hang out in good weather. The market itself no longer offers a lot for the traveler except for a few eateries (better options are the pubs in the plaza outside the market) though it remains busy with a four-screen cinema and an **IMAX Theatre** (℗ 403/974-4629), with its five-story domed screen.

750 9th Ave. SE. ℗ **403/264-6450.** Free admission. Market building 9am–9pm; shops and restaurants have varying hours. LRT: 3rd St. W.

Fort Calgary Historic Park ★★ (Kids)   On the occasion of the city's centennial in 1975, Fort Calgary became a public park of 16 hectares (40 acres), spread around the ruins of the original Mounted Police stronghold. In 2001, volunteers completed a replica of the 1888 barracks using traditional methods and building materials. The Interpretive Centre captures the history of Calgary, from its genesis as a military fort to the beginnings of 20th-century hegemony as an agricultural and oil boomtown. There are a number of interesting videos and docent-led displays; always in focus are the adventures and hardships of the Mounties a century ago.

If all this history whets your appetite, cross the Elbow River on 9th Avenue and head to the Deane House. This historic home was built by a Fort Calgary superintendent nearly 100 years ago and is now the **Deane House Restaurant** operated by Fort Calgary (℗ **403/269-7747**), open Monday to Friday from 11am to 3pm, Saturday and Sunday from 10am to 3pm.

750 9th Ave. SE. ℗ **403/290-1875.** www.fortcalgary.ab.ca. Admission C$11 adults, C$10 seniors and post-secondary students, C$7 youths 7–17, C$5 children 3–6. Daily 9am–5pm. LRT: Bridgeland.

Glenbow Museum ★★   One of the country's finest museums, the Glenbow is a must for anyone with an interest in the history and culture of western Canada. What sets it apart from other museums chronicling the continent's Native cultures and pioneer settlement is the excellence of its interpretation. Especially notable is the third floor, with its vivid evocation of Native cultures—particularly of the local Blackfeet—and compelling descriptions of western Canada's exploration and settlement. You'll enjoy the brief asides into whimsy, such as the display of early washing machines. Other floors contain displays of West African carvings, gems and minerals, and a cross-cultural look at arms and warfare.

130 9th Ave. SE (at 1st St.). ℗ **403/268-4100.** www.glenbow.org. Admission C$14 adults, C$10 seniors, C$9 students and children 7–17, free for children 6 and under. Mon–Sat 9am–5pm; Sun noon–5pm. LRT: 1st St. E.

Telus World of Science (Kids)   Formerly the Calgary Science Centre, this science center features a fascinating kid-oriented combination of exhibitions, a planetarium, films, laser shows, and live theater, all under one roof. The hands-on, science-oriented exhibits change, but always invite visitors to push, pull, talk, listen, and play. The 360-degree Discovery Dome Theatre offers a number of filmed presentations that engulf the senses (additional C$3.50 charge). A new home for the Telus World of Science is under construction, a 14,214-sq.-m (153,000 sq.-ft.) structure north of the Calgary Zoo that's due for completion in 2011.

701 11th St. SW. ℗ **403/221-3700.** www.calgaryscience.ca. Admission (exhibits and star shows) C$14 adults, C$10 seniors and children 3–17, free for children 2 and under. Mon–Thurs 10am–4pm; Fri 10am–5pm; Sat–Sun and holidays 10am–5pm. LRT: 10th St. W.

More Attractions

Art Gallery of Calgary This contemporary art gallery, housed in two renovated downtown buildings, places a special emphasis on local and regional art, and is a good place to check out Calgary's modern-art scene. The gallery also hosts national and regional exhibits.

117 8th Ave. SW. ℭ **403/770-1350.** www.artgallerycalgary.org. C$5 adults, C$2.50 seniors and students, free for children 11 and under. Tues–Sat 10am–5pm. LRT: 1st St. E.

Devonian Gardens These indoor gardens are a patch of paradise in downtown, especially in the chill of winter: Encompassing 1 hectare (2½ acres) and rising three stories, this is one of the world's largest indoor parks. Laid out in natural contours with 1.5km (1 mile) of pathways, the gardens contain 20,000 plants (a mix of native Alberta and tropical plants), a reflecting pool, sun garden, children's playground, sculpture court, water garden, and a central stage for musical performances.

8th Ave. and 3rd St. SW, 4th floor. ℭ **403/268-3830.** Free admission. Daily 9am–9pm. LRT: 3rd St. W.

Military Museums Formerly the Museum of the Regiments, this complex has expanded to include seven museums on 5.2 hectares (13 acres), encompassing 9,940 sq. m (106,993 sq. ft.) of viewing area dedicated to Canadian Forces' history and heritage. As the largest military museum in western Canada, the Military Museums focus on the story of four famous Canadian regiments from the early 1900s to the present. A series of lifelike miniature and full-size displays re-create scenes from the Boer War in 1900 to World War II; contemporary peacekeeping operations are also depicted. Videos, weapons, uniforms, medals, and photographs relating the history of the regiments round out the exhibits; you can also hear the actual voices of the combatants describing their experiences.

4520 Crowchild Trail SW (at Flanders Ave.). ℭ **403/974-2850.** http://themilitarymuseums.ca. Admission C$6 adults, C$4 seniors, C$3 students and children 7–17, free for military personnel and veterans. Mon–Fri 9am–5pm; Sat–Sun 9:30am–4pm. Bus: 20 to Flanders Ave., then 1 block south.

Tours & Excursions

Brewster Transportation (ℭ **877/791-5500;** www.brewster.ca), in conjunction with Gray Line Bus Lines (ℭ **800/661-4919;** www.grayline.ca), leads a wide variety of bus tours. In addition to a 4-hour Calgary tour for C$49, destinations include Banff, Lake Louise, Jasper, the Columbia Icefield, and Waterton Lakes.

Hammer Head Scenic Tours (ℭ **403/260-0940;** www.hammerheadtours.com) offers year-round 3½-hour Calgary tours (C$45), as well as tours to more distant destinations such as 9-hour tours to the Drumheller badlands and the Royal Tyrrell Museum for C$90, and Head-Smashed-in Buffalo Jump for C$97.

Shopping

The main shopping district is downtown along **8th Avenue SW,** between 5th and 1st streets SW. The lower part of 8th Avenue has been turned into a pedestrian zone called the **Stephen Avenue Mall.** Major centers lining 8th Avenue between 1st and 4th streets include the Hudson's Bay Company and Holt Renfrew. Check out **Art Central,** 100 7th Ave. SW, a visual arts complex with over 30 artists' studios and galleries. A hip hangout for the young at heart, **Kensington Village** is just northwest of downtown across the Bow River, centered at 10th Street NW and Kensington Road. The stretch of **17th Avenue SW** between 4th and 10th streets SW has developed a mix of specialty shops, boutiques, cafes, and bars that makes browsing a real pleasure.

Mountain Equipment Co-op, 830 10th Ave. SW (© **403/269-2420;** www.mec.ca), is the largest outdoors store in Calgary, with everything from kayaks to ice axes. Come here before you head to the backcountry. If you like the look of pearl-snap shirts and the cut of Wranglers jeans, head to **Riley & McCormick,** 209 8th Ave. SW (© **403/262-1556**), one of Calgary's original Western-apparel stores. If you're looking for cowboy boots, **Alberta Boot Company,** 50 50th Ave. S. (© **403/263-4623;** www.albertaboot. com), is Alberta's only remaining boot manufacturer.

WHERE TO STAY

Finding inexpensive lodging in Calgary can be difficult. The city's booming economy means that many of the older hotels that once offered perfectly pleasant but moderately priced accommodations have gentrified. If you enjoy B&Bs, try the **Bed and Breakfast Association of Calgary** (www.bbcalgary.com), which has several dozen listings for Calgary. The many hotels in **Motel Village** (see below), which link to the city center via the C-Train, are another option; you can often find these rooms at discount hotel websites.

Downtown
Very Expensive

The Fairmont Palliser ★★   This is the classiest address in all of Calgary. Opened in 1914 as one of the Canadian Pacific Railroad hotels, the Palliser is Calgary's landmark historic hotel. Guest rooms are sumptuously furnished and large for a hotel of this vintage. Fairmont Gold–class suites come with their own concierge and a private lounge with complimentary breakfast, drinks, and hors d'oeuvres. The vast marble-floored lobby, surrounded by columns and lit by gleaming chandeliers, is the very picture of Edwardian sumptuousness. You'll feel like an Alberta cattle king in the Rimrock Dining Room, with vaulted ceilings, period murals, a massive stone fireplace, and hand-tooled leather panels on teak beams.

133 9th Ave. SW, Calgary, AB T2P 2M3. © **800/441-1414** or 403/262-1234. Fax 403/260-1260. www. fairmont.com. 405 units. C$169–C$399 double; C$209–C$889 suite. AE, DC, DISC, MC, V. Valet parking C$32. **Amenities:** Restaurant; bar; babysitting; concierge; concierge-level rooms; health club; indoor pool; room service. *In room:* A/C, TV, hair dryer, minibar, Wi-Fi.

Hotel Le Germain Calgary ★★   A luxury outpost of the upscale Le Germain group from Quebec, this is Calgary's newest and most opulent hotel—and easily the most architecturally notable. The hotel tower is one leg of a three-part structure that looks like a postmodern Arc de Triomphe—very striking. Each room is a showcase of contemporary design, with stone floors, wood paneling, leather furniture, 42-inch high-definition TVs, and very comfortable beds complete with Frette linens. Oversized bathrooms feature white-tile-and-frosted-glass showers and rainfall shower heads. With friendly service and top-of-the-line amenities, Hotel Le Germain Calgary fairly exudes discrete elegance. The location is excellent, just steps from arts and culture at the Glenbow Museum and the performing arts center, and from shopping and dining along Stephen Avenue.

899 Centre St. SW, Calgary, AB T2G 1B8. © **877/362-8990** or 403/264-8990. www.germaincalgary.com. 143 units. From C$279 double. AE, MC, V. Valet parking C$30. **Amenities:** Restaurant; lounge; concierge; exercise room; room service; rooftop terrace. *In room:* A/C, TV, MP3 docking station, minibar, Wi-Fi, robes.

Hyatt Regency Calgary ★   Downtown's most upscale hotel, the Hyatt is linked to the Telus Convention Centre and is convenient to shopping and arts venues. Guest rooms are large, with comfy furniture and great views. Suites are truly spacious, with most of the comforts of home. The hotel's Stillwater Spa is a full-service day spa, with a combination of massage and hydro therapies, body wraps, and beauty treatments for both men and women. The fitness center and saline pool, located on the 18th floor, offer majestic views across the city skyline to the Rockies. The Hyatt flanks historic Stephen Avenue; rather than leveling the 1890s stone storefronts, the Hyatt cleverly incorporates them into the hotel's facade. Original art worth C$2 million is on display in the hotel lobby and corridors.

700 Center St. SE, Calgary, AB T2G 5P6. (✆) **800/233-1234** or 403/717-1234. Fax 403/537-4444. www. calgary.hyatt.com. 355 units. From C$269 double; from C$359 Regency Club suite. AE, DC, DISC, MC, V. Valet and self-parking, based on availability. **Amenities:** Restaurant; lounge; concierge; health club; indoor pool and Jacuzzi; room service; sauna; Stillwater Spa. *In room:* A/C, TV, hair dryer, Wi-Fi, voice mail.

Sheraton Suites Calgary ★

The Sheraton Suites overlooks the Eau Claire Market area, just steps away from both the Bow River Greenway and downtown business towers. As an all-suite hotel, the Sheraton offers large and thoughtfully designed rooms that put luxury and business ease foremost. Guest rooms are decorated with a striking modern aesthetic, with quality and notably comfortable furniture, plus easy access to all the high-tech tools necessary to get work done. The built-in cabinetry makes it feel very homelike, as do the Prairie-influenced art, houseplants, and two TVs found in all rooms. Corner king suites are especially nice, with a huge bathroom, tiled shower, and Jacuzzi tub.

255 Barclay Parade SW, Calgary, AB T2P 5C2. (✆) **888/784-8370** or 403/266-7200. Fax 403/266-1300. www.sheratonsuites.com. 323 units. C$149–C$519 double. Extra person C$30. AE, DC, DISC, MC, V. Valet parking C$35. **Amenities:** 2 restaurants; lounge; babysitting; concierge; exclusive club floors w/lounge; exercise room; lobby Internet stations; indoor pool w/water slide; room service; sauna; in-suite spa services. *In room:* A/C, TV w/movie channels, fridge, hair dryer, minibar, Wi-Fi, microwave, wet bar.

Westin Hotel ★★ (Kids)

Despite its anonymous business-hotel exterior, most guest rooms at the Westin have a subtle Western feel that's reflected in the mission-style furniture, sunny colors, and period photos. For business travelers, 126 rooms have been redesigned in a more contemporary style and with special features such as flatscreen TVs and all the technology to help a business traveler multitask, including large glass-topped working desks and two-line phones. While standard rooms are very comfortable, corner rooms come with balconies. For extra quiet, request one of the Tower rooms, which are normally reserved for business travelers. The hotel rolls out the welcome mat for kids, with a "kids club" offering children's furniture, babysitting, and a children's menu—and even games and special treats from room service. Even dogs, which are welcome, have specialty beds!

320 4th Ave. SW, Calgary, AB T2P 2S6. (✆) **800/937-8461** or 403/266-1611. Fax 403/233-7471. www.westin. com/calgary. 525 units. C$139–C$574 double. Extra person C$30. AE, DC, DISC, MC, V. Self-parking C$15; valet parking C$29 per day. **Amenities:** 2 restaurants; bar; coffee shop; concierge; health club; panoramic rooftop indoor pool; room service; sauna and whirlpool. *In room:* A/C, TV, hair dryer, minibar, Wi-Fi.

Expensive

Calgary Marriott Hotel ★

The Marriott is about as central as things get in Calgary. Linked to the convention center and convenient to the goings-on at the Centre for the Performing Arts and the Glenbow Museum, the Marriott is connected via skywalk with Palliser Square, Calgary Tower, and loads of downtown shopping. Its large guest rooms are subtly decorated and outfitted with niceties such as windows that open, lots of mirrors, and desks set up for business travelers. The even larger, tasteful suites are worth the extra money—especially the parlor suites, with lots of room to decompress. Yes, it's a convention hotel—but a lot nicer than the stereotype, and an excellent choice for leisure travelers.

110 9th Ave. SE (at Centre St.), Calgary, AB T2G 5A6. ✆ **800/228-9290** or 403/266-7331. Fax 403/269-1961. www.calgarymarriott.com. 384 units. C$129–C$269 double; C$239–C$439 suite. Extra person C$20. Weekend packages available. AE, DC, DISC, MC, V. Valet parking C$29 per day; self-parking C$18. **Amenities:** 2 restaurants; lounge; concierge; exercise room; Jacuzzi; indoor pool; room service; sauna. *In room:* A/C, TV, fridge, hair dryer, Wi-Fi, microwave.

Moderate

Best Western Suites Downtown   This well-maintained hotel started out as an apartment building, so the rooms are literally the size of apartments; some come with full kitchens. One- and two-bedroom suites are also available. While not exactly in the center of downtown, it's an easy walk to most sights, and this is one of the few lodgings near the trendy scene on 17th Avenue. All in all, considering the size and comfort of the rooms, and free parking, this is an excellent value in a very expensive town.

1330 Eighth St. SW, Calgary, AB T2R 1B3. ✆ **800/981-2555** or 403/228-6900. Fax 403/228-5535. www. bestwestern.com. 123 units. C$180–C$240 double. Extra person C$20. Senior, weekly, and monthly rates available. AE, DISC, MC, V. Free parking. **Amenities:** Restaurant; fitness room; Jacuzzi; convenience store. *In room:* A/C, TV, fridge, hair dryer, Wi-Fi, microwave.

Hotel Arts ★★   The longtime Holiday Inn just south of downtown Calgary has undergone a C$10-million renovation/upgrade, emerging as Hotel Arts, a one-of-a-kind boutique hotel that's a redoubt of contemporary chic style. The remodel increased the size of guest rooms and brought in such features as 42-inch plasma TVs, upscale linens, and luxury soaps and lotions; the lobby is filled with briskly modern visual art. Guest room decor is both swank and dramatic: Chocolate brown walls, blue velvet curtains, and strikingly modern furniture and lighting provide lots of pizazz; all rooms have balconies. If you're weary of identical corporate hotels but require excellent service and amenities, Hotel Arts is for you.

119 12th Ave. SW, Calgary, AB T2R 0G8. ✆ **800/661-9378** or 403/266-4611. Fax 403/237-0978. www. hotelarts.ca. 185 units. From C$129 double. AE, DC, DISC, MC, V. C$28 valet parking; C$18 self parking. **Amenities:** 2 restaurants; lounge; concierge; exercise room; heated outdoor pool w/patio; room service. *In room:* A/C, flatscreen plasma TV, hair dryer, Wi-Fi.

Sandman Hotel Downtown Calgary (Value)   This hotel on the west end of downtown is one of Calgary's best deals. The Sandman is conveniently located on the free rapid-transit mall, just west of the main downtown core. The standard rooms are a good size, but the real winners are the very large corner units, which feature small kitchens and great views. The Sandman is a popular place with corporate clients, due to its central location and good value. It also boasts a complete fitness facility.

888 7th Ave. SW, Calgary, AB T2P 3J3. ✆ **800/726-3626** or 403/237-8626. Fax 403/290-1238. www. sandmanhotels.com. 301 units. From C$109 double. Children 15 and under stay free in parent's room. AE, DC, DISC, MC, V. Parking C$18. **Amenities:** Restaurant; bar; health club; indoor pool; room service. *In room:* A/C, TV, fridge, hair dryer, Wi-Fi, microwave.

Inexpensive

Calgary City Center Hostel   This newly upgraded hostel at the edge of downtown Calgary offers some of the city's most affordable lodgings—but there are reasons beyond economy to stay here. The hostel is centrally located (right on the C-Train), and convenient to bars and restaurants along Stephen Avenue and theaters near the performing-arts center. Facilities include two private rooms, a self-catering kitchen, and a small convenience store.

520 Seventh Ave. SE, Calgary, AB T2G 0J6. ✆ **403/269-8239.** Fax 403/266-6227. www.hihostels.ca. 94 beds. C$27–C$44 dorm single; C$69–C$100 private double. MC, V. **Amenities:** Wi-Fi; kitchen; library; TV room; bike and ski storage. *In room:* A/C.

In Inglewood

Inglewood Bed & Breakfast ★ (Finds) It's a great location: minutes from downtown, on a quiet residential street backed up to a park and the swift waters of the Bow River. The Inglewood is a rambling modern structure in Queen Anne style built as a B&B. The three guest rooms are simply but stylishly furnished with handmade pine furniture and antiques; all have private bathrooms. Two of the turret rooms have great views over the river. Both owners are professional chefs, so expect an excellent breakfast.

1006 8th Ave. SE, Calgary, AB T2G 0M4. (C) **403/262-6570.** www.inglewoodbedandbreakfast.com. 3 units. C$90–C$135 double. Rates include breakfast. MC, V. Free parking. *In room:* TV/VCR.

Kensington

Kensington Riverside Inn ★★ (Finds) Discriminating travelers, look no further. Just across the Bow River from downtown is the hip Kensington neighborhood, with lots of boutique shops, pubs, coffee shops, and restaurants, a quick 5 minutes from the city center on the C-train. (Kensington is the first stop north of the river.) Facing downtown is the Kensington Riverside Inn, a beautifully furnished small boutique hotel that's a cross between a luxurious country inn and a hip urban getaway. Each of the expansive guest rooms is uniquely decorated and comes with a balcony or patio and a fireplace. Expect uniformly top-notch service here. The inn also houses the highly regarded Chef's Table restaurant (see below).

1126 Memorial Dr. NW, Calgary, AB T2N 3E3. (C) **403/228-4442** or 877/313-3733. Fax 403/228-9608. www.kensingtonriversideinn.com. 19 rooms. C$319–C$419 double. Rates include morning coffee delivery, newspaper, gourmet breakfast, evening turndown service, hors d'oeuvres, and parking. AE, DC, MC, V. **Amenities:** Restaurant; bar; video/DVD library; private meeting room. *In room:* A/C, TV/DVD, hair dryer, Wi-Fi.

Motel Village

Northwest of downtown, Motel Village is a triangle of more than 20 large motels, plus restaurants, stores, and gas stations forming a self-contained hamlet near the University of Calgary. Enclosed by Crowchild Trail, the Trans-Canada Highway, and Hwy. 1A, the village is arranged so that most of the costlier establishments flank the highway; the cheaper ones lie off Crowchild Trail, offering a wide choice of accommodations in a small area with good transportation connections. If you're driving and don't want to deal with downtown traffic, just head here to find a room.

Except during the Stampede, you'll be able to find a vacancy without reservations; on the C-Train, use either Lions Park or Banff Park stops. Use discount hotel websites such as Travelocity to find deals. Popular chain hotels are located here, including **Comfort Inn Calgary Motel Village,** 2369 Banff Trail NW ((C) **800/228-5150** or 403/289-2581); **Best Western Village Park Inn,** 1804 Crowchild Trail NW ((C) **888/774-7716** or 403/289-4645); **Calgary North Thriftlodge,** 2304 16th Ave. NW ((C) **800/578-7878** or 403/289-0211); and the **Quality Inn University,** 2359 Banff Trail NW ((C) **800/661-4667** or 403/289-1973).

Camping

The **Calgary West Campground,** on the Trans-Canada Highway West, 221 101st St. SW ((C) **403/288-0411;** www.calgarycampground.com), allows tents and pets. Facilities include washrooms, toilets, laundry, a dumping station, hot showers, groceries, and a pool. The price for full hookup with two people is C$41 per night; tent sites are C$29 per night.

Calgary has very stylish and exciting restaurants. The city is going through an unparalleled period of prosperity, and the citizenry's average age is around 30. Put these two factors together and you've got the ingredients for a vibrant bar-and-restaurant scene. The focus for dining and revelry is downtown along Stephen Avenue (that is, 8th Ave. btw. 2nd St. SE and 4th St. SW), much of it a bustling pedestrian mall; the long 17th Avenue strip with an abundance of small independent restaurants; and the Kensington area, across the Bow River from downtown, with a number of upbeat dining choices in a tony shopping district. In addition, several formal, chef-owned restaurants with outsize local reputations have set down roots in Inglenook, just south of downtown.

Downtown
Expensive

Belvedere ★★ NEW CANADIAN   The very stylish Belvedere is one of the most impressive of Calgary's restaurants. The dining room exudes a darkly elegant, 1930s atmosphere. The menu blends traditional favorites with stand-up-and-take-notice preparations. Foie gras frequently appears as an appetizer, perhaps seared with fig brioche and caramelized shallot puree. Main courses feature local meats and seasonal produce; favorite main courses include free-range pheasant breast with confit pheasant ravioli and fennel broth, and rack of lamb with celery root puree and olive and brandy demi glace. Vegetarians have the option of a seasonal tasting menu. The bar is a quiet and sophisticated spot for a drink.

107 8th Ave. SW. ✆ **403/265-9595.** www.thebelvedere.ca. Reservations recommended. Main courses C$28–C$49. AE, DC, MC, V. Mon–Fri 11:30am–10pm; Sat 5:30–10pm.

Catch ★ SEAFOOD   Calgary's top seafood restaurant has hooked a creel-full of awards under the direction of executive chef Hayato Okamitsu (including the 2009 Canadian Culinary Championships gold medal), so forget that Calgary is landlocked and explore the remarkable cooking at this two-story dining room in the Calgary Hyatt. The main floor is dedicated to cocktails, light dining, and an oyster bar; the upscale second floor is reserved for fine dining (and adults), where selections change daily, based on what's fresh and available. Expect innovative, even startling preparations here. A dish like Dungeness crab cake with saffron and vanilla sauce, topped with lime caviar, could drive a serious foodie to gastronomic delirium. Quality lamb, steaks, and beef tenderloin are also available, often matched with seafood as reborn surf-and-turf extravaganzas.

100 8th Ave. SE. ✆ **403/206-0000.** www.catchrestaurant.ca. Reservations recommended. Oyster bar main courses C$16–C$28; dining room main courses C$34–C$50; 5-course tasting menu C$95. AE, MC, V. Oyster bar Mon–Fri 11:30am–10pm, Sat 4–10pm; dining room Mon–Fri 11:30am–9:30pm and Sat 5:30–9:30pm.

CHARCUT Roast House ★ STEAKHOUSE   At the base of the Hotel Le Germain Calgary, this attractive dining room is modern but low-key, a mix that's best described as urban rustic. The menu focuses on locally sourced ingredients, particularly meat from Alberta farms and ranches. As you'd expect from the name, the restaurant makes its own cured meats and charcuterie using local pork and game. It also seeks out the finest and most flavorful of grass-fed beef, lamb, and other meats for transformation on the grill and in the wood-fired rotisserie oven. If you're just looking for a glass of wine and something light, take a seat at the charcuterie bar and sample such delicacies as duck breast prosciutto and wild hare rillettes.

899 Centre St. ✆ **403/984-2180.** www.charcut.com. Main courses C$21–C$42. AE, MC, V. Mon–Tues, 11am–11pm; Wed–Fri 11am–1am; Sat 5pm–1am; Sun 5–10pm.

Murrietta's West Coast Grill WESTERN CANADIAN   Just around the corner from the vibrant Stephen Avenue restaurant scene, Murrietta's is a popular and stylish bar and dining room that combines the best of historic and contemporary Calgary. Located on the second story of the 1890s Alberta Hotel, Murrietta's huge bar is a favorite watering hole for urban professionals, and the art-filled, two-story stone-walled dining room is the place for Alberta steaks and local lamb, pork, and game. For appetizers, choose fresh oysters or tuna tartar, and if excellent, locally sourced red meat's not your thing, Murrietta's offers pasta and a daily changing selection of fresh fish with a choice of sauces—perhaps spicy maple ginger sauce on seared wild Pacific salmon.

808 1st St. SW. ✆ **403/269-7707.** Reservations suggested. Main courses C$16–C$46. AE, DC, MC, V. Mon–Sat 11am–11pm; Sun 11am–10pm.

River Café ★★★ CONTEMPORARY CANADIAN   If you have just one meal in Calgary, it should be here. To reach the aptly named River Café, it takes a short walk through the Eau Claire Market area, then over the footbridge to lovely Prince's Island Park in the Bow River. On a summer evening, the walk is a plus, as are the restaurant's park-side decks (no vehicles hurtling by). The River Café has an elegant fishing lodge atmosphere, and the seasonal menu (which reads like a tasty adventure novel for gourmets) features products from small Alberta farms and ranches, and includes smoked fish and game and hearth-baked breads. There's a wide range of appetizers and light dishes— many vegetarian—as well as pizza-like flatbreads topped with zippy cheese, vegetables, and fruit. An excellent choice for a shared appetizer is the fish and game platter, with house-made cured meats and preserved vegetables. Specialties may include oven-roasted mussels with wild boar chorizo and roast apple cream, or lamb sweetbreads with pumpkin seed romesco.

Prince's Island Park. ✆ **403/261-7670.** www.river-cafe.com. Reservations recommended. Main courses C$36–C$50. AE, MC, V. Mon–Fri 11am–3pm and 5–11pm (till 10pm in winter); Sat–Sun 10am–3pm and 5–11pm (till 10pm in winter). Closed Jan.

Rush ★★ CONTEMPORARY CANADIAN   While the decor in most Calgary restaurants exalts the city's Western past, the C$6-million makeover at Rush is all space-age deluxe. The well-dressed crowds that frequent this popular restaurant and bar look lovely in the *Blade Runner*-esque chiaroscuro. Thankfully, the menu is deeply rooted in the here and now, with local ingredients treated to boundary-pushing levels by chef Justin Leboe, who melds together traditional French cuisine and the kind of technical bravura usually reserved for the science lab. For starters, try a fricassee of calamari served with edamame, jus of Basque peppers, and squid ink gremolata. Veal striploin comes with sweetbread ravioli and fresh chanterelles. The unusual combinations are always worth trying, and the prices are very reasonable for food this sophisticated.

207 9th Ave. SW. ✆ **403/271-7874.** www.rushrestaurant.com. Reservations required. Main courses C$19–C$34. 6-course tasting menu C$95. MC, V. Mon–Fri 11:30am–10pm; Sat 5–10pm.

Téatro ★★★ ITALIAN   Located in the historic Dominion Bank building just across from the Centre for the Performing Arts, Téatro delivers the best New Italian cooking in Calgary, courtesy of chef Romuald Coladon. The high-ceilinged dining room is dominated by columns and huge panel windows, bespeaking class and elegance. The extensive menu is based on "Italian Market Cuisine," featuring what's seasonally best and freshest, which is then cooked skillfully and simply to preserve natural flavors. The handmade pastas are marvelous, ranging from linguini with braised lamb shoulder and mint, to house-made spaghetti tossed with duck meatballs. Main courses, which feature Alberta beef, veal, game, and seafood, are prepared with flair and innovation—spice-rubbed bison tenderloin is served with celery root puree and orange-and-thyme-glazed endive. The broad, marble-topped bar is a marvelous spot for a drink. Service is extremely professional, but friendly without undue formality.

200 8th Ave. SE. ✆ **403/290-1012.** www.teatro-rest.com. Reservations recommended. Main courses C$22–C$52. AE, DC, MC, V. Mon–Thurs 11:30am–2pm and 5–10pm; Fri 11:30am–2pm and 5pm–midnight; Sat 5pm–midnight; Sun 5–10pm.

Moderate

Divino ★ BISTRO   This estimable bar and restaurant calls itself a "wine and cheese bistro," and while a casual spot for a drink and cheese platter is welcome on busy Stephen Avenue, Divino offers a lot more. This bustling, stylish gathering spot offers intriguing light entrees and small plates from seafood (Dungeness crab salad canoli with green apple rémoulade) to pasta (gnocchi with porcini mushrooms and watercress) in addition to full-flavored and satisfying main courses such as roast chicken with risotto Bourguignon and double smoked bacon. And whether you start or end your meal with cheese, you'll appreciate a choice of over two dozen cheeses ordered from a sushi-style checklist. A class act.

113 8th Ave. SW. ✆ **403/234-0403.** www.crmr.com/divino. Reservations recommended. Main courses C$21–C$36. AE, DC, MC, V. Mon–Thurs 11am–10pm; Fri 11am–11pm; Sat 5–11pm.

Gypsy Bistro & Wine Bar BISTRO   A small jewel box of a restaurant, the Gypsy Bistro is in the historic Grain Exchange building, and features deep red walls, odd nooks and crannies, and a soft-focus bordello ambience. The menu is extensive and Mediterranean-focused. For light appetites, there's a broad selection of pizzas, entree salads, and specialty sandwiches, such as a lamb and dried cranberry burger. The Gypsy is also the spot for a chic, low-key dinner with main courses such as roast lamb with lavender honey mustard and pancetta-wrapped salmon. The wine list is beguiling and the service friendly—this is the perfect spot for leisurely dinner and conversation.

817 1st St. SW. ✆ **403/263-5869.** Reservations recommended. Main courses C$15–C$33. AE, MC, V. Daily 11am–10pm.

Olives ITALIAN/DELI   Just south of the downtown core, near the Saddle Dome, Olives is an informal but classy spot for full-flavored Italian comfort food. Visually, it's quite striking: The vast dining room and bar is filled with briskly modern decor, which is at counterpoint to wall-sized mosaics of classical sculpture heads. Happily, the menu is more traditional than the surroundings, and many people come here for cocktails and a selection of antipasto while enjoying the scene. Pasta dishes are noteworthy, particularly ravioli stuffed with truffled parsnip and served with mascarpone and wild mushroom cream, and if you're looking for a full meal, a number of meaty main courses round out the menu. If you're on the go, you can pick up a sandwich or salad from the adjacent deli.

1129 Olympic Way. ✆ **403/984-5000.** Reservations recommended. Main courses C$19–C$40. MC, V. Dining room Mon–Fri 11am–2pm and 5–11pm; Sat 5–11pm. Deli daily 7am–5pm.

Inexpensive

There are dozens of inexpensive restaurants in **Chinatown,** not all Chinese; check out Vietnamese and Thai options. Dim sum is widely available and inexpensive. There's also a **food court** in the TD Square mall at 8th Avenue and 3rd Street SW.

On 17th Avenue

Roughly between 4th Street SW and 10th Street SW, 17th Avenue is home to many casual restaurants and bistros (and the scene has recently edged south along 4th St. SW).

Take a cab or drive over and walk the busy cafe-lined streets, perusing the menus; the restaurants listed below are just the beginning.

A good place to get a feel for the avenue is **Melrose Café & Bar,** 730 17th Ave. SW (© **403/228-3566**), a bar/restaurant that has the best deck seating in the area (sit by a waterfall).

Brava Bistro ★ CONTEMPORARY CANADIAN   Brava began as an offshoot of a successful catering company, and has now evolved into a well-loved North American–style bistro. In the relaxed, beautifully lit dining room, you can try a variety of dishes, from elegant appetizers and boutique pizzas to traditional main courses with contemporary zest. A goal of the restaurant is to serve high-quality, approachable food that matches well with wine—30 different bottles are usually available by the glass. For an appetizer, try lobster gnocchi or spicy prawns with chipotle pumpkin seed salsa. Among the entrees, the sautéed salmon with beets and horseradish is deliciously complex and colorful, while the homey rotisserie chicken or beef ribs with creamy polenta are tempting when comfort food feels more appropriate. The wine list is large and well priced.

723 17th Ave. SW. © **403/228-1854.** www.bravabistro.com. Reservations recommended. Main courses C$19–C$32. AE, DC, MC, V. Mon–Wed 11:30am–3pm and 5–10pm; Thurs–Sat 11:30am–3pm and 5pm–midnight; Sun 5–10pm.

Cilantro INTERNATIONAL   Cilantro has a forlorn stucco storefront that would look New Mexican if it weren't on an urban strip of 17th Avenue. The walls hide a tucked-away garden courtyard with a veranda bar. The food here is eclectic with feints toward California and Santa Fe. You can snack on sandwiches, homemade pasta, or salads, such as spinach in creamy tarragon vinaigrette with crispy pancetta, fresh figs, toasted pecans, and goat cheese. Or have a full meal of roast free-range chicken with whole-grain mustard demi glace or grilled sea bass with grilled peppers and citrus ancho chile sauce. The wood-fired pizzas—with mostly Mediterranean ingredients—are great for lunch. The food is always excellent, and the setting casual and friendly.

338 17th Ave. SW. © **403/229-1177.** Reservations recommended on weekends. Main courses C$14–C$39. AE, DC, MC, V. Mon–Thurs 11am–10pm; Fri 11am–11pm; Sat 5–11pm; Sun 5–10pm.

FARM DELI/WINE BAR   This small, homey spot combines features of a wine bar, deli, and local food emporium. FARM specializes in locally produced charcuterie, cheeses, pickles, fruits, and vegetables. Make your choices from the ever-changing chalkboard menu, take a seat at the communal table, and enjoy your selection of preserved meats and cheeses along with excellent bread and chutney (salads and main courses are also available). This is a great place to go if you're feeling social and looking for a light meal and a chance to try out local products with a glass of wine.

1006 17th Ave. SW. © **403/245-2276.** www.farm-restaurant.com. Reservations available for 6 or more. Main courses C$12–C$18. MC, V. Mon–Fri 11:30am–2pm and 5–10pm; Sat–Sun 10am–2pm and 5–10pm.

Living Room ★ CONTEMPORARY CANADIAN   The antithesis of a small-plates tapas bar, Living Room is located in a heritage home fronting 17th Avenue, with tables inside and on a lovely shaded patio (heated by outdoor fireplaces in chilly weather). It specializes in "contemporary interactive cuisine," which translates as those classics of French, Italian, and Canadian cooking meant to be shared. Most beguiling are the many dishes designed for two: double-size portions of fondues, whole roast chicken, bouillabaisse, or veal loin pot roast. Of course, individual portions are also served (the likes of roasted pork prime rib with cranberry mustard and quince butter), though in the same spirit of contemporary interactive dining. A five-course chef's tasting menu (C$90) lets the chef showcase what's absolutely up-to-the-moment.

514 17th Ave. SW. ✆ **403/228-9830.** Reservations suggested. Main courses C$20–C$42. MC, V. Tues–Fri 11:30am–2:30pm and 5pm–midnight; Sat–Mon 5pm–midnight.

Wildwood Grill & Brewing Company ★ BREWPUB   A few blocks south of 17th Avenue's street scene is this nouveau hunting lodge–style brewpub. Don't think pub grub—though you can get a good burger here—because Wildwood Grill offers high-end cuisine to match their house-made ales. In addition to pasta, wood-fired pizza, and upscale standards such as pork chops sautéed with figs and chanterelles, the pub specializes in game dishes. Elk loin medallions with spiced chocolate sauce are a standout for adventurous meat eaters. In good weather, the covered patio is a great spot to sample the brewery's excellent drafts.

2417 4th St. SW. ✆ **403/228-0100.** Reservations suggested. Main courses C$13–C$36. AE, MC, V. Mon–Thurs 11am–midnight; Fri 11am–2am; Sat 5–11pm; Sun 5–10pm.

Inglewood

Capo ★ ITALIAN   Just a short drive or cab ride south of downtown is Capo, one of the most lauded new restaurants in Calgary. Chef Guiseppe di Gennaro worked his way up through a handful of other Calgary restaurants, finally moving to Inglewood and his own modern and stylish dining room. The huzzahs were almost immediate, garnering several national accolades and drawing foodies from near and far to sample Capo's updated but tradition-based Italian cuisine. A standout is the pillowy ricotta gnocchi, served with lobster, black truffle oil, and a touch of tomato. The house specialty is roasted pheasant breast, served with a reduction of Muscat wine and rosemary. The dining room is tiny, seating just 35, so reservations are a must; on weekends, there are two seatings, at 5:30 and 8:30pm, so plan ahead.

1420 9th Ave. SE. ✆ **403/264-2276.** www.caporestaurant.ca. Reservations required. Main courses C$18–C$44. AE, MC, V. Tues 5:30–10pm; Wed–Fri 11:30am–2pm and 5:30–10pm; Sat 5:30–10pm.

Rouge FRENCH   Located in a historic home, Rouge serves upscale French cuisine in a quiet, almost rural setting. In summer, the dining room extends into the shaded yard, where the bustle of Calgary feels far away. The menu emphasizes contemporary French cuisine zestily translated to western Canada. Diners have a choice of a la carte selections or the chef's six-course tasting menu (C$95). For appetizers, try the elk cannelloni with nasturtium vinaigrette, or tomato gazpacho with olive oil ice cream. For a main course, pan-seared halibut, with garden sorrel pesto and white bean puree, is a standout.

1240 8th Ave. SE. ✆ **403/531-2767.** www.rougecalgary.com. Reservations recommended. Main courses C$34–C$44. MC, V. Mon–Fri 11:30am–2pm and 5–10pm; Sat 5–10pm.

Kensington

Chef's Table ★ CONTEMPORARY CANADIAN   Sophisticated and intimate, Chef's Table is in the upscale Kensington Riverside Inn. The food is very refined, a perfect match for the art-filled dining room and the inn's sumptuous furnishings. Start your meal with creamy butternut squash soup, afloat with truffled ricotta dumplings and curry oil. The main courses reflect French traditions with Canadian brio: Pan-seared pheasant breast is served with spaetzle, black trumpet mushrooms, and carrot puree; halibut comes with creamed chestnuts and orange fennel marmalade. A five-course tasting menu is C$95.

1126 Memorial Dr. NW. ✆ **403/228-4442.** Reservations required. Main courses C$32–C$43. AE, DC, MC, V. Mon–Sat 5–9:30pm.

Muse ★★ FRENCH   Appropriately set in the trendy Kensington neighborhood, Muse serves very up-to-date and stylish food based on French cooking, but deconstructed and reimagined as an extravagant dining adventure. There's playfulness and urbanity to the food, and it seems clear that the cooks are having fun in the kitchen. Start your meal with a blue cheese waffle topped with a salad spiked with poached pears and maple vinaigrette. Main courses are complex creations that verge temptingly on decadence: Potato lobster lasagna features buttery lobster between thin layers of Yukon gold potatoes, topped with seared scallops and flying fish roe. The dining room is a three-story maze curved around an atrium; the various levels and nooks only add to the sense of discovery.

107 10A St. NW. ✆ **403/670-6873.** www.muserestaurant.ca. Reservations recommended. Main courses C$29–C$39. AE, MC, V. Tues–Thurs and Sun 5–10pm; Fri–Sat 5–11pm.

CALGARY AFTER DARK

THE PERFORMING ARTS   The sprawling **EPCOR Centre for the Performing Arts,** 205 8th Ave. SE (✆ **403/294-7455;** www.epcorcentre.org), houses the Jack Singer Concert Hall, home of the **Calgary Philharmonic Orchestra** (✆ **403/571-0849;** www. cpo-live.com); the Max Bell Theatre, home of **Theatre Calgary** (✆ **403/294-7440;** www.theatrecalgary.com); and the Martha Cohen Theatre, home of **Alberta Theatre Projects** (✆ **403/294-7402;** www.atplive.com).

An acoustic marvel, **Jubilee Auditorium,** 14th Avenue and 14th Street NW, on the Southern Alberta Institute of Technology campus (✆ **403/297-8000;** www.jubilee auditorium.com), is located high on a hill with a panoramic view of downtown Calgary. The **Calgary Opera** (✆ **403/262-7286;** www.calgaryopera.com) and the **Alberta Ballet** (✆ **403/254-4222;** www.albertaballet.com) both stage performances here.

Calgary loves dinner theater, and **Stage West,** 727 42nd Ave. SE (✆ **403/243-6642;** www.stagewestcalgary.com), puts on polished performances as well as delectable buffet fare. Tickets for evening performances and dinner start at C$89. Performances are Tuesday to Sunday.

BARS & CLUBS   Cover charges at most clubs are C$5 to C$10 for live music. Pick up a copy of *Ffwd* (www.ffwdweekly.com) for up-to-date listings.

Eau Claire Market is the home of the **Garage** (✆ **403/262-67620**), a warehouse-of-a-sports-bar for playing billiards and listening to loud indie rock. A number of pubs and late-night watering holes are just outside the market on the Barclay Parade plaza. Check out **Barleymill Neighbourhood Pub,** 201 Barclay Parade SW (✆ **403/290-1500**), an Old World pub plunked down in the plaza across from the Eau Claire Market.

If you're just looking for a convivial drink, **Bottlescrew Bill's Old English Pub,** 1st Street and 10th Avenue SW (✆ **403/263-7900**), is a great choice. This friendly neighborhood pub is just on the edge of downtown, has lots of outdoor seating, and pours Alberta's widest selection of microbrewed beers.

If you're looking for dance clubs, head south of downtown. **Warehouse Nightclub,** 731 10th Ave. SW (✆ **403/264-0535**), offers straightforward rock with Calgary's top DJs. **Hi-Fi Club,** 219 10th Ave. SW (✆ 403/263-5222), hosts more alternative music and occasional live music and entertainment. **Broken City,** 613 11th Ave. SW (✆ **403/262-9976**), is a hipster hangout with live local bands on Tuesdays, Thursdays, and Saturdays.

Calgary isn't really a jazz town, but there's one good club to check out: **Beatniq Jazz & Social Club,** downstairs at the Piqniq Café, 811 1st St. SW (✆ **403/263-1650**), has great atmosphere and the best of local bands.

Twisted Element, 1006 11th Ave. SW (© **403/802-0230**), is Calgary's largest gay bar and dance club. It has both a dance floor and a downstairs piano bar. It's at the center of the city's small gay-bar area.

2 EDMONTON: CAPITAL OF ALBERTA

283km (176 miles) N of Calgary; 361km (224 miles) E of Jasper

Edmonton, Alberta's capital city, is located on the banks of the North Saskatchewan River, which cuts a deep, wooded valley through the city. It's a civilized city of one million citizens that's known for its summer festivals and easygoing friendliness.

Established as a fur-trading post in 1786, Edmonton grew in spurts, following a boom-and-bust pattern as exciting as it was unreliable. The railroad arrived in 1912, bringing homestead farmers, many from eastern Europe. While Edmonton initially boomed as the market center for these emigrant farm communities, the farm economy went bust during the droughts and Great Depression of the 1930s. During World War II, the boom came in the form of the Alaska Highway, with Edmonton as the material base and temporary home of 50,000 American troops and construction workers.

The ultimate boom, however, gushed from the ground in February 1947, when oil was discovered southwest of the city. Edmonton soon found itself the capital not just of Alberta but of the Canadian oil industry. Today the city is filled with gleaming office towers and other monuments to wealth—enormous shopping centers, a wonderful park system, and excellent arts performance facilities.

However, the combination of oil industry workers and provincial bureaucrats doesn't exactly make for a scintillating civic culture, and despite the youthful energy of 17,000 University of Alberta students, Edmonton lacks the spark you'd expect of a city of this size. It's ironic—and somehow symptomatic—that a city with over 200 years of history considers a shopping center its proudest monument.

ESSENTIALS

Getting There

BY PLANE **Edmonton International Airport** (© **800/268-7134;** www.edmonton airports.com) is served by **Air Canada** (© **800/372-9500**) and **Northwest** (© 800/447-4747), among other airlines. The airport lies 29km (18 miles) south of the city on Hwy. 2, about 45 minutes away from city center. By cab, the trip costs about C$45; by Sky Shuttle van (© **780/465-8515;** www.edmontonskyshuttle.com), C$15.

BY TRAIN The **VIA Rail** (© **800/561-8630** or 780/422-6032; www.viarail.ca) station is at 104th Avenue and 100th Street.

BY BUS **Greyhound** (© **780/413-8747;** www.greyhound.ca) buses link Edmonton to points in Canada from the depot at 10324 103rd St.

BY CAR Edmonton straddles Hwy. 16, the Yellowhead Highway, an east-west interprovincial highway that links western Manitoba and Prince Rupert, B.C. Just west of Edmonton, the Yellowhead joins to the Alaska Highway. Hwy. 2 connects Edmonton to Calgary, which is a 3-hour drive south. Edmonton is 515km (320 miles) north of the U.S. border.

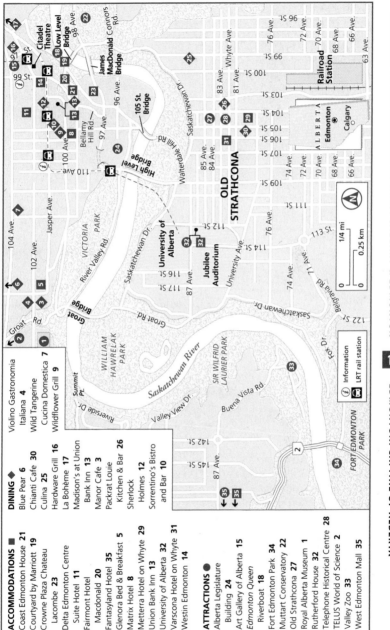

ACCOMMODATIONS ■
Coast Edmonton House **21**
Courtyard by Marriott **19**
Crowne Plaza Chateau
  Lacombe **23**
Delta Edmonton Centre
  Suite Hotel **11**
Fairmont Hotel
  Macdonald **20**
Fantasyland Hotel **35**
Glenora Bed & Breakfast **5**
Matrix Hotel **8**
Metterra Hotel on Whyte **29**
Union Bank Inn **13**
University of Alberta **32**
Varscona Hotel on Whyte **31**
Westin Edmonton **14**

DINING ◆
Blue Pear **6**
Chianti Cafe **30**
Culina **25**
Hardware Grill **16**
La Bohème **17**
Madison's at Union
  Bank Inn **13**
Manor Cafe **3**
Packrat Louie
  Kitchen & Bar **26**
Sherlock
  Holmes **12**
Sorrentino's Bistro
  and Bar **10**

Violino Gastronomia
  Italiana **4**
Wild Tangerine **7**
Cucina Domestica **9**
Wildflower Grill **9**

ATTRACTIONS ●
Alberta Legislature
  Building **24**
Art Gallery of Alberta **15**
Edmonton Queen
  Riverboat **18**
Fort Edmonton Park **34**
Muttart Conservatory **22**
Old Strathcona **27**
Royal Alberta Museum **1**
Rutherford House **32**
Telephone Historical Centre **28**
TELUS World of Science **2**
Valley Zoo **33**
West Edmonton Mall **35**

ⓘ Information
🚇 LRT rail station

Contact **Edmonton Tourism,** 9990 Jasper Ave. NW, Edmonton, AB T5J 1N9 (☎ **800/463-4667** or 780/496-8400; www.edmonton.com). There are also visitor centers located at City Hall and at Gateway Park, both open from 9am to 6pm, and on the Calgary Trail at the southern edge of the city, open from 9am to 9pm.

City Layout

The winding **North Saskatchewan River** flows right through the heart of the city, dividing it into roughly equal halves. Most of this steep-banked valley has been turned into public parklands. The downtown business district is on the north bank.

The street numbering system begins at the corner of 100th Street and 100th Avenue, which means that many downtown addresses have five digits and that suburban homes often have smaller addresses than businesses in the very center of town. Downtown Edmonton's main street is **Jasper Avenue** (actually 101st Ave.), running north of the river. The "A" designations you'll notice for certain streets and avenues downtown add to the confusion: They're essentially old service alleys between major streets, many of which are now pedestrian areas with sidewalk cafes.

At 97th Street, on Jasper Avenue, rises the massive pink **Canada Place,** the only completely planned government complex of its kind in Canada. Across the street is the **Edmonton Convention Centre,** which stair-steps down the hillside to the river.

Beneath the downtown core stretches a network of pedestrian walkways—called **Pedways**—connecting hotels, restaurants, and malls with the library, City Hall, and Citadel Theatre. These Pedways not only avoid the surface traffic, but are also climate-controlled—important in winter.

At the northern approach to the High Level Bridge stand the buildings of the **Alberta Legislature.** Across the bridge, to the south, is **Old Strathcona,** a bustling neighborhood of cafes, galleries, and hip shops that's now a haven for Edmonton's more alternative population. The main arterial through Old Strathcona is **Whyte Avenue,** or 82nd Avenue. Running south from here is 104th Street, which becomes the **Calgary Trail** and leads to the airport. Just west of Old Strathcona, and the source of much of the city's youthful energy, is the **University of Alberta.**

West of downtown, Jasper Avenue shifts and twists to eventually become Stony Plain Road, which passes near **West Edmonton Mall,** the world's largest shopping and entertainment center, before merging with Hwy. 16 on its way to Jasper National Park.

Getting Around

Edmonton Transit (☎ **780/496-1611**) operates the buses and the LRT (Light Rail Transit). This electric rail service connects downtown with Northlands Park to the north and the University of Alberta to the south. The LRT and buses have the same fares: C$2.50 for adults and C$2.25 for seniors and children; a day pass goes for C$7.50. Monday through Friday from 9am to 3pm, downtown LRT travel is free between Churchill, Central, Bay, Corona, and Grandin stations.

In addition to the following downtown locations, **National,** 10133 100A St. NW (☎ **780/422-6097**); **Budget,** 10016 106th St. (☎ **780/448-2000**); and **Hertz,** 10815 Jasper Ave. (☎ **780/423-3431**), all have bureaus at the airport.

Call **CO-OP Taxi** (☎ **780/425-2525** or 780/425-8310) for a ride in a driver/owner-operated cab.

(*Fast Facts* Edmonton

American Express The office at 10729 104th Ave. (© **780/496-7587;** LRT: Bay), is open Monday to Friday from 9am to 5pm.

Area Code Edmonton's area code is **780.**

Doctors If you need nonemergency medical care while in Edmonton, check the phone book for the closest branch of **Medicentre,** which offers walk-in medical services daily.

Emergency For fire, medical, or crime emergencies, dial © **911.**

Hospitals The closest hospital with emergency service to downtown Edmonton is the **Royal Alexandra Hospital,** 10240 Kingsway Ave. (© **780/477-4111;** bus: 9).

Newspapers The *Edmonton Journal* (www.edmontonjournal.com) and *Edmonton Sun* (www.fyiedmonton.com/htdocs/edmsun.shtml) are the local daily papers. Arts, entertainment, and nightlife listings can be found in the weekly *See* (www. seemagazine.com).

Pharmacies **Shoppers Drug Mart** has more than a dozen locations in Edmonton, most open until midnight. One central location is 8210 109th St. (© **780/433- 2424;** bus: 6).

Post Office The main post office is at 103A Avenue and 99th Street (LRT: Churchill).

Time Edmonton is on Mountain Time, the same as Calgary and Denver, and it observes daylight saving time.

SPECIAL EVENTS & FESTIVALS

Edmonton promotes itself as "the Festival City," and in summer almost every weekend brings another celebration. The citywide **Jazz City International Festival** (© 780/432-7166; www.edmontonjazz.com) takes over most music venues in Edmonton during the last week of June and first week of July.

The summer's biggest shindig is **Capital City Exposition,** also known as Capital EX (© **888/800-7275** or 780/471-7210; www.capitalex.ca), formerly Klondike Days. Capital EX has shed the previous event's Gold Rush trappings and focuses instead on midway rides, live music performances, and shopping promotions. Most events take place at Northlands Park, northeast of the city at 75th Street and 118th Avenue.

The **Edmonton Folk Music Festival** (© 780/429-1899; www.efmf.ab.ca) is the largest folk-music festival in North America. Held in early August, it brings in musicians from around the world, from the Celtic north to Indonesia, plus major rock stars playing "unplugged." All concerts are held outdoors.

For 11 days in mid-August, Old Strathcona is transformed into a series of stages for the renowned **Edmonton International Fringe Theatre Festival** ★★ (© 780/448-9000; www.fringetheatreadventures.ca). Only Edinburgh's fringe festival is larger than Edmonton's—more than 150 troupes attend from around the world, as does an audience of over 600,000. In addition to the hubbub of actors and theater, the Fringe Festival also plays host to food and crafts booths, beer tents, and innumerable buskers and street performers.

The Top Attractions

Fort Edmonton Park ★ (Kids)   Fort Edmonton Park is a complex of townscapes that reconstructs four distinct eras of Edmonton's history. As an open-air museum, the park is very impressive; the variety of activities and services here make this a great family destination. Perhaps most interesting is the complete reconstruction of the old Fort Edmonton fur-trading post from the turn of the 18th century. On 1885 Street, you'll see Frontier Edmonton, complete with saloons, general store, and Jasper House Hotel, which serves hearty pioneer meals. On 1905 Street, the agricultural boom years of the early 19th century are celebrated, when Edmonton thronged with new immigrants and was named provincial capital. On 1920 Street, sip an old-fashioned ice-cream soda at Bill's confectionery and see the changes wrought in the rural west by World War I. You can ride streetcar no. 1, a stagecoach, or a steam locomotive between the various streets.

If Fort Edmonton will appeal to your family, consider spending a night at the park's **Hotel Selkirk,** a handsome replica of a 1910s hotel, but with all modern comforts (© **888/962-2522** or 780/496-7227; www.hotelselkirk.com).

On Whitemud Dr. at Fox Dr. © **780/496-8787.** www.fortedmontonpark.ca. Admission C$14 adults, C$10 seniors and youths, C$6.75 children, C$41 families. Late May to late Sept daily 10am–6pm; call for off-season hours. LRT to University Station, then bus 32.

Old Strathcona ★★   This historic district used to be a separate township, but was amalgamated with Edmonton in 1912 and still contains some of the best-preserved landmarks in the city. It's best seen on foot, guided by the brochures given out at the **Old Strathcona Foundation,** 10324 82nd Ave., fourth floor (© **780/433-5866**). It's easy to spend an afternoon here, just wandering the shops, sitting at street-side cafes, and people-watching. This is hipster-central for Edmonton, where students, artists, and the city's alternative community come to hang out. In addition, if you're looking for good value in restaurants or for the city's prime spot for pubs and nightlife, Old Strathcona is ground zero: Come take in the sometimes rowdy evening scene. Be sure to stop by the **Old Strathcona Farmers Market** (© **780/439-1844**), at 83rd Avenue and 103rd Street, an open-air market with fresh produce, baked goods, and local crafts. It's open Saturday year-round, plus Tuesday and Thursday afternoons in summer.

Around 82nd Ave., btw. 103rd and 105th sts. Bus: 46 from downtown.

Royal Alberta Museum ★ (Kids)   Expertly curated, this 18,500-sq.-m (199,132-sq.-ft.) modern museum displays Alberta's natural and human history in three permanent galleries. The Wild Alberta exhibit represents Alberta's diverse natural history with astonishingly lifelike dioramas and interactive displays utilizing computers, microscopes, and other hands-on tools. The Gallery of Aboriginal Culture tells the 11,000-year story of Alberta's First Nations inhabitants, incorporating artifacts, film, interactive media, and Native interpreters; it's one of Canada's foremost exhibits on Native culture. The Natural History Gallery has fossils, minerals, and a live-bug room.

12845 102nd Ave. © **780/453-9100.** Fax 780/454-6629. www.royalalbertamuseum.ca. Admission C$10 adults, C$8 seniors, C$7 students, C$5 youths 7–17, C$28 families, free for children 6 and under; Sat–Sun half-price admission 9–11am. Daily 9am–5pm. Bus: 1.

West Edmonton Mall (Kids)   You won't find many shopping malls mentioned in this book, but the West Edmonton Mall is something else: *Guinness Book of World Records* recognizes this as the world's largest shopping mall. Although it contains 800 stores and services, including 110 eateries, it looks and sounds more like a large slice of Disneyland that has somehow broken loose and drifted north. The locals modestly call it the "Eighth Wonder of the World." More theme park than mall, it encompasses 480,000 sq. m (5.2 million sq. ft.)—that's 48 city blocks—and houses the world's largest indoor amusement park, including a titanic roller coaster, bungee-jumping platform, and enclosed wave-lake, complete with beach. It has a regulation size National Hockey League ice rink, 21 (count 'em, 21) movie theaters, a lagoon with performing sea lions, and several fabulous adventure rides (one of them by submarine to the "ocean floor"). In the middle of it all, an immense fountain with 19 computer-controlled jets weaves and dances in a musical performance.

Of course, you can shop here, too, and some of Edmonton's most popular restaurants are located in the mall. Roll your eyes all you want, but do go. You have to see the West Edmonton Mall to believe it.

8882 170th St. © **800/661-8890** or 780/444-5200. www.wem.ca. Bus: 10.

More Attractions
Art Gallery of Alberta Formerly the Edmonton Art Gallery, the Art Gallery of Alberta (AGA) has reopened in its former location but in a new postmodern, architectur-ally daring exhibition hall and art center designed by Los Angeles architect Randall Stout. The new gallery, with 7,900 sq. meters (85,035 sq. ft.) and a price tag of C$48 million, expands the role of the museum as a center for interdisciplinary media, such as film and performance-based programming, in addition to its traditional role as exhibition hall for painting, sculpture, crafts, and the graphic arts. The AGA also intends to increase its focus on touring shows, featuring more international exhibitions produced in partner-ship with Canadian and international museums. It's worth a visit just to view the perma-nent collection, which features a very strong collection of works by Alberta artists.

2 Sir Winston Churchill Sq. © **780/422-6223.** www.youraga.ca. Admission C$10, C$7 seniors and stu-dents, C$5 children 6–12, free for children 5 and under. Mon–Fri 10:30am–5pm (Thurs to 8pm); Sat–Sun and holidays 11am–5pm. LRT: Churchill.

Edmonton Queen Riverboat Moored just outside the convention center, this riv-erboat plies the North Saskatchewan River as it runs through the city's many parks. A number of packages are offered, usually the cruise itself or a meal package that includes lunch or dinner.

9734 98th Ave. © **780/424-2628.** www.edmontonqueen.com. Cruise only C$18; meal packages from C$48. Call for hours. Bus: 12 or 45.

Telephone Historical Centre North America's largest museum devoted to the his-tory of telecommunications is located in the 1912 Telephone Exchange Building. Multi-media displays tell the history of words over wire and hints at what your modem will get up to next.

10440 84th Ave. © **780/433-1010.** www.telephonehistoricalcentre.com. Admission by donation. Mon–Fri 10am–4pm. Bus: 44.

ESPECIALLY FOR KIDS
TELUS World of Science—Edmonton ★ (Kids) This is one of the most advanced facilities of its kind in the world. It contains, among other wonders, an **IMAX theater** (© **780/493-4250**), the largest planetarium theater in Canada, high-tech exhibits (including a virtual-reality showcase and a display on robotics), and an observatory open

on clear afternoons and evenings. Exhibits include a journey through the human body (including the Gallery of the Gross!) and Mystery Avenue, where young sleuths can collect clues at a crime scene, then analyze them at a crime lab.

11211 142nd St., Coronation Park. ✆ **780/451-3344.** www.edmontonscience.com. Admission C$14 adults, C$12 seniors and children 13–17, C$10 children 4–12, C$55 families. Exhibits daily 10am–5pm; observatory Fri–Sat till 10pm, weather permitting. Bus: 17 or 22. Free parking.

Valley Zoo (Kids) Edmonton's small zoo is home to over 400 animals, including 20 endangered species, such as Siberian tigers and snow leopards. Young children will like the pony and train rides, while older kids will be fascinated by falconry demonstrations.

13315 Buena Vista Rd., Laurier Park. ✆ **780/496-8787.** www.valleyzoo.ca. Admission May to mid-Oct C$9.75 adults, C$7.25 seniors and children 13–17, C$5 children 2–12, C$29 families; mid-Oct to May C$7.25 adults, C$5.50 seniors and children 13–17, C$3.75 children 2–12, C$21 families. Summer daily 9:30am–8pm; winter Mon–Fri 9:30am–4pm, Sat–Sun 9:30am–6pm.

WHERE TO STAY

For B&Bs, try the **Alberta Bed and Breakfast Association** (www.bbalberta.com).

Very Expensive

Delta Edmonton Centre Suite Hotel This all-suite establishment forms part of the upscale City Centre shopping complex in the heart of downtown. Without having to stir out-of-doors, you can access 170 shops in the mall, plus movie theaters and an indoor putting green. Four other malls are connected to the hotel via Pedway. Three-quarters of the windows look into the mall, so you can stand behind the tinted one-way glass (in your pajamas, if you like) and watch the shopping action outside. Most units are one-bedroom suites, each with a large sitting area (with TV and wet bar) and separate bedroom (with another TV and a plate-glass wall looking into the mall). If you need lots of room, or have work to do in Edmonton, these very spacious rooms are just the ticket.

10222 102nd St., Edmonton, AB T5J 4C5. ✆ **800/661-6655** or 780/429-3900. Fax 780/428-1566. www. deltahotels.com. 169 units. From C$199 standard room; from C$224 suite. AE, DC, MC, V. Parking C$18 per day; valet parking C$22 per day. **Amenities:** Restaurant; bar; concierge; exercise room; Jacuzzi; room service; sauna. *In room:* A/C, TV w/pay movies, hair dryer, Wi-Fi.

Fairmont Hotel Macdonald ★★★ From the outside, with its limestone facade and gargoyles, the Mac looks like a feudal château—it's no wonder that this is where Queen Elizabeth II stays when she's in town. Originally opened in 1915, the palatial Hotel Macdonald has undergone a masterwork of sensitive renovation and restoration. Everything, including the service, is absolutely top-notch. Rooms are beautifully furnished with luxurious upholstery, feather duvets, and original art. Rooms are large, and many have vistas across the river valley. Business-class suites each have a sitting area with a couch and two chairs, and a handy dressing area off the bathroom with a vanity table. The eight specialty suites, which take up the entire seventh and eighth floors, are simply magnificent. Needless to say, there aren't many hotels like this in Edmonton, or in Canada for that matter. As I rode the elevator, a guest broke the silence with the completely voluntary and effusive statement: "This is a *great* hotel."

10065 100th St., Edmonton, AB T5J 0N6. ✆ **800/441-1414** or 780/424-5181. Fax 780/429-6481. www. fairmont.com. 199 units. High season C$299–C$499 deluxe standard room; C$299–C$899 premier suite. Weekend and off-season discounts available. AE, DC, DISC, MC, V. Parking C$26 per day. **Amenities:** Restaurant; lounge; babysitting; concierge; concierge-level rooms; health club & spa; indoor pool; room service; squash court. *In room:* A/C, TV/VCR w/pay movies, hair dryer, minibar, Wi-Fi.

Fantasyland Hotel (Kids) From the outside, this solemn tower at the end of the huge West Edmonton Mall reveals little of the wildly decorated rooms found within. Fantasyland is a cross between a hotel and Las Vegas: It contains a total of 120 themed rooms decorated in 11 different styles (as well as over 230 large, well-furnished regular rooms). Take the Truck Room: Your bed is located in the back end of a real pickup, whose bench seats fold down into a child's bed, and the lights on the vanity are real stoplights. The themes continue, through the Canadian Rail Room (train berths for beds), the African Room, and more. All theme rooms come with four-person Jacuzzis and plenty of amenities.

It's not all fantasy here, though. The non-theme rooms are divided into superior rooms, with either a king-size or two queen-size beds, and executive rooms, with a king-size bed and Jacuzzi. The hotel's restaurant is quite good; of course, you have all-weather access to the world's largest mall and its many eateries as well.

17700 87th Ave., Edmonton, AB T5T 4V4. (C) **800/737-3783** or 780/444-3000. Fax 780/444-3294. www. fantasylandhotel.com. 355 units. From C$304–C$384 double. Extra person C$10. Weekend and off-season packages available. AE, MC, V. Free parking. **Amenities:** Restaurant; bar; babysitting; concierge; exercise room; room service. *In room:* A/C, TV w/pay movies, fridge, hair dryer, Wi-Fi.

Westin Edmonton ★★ Located in the heart of the downtown shopping and entertainment district, this modern hotel offers some of the city's largest and most comfortable rooms. Throughout the hotel, the rooms are decorated with a clean, contemporary look right out of *Architectural Digest*. Standard rooms come with one king-size bed or two double beds, while deluxe rooms are designed for business travelers, and come with two phone lines, a large desk, and upgraded amenities. Suites are gracious and large, with separate bedrooms, large dressing room and bathroom, and a very swank sitting room with black leather furniture. These stylish and comfortable rooms will quickly take the pain out of both business and leisure travel.

10135 100th St., Edmonton, AB T5J 0N7. (C) **800/228-3000** or 780/426-3636. Fax 780/428-1454. www. thewestinedmonton.com. 413 units. From C$214–C$329 double. AE, DC, DISC, MC, V. Parking C$19 per day; valet parking C$25 per day. **Amenities:** 2 restaurants; lounge; babysitting; concierge; exercise room; Jacuzzi; indoor pool; room service; sauna. *In room:* A/C, TV, fridge, hair dryer, minibar, Wi-Fi.

Expensive

Coast Edmonton House This is a great alternative to pricier downtown hotels: With a great location right above the North Saskatchewan River, the all-suite hotel has one of the best views in Edmonton. Each suite comes with a full kitchen and dining area, bedroom, separate sitting area with fold-out couch, balcony, and two phones. Edmonton House is within easy walking distance of most downtown office areas and public transport.

10205 100th Ave., Edmonton, AB T5J 4B5. (C) **800/661-6562** or 780/420-4000. Fax 780/420-4008. www. coasthotels.com. 305 units. C$129–C$239 1-bedroom suite. Extra person C$10. Weekend packages and weekly/monthly rates available. AE, DC, MC, V. C$10 parking. **Amenities:** Restaurant; lounge; exercise room; indoor pool; room service. *In room:* TV, hair dryer, kitchen, Wi-Fi, microwave.

Courtyard by Marriott ★ (Finds) Don't let the name fool you—this is anything but a could-be-anywhere business hotel. Located downtown on the cliff edge of the North Saskatchewan River, with vistas over city center and the breadth of the valley, this Courtyard (formerly the Warwick) must have the best views in the entire chain. The structure was built as an apartment building before conversion into a hotel, meaning that no two rooms are the same and many are very large—the two-bedroom, two-bathroom units are literally family-size. Rooms are comfortable and well furnished—business travelers will like the large work desks and free high-speed Internet access—but it's the setting and facilities at this that really stand out. Edmontonians have voted the three-tiered bar and restaurant patio—cantilevered hundreds of feet above the river—the city's top spot for outdoor drinks and dining.

One Thornton Court (99 St. and Jasper Ave.), Edmonton, AB T5J 2E7. (C) **866/441-7591** or 780/423-9999. Fax 780/423-9998. 177 units. C$129–C$259 double. Parking C$22 per day. AE, DC, DISC, MC, V. **Amenities:** Restaurant; lounge; fitness center. *In room:* A/C, TV, fridge, hair dryer, Wi-Fi.

Crowne Plaza Chateau Lacombe Centrally located downtown, the Crowne Plaza, a round 24-story tower sitting on the edge of a cliff overlooking the North Saskatchewan River, possesses some of the city's best views (best seen from **La Ronde,** the hotel's revolving restaurant; see below). The nicely furnished standard rooms aren't huge, though the wedge-shaped design necessitates that they are broadest toward the windows, where you'll spend time looking over the city. The Crowne Plaza's Sleep Advantage program focuses on extra-high-quality linens and pillows, plus interesting extras such as relaxation CDs and aromatherapeutic lavender atomizers for the sheets. For just a C$30 upgrade, executive suites offer twice the square footage of standard rooms, with a full living room with fold-out bed—a sweet deal.

10111 Bellamy Hill, Edmonton, AB T5J 1N7. (C) **800/661-8801** or 780/428-6611. Fax 780/425-6564. www. chateaulacombe.com. 307 units. From C$159 double. Extra person C$10. Weekend packages available. AE, DC, DISC, MC, V. Valet parking C$20; self-parking C$10 per day. **Amenities:** Revolving fine-dining restaurant; cafe; lounge; exercise room; room service. *In room:* A/C, TV, CD player, hair dryer, Wi-Fi, Sleep Advantage Program.

Glenora Bed & Breakfast ★ Located in the heart of the artsy High Street district, just west of downtown, the Glenora occupies the upper floors of a 1912 heritage apartment building that has been converted to B&B accommodations. The Glenora is an excellent value and fun to boot. It's a great option if you're weary of anonymous chain motels. While lots of care has been taken to retain the period character and charm of the rooms, the rooms have been thoroughly updated—all but three have private bathrooms, and some have full kitchen facilities. Most appealing is the happy mix of unique period furnishings and snappy interior design—every room is unique. There are five styles of rooms, from simple bedroom units with shared bathrooms to one-bedroom apartment suites with kitchens. Included is free parking and access to a handsome Edwardian common room and a second-story deck. Complimentary breakfast is offered in an adjacent restaurant.

12327 102nd Ave. NW, Edmonton, AB T5N 0I8. (C) **877/453-6672** or 780/488-6766. Fax 780/488-5168. www.glenorabnb.com. 18 units. C$90–C$175 double; specialty room packages available. Rates include continental breakfast. AE, MC, V. **Amenities:** Restaurant and bar on premises; parlor. *In room:* TV/VCR, hair dryer, minibar, Wi-Fi.

Matrix Hotel ★★ Located downtown on a quiet street between the Legislature Building and the heart of the city, the newly opened Matrix Hotel offers great value and a very chic design that combines mid-century and contemporary decor into a hybrid that's at once up-to-the-moment and very comfortable. The guest rooms are nicely furnished, with a palette of granite, walnut, and lots of chrome. While a standard guest room is perfectly nice, with pillow-top mattress, quality linens, and flatscreen TV, consider upgrading to a Platinum Suite, a truly large one-bedroom accommodation with wet bar and fireplace. Complimentary parking, breakfast, and wine-tasting (Mon–Sat) underscore that the Matrix represents a great value.

10640 100th Ave., Edmonton, AB T5J 1J1. ℂ **866/465-8150** or 780/429-2861. Fax 780/426-7225. www. matrixedmonton.com. 173 units. From C$140 double; from $240 suite. Rates include continental breakfast, parking, and wine tasting (Mon–Fri). AE, MC, V. **Amenities:** Exercise room. *In room:* A/C, TV, CD player, fridge, hair dryer, Wi-Fi, robes.

Metterra Hotel on Whyte ★★   The lively Old Strathcona neighborhood, filled with students and artists, now has a unique and stylish hotel. The Metterra is a redesigned former office building transformed into a swank boutique hotel, with a style that's contemporary and sleek but with homey warmth. The lobby sets the tone, with striking art, two-story rundlestone wall, and waterfall, while the guest rooms are large, with contemporary and Indonesian art adding a touch of humor and funk to the sleek modern decor. Some rooms offer a fireplace; others feature that ultimate symbol of comfort, a La-Z-Boy recliner. Rooms are all unique, reflecting the fact that this wasn't built as a hotel, including top-floor suites, with two balconies and more space than most apartments. The Metterra is also central for great nightlife and dining in Edmonton's hippest neighborhood.

10454 82 Ave., Edmonton, AB T6E 4Z7. ℂ **866/465-8150** or 780/465-8150. Fax 780/465-8174. www. metterra.com. 98 units. From C$175 double. Rates include continental breakfast and evening wine tasting (Mon–Sat). AE, MC, V. Free valet parking. *In room:* A/C, TV, hair dryer, Wi-Fi, robes.

Union Bank Inn ★★   If you're tired of unmemorable business hotels, this is a wonderful choice. The stylish Union Bank, built in 1910, now houses an elegant restaurant and intimate boutique hotel with each unique heritage guest room displaying its own charming style, rich colors, furniture, and fabrics. Joining the original inn are 20 contemporary business-class rooms in a new addition—each equally idiosyncratic and uniquely designed. All units, however, have the same amenities, including fireplaces, voice mail, feather duvets, and upscale toiletries. The older rooms vary in layout and aren't incredibly big; if you're in town with work to do, ask for one of the newer and larger units. Service is very friendly and professional. The restaurant/bar, Madison's, is a great place to meet friends (see "Where to Dine," below).

10053 Jasper Ave., Edmonton, AB T5J 1S5. ℂ **800/423-3601** or 780/423-3600. Fax 780/423-4623. www. unionbankinn.com. 34 units. C$199–C$349 double. Rates include full breakfast and in-room afternoon wine-and-cheese service. AE, DC, MC, V. Free parking. **Amenities:** Restaurant; bar; exercise room; access to nearby health club; room service. *In room:* A/C, TV, fridge, hair dryer, Wi-Fi, fireplace.

Varscona Hotel on Whyte ⓥalue   A sister boutique hotel to the boldly contemporary Metterra just down the street, the Varscona offers the same excellent quality of lodging and service but with a choice of more traditional hotel rooms. All rooms are nicely appointed; the real values here are the one-bedroom suites, with work desk, efficiency kitchen, dining room, Bose CD player, and sitting area. Old Strathcona shopping, dining, and nightlife are just outside your door.

8208 106 St., Edmonton, AB T6E 6R9. ℂ **866/465-8150** or 780/434-6111. Fax 780/439-1195. www. varscona.com. 89 units. From C$155 double. Rates include continental breakfast. AE, MC, V. Free valet parking. *In room:* A/C, TV, hair dryer, high-speed Internet, robes.

Inexpensive

University of Alberta   In May through August, dormitory rooms in Lister and Schäffer Halls at the University of Alberta are thrown open to visitors. Some are standard bathroom-down-the-hall dorm rooms, single or twin, while others are singles or twins with private washroom. In addition, the University offers a number of hotel-style guest rooms with private bathrooms (C$119) in the university's conference center. The university is right on the LRT line and not far from trendy Old Strathcona.

87th Ave. and 116th St. ℭ **780/492-4281.** Fax 780/492-0064. www.uofaweb.ualberta.ca/conference services/accommodation.cfm. C$49 single without private bathroom; C$59 twin without private bathroom; C$65 single with private bathroom. MC, V. Parking C$5 per day. **Amenities:** Food service nearby.

WHERE TO DINE

Edmonton has a vigorous dining scene, with hip new eateries joining traditional steak and seafood restaurants. In general, fine dining is found downtown and on High Street, close to the centers of politics and business. Over in Old Strathcona, south of the river, are trendy—and less expensive—cafes and bistros.

Downtown
Expensive

Hardware Grill ★★★ CONTEMPORARY CANADIAN This is easily one of western Canada's most exciting restaurants. The building may be historic (and within walking distance of most downtown hotels), but there's nothing antique about the dining room. Postmodern without being stark, the room is edged with glass partitions and exposed pipes and ducts painted a smoky rose. There are as many appetizers as entrees, making it tempting to graze through a series of smaller dishes. Bison carpaccio is served with Quebec Migneron cheese, and poached foie gras comes with onion marmalade and blackberry gastrique. But it's hard to resist entrees such as applewood-smoked pork chop with bourbon-molasses glaze, house-made sauerkraut, and truffled mac 'n' cheese, or porcini-crusted sea bass served with potato crêpes filled with white corn, arugula, and truffled lobster, all drizzled with warm portobello vinaigrette.

9698 Jasper Ave. ℭ **780/423-0969.** www.hardwaregrill.com. Reservations suggested. Main courses C$30–C$49. AE, DC, MC, V. Mon–Fri 11:30am–2pm; Mon–Thurs 5–9:30pm; Fri–Sat 5–10pm. Closed 1st week of July.

La Bohème FRENCH La Bohème consists of two small, lace-curtained dining rooms in a historic building northeast of downtown (at the turn of the 20th century, this structure was a luxury apartment building—the upper floors are now available as B&B accommodations). The cuisine is French, and so is the wine, with the accent on Rhône Valley vintages. There's a wide selection of appetizers and light dishes, including a number of good salads. The entrees are hearty, classically French preparations of lamb, chicken, and seafood; there's also a five-course table d'hôte menu for C$70. The restaurant also features daily vegetarian entrees. Desserts are outstanding.

6427 112th Ave. ℭ **780/474-5693.** www.laboheme.ca. Reservations required. Main courses C$25–C$35; table d'hôte menu C$70. AE, MC, V. Daily 5–10pm; Sun 10:30am–2:30pm.

La Ronde ★ REGIONAL CANADIAN On the 24th floor of the Crowne Plaza, the revolving La Ronde offers the best views of any restaurant in Edmonton. The Alberta-focused menu also puts on quite a show—chef Jasmin Kobajica is passionate about local organic meats and produce, and his menu is rich in Alberta-raised beef, lamb, and game prepared with a focus on indigenous flavors. Local bison rib-eye is served with sage spaetzle and sweet grass jus, while sirloin steak comes with wild-rice-and-onion cake and truffle bacon sauce. The intensely regional menu makes a brilliant companion to the ever-changing, revolving vista of city towers and river valley.

10111 Bellamy Hill. ℭ **780/428-6611.** Reservations required. Main courses C$28–C$39. AE, MC, V. Daily 5:30–11pm; Sun 10:30am–2pm.

Madison's at Union Bank Inn ★ CONTEMPORARY CANADIAN   One of the loveliest dining rooms and casual cocktail bars in Edmonton is Madison's. Once an early-20th-century bank, the building's formal architectural details remain, but they share the light and airy space with modern art and excellent food. The menu is up-to-date, bridging Continental European cooking with regional Canadian ingredients. The menu features grilled and roast fish and meats, plus pasta dishes, and interesting salads (one special featured rose petals, baby lettuce, and shaved white chocolate). For meat eaters, beef tenderloin with mushroom-shallot compote and Guinness hollandaise is a standout, while lighter appetites will enjoy intriguing combinations such as pepper-crusted tuna carpaccio with Nicoise salsa and avocado-cucumber sorbet.

10053 Jasper Ave. ✆ **780/423-3600.** Reservations suggested. Main courses C$28–C$41. AE, MC, V. Mon–Thurs 7–10am, 11am–2pm, and 5–10pm; Fri 7–10am, 11am–2pm, and 5–11pm; Sat 8–11am and 5–11pm; Sun 8–11am and 5–10pm.

Red Ox Inn ★ CONTEMPORARY CANADIAN   Just a quick drive or taxi ride from downtown, the Red Ox Inn has a real neighborhood feel—and with just 15 tables, this intimate restaurant is bound to remain an insider's favorite. Not a lot of money has been spent on decor; in fact, the dining room, with black booths, white walls, and gleaming hardwood floors, is almost austere. The Red Ox keeps its focus on the food, producing subtly delicious dishes based on quality regional produce, meats, and fresh fish. Grilled chile prawns are served with crisp corn and scallion dumplings and chipotle mayonnaise dipping sauce. An autumn evening's special was leek-wrapped local pickerel stuffed with shrimp mousse served in a pool of red beet beurre blanc, a masterpiece of delicate flavors and startling visual élan. The Red Ox serves serious cuisine, but in a very relaxed and comfortable atmosphere.

9420 91st St. ✆ **780/465-5727.** www.theredoxinn.com. Reservations recommended. Main courses C$28–C$34. MC, V. Tues–Sun 5–10pm.

15

Sorrentino's Bistro and Bar ITALIAN   This upscale branch of a local chain is a good addition to the downtown scene. This handsome and sophisticated dining room is a popular meeting place for the city's business and social elite. The menu features the stalwarts of Italian fine dining—antipasti platters, crispy salads, and pasta—and local beef and bison in a number of main courses as well as traditional standards such as saltimbocca and osso buco. Lavish specialties—sea bass with walnut tomato chutney and lavender beurre blanc, or seared duck breast with honey lemon-grass glaze—match the dazzle of the setting.

10162 100th St. ✆ **780/424-7500.** www.sorrentinos.com. Reservations suggested. Main courses C$25–C$38. AE, DC, MC, V. Mon–Fri 11:30am–10:30pm; Sat 5–10:30pm.

Wildflower Grill ★ CONTEMPORARY CANADIAN   Hip and upscale, the Wildflower Grill brings very stylish, up-to-the-moment dining to downtown Edmonton. The dining room and bar are temples of chic high design, and the extravagantly plated food does its best to outshine the art on the walls. The menu is eclectic, with big, vivid flavors. Pomegranate-glazed rack of lamb comes with Yorkshire pudding and Fontina herb and garlic fondue dipping sauce, and herb-crusted venison medallions are served with ancho pepper sauce, roasted mango, and huckleberry compote. There's nothing ordinary about the food or the scene at this popular hot spot.

10009 107th St. NW. ✆ **780/990-1938.** www.wildfloweredmonton.com. Main courses C$31–C$49. Reservations required. MC, V. Sun–Thurs 11am–2pm and 5–9pm; Fri 11am–2pm and 5–10pm; Sat 5–11pm.

Sherlock Holmes ENGLISH   The Sherlock Holmes is a tremendously popular English-style pub with local and regional beers on tap (as well as Guinness) and a very good and well-executed bar menu. The pub is housed in a charming Tudor-style building with a picket fence around the outdoor patio, completely surrounded by high-rise towers. The menu has a few traditional English dishes—fish and chips, steak-and-kidney pie—but there's a strong emphasis on new pub grub—the tandoori chicken and goat cheese quesadilla are excellent.

10012 101A Ave. (C) 780/426-7784. www.thesherlockholmes.com. Reservations not accepted. Main courses C$7–C$15. AE, MC, V. Daily 11:30am–1am.

Wild Tangerine Cucina Domestica ★ FUSION   Wild Tangerine is one of many new restaurants springing up in the former rail yards—now condo eruption—just west of downtown. This very hip and colorful restaurant offers updated and addictive versions of traditional Asian cuisine—the flavors and textures are as bright and crisp as the decor. The five-spice octopus salad with peppers, taro, and lotus root with a citrus dressing is an explosion of color and flavor. Shrimp lollipops with wasabi yogurt start the meal off with a bang. The jocular owner wanders from table to table. Besides the friendly welcome and the wonderful and affordable food, the green tea–based cocktails are ample reason for a return visit.

10393 112th St. (entrance on 104th Ave.). (C) 780/429-3131. www.wildtangerine.com. Reservations not accepted. Main courses C$13–C$28. AE, MC, V. Mon–Thurs 11:30am–10pm; Fri 11:30am–11:30pm; Sat 5–11:30pm.

High Street

Blue Pear ★★ CONTEMPORARY CANADIAN   This is a must-eat destination for serious foodies and adventurous diners. Just up the road from the High Street scene, Blue Pear serves prix fixe–menu dinners in an intimate, art-filled dining room. The full dinner involves five courses, and includes a selection of choices for appetizer, main dish, and dessert; an abbreviated three-course version of the menu, called Baby Blue Pear, is available from 5 to 6pm and all evening on Sunday (C$59). The menu changes weekly to focus on what's fresh and in season. Preparations are complex: As an appetizer, slow braised escargots are served with tempura mushrooms over blanched garlic puree with two sauces, parsley butter and a reduction of sun-dried tomato and red wine. Though verging on Baroque, all the dishes on the menu are designed to complement each other; wine pairings are available for each course.

10643 123rd St. (C) 780/482-7178. www.thebluepear.com. Reservations required. 5-course prix fixe menu C$89. MC, V. Wed–Sun 5–9pm.

Manor Cafe ★ INTERNATIONAL   Housed in a stately home amid gardens, the Manor Cafe offers one of the most fashionable outdoor dining patios in Edmonton. This longtime Edmonton favorite offers fusion and international cuisine, ranging from Italian pastas—Manor Pasta with chicken, spinach, goat cheese, and tomato gin cream sauce is the signature dish—to a delicious Moroccan curry to traditional wiener schnitzel. The food is eclectic, but always delicious.

10109 125th St. (C) 780/482-7577. www.manorcafe.com. Reservations recommended on weekends. Main courses C$15–C$29. AE, MC, V. Daily 11am–2pm and 5–9pm.

Violino Gastronomia Italiana ITALIAN   Violino, located along High Street's gallery row in a 1913 heritage home, offers nouveau Italian fine dining with an emphasis

on fresh, stylish ingredients. There's a large selection of appetizers for starters or light 369
dining, including a trio of foie gras preparations. Pasta dishes are especially tempting, including tiger-stripped agnolotti with lobster, scallops, artichoke hearts, and goat cheese, or pear and pecorino cheese ravioli with reduced cream and a drizzle of port. The house specialty is *bistecca fiorentina,* a grilled T-bone steak for two. The dining room exudes a certain version of luxe, with floor-length brocaded curtains, velvet upholstered chairs, and granite tiled walls. In summer there is alfresco dining on a quiet, shady deck.

10133 125th St. © 780/757-8701. www.violinogastronomia.com. Reservations recommended on weekends. Main courses C$14–C$39. AE, MC, V. Mon–Sat 11am–2:30pm and 5–10:30pm; Sun 11am–2pm.

Old Strathcona

Chianti Cafe ITALIAN   Chianti is a rarity among Italian restaurants: very good and very inexpensive. Pasta dishes begin at C$9 and run to C$13 for fettuccine with scallops, smoked salmon, curry, and garlic; even veal dishes (over half a dozen are offered) and sea-food specials barely top C$16. Chianti is located in a handsomely remodeled post-office building; the restaurant isn't a secret, so it can be a busy and fairly crowded experience.

10501 82nd Ave. © 780/439-9829. www.chianticafe.ca. Reservations required. Main courses C$8–C$20. AE, DC, DISC, MC, V. Daily 11am–11pm.

Culina ★★ INTERNATIONAL   A few blocks north of Old Strathcona's busy Whyte Avenue is Culina, an intimate and coolly retro dining room with intriguing but casual fine dining. The cooking here is a celebration of international flavors, without the mud-died tastes so common with fusion cooking or the assertive exoticism of many global menus. Instead, this is what comfort food would taste like as if the whole world were your neighborhood. Grilled white salmon is glazed with honey, almonds, and goat cheese; and sirloin steak is topped with an unexpectedly rich and flavorful sauce of blue cheese and chocolate. All meats are from local Alberta farms and ranches, and fish is line-caught.

9914 89th Ave. © 780/437-5588. www.culinafamily.ca. Reservations recommended. Main courses C$13–C$31. MC, V. Mon–Fri 9am–3pm and 5–10pm; Sat 10am–2pm and 5–11pm; Sun 10am–2pm.

Packrat Louie Kitchen & Bar ★★ ITALIAN   Bright and lively, this very popular bistro has a somewhat unlikely name, given that it's one of the best casual Italian trat-torie in Edmonton. Menu choices range from specialty pizzas to fine entree salads—I loved the seared goat cheese salad with mushrooms, pumpkin seeds, and smoked pear dressing—to grilled meats, chicken, and pasta. Most dishes cast an eye toward light or healthy preparations without sacrificing complexity. Grilled salmon is dressed with maple-sage brown butter sauce, and is served with crab and quinoa pilaf.

10335 83rd Ave. © 780/433-0123. www.packratlouie.com. Reservations recommended on weekends. Main courses C$20–C$40. MC, V. Mon–Thurs 11:30am–10pm; Fri and Sat 11:30am–11pm.

EDMONTON AFTER DARK

Tickets to most events are available through **Ticketmaster** (© 780/451-8000). For list-ings of current happenings, check the Friday arts section of the *Edmonton Journal* (www.edmontonjournal.com) or the alternative weekly *See* (www.seemagazine.com).

THE PERFORMING ARTS   A masterpiece of theatrical architecture, the **Citadel Theatre,** 9828 101A Ave. (© 780/426-4811; www.citadeltheatre.com), looks like a gigantic greenhouse and takes up the entire city block adjacent to Sir Winston Churchill Square. It houses five different theaters, workshops, and classrooms; a restaurant; and a magnificent indoor garden with a waterfall. The Citadel is one of the largest, busiest theaters in Canada.

Home to the **Edmonton Opera** (© **780/424-4040;** www.edmontonopera.com) and the **Alberta Ballet** (© **780/428-6839;** www.albertaballet.com), the **Northern Alberta Jubilee Auditorium,** 11455 87th Ave. (© **780/427-2760;** fax 780/422-3750; www.jubileeauditorium.com), also plays host to traveling dance troupes, Broadway shows, and other acts that require a large stage and excellent acoustics.

BARS & CLUBS   The flashy, upscale country scene is very popular in Edmonton, and the hottest country-dance bar in town is the **Cook County Saloon,** 8010 103rd St. (© 780/432-2665).

An Edmonton institution, the **Sidetrack Café ★**, 10333 112th St. (© **780/421-1326**), is a holdover from the '60s, when live music was a way of life. This venerable club on the wrong side of the tracks sees a real variety of bands, from Australian rock to West Coast punk to progressive jazz. For something uniquely Edmonton without the twang, check it out.

It may not look like much (and that's usually a good sign) but the popular **Blues on Whyte,** 10329 82nd Ave. (© **780/439-5058**), in the vintage Commercial Hotel in Old Strathcona, is Edmonton's best blues club.

Downtown, the **New City,** 10081 Jasper Ave. (© **780/429-2582**), is a youthful hangout with something different every night, from live bands to DJs to drag shows. In Old Strathcona, the **Backroom Vodka Bar,** 10324 82nd Ave. (© **780/436-4418**), offers a similarly lively mix of live music, DJs, and performance. You'll find plenty of other nightclubs and music scenes along 82nd Avenue in Old Strathcona.

Looking for Edmonton's gay and lesbian scene? Start your investigation of the city's lively gay life at **Play Nightclub,** 10220 103rd St. NW (© **780/497-7529**), with dancing and cocktails, or **Buddy's,** 11725 Jasper Ave. (© **780/488-6636**), with dancing nightly and drag shows on Wednesday.

The Canadian Rockies: Banff & Jasper National Parks & More

The Canadian Rockies rise to the west of the Alberta prairies and contain some of the finest mountain scenery on Earth. Between them, Banff and Jasper national parks preserve much of this mountain beauty, but vast and equally spectacular regions of the Rockies (as well as portions of nearby British Columbia's Selkirk and Purcell mountain ranges; see chapter 14) are protected by other national and provincial parks. Because Banff and Jasper are so popular and expensive, these smaller, less thronged, but equally dramatic parks—which include Waterton Lakes, Yoho, and Kootenay national parks, as well as a host of provincial parks—are excellent destinations for those travelers who are looking for wilderness adventure, and not just luxury shopping and dining in a mountain setting.

Hiking, biking, and pack trips on horseback have long pedigrees in the parks, as does superlative skiing—the Winter Olympics were held in Calgary and on the eastern face of the Rockies in 1988. Outfitters throughout the region offer white-water and float trips on mighty rivers; calmer pursuits such as fishing and canoeing are also popular.

In addition, some of the country's finest and most famous hotels are in the Canadian Rockies. The incredible mountain lodges and châteaux built by early rail entrepreneurs are still in operation, offering unforgettable experiences in luxury and stunning scenery. If you're looking for a more rural holiday, head to one of the Rockies' many guest ranches, where you can saddle up, poke some doggies, and end the evening at a steak barbecue.

The Canadian Rockies boast an excellent network of paved roads, which makes exploring by car safe and easy—if slow, during the busy summer season. From Calgary, it's a stunning 1-hour drive up the Bow River to Banff on Hwy. 1, and driving from Edmonton to Jasper on the Yellowhead Highway (Hwy. 16) takes from 3 to 4 hours. Both these roads (which continue over the Rockies into British Columbia), along with the Icefields Parkway between Lake Louise and Jasper, remain open year-round.

---

1 EXPLORING THE CANADIAN ROCKIES

Few places in the world are more dramatically beautiful than the Canadian Rockies. Banff and Jasper national parks are famous for their mountain lakes, flower-spangled meadows, spirelike peaks choked by glaciers, and abundant wildlife. Nearly the entire spine of the Rockies—from the U.S. border north for 1,127km (700 miles)—is preserved as parkland or wilderness.

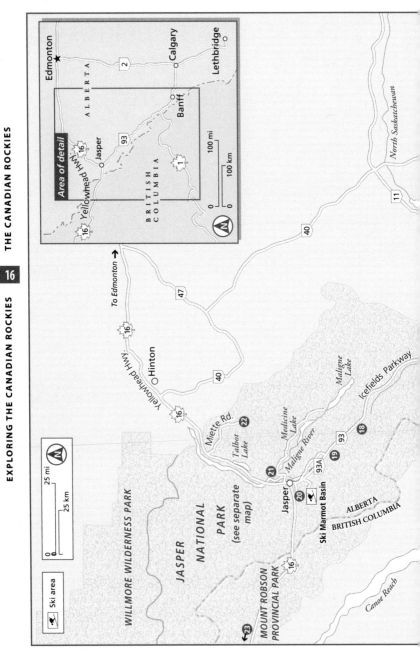

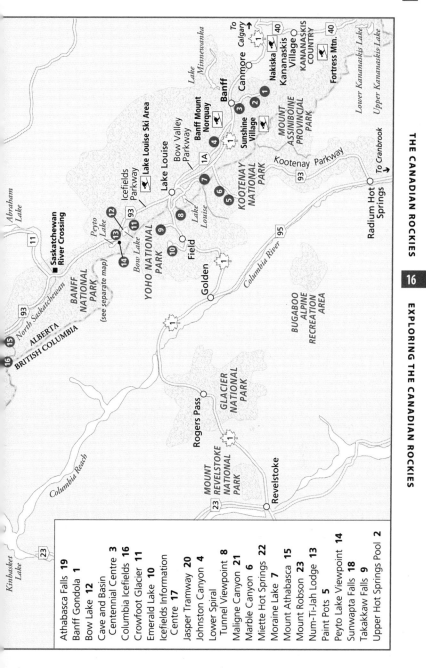

Athabasca Falls **19**
Banff Gondola **1**
Bow Lake **12**
Cave and Basin
Centennial Centre **3**
Columbia Icefields **16**
Crowfoot Glacier **11**
Emerald Lake **10**
Icefields Information
Centre **17**
Jasper Tramway **20**
Johnston Canyon **4**
Lower Spiral
Tunnel Viewpoint **8**
Maligne Canyon **21**
Marble Canyon **6**
Miette Hot Springs **22**
Moraine Lake **7**
Mount Athabasca **15**
Mount Robson **23**
Num-Ti-Jah Lodge **13**
Paint Pots **5**
Peyto Lake Viewpoint **14**
Sunwapta Falls **18**
Takakkaw Falls **9**
Upper Hot Springs Pool **2**

That's the good news. The bad news is that lovers of solitude who come here will find themselves surrounded by increasingly larger numbers of visitors. Advance planning is absolutely necessary if you're going to stay or eat where you want, or if you hope to evade the swarms of visitors who throng the parks during the high season, from mid-June to the end of August.

ORIENTATION

Canada's Rocky Mountain parks include Jasper and Banff, which together comprise 17,519 sq. km (6,764 sq. miles); the provincial parklands of the Kananaskis Country and Mount Robson; and Yoho and Kootenay national parks, to the west in British Columbia.

The parks are traversed by one of the most scenic highway systems in Canada, plus innumerable nature trails leading to more remote valleys and peaks. The two "capitals," Banff and Jasper, lie 287km (178 miles) apart, connected by Hwy. 93, one of the most scenic routes you'll ever drive. Banff is 128km (80 miles) from Calgary via Hwy. 1; Jasper, 375km (233 miles) from Edmonton on Route 16, the famous Yellowhead Highway.

Admission to Banff, Jasper, Yoho, and Kootenay parks costs C$9.80 adults, C$8.30 seniors, C$4.90 youths 6 to 16, or C$20 families per day.

VISITOR INFORMATION

For information on the entire province of Alberta, contact **Travel Alberta** (© **800/661-8888;** www.travelalberta.com). Ask for copies of the accommodations and visitors guides, as well as the excellent *Traveler's Guide* and a road map. There's a separate guide for campers as well.

Alberta has no provincial sales tax. There's only the 5% national goods and services tax (GST), plus a 4% accommodations tax (some communities, such as Banff, add on additional taxes). On the other side of the Rockies, the province of British Columbia levies a "harmonized" federal and provincial 12% tax on purchases and services.

TOURS & EXCURSIONS

You'll get used to the name Brewster, associated with many things in these parts. In particular, these folks operate the park system's principal tour-bus operation. **Brewster Transportation and Tours,** 100 Gopher St., Banff, AB T0L 0C0 (© **403/762-6767;** www.brewster.ca), covers most of the outstanding scenic spots in both parks. Call for a full brochure, or ask the concierge at your hotel to arrange a trip.

SEASONS

The parks have two peak seasons during which hotels charge top rates and restaurants are jammed. The first is summer, mid-June to late August, when it doesn't get terribly hot, rarely above 77°F (25°C), though the sun's rays are powerful at this altitude. The other peak time is winter, the skiing season from December to February; this is some of the finest skiing terrain in all Canada. March to May is decidedly off season: Hotels offer bargain room rates, and you can choose the best table in any eatery (note that many restaurants close for a week or two in the low seasons). There's plenty of rain in the warmer months, so don't forget to bring some suitable rainwear.

LODGING IN THE ROCKIES

On any given day in high season, up to 50,000 people wind through the Canadian Rocky national parks. Because growth in the parks is strictly regulated, there's not an abundance of hotel rooms waiting. The result is strong competition for a limited number of very expensive rooms. Adding to the squeeze is the fact that many hotels have 80% to 90% of their rooms reserved for coach tours in summer. To avoid disappointment, particularly if you want to stay in one of the landmark hotels, *reserve your room as far in advance as possible.*

On the other hand, if you don't mind uncertainty and are traveling with a laptop, the advent of discount hotel websites opens up possibilities for those who want to gamble on last-minute room availability. You can always take the chance that top-ranked hotels will have last-minute cancellations to sell over the Internet. In high season, the savings can be up to 50%, though there is no guarantee that you'll get the hotel or room type that you want.

Regarding price, it seems that lodgings can ask for and get just about any rate they want in high season. For the most part, hotels are well kept up in the parks, but few would justify these high prices anywhere else in the world. Knowing that, there are a few choices. You can decide whether or not to splurge on one of the world-class hotels here, actually only a bit more expensive than the midrange competition. Camping is another good option, because the parks have dozens of campgrounds with varying levels of facilities. There are also a number of hostels throughout the parks.

If you're having trouble locating a room, contact **Rocky Mountain Reservations** (© 877/902-9455; www.rockymountainreservations.com) for a free hotel and activities booking service.

In the off season, prices drop dramatically, often as much as 50%. Most hotels offer ski packages in winter, as well as other attractive getaway incentives. Ask about any special rates, especially at the larger hotels.

BED-AND-BREAKFASTS If you're looking for a B&B, try the **Alberta Bed and Breakfast Association** (www.bbalberta.com).

HOSTELS Hostels in the Rocky Mountain national parks are often the most affordable lodging option. Hostels aren't just for youths anymore; all **Hostelling International** properties welcome guests of any age. To find out more about Alberta hostels, check out **www.hihostels.ca**.

GUEST RANCHES Alberta has been ranch country for well over a century, and the Old West lifestyle is deeply ingrained in Albertan culture. Indulge in a cowboy fantasy and spend a few days at one of the many historic guest ranches.

At Seebe, in the Kananaskis Country near the entrance to Banff National Park, is **Rafter Six Ranch** (© 888/267-2624 or 403/673-3691; www.raftersix.com), with a beautiful old log lodge and a long menu of outdoor activities. The **Black Cat Guest Ranch** (© 800/859-6840 or 403/865-3084; www.blackcatguestranch.ca), near Hinton, was once a winter horse camp. At all these historic ranches, horseback riding and trail rides are the main focus, but other Western activities, such as rodeos, barbecues, and country dancing, are usually on the docket. Gentler pursuits, such as fishing, hiking, and lolling by the hot tub, are equally possible. Meals are usually served family-style in the central lodge, while accommodations are either in cabins or in the main lodge. A night at a guest ranch usually ranges from C$110 to C$200 and includes a ranch breakfast. Full bed-and-board packages are available for longer stays. There's usually an additional hourly fee for horseback riding.

Homestays at smaller working ranches are also possible. You can pitch in and help your hosts with their work or simply relax. For a stay on a real mom-and-pop farm or ranch, obtain a list of members from **Alberta Country Vacations Association** (© 403/722-3053; fax 403/625-3246; www.albertacountryvacation.com).

Banff and Jasper national parks have long been the center of mountain recreation for Alberta. If you're staying in Banff, Jasper, or Lake Louise, you'll find that outfitters and rental operations in these centers are pretty sophisticated and professional: They make it easy and convenient to get outdoors. Most hotels will offer a concierge service that can arrange activities for you; for many, you need little or no advance registration. Shuttle buses to more distant activities are usually available as well.

You don't even have to break a sweat to enjoy the magnificent scenery—hire a horse and ride to the backcountry, or take an afternoon trail ride. Jasper, Banff, and Lake Louise have gondolas to lift travelers from valley floor to mountaintop. Bring a picnic, or plan a ridge-top hike. If you're not ready for white water, the scenic cruises on Lake Minnewanka and Maligne Lake offer a more relaxed waterborne adventure.

BACKPACKING Backcountry trips through high mountain meadows and remote lakes provide an unforgettable experience; Banff Park alone has 3,059km (1,901 miles) of hiking trails.

BIKING Both parks provide free maps of local mountain-bike trails; the Bow Valley Parkway between Banff and Lake Louise and Parkway 93A in Jasper Park are both good, less trafficked roads for road biking. Bike rentals are easily available nearly everywhere in the parks.

ROCK CLIMBING, ICE CLIMBING & MOUNTAINEERING The sheer rock faces on Mount Rundle near Banff and the Palisades near Jasper are popular with rock climbers, and the area's many waterfalls become frozen ascents for ice climbers in winter. Instruction in mountaineering skills is offered by **Yamnuska Inc. Mountain School,** based in Canmore (© **403/678-4164;** www.yamnuska.com).

SKIING There are downhill areas at Banff, Lake Louise, Jasper, and the former Olympic site at Nakiska in the Kananaskis Country. Skiing can be superb here: The snowpack is copious, the scenery beautiful, après-ski festivities indulgent, and accommodations world-class. There's a lot of value in an Alberta ski holiday—lift tickets here are generally cheaper than at comparable ski areas in the United States.

Heli-skiing isn't allowed in the national parks but is popular in the adjacent mountain ranges near Golden in British Columbia. **CMH Heli-Skiing,** 217 Bear St., Banff (© **800/661-0252** or 403/762-7100; fax 403/762-5879; www.cmhski.com), is the leader in this increasingly popular sport, which uses helicopters to deposit skiers on virgin slopes far from the lift lines and runs of ski resorts. CMH offers 7- and 10-day trips to 12 locations; prices begin around C$6,685 for 1 week, including lodging, food, and transport from Calgary.

Cross-country skiers will find a lot to like in the Canadian Rockies. The 1988 Winter Olympic cross-country runs are now open as **Canmore Nordic Centre** ★ (© **403/678-2400**), and are administered as an all-season provincial park. A number of snowbound mountain lodges remain open throughout the winter and serve as bases for adventurous Nordic skiers. The historic **Emerald Lake Lodge,** in Yoho National Park (© **800/663-6336** or 250/343-6321), is one of the finest.

WHITE-WATER RAFTING & CANOEING The Rockies' many glaciers and snowfields are the source of mighty rivers. Outfitters throughout the region offer white-water rafting and canoe trips of varying lengths and difficulty—from a single morning on the river to a 5-day expedition. Jasper is central to a number of good white-water rivers. **Maligne**

Rafting Adventures Ltd. (© 780/852-3370; www.mra.ab.ca) offers packages for rafters
of all experience levels.

WILDLIFE-VIEWING   If you're thrilled by seeing animals in the wild, you've turned to
the right chapter. The Rocky Mountain national parks are all teeming with wildlife—bighorn sheep, grizzly and black bears, deer, mountain goats, moose, coyotes, lynxes, wolves,
and more. See "Park Wildlife & You," below, for important warnings on how to handle
wildlife encounters in the parks responsibly and safely.

PARK WILDLIFE & YOU

The parklands are swarming with wildlife, with some animals meandering along and
across highways and hiking trails, within easy camera range. However tempting, *don't feed
the animals and don't touch them!* For starters, you can be fined up to C$500 for feeding
any wildlife. There's also the distinct possibility you may end up paying more than cash
for disregarding this warning.

It isn't easy to resist the blithely fearless bighorn sheep, mountain goats, elk, soft-eyed
deer, and lumbering moose you meet. (You'll have very little chance of meeting the coyotes, lynxes, and occasional wolves, since they give humans a wide berth.) But the stuff
you feed them can kill them. Bighorns get accustomed to summer handouts of bread,
candy, potato chips, and marshmallows when they should be grazing on the high-protein
vegetation that'll help them survive through the winter.

Moose involve additional dangers. They've been known to take over entire picnics
after being given an initial snack, chase off the picnickers, and eat up everything in
sight—including cutlery, dishes, and the tablecloth.

Portions of the parks may sometimes be closed to hikers and bikers during elk calving
season. A mother elk can mistake your recreation for an imminent attack on her newborn; or an unsuspecting hiker could frighten a mother from her calf, separating the two
for good. Pay attention to—and obey—postings at trail heads.

Bears pose the worst problems. The parks contain two breeds: the big grizzly, standing
up to 2m (6½ ft.) on its hind legs, and the smaller black bear, about 1.5m (5 ft.) long.
The grizzly spends most of the summer in high alpine ranges, well away from tourist
haunts. As one of North America's largest carnivores, its appearance and reputation are
awesome enough to make you beat a retreat on sight. But the cuddly looks and circus
antics of the black bear tend to obscure the fact that these too are wild animals: powerful,
faster than a horse, and completely unpredictable.

Hiking in bear country (and virtually all parkland is bear country) necessitates certain
precautions. Never hike alone and never take a dog along (dogs often yap at bears, then
when the bear charges, they run toward their owners for protection, bringing the pursuer
with them). Above all, never go near a cub. The mother is usually close by, and a female
defending her young is ferocious.

2 KANANASKIS COUNTRY & CANMORE

31km (19 miles) E of Banff; 97km (60 miles) W of Calgary

Kananaskis Country is the name given to three Alberta provincial parks on the Rocky
Mountains' eastern slope, southeast of Banff National Park. Once considered only a
gateway region to more glamorous Banff, the Kananaskis has developed into a recreation
destination on a par with more famous brand-name resorts in the Rockies.

Located just west of the Kananaskis and just outside the eastern boundary of Banff National Park, **Canmore** is a sprawl of condominium and resort developments in a dramatic location beneath the soaring peaks of **Three Sisters Mountain.** Only 20 minutes from Banff, Canmore hasn't yet topped the list of Canadian resort destinations, but the scenery is magnificent and the accommodations generally much less expensive and considerably less overbooked than those in Banff.

Weather is generally warmer and sunnier here, which is conducive to great golf: The championship course at **Kananaskis** is considered one of the best in North America.

When the 1988 Olympics were held in Calgary, the national park service wouldn't allow the alpine ski events to be held inside the parks. **Nakiska,** in the Kananaskis, became the venue instead, vaulting it to international prominence.

The Kananaskis offers stunning scenery without Banff's crowds and high prices. Also, because Kananaskis Country isn't governed by national-park restrictions, there's better road access to out-of-the-way lakeside campgrounds and trail heads, which makes this a more convenient destination for family getaways (there are more than 3,000 campsites in the area!). This provincial parkland also allows "mixed use," including some traditional (though heavily regulated) ranching. Some of the best guest ranches in Alberta operate here.

The main road through Kananaskis Country is Hwy. 40, which cuts south from Hwy. 1 at the gateway to the Rockies and follows the Kananaskis River. **Kananaskis Village,** a collection of resort hotels and shops, is the center of activities in the Kananaskis and is convenient to most recreation areas. Hwy. 40 eventually climbs up to the 2,206m (7,238-ft.) Highwood Pass before looping around to meet Hwy. 22 south of Calgary.

ESSENTIALS

Canmore is served by **Greyhound Canada** (© **800/661-8747** or 403/260-0877; www. greyhound.ca) and **Brewster** (© **403/762-6767;** www.brewster.ca) buses and by private shuttle services that run between Banff and Calgary.

For information on Kananaskis and Canmore, contact **Kananaskis Country** (© **866/432-4322;** www.albertaskananaskis.com) or the **Barrier Lake Visitor Information Centre,** Box 32, Exshaw, AB G0L 2C0 (© **403/673-3985**). The **Travel Alberta Visitor Information Centre,** at the Bow Valley Trail exit off Hwy. 1 at Canmore (© **403/678-5277**), also has lots of information.

EXPLORING CANMORE

You could drive past Canmore many times—indeed, you could pull off the freeway and drive down the hotel- and mall-laden Bow Valley Trail—and think you've seen all the town has to offer. In fact, the booming modern development that you'll glimpse from the freeway started before the 1988 Olympics, when Canmore was the center for cross-country ski competition. The pace of development has greatly quickened in the last decade or so, as Canmore has become a retirement mecca, and vast subdivisions now rise from the slopes of the Bow Valley just outside the gates to Banff National Park. However, the old town center has been largely bypassed by this kind of "progress" and is pleasant to explore.

Canmore has actually been around since the 1880s, when it was the headquarters for the coal mines that fueled the Canadian Pacific Railroad's transcontinental trains as they climbed up over the Rockies. The old downtown area is on an island in the Bow River, and is reached by turning onto Main Street off Railway Avenue. Downtown is undeveloped by Banff standards, but three pleasant, pedestrian-friendly blocks are lined with shops, brewpubs, restaurants, and boutiques. The **Canmore Museum,** at Seventh Avenue and Ninth Street (℗ **403/678-2462**), tells the story of the community from its days as a coal-mining camp to its pinnacle as Olympic host.

ADVENTURE SPORTS

It's the excellent access to outdoor activities that makes Canmore and the Kananaskis such a prime destination. **Inside Out Experience** (℗ **877/999-7238** or 403/949-3305; www.insideoutexperience.com) represents most local outfitters. Check the website to find bike trips, trail rides, rafting, hiking, and sightseeing tours.

CROSS-COUNTRY SKIING & MORE   The **Canmore Nordic Centre** ★, south of town off Spray Lakes Road (1988 Olympic Way, Canmore, AB T1W 2T6; ℗ **403/678-2400**), was developed for the Olympics' cross-country skiing competition, though the facility is now open year-round. Today, it's administered as an all-season provincial park. In winter, the center offers 70km (43 miles) of scenic cross-country trails, plus the on-site **Trail Sports** shop (℗ **403/678-6764**) for rentals, repairs, and sales. In summer, hikers and mountain bikers take over the trails, and Trail Sports offers bike rentals, skill-building courses, and guided rides. In addition, there's an 18-hole disc golf course.

DOWNHILL SKIING   Kananaskis gained worldwide attention when it hosted the alpine ski events for the Winter Olympics in 1988, and skiing remains a primary attraction in the area. At **Nakiska** (℗ **800/258-7669** or 403/591-7777; www.skinakiska. com), skiers can follow in the tracks of past Winter Olympians. Adult lift tickets cost C$65.

HORSEBACK TRIPS   The Kananaskis is noted for its dude ranches, which offer a variety of horseback adventures from short trail rides to multiday pack trips. A 2-hour guided ride will generally cost C$60 to C$85. In addition, **Boundary Ranch,** just south of Kananaskis Village on Hwy. 40 (℗ **877/591-7177** or 403/591-7171; www.boundary ranch.com), offers a variety of trail rides, including a horseback lunch excursion.

RAFTING   The Kananaskis and Bow rivers are the main draw here. In addition to a range of half-day (C$49–C$85), full-day (C$119), and 2-day (C$259) white-water trips, there are excursions that combine a half-day of horseback riding with an afternoon of rafting (C$145). Contact **Inside Out Experience** (℗ **877/999-7238** or 403/949-3305; www.insideoutexperience.com) for information.

WHERE TO STAY
Kananaskis Village

Kananaskis was the site of the international G8 Summit in 2002, so you may well stay in a room once graced by a world leader.

Delta Lodge at Kananaskis ★   This resort hotel consists of three separate buildings that face each other across a pond at the center of Kananaskis Village. The Lodge is the largest building, with a more rustic facade, a shopping arcade, and a number of drinking and dining choices. Here, and in the Mount Kidd Manor, the guest rooms are large and well furnished; many have balconies and lofts, and some have fireplaces. The Signature Club rooms are in a smallest—and quietest—of the buildings. Rooms here are generally more spacious and even more sumptuously furnished. Additionally, the Signature Club rooms include deluxe continental breakfast, afternoon hors d'oeuvres, honor bar, and full concierge service. The new Summit Spa and Fitness Centre provides health and beauty treatments for both men and women.

Kananaskis Village, AB T0L 2H0. © **800/268-1133** or 403/591-7711. Fax 403/591-7770. www.deltahotels. com. 321 units. C$259–C$349 double. Ski/golf package rates and discounts available. AE, DC, MC, V. Parking C$15; valet parking C$19. **Amenities:** 4 restaurants; bar; babysitting; bike rental; concierge; concierge-level rooms; golf courses nearby; health club; indoor pool; room service; complete spa w/ saltwater pool, whirlpool, and beauty treatments; tennis courts. *In room:* A/C (Signature Club), TV/VCR w/ pay movies, fridge, hair dryer, minibar, Wi-Fi.

Kananaskis Wilderness Hostel   This is a great place for a recreation-loving traveler on a budget. The hostel is located at the Nakiska ski area, within walking distance of Kananaskis Village, and is close to 60 biking, hiking, and cross-country trails. Area outfitters offer special discounts to hostel guests. The hostel has a common room with a fireplace and four private family rooms.

At Nakiska Ski Area. © **866/762-4122** or 403/670-7580 for reservations, or 403/591-7333 for the hostel itself. www.hihostels.ca. 47 beds. Bunks C$20–C$23 members, C$24–C$27 nonmembers; private rooms C$58–C$60 members, C$66–C$68 nonmembers. MC, V. **Amenities:** Common room w/TV; kitchen; Wi-Fi. *In room:* No phone.

Canmore

About half of the hotel development in Canmore dates from the 1988 Olympics, and the rest dates from—oh, the last 15 minutes. Canmore is presently going through an intense period of growth, with new lodgelike hotels (the pine-timbered facades typically disguise standard hotel rooms inside) springing out of the forest like mushrooms. To a large degree, this is due to the restrictions on development within the national parks to the west: Hoteliers, outfitters, and other businesses designed to serve the needs of park visitors find Canmore, right on the park boundary, a much easier place to locate themselves than Banff. As a result, Canmore is booming, and is now a destination in its own right.

The main reason to stay in Canmore is the price of hotel rooms. Rates here are between a half and a third lower than in Banff, and the small downtown area is blossoming with interesting shops and good restaurants. However, be aware that some of the newer hotels and time-share complexes can be quite a ways from downtown, and many of the older properties, which are closer in, were built for the Olympics and generally have more facilities than today's batch of hotels. Canmore hotels can represent especially good deals on discount hotel websites.

For a complete list of B&Bs, contact the **Canmore–Bow Valley B&B Association,** P.O. Box 8005, Canmore, AB T1W 2T8 (www.bbcanmore.com).

Falcon Crest Lodge ★★   This beautifully equipped hotel is one of Canmore's newest, and is about a mile from the downtown core. The rooms here may be brand-new, but they don't have the build-'em-by-the-hundreds anonymity that can become so tedious in mass-constructed condo developments. There are four room types: The deluxe, usually with two queen-size beds, is pleasant but just a bit tight, though it does have a kitchenette. Step up to the studio or one-bedroom for lots of space, a full kitchen, and a fireplace; for larger families or groups, there are also two-bedroom units. All rooms have balconies. All in all, a delightful place to stay.

190 Kananaskis Way, Canmore, AB T1W 3K5. © **866/609-3222** or 403/678-6150. Fax 403/678-6148. www.falconcrestlodge.ca. 70 units. C$189–C$234 double. AE, MC, V. Free secured, indoor, heated parking. **Amenities:** Restaurant; lounge; exercise room; 2 outdoor hot tubs. *In room:* A/C, TV/DVD player, hair dryer, kitchen or kitchenette, Wi-Fi, fireplace.

Paintbox Lodge ★   One of the few lodgings in Canmore's charming town center, the Paintbox Lodge is a small and luxurious boutique inn that mingles rustic mountain charm and refined sophistication. The lodge offers seven guest rooms in the main building

Moments Riding Herd at a Guest Ranch

An old-time guest ranch with a long pedigree, **Rafter Six Ranch Resort,** P.O. Box 6, Seebe, AB T0L 1X0 (© **888/26-RANCH** [7264] or 403/673-3622; www. raftersix.com), is located in a meadow right on the banks of the Kananaskis River. This full-service resort is open year-round and accommodates guests in an especially inviting old log lodge (with restaurant, barbecue deck, and lounge), in various sizes of log cabins, and in large chalets that sleep up to six and have full kitchens (for a total of 30 units). All units have private bathrooms. Doubles go for C$179 to C$375 and include a ranch breakfast. Casual horseback and longer pack rides are offered, as well as raft and canoe trips. Seasonal special events might include rodeos, country dances, and hay or sleigh rides.

and a two-bedroom suite with a full kitchen in a separate lodge, all just steps from the Bow River and the lively cafes and shops of downtown Canmore.

701 Mallard Alley, Canmore, AB T1W 2A2. © **888/678-3100** or 403/609-0482. Fax 403/609-0481. www. paintboxlodge.com. 8 units. C$199–C$279 double. AE, MC, V. *In room:* TV w/movie channels, CD player, fridge, hair dryer, minibar, Wi-Fi, 2-person tubs.

Quality Resort Chateau Canmore ★ You can't miss this enormous complex along the hotel strip. Like a series of 10 four-story conjoined chalets, the all-suite Chateau Canmore offers some of the largest rooms in the area. The accommodations are very nicely decorated in a comfortable rustic style, while the lobby and common rooms look like they belong in a log lodge. Each standard suite has a fireplace and separate bedroom, while the deluxe one- or two-bedroom suites add a living room and dining area.

1720 Bow Valley Trail, Canmore, AB T1W 2X3. © **800/261-8551** or 403/678-6699. Fax 403/678-6954. www.chateaucanmore.com. 93 units. C$119–C$199 double. AE, DC, DISC, MC, V. **Amenities:** Restaurant; health club; outdoor Jacuzzi; indoor pool; sauna; day spa; lounge. *In room:* A/C, TV, fridge, hair dryer, Wi-Fi, microwave, toaster.

Camping

Kananaskis is a major camping destination for families, and the choice of **campgrounds** in Calgary is wide. There's a concentration of campgrounds at Upper and Lower Kananaskis Lakes, some 32km (20 miles) south of Kananaskis Village. A few campgrounds are scattered nearer to Kananaskis Village, around Barrier Lake and Ribbon Creek. For a full-service campground with RV hookups, go to **Mount Kidd RV Park** (© **403/591-7700**), just south of the Kananaskis golf course.

WHERE TO DINE

Pub dining in Canmore is noteworthy; most pubs have pleasant garden patios. **Grizzly Paw Pub,** 622 Main St. (© **403/678-9983**), makes its own excellent ales and serves good food. The **Rose and Crown,** 749 Railway Ave. (© **403/678-5168**), overlooking the river, wins for the best deck.

Crazyweed Kitchen ★★ CONTEMPORARY CANADIAN Crazyweed began as a little lunch spot in downtown Canmore then took the big step and moved into a brand-new building between downtown Canmore and Hwy. 1, where it's now open for both lunch and dinner. The dining room departs from the dark and woodsy look usually favored in the Canadian Rockies, with lots of windows, white walls, and modern art. The food is equally contemporary, with locally sourced ingredients enhanced with a touch of Asian, Italian, or Mexican zing. The menu is divided into small and large plates, with tempting full-flavored dishes like fresh fig salad with crispy prosciutto, grilled shrimp with mango and mint salsa, and chile-dusted rib-eye in red wine sauce.

1600 Railway Ave. ✆ **403/609-2530.** www.crazyweed.ca. Reservations required. Main courses C$22–C$38. MC, V. Daily noon–10pm.

Murrieta's Bar & Grill ★★ STEAKHOUSE/FISH   Residing a floor above Canmore's busy main street, Murrieta's is a stylish and lively steakhouse and bar with attractive lodge decor, and a soaring 7m (24-ft.) cathedral ceiling. The food is lofty as well—in addition to steak and chops, Murrieta's offers a broad selection of fresh fish and seafood. The grilled shrimp with vanilla saffron sauce is outstanding, and for a break from beef, try the chile-roasted pork rib-eye with red onion marmalade. On Friday and Saturday nights, the bar features live jazz.

200–737 Main St. ✆ **403/609-9500.** www.murrietas.ca. Reservations recommended. Main courses C$12–C$38. AE, MC, V. Mon–Thurs 11am–11pm; Fri–Sat 11am–1am; Sun 11am–10pm.

Tapas Restaurant ★ SPANISH/PORTUGUESE   Tapas Restaurant serves up over 40 authentically Spanish and Portuguese favorites including chile and cilantro mussels *escabeche*. The restaurant also focuses on dishes to be shared by two, including Cataplana, a Portuguese pork and seafood stew served in a copper pot. Three kinds of paella are also served for duo diners. With the scent of garlic and sausage in the air, you might just believe you're in Seville.

633 10th St. ✆ **403/609-0583.** www.tapascanmore.ca. Reservations suggested. Tapas C$5–C$12; main courses (for 2) C$30–C$40. AE, MC, V. Summer daily 8am–11pm; winter daily 5:30–11pm.

Trough Dining Company ★ INTERNATIONAL   In the case of Trough (to paraphrase the maxim) good things come in small, oddly named packages. This tiny restaurant, in a remodeled house just north of downtown Canmore, has developed an enormous following, and it's easy to see why: The food here is beautifully prepared and adventurous, but without the hoity-toity attitudes usually associated with fine dining. The menu is divided between small plates (Laurel) and main courses (Hardy), and although ingredients are from local farms and ranches, the preparations span the globe. Lamb short ribs are glazed with Indian tamarind sauce and served with onion and chick pea pakoras and cilantro-mint chutney; while duck confit comes with peashoots and orange-ginger slaw. With only a dozen or so tables, reservations are a must.

725 9th St. ✆ 403/678-2820. www.thetrough.ca. Reservations required. Main courses C$26–C$35. MC, V. Sun–Mon and Wed, Thurs 6–9:30pm; Fri–Sat 5:30–10pm.

3 BANFF NATIONAL PARK

Banff Townsite: 129km (80 miles) W of Calgary

Banff is Canada's oldest national park, founded in 1885 as a modest 26-sq.-km (10-sq.-mile) reserve by the country's first prime minister, Sir John A. Macdonald. The park is now 6,641 sq. km (2,564 sq. miles) of incredibly dramatic mountain landscape, glaciers, high morainal lakes, and rushing rivers. Its two towns, Lake Louise and Banff, are both

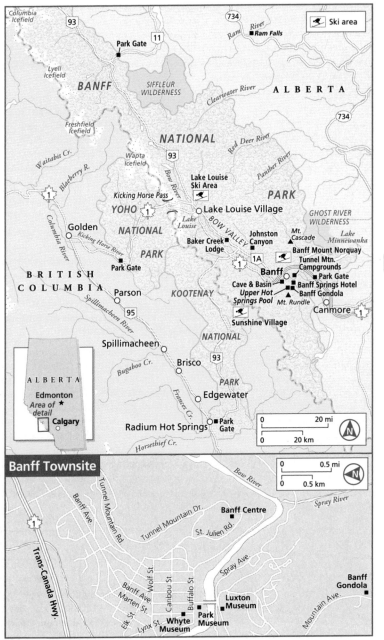

splendid counterpoints to the wilderness, with beautiful historic hotels, fine restaurants, and lively nightlife.

If there's a downside to all this sophisticated beauty, it's that Banff is incredibly popular—it's generally considered Canada's number-one tourist destination. About five million people visit Banff yearly, with the vast majority squeezing in during June, July, and August.

Happily, the wilderness invites visitors to get away from the crowds and from the congestion of the developed sites. Banff Park is blessed with a great many outfitters who make it easy to get on a raft, bike, or horse and find a little mountain solitude. Alternatively, consider visiting the park in the off season, when prices are lower, the locals are friendlier, and the scenery is just as stunning.

For more information on the park, contact **Banff National Park,** P.O. Box 900, Banff, AB T1L 1K2 (© **403/762-1550;** www.pc.gc.ca).

SPORTS & OUTDOOR ACTIVITIES IN THE PARK

Lots of great recreational activities are available in Banff National Park, so don't just spend your vacation shopping the boutiques on Banff Avenue. There are many more outfitters in Banff than the ones I list, but the offerings and prices below are typical of what's available.

BIKING The most popular cycling adventure in the Canadian Rockies is the 287km (178-mile) trip between Banff and Jasper along the Icefields Parkway, one of the world's most magnificent mountain roads.

If you're fit and ready for a high-elevation ride, but don't want to bother with the logistics yourself, consider signing on with a bike-touring outfitter. An Internet search will reveal dozens of tour operators; **Canusa Cycle Adventure Tours** (© **800/938-7986** or 403/703-5566; www.canusa-cat.com) offers 6-day supported trips starting at C$1,350.

If you'd prefer a self-guided tour, simply rent a bike in Banff or Lake Louise and peddle along the Bow Valley Parkway—Hwy. 1A—between Banff and Lake Louise, which makes an easy day trip for the average cyclist.

FISHING **Banff Fishing Unlimited** (© **403/762-4936;** www.banff-fishing.com) offers a number of fly-fishing expeditions on the Bow River as well as lake fishing at Lake Minnewanka. All levels of anglers are accommodated, and packages include part- or whole-day trips.

HIKING One of the great virtues of Banff is that many of its most scenic areas are easily accessible by day hikes. The park has more than 80 maintained trails, ranging from interpretive nature strolls to long-distance expeditions (you'll need a permit if you're planning on camping in the backcountry). For a good listing of popular hikes, pick up the free *Banff/Lake Louise Drives and Walks* brochure from the national park information center at 224 Banff Ave.

One of the best day hikes is up **Johnston Canyon** ★, 24km (15 miles) north of Banff on Hwy. 1A. This relatively easy hike up a limestone canyon passes seven waterfalls before reaching a series of jade-green springs known as the **Inkpots.** Part of the fun of this trail is the narrowness of the canyon—the walls are more than 30m (98 ft.) high, but only 5m (16 ft.) across; the path skirts the cliff face, tunnels through walls, and winds across wooden footbridges for more than a mile. The waterfalls plunge down through the canyon, soaking hikers with spray; watch for black swifts diving in the mist. The hike through the canyon to Upper Falls takes 1½ hours; all the way to the Inkpots will take at least 4.

It's easy to strike out from **Banff Townsite** and find any number of satisfying short hikes. Setting off on foot can be as simple as following the paths along both sides of the Bow River. From the west end of the Bow River Bridge, trails lead east to Bow Falls, past the Fairmont Banff Springs hotel to the Upper Hot Springs. Another popular hike just beyond town is the **Fenlands Trail,** which begins past the train station and makes a loop through marshland wildlife habitat near the Vermillion Lakes.

Two longer trails leave from the Cave and Basin Centennial Centre. The **Sundance Trail** follows the Bow River for nearly 5km (3.1 miles) past beaver dams and wetlands, ending at the entrance to Sundance Canyon. Keen hikers can continue up the canyon another 2.5km (1½ miles) to make a loop past Sundance Falls. The Marsh Loop winds 2.5km (1½ miles) past the Bow River and marshy lakes.

If you'd prefer a guided hike, Parks Canada offers several hikes daily. Ask at the Banff Information Centre or check the chalkboard outside to find out what hiking options are available. Some walks are free, while others (like the popular evening Wildlife Research Walks) charge a small fee; both require preregistration. For information and preregistration, call ✆ **403/762-9818.**

HORSEBACK RIDING See Banff on horseback with **Warner Guiding and Outfitting** (✆ **800/661-8352** or 403/762-4551; fax 403/762-8130; www.horseback.com). Multi-day trail rides, which start at C$729 for a 3-day lodge-to-lodge trip and include a 6-day backcountry tenting trip for C$1,446, explore some of the most remote areas of the park. Some rides climb up to backcountry lodges, which serve as base camps for further exploration; other trips involve a backcountry circuit, with lodging in tents. Shorter day rides are also offered from two stables near the townsite. A morning ride with brunch goes for C$102.

Operating out of Lake Louise, **Timberline Tours** (✆ **888/858-3388** or 403/522-3743; www.timberlinetours.ca) offers day trips to some of the area's more prominent beauty sites, starting at C$65 for 90 minutes of riding. Three- to 10-day pack trips are also offered.

RAFTING & CANOEING Family float trips on the Bow River just below Banff are popular 2-hour diversions, available from **Canadian Rockies Rafting Company** (✆ **877/226-7625** or 403/678-6535; www.rafting.ca). Trips are C$55 for adults, C$50 for seniors, and C$45 for children ages 3 to 16, with free pickup at Banff and Canmore hotels. Longer, more challenging trips on area rivers are also available.

For serious white water, the closest option is the **Kicking Horse River** ★, past Lake Louise just over the Continental Divide near Field, British Columbia. **Wet 'n' Wild Adventures** (✆ **800/668-9119** or 250/344-6546; www.wetnwild.bc.ca) offers Kicking Horse trips from Banff and Lake Louise (the shuttle to the Kicking Horse costs C$16 round-trip). The standard day trip is C$99, including lunch. If you just want to shoot the rapids of the lower canyon, a half-day trip is available for C$69. For beginners, a morning introduction to white water, with lunch, is available (C$60 adults, C$40 children 12 and under).

SKIING Banff Park has three ski areas, which together have formed a partnership for booking and promotional purposes. For information on all of the following, contact **Ski Banff/Lake Louise,** Box 1085, Banff, AB T0l 0C0 (✆ **403/762-4561;** fax 403/762-8185; www.skibig3.com).

Banff Mount Norquay (*✆* **403/762-4421;** www.banffnorquay.com) has twin runs just above the town of Banff. They cater to family skiing and offer day care, instruction, and night skiing.

Skiers must ski or take a gondola to the main lifts at **Sunshine Village** (*✆* **403/762-6500;** www.skibanff.com) and the Sunshine Inn, a ski-in/ski-out hotel. Sunshine, located 15 minutes west of Banff off Hwy. 1, receives more snow than any ski area in the Canadian Rockies (more than 9m/30 ft. per year!).

Lake Louise Ski Area (*✆* **800/258-SNOW** [7669] in North America, or 403/552-3555) has been named the most scenic ski resort in North America by *Ski* magazine. Snow machines keep the lifts running November to early May.

A single lift pass allows skiers unlimited access to all three resorts (and free rides on shuttle buses btw. the ski areas). Passes for 3 days (minimum) start at C$239 for adults and C$71 for youths 13 to 17.

BANFF TOWNSITE

Few towns in the world boast as beautiful a setting as Banff. The mighty Bow River courses right through town, while massive mountain blocks rear up on Banff's outskirts. Mount Rundle, a finlike mountain that somehow got tipped over on its side, parades off to the south. Mount Cascade rises up immediately north of downtown.

This is a stunning, totally unlikely place for a town, and Banff has been trading on its beauty for more than a century. The Fairmont Banff Springs hotel was built in 1888 as a destination resort by the Canadian Pacific Railroad. As outdoor-recreation enthusiasts began to frequent the area, the little town of Banff grew up to service their needs.

While the setting hasn't changed since the early days of the park, the town certainly has. Today, the streets of Banff are lined with exclusive boutiques, trendy cafes spill out onto the sidewalks, and buses filled with tourists choke the streets. There's a vital and cosmopolitan feel to the town; just don't come here expecting a bucolic alpine village—Banff in summer is a very busy place.

Essentials

GETTING THERE If you're flying into Calgary and heading straight to Banff, call and reserve a seat on the **Banff Airporter** (*✆* **403/762-3330;** www.banffairporter.com). Vans depart from Calgary Airport roughly every 2 hours; a one-way ticket costs C$56.

Greyhound (*✆* **800/661-8747** or 403/260-0877; www.greyhound.ca) operates **buses** that pass through Banff on the way from Calgary to Vancouver. One-way fare between Banff and Calgary is C$26. The depot is at 327 Railway Ave. (*✆* **403/762-1091**).

If you're **driving,** the Trans-Canada Highway takes you right to Banff's main street; the town is 129km (80 miles) west of Calgary.

VISITOR INFORMATION The **Banff Information Centre,** at 224 Banff Ave., houses both the Banff Tourism Bureau and a national-park information center. Contact the office at P.O. Box 1298, Banff, AB T0L 0C0 (*✆* **403/762-0270;** fax 403/762-8545; www.banfflakelouise.com). The center is open daily June 15 to October 15 from 9am to 9pm and the rest of the year from 9am to 5pm. Be sure to ask for the *Official Visitors Guide,* which is packed with information about local businesses and recreation. For information on the park, go to **www.pc.gc.ca**.

ORIENTATION Getting your bearings is easy. The main street—Banff Avenue—starts at the southern end of town at the Bow River and runs north until it's swallowed by the Trans-Canada Highway.

Just beyond the river, amid a beautifully landscaped garden, stands the park administration building. Here the road splits: **Fairmont Banff Springs** hotel and the **Banff Gondola** are to the left; to the right are the **Cave and Basin Hot Springs,** Banff National Park's original site. At the northwestern edge of town is the old railroad station, and a little farther northwest the road branches off to Lake Louise and Jasper. In the opposite direction, northeast, is the highway going to Calgary.

GETTING AROUND   Banff offers local bus service along two routes designed to pass through downtown and by most hotels. Service on the **Roam Bus** (✆ 403/762-6770) is pretty informal, but there's generally a bus every half-hour. One route runs from the Fairmont Banff Springs hotel down Banff Avenue to the northern end of town; the other runs between the train station and the Banff Hostel on Tunnel Mountain; the fare is C$2. The bus operates in summer only.

For a taxi, call Banff Taxi and Limousine at ✆ **403/762-4444.**

For a rental car, contact **National,** at the bus depot, 327 Railway Ave. (✆ **403/522-3870**). Avis, Budget, and Hertz also have offices in Banff. Reserve well in advance as cars are frequently sold out.

Exploring the Area

Banff Gondola ★   Apart from helicopter excursions (p. 376), the best way to get an overall view of Banff's landscape is this high-wire act (formerly the Sulphur Mountain Gondola). In 8 minutes, the enclosed gondolas lift you 698m (2,290 ft.) from the valley floor up to the top of Sulphur Mountain, at 2,281m (7,484 ft.). Up here, at the crest of the mountains behind Banff, the panoramas are stunning. Trails lead out along the mountain ridges; hike back to the bottom of the mountain, or spend the day exploring the subarctic zone along the mountaintop. Also, the upper terminal has two restaurants, a snack bar, and gift shop. Lines to get on the gondola can be very long in summer; if you are set on riding up to the high country, try to go as early as possible.

The lower terminal is 6km (3³/₄ miles) southeast of town on Mountain Ave. ✆ 403/762-5438. www. banffgondola.com. Admission C$28 adults, C$13 children 6–15. Late May to late Aug daily 8:30am–9pm; check website for off-season schedule.

Cave and Basin National Historic Site   Although most people now associate Banff with skiing or hiking, in the early days of the park, travelers streamed in to visit the curative hot springs. In fact, it was the discovery of the hot springs now preserved at this historic site that spurred the creation of the national park in 1888. During the 1910s, these hot mineral waters, which rise in a limestone cave, were piped into a rather grand Bathing Pavilion. Although the Cave and Basin springs are no longer open for swimming or soaking, the old pool area and the original cave have been preserved; interpretive displays and films round out the experience. *Note:* The 1914 Bathing Pavilion will be closed to visitors until November 2011 for upgrades. The rest of the site remains open.

1.5km (1 mile) west of Banff; turn right at the west end of the Bow River Bridge. ✆ 403/762-1566. Admission C$4 adults, C$3.50 seniors and students, C$2 children 6–12. May 15–Sept 30 daily 9am–6pm; Oct 1–May 14 Mon–Fri 11am–4pm, Sat–Sun 9:30am–5pm.

Lake Minnewanka Boat Tours   These very popular scenic and wildlife-viewing trips in glassed-in motor cruisers take place on Lake Minnewanka, a glacial lake wedged between two mountain ranges. These trips—usually 2 hours long—are among those excursions that nearly every visitor to Banff ends up taking, so unless you want to be part of a huge shuffling throng, try to go early in the day. Reservations are suggested. In high season, there are five sailings a day, and buses depart daily from Banff to meet these departures, both from the bus station and from most hotels.

24km (15 miles) north of Banff. © 403/762-3473. Fax 403/762-2800. www.minnewankaboattours.com. Tickets C$44 adults, C$19 children 6–15. Mid-May to early Oct.

Upper Hot Springs Pool If visiting the Cave and Basin makes you long for a soak in mountain hot springs, then drive up Mountain Avenue to this spa. In addition to the redesigned 1930s bath house and swimming pool filled with hot, sulfurous waters, you'll find a restaurant, snack bar, and home spa boutique. If you're looking more for a cure than a splash, try the adjacent **Pleiades Massage and Spa** (© **403/760-2500;** www. hotspring.ca) with a steam room, massage, plunge pools, and wellness and aromatherapy treatments.

At the top of Mountain Ave., 5km (3 miles) west of Banff. © **403/762-1515.** Pool admission C$7.30 adults, C$6.30 seniors and children 3–17, C$23 family. Daily 9am–11pm with reduced hours in winter.

Whyte Museum of the Canadian Rockies Part art gallery, part local-history museum, this is the only museum in North America that collects, exhibits, and interprets the history and culture of the Canadian Rockies. Two furnished heritage homes on the grounds are open in summer and stand as a memorial to the pioneers of the Rockies. Interpretive programs and tours are offered year-round. The Elizabeth Rummel Tea Room is open from mid-May to mid-October and serves light lunches, desserts, and coffee.

111 Bear St. © **403/762-2291.** www.whyte.org. Admission C$7 adults, C$4 seniors and students, C$16 family, free for children 4 and under. Daily 10am–5pm.

Shopping

The degree to which you like the town of Banff will depend largely upon your taste for shopping. **Banff Avenue** is increasingly an open-air boutique mall, with throngs of shoppers milling around. Of course, you would expect to find excellent outdoor-gear and sporting-goods stores here, as well as the usual T-shirt and gift emporiums. What's more surprising are the boutiques devoted to Paris and New York designers, the upscale jewelry stores, and the high-end galleries. What's most surprising of all is that many visitors seem to actually prefer to while away their time in this masterpiece of nature called Banff by shopping for English soaps or Italian shoes. There are no secrets to shopping here: Arcade after arcade opens onto Banff Avenue, where you'll find everything you need. Quality and prices are both quite high.

Where to Stay

Banff National Park offers hundreds of campsites within easy commuting distance of Banff. The closest are the three **Tunnel Mountain campgrounds** ★ just past the youth hostel west of town. Two of the campgrounds are for RVs only and have both partial and full hookups (C$32–C$38); the third has showers and is usually reserved for tenters (C$27). Some campsites in each section can be reserved by contacting © **877/737-3783** or by visiting www.pccamping.ca; others are available first-come, first-served only. One of the RV campgrounds remains open year-round; the rest are open May through September.

All accommodations prices listed are for high season, normally mid-May to mid-October; nearly all hotels have discounts for late fall, holidays, winter, late winter, and spring lodging. If you're having trouble finding affordable lodgings in Banff, try properties in Canmore, located 20 minutes away (see "Kananaskis Country & Canmore," earlier in this chapter).

Banff Caribou Lodge

The Caribou, with its gabled green roof, outdoor patio, bay windows, and wooden balconies, has a Western-lodge look that blends well with the alpine landscape. The interior is equally impressive, especially the vast lobby with slate-tile floor, peeled-log woodwork, and huge stone fireplace. The finely furnished bedrooms continue the Western theme with rustic pine chairs and beds decked out with snug down comforters. The bathrooms are spacious; some of the rooms have balconies. The Red Earth Spa, a full-service spa with a large fitness area adjacent, offers aesthetic and massage treatments, a Vichy shower table, and a couples treatment room. The Keg is a local favorite for steaks. Although it's not in the absolute center of town (about 10 min. on foot), a free shuttle bus ferries guests to destinations throughout Banff.

521 Banff Ave., Banff, AB T1L 1A4. ℂ **800/563-8764** or 403/762-5887. Fax 403/762-5918. www.bestofbanff. com. 185 units. C$129–C$239 double; from C$300 suite. Up to 2 children 15 and under stay free in parent's room. AE, DC, DISC, MC, V. Free heated parking. **Amenities:** Restaurant; bar; concierge; exercise room; 30-person indoor hot pool; room service; sauna; steam room. *In room:* TV w/pay movies, hair dryer, Wi-Fi.

Banff Park Lodge Resort Hotel and Conference Centre ★

A handsome cedar-and-oak structure with a cosmopolitan air, the Banff Park Lodge is a quiet block-and-a-half off the town's main street, near the Bow River. Calm and sophisticated are the key words here: All rooms are soundproof, and wild, après-ski cavorting isn't the norm. The lodge will feel like a tranquil retreat after a day in frantic Banff. The standard rooms are spacious and exceptionally well furnished, all with balconies. Most suites have a whirlpool, jetted tub, and fireplace. With its abundant ground-floor rooms and wide hallways, this lodging is popular with travelers with accessibility or mobility concerns.

222 Lynx St., Banff, AB T1L 1K5. ℂ **800/661-9266** or 403/762-4433. Fax 403/762-3553. www.banffpark lodge.com. 211 units. C$275 double; from C$395 suite. Extra person C$20. Children 16 and under stay free in parent's room. Off-season and ski packages available. AE, DC, MC, V. **Amenities:** Formal and family restaurants; bar; babysitting; concierge; Jacuzzi; indoor pool; room service; spa; steam room. *In room:* A/C, TV w/movie channels, fridge, hair dryer, Wi-Fi, voice mail.

Brewster's Mountain Lodge ★

All in all, for the comfort, convenience, and moderately priced (by Banff standards) rooms, this is one of the top picks in central Banff. This handsome lodgelike hotel, right in the heart of Banff, is operated by the Brewster family, who dominate much of the local recreation, guest ranching, and transportation. The modern hotel does its best to look rustic: Peeled log posts and beams fill the lobby and foyer, while quality pine furniture and paneling grace the spacious guest rooms. Wheelchair-accessible rooms are available. Although there's no fine dining in the hotel, you'll find plenty adjacent in central Banff. The Brewster affiliation makes it simple to take advantage of a number of lodging and adventure packages.

208 Caribou St., Banff, AB T1L 1C1. ℂ **888/762-2900** or 403/762-2900. Fax 403/762-2970. www. brewstermountainlodge.com. 77 units. From C$251 double. Rates include breakfast. AE, MC, V. Self-parking C$10. **Amenities:** Breakfast room; exercise room; Jacuzzi; sauna. *In room:* TV/VCR, hair dryer, Wi-Fi.

Buffaloberry Bed and Breakfast ★

Newly built and centrally located, the Buffaloberry offers the hominess of a B&B with the upscale touches of a fine hotel. The inn was purpose built, so rooms are expansive and have large, beautifully fitted bathrooms, plus in-floor heating and sound-proofed walls. The bedrooms, all with private bathrooms, have a relaxed formality with country touches in the furniture and fabrics. You'll also find the kind of extras that you'd expect at a hotel: turn-down service, bathrobes, slippers, pillow-top mattresses, and 800-thread-count linens. Guests share a two-story

Great Room with wood-burning fireplace, leather couches, loads of reading material, and a dining nook, where extravagant breakfasts begin the day for lucky guests. The friendly innkeepers are avid outdoors-people and bird-watchers, and are happy to share their experience.

417 Marten St. (Box 5443) Banff, AB T1L 1G5. *C* **403/762-3750.** Fax 403/762-3752. www.buffaloberry. com. 4 units. C$325 double. Lower off-season rates. MC, V. Free underground heated parking. *In room:* TV/ DVD, stereo, hair dryer.

Buffalo Mountain Lodge ★★ The most handsome of the properties on Tunnel Mountain, 1.6km (1 mile) northeast of Banff, this is the perfect choice if you'd rather avoid the frenetic pace of downtown and yet remain central to restaurants and activities. Its quiet location and beautiful lodge make this a good alternative to equally priced hotels in the heart of town (the Banff Bus stops right outside the front door). The lodge building, with recommended restaurant and lounge (see "Where to Dine," below), is an enormous log cabin, with a lobby supported by massive rafters. Accommodations are scattered around the forested 3-hectare (7-acre) property. They range from one-bedroom suites with kitchens to the exceptionally handsome Premier rooms, which feature slate-tiled bathrooms with both claw-foot tubs and slate-walled showers. The pine-and-twig furniture lends a rustic look to the otherwise sophisticated decor. A 25-person hot tub sits between the lodge and the guest rooms.

1.6km (1 mile) northeast of Banff on Tunnel Mountain Rd., P.O. Box 1326, Banff, AB T1L 1B3. *C* **800/661-1367** or 403/762-2400. Fax 403/760-4492. www.crmr.com. 108 units. C$169–C$269 double. AE, MC, V. Follow Otter St. from downtown. **Amenities:** 2 restaurants; lounge; exercise room; Jacuzzi; steam room. *In room:* TV, VCR or DVD players, hair dryer, Wi-Fi.

The Fairmont Banff Springs ★★ Standing north of Bow River Falls like an amazing Scottish baronial fortress, the Banff Springs is one of the most beautiful and famous hotels in North America. Founded in 1888 as an opulent destination resort by the Canadian Pacific Railroad, this stone castle of a hotel is still the best address in Banff—especially after the renovation of all guest rooms and a C$75-million face-lift that transformed many of the public and reception spaces. The Willow Stream spa is one of Canada's top spas, with 3,530 sq. m (37,997 sq. ft.) devoted to treatment, relaxation, and fitness. This venerable hotel doesn't offer the largest rooms in Banff, but the amenities are superlative. Expect sumptuous linens, fancy soaps and lotions, real art, and quality furniture. With the views, the spa, and the near pageantry of service, this is still the most amazing resort in an area blessed with beautiful accommodations.

405 Spray Ave. (P.O. Box 960), Banff, AB T1L 1J4. *C* **800/441-1414** or 403/762-2211. Fax 403/762-5755. www.fairmont.com. 778 units. C$449–C$529 double; C$609–C$1,089 suite. AE, DC, DISC, MC, V. Valet parking C$31; self-parking C$24. **Amenities:** 12 restaurants; 4 lounges; babysitting; bike rental; concierge; the famed Banff Springs golf course; hot tubs; Olympic-size pool; room service; the Willow Stream Spa; 4 tennis courts; ski rental; horseback riding. *In room:* A/C, TV/VCR w/pay movies and video games, hair dryer, Wi-Fi.

Hidden Ridge Resort Located up on Tunnel Mountain, a 5-minute drive from downtown Banff, is a collection of well-traveled condo developments. These properties are popular because they are out of the busy center of town, and they offer large units that can accommodate families and groups. One of these, Hidden Ridge Resort, has just undergone a major renovation and general spiffing up and offers some excellent deals for travelers who want self-catering accommodations. Condos range from king one-bedroom units to two-bedroom condos with lofts that comfortably sleep eight—even before opening out the sofa bed. All units have full maple-wood kitchens with granite counters, stone fireplace, dining area, living room, and balcony or patio. Added features include a giant outdoor hot tub, a covered barbecue area, and incredible views.

901 Hidden Ridge Way, Banff, AB T1L 1H8. © **800/661-1372** or 403/762-3544. www.bestofbanff.com/hrr. 94 units. C$199–C$259 double. AE, MC, V. Free parking. **Amenities:** Hot tub; barbecue. *In room:* TV, hair dryer, kitchen, Wi-Fi.

Rimrock Resort Hotel ★★ If you seek modern luxury and great views, this is your hotel. From its roadside lobby entrance, the enormous, stunningly beautiful Rimrock drops nine floors down a steep mountain slope, affording tremendous views from nearly all of its rooms. Aiming for the same quality of architecture and majesty of scale as venerable older lodges, the Rimrock offers a massive glass-fronted lobby that's lined with cherrywood, tiled with unpolished marble floors, and filled with inviting chairs and Oriental rugs. The stone fireplace, open on two sides, is so large that staff members step inside it to ready the kindling. Guest rooms are large and well-appointed with handsome furnishings; some have balconies. Standard rooms are all the same size; their prices vary only depending on the view. The suites are truly large, with balconies, wet bars, and loads of cozy couches. The fitness and recreational facilities here are superlative.

Mountain Ave. (5km/3 miles south of Banff), P.O. Box 1110, Banff, AB T1L 1J2. © **800/661-1587** or 403/762-3356. www.rimrockresort.com. 346 units. C$385–C$550 double; C$550–C$950 suite. AE, DC, DISC, MC, V. Valet parking C$25; C$15 self-parking in heated garage. **Amenities:** 2 restaurants; 2 bars; cafe; babysitting; concierge; gym w/weight training and exercise machines; hot tub; pool; room service; sauna and steam rooms; full service spa; squash court; yoga. *In room:* A/C, TV w/pay movies and video games, hair dryer, minibar, Wi-Fi.

Thea's House ★★ The most upscale and elegant bed-and-breakfast in Banff, Thea's is a modern home that was designed as a B&B. Just a 2-minute walk from downtown, this striking log-and-stone structure boasts 8m (26-ft.) ceilings, antiques and exquisite artwork, and discreet and friendly service. Guest rooms are all very large and beautifully outfitted, with vaulted pine ceilings, fir floors, rustic pine and antique furniture, fireplaces, sitting areas, cassette and CD players, and private balconies. All guests have access to a lounge area with a stocked minibar and refrigerator and a coffee and tea service; a full breakfast is included in the rates; ski packages are also available. "Elegant Alpine" is how Thea's describes itself, and you'll have no trouble imagining yourself in a fairy-tale mountain lodge. It is the perfect spot for a romantic getaway.

138 Otter St. (Box 1237), Banff, AB T1L 1B2. © **403/762-2499.** Fax 403/762-2496. www.theashouse.com. 3 units. C$225–C$250. 3-night minimum stay in summer and winter holidays. Rates include full breakfast. MC, V. **Amenities:** Complimentary use of mountain bikes; tea and coffee service; CD and DVD library. *In room:* TV/DVD, CD player, hair dryer, Wi-Fi, gas fireplace.

Expensive

Banff Aspen Lodge ★ (Value) Located a 5-minute walk from downtown, the Banff Aspen is a very well-maintained motel that offers good value for the dollar. Rooms are quite large and pleasantly decorated (particularly after a full upgrade completed in 2010), all with twin vanities and king- or queen-size beds. Some are divided into two sleeping areas by the bathroom, a great configuration for families or groups. All units have balconies or patio access.

401 Banff Ave., Banff, AB T1L 1A9. © **877/886-6660** or 403/762-4401. Fax 403/762-5905. www.banffaspenlodge.com. 89 units. C$169–C$241 double. Rates include continental breakfast. AE, MC, V. **Amenities:** 2 outdoor hot tubs; sauna; steam room. *In room:* TV, hair dryer, Wi-Fi.

Banff Boutique Inn   Formerly the Pensione Tannenhof, this rambling historic home in a quiet neighborhood is just an 8-minute stroll along the Bow River from downtown. Most rooms are quite large, with a mix of bed configurations, from one king-size to a queen-size and a single and everything in between, making this a good choice for families, which are welcome. Two rooms have fireplaces, and all but two have either en suite or private bathrooms. In a separate chalet at the back of the inn are two large rooms each with two queen-size beds, both with a fireplace and jetted tub. The home's original living room, an expansive room with fireplace and comfy couches, is a great place to relax and trade stories with other travelers.

121 Cave Ave. (P.O. Box 1870), Banff, AB T1L 1B7. ✆ **403/762-4636.** Fax 403/762-5660. www.banff boutiqueinn.com. 10 units. C$135–C$310 double. Extra person C$20. Rates include full breakfast. MC, V. **Amenities:** Jacuzzi; sauna. *In room:* Plasma TV.

Homestead Inn (Value)   One of the best lodging deals in Banff is the Homestead Inn, only a block from all the action on Banff Avenue. Though the amenities are modest, the rooms are tastefully furnished and equipped with armchairs and stylish bathrooms. Factor in the free downtown parking and this well-maintained older motel seems all the more enticing.

217 Lynx St., Banff, AB T1L 1A7. ✆ **800/661-1021** or 403/762-4471. Fax 403/762-8877. www.homestead innbanff.com. 27 units. C$149 double. Extra person C$15. Children 15 and under stay free in parent's room. AE, MC, V. **Amenities:** Family restaurant. *In room:* TV, fridge, hair dryer, Wi-Fi.

Red Carpet Inn (Value)   A handsome brick building with a balcony along the top floors, the Red Carpet Inn is located on the long, main street leading to downtown. Well maintained and more than adequately furnished, this is one of the best deals in Banff. Guest rooms are furnished with easy chairs and desks. There's an excellent restaurant next door. The entire facility is shipshape and very clean—just the thing if you don't want to spend a fortune.

425 Banff Ave., Banff, AB T1L 1B6. ✆ **800/563-4609** or 403/762-4184. www.banffredcarpet.com. Fax 403/762-4894. 52 units. C$149–C$179 double. Rates include continental breakfast. AE, MC, V. Free parking. **Amenities:** Hot tub. *In room:* A/C, TV, fridge, hair dryer, Wi-Fi.

Moderate

Blue Mountain Lodge   **(Value)** This rambling place east of downtown began its life in 1908 as a boardinghouse. As you may expect in an older building constructed at the edge of the wilderness, the bedrooms were never exactly palatial to begin with—and when the rooms were redesigned to include private bathrooms, they got even smaller. That's the bad news. The good news is that the lodge is full of charm and funny nooks and crannies. Those small rooms just mean that you'll be spending time with new friends in the lounge and common kitchen. Think of Blue Mountain Lodge as an upscale hostel, but whatever you call it, it's one of the least expensive and friendliest places to stay in central Banff. Many guests here are avid outdoorsy types, making this a great place to stay if you're on your own and would appreciate meeting other people to hike with. The staff is young, friendly, and eager to help you get out on the trails.

327 Caribou St. (Box 2763), Banff, AB T1L 1C4. ✆ **403/762-5134.** Fax 403/762-8081. www.bluemtnlodge. com. 10 units. From C$119–C$179 double. Extra person C$15. Rates include deluxe continental breakfast and afternoon hot beverages and homemade cookies. Extended-stay discounts available. MC, V. Free off-street parking. **Amenities:** Wi-Fi, guest kitchen; common room. *In room:* TV.

Mountain Home Bed & Breakfast   If you're looking for a bit of historical charm coupled with modern comforts, this excellent B&B may be it. It was originally built as a tourist lodge in the 1940s, and then served as a private home for years before being restored and turned back into a guesthouse. The present decor manages to be evocative without being too fussy. The bedrooms are airy and nicely furnished with quality furniture and antiques; all have an en suite bathroom and telephone. Especially nice is the cozy Rundle Room, with its own slate fireplace. Breakfast is a full, cooked meal with homemade baked goods. Downtown Banff is just a 2-minute walk away.

129 Muskrat St. (P.O. Box 272), Banff, AB T1L 01A4. ℂ **403/762-3889.** Fax 403/762-3254. www.mountain homebb.com. 4 units. C$135–C$175 double. Rates include full breakfast. MC, V. *In room:* HDTV, hair dryer, Wi-Fi.

Rocky Mountain B&B (**Kids**)   A former boardinghouse converted into a B&B, this pleasant and rambling inn offers comfortable, clean, cozy rooms and is just a few minutes from downtown. Accommodations are a mix of private and shared bathrooms. Four units have kitchenettes. Families are welcome.

223 Otter St. (Box 2528), Banff, AB T1L 1C3. ℂ/fax **403/762-4811.** www.rockymtnbb.com. 10 units. C$100–C$170 double. Extra person C$15. Rates include breakfast. MC, V. *In room:* TV.

Inexpensive

HI-Banff Alpine Centre   With a mix of two-, four-, and six-bed rooms, this hostel is the most pleasant budget lodging in Banff. Couple and family rooms are available. Facilities include a recreation room, kitchen, laundry, and lounge with fireplace. Meals are available at Cougar Pete's Kitchen and Lookout; there's also an on-site pub. Reserve at least a month in advance in summer.

On Tunnel Mountain Rd., 1.6km (1 mile) west of Banff (P.O. Box 1358), Banff, AB T1L 1B3. ℂ **866/762-4122** or 403/760-7580. Fax 403/762-3441. www.hihostels.ca. 216 beds. Bunks C$28–C$34 members, C$32–C$38 nonmembers; private rooms C$89–C$132 members, C$97–C$140 nonmembers. MC, V. **Amenities:** Restaurant; bike rental; access to health club across the street; Wi-Fi. *In room:* No phone.

Where to Dine

Food is generally good in Banff, although you pay handsomely for what you get. The difference in price between a simply okay meal in a theme restaurant and a nice meal in a classy dining room can be quite small. Service is often indifferent, as many restaurant staff members have become used to waiting on the in-and-out-in-a-hurry tour-bus crowds. An abundance of eateries line **Banff Avenue,** and most hotels have at least one dining room. The following recommendations are just the beginning of what's available in a very concentrated area.

Expensive

Bison Mountain Bistro & General Store CANADIAN   This recently opened two-story restaurant in downtown Banff has developed a loyal following for its "Rocky Mountain comfort food." On the ground floor is the "general store," a small deli with a good selection of meats and cheeses plus a variety of canned house-made pickles and relishes to purchase as gifts: This is a good spot for a lunchtime sandwich. The atmosphere changes as you climb the stairs to the dining room, dominated by an open kitchen and cathedral ceilings, with a pleasant side deck. As you'd expect in a restaurant named Bison, game meat reigns. There's a choice of bison striploin or a daily venison special, in addition to a smoked bison pizza and ginger venison wontons, though for those interested in sources of protein that didn't start off as wildlife, there are lighter dishes. Grilled halibut is served with roasted forest mushrooms, and roast chicken *suprêmes* come with honeyed carrot puree and toasted almond and apple salad.

211 Bear St. ℂ **403/762-5550.** www.thebison.ca. Reservations available. Main courses C$25–C$45. MC, V. Mon–Fri 5–10pm; Sat–Sun 10am–10pm.

Maple Leaf Grille & Lounge ★★★NEW CANADIAN   This excellent restaurant serves innovative Pan-Canadian cuisine based on Canadian produce and meats, particularly game. For regionally focused fine dining, the Maple Leaf is tops in Banff. The dining rooms and bar, all wood-paneled with river-rock columns, occupy two stories in the very center of Banff, and are linked by a long, open staircase. The seasonally changing menu is large and, unlike the meat-heavy lists typical in the Rockies, offers plenty of fish, seafood, and options for smaller appetites. The highly recommended house specialty is seared organic bison tenderloin, wrapped with double-smoked bacon and sprinkled with local blue cheese crumbles. Vegetarians aren't forgotten, either: Eggplant with forest mushroom ragout is a hearty match for any of the meat dishes. The 600-vintage-strong wine list is equally impressive.

137 Banff Ave. ✆ **403/760-7680.** www.banffmapleleaf.com. Reservations suggested. C$17–C$42. AE, MC, V. Daily 11am–4pm and 5–10pm.

Sleeping Buffalo Restaurant ★★NEW CANADIAN   One of the most pleasing restaurants in Banff, the dining room at the Buffalo Mountain Lodge occupies half of the lodge's soaring, three-story lobby, set in a quiet wooded location just outside town. As satisfying as all this is to the eye and the spirit, the food here is even more notable. The chef brings together the best of regional ingredients—Alberta beef, lamb, pheasant, venison, trout, and B.C. salmon—and prepares each in a seasonally changing, contemporary style. Roasted wild salmon with rhubarb maple compote and citrus couscous was one evening's standout. The fireplace-dominated bar is a lovely place for an intimate cocktail.

1.5km (1 mile) west of Banff on Tunnel Mountain Rd. ✆ **403/762-2400.** www.buffalomountainlodge. com. Reservations recommended on weekends. Main courses C$26–C$39. AE, DC, MC, V. Daily 7am–10pm.

Moderate

Balkan Restaurant GREEK   You'll find this airy blue-and-white dining room up a flight of stairs, with windows overlooking the street below. The fare consists of reliable Hellenic favorites, well prepared and served with a flourish; pasta and steaks are available as well. The Greek platter for two consists of a small mountain of beef souvlaki, ribs, moussaka, lamb chops, tomatoes, and salad. If you're dining alone, you can't do better than the *lagos stifado* (rabbit stew) with onions and red wine.

120 Banff Ave. ✆ **403/762-3454.** www.banffbalkan.ca. Reservations recommended. Main courses C$12–C$25. AE, MC, V. Daily 11am–11pm.

Coyotes Deli & Grill ★ SOUTHWEST/MEDITERRANEAN   One of the few places in Banff where you can find lighter, healthier food, Coyotes is an attractive bistro-like restaurant with excellent contemporary Southwestern cuisine. There's a broad selection of vegetarian dishes, as well as fresh fish, grilled meats, and multiethnic dishes prepared with an eye to spices and full flavors. There's also a deli, where you can get the makings for a picnic and head to the park. This is a very popular place, so go early or make reservations if you don't want to stand in line.

206 Caribou St. ✆ **403/762-3963.** http://coyotesbanff.com. Reservations recommended. Main courses C$14–C$25. AE, DC, MC, V. Daily 7:30am–11pm.

Magpie & Stump Restaurant & Cantina MEXICAN   The false-fronted Magpie & Stump doesn't really match up architecturally with the rest of smart downtown Banff—and neither do the food and atmosphere, thank goodness. The food here is traditional Mexican and Tex-Mex, done up with style and heft: Someone in the kitchen sure knows how to handle a tortilla. This isn't high cuisine, just well-prepared favorites such as enchiladas, tamales, tacos, and the like. Barbecued ribs and chicken are also delicious. Meals are well-priced for Banff, and you won't leave hungry. The interior looks like a dark and cozy English pub, except for the buffalo heads and cactus plants everywhere—plus a lot of Southwest kitsch. The Cantina is a good place for a lively late-night drink, as the town's young summer waitstaff likes to pack in here to unwind with an after-shift beverage—usually a beer served in a jam jar.

203 Caribou St. (C) **403/762-4067.** Reservations accepted for groups of 10 or more. Main courses C$10–C$24. AE, MC, V. Daily noon–2am.

Inexpensive

If you're really on a budget, you'll probably get used to the deli case at **Safeway,** at Martin and Elk streets, as even inexpensive food is costly here. There's also a food court in the basement of **Cascade Plaza Mall,** at Banff and Wolf streets. Another favorite for cheap and quick food is **Evelyn's Coffee Bar,** 201 Banff Ave. ((C) **403/762-0352**), for great home-baked muffins and rolls. The **Jump Start Coffee and Sandwich Place,** 206 Buffalo St. ((C) **403/762-0332**), offers sandwiches, soup, salads, pastries, and picnics to go. For all-day and all-night pizza, head to **Aardvark Pizza,** 304A Caribou St. ((C) **403/762-5500**), open daily to 4am.

Bruno's Cafe and Grill CANADIAN   Named for Bruno Engler, a famed outdoor guide and photographer, Bruno's serves burgers, pizza, wraps, and hearty Canadian-style entrees—all best washed down with locally brewed draft beer. This cozy and casual little joint is open late, a rarity in Banff.

304 Caribou St. (C) **403/762-8115.** Reservations not accepted. Main courses C$8–C$15. MC, V. Daily 7am–1am.

Melissa's Restaurant and Bar CANADIAN   Banff's original hostelries weren't all as grand as the Banff Springs hotel. There was also the Homestead Inn, established in the 1910s, with its much-loved restaurant, Melissa's. The original hotel has been replaced with a more modern structure, but the half-timbered cabin that houses Melissa's remains. The food has been updated over the course of the last century, but old-fashioned, traditionally Canadian foods still dominate the menu. Breakfasts are famed, especially the apple hot cakes. Lunch and dinner brings burgers, sandwiches, local trout, and steaks.

218 Lynx St. (C) **403/762-5511.** Reservations recommended. Main courses C$8–C$27. AE, MC, V. Daily 7am–10pm.

Banff After Dark

Most larger hotels and restaurants offer some form of nightly entertainment. However, for a more lively selection, head to downtown's Banff Avenue.

One of the best spots is the legendary **Wild Bill's Saloon,** 203 Banff Ave. ((C) **403/762-0333**), where you can watch tourists in cowboy hats learning to line dance. Alt-rock bands dominate on Monday and Tuesday evenings; Wednesday to Saturday, it's all country rock, all the time. The venerable **Rose and Crown Pub,** 202 Banff Ave. ((C) **403/762-2121**), used to be the only place to hear live music in Banff. It's still one of the best. Bands range from Celtic to folk to rock. In summer, sit on the rooftop bar and watch the stars. Another popular spot is the **Elk and Oarsman,** upstairs at 119 Banff Ave. ((C) **403/762-4616**), a friendly pub with a good selection of draught beers and live music on the weekends.

It took the ultra-cool cocktail lounge format a while to reach Banff, but here it is: **Aurora,** 110 Banff Ave. (© **403/760-5300**). Dance nightly to DJ-spun rock while sipping something delicious in a martini glass. Banff's most popular dance club, **HooDoo Lounge,** 137 Banff Ave. (© **403/762-8434**), is in the basement of the old King Eddy Hotel. DJs spin the tunes while young white-water guides chat and dance with impressionable young tourists. Thursday night is ladies' night.

LAKE LOUISE ★★★

Deep-green Lake Louise, 56km (35 miles) northwest of Banff and surrounded by snow-capped mountains, is one of the most famed beauty spots in a park renowned for its scenery. Lake Louise, in the valley below, boasts the largest ski area in Canada and easy hiking access to the remote high country along the Continental Divide.

The lake and the skiing may be spectacular, but probably as many people wind up the road to Lake Louise to see its most famous resort, the **Chateau Lake Louise** (p. 397). Built by the Canadian Pacific Railroad, the Chateau is, along with the **Fairmont Banff Springs** hotel (p. 390), one of the most celebrated hotels in Canada. More than just a lodging, this storybook castle—perched a mile high in the Rockies—is the center of recreation, dining, shopping, and entertainment for the Lake Louise area.

In case you were wondering, there's a reason the water in Lake Louise is so green: The stream water that tumbles into the lake is filled with minerals, ground by the glaciers that hang above the lake. Sunlight refracts off the glacial "flour," creating vivid colors. You'll want to at least stroll around the shore and gawk at the glaciers and the massive Chateau. The gentle **Lakeshore Trail** follows the northern shore to the end of Lake Louise. If you're looking for more exercise and even better views, continue on the trail as it begins to climb. Now called the **Plain of Six Glaciers Trail** ★ it passes a teahouse 5km (3.1 miles) from the Chateau, and is open in summer only, on its way to a tremendous viewpoint over Victoria Glacier and Lake Louise.

Seeing the Sights

The **Lake Louise Summer Sightseeing Lift** (© 403/522-3555) offers a 14-minute ride up to 2,088m (6,850 ft.) on Mt. Whitehorn, midway up the Lake Louise Ski Area. From here, the views of Lake Louise and the mountains along the Continental Divide are magnificent. Hikers can follow one of many trails into alpine meadows, visit the Wildlife Interpretation Centre, or join a free naturalist-led walk to explore the delicate ecosystem. Round-trip on the lift costs C$26 for adults, and C$13 for children ages 6 to 15. The lift operates from mid-May to late September. At the base, the Lodge of Ten Peaks offers buffet dining: Ride-and-dine packages are available.

To many visitors, **Moraine Lake** ★★is even more beautiful than Lake Louise, its more famous twin. Ten spirelike peaks, each over 3,000m (9,843 ft.) high, rise precipitously from the shores of this tiny gem-blue lake. It's an unforgettable sight, and definitely worth the short 13km (8-mile) drive from Lake Louise. A trail follows the lake's north shore to the mountain cliffs. There's also the **Moraine Lake Lodge** (© 403/522-3733; fax 403/522-3719; www.morainelake.com), which offers rooms, meals, and canoe rentals.

Where to Stay

Lake Louise is an expensive place to spend the night—let's face it: It's costly to run a hotel within view of the Continental Divide. A lesser-priced option is the **Lake Louise Hostel,** on Village Road, Box 115, Lake Louise, AB T0L 1E0 (© **866/762-4122** or 403/522-2202; www.hihostels.ca). Jointly owned by Hostelling International and the Alpine Club

Baker Creek Lodge ★   Secluded and rustic, Baker Creek Lodge offers log-built lodge, cabin, and chalet accommodations just off the quiet Bow Valley Parkway (Hwy. 1A). This very charming, family-owned resort sits right on the banks of Baker Creek amid firs and pines, and is the perfect destination for families who want their memories of Banff park to be of mountains and woods, not the shops of Banff townsite. Accommodations range from top-of-the-line one-bedroom Trapper's Cabins with wood-burning fireplace, double Jacuzzi, and a gas barbecue on the porch, to a selection of large chalets and suites that can comfortably sleep six. Call ahead and discuss your needs with the staff, as there are a number of room configurations; all have fireplaces, full or efficiency kitchens, decks, and locally built pine furniture.

Hwy. 1A, 15km (9¹/₃ miles) east of Lake Louise, P.O. Box 66, Lake Louise, AB T0L 1E0. ✆ **403/522-3761.** Fax 403/522-2270. www.bakercreek.com. 33 units. C$290–C$365 double cabin or chalet; C$235–C$335 suite. Reduced off-season rates. AE, MC, V. **Amenities:** Restaurant; lounge; exercise room; sauna; steam room. *In room:* Kitchen, no phone, fireplace.

Deer Lodge   Built in the 1920s, the original Deer Lodge was a teahouse for the early mountaineers who came to the area to hike (the original tearoom is now the Mount Fairview Dining Room and bar, offering Northwest cuisine). Although Lake Louise itself is a 3-minute stroll away, the charming Deer Lodge features a sense of privacy and solitude that the busy Chateau Lake Louise can't offer. Choose from three eras of rooms: small, basic rooms in the original lodge; larger rooms in the newer Tower Wing; and Heritage Rooms, the largest rooms in the newest wing. All are unfussy and comfortable, though it's the handsome common rooms, particularly the bar and the log-and-stone sitting room, that will create memories.

109 Lake Louise Dr., Lake Louise (P.O. Box 1598), Banff, AB T0L 0C0. ✆ **800/661-1595** or 403/522-3747. Fax 403/522-4222. www.crmr.com. 73 units. C$100–C$195 double. AE, MC, V. **Amenities:** Restaurant; lounge; rooftop Jacuzzi; sauna.

The Fairmont Chateau Lake Louise ★★★   The Chateau Lake Louise is one of the best-loved hotels in North America—and one of the most expensive. If you want to splurge on only one place in the Canadian Rockies, make it this one—you won't be sorry. This massive, formal structure is blue-roofed and turreted, furnished with Edwardian sumptuousness and alpine charm. Built in stages over the course of a century by the Canadian Pacific Railroad, the entire hotel was remodeled and upgraded in 1990, and now stays open year-round. The cavernous grand lobby, with its curious figurative chandeliers, gives way to a sitting room filled with overstuffed chairs and couches; these and other common areas overlook the Chateau's gardens and the deep blue-green lake in its glacier-hung cirque. The guest rooms' marble-tiled bathrooms, crystal barware, and comfy down duvets are indicative of the attention to detail and luxury you can expect here. The Chateau can sometimes feel like Grand Central Station—so many guests and so many visitors crowding into the hotel. But the guest rooms are truly sumptuous and the service highly professional.

Lake Louise, AB T0L 1E0. ✆ **800/441-1414** or 403/522-3511. Fax 403/522-3834. www.fairmont.com. 513 units. High season C$449–C$599 double; C$649–C$1,449 suite. Rates vary depending on whether you want a view of the lake or mountains. Off-season rates and packages available. Children 16 and under stay free in parent's room. AE, DC, DISC, MC, V. Parking C$24 per day. **Amenities:** 9 restaurants in high season, including the exquisite Fairview Room and the jolly Walliser Stube Wine Bar (see "Where to Dine," below); 2 bars; babysitting; bike rental; concierge; concierge-level rooms; exercise room; health club; Jacuzzi; indoor pool; room service; sauna; canoe rental. *In room:* A/C, TV, hair dryer, minibar, Wi-Fi.

Lake Louise Inn (Value)   The Lake Louise Inn stands in a wooded 3-hectare (7-acre) estate at the base of the moraine, 7 driving minutes from the fabled lake, with some of the most affordable rooms in the area. The inn consists of five different buildings—a central lodge with pool, whirlpool, steam room, restaurant, bar, and lounge, and four additional lodging units. There are nine different room types, starting with standard units with double beds and moving up to luxurious suites. All the rooms are nicely furnished, but the Economy Twin and the Superior Queen rooms are eminently affordable, particularly if booked in advance. For families, the loft suites are capable of sleeping up to eight, with two separate bedrooms, two bathrooms, full kitchen, living room, fireplace, and a fold-out couch—just the ticket for a big group.

210 Village Rd. (P.O. Box 209), Lake Louise, AB T0L 1E0. (*) **800/661-9237** or 403/522-3791. Fax 403/522-2018. www.lakelouiseinn.com. 247 units. High season C$139–C$319 double. AE, DC, MC, V. Free parking. **Amenities:** Restaurant; bar; Jacuzzi; pool; sauna. *In room:* TV, fridge, hair dryer, Wi-Fi, microwave.

Post Hotel and Spa ★★★   Discreetly elegant and beautifully furnished, this wonderful log hotel with a distinctive red roof began its life in 1942 as a humble ski lodge. In the 1990s, new owners completely rebuilt the old lodge, transforming it into one of the most luxurious getaways in the Canadian Rockies, and a member of the French network, Relais & Châteaux. Hospitality and service here are top-notch. The entire lodge is built of traditional log-and-beam construction, preserving the rustic flavor of the old structure and its mountain setting. The public rooms are lovely, from the renowned dining room (preserved intact from the original hotel) to the arched, two-story, wood-paneled library to the full-service Temple Mountain Spa.

Accommodations throughout are beautifully furnished with rustic pine pieces and rich upholstery. Most units have stone fireplaces, balconies, and whirlpool tubs. Due to the rambling nature of the property, there are a bewildering 14 different layouts available, so call and discuss your needs to ensure you get the perfect room.

P.O. Box 69, Lake Louise, AB T0L 1E0. (*) **800/661-1586** or 403/522-3989. Fax 403/522-3966. www.posthotel.com. 98 units. High season C$345–C$455 double; C$585–C$850 suite; C$390–C$760 cabin. AE, MC, V. Closed mid-Oct to late Nov. **Amenities:** Restaurant (see "Where to Dine," below); 2 bars; Jacuzzi; indoor pool; sauna; full spa. *In room:* TV/VCR, hair dryer, Wi-Fi.

Where to Dine

Lake Louise Station STEAKS/SEAFOOD   This handsome and historic log building served as the Lake Louise train station for nearly a century, before rail service ceased in the 1980s. Guests now dine in the old waiting room, or enjoy a quiet drink in the old ticketing lobby. Two dining cars sit on the sidings beside the station and are open for fine dining in the evening (usually weekends only). The most popular dish is New York steak with Cognac and green peppercorn sauce, though seared salmon filet Provençal provides a delicious change of pace.

200 Sentinel Rd. (*) **403/522-2600.** Reservations recommended on weekends. Pizzas C$15; steaks and seafood C$16–C$34. AE, MC, V. Daily 11:30am–midnight.

Post Hotel Dining Room ★★★ INTERNATIONAL   Let's face it: Your trip through the Canadian Rockies is costing you a lot more than you planned. But don't start economizing on food just yet because the Post Hotel offers some of the finest dining in western Canada. Guests dine in a long, rustic room with wood beams and windows looking out onto glaciered peaks. The menu focuses on full-flavored meat and fish preparations. For an appetizer, you might try carpaccio of ahi tuna and sea scallops, and move on to buffalo strip loin with blackberry maple-syrup butter and corn fritters. Desserts are equally imaginative, and service is excellent. With 30,000 bottles in the wine cellar, some good values are discreetly hidden in the (mostly French) selection (the 1,800-bottle wine list received the "Grand Award" from *Wine Spectator,* one of only a handful of Canadian restaurants to win such an honor).

In the Post Hotel, Lake Louise. ✆ **403/522-3989.** www.posthotel.com. Reservations required. Main courses C$36–C$49. AE, MC, V. Daily 7–11am, 11:30am–2pm, and 5–10pm.

Walliser Stube Wine Bar ★ SWISS   While the Chateau Lake Louise operates four major restaurants, including the formal Fairview Room, the most fun and relaxing place to eat is the Walliser Stube, a small dining room that serves excellent Swiss-style food and some of the best fondue ever. The back dining room is called the Library, and is indeed lined with tall and imposing wood cases and rolling library ladders. Happily, the cases are filled with wine, not books. A meal in the Walliser Stube is an evening's worth of eating and drinking, as the best foods—a variety of fondues and raclettes—make for convivial and communal dining experiences. The cheese fondue is fabulous; forget the stringy glutinous experience that was a hallmark of the 1970s and give it another chance. Raclettes are another communal operation, involving heat lamps that melt chunks of cheese until bubbly; the aromatic, molten result is spread on bread. If hot cheese isn't your thing, the Walliser Stube also offers more traditional meat and chicken preparations. It's all great fun in a great atmosphere—go with friends and have a blast.

In Chateau Lake Louise. ✆ **403/522-1817.** Reservations required. Main courses C$18–C$36; fondues for 2 C$33–C$48. AE, DISC, MC, V. Daily 5–11:30pm.

THE ICEFIELDS PARKWAY ★★★

Between Lake Louise and Jasper winds one of the most spectacular mountain roads in the world. Called the Icefields Parkway, the road climbs through three deep river valleys, beneath soaring, glacier-notched mountains, and past dozens of hornlike peaks shrouded with permanent snowfields. Capping this 287km (178-mile) route is the **Columbia Icefield,** a massive dome of glacial ice and snow straddling the top of the continent. From this mighty cache of ice—the largest nonpolar ice cap in the world—flow the Columbia, the Athabasca, and the North Saskatchewan rivers.

Although you can drive the Icefields Parkway in 3 hours, plan to take enough time to stop at eerily green lakes, hike to a waterfall, and take an excursion up onto the Columbia Icefields. There's also a good chance that you'll see wildlife: ambling bighorn sheep, mountain goats, elks with huge shovel antlers, and mama bears with cubs—all guaranteed to halt traffic and set cameras clicking.

After Lake Louise, the highway divides: Hwy. 1 continues west toward Golden, British Columbia, while Hwy. 93 (the Icefields Pkwy.) continues north along the Bow River. **Bow Lake,** the river's source, glimmers below enormous **Crowfoot Glacier;** when the glacier was named, a third "toe" was more in evidence, lending a resemblance to a bird's claw. **Num-Ti-Jah Lodge,** on the shores of Bow Lake, is a good place to stop for lunch and to take some photographs; it also offers accommodations in traditional guest rooms.

The road mounts Bow Summit and drops into the North Saskatchewan River drainage. Stop at the **Peyto Lake Viewpoint** and hike up a short but steep trail to glimpse this startling blue-green body of water.

The parkway then begins to climb up in earnest toward the Sunwapta Pass. Here, in the shadows of 3,490m (11,450-ft.) **Mount Athabasca,** the icy tendrils of the **Columbia Icefields** come into view. However impressive these glaciers may seem from the road, they're nothing compared to the massive amounts of centuries-old ice and snow hidden by mountain peaks; the Columbia Icefields cover nearly 518 sq. km (200 sq. miles) and are more than 760m (2,493 ft.) thick. From the parkway, the closest fingers of the icefield are **Athabasca Glacier,** which fills the horizon to the west of the **Columbia Icefields Centre** (© 780/852-7032), a recently rebuilt lodge with a restaurant open from 8am to 10pm and the **Glaicier View Inn** (© 780/852-6550 Apr–Oct; © 403/762-7431 Nov–Mar) with double rooms starting at C$235. The **Icefields Information Centre** (© 780/852-7030), a park service office that answers questions about the area, stands beside the lodge. It's open May 1 to June 14 daily from 9am to 5pm, June 15 to September 7 daily from 9am to 6pm, and September 8 to October 15 daily from 9am to 5pm. It is closed October 16 to April 30.

From the **Brewster Snocoach Tours** ticket office (© 403/762-6735), specially designed buses take visitors out onto the glacier. The 90-minute excursion includes a chance to hike the surface of Athabasca Glacier. The Snocoach Tour is C$49 for adults and C$24 for children. If you don't have the time for the tour, you can drive to the toe of the glacier and walk up onto its surface. Use extreme caution when on the glacier; accidents can result in broken limbs or even death.

From the Columbia Icefields, the parkway descends steeply into the Athabasca River drainage. From the parking area for **Sunwapta Falls,** travelers can choose to crowd around the chain-link fence and peer at this turbulent falls, or take the half-hour hike to equally impressive but less crowded Lower Sunwapta Falls. **Athabasca Falls,** farther north along the parkway, is another must-see. Here, the wide and powerful Athabasca River constricts into a roaring torrent before dropping 25m (82 ft.) into a narrow canyon. A mist-covered bridge crosses the chasm just beyond the falls; a series of trails leads to more viewpoints. The parkway continues along the Athabasca River, through a landscape of meadows and lakes, before entering the Jasper Townsite.

Where to Stay

Facilities are few along the parkway. Hikers and bikers will be pleased to know that there are **rustic hostels** at Mosquito Creek, Rampart Creek, Hilda Creek, Beauty Creek, Athabasca Falls, and Mount Edith Cavell. Reservations for all Icefields Parkway hostels can be made by calling © 866/762-4122. A shuttle runs between the Calgary International Hostel and hostels in Banff, Lake Louise, and along the Icefields Parkway to Jasper. You must have reservations at the destination hostel to use the service. Call © 403/283-5551 for details.

Simpson's Num-Ti-Jah Lodge Many Rocky Mountain hotels are newly constructed to look vintage—Num-Ti-Jah Lodge is the real thing. Sitting on the edge of Bow Lake, with a view of glaciers and soaring peaks to rival that at Lake Louise, this beloved lodge with a bright red roof had its beginnings when pioneering outfitter Jimmy Simpson stood on this site in 1898 and vowed one day to "build a shack here." Over the next 50 years, Simpson and his family did just that, though the handsome log-and-stone lodge now presiding over this astonishing vista is quite a bit more than a shack. Num-Ti-Jah Lodge (from a First Nations word for pine marten) breathes frontier tradition with its huge stone fireplaces, stuffed moose heads and antlers on the log walls, and cozy library and lounge areas amply supplied with comfy chairs and couches. Num-Ti-Jah is best for those who appreciate the heritage of a traditional lodge: Some will be charmed; others will consider this roughing it. Don't expect upscale guest rooms; though they are clean and nicely furnished, they are authentic to the period in which they were built. All but five rooms have private bathrooms. The dining room is a wonderful spot for lunch, and three-course dinners are available for C$65 in addition to a la carte dining.

40km (25 miles) north of Lake Louise on Hwy. 93 (P.O. Box 39), Lake Louise, AB T0L 1E0. © **403/522-2167.** Fax 403/522-2425. www.num-ti-jah.com. 25 units. C$195–C$300 double. Extra person C$15. MC, V. Closed mid-Oct to early Dec. **Amenities:** Restaurant; lounge w/pool table. *In room:* No phone.

4 JASPER NATIONAL PARK

Jasper Townsite: 287km (178 miles) NW of Banff

Jasper, now Canada's largest mountain park, was established in 1907, although it already boasted a "guesthouse" of sorts in the 1840s. A visiting painter described it as "composed of two rooms of about 14 and 15 feet square. One of them is used by all comers and goers, Indians, voyageurs and traders, men, women, and children being huddled together indiscriminately, the other room being devoted to the exclusive occupation of Colin Fraser (postmaster) and his family."

Things have changed. Slightly less busy than Banff to the south, Jasper National Park attracts a much more outdoors-oriented crowd, with hiking, biking, climbing, horseback riding, and rafting the main activities. Sure, there's shopping and fine dining in Jasper, but it's not the focus of activity as it is in Banff. Travelers seem a bit more determined and rugged-looking, as if they've just stumbled in from a long-distance hiking trail or off the face of a rock.

For more information on the park, contact **Jasper National Park,** P.O. Box 10, Jasper, AB T0E 1E0 (© **780/852-6176;** www.pc.gc.ca).

SPORTS & OUTDOOR ACTIVITIES IN THE PARK

The **Jasper Adventure Centre,** 604 Connaught Dr. (© **800/565-7547** in western Canada, or 780/852-5595; www.jasperadventurecentre.com), is a clearinghouse of local outfitters and guides. White-water rafting and canoeing trips, horseback rides, guided hikes, and other activities can be arranged out of this office, which is open June 1 to October 1 daily from 9am to 9pm.

A number of shops rent most of the equipment you'll need. Mountain bikes, canoes and rafts, tents, fishing gear, and skis are available for rent from **On-Line Sport and Tackle,** 600 Patricia St. (© **780/852-3630**), which can also set you up on guided rafting and fishing trips. Snowboards, cross-country ski equipment, and more bikes are available from **Freewheel Cycle,** 618 Patricia St. (© **780/852-3898**).

FISHING **Currie's Guiding** (© **780/852-5650;** www.curriesguidingjasper.com) conducts fishing trips to Maligne Lake; the trips begin at C$189 per person (minimum two persons) for an 8-hour day. Tackle, bait, boat, and lunch are included. Ask about special single and group rates. Patricia and Pyramid lakes, north of Jasper, are more convenient to Jasper-based anglers who fancy trying their luck at trout fishing.

HIKING Overnight and long-distance hikers will find an abundance of backcountry trails around Jasper, reaching into some of the most spectacular scenery in the Canadian Rockies. Day hikers have fewer, but still good, choices.

The complex of trails around **Maligne Canyon** ★ makes a good choice for a group, as there are a number of access points (across six different footbridges). The less keen can make the loop back and meet fellow hikers (after getting the car) farther down the canyon. Trails ring parklike Beauvert and Annette lakes (the latter is wheelchair accessible), both near Jasper Park Lodge. Likewise, Pyramid and Patricia lakes just north of town have loop trails but more of a backcountry atmosphere.

The brochure *Day Hikers' Guide to Jasper National Park* details dozens of hikes throughout the park. It costs C$2 at the visitor center. Several outfitters lead guided hikes; contact **Jasper Park Lodge Mountaineering and Interpretive Hiking** (© 780/852-3301) or **Walk and Talks Jasper** (© 780/852-4945; www.walksntalks. com) for a selection of half- and full-day hikes.

HORSEBACK RIDING One of the most exhilarating experiences the park can offer is trail riding. Guides take your riding prowess (or lack of it) into account and select trails slow enough to keep you mounted. The horses used are steady, reliable animals not given to sudden antics. For a short ride, call **Pyramid Stables** (© 780/852-7433), which offers 1- to 3-hour trips (C$40–C$85) around Pyramid and Patricia lakes.

Long-distance trail rides take you into the backcountry. **Skyline Trail Rides** (© 888/582-7787 or 780/852-4215; www.skylinetrail.com) offers a number of short day trips costing roughly C$40 per hour, as well as 3- to 4-day trips to a remote, albeit modernized, lodge. Sleigh rides are offered in winter.

RAFTING Jasper is the jumping-off point for float and white-water trips down several rivers. A raft trip is a good option for that inevitable drizzly day, as you're going to get wet anyway. The mild rapids (Class II–III) of the Athabasca River make a good introductory trip, with rates starting at C$55 for adults, children under 13 half price. Wilder runs down the Maligne River (Class III) will appeal to those needing something to brag about. Jasper is loaded with rafting outfitters; ask your hotel concierge for assistance, or call **Maligne River Adventures** (© 780/852-3370; www.mra.ab.ca), which offers trips down both rivers, as well as a 3-day wilderness trip on the Kakwa River (Class IV-plus). Most trips include equipment and transportation.

SKIING Jasper's downhill ski area is **Ski Marmot Basin** (© 780/852-3816; www. skimarmot.com), located 19km (12 miles) west of Jasper on Hwy. 93. Marmot is generally underrated as a ski resort; it doesn't get the crowds of Banff, nor does it get the infamous Chinook winds. The resort has 86 runs and eight lifts, and rarely any lines. Lift tickets start at C$72.

GETTING AROUND THE PARK

Some of the principal outfitters and guides also offer transportation to outlying park beauty spots. Leaving from Jasper, organized tours of the park's major sites—notably the Athabasca snowfields (C$110) and a Maligne Lake cruise (C$85)—are offered by **Brewster** (© 780/852-3332; www.brewster.ca) and **Maligne Tours** (© 780/852-3370; www.malignelake.com).

JASPER TOWNSITE

Jasper isn't Banff, and to listen to most residents of Jasper, that's just fine with them. Born as a railroad division point, Jasper Townsite lacks its southern neighbor's glitz and slightly precious air of an internationalized alpine fantasyland. Instead, it gives off a lived-in, community-oriented feel that's largely lacking in Banff. The streets are thronged with avid young hikers and mountain bikers rather than the shopping hordes. The people you meet in town may be a little muddy or wet, as if they've just gotten in from the river or the mountain. Chances are they have.

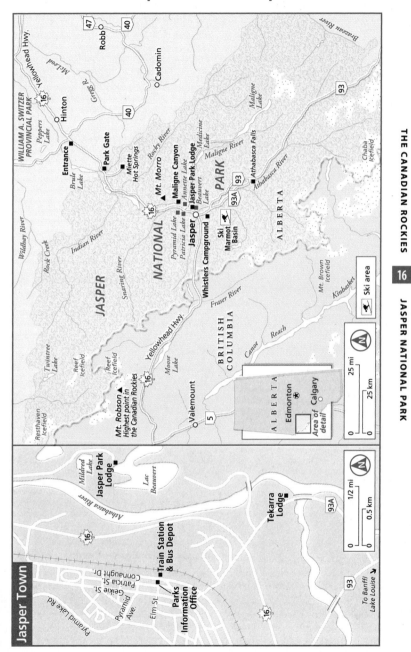

However, development is rapidly approaching: New nightclubs, restaurants, and shops geared toward tourists are springing up along Patricia Street, and that sound you hear in the distance is the thunder of tour buses.

Essentials

GETTING THERE Jasper is on the Yellowhead Highway System, linking it with Vancouver, Prince George, and Edmonton—and is therefore an important transportation hub. The town is 287km (178 miles) northwest of Banff.

VIA Rail connects Jasper to Vancouver and Edmonton with three trains weekly; the *Skeena* line connects with Prince George and Prince Rupert on the Pacific coast. The train station (② 780/852-4102) is at the town center, along Connaught Street. Also headquartered at the train station is the **Greyhound** bus station (② 780/852-3926) and **Brewster Transportation** (② 780/852-3332), which offers express service to Banff, as well as a large number of sightseeing excursions.

VISITOR INFORMATION For information on the townsite, contact **Jasper Tourism and Commerce,** P.O. Box 98, Jasper, AB T0E 1E0 (② 780/852-3858; www.jasper canadianrockies.com).

TOWN LAYOUT Jasper Townsite is much smaller than Banff. The main street, **Connaught Drive,** runs alongside the Canadian National Railway tracks, and is the address of the majority of Jasper's hotels. **Patricia Street,** a block west, is the boutique street, lined with shops and cafes. Right in the center of town, surrounded by delightful shady gardens, is the **Parks Information Offices** (② 780/852-6146). The post office is at the corner of Patricia and Elm streets. At the northern end of Connaught and Geike streets, a half-kilometer (⅓-mile) from downtown, is another complex of hotels.

GETTING AROUND For a rental car, contact **National,** 607 Connaught Dr. (② 780/852-1117). Call a taxi at ② 780/852-5558 or 780/852-3600.

Exploring Jasper & Environs

Just northeast of Jasper, off the Jasper Park Lodge access road, the Maligne River drops from its high mountain valley to cut an astounding canyon into a steep limestone face on its way to meet the Athabasca River. The chasm of **Maligne Canyon** is up to 46m (151 ft.) deep at points, yet only 3m (9¾ ft.) across. A sometimes-steep trail follows the canyon down the mountainside, bridging the gorge six times. In summer, a teahouse operates at the top.

An incredibly blue mountain lake buttressed by a ring of high-flying peaks, **Maligne Lake** is 45 minutes east of Jasper and is one of the park's great beauty spots. Maligne is the largest glacier-fed lake in the Rockies, and the second largest in the world. The local First Nations people, who called the lake Chaba Imne, had a superstitious awe of the region. White settlers didn't discover Maligne until 1908.

Today, droves of tour buses go to the "hidden lake," and the area is a popular destination for hikers, anglers, trail riders, and rafters. No matter what else they do, most visitors take a boat cruise to **Spirit Island,** at the head of the lake. The 90-minute cruise leaves from below the **Maligne Lake Lodge,** an attractive summer-only facility with a restaurant, bar, and gift shop (but no lodging). Cruise tickets cost C$55 for adults, half-price for kids 6 to 12.

Maligne Lake waters are alive with rainbow and eastern brook trout, and the Maligne Lake Boathouse is stocked with licenses, tackle, bait, and boats. Guided **fishing** trips include equipment, lunch, and hotel transportation, with half-day excursions starting at

C$199 per person for two or more, or C$349 solo. You can rent a boat, canoe, or sea kayak to ply the waters. All facilities at Maligne Lake, including lake cruises, fishing, trail rides, and a white-water raft outfitter that offers trips down three Jasper Park rivers, are operated by **Maligne Tours** (www.malignelake.com). Offices are located at the lake, next to the lodge in Jasper at 626 Connaught Dr. (© **780/852-3370**) and at the Jasper Park Lodge (© **780/852-4779**). Maligne Tours also operates a shuttle bus between Jasper and the lake.

Downstream from Maligne Lake, the Maligne River flows into **Medicine Lake.** This large body of water appears regularly every spring, grows 8km (5 miles) long and 18m (59 ft.) deep, and then vanishes in fall through a system of underground drainage caves, leaving only a dry gravel bed through the winter. According to First Nations belief, spirits were responsible for the lake's annual disappearance, hence the name.

Jasper Tramway ★   This aerial gondola tour starts at the foot of Whistler's Mountain, 6km (3¾ miles) south of Jasper off Hwy. 93. Each car takes 30 passengers (plus baby carriages, wheelchairs, and the family dog) and hoists them 2km (1¼ miles) up to the 2,250m (7,382-ft.) summit in a breathtaking sky ride. At the upper terminal, you'll step out into alpine tundra, the region above the tree line where some flowers take 25 years to blossom. A wonderful picnic area carpeted with mountain grass is alive with squirrels. You'll also see the "whistlers"—actually hoary marmots—that the mountain is named for. Combo tickets that include meals at the upper terminal's Treeline Restaurant are also available.

Off Hwy. 93, south of Jasper. © **780/852-3093.** www.jaspertramway.com. Tickets C$29 adults, C$15 children. Mid-Apr to mid-May and late Aug to mid-Oct daily 10am–5pm; mid-May to late June daily 9:30am–6:30pm; late June to late Aug daily 9am–8pm. Cars depart every 10–15 min. Closed mid-Oct to Apr.

Miette Hot Springs   The hot mineral water pools are only one reason to make the side trip to Miette Hot Springs. The drive is also one of the best wildlife-viewing routes in the park. Watch for elk, deer, coyotes, and moose en route. The springs can be enjoyed in a beautiful swimming pool or in two soaker pools (one is wheelchair accessible) surrounded by forest and an imposing mountain backdrop. Campgrounds and an attractive lodge with refreshments are nearby.

60km (37 miles) northeast of Jasper off Hwy. 16. © **780/866-3939.** Admission C$6.05 adults, C$5.15 children and seniors, C$18 family. Late June to Labour Day daily 9am–11pm; mid-May to late June and the day after Labour Day to early Oct daily 1–8pm; early Oct to mid-May Fri 6–9pm, Sat–Sun 1–9pm.

Shopping

Weather can be unpredictable in Jasper. If it's raining, you can while away an afternoon in the town's shops and boutiques—the town is especially rich in shops for outdoor gear and recreation clothing. In Jasper itself, Patricia Street and Connaught Drive contain most of the high-quality choices. A number of galleries feature Inuit and Native arts and crafts: Check out **Our Native Land,** 601 Patricia St. (© **780/852-5592**). The arcade at the Jasper Park Lodge, called the **Beauvert Promenade,** has a number of clothing and gift shops.

Where to Stay

As in Banff, there's a marked difference in rates between high season and the rest of the year, so if you can avoid the June-to-September crush, you may save up to 50%. All prices listed below are for high season. Call for off-season rates, as they usually follow a complex price structure. Reserve well in advance if possible. If you can't find a room, contact

Rocky Mountain Reservations (© **877/902-9455** or 780/852-9455; www.rocky mountainreservations.com), which offers a free booking service for Jasper accommodations and activities.

If you find the prices too astronomical in Jasper, or just can't find a room, consider staying east of the park near Hinton (see below).

Very Expensive

Best Western Jasper Inn ★ The Jasper Inn, on the northern end of town but set back off the main road, is one of the nicest lodgings in town, particularly after an extensive renovation in 2009. Rooms are available in three different buildings and in many configurations. If you're looking for good value, look past the standard units (which are perfectly nice); instead, fork over C$10 more and reserve a spacious one-bedroom suite with fireplace and kitchen. Even nicer are the rooms in the separate Maligne Suites building, which come with marble-and-granite bathrooms, fireplaces, Jacuzzis, and balconies. Two-bedroom chalet-style rooms can sleep up to seven.

98 Geikie St. (P.O. Box 879), Jasper, AB T0E 1E0. © **800/661-1933** or 780/852-4461. Fax 780/852-5916. www.jasperinn.com. 143 units. C$191–C$230 double; C$199–C$600 suite. Extra person C$15. Children 17 and under stay free in parent's room. AE, DC, MC, V. Free parking. **Amenities:** Restaurant; babysitting; Jacuzzi; small indoor pool; sauna. *In room:* TV, fridge, hair dryer, Wi-Fi, microwave.

Chateau Jasper This is one of the nicest of the newer lodgings north of downtown along Geikie Street. The guest rooms are large and comfortably furnished, and the indoor pool area is a jewel. Chateau Jasper is under new management, and all rooms are receiving upgrades, which should be complete by summer of 2010.

96 Geikie St., Jasper, AB T0E 1E0. © **800/852-7737** or 780/852-5644. Fax 780/852-4860. www.mpljasper.com. 119 units. From C$234 double. AE, DC, DISC, MC, V. Parking C$10 per day. **Amenities:** Restaurant; bar; concierge; Jacuzzi; indoor pool. *In room:* A/C, TV, hair dryer, Wi-Fi.

Fairmont Jasper Park Lodge ★★ Jasper's most exclusive lodging, the Jasper Park Lodge was built by the Canadian Pacific Railroad and has an air of luxury and gentility, but with a more woodsy feel—sort of like an upscale summer camp. The hotel's wooded, elk-inhabited grounds—over 360 hectares (890 acres)!—are located along Lac Beauvert, about 8km (5 miles) east of Jasper proper. The central lodge's lofty great room offers huge fireplaces to snuggle by. Accommodations are very comfortable, though a bit hard to characterize, as there are a wide variety of cabins, lodge rooms, chalets, and cottages available—all from different eras, all set amid the forest. It's a good idea to call and find out what suits your budget and needs. Groups can opt for one of the wonderful housekeeping cabins (some have eight bedrooms).

P.O. Box 40, Jasper, AB T0E 1E0. © **800/441-1414** or 780/852-3301. Fax 780/852-5107. www.fairmont.com. 446 units. C$499–C$599 double; C$679–C$799 suite. AE, DC, DISC, MC, V. Free parking. **Amenities:** 9 restaurants, including the 4-star Edith Cavell Dining Room and the Moose's Nook Northern Grill (see "Where to Dine," later in this chapter, for more on the latter); 3 lounges; babysitting; bike rentals; children's center; concierge; 1 of Canada's finest golf courses (Jasper Park Lodge Golf Course); health club; heated outdoor pool; room service; tennis courts; canoe and paddle-boat rentals; horseback riding. *In room:* TV w/pay movies, hair dryer, high-speed Internet access.

Lobstick Lodge (Kids) The Lobstick Lodge is a longtime favorite for the discerning traveler with an eye to value, with some of the largest standard units in Jasper. Even more impressive are the huge kitchen units, which come with a full kitchen, a sitting room with sofa bed and easy chairs, plus a separate bedroom with either two doubles or a king-size bed. As large as most apartments, these kitchen units are perfect for families and go fast—reserve early. King suites are also large and very comfortably furnished.

96 Geikie St. (P.O. Box 1200), Jasper, AB T0E 1E0. ✆ **888/852-7737** or 780/852-4431. Fax 780/852-4142. www.mpljasper.com. 139 units. From C$245 double; C$265 kitchen unit. Children 14 and under stay free in parent's room. AE, DC, MC, V. Free parking. **Amenities:** Restaurant; coffeeshop; lounge; exercise room; 3 Jacuzzis; indoor pool; 2 saunas. *In room:* TV, hair dryer, Wi-Fi.

Marmot Lodge ★ At the northern end of Jasper's main street, the Marmot Lodge offers pleasant rooms in three different buildings. One building contains large kitchen units with fireplaces, living area, and separate bedrooms with two queen-size beds or a king-size bed. These units are deservedly popular with families—ask for units with balconies off the back and you may see elk grazing on the back lawn. The building facing the street offers smaller, less expensive rooms; the third building features very large deluxe units. All are comfortable, with a relaxing, unfussy aesthetic that's restful after a day of sightseeing.

86 Connaught Dr., Jasper, AB T0E 1E0. ✆ **800/661-6521** or 780/852-4471. Fax 780/852-3280. www. mpljasper.com. 107 units. C$235 double; from C$265 suite. Children 14 and under stay free in parent's room. AE, DC, MC, V. **Amenities:** Restaurant; lounge; Jacuzzi; indoor pool; sauna. *In room:* TV w/pay movies, hair dryer, Wi-Fi.

Sawridge Inn and Conference Centre ★★ The three-story lobby of this hotel is large and airy, opening onto a central atrium lit with skylights and filled with tropical plants. The Sawridge is the classiest of all the Jasper Townsite hotels—the entire hotel was recently renovated, and offers large and beautifully furnished rooms. Half the rooms (most with one queen-size bed) overlook the jungle-like atrium, which also contains the restaurant, lounge, and pool. The other rooms (most with two queen-size beds) overlook the town and offer large private balconies as well. The king-size-bed corner suites are truly large, with two balconies and a jetted tub. The European Beauty and Wellness Centre is a day spa with a selection of beauty, aromatherapy, and massage treatments. The Sawridge, on the northern edge of Jasper, is unique in that it's owned by the Sawridge Cree Indian Band.

82 Connaught Dr. (P.O. Box 2080), Jasper, AB T0E 1E0. ✆ **888/729-7343** or 780/852-5111. Fax 780/852-5942. www.sawridge.com. 153 units. From C$261 double; from C$301 suite. B&B and other packages available. AE, DISC, MC, V. **Amenities:** Restaurant; 2 lounges; exercise room; Jacuzzi; indoor pool; room service; sauna; day spa. *In room:* A/C, TV w/movie channels, fridge, hair dryer, Wi-Fi, robes.

Expensive

If you are really just looking for a motel room, Jasper has a few standard motor lodges to accommodate your needs. The **Maligne Lodge,** on the western edge of Jasper at 900 Connaught Dr. (✆ **800/661-1315** or 780/852-3143), offers an indoor pool, restaurant, lounge, and clean unfussy rooms starting at C$190 double.

Becker's Chalets ★ This attractive log-cabin resort offers a variety of lodging options in free-standing chalets, set in a glade of trees along the Athabasca River. While the resort dates from the 1940s and retains the feel of an old-fashioned mountain retreat, most of the chalets have been built in the last 10 years or so, and thus are thoroughly modernized. Cabins come in a wide variety of sizes and styles, ranging from one-room cottages to four-bedroom chalets, with everything in between. Most cabins come with river-stone fireplaces and kitchens. My favorite? Ask for a deluxe one-bedroom log chalet (C$185) and live your log-cabin fantasies. The dining room at Becker's is also one of Jasper's best.

Hwy. 95, 5km (3 miles) south of Jasper (P.O. Box 579), Jasper, AB T0E 1E0. ✆ **780/852-3779.** Fax 780/852-7202. www.beckerschalets.com. 118 chalets. C$160–C$190 1-bedroom cabin; C$185–C$255 2-bedroom cabin; C$205–C$400 3-bedroom cabin. AE, MC, V. Closed early Oct to Apr 30. **Amenities:** Restaurant; playground. *In room:* TV, fridge, hair dryer, no phone.

Patricia Lake Bungalows ★

If you're looking for a bit of lakefront solitude and comfortable, unfussy lodgings, these cottages and motel rooms on Patricia Lake, just 10 minutes from downtown Jasper, are highly recommended. Lodgings are in a mix of vintage one-bed cottages, motel rooms, newly built suites, and a log cabin. Most of the cottages and all of the suites have kitchens; many have fireplaces.

7km (4¹⁄₃ miles) west of Jasper (P.O. Box 657), Jasper AB T0E 1E0. ✆ **888/499-6848** or 780/852-3560. Fax 780/852-4060. www.patricialakebungalows.com. 38 units. C$85–C$170 motel units; C$180–C$190 cottage; C$210 log cabin; C$170–C$260 suite. MC, V. Closed Nov–Apr. **Amenities:** Bike rentals; hot tub; boat rentals; playground; barbecues. *In room:* Kitchen (in some), no phone.

Tekarra Lodge ★

Just east of Jasper, this venerable log-cabin resort is situated above the confluence of the Miette and Athabasca rivers. Accommodations are in the lodge or in vintage cabins that can sleep from two to seven people; the lodge room rates include breakfast. The log cabins are nicely furnished (all with kitchens and private bathrooms), but it's the location that really sets Tekarra apart. Just far enough from the bustle of Jasper, off a quiet road in the forest, it offers the kind of charm that you dream of in a classic mountain-cabin resort. One of Jasper's best restaurants is located in the lodge, making this a great place for a family seeking solitude yet access to good food. Pets welcome.

1.5km (1 mile) east of Jasper off Hwy. 93A (P.O. Box 669), Jasper, AB T0E 1E0. ✆ **888/962-2522** or 780/852-3058. Fax 780/852-4636. www.tekarralodge.com. 52 units. C$169 lodge room; C$229–C$289 cabin double. 2-night minimum for cabins in summer. Extra person C$15. Rates for lodge rooms include continental breakfast. AE, DC, MC, V. Closed early Oct to Apr 30. **Amenities:** Restaurant; bar; bike rental. *In room:* Hair dryer, kitchen (in cabins), no phone.

Moderate

In high season, it seems that nearly half the dwellings in Jasper let rooms, B&B-style; contact **Jasper Home Accommodation Association,** P.O. Box 758, Jasper, AB T0E 1E0 (www.stayinjasper.com), for a full list. B&Bs listed with the local visitor association have little signs in front; if you arrive early enough in the day, you can comb the streets looking for a likely suspect. Note that B&Bs here are much less grand than those in Banff, and less expensive as well. Double-occupancy accommodations are in the C$75-to-C$115 range at most homes. You'll need to pay cash for most.

Athabasca Hotel (Value)

This hotel's lobby is like a hunting lodge, with a stone fireplace and trophy heads of deer and elk. A gray-stone corner building with a homey, old-fashioned air, the Athabasca was built in 1929, and has long served as one of Jasper's principal gathering spots. Each guest room offers a mountain view, although only half have private bathrooms; while rooms are small, the furnishings are simple and tasteful. The place is really quite pleasant—it's the very image of venerable Canadian charm—and one of the few good values in Jasper.

510 Patricia St., Jasper, AB T0E 1E0. ✆ **877/542-8422** or 780/852-3386. Fax 780/852-4955. www.athabascahotel.com. 61 units, 39 with private bathroom. C$99 double with shared bathroom; C$149–C$175 double with private bathroom. AE, DC, MC, V. **Amenities:** Restaurant; 2 bars; concierge; room service. *In room:* TV, hair dryer, Wi-Fi.

Austrian Haven

This large home in a quiet residential section of Jasper offers two very comfortable and spacious suites that are essentially full apartments. The large

Family Suite offers two queen-size beds, living room, kitchen, and dining area. The Honeymoon Suite is opulently decorated and has a king-size bed, cozy down duvet, and private sunroom with outstanding views. Both suites have private bathrooms, fridges, microwaves, TVs and VCRs, and private entrances. Both suites share a mountain-view deck with barbecue.

812 Patricia St. (Box 1856), Jasper, AB T0E 1E0. Ⓒ/fax **780/852-4259.** www.austrianhaven.ca. 2 units. C$140–C$160. Rates include continental breakfast. No credit cards. **Amenities:** Barbecue deck. *In room:* TV/VCR, fridge, microwave, toaster.

Inexpensive

Two Hostelling International **hostels,** both reachable at P.O. Box 387, Jasper, AB T0E 1E0 (Ⓒ **780/852-3215;** www.hihostels.ca), are the best alternatives for the budget traveler. Advance reservations are strongly advised in summer. The 80-bed **Jasper International Hostel,** on Skytram Road, 6km (3¾ miles) west of Jasper, charges C$26 for members and C$30 for nonmembers. The closest hostel to Jasper, it's open year-round. Two family rooms, a barbecue area, indoor plumbing, hot showers, and bike rentals are available. In winter, ask about ski packages. The **Maligne Canyon Hostel,** off Maligne Lake Road, 18km (11 miles) east of Jasper, sleeps 24; rates are C$23 for members and C$27 for nonmembers. This "wilderness" hostel is just above the astonishing Maligne Canyon. Facilities at this rustic facility include a self-catering kitchen and dining area, but no running water, showers, or flush toilets.

In & Around Hinton

Just east of the park gate in and near Hinton are a number of options that offer high-quality accommodations at significantly lower prices than you'll find in Jasper. Downtown Jasper is a 30- to 45-minute drive away from the choices listed below.

Hinton has a number of motel complexes with standard, no-nonsense rooms. The **Best Western White Wolf Inn,** 828 Carmichael Lane (Ⓒ **800/220-7870** in Canada, or 780/865-7777), has 42 air-conditioned rooms, most with kitchenettes. The **Black Bear Inn,** 571 Gregg Ave. (Ⓒ **888/817-2888** or 780/817-2000), features an exercise room, hot tub, and restaurant. The **Howard Johnson Plaza Hotel,** 678 Carmichael Lane (Ⓒ **800/661-7288** or 780/865-4001), has a pool and restaurant. Doubles at these motels cost between C$120 and C$150.

Overlander Mountain Lodge ★ The Overlander is a historic lodge on the edge of Jasper National Park. The original lodge building houses the Stone Peak Restaurant, a handsome dining room, and a bar with tremendous views of the Rockies, plus cozy guest rooms with queen- or twin-size beds. A newer wing features rooms with gas fireplaces and jetted tubs. The four-plex cabins have two double beds and a gas fireplace. Most of the chalets, which are scattered in the forest behind the lodge, contain a fireplace or wood-burning stove, full kitchen, washer/dryer, and patio. Accommodations throughout have private bathrooms and are decorated handsomely and furnished with country flair. The dining room serves notable tasty international and regional cuisine, with specialties of rack of lamb, venison, and fish. The Overlander's staff is friendly and helpful. This property offers excellent value and makes a charming base for exploring the park.

1km (²/₃ mile) from Jasper Park East Gate (Box 6118), Hinton, AB T7V 1X5. Ⓒ **877/866-2330** or 780/866-2330. Fax 780/866-2332. www.overlandermountainlodge.com. 29 units. C$173–C$238 lodge room; C$173 cabin room; C$413 2-bedroom chalet; C$522 3-bedroom chalet. AE, MC, V. **Amenities:** Restaurant; lounge; Wi-Fi; horseback riding; hiking trails. *In room:* Hair dryer, no phone.

Wyndswept Bed & Breakfast ★   This excellent B&B has a hostess who will make you feel like family. The main-floor guest rooms have private bathrooms, robes, hair dryers, handmade soaps, kettles, and other extras. The suite, which gives out onto a deck, measures 110 sq. m (1,184 sq. ft.) and has a full kitchen, large bathroom, and sitting area; it can sleep up to five. Breakfast is delicious and substantial—there's even a dessert course. Chances are good you'll see wildlife while here: Bears, coyotes, wolves, and deer have all been spotted from the deck. The owner will outfit you with a Wyndswept backpack upon arrival that contains books about hiking, wildlife, mosquito spray, band aids, and other incidentals that make your stay more comfortable and interesting—items that you won't need to purchase for your stay.

4km (2½ miles) east of Jasper Park gates (Box 2683), Hinton, AB T7V 1Y2. ℂ **780/866-3950.** Fax 780/866-3951. www.wyndswept.com. 3 units. C$165–C$199 double. Extra person C$35. MC, V. *In room:* A/C, TV w/movie channels, hair dryer, Wi-Fi.

Guest Ranch

Black Cat Guest Ranch   This venerable and historic wilderness retreat, established in 1935, sits in a superb mountain setting just outside the park boundaries in the foothills, with the Rockies filling up the western horizon. The rustic two-story lodge, built in 1978—guests don't stay in the original old cabins—offers 16 unfussy units, each with private bathroom, large windows, and an unspoiled view of the crags in Jasper Park across a pasture filled with horses and chattering birds. There's a large central fireplace room with couches, easy chairs, and game tables scattered about. Three home-cooked meals per day, served family-style by the friendly, welcoming staff, are available for C$46 adults, C$33 children per day. Activities include hiking, horseback riding, canoe rentals, murder-mystery weekends, and fishing. The ranch staff will meet your train or bus at Hinton.

56km (35 miles) northeast of Jasper, P.O. Box 6267, Hinton, AB T7V 1X6. ℂ **800/859-6840** or 780/865-3084. Fax 780/865-1924. www.blackcatguestranch.ca. C$110 per person, based on double occupancy. MC, V. **Amenities:** Large outdoor hot tub.

Camping

There are 10 campgrounds in Jasper National Park. You need a special permit to camp anywhere in the parks outside the regular campgrounds—a regulation necessary due to fire hazards. Contact the parks information office (ℂ **780/852-6176**) for permits. The campgrounds range from completely unserviced sites to those providing water, power, sewer connections, laundry facilities, gas, and groceries. The closest to Jasper Townsite is **The Whistlers,** up the road toward the gondola, providing a total of some 700 campsites for C$22 to C$36.

Where to Dine

Expensive

Andy's Bistro ★ CONTINENTAL/CANADIAN   This resourceful little restaurant's dining room looks like a wine cellar, and indeed the wine list is noteworthy. The food is classic Continental with a sprinkling of New-World specialties thrown in for spice. Starters may feature mussels steamed in white wine and cream. Main courses range from orange-and-vermouth-glazed lamb sirloin to chicken piccata with sun-dried tomatoes. Though the menu may seem highbrow, the atmosphere is casual and friendly—one communal table for six is saved for first-come, first-served diners.

606 Patricia St. ℂ **780/852-4559.** www.andysbistro.com. Reservations recommended. Main courses C$21–C$36. MC, V. Mid-May to mid-Oct daily 5–11pm; mid-Oct to mid-May Tues–Sat 5–11pm.

Becker's Gourmet Restaurant FRENCH/CANADIAN   Although the name's not very elegant, it's highly descriptive. This inventive restaurant serves what could only be termed gourmet food, observing the mandate to serve what's fresh and local without turning the menu into a list of endangered game animals. Samples include roasted chicken breast served with apples and maple-whiskey cream, and pan-seared veal tenderloin dusted with crushed juniper berries and napped with brandied cherry reduction. The dining room is an intimate log-and-glass affair that overlooks the Athabasca River.

At Becker's Chalets, Hwy. 93, 5km (3 miles) south of Jasper. ✆ **780/852-3779.** Reservations required. Main courses C$18–C$40. MC, V. Daily 8–11am and 5:30–9pm. Closed early Oct to Apr 30.

Evil Dave's Grill ★ CANADIAN   This recent addition to Jasper's food scene offers not just upscale comfort food but droll wit. Of course, there's nothing evil about the well-prepared food here, unless you count temptation: Malicious Salmon is blackened salmon topped with yogurt curry sauce, and Malevolent Meatloaf, made from ground beef and bacon, is served with cheddar mashed potatoes. Vegetarians get to smile too, with dishes like Vicious Hippie (artichoke-stuffed portobello mushroom cap on grilled tofu) and Glad Cow, which is vegetarian lasagna. The dining room is hip and full of youthful energy, fueled in part by Wicked Wines and Magic Elixirs, such as the Forbidden Fruit cocktail.

622 Patricia St. ✆ **780/852-3323.** www.evildavesgrill.com. Reservations suggested. Main courses C$19–C$35. MC, V. June–Sept daily 4–11pm; Oct–May daily 5–11pm.

Fiddle River Seafood ★ SEAFOOD   This rustic-looking retreat has panoramic windows facing the Jasper railroad station and the mountains beyond. The specialty here is fresh fish, though a number of pasta dishes and red-meat entrees will complicate your decision-making process. While there are plenty of good selections on the menu, Fiddle River offers as many daily specials (presented at the table on an easel-propped blackboard). At least 8 or 10 fresh fish and seafood specials are featured, including oysters and several preparations of Pacific salmon, such as pan-seared steelhead salmon filet with a honey, lime, and tarragon butter sauce. For "landlubbers," as the menu denotes the non-fish eaters, there are also excellent steaks. The wine list is short but interesting.

620 Connaught Dr. ✆ **780/852-3032.** Reservations required. Main courses C$18–C$38. AE, MC, V. Daily 5–10pm.

Moose's Nook Northern Grill ★ CANADIAN   This atmospheric restaurant off the great room of the Jasper Park Lodge features "Canadiana" specialties. With equal parts tradition and innovation, the Moose's Nook offers hearty presentations of native meats, fish, and game. Grilled duck breast is served with figs and celery root, and venison loin comes with a sauce of wild mushrooms and leeks. Lighter appetites will enjoy the vegetarian cabbage rolls.

In the Fairmont Jasper Park Lodge, 8km (5 miles) east of Jasper. ✆ **780/852-6052.** Reservations recommended. Main courses C$24–C$40. AE, DISC, MC, V. Daily 6–9pm; call to confirm hours during shoulder seasons.

Tekarra Lodge Restaurant STEAK/INTERNATIONAL   This local favorite offers excellent international cuisine, as well as steaks and other intriguing dishes such as macadamia-nut-crusted rack of lamb with mustard and chutney glaze. Lighter dishes such as salads and pastas are also available. The charming lodge dining room is one of Jasper's hidden gems; the service is friendly, and the fireplace-dominated room intimate.

Hwy. 93A, 1.6km (1 mile) east of Jasper (call for directions). ✆ **780/852-3058.** Reservations recommended on weekends. Main courses C$22–C$56. AE, DC, MC, V. Daily 8–11am and 5:30–10pm.

Jasper Brewing Company BREWPUB   A welcome addition to Jasper's youthful eating and nightlife scene, this brewpub made its debut on Food Network's *Opening Soon* series. All the attention has made this a very popular place, though the excellent ales and food—upscale pub grub with a Creole twist—are reason enough to make this your home-away-from-home in Jasper.

624 Connaught Dr. ℂ **780/852-4111.** Reservations accepted. Main courses C$10–C$26. MC, V. Daily 11am–midnight.

Something Else INTERNATIONAL/PIZZA   Something Else is accurately named: Fold together a good Greek restaurant and a pizza parlor, to which a high-quality Canadian-style restaurant has been added. Stir in a Creole bistro. In short, if you're with a group that can't decide where to eat, this is the place to go. Prime Alberta steaks, fiery Louisiana jambalaya and mesquite chicken, Greek saganaki and moussaka, an array of 21 pizzas—no matter what you choose, it's all well prepared and fresh, and the welcome is friendly.

621 Patricia St. ℂ **780/852-3850.** Reservations not needed. Main courses C$15–C$24. AE, DC, MC, V. Daily 11am–11pm.

Inexpensive

For muffins, sandwiches, coffee, desserts, soups, and salads, go to **Soft Rock Cafe,** 632 Connaught Dr. (ℂ **780/852-5850**), in the Connaught Square Mall. You can log onto the Internet from one of its computers. Another casual spot is **Spooner's Coffee Bar,** upstairs at 610 Patricia St. (ℂ **780/852-4046**), with a juice bar, coffee drinks, burritos, soups, sandwiches, and other deli items.

Jasper Pizza Place PIZZA   One of Jasper's most popular eateries, the redesigned Pizza Place agreeably combines the features of an upscale boutique pizzeria with a traditional Canadian bar. The excellent thin-crust pizzas are baked in a 1,000°F (538°C) wood-fired oven, and come in some very unusual—some would say unlikely—combinations. If you're not hungry for pizza, you'll also find inexpensive burgers, pasta, and even the French-Canadian specialty poutine. The bar side of things is lively, with pool tables and a crowd of summer resort workers on display.

402 Connaught Dr. ℂ **780/852-3225.** Reservations not accepted. Pizza C$7–C$18. MC, V. Daily 11am–11pm.

Jasper After Dark

Nearly all of Jasper's nightlife can be found in the bars and lounges of the hotels, motels, and inns.

O'Shea's, Athabasca Hotel, 510 Patricia St. (ℂ **780/852-3386**), is a longtime favorite party den, usually just called the Atha'B, or simply The B. It caters to a young clientele with its changing lineup of Top 40 bands, dance floor, and movies shown on the large-screen TV. O'Shea's is in action Monday to Saturday until 2am. If it's a straightforward and straight-head party scene that you're looking for, consider the **D'ed Dog Bar and Grill,** 404 Connaught Dr. (ℂ **780/852-3351**). This is where the young river and hiking guides who work in Jasper every summer gather to compare exploits by shouting above the din of country rock. Jasper's hottest club for music, **Pete's on Patricia,** upstairs at 614 Patricia St. (ℂ **780/852-6262**), presents live alternative and blues bands.

It's a little bit anomalous—Jasper's most exclusive and expensive hotel providing shelter for one of Jasper's most popular 20-something hangouts. **Tent City** is a youthful music, and a preponderance of the JPL's 650 employees.

You may think of most basement bars as dank and airless, but pleasant **Downstream Bar,** 620 Connaught Dr. (© **780/852-9449**), is a friendly place for a late evening drink, and you won't feel out of place if you're not 25 and totally tan.

---

5 BRITISH COLUMBIA'S ROCKIES: MOUNT ROBSON PROVINCIAL PARK & YOHO & KOOTENAY NATIONAL PARKS

MOUNT ROBSON PROVINCIAL PARK

24km (15 miles) W of Jasper

The highlight of this beautiful park, just west of Jasper National Park along the Yellowhead Highway, is 3,954m (12,972-ft.) Mount Robson, the highest peak in the Canadian Rockies. This massive sentinel fills the sky from most vantage points, making it a certainty that you'll easily overload your camera with images if the weather's good.

The mighty Fraser River rises in the park, offering a white-water adventure for experienced rafters. A number of Jasper-area outfitters offer trips down the Fraser; see "Sports & Outdoor Activities in the Park" under "Jasper National Park," earlier in this chapter.

Just 5km (3 miles) west of the park on Hwy. 16, **Mount Robson Lodge** (© **888/566-4821** or 250/566-4821) offers half-day white-water trips down the Fraser for C$89 in addition to campsites and accommodations in log cabins (C$79–C$139). For additional information on the park, call © **250/566-4325** or follow the links from **www.env.gov. bc.ca/bcparks**.

YOHO NATIONAL PARK

East gate is 60km (37 miles) W of Banff, west gate is 20km (12 miles) E of Golden

Located just east of Golden on the western slopes of the Rockies in British Columbia, Yoho National Park preserves some of the most famous rocks in Canada, as well as a historic rail line and the nation's second-highest waterfall. The park is essentially the drainage of the Kicking Horse River—famed for its white-water rafting—and is traversed by the Trans-Canada Highway.

The first white exploration of this area was by scouts looking for a pass over the Rockies that would be suitable for the Canadian Pacific's transcontinental run. Kicking Horse Pass, at 1,626m (5,335 ft.), was surveyed, and the railroad began its service in 1884. However, the first train to attempt the 4½%-grade descent lost control and crashed, killing three men. In 1909, after decades of accidents, the Canadian Pacific solved its problem by curling two spiral rail tunnels into the mountains facing Big Hill. Together, the two tunnels are more than 1,859m (6,099 ft.) long. At the Lower Spiral Tunnel Viewpoint, interpretive displays explain this engineering feat, and you can still watch trains enter and emerge from the tunnels.

Essentials

The service center for Yoho National Park is the little town of **Field,** with a half-dozen modest accommodations and a few casual restaurants. The park's **visitor center** is just off

Hwy. 1 near the entrance to town. For advance information, contact **Yoho National Park** (*℗* **250/343-6324;** www.pc.gc.ca).

The daily entrance fee is C$9.80 adults, C$8.30 seniors, C$4.90 youths 6 to 16, or C$20 families per day. The pass is good for entry at all of the four contiguous Rocky Mountain national parks.

Exploring the Park

Thirteen kilometers (8 miles) from the Kicking Horse Pass, turn north onto Yoho Valley Road to find some of the park's most scenic areas. Past another viewpoint of the Spiral Tunnels, continue 13km (8 miles) to **Takakkaw Falls ★**, Canada's second highest, which cascades 380m (1,247 ft.) in two drops. A short trail leads from the road's end to a picnic area, where views of this waterfall are even more eye-popping.

Another impressive waterfall is **Wapta Falls,** on the rushing Kicking Horse River. The falls is reached by an easy 2.4km (1.5-mile) hike near the park's western entrance.

The Kicking Horse River descends between Mount Field and Mount Stephen, famous in paleontological circles for the **Burgess Shale,** fossil-rich deposits from the Cambrian era. Interpretive displays on these fossil digs, which have produced organisms that seem to challenge some established evolutionary tenets, are found at the visitor center in Field.

Emerald Lake, a jewel-toned lake in a glacial cirque, is one of the park's most popular stops. Hiking trails ring the lake; the destination is popular for cross-country skiing as well. **The Emerald Lake Lodge ★** (*℗* **250/343-6321**) is open for meals and lodging year-round (see "Where to Stay & Dine," below). In summer, this is a very busy place, but it's worth the drive.

Lake O'Hara is another beautiful mountain lake nestled below the soaring peaks of the Continental Divide. To protect the fragile alpine ecosystem, access to the lake is restricted. Although you can hike into the lake basin—13km (8 miles) one-way—most people reserve a seat on the bus that travels the gravel road leading to the lake, four times per day. Reservations are essential, and in high season difficult to obtain. The buses run mid-June through the first weekend in October; tickets are C$15, and the reservation fee is another C$12. For reservations, call *℗* **250/343-6433.** Check out the Parks Canada website listed above for the most recent information on this area; the restrictions and options are fairly complex. Lake O'Hara is very popular with backcountry hikers, as the wilderness **campground** (C$10 per adult) here serves as a hub for a great many trails. Sitting on the shores is **Lake O'Hara Lodge** (*℗* **250/343-6418;** www.lakeohara.com), a rustic resort with lodge rooms and cabins starting at C$516 double, including all meals and bus transport.

Hiking

The trails that lead out from Emerald Lake are among the most popular in the park. The **Emerald Lake Trail** is a 5.2km (3.2-mile), all-abilities nature loop that leads from the parking area to the bridge at the back of the lake. At the end of the lake, it connects to the **Emerald Basin Trail,** an 8.6km (5.3-mile) round-trip hike ending dramatically in a natural amphitheater of hanging glaciers and avalanche paths. The Emerald Lake circuit alone will take 1 to 2 hours; the Emerald Basin Trail is a half-day hike taking from 3 to 4 hours.

The **Yoho Glacier Moraine Trail** is a half-day hike, 8.2km (5.1 miles) in length that passes by Laughing Falls en route to Twin Falls, the most popular destination in the valley. Energetic folks can continue to the top of **Twin Falls,** then over the **Whaleback Trail** for some of the most incredible views of glaciers in the park. Returning to Takakkaw Falls via the Whaleback and Laughing falls is a 20km (12-mile) circuit.

Heading up to the **Burgess Shale** formations is limited to guided hikes. The exquisitely preserved fossils discovered here were like none seen before, and even today are still reshaping our understanding of early evolution of modern animal life. The **Yoho–Burgess Shale Foundation** (📞 800/343-3006; www.burgess-shale.bc.ca) offers educational hikes from July to mid-September. The Burgess Shale Hike is 20km (12 miles) round-trip, a moderately difficult 10-hour trek. The cost is C$100 adults, C$50 for students, and C$25 for children under 12. The Mount Stephen Fossil Beds hike is a moderately difficult 6km (3.7 miles), lasting about 6 hours. The cost is C$75 adults, C$50 for students, and C$25 for children under 12. Other options include a special hike for seniors and the Mary Vaux Interpretive Hike. Call ahead for reservations.

Where to Stay & Dine

Cathedral Mountain Lodge ★ Luxurious log cabins characterize this recently upgraded resort property on the road to Takakkaw Falls, just east of Field. Each of the cabins is lovingly furnished with handcrafted pine furniture, stone-built fireplaces, and rustic Canadiana decor (and no TVs, phones, or Internet to break the woodsy spell). The newly constructed central lodge has a central great room with a fireplace and comfy chairs, plus a dining room with fine dining (open for dinner nightly; reservations for non-guests required). This is a top choice for a romantic vacation; children must be 8 or older.

Yoho Valley Rd., 5km (3 miles) east of Field (P.O. Box 40, Field, BC V0A 1G0). 📞 866/619-6442 or 250/343-6442. Fax 250/343-6424. www.cathedralmountain.com. 31 units. C$275–C$550. Rates include breakfast. AE, DC, MC, V. Children must be 8 or older. **Amenities:** Restaurant; bar; central lodge. *In room:* Hair dryer, fireplace.

The Emerald Lake Lodge ★ The Emerald Lake Lodge sits at the base of a placid aquamarine lake beneath towering cliff-faced mountains. The lake was discovered in 1882, when the Canadian Pacific Railway pushed over Kicking Horse Pass; by 1902, the railway had built a lodge on the lakeshore. The original lodge has expanded since then, but retains a marvelous sense of woodsy venerability and rustic charm. The main lodge houses a formal dining room, a bar, and conference facilities. Guest accommodations are in 24 newly built, cabin-style buildings, designed to harmonize with the historic lodge. Each unit features a fieldstone fireplace, bent-willow chairs, down comforters, and a balcony (most overlook the lake). There's fine dining in the elegant restaurant and lighter cuisine at Cilantro. The lounge features an oak bar salvaged from an 1890s Yukon saloon.

Box 10, Field, BC V0A 1G0. 📞 800/663-6336 or 250/343-6321. www.crmr.com. 85 units. C$180–$375 double. Extra person C$25. Children 17 and under stay free in parent's room. AE, MC, V. Free parking. **Amenities:** 2 restaurants; lounge; Jacuzzi; sauna; canoe and cross-country ski rentals. *In room:* Fridge (in some), hair dryer.

Camping

There are five campgrounds in Yoho National Park. East of Field, sites go for C$17 at **Monarch** and C$26 at **Kicking Horse.** Near the park's western gate, **Hoodoo Creek** charges C$21 per site. There's also a walk-in campground near **Takakkaw Falls,** where sites are C$17. For information, contact the visitor center at 📞 250/343-6783.

KOOTENAY NATIONAL PARK & RADIUM HOT SPRINGS

Radium Hot Springs is 105km (65 miles) SE of Golden; Vermillion Pass is 38km (24 miles) SW of Banff

Kootenay National Park ★ just west of Banff on the western slopes of the Canadian Rockies, preserves the valleys of the Kootenay and Vermillion rivers. The park contains prime wildlife habitats and a number of hiking trails. Although Kootenay's scenery is as grand as can be found anywhere else in the Rockies, its trails are considerably less crowded than those in the neighboring parks.

Essentials

Kootenay National Park is linked to the other Canadian Rockies parks by Hwy. 93, which departs from Hwy. 1 at Castle Junction to climb over the Vermillion Pass and descend to **Radium Hot Springs,** the park's western entrance. The town of Radium Hot Springs sits at the junction of highways 93 and 95. Not an especially attractive place, it nonetheless offers ample motel rooms along the stretch of Hwy. 93 just before the park gates.

For information on the town, contact **Radium Hot Springs Visitor Information Centre,** Unit #4, Radium Plaza, 7556 Main St. E. (© **888/347-9331** or 250/347-9331; www.radiumhotsprings.com). For information on the park, contact **Kootenay National Park** (© **250/347-9505;** www.pc.gc.ca).

The daily entrance fee is C$9.80 adults, C$8.30 seniors, C$4.90 youths 6 to 16, or C$20 families per day. The pass is good for entry at all of the four contiguous Rocky Mountain national parks.

Exploring the Park & Radium Hot Springs

Kootenay National Park is on the west side of the Continental Divide, just west of Banff. Kootenay has the fewest facilities of the four major Rocky Mountain national parks, and day-hiking options are limited. The drive through the park on Hwy. 93 does offer spectacular scenery.

Much of the area around **Vermillion Pass,** the eastern entrance to the park, was burned in a massive forest fire in 1968; from the parking area at the pass, the interpretive 15-minute Fireweed Trail leads into the still-devastated forest, describing the process of revegetation.

Seven kilometers (4⅓ miles) into the park is another dramatic stop. **Marble Canyon** is a narrow 61m-deep (200-ft.) chasm cut through a formation of limestone. A short trail winds over and through the canyon, bridging the canyon in several places. Just 5 minutes down the road are the **Paint Pots.** Here, cold spring water surfaces in an iron-rich deposit of red and yellow clay, forming intense colored pools.

The highway leaves the Vermillion River valley and climbs up to a viewpoint above the **Hector Gorge,** into which the river flows before meeting the Kootenay River. From here, look out for mountain goats, which can often be seen on the rocky cliffs of Mount Wardle to the north.

The highway passes through one of these narrow limestone canyons after it mounts Sinclair Pass and descends toward Radium Hot Springs. Called **Sinclair Canyon,** the chasm is about 10km (6¼ miles) long, and in places is scarcely wide enough to accommodate the roadbed.

Radium Hot Springs Pool (© **250/347-9485**), a long-established hot springs spa and resort, sits at the mouth of Sinclair Canyon. It's open from mid-May to mid-October daily from 9am to 11pm, and mid-October to mid-May weekdays from noon to 9pm (weekends until 10pm). Day passes are C$6.30 for adults, C$5.40 for seniors and children, and C$19 per family. Also here is the **Radium Hot Springs Massage Clinic** (© **250/347-9714**) and other spa services.

There's not much to keep you in the town of Radium Hot Springs unless you need an inexpensive motel room. Though if you're a golfer, the town does boast two new championship 18-hole courses, the **Springs Course,** along the Columbia just west of town with summer season greens fees of C$79 to C$110, and the **Resort Course,** south of

Radium, with summer fees of C$47 to C$59. Both are operated by **Radium Golf Resort**
(📞 **250/347-9311;** www.radiumresort.com), which offers restaurants, clubhouses, pro shops, and luxury accommodations.

Where to Stay

The Chalet Europe ★ One of the few places to stay in Radium that doesn't have busy Hwy. 93 as its front yard, the Chalet is perched high above the Columbia Valley, just above the entrance to Kootenay Park. Each of the property's suites has a galley kitchen and private balcony with superlative views of the Rockies and Columbia Valley.

5063 Madsen Rd., Radium Hot Springs, BC V0A 1M0. 📞 **888/428-9998** or 250/347-9305. Fax 250/347-9316. www.chaleteurope.com. 17 units. C$129–C$189 double. Extra person C$10. AE, DISC, MC, V. Free parking. **Amenities:** Exercise room; Jacuzzi; sauna; barbecue. In room: A/C, TV/DVD, hair dryer, kitchenette, microwave, Wi-Fi.

Prestige Radium Hot Springs ★ This recently built upscale hotel offers very comfortable rooms, perfect for travelers looking for an upgrade from the many older motels in Radium Hot Springs. Kitchen units are also available. This is a full-service hotel, with lots of extras such as a day spa, athletic club, and meeting and conference facilities. If you're looking for a splurge, or just need more room, the one-bedroom executive suites are very large and nicely furnished; the theme rooms, decorated with African, New York, or Egyptian motifs, may tantalize if you feel you've been in the Rockies too long.

7493 Main St., Radium Hot Springs, BC V0A 1M0. 📞 **877/737-8443** or 250/347-2300. Fax 250/347-2345. 87 units. C$170–C$210 double; C$240–C$250 executive suite; C$329 theme suite. AE, DC, MC, V. **Amenities:** Restaurant; lounge; athletic club; hot tub; indoor pool; day spa. In room: A/C, TV, fridge, hair dryer, Wi-Fi, voice mail.

Where to Dine

In addition to the following, consider stopping in for a beer and a light meal at **Horsethief Creek Pub & Eatery,** 7538 Main St. (📞 **250/347-6400**).

Old Salzburg Restaurant AUSTRIAN This is one of the most authentic-looking of Radium's ersatz Alpine structures, flanked by filigreed balconies, gables, and flowerpots. The menu features six varieties of schnitzel, but thankfully also contains a broad selection of other Austrian and Continental dishes. *Jagerrostbraten* is grilled beef loin in red wine, bacon, mushroom, and cranberry sauce. Homemade sausages, fish, and steaks round out the menu.

4943 Hwy. 93. 📞 **250/347-6553.** Reservations recommended. Main courses C$13–C$25. AE, MC, V. Mid-May to mid-Oct daily 11am–10pm; the rest of the year daily 5–10pm.

---

6 WATERTON LAKES NATIONAL PARK ★

264km (164 miles) S of Calgary

In the southwestern corner of the province, Waterton Lakes National Park is linked with Glacier National Park in neighboring Montana; together these two beautiful tracts of wilderness compose Waterton-Glacier International Peace Park. Once the hunting ground of the Blackfoot, Waterton Park contains superb mountain, prairie, and lake scenery and is home to abundant wildlife.

The transition from plains to mountains in Waterton and Glacier parks is abrupt: The formations that now rise above the prairie were once under the primal Pacific Ocean, but wedges of the ocean's basement rock broke along deep horizontal faults, cutting these rock layers free. The continued impact of the plate tectonics gouged these rocks out and pushed them 56km (35 miles) east over the prairies. Thus, almost 5km (3 miles) high, the rock block of Waterton Park—an overthrust in geological terms—is a late arrival, now sitting on top of the plains.

During the last ice age, the park was filled with glaciers, which deepened and straightened river valleys; those peaks that remained above the ice were carved into distinctive thin, finlike ridges. The park's famous lakes also date from the Ice Age; all three of the Waterton Lakes nestle in glacial basins.

ESSENTIALS

Waterton Park is 264km (164 miles) south of Calgary and 130km (81 miles) west of Lethbridge. From Waterton, it's 100km (62 miles) south across the U.S.-Canada border to St. Mary, at the entrance to Montana's Glacier National Park. **Greyhound Canada** (© 800/661-8747; www.greyhound.ca) runs buses between Lethbridge and Waterton Townsite.

For more information, contact the **Waterton Park Chamber of Commerce and Visitors Association,** P.O. Box 5599, Waterton Lakes National Park, AB T0K 2M0 (© 403/859-5133 summer, or 403/859-2224 winter; www.pc.gc.ca and www.my waterton.ca). The per-day park entry fee is C$7.80 for adults, C$6.80 for seniors, and C$3.90 for children.

EXPLORING THE PARK

The park's main entrance road leads to **Waterton Townsite,** the only commercial center, with a number of hotels, restaurants, and tourist facilities. Other roads lead to more remote lakes and trail heads. Akamina Parkway leads from the townsite to Cameron Lake, glimmering beneath the crags of the Continental Divide. Red Rock Parkway follows Blackiston Creek past the park's highest peaks to Red Rock Canyon. From here, three trails lead up deep canyons to waterfalls.

The most popular activity in the park is the **Inter-Nation Shoreline Cruise** (© 403/859-2362; www.watertoncruise.com), which leaves from the townsite and sails Upper Waterton Lake past looming peaks to the ranger station at Goat Haunt, Montana, in Glacier Park. The tour boat operates from early May through early October. In the high season, from the last weekend of June through August, there are three or four tour boat departures daily, with two daily in the shoulder seasons (check the website for exact schedules). Only during the high season does the boat land in Montana. The cruise usually takes just over 2 hours, including the stop in Montana. The price is C$34 for adults, C$17 for youths ages 13 to 17, and C$11 for children ages 4 to 12.

OUTDOOR PURSUITS

BIKING   Unusual in a national park, mountain biking is allowed on a number of trails. Cameron Lake is a good trail head, offering three different options. Two short but steep trails climb up to Wall and Forum lakes; the Akimina Creek Trail follows an old forestry road 14km (8.7 miles) up Akimina Creek. For rentals, contact **Pat's Cycle Rental** (© 403/859-2266).

GOLF   The **Waterton Park Golf Course** ★ (© 403/859-2114) is one of the oldest courses in Alberta. An original Stanley Thompson design (he designed the famed courses at Banff and Jasper), its hazards include incredible Rocky Mountain vistas and meandering elk, bear, and moose.

HIKING A 3km (1.9-mile) loop trail rings the peninsula that holds Waterton Townsite and links to long-distance trails. **Cameron Falls,** just above the Evergreen Avenue Bridge, is a good place to pick up the trail. From the Red Rock Canyon Trail Head, follow the main trail a mile up the canyon to see rust-red cliffs. From the same trail head, turn south and follow Blackiston Creek to Blackiston Falls, a 1km (.6-mile) leg-stretcher.

The most famous day hike is to **Crypt Lake.** This 17km (11-mile) round-trip is strenuous, but worth the effort for those in shape. The International Shoreline Cruise to Goat Haunt (see above) makes eight stops daily at the trail head.

Long-distance hiking trails skirt the edge of Upper Waterton Lake and link to the trail system in Glacier National Park.

HORSEBACK RIDING **Alpine Stables,** across from the golf course on Entrance Road (✆ **403/859-2462**), offers a variety of guided rides on more than 250km (155 miles) of trails.

WHERE TO STAY

Aspen Village Inn ★ Aspen Village offers motel rooms in the Wildflower building, suites in the Aspen building, and duplex cottages. The suites are the newest, and can accommodate up to eight persons each. The entire complex, located 2 blocks from the lake, is hung with flower boxes and is well maintained.

P.O. Box 100, Waterton Lake, AB T0K 2M0. ✆ **888/859-8669** or 403/859-2255. Fax 403/859-2033. www.theaspenvillageinn.com. 51 units. C$175–C$255 double; C$179–C$295 suite; C$175–C$265 cottage. Extra person C$20. Children 15 and under stay free in parent's room. AE, DISC, MC, V. Free parking. Closed Oct–May. **Amenities:** Jacuzzi; playground; barbecue and picnic area. *In room:* TV, hair dryer.

Crandell Mountain Lodge A Bavarian guesthouse look-alike, the Crandell is one of the park's original lodges. It has the feel of a charming country inn, with individually decorated rooms ranging from small units under the eaves to suites with kitchens and fireplaces. Two wheelchair-accessible units are available as well. The inn is noted for its friendly staff.

P.O. Box 114, Waterton Lake, AB T0K 2M0. ✆ **866/859-2288.** ✆/fax 403/859-2288. www.crandellmountainlodge.com. 17 units. C$140–C$220 double. Lower off-season rates. Extra person C$10. DC, MC, V. Free parking. *In room:* TV, fridge, hair dryer.

Prince of Wales Hotel Overrated Built in 1927 by the Great Northern Railway, this beautiful mountain lodge, perched on a bluff above Upper Waterton Lake, is reminiscent of the historic resorts in Banff. Rooms have been renovated, though many are historically authentic in that they're rather small. Operated by the same dilatory consortium that manages the historic lodges in Glacier National Park in Montana, the Prince of Wales is in need of some serious reinvestment. You'll want to at least visit this landmark for the view and perhaps for a meal at the Garden Court restaurant. Historic-monument status aside, however, there are better places to stay than this handsome doyen—until someone who values these grand lodges pries them away from their corporate owners.

P.O. Box 33, Waterton Lakes National Park, AB T0K 2M0. ✆ **403/236-3400.** www.glacierparkinc.com. 86 units. C$219–C$259 double. Extra person C$15. Children 11 and under stay free in parent's room. AE, MC, V. Closed late Sept to early June. **Amenities:** 2 restaurants; 2 bars.

Waterton Glacier Suites ★ These attractive suites are some of the nicest accommodations in Waterton, particularly if you're able to step up and pay for a top-end loft unit. Most expensive are town house–style suites with two bathrooms and a two-person Jacuzzi; one has vaulted ceilings. All units are attractively furnished, with both fireplaces and balconies. Extras include the Serenity Spa, with beauty treatments and massage. Open year-round.

P.O. Box 51, Waterton Park, AB T0K 2M0. ✆ **866/621-3330** or 403/859-2004. Fax 403/859-2118. www.watertonsuites.com. 26 units. C$225–C$289 double. Extra person C$15. Lower off-season rates. AE, MC, V. Free parking. **Amenities:** Jacuzzi. *In room:* A/C, TV/DVD, fridge, hair dryer, jetted tub, microwave.

Waterton Lakes Lodge ★ This new and classy complex sits on 1.5 hectares (3¾ acres) in the heart of Waterton Townsite. The 80 rooms are in nine separate lodgelike buildings that flank a central courtyard. All are decorated with an environmental theme and appointed with handsome pine furniture. Vimy's Lounge and Grill is part of the resort complex. Also on the property are a guest and community sports facility with a large pool, fitness center, and spa.

P.O. Box 4, Waterton Park, AB T0K 2M0. ✆ **888/985-6343** or 403/859-2150. Fax 403/859-2229. www.watertonlakeslodge.com. 80 units. C$185–C$215 double. Extra person C$20. Off-season rates available. AE, MC, V. Closed Jan–Apr. **Amenities:** 2 restaurants; bar; health club w/pool; fitness center & spa. *In room:* A/C, TV, fridge, hair dryer, Wi-Fi.

WHERE TO DINE

Note that the Kilmorey Lodge, with its beloved Lamp Post Dining Room, was destroyed by fire in 2009. Plans are moving forward to rebuild the structure.

Garden Court PACIFIC NORTHWEST This elegant dining room overlooks stunning Waterton Lake, with the towering peaks of Glacier National Park incising the southern horizon. By and large, the food is up to the challenge of competing with the vista. Appetizers include baked brie with sliced apples, crostini, and cranberry coulis; and scallops in chives, mushrooms, and cream in a puff-pastry shell. Entrees range from prime rib to the house specialty Princess chicken, a spinach-and-feta-stuffed breast with a pine-nut crust, served with saskatoonberry-and-onion chutney.

In Prince of Wales Hotel. ✆ **403/859-2231.** Reservations required. Main courses C$18–C$42. MC, V. Early June to mid-Sept daily 6:30–9:30am, 11:30am–2pm, and 5–9pm.

Fast Facts

AREA CODES The area code for Vancouver and the surrounding area is 604; for Victoria and the rest of the B.C., it's 250. In Alberta, the area code for Calgary and Banff is 403, while the area code for Edmonton and Jasper is 780.

AUTOMOBILE ORGANIZATIONS Members of the **American Automobile Association (AAA)** should remember to take their membership cards since the **Canadian Automobile Association (CAA; ✆ 800/222-4357; www.caa.ca)** extends privileges to them in Canada.

BUSINESS HOURS Standard business hours in Canada are similar to those in the U.S., usually 10am to 6pm. It is common for stores to be closed on Sundays, particularly outside of the larger cities and major tourist areas.

DRINKING LAWS In British Columbia, all beer, wine, and spirits are sold only in government liquor stores, which keep restricted hours and charge extortionate prices. Alberta's liquor laws more resemble those in the United States, and the minimum drinking age there is 18 (in British Columbia, it's 19), though you still need to go to liquor stores for all forms of alcohol, including beer and wine.

Proof of age is required and often requested at bars, nightclubs, and restaurants, so it's always a good idea to bring ID when you go out.

Do not carry open containers of alcohol in your car or any public area that isn't zoned for alcohol consumption. The police can fine you on the spot. Don't even think about driving while intoxicated.

DRIVING RULES See "Getting There and Getting Around," p. 36.

ELECTRICITY Canada uses the same plug configuration and 110–120 volts AC (60 cycles) as the U.S., compared to 220–240 volts AC (50 cycles) in most of Europe, Australia, and New Zealand. Downward converters that change 220–240 volts to 110–120 volts can be difficult to find in the United States and Canada, so bring one with you.

EMBASSIES & CONSULATES All embassies are in Ottawa, the national capital; the **U.S. Embassy** is at 490 Sussex Dr., Ottawa, ON K1N 1G8 (✆ **613/688-5335;** http://ottawa.usembassy.gov). You'll find U.S. consulates in Alberta at 615 Macleod Trail SE, 10th Floor, Calgary (✆ **403/266-8962**), and in British Columbia at Mezzanine, 1095 W. Pender St., Vancouver (✆ **604/685-4311**). Visit the American Citizen Information Services website (www.amcits.com) for further U.S. consular services information.

There's a **British consulate general** at 777 Bay St., Ste. 2800, Toronto, ON M5G 2G2 (✆ **416/593-1290;** for more information see http://ukincanada.fco.gov.uk/en), and an **Australian consulate general** at 175 Bloor St. E., Ste. 1100, South Tower, Toronto, ON M4W 3R8 (✆ **416/323-1155;** for more information see www.ahc-ottawa.org).

EMERGENCIES Dial ✆ **911** for emergencies.

GASOLINE (PETROL) Gas sells by the liter and pumps for anywhere from about C85¢ to C$1.10 per liter, or about C$3.80 to C$4.30 per U.S. gallon. (Note that the term "gallon" in Canada usually refers to the imperial gallon, which amounts to about 1.2 U.S. gal.) Gasoline prices vary from region to region.

HOLIDAYS Most banks, government offices, post offices, and many stores, restaurants, and museums are closed on the following legal national holidays: January 1 (New Year's Day), Good Friday, Easter, the Monday on or before May 24 (Victoria Day), July 1 (Canada Day), the first Monday in September (Labour Day), the second Monday in October (Thanksgiving), November 11 (Remembrance Day), and December 25 and 26 (Christmas and Boxing Day).

Travelers should note that most Canadians consider their high summer season to run between Victoria Day (a week before Memorial Day in the U.S.) and Labour Day (the same date as in the U.S.). Seasonal destinations often close the weekend before Canadian Thanksgiving, in early October.

LANGUAGE English is spoken throughout B.C. and the Canadian Rockies.

LEGAL AID If you are "pulled over" for a minor infraction (such as speeding), never attempt to pay the fine directly to a police officer; this could be construed as attempted bribery, a much more serious crime. Pay fines by mail, or directly into the hands of the clerk of the court. If accused of a more serious offense, say and do nothing before consulting your embassy or consulate.

MAIL Standard mail in Canada is carried by **Canada Post** (✆ **800/267-1177** in Canada, or 416/979-8822 in the U.S.; www.canadapost.ca). At press time, it costs C57¢ to send a first-class letter or postcard within Canada and C$1.03 to send a first-class letter or postcard from Canada to the United States. First-class airmail service to other countries is C$1.73 for the first 30 grams (1 oz.). Rates go up frequently. If you put a return address on your letter, make sure it's Canadian; otherwise, leave it without.

PASSPORTS See www.frommers.com/planning for information on how to obtain a passport. See "Embassies & Consulates," above, for whom to contact if you lose yours while traveling in Canada. For other information, please contact the following agencies:

For Residents of Australia Contact the **Australian Passport Information Service** at ✆ **131-232,** or visit the government website at www.passports.gov.au.

For Residents of Ireland Contact the **Passport Office,** Setanta Centre, Molesworth Street, Dublin 2 (✆ **01/671-1633;** www.irlgov.ie/iveagh).

For Residents of New Zealand Contact the **Passports Office** at ✆ **0800/225-050** in New Zealand or 04/474-8100, or log on to www.passports.govt.nz.

For Residents of the United Kingdom Visit your nearest passport office, major post office, or travel agency, or contact the **United Kingdom Passport Service** at ✆ **0870/521-0410** or search its website at www.ukpa.gov.uk.

For Residents of the United States To find your regional passport office, either check the U.S. State Department website or call the **National Passport Information Center**'s toll-free number (✆ **877/487-2778**) for automated information.

POLICE To contact the police in an emergency, dial ✆ **911.**

SMOKING Canada is considered to be at the forefront of anti-smoking legislation. Eleven of the country's 13 provinces and territories have now passed smoking bans prohibiting cigarettes in the workplace and public buildings, bars, and restaurants. In Alberta, no smoking is allowed in public places and workplaces where minors are allowed. Casinos, bingo halls, and bars don't fall under these restrictions. In B.C., you can't smoke in public places like restaurants, bars, bingo halls, bowling alleys, and casinos. Restaurant and bar owners may construct open smoking rooms where staff may volunteer to serve. Traveling smokers should be aware that in B.C., it is illegal to light a cigarette in a motor vehicle in the presence of a person under the age of 16.

TAXES Throughout Canada, you will be charged a federal **goods and service tax (GST),** a 5% tax on virtually all goods and services. In all provinces except Alberta, there is an additional provincial sales tax added to purchases and financial transactions. British Columbia levies a "harmonized" federal and provincial 12% tax on purchases and services.

All provinces and some municipalities levy a hotel room tax (5% in Alberta; 8% in B.C.).

Some hotels and shops include the GST in their prices; others add it on separately. When included, the tax accounts for the odd hotel rates, such as C$96.05 per day, that you may find on your final bill.

As of 2007, **the Canadian government no longer offers GST or HST rebates** of hotel bills or the cost of goods you've purchased in Canada.

TELEPHONES The Canadian phone system is exactly the same as the 10-digit system in the United States. (See "Staying Connected," in chapter 3, for more information). Many stores sell **prepaid calling cards** in denominations up to $50; for international visitors these can be the least expensive way to call home. Many public pay phones at airports now accept American Express, MasterCard, and Visa credit cards. **Local calls** made from pay phones in most locales cost C50¢. Most long-distance and international calls can be dialed directly from any phone.

For calls within Canada to the United States, dial 1 followed by the area code and the seven-digit number. **For other international calls,** dial 011 followed by the country code, city code, and the number you are calling. The country code from Canada to the U.K. is 44; Australia is 61; the country code for New Zealand is 64.

Calls to area codes **800, 888, 877,** and **866** are toll-free. However, calls to area codes **700** and **900** (chat lines, bulletin boards, "dating" services, and so on) can be very expensive—usually a charge of C$3 or more per minute, and they sometimes have minimum charges that can run as high as C$15 or more.

For **reversed-charge or collect calls,** and for person-to-person calls, dial the number 0, then the area code and number; an operator will come on the line, and you should specify whether you are calling collect, person-to-person, or both. If your operator-assisted call is international, ask for the overseas operator.

TIME Most of British Columbia is in the Pacific Time zone, 3 hours earlier than Eastern Standard Time. A sliver of British Columbia, stretching from Golden down to Cranbrook, and all of Alberta are on Mountain Time, an hour later than the rest of the province. So when it's noon in New York City, it's 9am in Victoria and 10am in Calgary. Each year, on the second Sunday in March, daylight saving time comes into effect in most of Canada, and clocks are advanced by 1 hour. On the first Sunday in November, Canada reverts to standard time.

TIPPING The rules for tipping in Canada parallel those in the United States.

In hotels, tip **bellhops** at least C$1 per bag (C$2–C$3 if you have a lot of luggage) and tip the **chamber staff** C$1 to C$2 per day (more if you've left a disaster area for him or her to clean up). Tip the **doorman** or **concierge** only if he or she has provided you with some specific service (for example, calling a cab for you or obtaining difficult-to-get theater tickets). Tip the **valet-parking attendant** C$1 every time you get your car.

In restaurants, bars, and nightclubs, tip **service staff** and **bartenders** 15% to 20% of the check, tip **checkroom attendants** C$1 per garment, and tip **valet-parking attendants** C$1 per vehicle.

As for other service personnel, tip **cab drivers** 10% to 15% of the fare; tip **skycaps** at airports at least C$1 per bag (C$2–C$3 if you have a lot of luggage); and tip **hairdressers** and **barbers** 15% to 20%.

TOILETS You won't find public toilets or "washrooms" on the streets in most Canadian cities, but they can be found in hotel lobbies, bars, restaurants, museums, department stores, railway and bus stations, and service stations. Large hotels and fast-food restaurants are often the best bet for clean facilities. Restaurants and bars in resorts or heavily visited areas may reserve their washrooms for patrons.

VISAS Citizens of the U.S., most European countries, most former British colonies and certain other countries (Israel, Korea, and Japan, for instance) do not need visas but must carry passports to enter Canada. Entry visas are required for citizens of more than 130 countries. Entry visas must be applied for and received from the Canadian embassy in your home country. For more information on entry requirements to Canada, see the Citizenship and Immigration website visitors' services page at **www.cic.gc.ca/english/visit/index.asp**.

VISITOR INFORMATION For advance information on British Columbia, contact **Tourism British Columbia,** P.O. Box 9830, Stn. Prov. Govt., 1803 Douglas St., Third Floor, Victoria, BC V8W 9W5 (✆ **800/HELLO-BC** [435-5622] or 250/387-1642; www.hellobc.com).

To request information on Alberta, contact **Travel Alberta,** Box 2500, Edmonton, AB T5J 2Z4 (✆ **800/252-3782;** www.travelalberta.com).

For general information about Canada's national parks, contact **Parks Canada National Office,** 25 Eddy St., Hull, PQ K1A 0M5 (✆ **888/773-8888;** www.pc.gc.ca). For Canada-wide travel information, see the official tourism site for Canada at www.canada.travel.

Here are some other useful provincial and city sites:

- **British Columbia:** www.bc.worldweb.com; www.travel.bc.ca
- **Alberta:** www.discoveralberta.com
- **Vancouver:** www.tourismvancouver.com
- **Whistler:** www.whistler.com, www.whistlerblackcomb.com
- **Victoria:** www.tourismvictoria.com, www.victoriabc.com
- **Banff:** www.bannflakelouise.com, www.banff.com
- **Calgary:** www.tourismcalgary.com, www.discovercalgary.com
- **Edmonton:** www.edmonton.ca, www.discoveredmonton.com, www.edmonton.com

If you enjoy blogs, there are a number dedicated to food and travel in Canada. Try www.canadatravelblog.ca, which offers a compendium of private blogs of travelers as they make their way across the country; you can blog about your trip to Canada here, too.

INDEX